COLOR ME JUSTICE

KENNETH F. MC LAUGHLIN

Volume 1

Printed by

EQUITY PUBLISHING CORPORATION

ORFORD, NEW HAMPSHIRE

Contents

VOLUME II

Preface

It is hoped that this work will provide the discerning reader with an insight into recent Supreme Court opinions by allowing him to read entire unabridged decisions. Having done so, he will be better able to understand the extent and the significance of the Court's rulings. This work isn't being written with the hope of changing anyone's views but rather to furnish means by which the reader may make intelligent appraisals and appropriate inquiries relative to the role of the Supreme Court in our society.

The Warren Court just prior to his retirement. Seated left to right, John M. Harlan, Hugo L. Black, Earl Warren, William O. Douglas, William J. Brennan, Jr. Standing left to right, Abe Fortas, Potter Stewart, Byron White and Thurgood Marshall.

Introduction

Mr. Justice Holmes' statement that a page of history is worth a volume of logic is the basis for the format of this work. In these volumes are presented selected Supreme Court decisions in an unabridged form.

These cases are history. The logic of the cases (if it exists) is much more difficult to understand than their holdings. The reader will soon be aware that from the same set of facts different members of the court will deduce an entirely different theory and in many cases a different determination. This results from the application of their "logic" to the facts and the Constitution as they see it.

Since the members of the Court generally cannot agree amongst themselves, it is important to determine reasons for their disagreement. The author has chosen not to attempt an explanation of the disagreements but to let the Justices do so themselves in this publication. Accordingly, all concurring and dissenting opinions are reported along with the majority opinion in every instance.

It is left to the reader to determine (with the help of history) possible answers to many of the fundamental questions in the area of constitutional law. What is the function of the Supreme Court in analyzing the facts of the case? Is it, as Warren says, to determine "what is fair?" Is it to determine what the framers of the Constitution meant? Is it a matter of interpretation of the Constitution in light of the social problems of today, taking into consideration the evolution of the democratic system as we know it? These matters and many others, I am sure, will concern the reader as he reads through these different decisions and the myriad of dissenting opinions.

The reader will note that with very few exceptions, these decisions are not unanimous. The usual case is apt to have from one to four dissenting justices. In view of the fact that the Justices themselves cannot agree unanimously on the conclusion to be reached from the application of the law to a set of facts, it is anticipated and assumed that the reader may frequently find himself perplexed by the logic of some of the justices, and the head-on inconsistencies contained in the reasonings of some of the dissents in these very important cases.

This is not an exhaustive collection, but rather cases of consequence which are landmark cases, either in and of themselves, or because they have altered, changed, abrogated, overruled, or otherwise rearranged the relationships which had existed prior to their application. These are cases which have directly affected the social infrastructure of our times. The author has not included cases involving mineral rights, anti-trust matters—tax disputes, maritime matters, etc. Certainly such cases have a considerable social effect on our society. But their impact is more of an indirect one. This work is confined to those cases which have a dynamic impact or a direct and immediate effect on society.

No attempt has been made by the author to prepare or present a comprehensive analysis of the cases reported. That task is left to the reader. This is not meant to be a work of law, but rather a work about laws.

During the period commencing with the 1953 Term of the Supreme Court in which the Court rendered its historic decision in the case of *Brown v Board of Education of Topeka*[1] and ending with the date of this work, 33,888 matters[2] were disposed of by the Supreme Court. In many of these cases, the Court decided not to render any further judgment in the particular matter after studying the record of appeal. In the others, the Court was either required to render a judgment or in its discretion decided that this was the type of case that warranted its attention. The author has selected for inclusion in this work twenty-six of those cases, from this period, in which the Supreme Court rendered a judgment. Whether these twenty-six cases are the most important decisions of the period from a philosophical and sociological viewpoint is a judg-

---

[1] 347 U.S. 483 (May 17, 1954).

[2] Figure arrived at by analyzing Court docket from 1953 Term through 1968 Term. Statistics on Court docket obtained from Harvard Law Review and United States Law Week. The Harvard Law Review each fall publishes an article on the Supreme Court containing statistics for the previous Term. United States Law Week each summer publishes similar statistics.

ment for future historians. Certainly they will number among the most significant opinions rendered by the Court during the span of years in question.

No attempt is made by the author to influence the reader by superimposing the author's opinion over that of the Justices of the Supreme Court. Whenever applicable, an attempt has been made to explain the previous legal doctrine that was changed by the case reported here if the case itself has not clearly set forth how it has changed the law or the interpretation of the law. Where the case has made it clear, then the author will make no attempt to further explain the law as it existed prior to the decisions cited herein.

Teachers in the field of Constitutional law, American politics, U.S. history, comparative government, political science and sociology, all have occasion to refer to and study these cases because of their relevance to the teaching of their disciplines. Law enforcement officials, sociologists, social workers, legislators, and many others must possess a basic understanding of many of these cases if they are to be knowledgeable members of their chosen profession. In order that these individuals may have the benefits not only of the holding or rule of law in a given case, but also the benefit of the logic and the reasonings of the various Justices participating in the decision of the Court, concurring and dissenting opinions are all included in the reports of the cases. It is felt that the entire case with all opinions should be presented in its unabridged form, to enable the reader to make intelligent appraisals of the cases and their ramifications.

It is true that law libraries contain the entire reported decisions of the Supreme Court. But most law libraries are unavailable to individuals not members of the legal profession. Even when available, although the cataloging processes are much simpler than the Dewey Decimal and the Library of Congress Systems, to the uninitiated, they present a formidable obstacle. Consequently, this work contains without any alteration whatsoever, the entire decision in each of the reported cases.

In addition since these cases involve constitutional interpretation, the Constitution and its amendments have been reproduced in their entirety for easy reference by the reader.

This collection of cases is being published at that point in history when the Warren Court has come to an end. Mr. Chief Justice Earl Warren retired on June 23, 1969. When the Court commences its 1969–1970 Term, this coming October, it will be headed by its new Chief Justice, Warren Earl Burger. In addition to this shift, there will be an additional change in the personnel of the Supreme Court this coming Term. President Richard M. Nixon has to appoint a replacement for Justice Abe Fortas who resigned May 14, 1969. These changes should be of particular interest to the student of the Supreme Court for the evolution of the law in our country is directly affected by the judicial complexion of the Supreme Court as an examination of the cases included in this work will reveal. How the impending change on the bench of the Court might affect our law is a consideration which the reader should keep in mind when reading the cases which follow.

It should be noted that the value of this work is not lessened by this impending change of Court personnel. The only thing constant about the law is change as the cases in this work illustrate. Hopefully, one of the chief assets of this work is its portrayal of this phenomena. The shift in Court personnel will merely further this evolutionary process.

The cases reported herein are important cases. They are decisions which have greatly affected, and will continue to affect, our human relationships and our individual freedoms. More often than not, these cases seem to be decided on the basis of Chief Justice Warren's oft asked question, "What is fair?" This concept of fairness appears to play as significant a role in the decision making process of the Court as does the age old "Stare Decisis" Doctrine (like cases should be treated alike). It is left to the historians to pass on the wisdom or correctness of these decisions. But until altered or changed, they are the law of the land. As such, these decisions are cogent to our everyday considerations whether in or out of the classroom.

Kenneth F. McLaughlin
Nashua, New Hampshire

Rights of an Accused

The Warren Court was often the subject of considerable attack with its opinions in many areas causing storms of controversy. In no area was this more prevalent than in those decisions involving criminal law. Some view the court as having shackled the hands of law enforcement officials at a considerable expense to law abiding members of society, while others view these controversial opinions as recognizing basic rights of an accused which have long been trampled upon. Included in this chapter are some of the most significant cases decided by the Court in this area, an examination of which will enable the reader to determine where he stands in this all important debate.

Gideon v. Wainwright*

THE *Gideon Case* is important in that it nationalized the right of an indigent defendant to appointed counsel in any felony prosecution. Before this decision the law of most states provided that a defendant, unable to retain counsel, had to represent himself in all but capital cases. Such state law differed from the federal law. In federal proceedings, counsel have been appointed for indigents since the 1938 Supreme Court decision of *Johnson v Zerbst*.[1] After *Gideon* it was clear that state law must conform to the federal law in this area. The Supreme Court ruled that a defendant in any felony prosecution, federal or state, is entitled to appointed counsel.

Gideon was financially destitute. He was charged with breaking into a poolroom. At his Florida trial he made a pathetic plea to the court. "Your Honor, the United States Constitution says I am

---

* 372 U.S. 335, 83 S.Ct. 792 (March 18, 1963)
[1] 304 U.S. 458, 58 S. Ct. 1019 (1938)

entitled to be represented by a counsel." The trial judge responded, "I am sorry but I cannot appoint counsel to represent you in this case." His response was a proper one under the then existing Florida law. Gideon was tried without the advantage of counsel. He was convicted and sentenced to a term of five years in the state penitentiary at Raiford, Florida.

The case reached the Supreme Court as the result of a petition, handwritten in pencil, and mailed by Gideon from his Florida prison cell.[2] Mr. Justice Abe Fortas, then a prominent Washington attorney, was appointed to argue on Gideon's behalf. He was most persuasive. Without a dissent, the Court overruled one of its prior decisions, *Betts v Brady*.[3]

The *Betts Case,* which had been the law of the land for some twenty-one years, held that the constitution only required that an indigent be furnished counsel in capital cases. In *Gideon* the Court ruled squarely that a state's failure to appoint counsel in a noncapital felony deprived the indigent defendant of due process of law under the Fourteenth Amendment. Gideon's conviction was reversed.

This case was one of the first in a line of recent Supreme Court decisions liberalizing the right to counsel concept. The concept was further expanded in the *Escobedo*,[4] *Miranda*[5] and *Wade*[6] decisions, which are also included in this collection of cases.

The State of Florida decided to prosecute Gideon a second time. A leading Florida attorney specializing in criminal law, W. Fred Turner, defended him. The advantage to be gained through representation by counsel soon became apparent. The state's star witness at both trials was a twenty year old youth named Henry Cook. His eye witness testimony placed Gideon at the scene of the crime. But one very important point was not made at the first trial. Cook had a criminal record himself. At the second trial Turner was quick to capitalize on this fact. Indeed, in his closing argument he suggested that Cook was the real culprit! The jury took only one hour and five minutes to render its verdict: not guilty. After having served nearly two years in the state penitentiary Gideon was at last free.[7]

Text of Case

Charged in a Florida State Court with a noncapital felony, petitioner appeared without funds and without counsel and asked the Court to appoint counsel for him; but this was denied on the

---

[2] N.Y. Times, Aug. 6, 1963, p. 21, col. 2.

[3] 316 U.S. 445 (1942)

[4] 378 U.S. 478, 84 S. Ct. 1758 (1964)

[5] 384 U.S. 436, 86 S. Ct. 1602 (1966)

[6] 388 U.S. 218, 87 S. Ct. 1926 (1967)

[7] N.Y. Times, *supra* note 2.

ground that the state law permitted appointment of counsel for indigent defendants in capital cases only. Petitioner conducted his own defense about as well as could be expected of a layman; but he was convicted and sentenced to imprisonment. Subsequently, he applied to the State Supreme Court for a writ of habeas corpus, on the ground that his conviction violated his rights under the Federal Constitution. The State Supreme Court denied all relief.

Abe Fortas, by appointment of the Court, 370 U.S. 932, argued the cause for petitioner. With him on the brief were *Abe Krash* and *Ralph Temple*.

Bruce R. Jacob, Assistant Attorney General of Florida, argued the cause for respondent. With him on the brief were *Richard W. Ervin*, Attorney General, and *A. G. Spicola, Jr.*, Assistant Attorney General.

J. Lee Rankin, by special leave of Court, argued the cause for the American Civil Liberties Union et al., as *amici curiae*, urging reversal. With him on the brief were *Norman Dorsen, John Dwight Evans, Jr., Melvin L. Wulf, Richard J. Medalie, Howard W. Dixon* and *Richard Yale Feder*.

George D. Mentz, Assistant Attorney General of Alabama, argued the cause for the State of Alabama, as *amicus curiae*, uring affirmance. With him on the brief were *MacDonald Gallion*, Attorney General of Alabama, *T. W. Bruton*, Attorney General of North Carolina, and *Ralph Moody*, Assistant Attorney General of North Carolina.

A brief for the state governments of twenty-two States and Commonwealths, as *amici curiae*, urging reversal, was filed by *Edward J. McCormack, Jr.*, Attorney General of Massachusetts, *Walter F. Mondale*, Attorney General of Minnesota, *Duke W. Dunbar*, Attorney General of Colorado, *Albert L. Coles*, Attorney General of Connecticut, *Eugene Cook*, Attorney General of Georgia, *Shiro Kashiwa*, Attorney General of Hawaii, *Frank Benson*, Attorney General of Idaho, *William G. Clark*, Attorney General of Illinois, *Evan L. Hultman*, Attorney General of Iowa, *John B. Breckinridge*, Attorney General of Kentucky, *Frank E. Hancock*, Attorney General of Maine, *Frank J. Kelley*, Attorney General of Michigan, *Thomas F. Eagleton*, Attorney General of Missouri, *Charles E. Springer*, Attorney General of Nevada, *Mark McElroy*, Attorney General of Ohio, *Leslie R. Burgum*, Attorney General of North Dakota, *Robert Y. Thornton*, Attorney General of Oregon, *J. Joseph Nugent*, Attorney General of Rhode Island, *A. C. Miller*, Attorney General of South Dakota, *John J. O'Connell*, Attorney General of Washington, *C. Donald Robertson*, Attorney General of West Virginia, and *George N. Hayes*, Attorney General of Alaska.

3

Robert Y. Thornton, Attorney General of Oregon, and *Harold W. Adams,* Assistant Attorney General, filed a separate brief for the State of Oregon, as *amicus curiae.*

Mr. Justice BLACK delivered the opinion of the Court.

Petitioner was charged in a Florida state court with having broken and entered a poolroom with intent to commit a misdemeanor. This offense is a felony under Florida law. Appearing in court without funds and without a lawyer, petitioner asked the court to appoint counsel for him, whereupon the following colloquy took place:

"The COURT: Mr. Gideon, I am sorry, but I cannot appoint Counsel to represent you in this case. Under the laws of the State of Florida, the only time the Court can appoint Counsel to represent a Defendant is when that person is charged with a capital offense. I am sorry, but I will have to deny your request to appoint Counsel to defend you in this case.

"The DEFENDANT: The United States Supreme Court says I am entitled to be represented by Counsel."

Put to trial before a jury, Gideon conducted his defense about as well as could be expected from a layman. He made an opening statement to the jury, cross-examined the State's witnesses, presented witnesses in his own defense, declined to testify himself, and made a short argument "emphasizing his innocence to the charge contained in the Information filed in this case." The jury returned a verdict of guilty, and petitioner was sentenced to serve five years in the state prison. Later, petitioner filed in the Florida Supreme Court this habeas corpus petition attacking his conviction and sentence on the ground that the trial court's refusal to appoint counsel for him denied him rights "guaranteed by the Constitution and the Bill of Rights by the United States Government."[1] Treating the petition for habeas corpus as properly before it, the State Supreme Court, "upon consideration thereof" but without an opinion, denied all relief. Since 1942, when Betts v. Brady, 316 U.S. 455, 62 S.Ct. 1252, 86 L.Ed. 1595, was decided by a divided Court, the problem of a defendant's federal constitutional right to counsel in a state court has been a continuing source of controversy and litigation in both state and federal courts.[2] To give this problem

---

[1] Later in the petition for habeas corpus, signed and apparently prepared by petitioner himself, he stated, "I, Clarence Earl Gideon, claim that I was denied the rights of the 4th, 5th and 14th amendments of the Bill of Rights."

[2] Of the many such cases to reach this court, recent examples are Carnley v. Cochran, 369 U.S. 506, 82 S.Ct. 884, 8 L.Ed.2d 70 (1962); Hudson v. North Carolina, 363 U.S. 697, 80 S.Ct. 1314, 4 L.Ed.2d 1500 (1960); Moore v. Michigan, 355 U.S. 155, 78 S.Ct. 191, 2 L.Ed.2d 167 (1957). Illustrative cases in the state courts are Artrip v. State, 41 Ala.App.

another review here, we granted certiorari, 370 U.S. 908, 82 S.Ct. 1259, 8 L.Ed.2d 403. Since Gideon was proceeding *in forma pauperis,* we appointed counsel to represent him and requested both sides to discuss in their briefs and oral arguments the following: "Should this Court's holding in Betts v. Brady, 316 U.S. 455, 62 S.Ct. 1252, 86 L.Ed. 1595, be reconsidered?"

I.

The facts upon which Betts claimed that he had been unconstitutionally denied the right to have counsel appointed to assist him are strikingly like the facts upon which Gideon here bases his federal constitutional claim. Betts was indicted for robbery in a Maryland state court. On arraignment, he told the trial judge of his lack of funds to hire a lawyer and asked the court to appoint one for him. Betts was advised that it was not the practice in that county to appoint counsel for indigent defendants except in murder and rape cases. He then pleaded not guilty, had witnesses summoned, cross-examined the State's witnesses, examined his own, and chose not to testify himself. He was found guilty by the judge, sitting without a jury, and sentenced to eight years in prison. Like Gideon, Betts sought release by habeas corpus, alleging that he had been denied the right to assistance of counsel in violation of the Fourteenth Amendment. Betts was denied any relief, and on review this Court affirmed. It was held that a refusal to appoint counsel for an indigent defendant charged with a felony did not necessarily violate the Due Process Clause of the Fourteenth Amendment, which for reasons given the Court deemed to be the only applicable federal constitutional provision. The Court said:
"Asserted denial [of due process] is to be tested by an appraisal of the totality of facts in a given case. That which may, in one setting, constitute a denial of fundamental fairness, shocking to the universal sense of justice, may, in other circumstances, and in the light of other considerations, fall short of such denial." 316 U.S., at 462, 62 S.Ct., at 1256, 86 L.Ed. 1595.

Treating due process as "a concept less rigid and more fluid than those envisaged in other specific and particular provisions of the Bill of Rights," the Court held that refusal to appoint counsel under the particular facts and circumstances in the Betts case was not so

492, 136 So.2d 574 (Ct.App.Ala. 1962); Shaffer v. Warden, 211 Md. 635, 126 A.2d 573 (1956). For examples of commentary, see Allen, The Supreme Court, Federalism, and State Systems of Criminal Justice, 8 De Paul L.Rev. 213 (1959); Kamisar, The Right to Counsel and the Fourteenth Amendment: A Dialogue on "The Most Pervasive Right" of an Accused, 30 U. of Chi.L.Rev. 1 (1962); The Right to Counsel, 45 Minn.L.Rev. 693 (1961).

"offensive to the common and fundamental ideas of fairness" as to amount to a denial of due process. Since the facts and circumstances of the two cases are so nearly indistinguishable, we think the Betts v. Brady holding if left standing would require us to reject Gideon's claim that the Constitution guarantees him the assistance of counsel. Upon full reconsideration we conclude that Betts v. Brady should be overruled.

II.

The Sixth Amendment provides, "In all criminal prosecutions, the accused shall enjoy the right * * * to have the Assistance of Counsel for his defence." We have construed this to mean that in federal courts counsel must be provided for defendants unable to employ counsel unless the right is competently and intelligently waived.[3] Betts argued that this right is extended to indigent defendants in state courts by the Fourteenth Amendment. In response the Court stated that, while the Sixth Amendment laid down "no rule for the conduct of the states, the question recurs whether the constraint laid by the amendment upon the national courts expresses a rule so fundamental and essential to a fair trial, and so, to due process of law, that it is made obligatory upon the states by the Fourteenth Amendment." 316 U.S., at 465, 62 S.Ct., at 1257, 86 L.Ed. 1595. In order to decide whether the Sixth Amendment's guarantee of counsel is of this fundamental nature, the Court in Betts set out and considered "[r]elevant data on the subject * * * afforded by constitutional and statutory provisions subsisting in the colonies and the states prior to the inclusion of the Bill of Rights in the national Constitution, and in the constitutional, legislative, and judicial history of the states to the present date." 316 U.S., at 465, 62 S.Ct., at 1257. On the basis of this historical data the Court concluded that "appointment of counsel is not a fundamental right, essential to a fair trial." 316 U.S. at 471, 62 S.Ct., at 1261. It was for this reason the Betts Court refused to accept the contention that the Sixth Amendment's guarantee of counsel for indigent federal defendants was extended to or, in the words of that Court, "made obligatory upon the states by the Fourteenth Amendment". Plainly, had the Court concluded that appointment of counsel for an indigent criminal defendant was "a fundamental right, essential to a fair trial," it would have held that the Fourteenth Amendment requires appointment of counsel in a state court, just as the Sixth Amendment requires in a federal court.

---

[3] Johnson v. Zerbst, 304 U.S. 458, 58 S.Ct. 1019, 82 L.Ed. 1461 (1938).

We think the Court in Betts had ample precedent for acknowledging that those guarantees of the Bill of Rights which are fundamental safeguards of liberty immune from federal abridgment are equally protected against state invasion by the Due Process Clause of the Fourteenth Amendment. This same principle was recognized, explained, and applied in Powell v. Alabama, 287 U.S. 45, 53 S.Ct. 55, 77 L.Ed. 158 (1932), a case upholding the right of counsel, where the Court held that despite sweeping language to the contrary in Hurtado v. California, 110 U.S. 516, 4 S.Ct. 292, 28 L.Ed. 232 (1884), the Fourteenth Amendment "embraced" those " 'fundamental principles of liberty and justice which lie at the base of all our civil and political institutions,' " even though they had been "specifically dealt with in another part of the Federal Constitution." 287 U.S., at 67, 53 S.Ct., at 63, 77 L.Ed. 158. In many cases other than Powell and Betts, this Court has looked to the fundamental nature of original Bill of Rights guarantees to decide whether the Fourteenth Amendment makes them obligatory on the States. Explicitly recognized to be of this "fundamental nature" and therefore made immune from state invasion by the Fourteenth, or some part of it, are the First Amendment's freedoms of speech, press, religion, assembly, association, and petition for redress of grievances.[4] For the same reason, though not always in precisely the same terminology, the Court has made obligatory on the States the Fifth Amendment's command that private property shall not be taken for public use without just compensation,[5] the Fourth Amendment's prohibition of unreasonable searches and seizures,[6] and the Eighth's ban on cruel and unusual punishment.[7] On the

---

[4] E. g., Gitlow v. New York, 268 U.S. 652, 666, 45 S.Ct. 625, 629, 69 L.Ed. 1138 (1925) (speech and press); Lovell v. City of Griffin, 303 U.S. 444, 450, 58 S.Ct. 666, 668, 82 L.Ed. 949 (1938) (speech and press); Staub v. City of Baxley, 355 U.S. 313, 321, 78 S.Ct. 277, 281, 2 L.Ed. 2d 302 (1958) (speech); Grosjean v. American Press Co., 297 U.S. 233, 244, 56 S.Ct. 444, 446, 80 L.Ed. 660 (1936) (press); Cantwell v. Connecticut, 310 U.S. 296, 303, 60 S.Ct. 900, 903, 84 L.Ed. 1213 (1940) (religion); De Jonge v. Oregon, 299 U.S. 353, 364, 57 S.Ct. 255, 259, 81 L.Ed. 278 (1937) (assembly); Shelton v. Tucker, 364 U.S. 479, 486, 488, 81 S.Ct. 247, 251, 252, 5 L.Ed.2d 231 (1960) (association); Louisiana ex rel. Gremillion v. NAACP, 366 U.S. 293, 296, 81 S.Ct. 1333, 1335, 6 L.Ed.2d 301 (1961) (association); Edwards v. South Carolina, 372 U.S. 229, 83 S.Ct. 680 (1963) (speech, assembly, petition for redress of grievances).

[5] E. g., Chicago, B. & Q. R. Co. v. Chicago, 166 U.S. 226, 235–241, 17 S.Ct. 581, 584–586, 41 L.Ed. 979 (1897); Smyth v. Ames, 169 U.S. 466, 522–526, 18 S.Ct. 418, 424–426, 42 L.Ed. 819 (1898).

[6] E. g., Wolf v. Colorado, 338 U.S. 25, 27–28, 69 S.Ct. 1359, 1361, 93 L.Ed. 1782 (1949); Elkins v. United States, 364 U.S. 206, 213, 80 S.Ct. 1437, 1441, 4 L.Ed.2d 1669 (1960); Mapp v. Ohio, 367 U.S. 643, 655, 81 S.Ct. 1684, 1691, 6 L.Ed.2d 1081 (1961).

[7] Robinson v. California, 370 U.S. 660, 666, 82 S.Ct. 1417, 1420, 8 L.Ed.2d 758 (1962).

other hand, this Court in Palko v. Connecticut, 302 U.S. 319, 58 S.Ct. 149, 82 L.Ed. 288 (1937), refused to hold that the Fourteenth Amendment made the double jeopardy provision of the Fifth Amendment obligatory on the States. In so refusing, however, the Court, speaking through Mr. Justice Cardozo, was careful to emphasize that "immunities that are valid as against the federal government by force of the specific pledges of particular amendments have been found to be implicit in the concept of ordered liberty, and thus, through the Fourteenth Amendment, become valid as against the states" and that guarantees "in their origin * * * effective against the federal government alone" had by prior cases "been taken over from the earlier articles of the Federal Bill of Rights and brought within the Fourteenth Amendment by a process of absorption." 302 U.S., at 324–325, 326, 58 S.Ct., at 152.

We accept Betts v. Brady's assumption, based as it was on our prior cases, that a provision of the Bill of Rights which is "fundamental and essential to a fair trial" is made obligatory upon the States by the Fourteenth Amendment. We think the Court in Betts was wrong, however, in concluding that the Sixth Amendment's guarantee of counsel is not one of these fundamental rights. Ten years before Betts v. Brady, this Court, after full consideration of all the historical data examined in Betts, had unequivocally declared that "the right to the aid of counsel is of this fundamental character." Powell v. Alabama, 287 U.S. 45, 68, 53 S.Ct. 55, 63, 77 L.Ed. 158 (1932). While the Court at the close of its Powell opinion did by its language, as this Court frequently does, limit its holding to the particular facts and circumstances of that case, its conclusions about the fundamental nature of the right to counsel are unmistakable. Several years later, in 1936, the Court re-emphasized what it had said about the fundamental nature of the right to counsel in this language:

"We concluded that certain fundamental rights, safeguarded by the first eight amendments against federal action, were also safeguarded against state action by the due process of law clause of the Fourteenth Amendment, and among them the fundamental right of the accused to the aid of counsel in a criminal prosecution." Grosjean v. American Press Co., 297 U.S. 233, 243–244, 56 S.Ct. 444, 446, 80 L.Ed. 660 (1936).

And again in 1938 this Court said:

"[The assistance of counsel] is one of the safeguards of the Sixth Amendment deemed necessary to insure fundamental human rights of life and liberty. * * * The Sixth Amendment stands as a constant admonition that if the constitutional safeguards it provides be lost, justice will not 'still be done.' " Johnson v. Zerbst, 304

8

U.S. 458, 462, 58 S.Ct. 1019, 1022, 82 L.Ed. 1461 (1938). To the same effect, see Avery v. Alabama, 308 U.S. 444, 60 S.Ct. 321, 84 L.Ed. 377 (1940), and Smith v. O'Grady, 312 U.S. 329, 61 S.Ct. 572, 85 L.Ed. 859 (1941).

In light of these and many other prior decisions of this Court, it is not surprising that the Betts Court, when faced with the contention that "one charged with crime, who is unable to obtain counsel, must be furnished counsel by the state," conceded that "[e]xpressions in the opinions of this court lend color to the argument * * *" 316 U.S., at 462–463, 62 S.Ct., at 1256, 86 L.Ed. 1595. The fact is that in deciding as it did—that "appointment of counsel is not a fundamental right, essential to a fair trial"—the Court in Betts v. Brady made an abrupt break with its own well-considered precedents. In returning to these old precedents, sounder we believe than the new, we but restore constitutional principles established to achieve a fair system of justice. Not only these precedents but also reason and reflection require us to recognize that in our adversary system of criminal justice, any person haled into court, who is too poor to hire a lawyer, cannot be assured a fair trial unless counsel is provided for him. This seems to us to be an obvious truth. Governments, both state and federal, quite properly spend vast sums of money to establish machinery to try defendants accused of crime. Lawyers to prosecute are everywhere deemed essential to protect the public's interest in an orderly society. Similarly, there are few defendants charged with crime, few indeed, who fail to hire the best lawyers they can get to prepare and present their defenses. That government hires lawyers to prosecute and defendants who have the money hire lawyers to defend are the strongest indications of the widespread belief that lawyers in criminal courts are necessities, not luxuries. The right of one charged with crime to counsel may not be deemed fundamental and essential to fair trials in some countries, but it is in ours. From the very beginning, our state and national constitutions and laws have laid great emphasis on procedural and substantive safeguards designed to assure fair trials before impartial tribunals in which every defendant stands equal before the law. This noble ideal cannot be realized if the poor man charged with crime has to face his accusers without a lawyer to assist him. A defendant's need for a lawyer is nowhere better stated than in the moving words of Mr. Justice Sutherland in Powell v. Alabama:

"The right to be heard would be, in many cases, of little avail if it did not comprehend the right to be heard by counsel. Even the intelligent and educated layman has small and sometimes no skill in the science of law. If charged with crime, he is incapable, generally, of determining for himself whether the indictment is

9

good or bad. He is unfamiliar with the rules of evidence. Left without the aid of counsel he may be put on trial without a proper charge, and convicted upon incompetent evidence, or evidence irrelevant to the issue or otherwise inadmissible. He lacks both the skill and knowledge adequately to prepare his defense, even though he have a perfect one. He requires the guiding hand of counsel at every step in the proceedings against him. Without it, though he be not guilty, he faces the danger of conviction because he does not know how to establish his innocence." 287 U.S., at 68–69, 53 S.Ct., at 64, 77 L.Ed. 158.

The Court in Betts v. Brady departed from the sound wisdom upon which the Court's holding in Powell v. Alabama rested. Florida, supported by two other States, has asked that Betts v. Brady be left intact. Twenty-two States, as friends of the Court, argue that Betts was "an anachronism when handed down" and that it should now be overruled. We agree.

The judgment is reversed and the cause is remanded to the Supreme Court of Florida for further action not inconsistent with this opinion.

Reversed.

Mr. Justice DOUGLAS.

While I join the opinion of the Court, a brief historical résumé of the relation between the Bill of Rights and the first section of the Fourteenth Amendment seems pertinent. Since the adoption of that Amendment, ten Justices have felt that it protects from infringement by the States the privileges, protections, and safeguards granted by the Bill of Rights.

Justice Field, the first Justice Harlan, and probably Justice Brewer, took that position in O'Neil v. Vermont, 144 U.S. 323, 362–363, 370–371, 12 S.Ct. 693, 708, 711, 36 L.Ed. 450, as did Justices Black, Douglas, Murphy and Rutledge in Adamson v. California, 332 U.S. 46, 71–72, 124, 67 S.Ct. 1672, 1683, 1686, 91 L.Ed. 1903. And see Poe v. Ullman, 367 U.S. 497, 515–522, 81 S.Ct. 1752, 6 L.Ed. 2d 989 (dissenting opinion). That view was also expressed by Justices Bradley and Swayne in the Slaughter-House Cases, 16 Wall. 36, 118–119, 122, 21 L.Ed. 394, and seemingly was accepted by Justice Clifford when he dissented with Justice Field in Walker v. Sauvinet, 92 U.S. 90, 92, 23 L.Ed. 678.[1] Unfortunately it has

---

[1] Justices Bradley, Swayne and Field emphasized that the first eight Amendments granted citizens of the United States certain privileges and immunities that were protected from abridgment by the States by the Fourteenth Amendment. See Slaughter-House Cases, supra. 16 Wall. at 118-119, 21 L.Ed. 394; O'Neil v. Vermont, supra, 144 U.S.

never commanded a Court. Yet, happily, all constitutional questions are always open. Erie R. Co. v. Tompkins, 304 U.S. 64, 58 S.Ct. 817, 82 L.Ed. 1188. And what we do today does not foreclose the matter.

My Brother HARLAN is of the view that a guarantee of the Bill of Rights that is made applicable to the States by reason of the Fourteenth Amendment is a lesser version of that same guarantee as applied to the Federal Government.[2] Mr. Justice Jackson shared that view.[3] But that view has not prevailed[4] and rights protected against state invasion by the Due Process Clause of the Fourteenth Amendment are not watered-down versions of what the Bill of Rights guarantees.

Mr. Justice CLARK, concurring in the result.

In Bute v. Illinois, 333 U.S. 640, 68 S.Ct. 763, 92 L.Ed. 986 (1948) this Court found no special circumstances requiring the appointment of counsel but stated that "if these charges had been capital charges, the court would have been required, both by the state statute and the decisions of this Court interpreting the Fourteenth Amendment, to take some such steps." Id., at 674, 68 S.Ct., at 780. Prior to that case I find no language in any cases in this Court indicating that appointment of counsel in all capital cases was required by the Fourteenth Amendment.[1] At the next Term of the

---

at 363, 12 S.Ct. 708, 36 L.Ed. 450. Justices Harlan and Brewer accepted the same theory in the O'Neil case (see id., at 370–371, 12 S.Ct. at 711), though Justice Harlan indicated that all "persons," not merely "citizens," were given this protection. Ibid. In Twining v. New Jersey, 211 U.S. 78, 117, 29 S.Ct. 14, 27, 53 L.Ed. 97, Justice Harlan's position was made clear: "In my judgment, immunity from self-incrimination is protected against hostile state action, not only by * * * [the Privileges and Immunities Clause], but [also] by * * * [the Due Process Clause]." Justice Brewer, in joining the opinion of the Court, abandoned the view that the entire Bill of Rights applies to the States in Maxwell v. Dow, 176 U.S. 581, 20 S.Ct. 448, 44 L.Ed. 597.

[2] See Roth v. United States, 354 U.S. 476, 501, 506, 77 S.Ct. 1304, 1317, 1320, 1 L.Ed.2d 1498; Smith v. California, 361 U.S. 147, 169, 80 S.Ct. 215, 227, 4 L.Ed.2d 205.

[3] Beauharnais v. Illinois, 343 U.S. 250, 288, 72 S.Ct. 725, 746, 96 L.Ed. 919. Cf. the opinions of Justices Holmes and Brandeis in Gitlow v. New York, 268 U.S. 652, 672, 45 S.Ct. 625, 632, 69 L.Ed. 1138, and Whitney v. California, 274 U.S. 357, 372, 47 S.Ct. 641, 647, 71 L.Ed. 1095.

[4] The cases are collected by Mr. Justice Black in Speiser v. Randall, 357 U.S. 513, 530, 78 S.Ct. 1332, 1552, 2 L.Ed.2d 1460. And see, Ohio ex rel. Eaton v. Price, 364 U.S. 263, 274–276, 80 S.Ct. 1463, 1469–1470, 4 L.Ed.2d 1708.

[1] It might, however, be said that there is such an implication in Avery v. Alabama, 308 U.S. 444, 60 S.Ct. 321, 84 L.Ed. 377 (1940), a capital case in which counsel had been appointed but in which the petitioner claimed a denial of "effective" assistance. The Court in affirming noted that "[h]ad petitioner been denied any representation of counsel at all, such a clear violation of the Fourteenth Amendment's guarantee of assistance of counsel would have required reversal of his conviction." Id., at 445, 60 S.Ct.

11

Court Mr. Justice Reed revealed that the Court was divided as to noncapital cases but that "the due process clause * * * requires counsel for all persons charged with serious crimes * * *." Uveges v. Pennsylvania, 335 U.S. 437, 441, 69 S.Ct. 184, 186, 93 L.Ed. 127 (1948). Finally, in Hamilton v. Alabama, 368 U.S. 52, 82 S.Ct. 157, 7 L.Ed.2d 114 (1961), we said that "[w]hen one pleads to a capital charge without benefit of counsel, we do not stop to determine whether prejudice resulted." Id., at 55, 82 S.Ct., at 159.

That the Sixth Amendment requires appointment of counsel in "all criminal prosecutions" is clear, both from the language of the Amendment and from this Court's interpretation. See Johnson v. Zerbst, 304 U.S. 458, 58 S.Ct. 1019, 82 L.Ed. 1461 (1938). It is equally clear from the above cases, all decided after Betts v. Brady, 316 U.S. 455, 62 S.Ct. 1252, 86 L.Ed. 1595 (1942), that the Fourteenth Amendment requires such appointment in all prosecutions for capital crimes. The Court's decision today, then, does no more than erase a distinction which has no basis in logic and an increasingly eroded basis in authority. In Kinsella v. United States ex rel. Singleton, 361 U.S. 234, 80 S.Ct. 297, 4 L.Ed.2d 268 (1960), we specifically rejected any constitutional distinction between capital and noncapital offenses as regards congressional power to provide for court-martial trials of civilian dependents of armed forces personnel. Having previously held that civilian dependents could not constitutionally be deprived of the protections of Article III and the Fifth and Sixth Amendments in capital cases, Reid v. Covert, 354 U.S. 1, 77 S.Ct. 1222, 1 L.Ed.2d 1148 (1957), we held that the same result must follow in noncapital cases. Indeed, our opinion there foreshadowed the decision today,[2] as we noted that:

"Obviously Fourteenth Amendment cases dealing with state action have no application here, but if they did, we believe that to

---

at 322. No "special circumstances" were recited by the Court, but in citing Powell v. Alabama, 287 U.S. 45, 53 S.Ct. 55, 77 L.Ed. 158 (1932), as authority for its dictum it appears that the Court did not rely solely on the capital nature of the offense.

[2] Portents of today's decision may be found as well in Griffin v. Illinois, 351 U.S. 12, 76 S.Ct. 585, 100 L.Ed. 891 (1956), and Ferguson v. Georgia, 365 U.S. 570, 81 S.Ct. 756, 5 L.Ed.2d 783 (1961). In Griffin, a noncapital case, we held that the petitioner's constitutional rights were violated by the State's pro-cedure, which provided free transcripts for indigent defendants only in capital cases. In Ferguson we struck down a state practice denying the appellant the effective assistance of counsel, cautioning that "[o]ur decision does not turn on the facts that the appellant was tried for a capital offense and was represented by employed counsel. The command of the Fourteenth Amendment also applies in the case of an accused tried for a noncapital offense, or represented by appointed counsel." 365 U.S., at 596, 81 S.Ct. at 770.

deprive civilian dependents of the safeguards of a jury trial here * * * would be as invalid under those cases as it would be in cases of a capital nature." 361 U.S., at 246–247, 80 S.Ct., at 304, 4 L.Ed.2d 268.

I must conclude here, as in Kinsella, supra, that the Constitution makes no distinction between capital and noncapital cases. The Fourteenth Amendment requires due process of law for the deprival of "liberty" just as for deprival of "life," and there cannot constitutionally be a difference in the quality of the process based merely upon a supposed difference in the sanction involved. How can the Fourteenth Amendment tolerate a procedure which it condemns in capital cases on the ground that deprival of liberty may be less onerous than deprival of life—a value judgment not universally accepted[3]—or that only the latter deprival is irrevocable? I can find no acceptable rationalization for such a result, and I therefore concur in the judgment of the Court.

Mr. Justice HARLAN, concurring.

I agree that Betts v. Brady should be overruled, but consider it entitled to a more respectful burial than has been accorded, at least on the part of those of us who were not on the Court when that case was decided.

I cannot subscribe to the view that Betts v. Brady represented "an abrupt break with its own well-considered precedents." Ante, p. 344. In 1932, in Powell v. Alabama, 287 U.S. 45, 53 S.Ct. 55, 77 L.Ed. 158, a capital case, this Court declared that under the particular facts there presented—"the ignorance and illiteracy of the defendants, their youth, the circumstances of public hostility * * * and above all that they stood in deadly peril of their lives" (287 U.S., at 71, 53 S.Ct., at 65)— the state court had a duty to assign counsel for the trial as a necessary requisite of due process of law. It is evident that these limiting facts were not added to the opinion as an afterthought; they were repeatedly emphasized, see 287 U.S., at 52, 57–58, 71, 53 S.Ct., at 58, 59–60, 65 and were clearly regarded as important to the result.

Thus when this Court, a decade later, decided Betts v. Brady, it did no more than to admit of the possible existence of special circumstances in noncapital as well as capital trials, while at the same time insisting that such circumstances be shown in order to establish a denial of due process. The right to appointed counsel had been recognized as being considerably broader in federal prose-

---

[3] See, e. g., Barzun, In Favor of Capital Punishment, 31 American Scholar 181, 188–189 (1962).

cutions, see Johnson v. Zerbst, 304 U.S. 458, 58 S.Ct. 1019, 82 L.Ed. 1461, but to have imposed these requirements on the States would indeed have been "an abrupt break" with the almost immediate past. The declaration that the right to appointed counsel in state prosecutions, as established in Powell v. Alabama, was not limited to capital cases was in truth not a departure from, but an extension of, existing precedent.

The principles declared in Powell and in Betts, however, have had a troubled journey throughout the years that have followed first the one case and then the other. Even by the time of the Betts decision, dictum in at least one of the Court's opinions had indicated that there was an absolute right to the services of counsel in the trial of state capital cases.[1] Such dicta continued to appear in subsequent decisions,[2] and any lingering doubts were finally eliminated by the holding of Hamilton v. Alabama, 368 U.S. 52, 82 S.Ct. 157, 7 L.Ed.2d 114.

In noncapital cases, the "special circumstances" rule has continued to exist in form while its substance has been substantially and steadily eroded. In the first decade after Betts, there were cases in which the Court found special circumstances to be lacking, but usually by a sharply divided vote.[3] However, no such decision has been cited to us, and I have found none, after Quicksall v. Michigan, 339 U.S. 660, 70 S.Ct. 910, 94 L.Ed. 1188 decided in 1950. At the same time, there have been not a few cases in which special circumstances were found in little or nothing more than the "complexity" of the legal questions presented, although those questions were often of only routine difficulty.[4] The Court has come to recognize, in other words, that the mere existence of a serious criminal charge constituted in itself special circumstances requiring the services of counsel at trial. In truth the Betts v. Brady rule is no longer a reality.

This evolution, however, appears not to have been fully recognized by many state courts, in this instance charged with the front-line responsibility for the enforcement of constitutional rights.[5] To con-

---

[1] Avery v. Alabama, 308 U.S. 444, 445, 60 S.Ct. 321, 84 L.Ed. 377.

[2] E. g., Bute v. Illinois, 333 U.S. 640, 674, 68 S.Ct. 763, 780, 92 L.Ed. 986; Uveges v. Pennsylvania, 335 U.S. 437, 441, 69 S.Ct. 184, 185, 93 L.Ed. 127.

[3] E. g., Foster v. Illinois, 332 U.S. 134, 67 S.Ct. 1716, 91 L.Ed. 1955; Bute v. Illinois, 333 U.S. 640, 68 S.Ct. 763, 92 L.Ed. 986; Gryger v. Burke, 334 U.S. 728, 68 S.Ct. 1256, 92 L.Ed. 1683.

[4] E. g., Williams v. Kaiser, 323 U.S. 471, 65 S.Ct. 363, 89 L.Ed. 398; Hudson v. North Carolina, 363 U.S. 697, 80 S.Ct. 1314, 3 L.Ed.2d 1500; Chewning v. Cunningham, 368 U.S. 443, 82 S.Ct. 498, 7 L.Ed.2d 442.

[5] See, e. g., Commonwealth ex rel. Simon v. Maroney, 405 Pa. 562, 176 A.2d 94 (1961); Shaffer v. Warden, 211 Md. 635, 126 A.2d 573 (1956); Henderson v. Bannan, 256 F.2d 363 (C.A.6th Cir. 1958).

tinue a rule which is honored by this Court only with lip service is not a healthy thing and in the long run will do disservice to the federal system.

The special circumstances rule has been formally abandoned in capital cases, and the time has now come when it should be similarly abandoned in noncapital cases, at least as to offenses which, as the one involved here, carry the possibility of a substantial prison sentence. (Whether the rule should extend to *all* criminal cases need not now be decided.) This indeed does no more than to make explicit something that has long since been foreshadowed in our decisions.

In agreeing with the Court that the right to counsel in a case such as this should now be expressly recognized as a fundamental right embraced in the Fourteenth Amendment, I wish to make a further observation. When we hold a right or immunity, valid against the Federal Government, to be "implicit in the concept of ordered liberty"[6] and thus valid against the States, I do not read our past decisions to suggest that by so holding, we automatically carry over an entire body of federal law and apply it in full sweep to the States. Any such concept would disregard the frequently wide disparity between the legitimate interests of the States and of the Federal Government, the divergent problems that they face, and the significantly different consequences of their actions. Cf. Roth v. United States, 354 U.S. 476, 496–508, 77 S.Ct. 1304, 1315–1321, 1 L.Ed.2d 1498 (separate opinion of this writer). In what is done today I do not understand the Court to depart from the principles laid down in Palko v. Connecticut, 302 U.S. 319, 58 S.Ct. 149, 82 L.Ed. 288, or to embrace the concept that the Fourteenth Amendment "incorporates" the Sixth Amendment as such.

On these premises I join in the judgment of the Court.

Escobedo v. Illinois*

The *Escobedo Case* concerns itself with ascertaining the point in time when an individual's right to counsel attaches. It is a significant decision in that the opinion establishes guidelines for making such a determination.

Suspected of having participated in a murder, Danny Escobedo was brought to the police station where a lengthy interrogation began. For a considerable time, his repeated response to the police

---

6 Palko v. Connecticut, 302 U.S. 319, 325, 58 S.Ct. 149, 152, 82 L.Ed. 288.
* 378 U.S. 478, 84 S.Ct. 1758 (June 22, 1964)

was "I am sorry, but I would like to have advice from my lawyer". Denied access to his attorney, who was present at the station house attempting in vain to see his client, Escobedo made damaging statements. These damaging statements were admitted at his trial and Escobedo was convicted.

In a close five to four decision written by Mr. Justice Goldberg the Court held that the right to counsel attaches when "the investigation is no longer a general inquiry into an unsolved crime but has begun to focus upon a particular suspect." The Supreme Court reversed Escobedo's conviction holding that he had been denied assistance of counsel in violation of the due process clause of the Fourteenth Amendment.

The four dissenting justices (White, Clark, Stewart and Harlan) express an opinion, supported by many in this country, that the decision unnecessarily hampers effective law enforcement. This view is succinctly stated by Harlan in his dissent where he states that the majority rule is "ill conceived and that it seriously and unjustifiably fetters perfectly legitimate methods of criminal law enforcement."

So begins a new struggle of liberal versus conservative views in the Supreme Court, a struggle focusing on the Constitutional right of an accused to counsel. In the case of *Gideon v Wainwright*[1] the Supreme Court unanimously ruled that the right to counsel exists in all felony prosecutions. The *Escobedo case* expands the concept of right to counsel to a considerable extent, but unanimity is absent. The liberal view prevails but by the narrowest of margins. The next significant battle in this struggle was waged in *Miranda v Arizona*[2] which is the next reported decision in this collection of cases.

Upon the reversal of Escobedo's conviction, he was permitted to go free. Unable to use the now inadmissible statements of the accused, the State of Illinois declined to prosecute him again. But Escobedo did not remain out of trouble for long. Since his release he has had several clashes with the law, the most serious of these encounters involving violations of the Federal Narcotic laws. On February 20, 1968, Escobedo was sentenced to 22 years in federal prison on charges of selling heroin to an undercover agent of the Federal Bureau of Narcotics.[3] On May 29, 1968, Escobedo was given another 20 year sentence to federal prison for selling marijuana.[4] Escobedo is presently serving these sentences concurrently.

---

[1] Gideon v. Wainwright, 372 U.S. 335, 83 S.Ct. 792 (March 18, 1963).

[2] Miranda v. Arizona, 384 U.S. 436, 86 S.Ct. 1602 (June 13, 1966).

[3] N.Y. Times, Feb. 21, 1968, p. 33, col. 8.

[4] N.Y. Times, May 30, 1968, p. 22, col. 1.

Text of Case

Petitioner, a 22-year-old of Mexican extraction, was arrested with his sister and taken to police headquarters for interrogation in connection with the fatal shooting, about 11 days before, of his brother-in-law. He had been arrested shortly after the shooting, but had made no statement, and was released after his lawyer obtained a writ of habeas corpus from a state court. Petitioner made several requests to see his lawyer, who, though present in the building, and despite persistent efforts, was refused access to his client. Petitioner was not advised by the police of his right to remain silent and, after persistent questioning by the police, made a damaging statement to an Assistant State's Attorney which was admitted at the trial. Convicted of murder, he appealed to the State Supreme Court, which affirmed the conviction.

Barry L. Kroll argued the cause for petitioner. With him on the brief was *Donald M. Haskell.*

James R. Thompson argued the cause for respondent. With him on the brief were *Daniel P. Ward* and *Elmer C. Kissane.*

Bernard Weisberg argued the cause for the American Civil Liberties Union, as *amicus curiae,* urging reversal. With him on the brief was *Walter T. Fisher.*

Mr. Justice GOLDBERG delivered the opinion of the Court.

The critical question in this case is whether, under the circumstances, the refusal by the police to honor petitioner's request to consult with his lawyer during the course of an interrogation constitutes a denial of "the Assistance of Counsel" in violation of the Sixth Amendment to the Constitution as "made obligatory upon the States by the Fourteenth Amendment," Gideon v. Wainwright, 372 U.S. 335, 342, 83 S.Ct. 792, 795, 9 L.Ed.2d 799, and thereby renders inadmissible in a state criminal trial any incriminating statement elicited by the police during the interrogation.

On the night of January 19, 1960, petitioner's brother-in-law was fatally shot. In the early hours of the next morning, at 2:30 a.m., petitioner was arrested without a warrant and interrogated. Petitioner made no statement to the police and was released at 5 that afternoon pursuant to a state court writ of habeas corpus obtained by Mr. Warren Wolfson, a lawyer who had been retained by petitioner.

On January 30, Benedict DiGerlando, who was then in police custody and who was later indicted for the murder along with petitioner, told the police that petitioner had fired the fatal shots. Between 8 and 9 that evening, petitioner and his sister, the widow of the deceased, were arrested and taken to police headquarters.

17

En route to the police station, the police "had handcuffed the defendant behind his back," and "one of the arresting officers told defendant that DiGerlando had named him as the one who shot" the deceased. Petitioner testified, without contradiction, that the "detectives said they had us pretty well, up pretty tight, and we might as well admit to this crime," and that he replied, "I am sorry but I would like to have advice from my lawyer." A police officer testified that although petitioner was not formally charged "he was in custody" and "couldn't walk out the door."

Shortly after petitioner reached police headquarters, his retained lawyer arrived. The lawyer described the ensuing events in the following terms:

"On that day I received a phone call [from 'the mother of another defendant'] and pursuant to that phone call I went to the Detective Bureau at 11th and State. The first person I talked to was the Sergeant on duty at the Bureau Desk, Sergeant Pidgeon. I asked Sergeant Pidgeon for permission to speak to my client, Danny Escobedo. * * * Sergeant Pidgeon made a call to the Bureau lockup and informed me that the boy had been taken from the lockup to the Homicide Bureau. This was between 9:30 and 10:00 in the evening. Before I went anywhere, he called the Homicide Bureau and told them there was an attorney waiting to see Escobedo. He told me I could not see him. Then I went upstairs to the Homicide Bureau. There were several Homicide Detectives around and I talked to them. I identified myself as Escobedo's attorney and asked permission to see him. They said I could not. * * * The police officer told me to see Chief Flynn who was on duty. I identified myself to Chief Flynn and asked permission to see my client. He said I could not. * * * I think it was approximately 11:00 o'clock. He said I couldn't see him because they hadn't completed questioning. * * * [F]or a second or two I spotted him in an office in the Homicide Bureau. The door was open and I could see through the office. * * * I waved to him and he waved back and then the door was closed, by one of the officers at Homicide.[1] There were four or five officers milling around the Homicide Detail that night. As to whether I talked to Captain Flynn any later that day, I waited around for another hour or two and went back again and renewed by [sic] request to see my client. He again told me I could not. * * * I filed an official complaint with Commissioner Phelan of the Chicago Police Department. I had a conversation with every police officer I could find. I was told at Homicide that I couldn't see him

---

[1] Petitioner testified that this ambiguous gesture "could have meant most anything," but that he "took it upon [his] own to think that [the lawyer was telling him] not to say anything," and that the lawyer "wanted to talk" to him.

18

and I would have to get a writ of habeas corpus. I left the Homicide Bureau and from the Detective Bureau at 11th and State at approximately 1:00 A.M. [Sunday morning] I had no opportunity to talk to my client that night. I quoted to Captain Flynn the Section of the Criminal Code which allows an attorney the right to see his client."[2]

Petitioner testified that during the course of the interrogation he repeatedly asked to speak to his lawyer and that the police said that his lawyer "didn't want to see" him. The testimony of the police officers confirmed these accounts in substantial detail.

Notwithstanding repeated requests by each, petitioner and his retained lawyer were afforded no opportunity to consult during the course of the entire interrogation. At one point, as previously noted, petitioner and his attorney came into each other's view for a few moments but the attorney was quickly ushered away. Petitioner testified "that he heard a detective telling the attorney the latter would not be allowed to talk to [him] 'until they were done' " and that he heard the attorney being refused permission to remain in the adjoining room. A police officer testified that he had told the lawyer that he could not see petitioner until "we were through interrogating" him.

There is testimony by the police that during the interrogation, petitioner, a 22-year-old of Mexican extraction with no record of previous experience with the police, "was handcuffed"[3] in a standing position and that he "was nervous, he had circles under his eyes and he was upset" and was "agitated" because "he had not slept well in over a week."

It is undisputed that during the course of the interrogation Officer Montejano, who "grew up" in petitioner's neighborhood, who knew his family, and who uses "Spanish language in [his] police work," conferred alone with petitioner "for about a quarter of an hour * * *." Petitioner testified that the officer said to him "in Spanish that my sister and I could go home if I pinned it on Benedict DiGerlando," that "he would see to it that we would go home and be held only as witnesses, if anything, if we had made a statement against DiGerlando * * *, that we would be able to go home that night." Petitioner testified that he made the statement in issue

---

[2] The statute then in effect provided in pertinent part that: "All public officers * * * having the custody of any person * * * restrained of his liberty for any alleged cause whatever, shall, except in cases of imminent danger of escape, admit any practicing attorney * * * whom such person * * * may desire to see or consult * * *." Ill.Rev.Stat. (1959), c. 38, § 477. Repealed as of Jan. 1, 1964, by Act approved Aug. 14, 1963, H.B. No. 851.

[3] The trial judge justified the handcuffing on the ground that it "is ordinary police procedure."

because of this assurance. Officer Montejano denied offering any such assurance.

A police officer testified that during the interrogation the following occurred:

"I informed him of what DiGerlando told me and when I did, he told me that DiGerlando was [lying] and I said, 'Would you care to tell DiGerlando that?' and he said, 'Yes, I will.' So, I brought * * * Escobedo in and he confronted DiGerlando and he told him that he was lying and said, 'I didn't shoot Manuel, you did it.' "

In this way, petitioner, for the first time admitted to some knowledge of the crime. After that he made additional statements further implicating himself in the murder plot. At this point an Assistant State's Attorney, Theodore J. Cooper, was summoned "to take" a statement. Mr. Cooper, an experienced lawyer who was assigned to the Homicide Division to take "statements from some defendants and some prisoners that they had in custody," "took" petitioner's statement by asking carefully framed questions apparently designed to assure the admissibility into evidence of the resulting answers. Mr. Cooper testified that he did not advise petitioner of his constitutional rights, and it is undisputed that no one during the course of the interrogation so advised him.

Petitioner moved both before and during trial to suppress the incriminating statement, but the motions were denied. Petitioner was convicted of murder and he appealed the conviction.

The Supreme Court of Illinois, in its original opinion of February 1, 1963, held the statement inadmissible and reversed the conviction. The court said:

"[I]t seems manifest to us, from the undisputed evidence and the circumstances surrounding defendant at the time of his statement and shortly prior thereto, that the defendant understood he would be permitted to go home if he gave the statement and would be granted an immunity from prosecution."

Compare Lynumn v. Illinois, 372 U.S. 528, 83 S.Ct. 917, 9 L.Ed.2d 922.

The State petitioned for, and the court granted, rehearing. The court then affirmed the conviction. It said: "[T]he officer denied making the promise and the trier of fact believed him. We find no reason for disturbing the trial court's finding that the confession was voluntary."[4] 28 Ill.2d 41, 45–46, 190 N.E.2d 825, 827. The court

---

4 Compare Haynes v. Washington, 373 U.S. 503, 515, 83 S.Ct. 1336, 1344, 10 L.Ed.2d 513 (decided on the same day as the decision of the Illinois Supreme Court here), where we said:

"Our conclusion is in no way foreclosed, as the State contends, by the fact that the state trial judge or the jury may have reached a different result on this issue.

"It is well settled that the duty

also held, on the authority of this Court's decisions in Crooker v. California, 357 U.S. 433, 78 S.Ct. 1287, 2 L.Ed.2d 1448, and Cicenia v. Lagay, 357 U.S. 504, 78 S.Ct. 1297, 2 L.Ed.2d 1523, that the confession was admissible even though "it was obtained after he had requested the assistance of counsel, which request was denied." 28 Ill.2d, at 46, 190 N.E.2d, at 827. We granted a writ of certiorari to consider whether the petitioner's statement was constitutionally admissible at his trial. 375 U.S. 902, 84 S.Ct. 203, 11 L.Ed.2d 143. We conclude, for the reasons stated below, that it was not and, accordingly, we reverse the judgment of conviction.

In Massiah v. United States, 377 U.S. 201, 84 S.Ct. 1199, this Court observed that "a Constitution which guarantees a defendant the aid of counsel at * * * trial could surely vouchsafe no less to an indicted defendant under interrogation by the police in a completely extrajudicial proceeding. Anything less * * * might deny a defendant 'effective representation by counsel at the only stage when legal aid and advice would help him.'" Id., 377 U.S., at 204, 84 S.Ct., at 1202, quoting DOUGLAS, J., concurring in Spano v. New York, 360 U.S. 315, 326, 79 S.Ct. 1202, 1209, 3 L.Ed.2d 1265.

The interrogation here was conducted before petitioner was formally indicted. But in the context of this case, that fact should make no difference. When petitioner requested, and was denied, an opportunity to consult with his lawyer, the investigation had ceased to be a general investigation of "an unsolved crime." Spano v. New York, 360 U.S. 315, 327, 79 S.Ct. 1202, 1209 (STEWART, J., concurring). Petitioner had become the accused, and the purpose of the interrogation was to "get him" to confess his guilt despite his constitutional right not to do so. At the time of his arrest and throughout the course of the interrogation, the police told petitioner that they had convincing evidence that he had fired the fatal shots. Without informing him of his absolute right to remain silent in the face of this accusation, the police urged him to make a statement.[5] As this Court observed many years ago:

---

of constitutional adjudication resting upon this Court requires that the question whether the Due Process Clause of the Fourteenth Amendment has been violated by admission into evidence of a coerced confession be the subject of an *independent* determination here, see, e. g., Ashcraft v. Tennessee, 322 U.S. 143, 147–148, 64 S.Ct. 921, 923, 88 L.Ed. 1192; 'we cannot escape the responsibility of making our own examination of the record,'

Spano v. New York, 360 U.S. 315, 316, 79 S.Ct. 1202, 1203." (Emphasis in original.)

[5] Although there is testimony in the record that petitioner and his lawyer had previously discussed what petitioner should do in the event of interrogation, there is no evidence that they discussed what petitioner should, or could, do in the face of a false accusation that he had fired the fatal bullets.

21

"It cannot be doubted that, placed in the position in which the accused was when the statement was made to him that the other suspected person had charged him with crime, the result was to produce upon his mind the fear that if he remained silent it would be considered an admission of guilt, and therefore render certain his being committed for trial as the guilty person, and it cannot be conceived that the converse impression would not also have naturally arisen that, by denying, there was hope of removing the suspicion from himself." Bram v. United States, 168 U.S. 532, 562, 18 S.Ct. 183, 194, 42 L.Ed. 568.

Petitioner, a layman, was undoubtedly unaware that under Illinois law an admission of "mere" complicity in the murder plot was legally as damaging as an admission of firing of the fatal shots. Illinois v. Escobedo, 28 Ill.2d 41, 190 N.E.2d 825. The "guiding hand of counsel" was essential to advise petitioner of his rights in this delicate situation. Powell v. Alabama, 287 U.S. 45, 69, 53 S.Ct. 55, 64, 77 L.Ed. 158. This was the "stage when legal aid and advice" were most critical to petitioner. Massiah v. United States, supra, 377 U.S., at 204, 84 S.Ct. at 1202. It was a stage surely as critical as was the arraignment in Hamilton v. Alabama, 368 U.S. 52, 82 S.Ct. 157, 7 L.Ed.2d 114, and the preliminary hearing in White v. Maryland, 373 U.S. 59, 83 S.Ct. 1050, 10 L.Ed.2d 193. What happened at this interrogation could certainly "affect the whole trial," Hamilton v. Alabama, supra, 368 U.S. at 54, 82 S.Ct. at 159 since rights "may be as irretrievably lost, if not then and there asserted, as they are when an accused represented by counsel waives a right for strategic purposes." Ibid. It would exalt form over substance to make the right to counsel, under these circumstances, depend on whether at the time of the interrogation, the authorities had secured a formal indictment. Petitioner had, for all practical purposes, already been charged with murder.

The New York Court of Appeals, whose decisions this Court cited with approval in Massiah, 377 U.S. 201, at 205, 84 S.Ct. 1199, at 1202, has recently recognized that, under circumstances such as those here, no meaningful distinction can be drawn between interrogation of an accused before and after formal indictment. In People v. Donovan, 13 N.Y.2d 148, 243 N.Y.S.2d 841, 193 N.E.2d 628, that court, in an opinion by Judge Fuld, held that a "confession taken from a defendant, during a period of detention [prior to indictment], after his attorney had requested and been denied access to him" could not be used against him in a criminal trial.[6]

---

[6] The English Judges' Rules also recognize that a functional rather than a formal test must be applied and that, under circumstances such as those here, no special significance should be attached to formal indictment. The applicable Rule does not permit the police to question an

Id., 13 N.Y.2d at 151, 243 N.Y.S.2d at 842, 193 N.E.2d at 629. The court observed that it "would be highly incongruous if our system of justice permitted the district attorney, the lawyer representing the State, to extract a confession from the accused while his own lawyer, seeking to speak with him was kept from him by the police." Id., 13 N.Y.2d at 152, 243 N.Y.S.2d at 842, 193 N.E.2d at 629.[7]

In Gideon v. Wainwright, 372 U.S. 335, 83 S.Ct. 792, 9 L.Ed.2d 799, we held that every person accused of a crime, whether state or federal, is entitled to a lawyer at trial.[8] The rule sought by the State here, however, would make the trial no more than an appeal from the interrogation; and the "right to use counsel at the formal trial [would be] a very hollow thing [if], for all practical purposes, the conviction is already assured by pretrial examination." In re Groban, 352 U.S. 330, 344, 77 S.Ct. 510, 519, 1 L.Ed.2d 376 (BLACK, J., dissenting).[9] "One can imagine a cynical prosecutor saying: 'Let them have the most illustrious counsel, now. They can't escape the noose. There is nothing that counsel can do for them at the trial.'" Ex parte Sullivan, D.C., 107 F.Supp. 514, 517–518.

It is argued that if the right to counsel is afforded prior to indictment, the number of confessions obtained by the police will diminish significantly, because most confessions are obtained during the period between arrest and indictment,[10] and "any lawyer worth his salt will tell the suspect in no uncertain terms to make no state-

accused, except in certain extremely limited situations not relevant here, at any time after the defendant "has been charged *or informed that he may be prosecuted.*" [1964] Crim.L.Rev. 166–170 (emphasis supplied). Although voluntary statements obtained in violation of these rules are not automatically excluded from evidence the judge may, in the exercise of his discretion, exclude them. "Recent cases suggest that perhaps the judges have been tightening up [and almost] inevitably, the effect of the new Rules will be to stimulate this tendency." Id., at 182.

[7] Canon 9 of the American Bar Association's Canons of Professional Ethics provides that:
"A lawyer should not in any way communicate upon the subject of controversy with a party represented by counsel; much less should he undertake to negotiate or compromise the matter with him, but should deal only with his counsel. It is incumbent upon the lawyer most particularly to avoid everything that may tend to mislead a party not represented by counsel, and he should not undertake to advise him as to the law." See Broeder, Wong Sun v. United States: A Study in Faith and Hope, 42 Neb.L.Rev. 483, 599–604.

[8] Twenty-two States, including Illinois, urged us so to hold.

[9] The Soviet criminal code does not permit a lawyer to be present during the investigation. The Soviet trial has thus been aptly described as "an appeal from the pretrial investigation." Feifer, Justice in Moscow (1964), 86.

[10] See Barrett, Police Practices and the Law—From Arrest to Release or Charge, 50 Cal.L.Rev. 11, 43 (1962).

ment to police under any circumstances." Watts v. Indiana, 338, U.S. 49, 59, 69 S.Ct. 1347, 1357, 93 L.Ed. 1801 (Jackson, J., concurring in part and dissenting in part). This argument, of course, cuts two ways. The fact that many confessions are obtained during this period points up its critical nature as a "stage when legal aid and advice" are surely needed. Massiah v. United States, supra, 377 U.S. at 204, 84 S.Ct. at 1202; Hamilton v. Alabama, supra; White v. Maryland, supra. The right to counsel would indeed be hollow if it began at a period when few confessions were obtained. There is necessarily a direct relationship between the importance of a stage to the police in their quest for a confession and the criticalness of that stage to the accused in his need for legal advice. Our Constitution, unlike some others, strikes the balance in favor of the right of the accused to be advised by his lawyer of his privilege against self-incrimination. See Note, 73 Yale L.J. 1000, 1048–1051 (1964).

We have learned the lesson of history, ancient and modern, that a system of criminal law enforcement which comes to depend on the "confession" will, in the long run, be less reliable[11] and more subject to abuses[12] than a system which depends on extrinsic evidence independently secured through skillful investigation. As Dean Wigmore so wisely said:

"*[A]ny system of administration which permits the prosecution to trust habitually to compulsory self-disclosure as a source of proof must itself suffer morally thereby.* The inclination develops to rely mainly upon such evidence, and to be satisfied with an incomplete investigation of the other sources. The exercise of the power to extract answers begets a forgetfulness of the just limitations of that power. The simple and peaceful process of questioning breeds a readiness to resort to bullying and to physical force and torture. If there is a right to an answer, there soon seems to be a right to the expected answer,—that is, to a confession of guilt. Thus the legitimate use grows into the unjust abuse; ultimately, the innocent are jeopardized by the encroachments of a bad system. Such seems to have been the course of experience in

---

[11] See Committee Print, Subcommittee to Investigate Administration of the Internal Security Act, Senate Committee on the Judiciary, 85th Cong., 1st Sess., reporting and analyzing the proceedings at the XXth Congress of the Communist Party of the Soviet Union, February 25, 1956, exposing the false confessions obtained during the Stalin purges of the 1930's. See also Miller v. United States, 320 F.2d 767, 772–

773 (opinion of Chief Judge Bazelon); Lifton, Thought Reform and the Psychology of Totalism (1961); Rogge, Why Men Confess (1959); Schein, Coercive Persuasion (1961).

[12] See Stephen, History of the Criminal Law, quoted in 8 Wigmore, Evidence (3d ed. 1940), 312; Report and Recommendations of the Commissioners' Committee on Police Arrests for Investigation, District of Columbia (1962).

those legal systems where the privilege was not recognized." 8 Wigmore, Evidence (3d ed. 1940), 309. (Emphasis in original.) This Court also has recognized that "history amply shows that confessions have often been extorted to save law enforcement officials the trouble and effort of obtaining valid and independent evidence * * *." Haynes v. Washington, 373 U.S. 503, 519, 83 S.Ct. 1336, 1346.

We have also learned the companion lesson of history that no system of criminal justice can, or should, survive if it comes to depend for its continued effectiveness on the citizens' abdication through unawareness of their constitutional rights. No system worth preserving should have to *fear* that if an accused is permitted to consult with a lawyer, he will become aware of, and exercise, these rights.[13] If the exercise of constitutional rights will thwart the effectiveness of a system of law enforcement, then there is something very wrong with that system.[14]

We hold, therefore, that where, as here, the investigation is no longer a general inquiry into an unsolved crime but has begun to focus on a particular suspect, the suspect has been taken into police custody, the police carry out a process of interrogations that lends itself to eliciting incriminating statements, the suspect has requested and been denied an opportunity to consult with his lawyer, and the police have not effectively warned him of his absolute constitutional right to remain silent, the accused has been denied "the Assistance of Counsel" in violation of the Sixth Amendment to the Constitution as "made obligatory upon the States by the Fourteenth Amendment," Gideon v. Wainwright, 372 U.S., at 342, 83 S.Ct., at 795, and that no statement elicited by the police during the interrogation may be used against him at a criminal trial.

---

[13] Cf. Report of Attorney General's Committee on Poverty and the Administration of Federal Criminal Justice (1963), 10–11: "The survival of our system of criminal justice and the values which it advances depends upon a constant, searching, and creative questioning of official decisions and assertions of authority at all stages of the process. * * * Persons [denied access to counsel] are incapable of providing the challenges that are indispensable to satisfactory operation of the system. The loss to the interests of accused individuals, occasioned by these failures, are great and apparent. It is also clear that a situation in which persons are required to contest a serious accusation but are denied access to the tools of contest is offensive to fairness and equity. Beyond these considerations, however, is the fact that [this situation is] detrimental to the proper functioning of the system of justice and that the loss in vitality of the adversary system, thereby occasioned, significantly endangers the basic interests of a free community."

[14] The accused may, of course, intelligently and knowingly waive his privilege against self-incrimination and his right to counsel either at a pretrial stage or at the trial. See Johnson v. Zerbst, 304 U.S. 458, 58 S.Ct. 1019, 82 L.Ed. 1461. But no knowing and intelligent waiver of any constitutional right can be said to have occurred under the circumstances of this case.

Crooker v. California, 357 U.S. 433, 78 S.Ct. 1287, does not compel a contrary result. In that case the Court merely rejected the absolute rule sought by petitioner, that "every state denial of a request to contact counsel [is] an infringement of the constitutional right *without regard to the circumstances of the case.*" Id., 357 U.S., at 440, 78 S.Ct., at 1292. (Emphasis in original.) In its place, the following rule was announced:
"[S]tate refusal of a request to engage counsel violates due process not only if the accused is deprived of counsel at trial on the merits, * * * *but also if he is deprived of counsel for any part of the pretrial proceedings,* provided that he is so prejudiced thereby as to infect his subsequent trial with an absence of 'that fundamental fairness essential to the very concept of justice. * * *'
The latter determination necessarily depends upon all the circumstances of the case." 357 U.S., at 439–440, 78 S.Ct., at 1292. (Emphasis added.)
The Court, applying "these principles" to "the sum total of the circumstances [there] during the time petitioner was without counsel," id., 357 U.S., at 440, 78 S.Ct., at 1292, concluded that he had not been fundamentally prejudiced by the denial of his request for counsel. Among the critical circumstances which distinguish that case from this one are that the petitioner there, but not here, was explicitly advised by the police of his constitutional right to remain silent and not to "say anything" in response to the questions, id., 357 U.S., at 437, 78 S.Ct., at 1290, and that petitioner there, but not here, was a well-educated man who had studied criminal law while attending law school for a year. The Court's opinion in Cicenia v. Lagay, 357 U.S. 504, 78 S.Ct. 1297, 2 L.Ed.2d 1523, decided the same day, merely said that the "contention that petitioner had a constitutional right to confer with counsel is disposed of by Crooker v. California * * *." That case adds nothing, therefore, to Crooker. In any event, to the extent that Cicenia or Crooker may be inconsistent with the principles announced today, they are not to be regarded as controlling.[15]

Nothing we have said today affects the powers of the police to investigate "an unsolved crime," Spano v. New York, 360 U.S. 315, 327, 79 S.Ct. 1202, 1209 (STEWART, J., concurring), by gathering information from witnesses and by other "proper investigative efforts." Haynes v. Washington, 373 U.S. 503, 519, 83 S.Ct.

---

[15] The authority of Cicenia v. Lagay, 357 U.S. 504, 78 S.Ct. 1297, and Crooker v. California, 357 U.S. 433, 78 S.Ct. 1287, was weakened by the subsequent decisions of this Court in Hamilton v. Alabama, 368 U.S. 52, 82 S.Ct. 157, White v. Maryland, 373 U.S. 59, 83 S.Ct. 1050, and Massiah v. United States, 377 U.S. 201, 84 S.Ct. 1199 (as the dissenting opinion in the last-cited case recognized).

26

1336, 1346. We hold only that when the process shifts from investigatory to accusatory—when its focus is on the accused and its purpose is to elicit a confession—our adversary system begins to operate, and, under the circumstances here, the accused must be permitted to consult with his lawyer.

The judgment of the Illinois Supreme Court is reversed and the case remanded for proceedings not inconsistent with this opinion.

Reversed and remanded.

Mr. Justice HARLAN, dissenting.

I would affirm the judgment of the Supreme Court of Illinois on the basis of Cicenia v. Lagay, 357 U.S. 504, 78 S.Ct. 1297, decided by this Court only six years ago. Like my Brother White, post, p. 495, I think the rule announced today is most ill-conceived and that it seriously and unjustifiably fetters perfectly legitimate methods of criminal law enforcement.

Mr. Justice STEWART, dissenting.

I think this case is directly controlled by Cicenia v. Lagay, 357 U.S. 504, 78 S.Ct. 1297, 2 L.Ed.2d 1523, and I would therefore affirm the judgment.

Massiah v. United States, 377 U.S. 201, 84 S.Ct. 1199, is not in point here. In that case a federal grand jury had indicted Massiah. He had retained a lawyer and entered a formal plea of not guilty. Under our system of federal justice an indictment and arraignment are followed by a trial, at which the Sixth Amendment guarantees the defendant the assistance of counsel.* But Massiah was released on bail, and thereafter agents of the Federal Government deliberately elicited incriminating statements from him in the absence of his lawyer. We held that the use of these statements against him at his trial denied him the basic protections of the Sixth Amendment guarantee. Putting to one side the fact that the case now before us is not a federal case, the vital fact remains that this case does not involve the deliberate interrogation of a defendant after the initiation of judicial proceedings against him. The Court disregards this basic difference between the present case and Massiah's, with the bland assertion that "that fact should make no difference." Ante, p. 485.

It is "that fact," I submit, which makes all the difference. Under our system of criminal justice the institution of formal, meaningful judicial proceedings, by way of indictment, information, or ar-

---

* "In all criminal prosecutions, the accused shall enjoy the right * * * to have the Assistance of Counsel for his defence."

raignment, marks the point at which a criminal investigation has ended and adversary proceedings have commenced. It is at this point that the constitutional guarantees attach which pertain to a criminal trial. Among those guarantees are the right to a speedy trial, the right of confrontation, and the right to trial by jury. Another is the guarantee of the assistance of counsel. Gideon v. Wainwright, 372 U.S. 335, 83 S.Ct. 792; Hamilton v. Alabama, 368 U.S. 52, 82 S.Ct. 157; White v. Maryland, 373 U.S. 59, 83 S.Ct. 1050.

The confession which the Court today holds inadmissible was a voluntary one. It was given during the course of a perfectly legitimate police investigation of an unsolved murder. The Court says that what happened during this investigation "affected" the trial. I had always supposed that the whole purpose of a police investigation of a murder was to "affect" the trial of the murderer, and that it would be only an incompetent, unsuccessful, or corrupt investigation which would not do so. The Court further says that the Illinois police officers did not advise the petitioner of his "constitutional rights" before he confessed to the murder. This Court has never held that the Constitution requires the police to give any "advice" under circumstances such as these.

Supported by no stronger authority than its own rhetoric, the Court today converts a routine police investigation of an unsolved murder into a distorted analogue of a judicial trial. It imports into this investigation constitutional concepts historically applicable only after the onset of formal prosecutorial proceedings. By doing so, I think the Court perverts those precious constitutional guarantees, and frustrates the vital interests of society in preserving the legitimate and proper function of honest and purposeful police investigation.

Like my Brother CLARK, I cannot escape the logic of my Brother WHITE's conclusions as to the extraordinary implications which emanate from the Court's opinion in this case, and I share their views as to the untold and highly unfortunate impact today's decision may have upon the fair administration of criminal justice. I can only hope we have completely misunderstood what the Court has said.

Mr. Justice WHITE, with whom Mr. Justice CLARK and Mr. Justice STEWART join, dissenting.

In Massiah v. United States, 377 U.S. 201, 84 S.Ct. 1199, the Court held that as of the date of the indictment the prosecution is disentitled to secure admissions from the accused. The Court now moves that date back to the time when the prosecution begins to "focus" on the accused. Although the opinion purports to be limited to the facts of this case, it would be naive to think that the

28

new constitutional right announced will depend upon whether the accused has retained his own counsel, cf. Gideon v. Wainwright, 372 U.S. 335, 83 S.Ct. 792, 9 L.Ed.2d 799; Griffin v. Illinois, 351 U.S. 12, 76 S.Ct. 585, 100 L.Ed. 891; Douglas v. California, 372 U.S. 353, 83 S.Ct. 814, 9 L.Ed.2d 899, or has asked to consult with counsel in the course of interrogation. Cf. Carnley v. Cochran, 369 U.S. 506, 82 S.Ct. 884, 8 L.Ed.2d 70. At the very least the Court holds that once the accused becomes a suspect and, presumably, is arrested, any admission made to the police thereafter is inadmissible in evidence unless the accused has waived his right to counsel. The decision is thus another major step in the direction of the goal which the Court seemingly has in mind—to bar from evidence all admissions obtained from an individual suspected of crime, whether involuntarily made or not. It does of course put us one step "ahead" of the English judges who have had the good sense to leave the matter a discretionary one with the trial court.*
I reject this step and the invitation to go farther which the Court has now issued.

By abandoning the voluntary-involuntary test for admissibility of confessions, the Court seems driven by the notion that it is uncivilized law enforcement to use an accused's own admissions against him at his trial. It attempts to find a home for this new and nebulous rule of due process by attaching it to the right to counsel guaranteed in the federal system by the Sixth Amendment and binding upon the States by virtue of the due process guarantee of the Fourteenth Amendment. Gideon v. Wainwright, supra. The right to counsel now not only entitles the accused to counsel's advice and aid in preparing for trial but stands as an impenetrable barrier to any interrogation once the accused has become a suspect. From that very moment apparently his right to counsel attaches, a rule wholly unworkable and impossible to administer unless police cars are equipped with public defenders and undercover agents and police informants have defense counsel at their side. I would not

---

* "[I]t seems from reported cases that the judges have given up enforcing their own rules, for it is no longer the practice to exclude evidence obtained by questioning in custody. * * * A traditional principle of 'fairness' to criminals, which has quite possibly lost some of the reason for its existence, is maintained in words while it is disregarded in fact. * * *

"The reader may be expecting at this point a vigorous denunciation of the police and of the judges, and a plea for a return to the Judges' Rules as interpreted in 1930. What has to be considered, however, is whether these Rules are a workable part of the machinery of justice. Perhaps the truth is that the Rules have been abandoned, by tacit consent, just because they are an unreasonable restriction upon the activities of the police in bringing criminals to book." Williams, Questioning by the Police: Some Practical Considerations, [1960] Crim. L.Rev. 325, 331–332. See also [1964] Crim.L.Rev. 161–182.

abandon the Court's prior cases defining with some care and analysis the circumstances requiring the presence or aid of counsel and substitute the amorphous and wholly unworkable principle that counsel is constitutionally required whenever he would or could be helpful. Hamilton v. Alabama, 368 U.S. 52, 82 S.Ct. 157, 7 L.Ed.2d 114; White v. Maryland, 373 U.S. 59, 83 S.Ct. 1050, 10 L.Ed2d 193; Gideon v. Wainwright, supra. These cases dealt with the requirement of counsel at proceedings in which definable rights could be won or lost, not with stages where probative evidence might be obtained. Under this new approach one might just as well argue that a potential defendant is constitutionally entitled to a lawyer before, not after, he commits a crime, since it is then that crucial incriminating evidence is put within the reach of the Government by the would-be accused. Until now there simply has been no right guaranteed by the Federal Constitution to be free from the use at trial of a voluntary admission made prior to indictment.

It is incongruous to assume that the provision for counsel in the Sixth Amendment was meant to amend or supersede the self-incrimination provision of the Fifth Amendment, which is now applicable to the States. Malloy v. Hogan, 378 U.S. 1, 84 S.Ct. 1489. That amendment addresses itself to the very issue of incriminating admissions of an accused and resolves it by proscribing only compelled statements. Neither the Framers, the constitutional language, a century of decisions of this Court nor Professor Wigmore provides an iota of support for the idea that an accused has an absolute constitutional right not to answer even in the absence of compulsion—the constitutional right not to incriminate himself by making voluntary disclosures.

Today's decision cannot be squared with other provisions of the Constitution which, in my view, define the system of criminal justice this Court is empowered to administer. The Fourth Amendment permits upon probable cause even compulsory searches of the suspect and his possessions and the use of the fruits of the search at trial, all in the absence of counsel. The Fifth Amendment and state constitutional provisions authorize, indeed require, inquisitorial grand jury proceedings at which a potential defendant, in the absence of counsel, is shielded against no more than compulsory incrimination. Mulloney v. United States, 79 F.2d 566, 578 (C.A. 1st Cir.); United States v. Benjamin, 120 F.2d 521, 522 (C.A. 2d Cir.); United States v. Scully, 225 F.2d 113, 115 (C.A.2d Cir.); United States v. Gilboy, 160 F.Supp. 442 (D.C.M.D.Pa.). A grand jury witness, who may be a suspect, is interrogated and his answers, at least until today, are admissible in evidence at trial. And these provisions have been thought of as constitutional safeguards to persons suspected of an offense. Furthermore, until now, the Constitution has permitted the accused to be fingerprinted and to be identified in a line-up or in the courtroom itself.

The Court chooses to ignore these matters and to rely on the virtues and morality of a system of criminal law enforcement which does not depend on the "confession." No such judgment is to be found in the Constitution. It might be appropriate for a legislature to provide that a suspect should not be consulted during a criminal investigation; that an accused should never be called before a grand jury to answer, even if he wants to, what may well be incriminating questions; and that no person, whether he be a suspect, guilty criminal or innocent by-stander, should be put to the ordeal of responding to orderly noncompulsory inquiry by the State. But this is not the system our Constitution requires. The only "inquisitions" the Constitution forbids are those which compel incrimination. Escobedo's statements were not compelled and the Court does not hold that they were.

This new American judges' rule, which is to be applied in both federal and state courts, is perhaps thought to be a necessary safeguard against the possibility of extorted confessions. To this extent it reflects a deep-seated distrust of law enforcement officers everywhere, unsupported by relevant data or current material based upon our own experience. Obviously law enforcement officers can make mistakes and exceed their authority, as today's decision shows that even judges can do, but I have somewhat more faith than the Court evidently has in the ability and desire of prosecutors and of the power of the appellate courts to discern and correct such violations of the law.

The Court may be concerned with a narrower matter: the unknowing defendant who responds to police questioning because he mistakenly believes that he must and that his admissions will not be used against him. But this worry hardly calls for the broadside the Court has now fired. The failure to inform an accused that he need not answer and that his answers may be used against him is very relevant indeed to whether the disclosures are compelled. Cases in this Court, to say the least, have never placed a premium on ignorance of constitutional rights. If an accused is told he must answer and does not know better, it would be very doubtful that the resulting admissions could be used against him. When the accused has not been informed of his rights at all the Court characteristically and properly looks very closely at the surrounding circumstances. See Ward v. Texas, 316 U.S. 547, 62 S.Ct. 1139, 86 L.Ed. 1663; Haley v. Ohio, 332 U.S. 596, 68 S.Ct. 302, 92 L.Ed. 224; Payne v. Arkansas, 356 U.S. 560, 78 S.Ct. 844, 2

L.Ed.2d 975. I would continue to do so. But, in this case Danny Escobedo knew full well that he did not have to answer and knew full well that his lawyer had advised him not to answer.

I do not suggest for a moment that law enforcement will be destroyed by the rule announced today. The need for peace and order is too insistent for that. But it will be crippled and its task made a great deal more difficult, all in my opinion, for unsound, unstated reasons, which can find no home in any of the provisions of the Constitution.

Miranda v. Arizona*

The *Miranda case*[1] concerns two fundamental rights of an accused, the right to counsel and the right to remain silent. The significance of the decision is best stated in the Court's own words. The opinion sets forth "concrete constitutional guidelines for law enforcement agencies and courts to follow",[2] in the implementation of the above rights.

Ernesto Miranda was taken from his home and brought to the police station where a complaining witness identified him as the man that had raped her. Without advising him that he had a right to have an attorney present, the police began an interrogation which within two hours produced a signed confession. On the basis of this confession, Miranda was convicted.

In overturning Miranda's conviction, the Supreme Court used the opportunity presented to set forth specific constitutional standards to be followed by law enforcement officials. As a result, nearly all policemen and other law enforcement officials now carry a little card in their wallet which contains the "Miranda Warnings", which they read any suspect before questioning him. The necessity of having to give such warnings has opened the floodgates of controversy.

What are the warnings? Prior to any questioning the accused must be warned that he has a right to remain silent and that anything he does say may be used against him. He must also be

---

* 384 U.S. 436, 86 S.Ct. 1602 (June 13, 1966)

Together with No. 760, *Vignera* v. *New York*, on certiorari to the Court of Appeals of New York and No. 761, *Westover* v. *United States*, on certiorari to the United States Court of Appeals for the Ninth Circuit, both argued February 28–March 1, 1966; and No. 584, *California* v. *Stewart*, on certiorari to the Supreme Court of California, argued February 28–March 2, 1966.

[1] The Miranda decision is based on a consideration of four separate cases accepted for review by the Supreme Court. In the interest of simplicity the opinion is generally identified by the name of the first of these cases, *Miranda v. Arizona*.

[2] 384 U.S. 436, at 442, 86 S.Ct. 1602 at 1611.

warned that he has the right to have an attorney present and further, he must be told that if he desires an attorney but cannot afford one, counsel can be appointed to represent him. In addition, it must be made clear that he may elect to exercise these rights at any point after the warnings are given, either before or during any questioning process.[3]

A struggle within the court, between liberal and conservative views on the right to counsel, continues in this case. This struggle commenced in the Escobedo[4] decision where the liberal view prevailed by the narrowest of margins, a five to four decision. In Miranda the liberal view prevails again as the right to counsel concept is expanded even further. However, as in Escobedo, the margin of victory is but one vote with Justices Harlan, Stewart, White and Clark dissenting in Miranda as they did in Escobedo.

It is undisputable that these and similar Supreme Court decisions have had a profound impact on the administration of criminal justice. It is interesting to observe that in many of these cases the law of the land would have evolved in a different direction but for one vote. Had the decisions in Escobedo and Miranda been five to four in favor of sustaining the convictions much of the controversy concerning the present Supreme Court would have been avoided.

Because of the ages of the present Supreme Court justices, coupled with the possibility of resignation for reasons other than retirement,[5] it is likely that there will be a few vacancies on the Supreme Court within a short period of time. The importance of the President's personnel decision—whom he should nominate to fill such vacancies—is readily apparent. The appointment of a man who sides with the conservative views on the Court could change the whole complexion of the law as it is presently evolving.

Text of Case

In each of these cases the defendant while in police custody was questioned by police officers, detectives, or a prosecuting attorney

---

[3] The Supreme Court decision in *Application of Gault*, 387 U.S. 1, 87 S.Ct. 1428 (1967), should be read in connection with the *Miranda case* relative to the extent that these safeguards are applicable to juveniles. The *Gault case* is included in this work and begins on page 142.

[4] *Escobedo v. Illinois*, 378 U.S. 478, 84 S.Ct. 1758 (1964).

[5] Mr. Justice Goldberg resigned July 25, 1965 to accept the United States Ambassadorship to the United Nations. Mr. Justice Tom Clark retired June 12, 1967 to enable his son, Ramsey Clark, to accept an appointment as the Attorney General of the United States. Mr. Justice Abe Fortas resigned May 14, 1969 under pressure from the United States Congress because of certain extra judicial activities he had been engaged in.

in a room in which he was cut off from the outside world. None of the defendants was given a full and effective warning of his rights at the outset of the interrogation process. In all four cases the questioning elicited oral admissions, and in three of them signed statements as well, which were admitted at their trials. All defendants were convicted and all convictions, except in No. 584, were affirmed on appeal.

John J. Flynn argued the cause for petitioner in No. 759. With him on the brief was *John P. Frank. Victor M. Earle III* argued the cause and filed a brief for petitioner in No. 760. *F Conger Fawcett* argued the cause and filed a brief for petitioner in No. 761. *Gordon Ringer*, Deputy Attorney General of California, argued the cause for petitioner in No. 584. With him on the briefs were *Thomas C. Lynch*, Attorney General, and *William E. James*, Assistant Attorney General.

Gary K. Nelson, Assistant Attorney General of Arizona, argued the cause for respondent in No. 759. With him on the brief was *Darrell F. Smith*, Attorney General. *William I. Siegel* argued the cause for respondent in No. 760. With him on the brief was *Aaron E. Koota. Solicitor General Marshall* argued the cause for the United States in No. 761. With him on the brief were *Assistant Attorney General Vinson, Ralph S. Spritzer, Nathan Lewin, Beatrice Rosenberg* and *Ronald L. Gainer. William A. Norris*, by appointment of the Court, 382 U.S. 952, argued the cause and filed a brief for respondent in No. 584.

Telford Taylor, by special leave of Court, argued the cause for the State of New York, as *amicus curiae*, in all cases. With him on the brief were *Louis J. Lefkowitz*, Attorney General of New York, *Samuel A. Hirshowitz*, First Assistant Attorney General, and *Barry Mahoney* and *George D. Zuckerman*, Assistant Attorneys General, joined by the Attorneys General for their respective States and jurisdictions as follows: *Richmond M. Flowers* of Alabama, *Darrell F. Smith* of Arizona, *Bruce Bennett* of Arkansas, *Duke W. Dunbar* of Colorado, *David P. Buckson* of Delaware, *Earl Faircloth* of Florida, *Arthur K. Bolton* of Georgia, *Allan G. Shepard* of Idaho, *William G. Clark* of Illinois, *Robert C. Londerholm* of Kansas, *Robert Matthews* of Kentucky, *Jack P. F. Gremillion* of Louisiana, *Richard J. Dubord* of Maine, *Thomas B. Finan* of Maryland, *Norman H. Anderson* of Missouri, *Forrest H. Anderson* of Montana, *Clarence A. H. Meyer* of Nebraska, *T. Wade Bruton* of North Carolina, *Helgi Johanneson* of North Dakota, *Robert Y. Thornton* of Oregon, *Walter E. Alessandroni of* Pennsylvania, *J. Joseph Nugent* of Rhode Island, *Daniel R. McLeod* of South Carolina, *Waggoner Carr* of Texas, *Robert Y. Button* of Virginia, *John J. O'Connell* of Washington, *C. Donald Robertson of*

West Virginia, *John F. Raper* of Wyoming, *Rafael Hernandez Colon* of Puerto Rico and *Francisco Corneiro* of the Virgin Islands.

Duane R. Nedrud, by special leave of Court, argued the cause for the National District Attorneys Association, as *amicus curiae,* urging affirmance in Nos. 759 and 760, and reversal in No. 584. With him on the brief was *Marguerite D. Oberto.*

Anthony G. Amsterdam, Paul Mishkin, Raymond L. Bradley, Peter Hearn and *Melvin L. Wulf* filed a brief for the American Civil Liberties Union, as *amicus curiae,* in all cases.

Mr. Chief Justice WARREN delivered the opinion of the Court.

The cases before us raise questions which go to the roots of our concepts of American criminal jurisprudence: the restraints society must observe consistent with the Federal Constitution in prosecuting individuals for crime. More specifically, we deal with the admissibility of statements obtained from an individual who is subjected to custodial police interrogation and the necessity for procedures which assure that the individual is accorded his privilege under the Fifth Amendment to the Constitution not to be compelled to incriminate himself.

We dealt with certain phases of this problem recently in Escobedo v. State of Illinois, 378 U.S. 478, 84 S.Ct. 1758, 12 L.Ed.2d 977 (1964). There, as in the four cases before us, law enforcement officials took the defendant into custody and interrogated him in a police station for the purpose of obtaining a confession. The police did not effectively advise him of his right to remain silent or of his right to consult with his attorney. Rather, they confronted him with an alleged accomplice who accused him of having perpetrated a murder. When the defendant denied the accusation and said "I didn't shoot Manuel, you did it," they handcuffed him and took him to an interrogation room. There, while handcuffed and standing, he was questioned for four hours until he confessed. During this interrogation, the police denied his request to speak to his attorney, and they prevented his retained attorney, who had come to the police station, from consulting with him. At his trial, the State, over his objection, introduced the confession against him. We held that the statements thus made were constitutionally inadmissible.

This case has been the subject of judicial interpretation and spirited legal debate since it was decided two years ago. Both state and federal courts, in assessing its implications, have arrived at varying conclusions.[1] A wealth of scholarly material has

---

[1] Compare United States v. Childress, 347 F.2d 448 (C.A. 7th Cir. 1965), with Collins v. Beto, 348 F.2d 823 (C.A. 5th Cir. 1965). Compare People v. Dorado, 62 Cal.2d 338, 42 Cal.Rptr. 169, 398 P.2d 361 (1964) with People v. Hartgraves, 31 Ill.2d 375, 202 N.E.2d 33 (1964).

been written tracing its ramifications and underpinnings.[2] Police and prosecutor have speculated on its range and desirability.[3] We granted certiorari in these cases, 382 U.S. 924, 925, 937, 86 S.Ct. 318, 320, 395, 15 L.Ed.2d 338, 339, 348, in order further to explore some facets of the problems, thus exposed, of applying the privilege against self-incrimination to in-custody interrogation, and to give concrete constitutional guidelines for law enforcement agencies and courts to follow.

We start here, as we did in *Escobedo*, with the premise that our holding is not an innovation in our jurisprudence, but is an application of principles long recognized and applied in other settings. We have undertaken a thorough re-examination of the *Esco-*

---

[2] See, e. g., Enker & Elsen, Counsel for the Suspect: Massiah v. United States, 377 U.S. 201, 84 S.Ct. 1199, 12 L.Ed.2d 246 and Escobedo v. State of Illinois, 49 Minn.L.Rev. 47 (1964); Herman, The Supreme Court and Restrictions on Police Interrogation, 25 Ohio St.L.J. 449 (1964); Kamisar, Equal Justice in the Gatehouses and Mansions of American Criminal Procedure, in Criminal Justice in Our Time 1 (1965); Dowling, Escobedo and Beyond: The Need for a Fourteenth Amendment Code of Criminal Procedure, 56 J.Crim.L., C. & P.S. 143, 156 (1965).

The complex problems also prompted discussions by jurists. Compare Bazelon, Law, Morality, and Civil Liberties, 12 U.C.L.A.L.Rev. 13 (1964), with Friendly, The Bill of Rights as a Code of Criminal Procedure, 53 Calif.L.Rev. 929 (1965).

[3] For example, the Los Angeles Police Chief stated that "If the police are required * * * to * * * establish that the defendant was apprised of his constitutional guarantees of silence and legal counsel prior to the uttering of any admission or confession, and that he intelligently waived these guarantees * * * a whole Pandora's box is opened as to under what circumstances * * * can a defendant intelligently waive these rights. * * * Allegations that modern criminal investigation can compensate for the lack of a confession or admission in every

criminal case is totally absurd!" Parker, 40 L.A.Bar Bull. 603, 607, 642 (1965). His prosecutorial counterpart, District Attorney Younger, stated that "[I]t begins to appear that many of these seemingly restrictive decisions are going to contribute directly to a more effective, efficient and professional level of law enforcement." L. A. Times, Oct. 2, 1965, p. 1. The former Police Commissioner of New York, Michael J. Murphy, stated of *Escobedo*: "What the Court is doing is akin to requiring one boxer to fight by Marquis of Queensbury rules while permitting the other to butt, gouge and bite." N. Y. Times, May 14, 1965, p. 39. The former United States Attorney for the District of Columbia, David C. Acheson, who is presently Special Assistant to the Secretary of the Treasury (for Enforcement), and directly in charge of the Secret Service and the Bureau of Narcotics, observed that "Prosecution procedure has, at most, only the most remote causal connection with crime. Changes in court decisions and prosecution procedure would have about the same effect on the crime rate as an aspirin would have on a tumor of the brain." Quoted in Herman, supra, n. 2, at 500, n. 270. Other views on the subject in general are collected in Weisberg, Police Interrogation of Arrested Person: A Skeptical View, 52 J.Crim.L., C. & P.S. 21 (1961).

bedo decision and the principles it announced, and we reaffirm it. That case was but an explication of basic rights that are enshrined in our Constitution—that "No person * * * shall be compelled in any criminal case to be a witness against himself," and that "the accused shall * * * have the Assistance of Counsel"—rights which were put in jeopardy in that case through official overbearing. These precious rights were fixed in our Constitution only after centuries of persecution and struggle. And in the words of Chief Justice Marshall, they were secured "for ages to come, and * * * designed to approach immortality as nearly as human institutions can approach it," Cohens v. Commonwealth of Virginia, 6 Wheat. 264, 387, 5 L.Ed. 257 (1821).

Over 70 years ago, our predecessors on this Court eloquently stated:

"The maxim *nemo tenetur seipsum accusare*, had its origin in a protest against the inquisitorial and manifestly unjust methods of interrogating accused persons, which [have] long obtained in the continental system, and, until the expulsion of the Stuarts from the British throne in 1688, and the erection of additional barriers for the protection of the people against the exercise of arbitrary power, [were] not uncommon even in England. While the admissions or confessions of the prisoner, when voluntarily and freely made, have always ranked high in the scale of incriminating evidence, if an accused person be asked to explain his apparent connection with a crime under investigation, the ease with which the questions put to him may assume an inquisitorial character, the temptation to press the witness unduly, to browbeat him if he be timid or reluctant, to push him into a corner, and to entrap him into fatal contradictions, which is so painfully evident in many of the earlier state trials, notably in those of Sir Nicholas Throckmorton, and Udal, the Puritan minister, made the system so odious as to give rise to a demand for its total abolition. The change in the English criminal procedure in that particular seems to be founded upon no statute and no judicial opinion, but upon a general and silent acquiescence of the courts in a popular demand. But, however adopted, it has become firmly embedded in English, as well as in American jurisprudence. So deeply did the iniquities of the ancient system impress themselves upon the minds of the American colonists that the States, with one accord, made a denial of the right to question an accused person a part of their fundamental law, so that a maxim, which in England was a mere rule of evidence, became clothed in this country with the impregnability of a constitutional enactment." Brown v. Walker, 161 U.S. 591, 596–597, 16 S.Ct. 644, 646, 40 L.Ed. 819 (1896).

37

In stating the obligation of the judiciary to apply these constitutional rights, this Court declared in Weems v. United States, 217 U.S. 349, 373, 30 S.Ct. 544, 551, 54 L.Ed. 793 (1910):
"* * * our contemplation cannot be only of what has been, but of what may be. Under any other rule a constitution would indeed be as easy of application as it would be deficient in efficacy and power. Its general principles would have little value, and be converted by precedent into impotent and lifeless formulas. Rights declared in words might be lost in reality. And this has been recognized. The meaning and vitality of the Constitution have developed against narrow and restrictive construction."

This was the spirit in which we delineated, in meaningful language, the manner in which the constitutional rights of the individual could be enforced against overzealous police practices. It was necessary in *Escobedo,* as here, to insure that what was proclaimed in the Constitution had not become but a "form of words," Silverthorne Lumber Co. v. United States, 251 U.S. 385, 392, 40 S.Ct. 182, 64 L.Ed. 319 (1920), in the hands of government officials. And it is in this spirit, consistent with our role as judges, that we adhere to the principles of *Escobedo* today.

Our holding will be spelled out with some specificity in the pages which follow but briefly stated it is this: the prosecution may not use statements, whether exculpatory or inculpatory, stemming from custodial interrogation of the defendant unless it demonstrates the use of procedural safeguards effective to secure the privilege against self-incrimination. By custodial interrogation, we mean questioning initiated by law enforcement officers after a person has been taken into custody or otherwise deprived of his freedom of action in any significant way.[4] As for the procedural safeguards to be employed, unless other fully effective means are devised to inform accused persons of their right of silence and to assure a continuous opportunity to exercise it, the following measures are required. Prior to any questioning, the person must be warned that he has a right to remain silent, that any statement he does make may be used as evidence against him, and that he has a right to the presence of an attorney, either retained or appointed. The defendant may waive effectuation of these rights, provided the waiver is made voluntarily, knowingly and intelligently. If, however, he indicates in any manner and at any stage of the process that he wishes to consult with an attorney before speaking there can be no questioning. Likewise, if the individual is alone and indicates in any manner that he does not wish to be interrogated, the po-

---

[4] This is what we meant in *Esco-bedo* when we spoke of an investigation which had focused on an accused.

lice may not question him. The mere fact that he may have answered some questions or volunteered some statements on his own does not deprive him of the right to refrain from answering any further inquiries until he has consulted with an attorney and thereafter consents to be questioned.

I.

The constitutional issue we decide in each of these cases is the admissibility of statements obtained from a defendant questioned while in custody or otherwise deprived of his freedom of action in any significant way. In each, the defendant was questioned by police officers, detectives, or a prosecuting attorney in a room in which he was cut off from the outside world. In none of these cases was the defendant given a full and effective warning of his rights at the outset of the interrogation process. In all the cases, the questioning elicited oral admissions, and in three of them, signed statements as well which were admitted at their trials. They all thus share salient features—incommunicado interrogation of individuals in a police-dominated atmosphere, resulting in self-incriminating statements without full warnings of constitutional rights.

An understanding of the nature and setting of this in-custody interrogation is essential to our decisions today. The difficulty in depicting what transpires at such interrogations stems from the fact that in this country they have largely taken place incommunicado. From extensive factual studies undertaken in the early 1930's, including the famous Wickersham Report to Congress by a Presidential Commission, it is clear that police violence and the "third degree" flourished at that time.[5] In a series of cases decided by this Court long after these studies, the police resorted to physical brutality—beatings, hanging, whipping—and to sustained and protracted questioning incommunicado in order to extort confessions.[6]

---

[5] See, for example, IV National Commission on Law Observance and Enforcement, Report on Lawlessness in Law Enforcement (1931) [Wickersham Report]; Booth, Confessions, and Methods Employed in Procuring Them, 4 So.Calif.L.Rev. 83 (1930); Kauper, Judicial Examination of the Accused—A Remedy for the Third Degree, 30 Mich.L.Rev. 1224 (1932). It is significant that instances of third-degree treatment of prisoners almost invariably took place during the period between arrest and preliminary examination.

Wickersham Report, at 169; Hall, The Law of Arrest in Relation to Contemporary Social Problems, 3 U.Chi.L.Rev. 345, 357 (1936). See also Foote, Law and Police Practice: Safeguards in the Law of Arrest, 52 NwU.L.Rev. 16 (1957).

[6] Brown v. State of Mississippi, 297 U.S. 278, 56 S.Ct. 461, 80 L.Ed. 682 (1936); Chambers v. State of Florida, 309 U.S. 227, 60 S.Ct. 472, 84 L.Ed. 716 (1940); Canty v. State of Alabama, 309 U.S. 629, 60 S.Ct. 612, 84 L.Ed. 988 (1940); White v. State of Texas, 310 U.S. 530, 60 S.Ct. 1032, 84 L.Ed. 1342

The Commission on Civil Rights in 1961 found much evidence to indicate that "some policemen still resort to physical force to obtain confessions," 1961 Comm'n on Civil Rights Rep., Justice, pt. 5, 17. The use of physical brutality and violence is not, unfortunately, relegated to the past or to any part of the country. Only recently in Kings County, New York, the police brutally beat, kicked and placed lighted cigarette butts on the back of a potential witness under interrogation for the purpose of securing a statement incriminating a third party. People v. Portelli, 15 N.Y.2d 235, 257 N.Y.S.2d 931, 205 N.E.2d 857 (1965).[7]

The examples given above are undoubtedly the exception now, but they are sufficiently widespread to be the object of concern. Unless a proper limitation upon custodial interrogation is achieved —such as these decisions will advance—there can be no assurance that practices of this nature will be eradicated in the foreseeable future. The conclusion of the Wickersham Commission Report, made over 30 years ago, is still pertinent:

"To the contention that the third degree is necessary to get the facts, the reporters aptly reply in the language of the present Lord Chancellor of England (Lord Sankey) : 'It is not admissible to do a great right by doing a little wrong. * * * It is not sufficient to do justice by obtaining a proper result by irregular or improper means.' Not only does the use of the third degree involve a fla-

---

(1940); Vernon v. State of Alabama, 313 U.S. 547, 61 S.Ct. 1092, 85 L.Ed. 1513 (1941); Ward v. State of Texas, 316 U.S. 547, 62 S.Ct. 1139, 86 L.Ed. 1663 (1942); Ashcraft v. State of Tennessee, 322 U.S. 143, 64 S.Ct. 921, 88 L.Ed. 1192 (1944); Malinski v. People of State of New York, 324 U.S. 401, 65 S.Ct. 781, 89 L.Ed. 1029 (1945); Leyra v. Denno, 347 U.S. 556, 74 S.Ct. 716, 98 L.Ed. 948 (1954). See also Williams v. United States, 341 U.S. 97, 71 S.Ct. 576, 95 L.Ed. 774 (1951).

[7] In addition, see People v. Wakat, 415 Ill. 610, 114 N.E.2d 706 (1953); Wakat v. Harlib, 253 F.2d 59 (C.A.7th Cir. 1958) (defendant suffering from broken bones, multiple bruises and injuries sufficiently serious to require eight months' medical treatment after being manhandled by five policemen); Kier v. State, 213 Md. 556, 132 A.2d 494 (1957) (police doctor told accused, who was strapped to a chair completely nude, that he proposed to take hair and skin scrapings from anything that looked like blood or sperm from various parts of his body); Bruner v. People, 113 Colo. 194, 156 P.2d 111 (1945) (defendant held in custody over two months, deprived of food for 15 hours, forced to submit to a lie detector test when he wanted to go to the toilet); People v. Matlock, 51 Cal.2d 682, 336 P.2d 505, 71 A.L.R.2d 605 (1959) (defendant questioned incessantly over an evening's time, made to lie on cold board and to answer questions whenever it appeared he was getting sleepy). Other cases are documented in American Civil Liberties Union, Illinois Division, Secret Detention by the Chicago Police (1959); Potts, The Preliminary Examination and "The Third Degree," 2 Baylor L.Rev. 131 (1950); Sterling, Police Interrogation and the Psychology of Confession, 14 J.Pub.L. 25 (1965).

grant violation of law by the officers of the law, but it involves also the dangers of false confessions, and it tends to make police and prosecutors less zealous in the search for objective evidence. As the New York prosecutor quoted in the report said, 'It is a short cut and makes the police lazy and unenterprising.' Or, as another official quoted remarked: 'If you use your fists, you are not so likely to use your wits.' We agree with the conclusion expressed in the report, that 'The third degree brutalizes the police, hardens the prisoner against society, and lowers the esteem in which the administration of justice is held by the public.' " IV National Commission on Law Observance and Enforcement, Report on Lawlessness in Law Enforcement 5 (1931).

Again we stress that the modern practice of in-custody interrogation is psychologically rather than physically oriented. As we have stated before, "Since Chambers v. State of Florida, 309 U.S. 227, 60 S.Ct. 472, 84 L.Ed. 716, this Court has recognized that coercion can be mental as well as physical, and that the blood of the accused is not the only hallmark of an unconstitutional inquisition." Blackburn v. State of Alabama, 361 U.S. 199, 206, 80 S.Ct. 274, 279, 4 L.Ed.2d 242 (1960). Interrogation still takes place in privacy. Privacy results in secrecy and this in turn results in a gap in our knowledge as to what in fact goes on in the interrogation rooms. A valuable source of information about present police practices, however, may be found in various police manuals and texts which document procedures employed with success in the past, and which recommend various other effective tactics.[8] These texts are used by law enforcement agencies themselves as guides.[9]

---

[8] The manuals quoted in the text following are the most recent and representative of the texts currently available. Material of the same nature appears in Kidd, Police Interrogation (1940); Mulbar, Interrogation (1951); Dienstein, Technics for the Crime Investigator 97–115 (1952). Studies concerning the observed practices of the police appear in LaFave, Arrest: The Decision To Take a Suspect Into Custody 244–437, 490–521 (1965); LaFave, Detention for Investigation by the Police: An Analysis of Current Practices, 1962 Wash.U.L.Q. 331; Barrett, Police Practices and the Law—From Arrest to Release or Charge, 50 Calif.L.Rev. 11 (1962); Sterling, supra, n. 7, at 47–65.

[9] The methods described in Inbau & Reid, Criminal Interrogation and Confessions (1962), are a revision and enlargement of material presented in three prior editions of a predecessor text, Lie Detection and Criminal Interrogation (3d ed. 1953). The authors and their associates are officers of the Chicago Police Scientific Crime Detection Laboratory and have had extensive experience in writing, lecturing and speaking to law enforcement authorities over a 20-year period. They say that the techniques portrayed in their manuals reflect their experiences and are the most effective psychological stratagems to employ during interrogations. Similarly, the techniques described in O'Hara, Fundamentals of Criminal Investigation (1956), were gleaned from long service as observer, lecturer in police science, and work

It should be noted that these texts professedly present the most enlightened and effective means presently used to obtain statements through custodial interrogation. By considering these texts and other data, it is possible to describe procedures observed and noted around the country.

The officers are told by the manuals that the "principal psychological factor contributing to a successful interrogation is privacy —being alone with the person under interrogation."[10] The efficacy of this tactic has been explained as follows:

"If at all practicable, the interrogation should take place in the investigator's office or at least in a room of his own choice. The subject should be deprived of every psychological advantage. In his own home he may be confident, indignant, or recalcitrant. He is more keenly aware of his rights and more reluctant to tell of his indiscretions or criminal behavior within the walls of his home. Moreover his family and other friends are nearby, their presence lending moral support. In his own office, the investigator possesses all the advantages. The atmosphere suggests the invincibility of the forces of the law."[11]

To highlight the isolation and unfamiliar surroundings, the manuals instruct the police to display an air of confidence in the suspect's guilt and from outward appearance to maintain only an interest in confirming certain details. The guilt of the subject is to be posited as a fact. The interrogator should direct his comments toward the reasons why the subject committed the act, rather than court failure by asking the subject whether he did it. Like other men, perhaps the subject has had a bad family life, had an unhappy childhood, had too much to drink, had an unrequited desire for women. The officers are instructed to minimize the moral seriousness of the offense,[12] to cast blame on the victim or on society.[13] These tactics are designed to put the subject in a psychological state where his story is but an elaboration of what the police purport to know already—that he is guilty. Explanations to the contrary are dismissed and discouraged.

---

as a federal criminal investigator. All these texts have had rather extensive use among law enforcement agencies and among students of police science, with total sales and circulation of over 44,000.

[10] Inbau & Reid, Criminal Interrogation and Confessions (1962), at 1.

[11] O'Hara, supra, at 99.

[12] Inbau & Reid, supra, at 34–43, 87. For example, in Leyra v. Denno, 347 U.S. 556, 74 S.Ct. 716, 98 L.Ed.

948 (1954), the interrogator-psychiatrist told the accused, "We do sometimes things that are not right, but in a fit of temper or anger we sometimes do things we aren't really responsible for," id., at 562, 74 S.Ct. at 719, and again, "We know that morally you were just in anger. Morally, you are not to be condemned," id., at 582, 74 S.Ct. at 729.

[13] Inbau & Reid, supra, at 43–55.

The texts thus stress that the major qualities an interrogator should possess are patience and perseverance. One writer describes the efficacy of these characteristics in this manner:

"In the preceding paragraphs emphasis has been placed on kindness and stratagems. The investigator will, however, encounter many situations where the sheer weight of his personality will be the deciding factor. Where emotional appeals and tricks are employed to no avail, he must rely on an oppressive atmosphere of dogged persistence. He must interrogate steadily and without relent, leaving the subject no prospect of surcease. He must dominate his subject and overwhelm him with his inexorable will to obtain the truth. He should interrogate for a spell of several hours pausing only for the subject's necessities in acknowledgment of the need to avoid a charge of duress that can be technically substantiated. In a serious case, the interrogation may continue for days, with the required intervals for food and sleep, but with no respite from the atmosphere of domination. It is possible in this way to induce the subject to talk without resorting to duress or coercion. The method should be used only when the guilt of the subject appears highly probable."[14]

The manuals suggest that the suspect be offered legal excuses for his actions in order to obtain an initial admission of guilt. Where there is a suspected revenge-killing, for example, the interrogator may say:

"Joe, you probably didn't go out looking for this fellow with the purpose of shooting him. My guess is, however, that you expected something from him and that's why you carried a gun—for your own protection. You knew him for what he was, no good. Then when you met him he probably started using foul, abusive language and he gave some indication that he was about to pull a gun on you, and that's when you had to act to save your own life. That's about it, isn't it, Joe?"[15]

Having then obtained the admission of shooting, the interrogator is advised to refer to circumstantial evidence which negates the self-defense explanation. This should enable him to secure the entire story. One text notes that "Even if he fails to do so, the inconsistency between the subject's original denial of the shooting and his present admission of at least doing the shooting will serve to deprive him of a self-defense 'out' at the time of trial."[16]

---

[14] O'Hara, supra, at 112.   [16] Ibid.

[15] Inbau & Reid, supra, at 40.

43

When the techniques described above prove unavailing, the texts recommend they be alternated with a show of some hostility. One ploy often used has been termed the "friendly-unfriendly" or the "Mutt and Jeff" act:

"* * * In this technique, two agents are employed. Mutt, the relentless investigator, who knows the subject is guilty and is not going to waste any time. He's sent a dozen men away for this crime and he's going to send the subject away for the full term. Jeff, on the other hand, is obviously a kindhearted man. He has a family himself. He has a brother who was involved in a little scrape like this. He disapproves of Mutt and his tactics and will arrange to get him off the case if the subject will cooperate. He can't hold Mutt off for very long. The subject would be wise to make a quick decision. The technique is applied by having both investigators present while Mutt acts out his role. Jeff may stand by quietly and demur at some of Mutt's tactics. When Jeff makes his plea for cooperation, Mutt is not present in the room."[17]

The interrogators sometimes are instructed to induce a confession out of trickery. The technique here is quite effective in crimes which require identification or which run in series. In the identification situation, the interrogator may take a break in his questioning to place the subject among a group of men in a line-up. "The witness or complainant (previously coached, if necessary) studies the line-up and confidently points out the subject as the guilty party."[18] Then the questioning resumes "as though there were now no doubt about the guilt of the subject." A variation on this technique is called the "reverse line-up":

"The accused is placed in a line-up, but this time he is identified by several fictitious witnesses or victims who associated him with different offenses. It is expected that the subject will become desperate and confess to the offense under investigation in order to escape from the false accusations."[19]

The manuals also contain instructions for police on how to handle the individual who refuses to discuss the matter entirely, or who

[17] O'Hara, supra, at 104, Inbau & Reid, supra, at 58–59. See Spano v. People of State of New York, 360 U.S. 315, 79 S.Ct. 1202, 3 L.Ed.2d 1265 (1959). A variant on the technique of creating hostility is one of engendering fear. This is perhaps best described by the prosecuting attorney in Malinski v. People of State of New York, 324 U.S. 401, 407, 65 S.Ct. 781, 784, 89 L.Ed. 1029 (1945): "Why this talk about being undressed? Of course, they had a right to undress him to look for bullet scars, and keep the clothes off him. That was quite proper police procedure. That is some more psychology— let him sit around with a blanket on him, humiliate him there for a while; let him sit in the corner, let him think he is going to get a shellacking."

[18] O'Hara, supra, at 105–106.

[19] Id., at 106.

44

asks for an attorney or relatives. The examiner is to concede him the right to remain silent. "This usually has a very undermining effect. First of all, he is disappointed in his expectation of an unfavorable reaction on the part of the interrogator. Secondly, a concession of this right to remain silent impresses the subject with the apparent fairness of his interrogator."[20] After this psychological conditioning, however, the officer is told to point out the incriminating significance of the suspect's refusal to talk:

"Joe, you have a right to remain silent. That's your privilege and I'm the last person in the world who'll try to take it away from you. If that's the way you want to leave this, O. K. But let me ask you this. Suppose you were in my shoes and I were in yours and you called me in to ask me about this and I told you, 'I don't want to answer any of your questions.' You'd think I had something to hide, and you'd probably be right in thinking that. That's exactly what I'll have to think about you, and so will everybody else. So let's sit here and talk this whole thing over."[21]

Few will persist in their initial refusal to talk, it is said, if this monologue is employed correctly.

In the event that the subject wishes to speak to a relative or an attorney, the following advice is tendered:

"[T]he interrogator should respond by suggesting that the subject first tell the truth to the interrogator himself rather than get anyone else involved in the matter. If the request is for an attorney, the interrogator may suggest that the subject save himself or his family the expense of any such professional service, particularly if he is innocent of the offense under investigation. The interrogator may also add, 'Joe, I'm only looking for the truth, and if you're telling the truth, that's it. You can handle this by yourself.' "[22]

From these representative samples of interrogation techniques, the setting prescribed by the manuals and observed in practice becomes clear. In essence, it is this: To be alone with the subject is essential to prevent distraction and to deprive him of any outside support. The aura of confidence in his guilt undermines his will to resist. He merely confirms the preconceived story the police seek to have him describe. Patience and persistence, at times relentless questioning, are employed. To obtain a confession, the interrogator must "patiently maneuver himself or his quarry into a position from which the desired objective may be attained."[23] When normal procedures fail to produce the needed result, the police may resort to deceptive stratagems such as giving false legal advice.

---

[20] Inbau & Reid, supra, at 111.
[21] Ibid.
[22] Inbau & Reid, supra, at 112.

[23] Inbau & Reid, Lie Detection and Criminal Interrogation 185 (3d ed. 1953).

It is important to keep the subject off balance, for example, by trading on his insecurity about himself or his surroundings. The police then persuade, trick, or cajole him out of exercising his constitutional rights.

Even without employing brutality, the "third degree" or the specific stratagems described above, the very fact of custodial interrogation exacts a heavy toll on individual liberty and trades on the weakness of individuals.[24] This fact may be illustrated simply by referring to three confession cases decided by this Court in the Term immediately preceding our *Escobedo* decision. In Townsend v. Sain, 372 U.S. 293, 83 S.Ct. 745, 9 L.Ed.2d 770 (1963), the defendant was a 19-year-old heroin addict, described as a "near mental defective," id., at 307–310, 83 S.Ct. at 754–755. The defendant in Lynumn v. State of Illinois, 372 U.S. 528, 83 S.Ct. 917, 9 L.Ed.2d 922 (1963), was a woman who confessed to the arresting officer after being importuned to "cooperate" in order to prevent her children from being taken by relief authorities. This Court as in those cases reversed the conviction of a defendant in Haynes v. State of Washington, 373 U.S. 503, 83 S.Ct. 1336, 10 L.Ed.2d 513 (1963), whose persistent request during his interrogation was to phone his wife or attorney.[25] In other settings, these individuals might have exercised their constitutional rights. In the incommunicado police-dominated atmosphere, they succumbed.

In the cases before us today, given this background, we concern ourselves primarily with this interrogation atmosphere and the evils it can bring. In No. 759, Miranda v. Arizona, the police arrested the defendant and took him to a special interrogation room where they secured a confession. In No. 760, Vignera v. New York,

---

[24] Interrogation procedures may even give rise to a false confession. The most recent conspicuous example occurred in New York, in 1964, when a Negro of limited intelligence confessed to two brutal murders and a rape which he had not committed. When this was discovered, the prosecutor was reported as saying: "Call it what you want—brain-washing, hypnosis, fright. They made him give an untrue confession. The only thing I don't believe is that Whitmore was beaten." N. Y. Times, Jan. 28, 1965, p. 1, col. 5. In two other instances, similar events had occurred N. Y. Times, Oct. 20, 1964, p. 22, col. 1; N. Y. Times, Aug. 25, 1965, p. 1, col. 1. In general, see Borchard, Convicting the Innocent (1932); Frank & Frank, Not Guilty (1957).

[25] In the fourth confession case decided by the Court in the 1962 Term, Fay v. Noia, 372 U.S. 391, 83 S.Ct. 822, 9 L.Ed.2d 837 (1963), our disposition made it unnecessary to delve at length into the facts. The facts of the defendant's case there, however, paralleled those of his co-defendants, whose confessions were found to have resulted from continuous and coercive interrogation for 27 hours, with denial of requests for friends or attorney. See United States ex rel. Caminito v. Murphy, 222 F.2d 698 (C.A.2d Cir. 1955) (Frank, J.); People v. Bonino, 1 N.Y.2d 752, 152 N.Y.S.2d 298, 135 N.E.2d 51 (1956).

the defendant made oral admissions to the police after interrogation in the afternoon, and then signed an inculpatory statement upon being questioned by an assistant district attorney later the same evening. In No. 761, Westover v. United States, the defendant was handed over to the Federal Bureau of Investigation by local authorities after they had detained and interrogated him for a lengthy period, both at night and the following morning. After some two hours of questioning, the federal officers had obtained signed statements from the defendant. Lastly, in No. 584, California v. Stewart, the local police held the defendant five days in the station and interrogated him on nine separate occasions before they secured his inculpatory statement.

In these cases, we might not find the defendants' statements to have been involuntary in traditional terms. Our concern for adequate safeguards to protect precious Fifth Amendment rights is, of course, not lessened in the slightest. In each of the cases, the defendant was thrust into an unfamiliar atmosphere and run through menacing police interrogation procedures. The potentiality for compulsion is forcefully apparent, for example, in *Miranda*, where the indigent Mexican defendant was a seriously disturbed individual with pronounced sexual fantasies, and in *Stewart*, in which the defendant was an indigent Los Angeles Negro who had dropped out of school in the sixth grade. To be sure, the records do not evince overt physical coercion or patent psychological ploys. The fact remains that in none of these cases did the officers undertake to afford appropriate safeguards at the outset of the interrogation to insure that the statements were truly the product of free choice.

It is obvious that such an interrogation environment is created for no purpose other than to subjugate the individual to the will of his examiner. This atmosphere carries its own badge of intimidation. To be sure, this is not physical intimidation, but it is equally destructive of human dignity.[26] The current practice of incommu-

---

[26] The absurdity of denying that a confession obtained under these circumstances is compelled is aptly protrayed by an example in Professor Sutherland's recent article, Crime and Confession, 79 Harv.L.Rev. 21, 37 (1965):

"Suppose a well-to-do testatrix says she intends to will her property to Elizabeth. John and James want her to bequeath it to them instead. They capture the testatrix, put her in a carefully designed room, out of touch with everyone but themselves and their convenient 'witnesses,' keep her secluded there for hours while they make insistent demands, weary her with contradictions of her assertions that she wants to leave her money to Elizabeth, and finally induce her to execute the will in their favor. Assume that John and James are deeply and correctly convinced that Elizabeth is unworthy and will make base use of the property if she gets her hands on it, whereas John and James have the noblest and most righteous intentions. Would any judge of probate accept the will so procured as the 'voluntary' act of the testatrix?"

nicado interrogation is at odds with one of our Nation's most cherished principles—that the individual may not be compelled to incriminate himself. Unless adequate protective devices are employed
to dispel the compulsion inherent in custodial surroundings, no
statement obtained from the defendant can truly be the product
of his free choice.

From the foregoing, we can readily perceive an intimate connection between the privilege against self-incrimination and police custodial questioning. It is fitting to turn to history and precedent
underlying the Self-Incrimination Clause to determine its applicability in this situation.

II.

We sometimes forget how long it has taken to establish the privilege against self-incrimination, the sources from which it came and
the fervor with which it was defended. Its roots go back into ancient
times.[27] Perhaps the critical historical event shedding light on its
origins and evolution was the trial of one John Lilburn, a vocal
anti-Stuart Leveller, who was made to take the Star Chamber Oath
in 1637. The oath would have bound him to answer to all questions
posed to him on any subject. The Trial of John Lilburn and John
Wharton, 3 How.St.Tr. 1315 (1637). He resisted the oath and de-
claimed the proceedings, stating:

"Another fundamental right I then contended for, was, that no
man's conscience ought to be racked by oaths imposed, to answer
to questions concerning himself in matters criminal, or pretended
to be so." Haller & Davies, The Leveller Tracts 1647–1653, p. 454
(1944).

On account of the Lilburn Trial, Parliament abolished the inquisitorial Court of Star Chamber and went further in giving him gen-
erous reparation. The lofty principles to which Lilburn had appealed during his trial gained popular acceptance in England.[28]
These sentiments worked their way over to the Colonies and were

---

[27] Thirteenth century commentators
found an analogue to the privilege
grounded in the Bible. "To sum
up the matter, the principle that
no man is to be declared guilty
on his own admission is a divine
decree." Maimonides, Mishneh
Torah (Code of Jewish Law),
Book of Judges, Laws of the San-
hedrin, c. 18, ¶ 6, III Yale Ju-
daica Series 52–53. See also Lamm,
The Fifth Amendment and Its
Equivalent in the Halakhah, 5 Ju-
daism 53 (Winter 1956).

[28] See Morgan, The Privilege
Against Self-Incrimination, 34
Min.L.Rev. 1, 9–11 (1949); 8
Wigmore, Evidence 289–295 (Mc-
Naughton rev. 1961). See also
Lowell, The Judicial Use of Tor-
ture, Parts I and II, 11 Harv.L.
Rev. 220, 290 (1897).

implanted after great struggle into the Bill of Rights.[29] Those who framed our Constitution and the Bill of Rights were ever aware of subtle encroachments on individual liberty. They knew that "illegitimate and unconstitutional practices get their first footing * * * by silent approaches and slight deviations from legal modes of procedure." Boyd v. United States, 116 U.S. 616, 635, 6 S.Ct. 524, 535, 29 L.Ed. 746 (1886). The privilege was elevated to constitutional status and has always been "as broad as the mischief against which it seeks to guard." Counselman v. Hitchcock, 142 U.S. 547, 562, 12 S.Ct. 195, 198, 35 L.Ed. 1110 (1892). We cannot depart from this noble heritage.

Thus we may view the historical development of the privilege as one which groped for the proper scope of governmental power over the citizen. As a "noble principle often transcends its origins," the privilege has come rightfully to be recognized in part as an individual's substantive right, a "right to a private enclave where he may lead a private life. That right is the hallmark of our democracy." United States v. Grunewald, 233 F.2d 556, 579, 581-582 (Frank, J., dissenting), rev'd, 353 U.S. 391, 77 S.Ct. 963, 1 L.Ed.2d 931 (1957). We have recently noted that the privilege against self-incrimination—the essential mainstay of our adversary system—is founded on a complex of values, Murphy v. Waterfront Comm. of New York Harbor, 378 U.S. 52, 55-57, n. 5, 84 S.Ct. 1594, 1596-1597, 12 L.Ed.2d 678 (1964); Tehan v. United States ex rel. Shott, 382 U.S. 406, 414-415, n. 12, 86 S.Ct. 459, 464, 15 L.Ed.2d 453 (1966). All these policies point to one overriding thought: the constitutional foundation underlying the privilege is the respect a government—state or federal—must accord to the dignity and integrity of its citizens. To maintain a "fair state-individual balance," to require the government "to shoulder the entire load," 8 Wigmore, Evidence 317 (McNaughton rev. 1961), to respect the inviolability of the human personality, our accusatory system of criminal justice demands that the government seeking to punish an individual produce the evidence against him by its own independent labors, rather than by the cruel, simple expedient of compelling it from his own mouth. Chambers v. State of Florida, 309 U.S. 227, 235-238, 60 S.Ct. 472, 476-477, 84 L.Ed. 716 (1940). In sum, the privilege is fulfilled only when the person is guaranteed the right "to remain silent unless he chooses to speak in the unfettered exercise of his own will." Malloy v. Hogan, 378 U.S. 1, 8, 84 S.Ct. 1489, 1493, 12 L.Ed.2d 653 (1964).

---

[29] See Pittman, The Colonial and Constitutional History of the Privilege Against Self-Incrimination in America, 21 Va.L.Rev. 763 (1935); Ullmann v. United States, 350 U.S. 422, 445-449, 76 S.Ct. 497, 510-512, 100 L.Ed. 511 (1956) (Douglas, J., dissenting).

The question in these cases is whether the privilege is fully applicable during a period of custodial interrogation. In this Court, the privilege has consistently been accorded a liberal construction. Albertson v. Subversive Activities Control Board, 382 U.S. 70, 81, 86 S.Ct. 194, 200, 15 L.Ed.2d 165 (1965); Hoffman v. United States, 341 U.S. 479, 486, 71 S.Ct. 814, 818, 95 L.Ed.2d 1118 (1951); Arndstein v. McCarthy, 254 U.S. 71, 72–73, 41 S.Ct. 26, 65 L.Ed. 138 (1920); Counselman v. Hitchcock, 142 U.S. 547, 562, 12 S.Ct. 195, 197, 35 L.Ed. 1110 (1892). We are satisfied that all the principles embodied in the privilege apply to informal compulsion exerted by law-enforcement officers during in-custody questioning. An individual swept from familiar surroundings into police custody, surrounded by antagonistic forces, and subjected to the techniques of persuasion described above cannot be otherwise than under compulsion to speak. As a practical matter, the compulsion to speak in the isolated setting of the police station may well be greater than in courts or other official investigations, where there are often impartial observers to guard against intimidation or trickery.[30]

This question, in fact, could have been taken as settled in federal courts almost 70 years ago, when, in Bram v. United States, 168 U.S. 532, 542, 18 S.Ct. 183, 187, 42 L.Ed. 568 (1897), this Court held:

"In criminal trials, in the courts of the United States, wherever a question arises whether a confession is incompetent because not voluntary, the issue is controlled by that portion of the fifth amendment * * * commanding that no person 'shall be compelled in any criminal case to be a witness against himself.' "

In *Bram*, the Court reviewed the British and American history and case law and set down the Fifth Amendment standard for compulsion which we implement today:

"Much of the confusion which has resulted from the effort to deduce from the adjudged cases what would be a sufficient quantum of proof to show that a confession was or was not voluntary, has arisen from a misconception of the subject to which the proof must address itself. The rule is not that in order to render a statement admissible the proof must be adequate to establish that the particular communications contained in a statement were voluntarily made, but it must be sufficient to establish that the making of the statement was voluntary; that is to say, that from the causes, which the law treats as legally sufficient to engender in the mind of the accused hope or fear in respect to the crime charged, the accused

---

[30] Compare Brown v. Walker, 161 U.S. 591, 16 S.Ct. 644, 40 L.Ed. 819 (1896); Quinn v. United States, 349 U.S. 155, 75 S.Ct. 668, 99 L.Ed. 964 (1955).

was not involuntarily impelled to make a statement, when but for the improper influences he would have remained silent. * * *" 168 U.S., at 549, 18 S.Ct. at 189. And see, id., at 542, 18 S.Ct. at 186.

The Court has adhered to this reasoning. In 1924, Mr. Justice Brandeis wrote for a unanimous Court in reversing a conviction resting on a compelled confession, Ziang Sung Wan v. United States, 266 U.S. 1, 45 S.Ct. 1, 69 L.Ed. 131. He stated: "In the federal courts, the requisite of voluntariness is not satisfied by establishing merely that the confession was not induced by a promise or a threat. A confession is voluntary in law if, and only if, it was, in fact, voluntarily made. A confession may have been given voluntarily, although it was made to police officers, while in custody, and in answer to an examination conducted by them. But a confession obtained by compulsion must be excluded whatever may have been the character of the compulsion, and whether the compulsion was applied in a judicial proceeding or otherwise. Bram v. United States, 168 U.S. 532, 18 S.Ct. 183, 42 L.Ed. 568." 266 U.S., at 14–15, 45 S.Ct. at 3. In addition to the expansive historical development of the privilege and the sound policies which have nurtured its evolution, judicial precedent thus clearly establishes its application to incommunicado interrogation. In fact, the Government concedes this point as well established in No. 761, Westover v. United States, stating: "We have no doubt * * * that it is possible for a suspect's Fifth Amendment right to be violated during in-custody questioning by a law-enforcement officer."[31]

Because of the adoption by Congress of Rule 5(a) of the Federal Rules of Criminal Procedure, and this Court's effectuation of that Rule in McNabb v. United States, 318 U.S. 332, 63 S.Ct. 608, 87 L.Ed. 819 (1943), and Mallory v. United States, 354 U.S. 449, 77 S.Ct. 1356, 1 L.Ed.2d 1479 (1957), we have had little occasion in the past quarter century to reach the constitutional issues in dealing with federal interrogations. These supervisory rules, requiring production of an arrested person before a commissioner "without unnecessary delay" and excluding evidence obtained in default of that statutory obligation, were nonetheless responsive to the same considerations of Fifth Amendment policy that unavoidably face us now as to the States. In McNabb, 318 U.S., at 343–344, 63 S.Ct. at 614, and in Mallory, 354 U.S., at 455–456, 77 S.Ct. at 1359–

---

[31] Brief for the United States, p. 28. To the same effect, see Brief for the United States, pp. 40–49, n. 44, Anderson v. United States, 318 U.S. 350, 63 S.Ct. 599, 87 L.Ed. 829 (1943); Brief for the United States, pp. 17–18, McNabb v. United States, 318 U.S. 332, 63 S.Ct. 608 (1943).

1360, we recognized both the dangers of interrogation and the appropriateness of prophylaxis stemming from the very fact of interrogation itself.[32]

Our decision in Malloy v. Hogan, 378 U.S. 1, 84 S.Ct. 1489, 12 L.Ed.2d 653 (1964), necessitates an examination of the scope of the privilege in state cases as well. In *Malloy*, we squarely held the privilege applicable to the States, and held that the substantive standards underlying the privilege applied with full force to state court proceedings. There, as in Murphy v. Waterfront Comm. of New York Harbor, 378 U.S. 52, 84 S.Ct. 1594, 12 L.Ed.2d 678 (1964), and Griffin v. State of California, 380 U.S. 609, 85 S.Ct. 1229, 14 L.Ed.2d 106 (1965), we applied the existing Fifth Amendment standards to the case before us. Aside from the holding itself, the reasoning in *Malloy* made clear what had already become apparent—that the substantive and procedural safegards surrounding admissibility of confessions in state cases had become exceedingly exacting, reflecting all the policies embedded in the privilege, 378 U.S., at 7–8, 84 S.Ct. at 1493.[33] The voluntariness doctrine in

---

[32] Our decision today does not indicate in any manner, of course, that these rules can be disregarded. When federal officials arrest an individual, they must as always comply with the dictates of the congressional legislation and cases thereunder. See generally, Hogan & Snee, The McNabb-Mallory Rule: Its Rise, Rationale and Rescue, 47 Geo.L.J. 1 (1958).

[33] The decisions of this Court have guaranteed the same procedural protection for the defendant whether his confession was used in a federal or state court. It is now axiomatic that the defendant's constitutional rights have been violated if his conviction is based, in whole or in part, on an involuntary confession, regardless of its truth or falsity. Rogers v. Richmond, 365 U.S. 534, 544, 81 S.Ct. 735, 741, 5 L.Ed.2d 760 (1961); Siang Sung Wan v. United States, 266 U.S. 1, 45 S.Ct. 1, 69 L.Ed. 131 (1924). This is so even if there is ample evidence aside from the confession to support the conviction, e. g., Malinski v. People of State of New York, 324 U.S. 401, 404, 65 S.Ct. 781, 783, 89 L.Ed. 1029 (1945); Bram v. United States, 168 U.S. 532, 540–542, 18 S.Ct. 183, 185–186

(1897). Both state and federal courts now adhere to trial procedures which seek to assure a reliable and clear-cut determination of the voluntariness of the confession offered at trial, Jackson v. Denno, 378 U.S. 368, 84 S.Ct. 1774, 12 L.Ed.2d 904 (1964); United States v. Carignan, 342 U.S. 36, 38, 72 S.Ct. 97, 98, 96 L.Ed. 48 (1951); see also Wilson v. United States, 162 U.S. 613, 624, 16 S.Ct. 895, 900, 40 L.Ed. 1090 (1896). Appellate review is exacting, see Haynes v. State of Washington, 373 U.S. 503, 83 S.Ct. 1336, 10 L.Ed.2d 513 (1963); Blackburn v. State of Alabama, 36 U.S. 199, 80 S.Ct. 274, 4 L.Ed.2d 242 (1960). Whether his conviction was in a federal or state court, the defendant may secure a postconviction hearing based on the alleged involuntary character of his confession, provided he meets the procedural requirements, Fay v. Noia, 372 U.S. 391, 83 S.Ct. 822, 9 L.Ed.2d 837 (1963); Townsend v. Sain, 372 U.S. 293, 83 S.Ct. 745, 9 L.Ed.2d 770 (1963). In addition, see Murphy v. Waterfront Comm. of New York Harbor, 378 U.S. 52, 84 S.Ct. 1594 (1964).

the state cases, as *Malloy* indicates, encompasses all interrogation practices which are likely to exert such pressure upon an individual as to disable him from making a free and rational choice.[34] The implications of this proposition were elaborated in our decision in Escobedo v. State of Illinois, 378 U.S. 478, 84 S.Ct. 1758, 12 L.Ed.2d 977, decided one week after *Malloy* applied the privilege to the States.

Our holding there stressed the fact that the police had not advised the defendant of his constitutional privilege to remain silent at the outset of the interrogation, and we drew attention to that fact at several points in the decision, 378 U.S., at 483, 485, 491, 84 S.Ct. at 1761, 1762, 1765. This was no isolated factor, but an essential ingredient in our decision. The entire thrust of police interrogation there, as in all the cases today, was to put the defendant in such an emotional state as to impair his capacity for rational judgment. The abdication of the constitutional privilege—the choice on his part to speak to the police—was not made knowingly or competently because of the failure to apprise him of his rights; the compelling atmosphere of the in custody interrogation, and not an independent decision on his part, caused the defendant to speak.

A different phase of the *Escobedo* decision was significant in its attention to the absence of counsel during the questioning. There, as in the cases today, we sought a protective device to dispel the compelling atmosphere of the interrogation. In *Escobedo*, however, the police did not relieve the defendant of the anxieties which they had created in the interrogation rooms. Rather, they denied his request for the assistance of counsel, 378 U.S., at 481, 488, 491, 84 S.Ct. at 1760, 1763, 1765.[35] This heightened his dilemma, and made his later statements the product of this compulsion. Cf. Haynes v. State of Washington, 373 U.S. 503, 514, 83 S.Ct. 1336, 1343 (1963). The denial of the defendant's request for his attorney thus undermined his ability to exercise the privilege—to remain si-

---

[34] See Lisenba v. People of State of California, 314 U.S. 219, 241, 62 S.Ct. 280, 292, 86 L.Ed. 166 (1941); Ashcraft v. State of Tennessee, 322 U.S. 143, 64 S.Ct. 921, 88 L.Ed. 1192 (1944); Malinski v. People of State of New York, 324 U.S. 401, 65 S.Ct. 781 (1945); Spano v. People of State of New York, 360 U.S. 315, 79 S.Ct. 1202, 3 L.Ed.2d 1265 (1959); Lynumn v. State of Illinois, 372 U.S. 528, 83 S.Ct. 917, 9 L.Ed.2d 922 (1963); Haynes v. State of Washington, 373 U.S. 503, 83 S.Ct. 1336, 10 L.Ed.2d 513 (1963).

[35] The police also prevented the attorney from consulting with his client. Independent of any other constitutional proscription, this action constitutes a violation of the Sixth Amendment right to the assistance of counsel and excludes any statement obtained in its wake. See People v. Donovan, 13 N.Y.2d 148, 243 N.Y.S.2d 841, 193 N.E. 2d 628 (1963) (Fuld, J.).

lent if he chose or to speak without any intimidation, blatant or subtle. The presence of counsel, in all the cases before us today, would be the adequate protective device necessary to make the process of police interrogation conform to the dictates of the privilege. His presence would insure that statements made in the government-established atmosphere are not the product of compulsion.

It was in this manner that *Escobedo* explicated another facet of the pre-trial privilege, noted in many of the Court's prior decisions: the protection of rights at trial.[36] That counsel is present when statements are taken from an individual during interrogation obviously enhances the integrity of the fact-finding processes in court. The presence of an attorney, and the warnings delivered to the individual, enable the defendant under otherwise compelling circumstances to tell his story without fear, effectively, and in a way that eliminates the evils in the interrogation process. Without the protections flowing from adequate warning and the rights of counsel, "all the careful safeguards erected around the giving of testimony, whether by an accused or any other witness, would become empty formalities in a procedure where the most compelling possible evidence of guilt, a confession, would have already been obtained at the unsupervised pleasure of the police." Mapp v. Ohio, 367 U.S. 643, 685, 81 S.Ct. 1684, 1707, 6 L.Ed.2d 1081 (1961) (Harlan, J., dissenting). Cf. Pointer v. State of Texas, 380 U.S. 400, 85 S.Ct. 1065, 1 3L.Ed.2d 923 (1965).

III.

Today, then, there can be no doubt that the Fifth Amendment privilege is available outside of criminal court proceedings and serves to protect persons in all settings in which their freedom of action is curtailed in any significant way from being compelled to incriminate themselves. We have concluded that without proper safeguards the process of in-custody interrogation of persons suspected or accused of crime contains inherently compelling pressures which work to undermine the individual's will to resist and to compel him to speak where he would not otherwise do so freely. In order to combat these pressures and to permit a full opportunity to exercise the privilege against self-incrimination, the accused must be adequately and effectively apprised of his rights and the exercise of those rights must be fully honored.

---

[36] In re Groban, 352 U.S. 330, 340–352, 77 S.Ct. 510, 517–523, 1 L. Ed.2d 376 (1957) (Black, J., dissenting); Note, 73 Yale L.J. 1000, 1048–1051 (1964); Comment, 31 U.Chi.L.Rev. 313, 320 (1964) and authorities cited.

It is impossible for us to foresee the potential alternatives for protecting the privilege which might be devised by Congress or the States in the exercise of their creative rule-making capacities. Therefore we cannot say that the Constitution necessarily requires adherence to any particular solution for the inherent compulsions of the interrogation process as it is presently conducted. Our decision in no way creates a constitutional straitjacket which will handicap sound efforts at reform, nor is it intended to have this effect. We encourage Congress and the States to continue their laudable search for increasingly effective ways of protecting the rights of the individual while promoting efficient enforcement of our criminal laws. However, unless we are shown other procedures which are at least as effective in apprising accused persons of their right of silence and in assuring a continuous opportunity to exercise it, the following safeguards must be observed.

At the outset, if a person in custody is to be subjected to interrogation, he must first be informed in clear and unequivocal terms that he has the right to remain silent. For those unaware of the privilege, the warning is needed simply to make them aware of it— the threshold requirement for an intelligent decision as to its exercise. More important, such a warning is an absolute prerequisite in overcoming the inherent pressures of the interrogation atmosphere. It is not just the subnormal or woefully ignorant who succumb to an interrogator's imprecations, whether implied or expressly stated, that the interrogation will continue until a confession is obtained or that silence in the face of accusation is itself damning and will bode ill when presented to a jury.[37] Further, the warning will show the individual that his interrogators are prepared to recognize his privilege should he choose to exercise it.

The Fifth Amendment privilege is so fundamental to our system of constitutional rule and the expedient of giving an adequate warn-

---

[37] See p. 1617, supra. Lord Devlin has commented:
"It is probable that even today, when there is much less ignorance about these matters than formerly, there is still a general belief that you must answer all questions put to you by a policeman, or at least that it will be the worse for you if you do not." Devlin, The Criminal Prosecution in England 32 (1958).

In accord with our decision today, it is impermissible to penalize an individual for exercising his Fifth Amendment privilege when he is under police custodial interrogation. The prosecution may not, therefore, use at trial the fact that he stood mute or claimed his privilege in the face of accusation. Cf. Griffin v. State of California, 380 U.S. 609, 85 S.Ct. 1229, 14 L.Ed.2d 106 (1965); Malloy v. Hogan, 378 U.S. 1, 8, 84 S.Ct. 1489, 1493, 12 L. Ed.2d 653 (1964); Comment, 31 U.Chi.L.Rev. 556 (1964); Developments in the Law—Confessions, 79 Harv.L.Rev. 935, 1041–1044 (1966). See also Bram v. United States, 168 U.S. 532, 562, 18 S.Ct. 183, 194, 42 L.Ed. 568 (1897).

ing as to the availability of the privilege so simple, we will not pause to inquire in individual cases whether the defendant was aware of his rights without a warning being given. Assessments of the knowledge the defendant possessed, based on information as to his age, education, intelligence, or prior contact with authorities, can never be more than speculation;[38] a warning is a clearcut fact. More important, whatever the background of the person interrogated, a warning at the time of the interrogation is indispensable to overcome its pressures and to insure that the individual knows he is free to exercise the privilege at that point in time.

The warning of the right to remain silent must be accompanied by the explanation that anything said can and will be used against the individual in court. This warning is needed in order to make him aware not only of the privilege, but also of the consequences of foregoing it. It is only through an awareness of these consequences that there can be any assurance of real understanding and intelligent exercise of the privilege. Moreover, this warning may serve to make the individual more acutely aware that he is faced with a phase of the adversary system—that he is not in the presence of persons acting solely in his interest.

The circumstances surrounding in-custody interrogation can operate very quickly to overbear the will of one merely made aware of his privilege by his interrogators. Therefore, the right to have counsel present at the interrogation is indispensable to the protection of the Fifth Amendment privilege under the system we delineate today. Our aim is to assure that the individual's right to choose between silence and speech remains unfettered throughout the interrogation process. A once-stated warning, delivered by those who will conduct the interrogation, cannot itself suffice to that end among those who most require knowledge of their rights. A mere warning given by the interrogators is not alone sufficient to accomplish that end. Prosecutors themselves claim that the admonishment of the right to remain silent without more "will benefit only the recidivist and the professional." Brief for the National District Attorneys Association as *amicus curiae*, p. 14. Even preliminary advice given to the accused by his own attorney can be swiftly overcome by the secret interrogation process. Cf. Escobedo v. State of Illinois, 378 U.S. 478, 485, n. 5, 84 S.Ct. 1758, 1762. Thus, the need for counsel to protect the Fifth Amendment privilege comprehends not merely a right to consult with counsel prior to questioning, but also to

---

[38] Cf. Betts v. Brady, 316 U.S. 455, 62 S.Ct. 1252, 86 L.Ed. 1595 (1942), and the recurrent inquiry into special circumstances it necessitated. See generally, Kamisar, Betts v. Brady Twenty Years Later: The Right to Counsel and Due Process Values, 61 Mich.L.Rev. 219 (1962).

have counsel present during any questioning if the defendant so desires.

The presence of counsel at the interrogation may serve several significant subsidiary functions as well. If the accused decides to talk to his interrogators, the assistance of counsel can mitigate the dangers of untrustworthiness. With a lawyer present the likelihood that the police will practice coercion is reduced, and if coercion is nevertheless exercised the lawyer can testify to it in court. The presence of a lawyer can also help to guarantee that the accused gives a fully accurate statement to the police and that the statement is rightly reported by the prosecution at trial. See Crooker v. State of California, 357 U.S. 433, 443–448, 78 S.Ct. 1287, 1293–1296, 2 L.Ed.2d 1448 (1958) (Douglas, J., dissenting).

An individual need not make a pre-interrogation request for a lawyer. While such request affirmatively secures his right to have one, his failure to ask for a lawyer does not constitute a waiver. No effective waiver of the right to counsel during interrogation can be recognized unless specifically made after the warnings we here delineate have been given. The accused who does not know his rights and therefore does not make a request may be the person who most needs counsel. As the California Supreme Court has aptly put it:

"Finally, we must recognize that the imposition of the requirement for the request would discriminate against the defendant who does not know his rights. The defendant who does not ask for counsel is the very defendant who most needs counsel. We cannot penalize a defendant who, not understanding his constitutional rights, does not make the formal request and by such failure demonstrates his helplessness. To require the request would be to favor the defendant whose sophistication or status had fortuitously prompted him to make it." People v. Dorado, 62 Cal.2d 338, 351, 42 Cal. Rptr. 169, 177–178, 398 P.2d 361, 369–370, (1965) (Tobriner, J.).

In Carnley v. Cochran, 369 U.S. 506, 513, 82 S.Ct. 884, 889, 8 L.Ed.2d 70 (1962), we stated: "[I]t is settled that where the assistance of counsel is a constitutional requisite, the right to be furnished counsel does not depend on a request." This proposition applies with equal force in the context of providing counsel to protect an accused's Fifth Amendment privilege in the face of interrogation.[39] Although the role of counsel at trial differs from the role during

---

[39] See Herman, The Supreme Court and Restrictions on Police Interrogation, 25 Ohio St. L.J. 449, 480 (1964).

interrogation, the differences are not relevant to the question whether a request is a prerequisite.

Accordingly we hold that an individual held for interrogation must be clearly informed that he has the right to consult with a lawyer and to have the lawyer with him during interrogation under the system for protecting the privilege we delineate today. As with the warnings of the right to remain silent and that anything stated can be used in evidence against him, this warning is an absolute prerequisite to interrogation. No amount of circumstantial evidence that the person may have been aware of this right will suffice to stand in its stead. Only through such a warning is there ascertainable assurance that the accused was aware of this right.

If an individual indicates that he wishes the assistance of counsel before any interrogation occurs, the authorities cannot rationally ignore or deny his request on the basis that the individual does not have or cannot afford a retained attorney. The financial ability of the individual has no relationship to the scope of the rights involved here. The privilege against self-incrimination secured by the Constitution applies to all individuals. The need for counsel in order to protect the privilege exists for the indigent as well as the affluent. In fact, were we to limit these constitutional rights to those who can retain an attorney, our decisions today would be of little significance. The cases before us as well as the vast majority of confession cases with which we have dealt in the past involve those unable to retain counsel.[40] While authorities are not required to relieve the accused of his poverty, they have the obligation not to take advantage of indigence in the administration of justice.[41] Denial of counsel to the indigent at the time of interrogation while allowing an attorney to those who can afford one would be no more supportable by reason or logic than the similar situation at

---

[40] Estimates of 50–90% indigency among felony defendants have been reported. Pollock, Equal Justice in Practice, 45 Minn.L.Rev. 737, 738–739 (1961); Birzon, Kasanof & Forma, The Right to Counsel and the Indigent Accused in Courts of Criminal Jurisdiction in New York State, 14 Buffalo L.Rev. 428, 433 (1965).

[41] See Kamisar, Equal Justice in the Gatehouses and Mansions of American Criminal Procedure, in Criminal Justice in Our Time 1, 64–81 (1965). As was stated in the Report of the Attorney General's Committee on Poverty and the Administration of Federal Criminal Justice 9 (1963):

"When government chooses to exert its powers in the criminal area, its obligation is surely no less than that of taking reasonable measures to eliminate those factors that are irrelevant to just administration of the law but which, nevertheless, may occasionally affect determinations of the accused's liability or penalty. While government may not be required to relieve the accused of his poverty, it may properly be required to minimize the influence of poverty on its administration of justice."

58

trial and on appeal struck down in Gideon v. Wainwright, 372 U.S. 335, 83 S.Ct. 792, 9 L.Ed.2d 799 (1963), and Douglas v. People of State of California, 372 U.S. 353, 83 S.Ct. 814, 9 L.Ed.2d 811 (1963).

In order fully to apprise a person interrogated of the extent of his rights under this system then, it is necessary to warn him not only that he has the right to consult with an attorney, but also that if he is indigent a lawyer will be appointed to represent him. Without this additional warning, the admonition of the right to consult with counsel would often be understood as meaning only that he can consult with a lawyer if he has one or has the funds to obtain one. The warning of a right to counsel would be hollow if not couched in terms that would convey to the indigent—the person most often subjected to interrogation—the knowledge that he too has a right to have counsel present.[42] As with the warnings of the right to remain silent and of the general right to counsel, only by effective and express explanation to the indigent of this right can there be assurance that he was truly in a position to exercise it.[43]

Once warnings have been given, the subsequent procedure is clear. If the individual indicates in any manner, at any time prior to or during questioning, that he wishes to remain silent, the interrogation must cease.[44] At this point he has shown that he intends to exercise his Fifth Amendment privilege; any statement taken after the person invokes his privilege cannot be other than the product of compulsion, subtle or otherwise. Without the right to cut off questioning, the setting of in-custody interrogation operates on the individual to overcome free choice in producing a statement after the privilege has been once invoked. If the individual states that he wants an attorney, the interrogation must cease until an attorney is present. At that time, the individual must have an opportunity to confer with the attorney and to have him present during any subsequent questioning. If the individual can-

---

[42] Cf. United States ex rel. Brow v. Fay, 242 F.Supp. 273, 277 (D.C.S.D. N.Y. 1965); People v. Witenski, 15 N.Y.2d 392, 259 N.Y.S.2d 413, 207 N.E.2d 358 (1965).

[43] While a warning that the indigent may have counsel appointed need not be given to the person who is known to have an attorney or is known to have ample funds to secure one, the expedient of giving a warning is too simple and the rights involved too important to engage in *ex post facto* inquiries into financial ability when there is any doubt at all on that score.

[44] If an individual indicates his desire to remain silent, but has an attorney present, there may be some circumstances in which further questioning would be permissible. In the absence of evidence of overbearing, statements then made in the presence of counsel might be free of the compelling influence of the interrogation process and might fairly be construed as a waiver of the privilege for purposes of these statements.

not obtain an attorney and he indicates that he wants one before speaking to police, they must respect his decision to remain silent.

This does not mean, as some have suggested, that each police station must have a "station house lawyer" present at all times to advise prisoners. It does mean, however, that if police propose to interrogate a person they must make known to him that he is entitled to a lawyer and that if he cannot afford one, a lawyer will be provided for him prior to any interrogation. If authorities conclude that they will not provide counsel during a reasonable period of time in which investigation in the field is carried out, they may refrain from doing so without violating the person's Fifth Amendment privilege so long as they do not question him during that time.

If the interrogation continues without the presence of an attorney and a statement is taken, a heavy burden rests on the government to demonstrate that the defendant knowingly and intelligently waived his privilege against self-incrimination and his right to retained or appointed counsel. Escobedo v. State of Illinois, 378 U.S. 478, 490, n. 14, 84 S.Ct. 1758, 1764, 12 L.Ed.2d 977. This Court has always set high standards of proof for the waiver of constitutional rights, Johnson v. Zerbst, 304 U.S. 458, 58 S.Ct. 1019, 82 L.Ed. 1461 (1938), and we reassert these standards as applied to in-custody interrogation. Since the State is responsible for establishing the isolated circumstances under which the interrogation takes place and has the only means of making available corroborated evidence of warnings given during incommunicado interrogation, the burden is rightly on its shoulders.

An express statement that the individual is willing to make a statement and does not want an attorney followed closely by a statement could constitute a waiver. But a valid waiver will not be presumed simply from the silence of the accused after warnings are given or simply from the fact that a confession was in fact eventually obtained. A statement we made in Carnley v. Cochran, 369 U.S. 506, 516, 82 S.Ct. 884, 890, 8 L.Ed.2d 70 (1962), is applicable here:

"Presuming waiver from a silent record is impermissible. The record must show, or there must be an allegation and evidence which show, that an accused was offered counsel but intelligently and understandingly rejected the offer. Anything less is not waiver." See also Glasser v. United States, 315 U.S. 60, 62 S.Ct. 457, 86 L.Ed. 680 (1942). Moreover, where in-custody interrogation is involved, there is no room for the contention that the privilege is waived if the individual answers some questions or gives some information on his own prior to invoking his right to remain silent when interrogated.[45]

Whatever the testimony of the authorities as to waiver of rights by an accused, the fact of lengthy interrogation or incommunicado incarceration before a statement is made is strong evidence that the accused did not validly waive his rights. In these circumstances the fact that the individual eventually made a statement is consistent with the conclusion that the compelling influence of the interrogation finally forced him to do so. It is inconsistent with any notion of a voluntary relinquishment of the privilege. Moreover, any evidence that the accused was threatened, tricked, or cajoled into a waiver will, of course, show that the defendant did not voluntarily waive his privilege. The requirement of warnings and waiver of rights is a fundamental with respect to the Fifth Amendment privilege and not simply a preliminary ritual to existing methods of interrogation.

The warnings required and the waiver necessary in accordance with our opinion today are, in the absence of a fully effective equivalent, prerequisites to the admissibility of any statement made by a defendant. No distinction can be drawn between statements which are direct confessions and statements which amount to "admissions" of part or all of an offense. The privilege against self-incrimination protects the individual from being compelled to incriminate himself in any manner; it does not distinguish degrees of incrimination. Similarly, for precisely the same reason, no distinction may be drawn between inculpatory statements and statements alleged to be merely "exculpatory." If a statement made were in fact truly exculpatory it would, of course, never be used by the prosecution. In fact, statements merely intended to be exculpatory by the defendant are often used to impeach his testimony at trial or to demonstrate untruths in the statement given under interrogation and thus to prove guilt by implication. These statements are incriminating in any meaningful sense of the word and may not be used without the full warnings and effective waiver required for any other statement. In *Escobedo* itself, the defendant fully intended his accusation of another as the slayer to be exculpatory as to himself.

---

[45] Although this Court held in Rogers v. United States, 340 U.S. 367, 71 S.Ct. 438, 95 L.Ed. 344 (1951), over strong dissent, that a witness before a grand jury may not in certain circumstances decide to answer some questions and then refuse to answer others, that decision has no application to the interrogation situation we deal with today. No legislative or judicial fact-finding authority is involved here, nor is there a possibility that the individual might make self-serving statements of which he could make use at trial while refusing to answer incriminating statements.

The principles announced today deal with the protection which must be given to the privilege against self-incrimination when the individual is first subjected to police interrogation while in custody at the station or otherwise deprived of his freedom of action in any significant way. It is at this point that our adversary system of criminal proceedings commences, distinguishing itself at the outset from the inquisitorial system recognized in some countries. Under the system of warnings we delineate today or under any other system which may be devised and found effective, the safeguards to be erected about the privilege must come into play at this point.

Our decision is not intended to hamper the traditional function of police officers in investigating crime. See Escobedo v. State of Illinois, 378 U.S. 478, 492, 84 S.Ct. 1758, 1765. When an individual is in custody on probable cause, the police may, of course, seek out evidence in the field to be used at trial against him. Such investigation may include inquiry of persons not under restraint. General on-the-scene questioning as to facts surrounding a crime or other general questioning of citizens in the fact-finding process is not affected by our holding. It is an act of responsible citizenship for individuals to give whatever information they may have to aid in law enforcement. In such situations the compelling atmosphere inherent in the process of in-custody interrogation is not necessarily present.[46]

In dealing with statements obtained through interrogation, we do not purport to find all confessions inadmissible. Confessions remain a proper element in law enforcement. Any statement given freely and voluntarily without any compelling influences is, of course, admissible in evidence. The fundamental import of the privilege while an individual is in custody is not whether he is allowed to talk to the police without the benefit of warnings and counsel, but whether he can be interrogated. There is no requirement that police stop a person who enters a police station and states that he wishes to confess to a crime,[47] or a person who calls the police to offer a confession or any other statement he desires to make. Volunteered statements of any kind are not barred by the Fifth

---

[46] The distinction and its significance has been aptly described in the opinion of a Scottish court: "In former times such questioning, if undertaken, would be conducted by police officers visiting the house or place of business of the suspect and there questioning him, probably in the presence of a relation or friend. However convenient the modern practice may be, it must normally create a situation very unfavourable to the suspect." Chalmers v. H. M. Advocate, [1954] Sess.Cas. 66, 78 (J.C.).

[47] See People v. Dorado, 62 Cal.2d 338, 354, 42 Cal.Rptr. 169, 179, 398 P.2d 361, 371 (1965).

Amendment and their admissibility is not affected by our holding today.

To summarize, we hold that when an individual is taken into custody or otherwise deprived of his freedom by the authorities in any significant way and is subjected to questioning, the privilege against self-incrimination is jeopardized. Procedural safeguards must be employed to protect the privilege, and unless other fully effective means are adopted to notify the person of his right of silence and to assure that the exercise of the right will be scrupulously honored, the following measures are required. He must be warned prior to any questioning that he has the right to remain silent, that anything he says can be used against him in a court of law, that he has the right to the presence of an attorney, and that if he cannot afford an attorney one will be appointed for him prior to any questioning if he so desires. Opportunity to exercise these rights must be afforded to him throughout the interrogation. After such warnings have been given, and such opportunity afforded him, the individual may knowingly and intelligently waive these rights and agree to answer questions or make a statement. But unless and until such warnings and waiver are demonstrated by the prosecution at trial, no evidence obtained as a result of interrogation can be used against him.[48]

IV.

A recurrent argument made in these cases is that society's need for interrogation outweighs the privilege. This argument is not unfamiliar to this Court. See, e. g., Chambers v. State of Florida, 309 U.S. 227, 240–241, 60 S.Ct. 472, 478–479, 84 L.Ed. 716 (1940). The whole thrust of our foregoing discussion demonstrates that the Constitution has prescribed the rights of the individual when confronted with the power of government when it provided in the Fifth Amendment that an individual cannot be compelled to be a witness against himself. That right cannot be abridged. As Mr. Justice Brandeis once observed:

"Decency, security, and liberty alike demand that government officials shall be subjected to the same rules of conduct that are commands to the citizen. In a government of laws, existence of the government will be imperilled if it fails to observe the law scrupulously. Our government is the potent, the omnipresent teacher.

---

[48] In accordance with our holdings today and in Escobedo v. State of Illinois, 378 U.S. 478, 492, 84 S.Ct. 1758, 1765; Crooker v. State of California, 357 U.S. 433, 78 S.Ct. 1287, 2 L.Ed.2d 1448 (1958) and Cicenia v. Lagay, 357 U.S. 504, 78 S. Ct. 1297, 2 L.Ed.2d 1523 (1958) are not to be followed.

For good or for ill, it teaches the whole people by its example. Crime is contagious. If the Government becomes a lawbreaker, it breeds contempt for law; it invites every man to become a law unto himself; it invites anarchy. To declare that in the administration of the criminal law the end justifies the means * * * would bring terrible retribution. Against that pernicious doctrine this court should resolutely set its face." Olmstead v. United States, 277 U.S. 438, 485, 48 S.Ct. 564, 575, 72 L.Ed. 944 (1928) (dissenting opinion).[49]

In this connection, one of our country's distinguished jurists has pointed out: "The quality of a nation's civilization can be largely measured by the methods it uses in the enforcement of its criminal law."[50]

If the individual desires to exercise his privilege, he has the right to do so. This is not for the authorities to decide. An attorney may advise his client not to talk to police until he has had an opportunity to investigate the case, or he may wish to be present with his client during any police questioning. In doing so an attorney is merely exercising the good professional judgment he has been taught. This is not cause for considering the attorney a menace to law enforcement. He is merely carrying out what he is sworn to do under his oath—to protect to the extent of his ability the rights of his client. In fulfilling this responsibility the attorney plays a vital role in the administration of criminal justice under our Constitution.

In announcing these principles, we are not unmindful of the burdens which law enforcement officials must bear, often under trying circumstances. We also fully recognize the obligation of all citizens to aid in enforcing the criminal laws. This Court, while protecting individual rights, has always given ample latitude to law enforcement agencies in the legitimate exercise of their duties. The limits we have placed on the interrogation process should not constitute an undue interference with a proper system of law enforcement. As we have noted, our decision does not in any way preclude police from carrying out their traditional investigatory functions. Although confessions may play an important role in some convictions, the cases before us present graphic examples of the overstatement of the "need" for confessions. In each case authorities conducted interrogations ranging up to five days in duration despite

---

[49] In quoting the above from the dissenting opinion of Mr. Justice Brandeis we, of course, do not intend to pass on the constitutional questions involved in the *Olmstead* case.

[50] Schaefer, Federalism and State Criminal Procedure, 70 Harv.L. Rev. 1, 26 (1956).

the presence, through standard investigating practices, of considerable evidence against each defendant.[51] Further examples are chronicled in our prior cases. See, e. g., Haynes v. State of Washington, 373 U.S. 503, 518–519, 83 S.Ct. 1336, 1345, 1346, 10 L.Ed. 2d 513 (1963) ; Rogers v. Richmond, 365 U.S. 534, 541, 81 S.Ct. 735, 739, 5 L.Ed.2d 760 (1961) ; Malinski v. People of State of New York, 324 U.S. 401, 402, 65 S.Ct. 781, 782 (1945).[52]

It is also urged that an unfettered right to detention for interrogation should be allowed because it will often redound to the benefit of the person questioned. When police inquiry determines that there is no reason to believe that the person has committed any crime, it is said, he will be released without need for further formal procedures. The person who has committed no offense, however, will be better able to clear himself after warnings with counsel present than without. It can be assumed that in such circumstances a lawyer would advise his client to talk freely to police in order to clear himself.

Custodial interrogation, by contrast, does not necessarily afford the innocent an opportunity to clear themselves. A serious consequence of the present practice of the interrogation alleged to be beneficial for the innocent is that many arrests "for investigation" subject large numbers of innocent persons to detention and interrogation. In one of the cases before us, No. 584, California v. Stewart, police held four persons, who were in the defendant's house at the time of the arrest, in jail for five days until defendant confessed. At that time they were finally released. Police stated that there was "no evidence to connect them with any crime." Available statistics on the extent of this practice where it is condoned indicate that these four are far from alone in being subjected to arrest, prolonged detention, and interrogation without the requisite probable cause.[53]

---

[51] Miranda, Vignera, and Westover were identified by eyewitnesses. Marked bills from the bank robbed were found in Westover's car. Articles stolen from the victim as well as from several other robbery victims were found in Stewart's home at the outset of the investigation.

[52] Dealing as we do here with constitutional standards in relation to statements made, the existence of independent corroborating evidence produced at trial is, of course, irrelevant to our decisions. Haynes v. State of Washington, 373 U.S. 503, 518–519, 83 S.Ct. 1336, 1345–

1346 (1963) ; Lynumn v. State of Illinois, 372 U.S. 528, 537–538, 83 S.Ct. 917, 922, 9 L.Ed.2d 922 (1963) ; Rogers v. Richmond, 365 U.S. 534, 541, 81 S.Ct. 735, 739 (1961) ; Blackburn v. State of Alabama, 361 U.S. 199, 206, 80 S.Ct. 274, 279, 4 L.Ed.2d 242 (1960).

[53] See, e. g., Report and Recommendations of the [District of Columbia] Commissioners' Committee on Police Arrests for Investigation (1962) ; American Civil Liberties Union, Secret Detention by the Chicago Police (1959). An extreme example of this practice occurred in

Over the years the Federal Bureau of Investigation has compiled an exemplary record of effective law enforcement while advising any suspect or arrested person, at the outset of an interview, that he is not required to make a statement, that any statement may be used against him in court, that the individual may obtain the services of an attorney of his own choice and, more recently, that he has a right to free counsel if he is unable to pay.[54] A letter received from the Solicitor General in response to a question from the Bench makes it clear that the present pattern of warnings and respect for the rights of the individual followed as a practice by the FBI is consistent with the procedure which we delineate today. It states:

"At the oral argument of the above cause, Mr. Justice Fortas asked whether I could provide certain information as to the practices followed by the Federal Bureau of Investigation. I have directed these questions to the attention of the Director of the Federal Bureau of Investigation and am submitting herewith a statement of the questions and of the answers which we have received.

" '(1) When an individual is interviewed by agents of the Bureau, what warning is given to him?

" 'The standard warning long given by Special Agents of the FBI to both suspects and persons under arrest is that the person has

---

the District of Columbia in 1958. Seeking three "stocky" young Negroes who had robbed a restaurant, police rounded up 90 persons of that general description. Sixty-three were held overnight before being released for lack of evidence. A man not among the 90 arrested was ultimately charged with the crime. Washington Daily News, January 21, 1958, p. 5, col. 1; Hearings before a Subcommittee of the Senate Judiciary Committee on H.R. 11477, S. 2970, S. 3325, and S. 3355, 85th Cong., 2d Sess. (July 1958), pp. 40, 78.

[54] In 1952, J. Edgar Hoover, Director of the Federal Bureau of Investigation, stated:

"Law enforcement, however, in defeating the criminal, must maintain inviolate the historic liberties of the individual. To turn back the criminal, yet, by so doing, destroy the dignity of the individual, would be a hollow victory.

* * * * *

"We can have the Constitution, the best laws in the land, and the most honest reviews by courts—but unless the law enforcement profession is steeped in the democratic tradition, maintains the highest in ethics, and makes its work a career of honor, civil liberties will continually—and without end—be violated. * * * The best protection of civil liberties is an alert, intelligent and honest law enforcement agency. There can be no alternative.

* * * * *

"* * * Special Agents are taught that any suspect or arrested person, at the outset of an interview, must be advised that he is not required to make a statement and that any statement given can be used against him in court. Moreover, the individual must be informed that, if he desires, he may obtain the services of an attorney of his own choice."
Hoover, Civil Liberties and Law Enforcement: The Role of the FBI, 37 Iowa L.Rev. 175, 177–182 (1952).

a right to say nothing and a right to counsel, and that any statement he does make may be used against him in court. Examples of this warning are to be found in the *Westover* case at 342 F.2d 684 (1965), and Jackson v. U.S., [119 U.S.App.D.C. 100] 337 F.2d 136 (1964), cert. den. 380 U.S. 935, 85 S.Ct. 1353.

" 'After passage of the Criminal Justice Act of 1964, which provides free counsel for Federal defendants unable to pay, we added to our instructions to Special Agents the requirement that any person who is under arrest for an offense under FBI jurisdiction, or whose arrest is contemplated following the interview, must also be advised of his right to free counsel if he is unable to pay, and the fact that such counsel will be assigned by the Judge. At the same time, we broadened the right to counsel warning to read counsel of his own choice, or anyone else with whom he might wish to speak.

" '(2) When is the warning given?

" 'The FBI warning is given to a suspect at the very outset of the interview, as shown in the *Westover* case, cited above. The warning may be given to a person arrested as soon as practicable after the arrest, as shown in the *Jackson* case, also cited above, and in U. S. v. Konigsberg, 336 F.2d 844 (1964), cert. den. [Celso v. United States] 379 U.S. 933 [85 S.Ct. 327, 13 L.Ed.2d 342] but in any event it must precede the interview with the person for a confession or admission of his own guilt.

" '(3) What is the Bureau's practice in the event that (a) the individual requests counsel and (b) counsel appears?

" 'When the person who has been warned of his right to counsel decides that he wishes to consult with counsel before making a statement, the interview is terminated at that point, Shultz v. U.S., 351 F.2d 287 ([10 Cir.] 1965). It may be continued, however, as to all matters *other* than the person's own guilt or innocence. If he is indecisive in his request for counsel, there may be some question on whether he did or did not waive counsel. Situations of this kind must necessarily be left to the judgment of the interviewing Agent. For example, in Hiram v. U.S., 354 F.2d 4 ([9 Cir.] 1965), the Agent's conclusion that the person arrested had waived his right to counsel was upheld by the courts.

" 'A person being interviewed and desiring to consult counsel by telephone must be permitted to do so, as shown in Caldwell v. U.S., 351 F.2d 459 ([1 Cir.] 1965). When counsel appears in person, he is permitted to confer with his client in private.

" '(4) What is the Bureau's practice if the individual requests counsel, but cannot afford to retain an attorney?

67

" 'If any person being interviewed after warning of counsel decides that he wishes to consult with counsel before proceeding further the interview is terminated, as shown above. FBI Agents do not pass judgment on the ability of the person to pay for counsel. They do, however, advise those who have been arrested for an offense under FBI jurisdiction, or whose arrest is contemplated following the interview, of a right to free counsel *if* they are unable to pay, and the availability of such counsel from the Judge.' "[55]

The practice of the FBI can readily be emulated by state and local enforcement agencies. The argument that the FBI deals with different crimes than are dealt with by state authorities does not mitigate the significance of the FBI experience.[56]

The experience in some other countries also suggests that the danger to law enforcement in curbs on interrogation is overplayed. The English procedure since 1912 under the Judges' Rules is significant. As recently strengthened, the Rules require that a cautionary warning be given an accused by a police officer as soon as he has evidence that affords reasonable grounds for suspicion; they also require that any statement made be given by the accused without questioning by police.[57] The right of the individual to con-

---

[55] We agree that the interviewing agent must exercise his judgment in determining whether the individual waives his right to counsel. Because of the constitutional basis of the right, however, the standard for waiver is necessarily high. And, of course, the ultimate responsibility for resolving this constitutional question lies with the courts.

[56] Among the crimes within the enforcement jurisdiction of the FBI are kidnapping, 18 U.S.C. § 1201 (1964 ed.), white slavery, 18 U.S.C. §§ 2421–2423 (1964 ed.), bank robbery, 18 U.S.C. § 2113 (1964 ed.), interstate transportation and sale of stolen property, 18 U.S.C. §§ 2311–2317 (1964 ed.), all manner of conspiracies, 18 U.S.C. § 371 (1964 ed.), and violations of civil rights, 18 U.S.C. §§ 241–242 (1964 ed.). See also 18 U.S.C. § 1114 (1964 ed.) (murder of officer or employee of the United States).

[57] [1964] Crim.L.Rev., at 166–170. These Rules provide in part:
"II. As soon as a police officer has evidence which would afford reasonable grounds for suspecting that a person has committed an offence, he shall caution that person or cause him to be cautioned before putting to him any questions, or further questions, relating to that offence.
"The caution shall be in the following terms:
" 'You are not obliged to say anything unless you wish to do so but what you say may be put into writing and given in evidence.'
"When after being cautioned a person is being questioned, or elects to make a statement, a record shall be kept of the time and place at which any such questioning or statement began and ended and of the persons present.

*   *   *   *   *

"III. * * *

*   *   *   *   *

"(b) It is only in exceptional cases that questions relating to the offence should be put to the accused person after he has been charged or informed that he may be prosecuted.

*   *   *   *   *

"IV. All written statements made after caution shall be taken in the following manner:
"(a) If a person says that he

68

sult with an attorney during this period is expressly recognized.[58]
The safeguards present under Scottish law may be even greater
than in England. Scottish judicial decisions bar use in evidence of
most confessions obtained through police interrogation.[59] In India,
confessions made to police not in the presence of a magistrate
have been excluded by rule of evidence since 1872, at a time when
it operated under British law.[60] Identical provisions appear in the

---

wants to make a statement he shall
be told that it is intended to make
a written record of what he says.

"He shall always be asked
whether he wishes to write down
himself what he wants to say; if
he says that he cannot write or that
he would like someone to write it
for him, a police officer may offer
to write the statement for him.
* * *

"(b) Any person writing his
own statement shall be allowed to
do so without any prompting as distinct from indicating to him what
matters are material.

 * * * * *

"(d) Whenever a police officer
writes the statement, he shall take
down the exact words spoken by
the person making the statement,
without putting any questions other
than such as may be needed to make
the statement coherent, intelligible
and relevant to the material matters: he shall not prompt him."
The prior Rules appear in Devlin,
The Criminal Prosecution in England 137–141 (1958).

Despite suggestions of some lax-
ity in enforcement of the Rules and
despite the fact some discretion as
to admissibility is invested in the
trial judge, the Rules are a significant influence in the English criminal law enforcement system. See,
e. g., [1964] Crim.L.Rev., at 182;
and articles collected in [1960]
Crim.L.Rev., at 298–356.

[58] The introduction to the Judges'
Rules states in part:
"These Rules do not affect the
principles

 * * * * *

"(c) That every person at any
stage of an investigation should be
able to communicate and to con-

sult privately with a solicitor. This
is so even if he is in custody provided that in such a case no unreasonable delay or hindrance is caused
to the processes of investigation or
the administration of justice by his
doing so. * * *" [1964] Crim.L.
Rev., at 166–167.

[59] As stated by the Lord Justice General in Chalmers v. H. M. Advocate, [1954] Sess.Cas. 66, 78 (J.C.):
"The theory of our law is that at
the stage of initial investigation the
police may question anyone with a
view to acquiring information
which may lead to the detection of
the criminal; but that, when the
stage has been reached at which
suspicion, or more than suspicion,
has in their view centered upon
some person as the likely perpetrator of the crime, further interrogation of that person becomes very
dangerous, and, if carried too far,
e. g., to the point of extracting a
confession by what amounts to
cross-examination, the evidence of
that confession will almost certainly be excluded. Once the accused has been apprehended and
charged he has the statutory right
to a private interview with a solicitor and to be brought before a magistrate with all convenient speed so
that he may, if so advised, emit
a declaration in presence of his solicitor under conditions which safeguard him against prejudice."

[60] "No confession made to a police officer shall be proved as against a
person accused of any offence." Indian Evidence Act § 25.

"No confession made by any person whilst he is in the custody of
a police officer unless it be made
in the immediate presence of a
Magistrate, shall be proved as
against such person." Indian Evi-

Evidence Ordinance of Ceylon, enacted in 1895.[61] Similarly, in our country the Uniform Code of Military Justice has long provided that no suspect may be interrogated without first being warned of his right not to make a statement and that any statement he makes may be used against him.[62] Denial of the right to consult counsel during interrogation has also been proscribed by military tribunals.[63] There appears to have been no marked detrimental effect on criminal law enforcement in these jurisdictions as a result of these rules. Conditions of law enforcement in our country are sufficiently similar to permit reference to this experience as assurance that lawlessness will not result from warning an individual of his rights or allowing him to exercise them. Moreover, it is consistent with our legal system that we give at least as much protection to these rights as is given in the jurisdictions described. We deal in our country with rights grounded in a specific requirement of the Fifth Amendment of the Constitution, whereas other jurisdictions arrived at their conclusions on the basis of principles of justice not so specifically defined.[64]

It is also urged upon us that we withhold decision on this issue until state legislative bodies and advisory groups have had an opportunity to deal with these problems by rule making.[65] We have already pointed out that the Constitution does not require any specific code of procedures for protecting the privilege against self-incrimination during custodial interrogation. Congress and the States are free to develop their own safegaurds for the privilege, so long as they are fully as effective as those described above in informing accused persons of their right of silence and in affording a continuous opportunity to exercise it. In any event, however, the issues presented are of constitutional dimensions and must

---

dence Act § 26. See 1 Ramaswami & Rajagopalan, Law of Evidence in India 553–569 (1962). To avoid any continuing effect of police pressure or inducement, the Indian Supreme Court has invalidated a confession made shortly after police brought a suspect before a magistrate, suggesting: "[I]t would, we think, be reasonable to insist upon giving an accused person at least 24 hours to decide whether or not he should make a confession." Sarwan Singh v. State of Punjab, 44 All India Rep. 1957, Sup.Ct. 637, 644.

[61] I Legislative Enactments of Ceylon 211 (1958).

[62] 10 U.S.C. § 831(b) (1964 ed.).

[63] United States v. Rose, 24 CMR 251 (1957): United States v. Gunnels, 23 CMR 354 (1957).

[64] Although no constitution existed at the time confessions were excluded by rule of evidence in 1872, India now has a written constitution which includes the provision that "No person accused of any offence shall be compelled to be a witness against himself." Constitution of India, Article 20(3). See Tope, The Constitution of India 63–67 (1960).

[65] Brief for United States in No. 761, Westover v. United States, pp. 44–47; Brief for the State of New York as *amicus curiae*, pp. 35–39. See also Brief for the National District Attorneys Association as *amicus curiae*, pp. 23–26.

be determined by the courts. The admissibility of a statement in the face of a claim that it was obtained in violation of the defendant's constitutional rights is an issue the resolution of which has long since been undertaken by this Court. See Hopt v. People of Territory of Utah, 110 U.S. 574, 4 S.Ct. 202, 28 L.Ed. 262 (1884). Judicial solutions to problems of constitutional dimension have evolved decade by decade. As courts have been presented with the need to enforce constitutional rights, they have found means of doing so. That was our responsibility when *Escobedo* was before us and it is our responsibility today. Where rights secured by the Constitution are involved, there can be no rule making or legislation which would abrogate them.

V.

Because of the nature of the problem and because of its recurrent significance in numerous cases, we have to this point discussed the relationship of the Fifth Amendment privilege to police interrogation without specific concentration on the facts of the cases before us. We turn now to these facts to consider the application to these cases of the constitutional principles discussed above. In each instance, we have concluded that statements were obtained from the defendant under circumstances that did not meet constitutional standards for protection of the privilege.

No. 759. Miranda v. Arizona.

On March 13, 1963, petitioner, Ernesto Miranda, was arrested at his home and taken in custody to a Phoenix police station. He was there identified by the complaining witness. The police then took him to "Interrogation Room No. 2" of the detective bureau. There he was questioned by two police officers. The officers admitted at trial that Miranda was not advised that he had a right to have an attorney present.[66] Two hours later, the officers emerged from the interrogation room with a written confession signed by Miranda. At the top of the statement was a typed paragraph stating that the confession was made voluntarily, without threats or promises of immunity and "with full knowledge of my legal rights,

---

[66] Miranda was also convicted in a separate trial on an unrelated robbery charge not presented here for review. A statement introduced at that trial was obtained from Miranda during the same interrogation which resulted in the confession involved here. At the robbery trial, one officer testified that during the interrogation he did not tell Miranda that anything he said would be held against him or that he could consult with an attorney. The other officer stated that they had both told Miranda that anything he said would be used against him and that he was not required by law to tell them anything.

understanding any statement I make may be used against me."[67]

At his trial before a jury, the written confession was admitted into evidence over the objection of defense counsel, and the officers testified to the prior oral confession made by Miranda during the interrogation. Miranda was found guilty of kidnapping and rape. He was sentenced to 20 to 30 years' imprisonment on each count, the sentences to run concurrently. On appeal, the Supreme Court of Arizona held that Miranda's constitutional rights were not violated in obtaining the confession and affirmed the conviction. 98 Ariz. 18, 401 P.2d 721. In reaching its decision, the court emphasized heavily the fact that Miranda did not specifically request counsel.

We reverse. From the testimony of the officers and by the admission of respondent, it is clear that Miranda was not in any way apprised of his right to consult with an attorney and to have one present during the interrogation, nor was his right not to be compelled to incriminate himself effectively protected in any other manner. Without these warnings the statements were inadmissible. The mere fact that he signed a statement which contained a typed-in clause stating that he had "full knowledge" of his "legal rights" does not approach the knowing and intelligent waiver required to relinquish constitutional rights. Cf. Haynes v. State of Washington, 373 U.S. 503, 512–513, 83 S.Ct. 1336, 1342, 10 L.Ed.2d 513 (1963); Haley v. State of Ohio, 332 U.S. 596, 601, 68 S.Ct. 302, 304, 92 L.Ed. 224 (1948) (opinion of Mr. Justice Douglas).

No. 760. Vignera v. New York.

Petitioner, Michael Vignera, was picked up by New York police on October 14, 1960, in connection with the robbery three days earlier of a Brooklyn dress shop. They took him to the 17th Detective Squad headquarters in Manhattan. Sometime thereafter he was taken to the 66th Detective Squad. There a detective questioned Vignera with respect to the robbery. Vignera orally admitted the robbery to the detective. The detective was asked on cross-examination at trial by defense counsel whether Vignera was warned of his right to counsel before being interrogated. The prosecution objected to the question and the trial judge sustained the objection. Thus, the defense was precluded from making any showing that warnings had not been given. While at the 66th Detective Squad, Vignera was identified by the store owner and a saleslady as the man who robbed the dress shop. At about 3 p.m. he was formally

---

[67] One of the officers testified that he read this paragraph to Miranda. Apparently, however, he did not do so until after Miranda had confessed orally.

arrested. The police then transported him to still another station, the 70th Precinct in Brooklyn, "for detention." At 11 p. m. Vignera was questioned by an assistant district attorney in the presence of a hearing reporter who transcribed the questions and Vignera's answers. This verbatim account of these proceedings contains no statement of any warnings given by the assistant district attorney. At Vignera's trial on a charge of first degree robbery, the detective testified as to the oral confession. The transcription of the statement taken was also introduced in evidence. At the conclusion of the testimony, the trial judge charged the jury in part as follows:

"The law doesn't say that the confession is void or invalidated because the police officer didn't advise the defendant as to his rights. Did you hear what I said? I am telling you what the law of the State of New York is."

Vignera was found guilty of first degree robbery. He was subsequently adjudged a third-felony offender and sentenced to 30 to 60 years' imprisonment.[68] The conviction was affirmed without opinion by the Appellate Division, Second Department, 21 A.D.2d 752, 252 N.Y.S.2d 19, and by the Court of Appeals, also without opinion, 15 N.Y.2d 970, 259 N.Y.S.2d 857, 207 N.E.2d 527, remittitur amended, 16 N.Y.2d 614, 261 N.Y.S.2d 65, 209 N.E.2d 110. In argument to the Court of Appeals, the State contended that Vignera had no constitutional right to be advised of his right to counsel or his privilege against self-incrimination.

We reverse. The foregoing indicates that Vignera was not warned of any of his rights before the questioning by the detective and by the assistant district attorney. No other steps were taken to protect these rights. Thus he was not effectively apprised of his Fifth Amendment privilege or of his right to have counsel present and his statements are inadmissible.

No. 761. Westover v. United States.

At approximately 9:45 p. m. on March 20, 1963, petitioner, Carl Calvin Westover, was arrested by local police in Kansas City as a suspect in two Kansas City robberies. A report was also received from the FBI that he was wanted on a felony charge in California. The local authorities took him to a police station and placed him in a line-up on the local charges, and at about 11:45 p. m. he was booked. Kansas City police interrogated Westover on the night of

---

[68] Vignera thereafter successfully attacked the validity of one of the prior convictions, Vignera v. Wilkins, Civ. 9901 (D.C.W.D.N.Y. Dec. 31, 1961) (unreported), but was then resentenced as a second-felony offender to the same term of imprisonment as the original sentence. R. 31–33.

his arrest. He denied any knowledge of criminal activities. The next day local officers interrogated him again throughout the morning. Shortly before noon they informed the FBI that they were through interrogating Westover and that the FBI could proceed to interrogate him. There is nothing in the record to indicate that Westover was ever given any warning as to his rights by local police. At noon, three special agents of the FBI continued the interrogation in a private interview room of the Kansas City Police Department, this time with respect to the robbery of a savings and loan association and a bank in Sacramento, California. After two or two and one-half hours, Westover signed separate confessions to each of these two robberies which had been prepared by one of the agents during the interrogation. At trial one of the agents testified, and a paragraph on each of the statements states, that the agents advised Westover that he did not have to make a statement, that any statement he made could be used against him, and that he had the right to see an attorney.

Westover was tried by a jury in federal court and convicted of the California robberies. His statements were introduced at trial. He was sentenced to 15 years' imprisonment on each count, the sentences to run consecutively. On appeal, the conviction was affirmed by the Court of Appeals for the Ninth Circuit. 342 F.2d 684.

We reverse. On the facts of this case we cannot find that Westover knowingly and intelligently waived his right to remain silent and his right to consult with counsel prior to the time he made the statement.[69] At the time the FBI agents began questioning Westover, he had been in custody for over 14 hours and had been interrogated at length during that period. The FBI interrogation began immediately upon the conclusion of the interrogation by Kansas City police and was conducted in local police headquarters. Although the two law enforcement authorities are legally distinct and the crimes for which they interrogated Westover were different, the impact on him was that of a continuous period of ques-

---

[69] The failure of defense counsel to object to the introduction of the confession at trial, noted by the Court of Appeals and emphasized by the Solicitor General, does not preclude our consideration of the issue. Since the trial was held prior to our decision in *Escobedo* and, of course, prior to our decision today making the objection available, the failure to object at trial does not constitute a waiver of the claim. See, e. g., United States ex rel. Angelet v. Fay, 333 F.2d 12, 16 (C.A.2d Cir. 1964), aff'd, 381 U.S. 654, 85 S.Ct. 1750, 14 L.Ed.2d 623 (1965). Cf. Ziffrin, Inc. v. United States, 318 U.S. 73, 78, 63 S.Ct. 465, 87 L.Ed. 621 (1943).

tioning. There is no evidence of any warning given prior to the FBI interrogation nor is there any evidence of an articulated waiver of rights after the FBI commenced its interrogation. The record simply shows that the defendant did in fact confess a short time after being turned over to the FBI following interrogation by local police. Despite the fact that the FBI agents gave warnings at the outset of their interview, from Westover's point of view the warnings came at the end of the interrogation process. In these circumstances an intelligent waiver of constitutional rights can not be assumed.

We do not suggest that law enforcement authorities are precluded from questioning any individual who has been held for a period of time by other authorities and interrogated by them without appropriate warnings. A different case would be presented if an accused were taken into custody by the second authority, removed both in time and place from his original surroundings, and then adequately advised of his rights and given an opportunity to exercise them. But here the FBI interrogation was conducted immediately following the state interrogation in the same police station—in the same compelling surroundings. Thus, in obtaining a confession from Westover the federal authorities were the beneficiaries of the pressure applied by the local in-custody interrogation. In these circumstances the giving of warnings alone was not sufficient to protect the privilege.

No. 584. California v. Stewart.

In the course of investigating a series of purse-snatch robberies in which one of the victims had died of injuries inflicted by her assailant, respondent, Roy Allen Stewart, was pointed out to Los Angeles police as the endorser of dividend checks taken in one of the robberies. At about 7:15 p. m., January 31, 1963, police officers went to Stewart's house and arrested him. One of the officers asked Stewart if they could search the house, to which he replied, "Go ahead." The search turned up various items taken from the five robbery victims. At the time of Stewart's arrest, police also arrested Stewart's wife and three other persons who were visiting him. These four were jailed along with Stewart and were interrogated. Stewart was taken to the University Station of the Los Angeles Police Department where he was placed in a cell. During the next five days, police interrogated Stewart on nine different occasions. Except during the first interrogation session, when he was confronted with an accusing witness, Stewart was isolated with his interrogators.

During the ninth interrogation session, Stewart admitted that he had robbed the deceased and stated that he had not meant to hurt her. Police then brought Stewart before a magistrate for the first time. Since there was no evidence to connect them with any crime, the police then released the other four persons arrested with him.

Nothing in the record specifically indicates whether Stewart was or was not advised of his right to remain silent or his right to counsel. In a number of instances, however, the interrogating officers were asked to recount everything that was said during the interrogations. None indicated that Stewart was ever advised of his rights.

Stewart was charged with kidnapping to commit robbery, rape, and murder. At his trial, transcripts of the first interrogation and the confession at the last interrogation were introduced in evidence. The jury found Stewart guilty of robbery and first degree murder and fixed the penalty as death. On appeal, the Supreme Court of California reversed. 62 Cal.2d 571, 43 Cal.Rptr. 201, 400 P.2d 97. It held that under this Court's decision in *Escobedo*, Stewart should have been advised of his right to remain silent and of his right to counsel and that it would not presume in the face of a silent record that the police advised Stewart of his rights.[70]

We affirm.[71] In dealing with custodial interrogation, we will not presume that a defendant has been effectively apprised of his rights and that his privilege against self-incrimination has been adequately safeguarded on a record that does not show that any warnings have been given or that any effective alternative has been employed. Nor can a knowing and intelligent waiver of these rights be assumed on a silent record. Furthermore, Stewart's stead-

---

[70] Because of this disposition of the case, the California Supreme Court did not reach the claims that the confession was coerced by police threats to hold his ailing wife in custody until he confessed, that there was no hearing as required by Jackson v. Denno, 378 U.S. 368, 84 S.Ct. 1774, 12 L.Ed.2 908 (1964), and that the trial judge gave an instruction condemned by the California Supreme Court's decision in People v. Morse, 60 Cal.2d 631, 36 Cal.Rptr. 201, 388 P.2d 33 (1964).

[71] After certiorari was granted in this case, respondent moved to dismiss on the ground that there was no final judgment from which the State could appeal since the judgment below directed that he be retried. In the event respondent was successful in obtaining an acquittal on retrial, however, under California law the State would have no appeal. Satisfied that in these circumstances the decision below constituted a final judgment under 28 U.S.C. § 1257(3) (1964 ed.), we denied the motion. 383 U.S. 903, 86 S.Ct. 885.

fast denial of the alleged offenses through eight of the nine interrogations over a period of five days is subject to no other construction than that he was compelled by persistent interrogation to forego his Fifth Amendment privilege.

Therefore, in accordance with the foregoing, the judgments of the Supreme Court of Arizona in No. 759, of the New York Court of Appeals in No. 760, and of the Court of Appeals for the Ninth Circuit in No. 761 are reversed. The judgment of the Supreme Court of California in No. 584 is affirmed.

It is so ordered.

Mr. Justice CLARK, dissenting in Nos. 759, 760, and 761, and concurring in the result in No. 584.

It is with regret that I find it necessary to write in these cases. However, I am unable to join the majority because its opinion goes too far on too little, while my dissenting brethren do not go quite far enough. Nor can I join in the Court's criticism of the present practices of police and investigatory agencies as to custodial interrogation. The materials it refers to as "police manuals"[1] are, as I read them, merely writings in this field by professors and some police officers. Not one is shown by the record here to be the official manual of any police department, much less in universal use in crime detection. Moreover, the examples of police brutality mentioned by the Court[2] are rare exceptions to the thousands of cases that appear every year in the law reports. The police agencies—all the way from municipal and state forces to the federal bureaus— are responsible for law enforcement and public safety in this country. I am proud of their efforts, which in my view are not fairly characterized by the Court's opinion.

I.

The *ipse dixit* of the majority has no support in our cases. Indeed, the Court admits that "we might not find the defendants' statements [here] to have been involuntary in traditional terms." Ante, p. 457. In short, the Court has added more to the requirements that the accused is entitled to consult with his lawyer and

---

[1] *E. g.*, Inbau & Reid, Criminal Interrogation and Confessions (1962); O'Hara, Fundamentals of Criminal Investigation (1956); Dienstein, Technics for the Crime Investigator (1952); Mulbar, Interrogation (1951); Kidd, Police Interrogation (1940).

[2] As developed by my Brother HARLAN, post, such cases, with the exception of the long-discredited decision in Bram v. United States, 168 U.S. 532, 18 S.Ct. 183, 42 L.Ed. 568 (1897), were adequately treated in terms of due process.

that he must be given the traditional warning that he may remain silent and that anything that he says may be used against him. Escobedo v. State of Illinois, 378 U.S. 478, 490–491, 84 S.Ct. 1758, 1764–1765, 12 L.Ed.2d 977 (1964). Now, the Court fashions a constitutional rule that the police may engage in no custodial interrogation without additionally advising the accused that he has a right under the Fifth Amendment to the presence of counsel during interrogation and that, if he is without funds, counsel will be furnished him. When at any point during an interrogation the accused seeks affirmatively or impliedly to invoke his rights to silence or counsel, interrogation must be foregone or postponed. The Court further holds that failure to follow the new procedures requires inexorably the exclusion of any statement by the accused, as well as the fruits thereof. Such a strict constitutional specific inserted at the nerve center of crime detection may well kill the patient.[3] Since there is at this time a paucity of information and an almost total lack of empirical knowledge on the practical operation of requirements truly comparable to those announced by the majority, I would be more restrained lest we go too far too fast.

II.

Custodial interrogation has long been recognized as "undoubtedly an essential tool in effective law enforcement." Haynes v. State of Washington, 373 U.S. 503, 515, 83 S.Ct. 1336, 1344, 10 L.Ed.2d

---

[3] The Court points to England, Scotland, Ceylon and India as having equally rigid rules. As my Brother Harlan points out, post, the Court is mistaken in this regard, for it overlooks counterbalancing prosecutorial advantages. Moreover, the requirements of the Federal Bureau of Investigation do not appear from the Solicitor General's letter, ante, to be as strict as those imposed today in at least two respects: (1) The offer of counsel is articulated only as "a right to counsel"; nothing is said about a right to have counsel present at the custodial interrogation. (See also the examples cited by the Solicitor General, Westover v. United States, 342 F.2d 684, 685 (9 Cir., 1965) ("right to consult counsel"); Jackson v. United States, 119 U.S.App.D.C. 100, 337 F.2d 136, 138 (1964) (accused "entitled to an attorney").) Indeed, the practice is that whenever the suspect "decides that he wishes to consult with counsel before making a statement, the interview is terminated at that point. * * * When counsel appears in person, he is permitted to confer with his client in private." This clearly indicates that the FBI does not warn that counsel may be present during custodial interrogation. (2) The Solicitor General's letter states: "[T]hose who have been arrested for an offense under FBI jurisdiction, or whose arrest is contemplated following the interview, [are advised] of a right to free counsel if they are unable to pay, and the availability of such counsel from the Judge." So phrased, this warning does not indicate that the agent will secure counsel. Rather, the statement may well be interpreted by the suspect to mean that the burden is placed upon himself and that he may have counsel appointed only when brought before the judge or at trial—but not at custodial interrogation. As I view the FBI practice, it is not as broad as the one laid down today by the Court.

513 (1963). Recognition of this fact should put us on guard against the promulgation of doctrinaire rules. Especially is this true where the Court finds that "the Constitution has prescribed" its holding and where the light of our past cases, from Hopt v. People of Territory of Utah, 110 U.S. 574, 4 S.Ct. 202, 28 L.Ed. 262 (1884), down to Haynes v. State of Washington, supra, is to the contrary. Indeed, even in *Escobedo* the Court never hinted that an affirmative "waiver" was a prerequisite to questioning; that the burden of proof as to waiver was on the prosecution; that the presence of counsel—absent a waiver—during interrogation was required; that a waiver can be withdrawn at the will of the accused; that counsel must be furnished during an accusatory stage to those unable to pay; nor that admissions and exculpatory statements are "confessions." To require all those things at one gulp should cause the Court to choke over more cases than Crooker v. State of California, 357 U.S. 433, 78 S.Ct. 1287, 2 L.Ed.2d 1448 (1958), and Cicenia v. Lagay, 357 U.S. 504, 78 S.Ct. 1297, 2 L.Ed.2d 1523 (1958), which it expressly overrules today.

The rule prior to today—as Mr. Justice Goldberg, the author of the Court's opinion in *Escobedo,* stated it in Haynes v. Washington —depended upon "a totality of circumstances evidencing an involuntary * * * admission of guilt." 373 U.S., at 514, 83 S.Ct. at 1343. And he concluded:

"Of course, detection and solution of crime is, at best, a difficult and arduous task requiring determination and persistence on the part of all responsible officers charged with the duty of law enforcement. And, certainly, we do not mean to suggest that all interrogation of witnesses and suspects is impermissible. Such questioning is undoubtedly an essential tool in effective law enforcement. The line between proper and permissible police conduct and techniques and methods offensive to do process is, at best, a difficult one to draw, particularly in cases such as this where it is necessary to make fine judgments as to the effect of psychologically coercive pressures and inducements on the mind and will of an accused. * * * We are here impelled to the conclusion, from all of the facts presented, that the bounds of due process have been exceeded." Id., at 514–515, 83 S.Ct. at 1344.

III.

I would continue to follow that rule. Under the "totality of circumstances" rule of which my Brother Goldberg spoke in *Haynes,* I would consider in each case whether the police officer prior to custodial interrogation added the warning that the suspect might have counsel present at the interrogation and, further, that a court would appoint one at his request if he was too poor to employ counsel. In the absence of warnings, the burden would be on the State to prove that counsel was knowingly and intelligently waived or that in the totality of the circumstances, including the failure to give the necessary warnings, the confession was clearly voluntary.

Rather than employing the arbitrary Fifth Amendment rule[4] which the Court lays down I would follow the more pliable dictates of the Due Process Clauses of the Fifth and Fourteenth Amendments which we are accustomed to administering and which we know from our cases are effective instruments in protecting persons in police custody. In this way we would not be acting in the dark nor in one full sweep changing the traditional rules of custodial interrogation which this Court has for so long recognized as a justifiable and proper tool in balancing individual rights against the rights of society. It will be soon enough to go further when we are able to appraise with somewhat better accuracy the effect of such a holding.

I would affirm the convictions in Miranda v. Arizona, No. 759; Vignera v. New York, No. 760; and Westover v. United States, No. 761. In each of those cases I find from the circumstances no warrant for reversal. In California v. Stewart, No. 584, I would dismiss the writ of certiorari for want of a final judgment, 28 U.S.C. § 1257(3) (1964 ed.); but if the merits are to be reached I would affirm on the ground that the State failed to fulfill its burden, in the absence of a showing that appropriate warnings were given, of proving a waiver or a totality of circumstances showing voluntariness. Should there be a retrial, I would leave the State free to attempt to prove these elements.

Mr. Justice HARLAN, whom Mr. Justice STEWART and Mr. Justice WHITE join, dissenting.

I believe the decision of the Court represents poor constitutional law and entails harmful consequences for the country at large. How serious these consequences may prove to be only time can tell. But the basic flaws in the Court's justification seem to me readily apparent now once all sides of the problem are considered.

I. INTRODUCTION.

At the outset, it is well to note exactly what is required by the Court's new constitutional code of rules for confessions. The foremost requirement, upon which later admissibility of a confession depends, is that a fourfold warning be given to a person in

---

[4] In my view there is "no significant support" in our cases for the holding of the Court today that the Fifth Amendment privilege, in effect, forbids custodial interrogation. For a discussion of this point see the dissenting opinion of my Brother WHITE, post.

custody before he is questioned, namely, that he has a right to remain silent, that anything he says may be used against him, that he has a right to have present an attorney during the questioning, and that if indigent he has a right to a lawyer without charge. To forego these rights, some affirmative statement of rejection is seemingly required, and threats, tricks, or cajolings to obtain this waiver are forbidden. If before or during questioning the suspect seeks to invoke his right to remain silent, interrogation must be foregone or cease; a request for counsel brings about the same result until a lawyer is procured. Finally, there are a miscellany of minor directives, for example, the burden of proof of waiver is on the State, admissions and exculpatory statements are treated just like confessions, withdrawal of a waiver is always permitted, and so forth.[1]

While the fine points of this scheme are far less clear than the Court admits, the tenor is quite apparent. The new rules are not designed to guard against police brutality or other unmistakably banned forms of coercion. Those who use third-degree tactics and deny them in court are equally able and destined to lie as skillfully about warnings and waivers. Rather, the thrust of the new rules is to negate all pressures, to reinforce the nervous or ignorant suspect, and ultimately to discourage any confession at all. The aim in short is toward "voluntariness" in a utopian sense, or to view it from a different angle, voluntariness with a vengeance.

To incorporate this notion into the Constitution requires a strained reading of history and precedent and a disregard of the very pragmatic concerns that alone may on occasion justify such strains. I believe that reasoned examination will show that the Due Process Clauses provide an adequate tool for coping with confessions and that, even if the Fifth Amendment privilege against self-incrimination be invoked, its precedents taken as a whole do not sustain the present rules. Viewed as a choice based on pure policy, these new rules prove to be a highly debatable, if not one-sided, appraisal of the competing interests, imposed over widespread objection, at the very time when judicial restraint is most called for by the circumstances.

II. Constitutional Premises.

It is most fitting to begin an inquiry into the constitutional precedents by surveying the limits on confessions the Court has evolved under the Due Process Clause of the Fourteenth Amendment. This

---

[1] My discussion in this opinion is directed to the main questions decided by the Court and necessary to its decision; in ignoring some of the collateral points, I do not mean to imply agreement.

is so because these cases show that there exists a workable and effective means of dealing with confessions in a judicial manner; because the cases are the baseline from which the Court now departs and so serve to measure the actual as opposed to the professed distance it travels; and because examination of them helps reveal how the Court has coasted into its present position.

The earliest confession cases in this Court emerged from federal prosecutions and were settled on a nonconstitutional basis, the Court adopting the common-law rule that the absence of inducements, promises, and threats made a confession voluntary and admissible. Hopt v. People of Territory of Utah, 110 U.S. 574, 4 S.Ct. 202, 28 L.Ed. 262; Pierce v. United States, 160 U.S. 355, 16 S.Ct. 321, 40 L.Ed. 454. While a later case said the Fifth Amendment privilege controlled admissibility, this proposition was not itself developed in subsequent decisions.[2] The Court did, however, heighten the test of admissiblity in federal trials to one of voluntariness "in fact," Ziang Sung Wan v. United States, 266 U.S. 1, 14, 45 S.Ct. 1, 3, 69 L.Ed. 131 (quoted, ante, p. 462), and then by and large left federal judges to apply the same standards the Court began to derive in a string of state court cases.

This new line of decisions, testing admissibility by the Due Process Clause, began in 1936 with Brown v. State of Mississippi, 297 U.S. 278, 56 S.Ct. 461, 80 L.Ed. 682, and must now embrace somewhat more than 30 full opinions of the Court.[3] While the voluntariness rubric was repeated in many instances, e. g., Lyons v. State of Oklahoma, 322 U.S. 596, 64 S.Ct. 1208, 88 L.Ed. 1481, the Court never pinned it down to a single meaning but on the contrary infused it with a number of different values. To travel quickly over the main themes, there was an initial emphasis on

---

[2] The case was Bram v. United States, 168 U.S. 532, 18 S.Ct. 183, 42 L.Ed. 568. Its historical premises were afterwards disproved by Wigmore, who concluded "that no assertions could be more unfounded." 3 Wigmore, Evidence § 823, at 250, n. 5 (3d ed. 1940). The Court in United States v. Carignan, 342 U.S. 36, 41, 72 S.Ct. 97, 100, 96 L.Ed. 48, declined to choose between *Bram* and Wigmore, and Stein v. People of State of New York, 346 U.S. 156, 191, n. 35, 73 S.Ct. 1077, 1095, 97 L.Ed. 1522, cast further doubt on *Bram*. There are, however, several Court opinions which assume in dicta the relevance of the Fifth Amendment privilege to confessions. Burdeau v. McDowell, 256 U.S. 465, 475, 41 S.Ct. 574, 576, 65 L.Ed. 1048; see Shotwell Mfg. Co. v. United States, 371 U.S. 341, 347, 83 S.Ct. 448, 453, 9 L.Ed.2d 357. On *Bram* and the federal confession cases generally, see Developments in the Law—Confessions, 79 Harv.L. Rev. 935, 959–961 (1966).

[3] Comment, 31 U.Chi.L.Rev. 313 & n. 1 (1964), states that by the 1963 Term 33 state coerced-confession cases had been decided by this Court, apart from *per curiams.* Spano v. People of State of New York, 360 U.S. 315, 321, n. 2, 79 S.Ct. 1202, 1206, 3 L.Ed.2d 1265, collects 28 cases.

reliability, e. g., Ward v. State of Texas, 316 U.S. 547, 62 S.Ct. 1139, 86 L.Ed. 1663, supplemented by concern over the legality and fairness of the police practices, e. g., Ashcraft v. State of Tennessee, 322 U.S. 143, 64 S.Ct. 921, 88 L.Ed. 1192, in an "accusatorial" system of law enforcement, Watts v. State of Indiana, 338 U.S. 49, 54, 69 S.Ct. 1347, 1350, 93 L.Ed. 1801, and eventually by close attention to the individual's state of mind and capacity for effective choice, e. g., Gallegos v. State of Colorado, 370 U.S. 49, 82 S.Ct. 1209, 8 L.Ed.2d 325. The outcome was a continuing re-evaluation on the facts of each case of *how much* pressure on the suspect was permissible.[4]

Among the criteria often taken into account were threats or imminent danger, e. g., Payne v. State of Arkansas, 356 U.S. 560, 78 S.Ct. 844, 2 L.Ed.2d 975, physical deprivations such as lack of sleep or food, e. g., Reck v. Pate, 367, U.S. 433, 81 S.Ct. 1541, 6 L.Ed.2d 948, repeated or extended interrogation, e. g., Chambers v. State of Florida, 309 U.S. 227, 60 S.Ct. 472, 84 L.Ed. 716, limits on access to counsel or friends, Crooker v. State of California, 357 U.S. 433, 78 S.Ct. 1287, 2 L.Ed.2d 1448; Cicenia v. Lagay, 357 U.S. 504, 78 S.Ct. 1297, 2 L.Ed.2d 1523, length and illegality of detention under state law, e. g., Haynes v. State of Washington, 373 U.S. 503, 83 S.Ct. 1336, 10 L.Ed.2d 513, and individual weakness or incapacities, Lynumn v. State of Illinois, 372 U.S. 528, 83 S.Ct. 917, 9 L.Ed.2d 922. Apart from direct physical coercion, however, no single default or fixed combination of defaults guaranteed exclusion, and synopses of the cases would serve little use because the overall gauge has been steadily changing, usually in the direction of restricting admissibility. But to mark just what point had been reached before the Court jumped the rails in Escobedo v. State of Illinois, 378 U.S. 478, 84 S.Ct. 1758, 12 L.Ed.2d 977, it is worth capsulizing the then-recent case of Haynes v. State of Washington, 373 U.S. 503, 83 S.Ct. 1336. There, Haynes had been held some 16 or more hours in violation of state law before signing the disputed confession, had received no warnings of any kind, and despite requests had been refused access to his wife or to counsel, the police indicating that access would be allowed after a confession. Emphasizing especially this last inducement and reject-

---

[4] Bator & Vorenberg, Arrest, Detention, Interrogation and the Right to Counsel, 66 Col.L.Rev. 62, 73 (1966): "In fact, the concept of involuntariness seems to be used by the courts as a shorthand to refer to practices which are repellent to civilized standards of decency or which, under the circumstances, are thought to apply a degree of pressure to an individual which unfairly impairs his capacity to make a rational choice." See Herman, The Supreme Court and Restrictions on Police Interrogation, 25 Ohio St.L.J. 449, 452–458 (1964); Developments, supra, n. 2, at 964–984.

ing some contrary indicia of voluntariness, the Court in a 5-to-4 decision held the confession inadmissible.

There are several relevant lessons to be drawn from this constitutional history. The first is that with over 25 years of precedent the Court has developed an elaborate, sophisticated, and sensitive approach to admissibility of confessions. It is "judicial" in its treatment of one case at a time, see Culombe v. Connecticut, 367 U.S. 568, 635, 81 S.Ct. 1860, 1896, 6 L.Ed.2d 1037 (concurring opinion of The Chief Justice), flexible in its ability to respond to the endless mutations of fact presented, and ever more familiar to the lower courts. Of course, strict certainty is not obtained in this developing process, but this is often so with constitutional principles, and disagreement is usually confined to that borderland of close cases where it matters least.

The second point is that in practice and from time to time in principle, the Court has given ample recognition to society's interest in suspect questioning as an instrument of law enforcement. Cases countenancing quite significant pressures can be cited without difficulty,[5] and the lower courts may often have been yet more tolerant. Of course the limitations imposed today were rejected by necessary implication in case after case, the right to warnings having been explicitly rebuffed in this Court many years ago. Powers v. United States, 223 U.S. 303, 32 S.Ct. 281, 56 L.Ed. 448; Wilson v. United States, 162 U.S. 613, 16 S.Ct. 895, 40 L.Ed. 1090. As recently as Haynes v. State of Washington, 373 U.S. 503, 515, 83 S.Ct. 1336, 1344, the Court openly acknowledged that questioning of witnesses and suspects "is undoubtedly an essential tool in effective law enforcement." Accord, Crooker v. State of California, 357 U.S. 433, 441, 78 S.Ct. 1287, 1292.

Finally, the cases disclose that the language in many of the opinions overstates the actual course of decision. It has been said, for example, that an admissible confession must be made by the suspect "in the unfettered exercise of his own will," Malloy v. Hogan, 378 U.S. 1, 8, 84 S.Ct. 1489, 1493, 12 L.Ed.2d 653, and that "a prisoner is not 'to be made the deluded instrument of his own conviction,'" Culombe v. Connecticut, 367 U.S. 568, 581, 81 S.Ct. 1860, 1867, 6 L.Ed.2d 1037 (Frankfurter, J., announcing the Court's judgment and an opinion). Though often repeated, such principles are rarely observed in full measure. Even the word "voluntary" may be deemed somewhat misleading, especially when one

---

[5] See the cases synopsized in Herman, supra, n. 4, at 456, nn. 36–39. One not too distant example is Stroble v. State of California, 343 U.S. 181, 72 S.Ct. 599, 96 L.Ed. 872, in which the suspect was kicked and threatened after his arrest, questioned a little later for two hours, and isolated from a lawyer trying to see him; the resulting confession was held admissible.

considers many of the confessions that have been brought under its umbrella. See, e. g., supra, n. 5. The tendency to overstate may be laid in part to the flagrant facts often before the Court; but in any event one must recognize how it has tempered attitudes and lent some color of authority to the approach now taken by the Court.

I turn now to the Court's asserted reliance on the Fifth Amendment, an approach which I frankly regard as a *trompe l'oeil*. The Court's opinion in my view reveals no adequate basis for extending the Fifth Amendment's privilege against self-incrimination to the police station. Far more important, it fails to show that the Court's new rules are well supported, let alone compelled, by Fifth Amendment precedents. Instead, the new rules actually derive from quotation and analogy drawn from precedents under the Sixth Amendment, which should properly have no bearing on police interrogation.

The Court's opening contention, that the Fifth Amendment governs police station confessions, is perhaps not an impermissible extension of the law but it has little to commend itself in the present circumstances. Historically, the privilege against self-incrimination did not bear at all on the use of extra-legal confessions, for which distinct standards evolved; indeed, "the *history* of the two principles is wide apart, differing by one hundred years in origin, and derived through separate lines of precedents. * * *" 8 Wigmore, Evidence § 2266, at 401 (McNaughton rev. 1961). Practice under the two doctrines has also differed in a number of important respects.[6] Even those who would readily enlarge the privilege must concede some linguistic difficulties since the Fifth Amendment in terms proscribes only compelling any person "in any criminal case to be a witness against himself." Cf. Kamisar, Equal Justice in the Gatehouses and Mansions of American Criminal Procedure, in Criminal Justice in Our Time 1, 25–26 (1965).

Though weighty, I do not say these points and similar ones are conclusive, for, as the Court reiterates, the privilege embodies basic principles always capable of expansion.[7] Certainly the priv-

---

[6] Among the examples given in 8 Wigmore, Evidence § 2266, at 401 (McNaughton rev. 1961), are these: the privilege applies to any witness, civil or criminal, but the confession rule protects only criminal defendants; the privilege deals only with compulsion, while the confession rule may exclude statements obtained by trick or promise; and where the privilege has been nul-lified—as by the English Bankruptcy Act—the confession rule may still operate.

[7] Additionally, there are precedents and even historical arguments that can be arrayed in favor of bringing extra-legal questioning within the privilege. See generally Maguire, Evidence of Guilt § 2.03, at 15–16 (1959).

ilege does represent a protective concern for the accused and an emphasis upon accusatorial rather than inquisitorial values in law enforcement, although this is similarly true of other limitations such as the grand jury requirement and the reasonable doubt standard. Accusatorial values, however, have openly been absorbed into the due process standard governing confessions; this indeed is why at present "the kinship of the two rules [governing confessions and self-incrimination] is too apparent for denial." McCormick, Evidence 155 (1954). Since extension of the general principle has already occurred, to insist that the privilege applies as such serves only to carry over inapposite historical details and engaging rhetoric and to obscure the policy choices to be made in regulating confessions.

Having decided that the Fifth Amendment privilege does apply in the police station, the Court reveals that the privilege imposes more exacting restrictions than does the Fourteenth Amendment's voluntariness test.[8] It then emerges from a discussion of *Escobedo* that the Fifth Amendment requires for an admissible confession that it be given by one distinctly aware of his right not to speak and shielded from "the compelling atmosphere" of interrogation. See ante, pp. 465–466. From these key premises, the Court finally develops the safeguards of warning, counsel, and so forth. I do not believe these premises are sustained by precedents under the Fifth Amendment.[9]

The more important premise is that pressure on the suspect must be eliminated though it be only the subtle influence of the atmosphere and surroundings. The Fifth Amendment, however, has never been thought to forbid *all* pressure to incriminate one's self in the situations covered by it. On the contrary, it has been held that failure to incriminate one's self can result in denial of removal of one's case from state to federal court, State of Maryland v. Soper, 270 U.S. 9, 46 S.Ct. 185, 70 L.Ed. 449; in refusal of

---

[8] This, of course, is implicit in the Court's introductory announcement that "[o]ur decision in Malloy v. Hogan, 378 U.S. 1, 84 S.Ct. 1489, 12 L.Ed.2d 653 (1964) [extending the Fifth Amendment privilege to the States] necessitates an examination of the scope of the privilege in state cases as well." Ante, p. 1622. It is also inconsistent with *Malloy* itself, in which extension of the Fifth Amendment to the States rested in part on the view that the Due Process Clause restriction on state confessions has in recent years been "the same standard" as that imposed in federal prosecutions assertedly by the Fifth Amendment. 378 U.S., at 7, 84 S.Ct., at 1493.

[9] I lay aside *Escobedo* itself; it contains no reasoning or even general conclusions addressed to the Fifth Amendment and indeed its citation in this regard seems surprising in view of *Escobedo's* primary reliance on the Sixth Amendment.

a military commission, Orloff v. Willoughby, 345 U.S. 83, 73 S.Ct. 534, 97 L.Ed. 842; in denial of a discharge in bankruptcy, Kaufman v. Hurwitz, 4 Cir., 176 F.2d 210; and in numerous other adverse consequences. See 8 Wigmore, Evidence § 2272, at 441–444, n. 18 (McNaughton rev. 1961); Maguire, Evidence of Guilt § 2.062 (1959). This is not to say that short of jail or torture any sanction is permissible in any case; policy and history alike may impose sharp limits. See, e. g., Griffin v. State of California, 380 U.S. 609, 85 S.Ct. 1229, 14 L.Ed.2d 106. However, the Court's unspoken assumption that *any* pressure violates the privilege is not supported by the precedents and it has failed to show why the Fifth Amendment prohibits that relatively mild pressure the Due Process Clause permits.

The Court appears similarly wrong in thinking that precise knowledge of one's rights is a settled prerequisite under the Fifth Amendment to the loss of its protections. A number of lower federal court cases have held that grand jury witnesses need not always be warned of their privilege, e. g., United States v. Scully, 2 Cir., 225 F.2d 113, 116, and Wigmore states this to be the better rule for trial witnesses. See 8 Wigmore, Evidence § 2269 (McNaughton rev. 1961). Cf. Henry v. State of Mississippi, 379 U.S. 443, 451–452, 85 S.Ct. 564, 569, 13 L.Ed.2d 408 (waiver of constitutional rights by counsel despite defendant's ignorance held allowable). No Fifth Amendment precedent is cited for the Court's contrary view. There might of course be reasons apart from Fifth Amendment precedent for requiring warning or any other safeguard on questioning but that is a different matter entirely. See infra, pp. 516–517.

A closing word must be said about the Assistance of Counsel Clause of the Sixth Amendment, which is never expressly relied on by the Court but whose judicial precedents turn out to be linchpins of the confession rules announced today. To support its requirement of a knowing and intelligent waiver, the Court cites Johnson v. Zerbst, 304 U.S. 458, 58 S.Ct. 1019, 82 L.Ed. 1461, ante, p. 475; appointment of counsel for the indigent suspect is tied to Gideon v. Wainwright, 372 U.S. 335, 83 S.Ct. 792, 9 L.Ed.2d 799, and Douglas v. People of State of California, 372 U.S. 353, 83 S.Ct. 814, 9 L.Ed.2d 811, ante, p. 473; the silent-record doctrine is borrowed from Carnley v. Cochran, 369, U.S. 506, 82 S.Ct. 884, 8 L.Ed.2d 70, ante, p. 475, as is the right to an express offer of counsel, ante, p. 471. All these cases imparting glosses to the Sixth Amendment concerned counsel at trial or on appeal. While the Court finds no pertinent difference between judicial proceedings and police interrogation, I believe the differences are so vast as to disqualify wholly the Sixth Amendment precedents as suitable analogies in the present cases.[10]

The only attempt in this Court to carry the right to counsel into the station house occurred in *Escobedo,* the Court repeating several times that that stage was no less "critical" than trial itself. See 378 U.S., 485–488, 84 S.Ct. 1762–1763. This is hardly persuasive when we consider that a grand jury inquiry, the filing of a certiorari petition, and certainly the purchase of narcotics by an undercover agent from a prospective defendant may all be equally "critical" yet provision of counsel and advice on that score have never been thought compelled by the Constitution in such cases. The sound reason why this right is so freely extended for a criminal trial is the severe injustice risked by confronting an untrained defendant with a range of technical points of law, evidence, and tactics familiar to the prosecutor but not to himself. This danger shrinks markedly in the police station where indeed the lawyer in fulfilling his professional responsibilities of necessity may become an obstacle to truthfinding. See infra, n. 12. The Court's summary citation of the Sixth Amendment cases here seems to me best described as "the domino method of constitutional adjudication * * * wherein every explanatory statement in a previous opinion is made the basis for extension to a wholly different situation." Friendly, supra, n. 10, at 950.

III. POLICY COSIDERATIONS.

Examined as an expression of public policy, the Court's new regime proves so dubious that there can be no due compensation for its weakness in constitutional law. The foregoing discussion has shown, I think, how mistaken is the Court in implying that the Constitution has struck the balance in favor of the approach the Court takes. Ante, p. 479. Rather, precedent reveals that the Fourteenth Amendment in practice has been construed to strike a different balance, that the Fifth Amendment gives the Court little solid support in this context, and that the Sixth Amendment should have no bearing at all. Legal history has been streched before to satisfy deep needs of society. In this instance, however, the Court has not and cannot make the powerful showing that its new rules are plainly desirable in the context of our society, something which is surely

[10] Since the Court conspicuously does not assert that the Sixth Amendment itself warrants its new police-interrogation rules, there is no reason now to draw out the extremely powerful historical and precedential evidence that the Amendment will bear no such meaning. See generally Friendly, The Bill of Rights as a Code of Criminal Procedure, 53 Calif.L.Rev. 929, 943–948 (1965).

demanded before those rules are engrafted onto the Constitution and imposed on every State and county in the land.

Without at all subscribing to the generally black picture of police conduct painted by the Court, I think it must be frankly recognized at the outset that police questioning allowable under due process precedents may inherently entail some pressure on the suspect and may seek advantage in his ignorance or weaknesses. The atmosphere and questioning techniques, proper and fair though they be, can in themselves exert a tug on the suspect to confess, and in this light "[t]o speak of any confessions of crime made after arrest as being 'voluntary' or 'uncoerced' is somewhat inaccurate, although traditional. A confession is wholly and incontestably voluntary only if a guilty person gives himself up to the law and becomes his own accuser." Ashcraft v. State of Tennessee, 322 U.S. 143, 161, 64 S.Ct. 921, 929, 88 L.Ed. 1192 (Jackson, J., dissenting). Until today, the role of the Constitution has been only to sift out *undue* pressure, not to assure spontaneous confessions.[11]

The Court's new rules aim to offset these minor pressures and disadvantages intrinsic to any kind of police interrogation. The rules do not serve due process interests in preventing blatant coercion since, as I noted earlier, they do nothing to contain the policeman who is prepared to lie from the start. The rules work for reliability in confessions almost only in the Pickwickian sense that they can prevent some from being given at all.[12] In short, the benefit of this new regime is simply to lessen or wipe out the inherent compulsion and inequalities to which the Court devotes some nine pages of description. Ante, pp. 448–456.

What the Court largely ignores is that its rules impair, if they will not eventually serve wholly to frustrate, an instrument of law enforcement that has long and quite reasonably been thought worth the price paid for it.[13] There can be little doubt that the

---

[11] See supra, n. 4, and text. Of course, the use of terms like voluntariness involves questions of law and terminology quite as much as questions of fact. See Collins v. Beto, 5 Cir., 348 F.2d 823, 832 (concurring opinion); Bator & Vorenberg, supra, n. 4, at 72–73.

[12] The Court's vision of a lawyer "mitigat[ing] the dangers of untrustworthiness" (ante, p. 470) by witnessing coercion and assisting accuracy in the confession is largely a fancy; for if counsel arrives, there is rarely going to be a police station confession. Watts v. State of Indiana, 338, U.S. 49, 59, 69 S.Ct.

1347, 1358, 93 L.Ed. 1801 (separate opinion of Jackson, J.): "[A]ny lawyer worth his salt will tell the suspect in no uncertain terms to make no statement to police under any circumstances." See Enker & Elsen, Counsel for the Suspect, 49 Minn. L.Rev. 47, 66–68 (1964).

[13] This need is, of course, what makes so misleading the Court's comparison of a probate judge readily setting aside as involuntary the will of an old lady badgered and beleaguered by the new heirs. Ante, n. 26. With wills, there is no public interest save in a totally free choice; with confessions, the solu-

Court's new code would markedly decrease the number of confessions. To warn the suspect that he may remain silent and remind him that his confession may be used in court are minor obstructions. To require also an express waiver by the suspect and an end to questioning whenever he demurs must heavily handicap questioning. And to suggest or provide counsel for the suspect simply invites the end of the interrogation. See, supra, n. 12.

How much harm this decision will inflict on law enforcement cannot fairly be predicted with accuracy. Evidence on the role of confessions is notoriously incomplete, see Developments, supra, n. 2, at 941–944, and little is added by the Court's reference to the FBI experience and the resources believed wasted in interrogation. See infra, n. 19, and text. We do know that some crimes cannot be solved without confessions, that ample expert testimony attests to their importance in crime control,[14] and that the Court is taking a real risk with society's welfare in imposing its new regime on the country. The social costs of crime are too great to call the new rules anything but a hazardous experimentation.

While passing over the costs and risks of its experiment, the Court portrays the evils of normal police questioning in terms which I think are exaggerated. Albeit stringently confined by the due process standards interrogation is no doubt often inconvenient and unpleasant for the suspect. However, it is no less so for a man to be arrested and jailed, to have his house searched, or to stand trial in court, yet all this may properly happen to the most innocent given probable cause, a warrant, or an indictment. Society has always paid a stiff price for law and order, and peaceful interrogation is not one of the dark moments of the law.

This brief statement of the competing considerations seems to me ample proof that the Court's preference is highly debatable at best and therefore not to be read into the Constitution. However, it may make the analysis more graphic to consider the actual facts of one of the four cases reversed by the Court. Miranda v. Arizona serves best, being neither the hardest nor easiest of the four under the Court's standards.[15]

---

tion of crime is a countervailing gain, however the balance is resolved.

[14] See, e. g., the voluminous citations to congressional committee testimony and other sources collected in Culombe v. Connecticut, 367 U.S. 568, 578–579, 81 S.Ct. 1860, 1865, 1866, 6 L.Ed.2d 1037, (Frankfurter, J., announcing the Court's judgment and an opinion).

[15] In Westover, a seasoned criminal was practically given the Court's full complement of warnings and did not heed them. The *Stewart* case, on the other hand, involves long detention and successive questioning. In *Vignera*, the facts are complicated and the record somewhat incomplete.

On March 3, 1963, an 18-year-old girl was kidnapped and forcibly raped near Phoenix, Arizona. Ten days later, on the morning of March 13, petitioner Miranda was arrested and taken to the police station. At this time Miranda was 23 years old, indigent, and educated to the extent of completing half the ninth grade. He had "an emotional illness" of the schizophrenic type, according to the doctor who eventually examined him; the doctor's report also stated that Miranda was "alert and oriented as to time, place, and person," intelligent within normal limits, competent to stand trial, and sane within the legal definition. At the police station, the victim picked Miranda out of a lineup, and two officers then took him into a separate room to interrogate him, starting about 11:30 a. m. Though at first denying his guilt, within a short time Miranda gave a detailed oral confession and then wrote out in his own hand and signed a brief statement admitting and describing the crime. All this was accomplished in two hours or less without any force, threats or promises and—I will assume this though the record is uncertain, ante, 491–492 and nn. 66–67—without any effective warnings at all.

Miranda's oral and written confessions are now held inadmissible under the Court's new rules. One is entitled to feel astonished that the Constitution can be read to produce this result. These confessions were obtained during brief, daytime questioning conducted by two officers and unmarked by any of the traditional indicia of coercion. They assured a conviction for a brutal and unsettling crime, for which the police had and quite possibly could obtain little evidence other than the victim's identifications, evidence which is frequently unreliable. There was, in sum, a legitimate purpose, no perceptible unfairness, and certainly little risk of injustice in the interrogation. Yet the resulting confessions, and the responsible course of police practice they represent, are to be sacrificed to the Court's own finespun conception of fairness which I seriously doubt is shared by many thinking citizens in this country.[16]

The tenor of judicial opinion also falls well short of supporting the Court's new approach. Although *Escobedo* has widely been interpreted as an open invitation to lower courts to rewrite the law of confessions, a significant heavy majority of the state and federal decisions in point have sought quite narrow interpretations.[17] Of the courts that have accepted the invitation, it is hard

---

[16] "[J]ustice, though due to the accused, is due to the accuser also. The concept of fairness must not be strained till it is narrowed to a filament. We are to keep the balance true." Snyder v. Commonwealth of Massachusetts, 291 U.S. 97, 122, 54 S.Ct. 330, 338, 78 L.Ed. 674 (Cardozo, J.).

[17] A narrow reading is given in: United States v. Robinson, 354 F.2d 109 (C.A.2d Cir.) ; Davis v. State of North Carolina, 339 F.2d 770

to know how many have felt compelled by their best guess as to this Court's likely construction; but none of the state decisions saw fit to rely on the state privilege against self-incrimination, and no decision at all has gone as far as this Court goes today.[18]

It is also instructive to compare the attitude in this case of those responsible for law enforcement with the official views that existed when the Court undertook three major revisions of prosecutorial practice prior to this case, Johnson v. Zerbst, 304 U.S. 458, 58 S.Ct. 1019, 82 L.Ed. 1461; Mapp v. Ohio, 367 U.S. 643, 81 S.Ct. 1684, 6 L.Ed.2d 1081, and Gideon v. Wainwright, 372 U.S. 335, 83 S.Ct. 792, 9 L.Ed.2d 799. In Johnson, which established that appointed counsel must be offered the indigent in federal criminal trials, the Federal Government all but conceded the basic issue, which had in fact been recently fixed as Department of Justice policy. See Beany, Right to Counsel 29–30, 36–42 (1955). In *Mapp,* which imposed the exclusionary rule on the States for Fourth Amendment violations, more than half of the States had themselves already adopted some such rule. See 367 U.S., at 651, 81 S.Ct., at 1689. In *Gideon,* which extended Johnson v. Zerbst to the States, in *amicus* brief was filed by 22 States and Commonwealths urging that course; only two States besides that of the respondent came forward to protest. See 372 U.S., at 345, 83 S.Ct., at 797. By contrast, in this case new restrictions on police questioning have been opposed by the United States and in an *amicus* brief signed by 27 States and Commonwealths, not including the three other States which are parties. No State in the country has urged this Court to impose the newly announced rules, nor has any State chosen to go nearly so far on its own.

(C.A.4th Cir.); Edwards v. Holman, 342 F.2d 679 (C.A.5th Cir.); United States ex rel. Townsend v. Ogilvie, 334 F.2d 837 (C.A.7th Cir.); People v. Hartgraves, 31 Ill.2d 375, 202 N.E.2d 33; State v. Fox, 131 N.W.2d 684 (Iowa); Rowe v. Commonwealth, 394 S.W.2d 751 (Ky.); Parker v. Warden, 236 Md. 236, 203 A.2d 418; State v. Howard, 383 S.W.2d 701 (Mo.); Bean v. State, 398 P.2d 251 (Nev.); State of New Jersey v. Hodgson, 44 N.J. 151, 207 A.2d 542; People v. Gunner, 15 N.Y.2d 226, 257 N.Y.S.2d 924, 205 N.E.2d 852; Commonwealth ex rel. Linde v. Maroney, 416 Pa. 331, 206 A.2d 288; Browne v. State, 24 Wis.2d 491, 129 N.W.2d 175, 131 N.W.2d 169.

An ample reading is given in: United States ex rel. Russo v. State of New Jersey, 351 F.2d 429 (C.A. 3d Cir.); Wright v. Dickson, 336 F.2d 878 (C.A.9th Cir.); People v. Dorado, 62 Cal.2d 338, 42 Cal.Rptr. 169, 398, P.2d 361; State v. Dufour, 206 A.2d 82 (R.I.); State v. Neely, 239 Or. 487, 395 P.2d 557, modified 398 P.2d 482.

The cases in both categories are those readily available; there are certainly many others.

[18] For instance, compare the requirements of the catalytic case of People v. Dorado, 62 Cal.2d 338, 42 Cal.Rptr. 169, 398 P.2d 361, with those laid down today. See also Traynor, The Devils of Due Process in Criminal Detection, Detention, and Trial, 33 U.Chi.L.Rev. 657, 670.

The Court in closing its general discussion invokes the practice in federal and foreign jurisdictions as lending weight to its new curbs on confessions for all the States. A brief résumé will suffice to show that none of these jurisdictions has struck so one-sided a balance as the Court does today. Heaviest reliance is placed on the FBI practice. Differing circumstances may make this comparison quite untrustworthy,[19] but in any event the FBI falls sensibly short of the Court's formalistic rules. For example, there is no indication that FBI agents must obtain an affirmative "waiver" before they pursue their questioning. Nor is it clear that one invoking his right to silence may not be prevailed upon to change his mind. And the warning as to appointed counsel apparently indicates only that one will be assigned by the judge when the suspect appears before him; the thrust of the Court's rules is to induce the suspect to obtain appointed counsel before continuing the interview. See ante, pp. 484–486. Apparently American military practice, briefly mentioned by the Court, has these same limits and is still less favorable to the suspect than the FBI warning, making no mention of appointed counsel. Developments, supra, n. 2, at 1084–1089.

The law of the foreign countries described by the Court also reflects a more moderate conception of the rights of the accused as against those of society when other data are considered. Concededly, the English experience is most relevant. In that country, a caution as to silence but not counsel has long been mandated by the "judges' Rules," which also place other somewhat imprecise limits on police cross-examination of suspects. However, in the court's discretion confessions can be and apparently quite frequently are admitted in evidence despite disregard of the Judges' Rules, so long as they are found voluntary under the common-law test. Moreover, the check that exists on the use of pretrial statements is counterbalanced by the evident admissibility of fruits of an illegal confession and by the judge's often-used authority to comment adversely on the defendant's failure to testify.[20]

India, Ceylon and Scotland are the other examples chosen by the Court. In India and Ceylon the general ban on police-adduced confessions cited by the Court is subject to a major exception: if

---

[19] The Court's *obiter dictum* notwithstanding, ante, there is some basis for believing that the staple of FBI criminal work differs importantly from much crime within the ken of local police. The skill and resources of the FBI may also be unusual.

[20] For citations and discussion covering each of these points, see Developments, supra, n. 2, at 1091–1097, and Enker & Elsen, supra, n. 12, at 80 & n. 94.

evidence is uncovered by police questioning, it is fully admissible at trial along with the confession itself, so far as it relates to the evidence and is not blatantly coerced. See Developments, supra, n. 2, at 1106–1110; Reg. v. Ramasamy [1965] A.C. 1 (P.C.). Scotland's limits on interrogation do measure up to the Court's; however, restrained comment at trial on the defendant's failure to take the stand is allowed the judge, and in many other respects Scotch law redresses the prosecutor's disadvantage in ways not permitted in this country.[21] The Court ends its survey by imputing added strength to our privilege against self-incrimination since, by contrast to other countries, it is embodied in a written Constitution. Considering the liberties the Court has today taken with constitutional history and precedent, few will find this emphasis persuasive.

In closing this necessarily truncated discussion of policy considerations attending the new confession rules, some reference must be made to their ironic untimeliness. There is now in progress in this country a massive re-examination of criminal law enforcement procedures on a scale never before witnessed. Participants in this undertaking include a Special Committee of the American Bar Association, under the chairmanship of Chief Judge Lumbard of the Court of Appeals for the Second Circuit; a distinguished study group of the American Law Institute, headed by Professors Vorenberg and Bator of the Harvard Law School; and the President's Commission on Law Enforcement and Administration of Justice, under the leadership of the Attorney General of the United States.[22] Studies are also being conducted by the District of Columbia Crime Commission, the Georgetown Law Center, and by others equipped to do practical research.[23] There are also signs that legislatures in some of the States may be preparing to re-examine the problem before us.[24]

---

[21] On Comment, see Hardin, Other Answers: Search and Seizure, Coerced Confession, and Criminal Trial in Scotland, 113 U.Pa.L.Rev. 165, 181 and nn. 96–97 (1964). Other examples are less stringent search and seizure rules and no automatic exclusion for violation of them, id., at 167–169; guilt based on majority jury verdicts, id., at 185; and pre-trial discovery of evidence on both sides, id., at 175.

[22] Of particular relevance is the ALI's drafting of a Model Code of Pre-Arraignment Procedure, now in its first tentative draft. While the ABA and National Commission studies have wider scope, the former is lending its advice to the ALI project and the executive director of the latter is one of the reporters for the Model Code.

[23] See Brief for the United States in Westover, p. 45. The N. Y. Times, June 3, 1966 p. 41 (late city ed.) reported that the Ford Foundation has awarded $1,100,000 for a five-year study of arrests and confessions in New York.

[24] The New York Assembly recently passed a bill to require certain warnings before an admissible confession is taken, though the rules are less strict than are the Court's. N. Y. Times, May 24, 1966, p. 35 (late city ed.).

It is no secret that concern has been expressed lest long-range and lasting reforms be frustrated by this Court's too rapid departure from existing constitutional standards. Despite the Court's disclaimer, the practical effect of the decision made today must inevitably be to handicap seriously sound efforts at reform, not least by removing options necessary to a just compromise of competing interests. Of course legislative reform is rarely speedy or unanimous, though this Court has been more patient in the past.[25] But the legislative reforms when they come would have the vast advantage of empirical data and comprehensive study, they would allow experimentation and use of solutions not open to the courts, and they would restore the initiative in criminal law reform to those forums where it truly belongs.

IV. CONCLUSIONS.

All four of the cases involved here present express claims that confessions were inadmissible, not because of coercion in the traditional due process sense, but solely because of lack of counsel or lack of warnings concerning counsel and silence. For the reasons stated in this opinion, I would adhere to the due process test and reject the new requirements inaugurated by the Court. On this premise my disposition of each of these cases can be stated briefly.

In two of the three cases coming from state courts, Miranda v. Arizona (No. 759) and Vignera v. New York (No. 760), the confessions were held admissible and no other errors worth comment are alleged by petitioners. I would affirm in these two cases. The other state case is California v. Stewart (No. 584), where the state supreme court held the confession inadmissible and reversed the conviction. In that case I would dismiss the writ of certiorari on the ground that no final judgment is before us, 28 U.S.C. § 1257 (1964 ed.) ; putting aside the new trial open to the State in any event, the confession itself has not even been finally excluded since the California Supreme Court left the State free to show proof of a waiver. If the merits of the decision in *Stewart* be reached, then I believe it should be reversed and the case remanded so the state supreme court may pass on the other claims available to respondent.

---

[25] The Court waited 12 years after Wolf v. People of State of Colorado, 338 U.S. 25, 69 S.Ct. 1359, 93 L.Ed. 1782, declared privacy against improper state intrusions to be constitutionally safeguarded before it concluded in Mapp v. Ohio, 367 U.S. 643, 81 S.Ct. 1684, 6 L.Ed.2d 1081, that adequate state remedies had not been provided to protect this interest so the exclusionary rule was necessary.

In the federal case, Westover v. United States (No. 761), a number of issues are raised by petitioner apart from the one already dealt with in this dissent. None of these other claims appears to me tenable, nor in this context to warrant extended discussion. It is urged that the confession was also inadmissible because not voluntary even measured by due process standards and because federal-state cooperation brought the McNabb-Mallory rule into play under Anderson v. United States, 318 U.S. 350, 63 S.Ct. 599, 87 L.Ed. 829. However, the facts alleged fall well short of coercion in my view, and I believe the involvement of federal agents in petitioner's arrest and detention by the State too slight to invoke *Anderson*. I agree with the Government that the admission of the evidence now protested by petitioner was at most harmless error, and two final contentions—one involving weight of the evidence and another improper prosecutor comment—seem to me without merit. I would therefore affirm Westover's conviction.

In conclusion: Nothing in the letter or the spirit of the Constitution or in the precedents squares with the heavy-handed and one-sided action that is so precipitously taken by the Court in the name of fulfilling its constitutional responsibilities. The foray which the Court makes today brings to mind the wise and far-sighted words of Mr. Justice Jackson in Douglas v. City of Jeannette, 319 U.S. 157, 181, 63 S.Ct. 877, 889, 87 L.Ed. 1324 (separate opinion): "This Court is forever adding new stories to the temples of constitutional law, and the temples have a way of collapsing when one story too many is added."

Mr. Justice WHITE, with whom Mr. Justice HARLAN and Mr. Justice STEWART join, dissenting.

I.

The proposition that the privilege against self-incrimination forbids in-custody interrogation without the warnings specified in the majority opinion and without a clear waiver of counsel has no significant support in the history of the privilege or in the language of the Fifth Amendment. As for the English authorities and the common-law history, the privilege, firmly established in the second half of the seventeenth century, was never applied except to prohibit compelled judicial interrogations. The rule excluding coerced confessions matured about 100 years later, "[b]ut there is nothing in the reports to suggest that the theory has its roots in the privilege against self-incrimination. And so far as the cases reveal, the privilege, as such, seems to have been given effect only in judicial proceedings, including the preliminary examinations by authorized magistrates." Morgan, The Privilege Against Self-Incrimination, 34 Minn.L.Rev. 1, 18, (1949).

Our own constitutional provision provides that no person "shall be compelled in any criminal case to be a witness against himself." These words, when "[c]onsidered in the light to be shed by grammar and the dictionary * * * appear to signify simply that nobody shall be compelled to give oral testimony against himself in a criminal proceeding under way in which he is defendant." Corwin, The Supreme Court's Construction of the Self-Incrimination Clause, 29 Mich.L.Rev. 1, 2. And there is very little in the surrounding circumstances of the adoption of the Fifth Amendment or in the provisions of the then existing state constitutions or in state practice which would give the constitutional provision any broader meaning. Mayers, The Federal Witness' Privilege Against Self-Incrimination: Constitutional or Common-Law? 4 American Journal of Legal History 107 (1960). Such a construction, however, was considerably narrower than the privilege at common law, and when eventually faced with the issues, the Court extended the constitutional privilege to the compulsory production of books and papers, to the ordinary witness before the grand jury and to witnesses generally. Boyd v. United States, 116 U.S. 616, 6 S.Ct. 524, 29 L.Ed. 746, and Counselman v. Hitchcock, 142 U.S. 547, 12 S.Ct. 195, 35 L.Ed. 1110. Both rules had solid support in common-law history, if not in the history of our own constitutional provision.

A few years later the Fifth Amendment privilege was similarly extended to encompass the then well-established rule against coerced confessions: "In criminal trials, in the courts of the United States, wherever a question arises whether a confession is incompetent because not voluntary, the issue is controlled by that portion of the Fifth Amendment to the Constitution of the United States, commanding that no person 'shall be compelled in any criminal case to be a witness against himself.'" Bram v. United States, 168 U.S. 532, 542, 18 S.Ct. 183, 187, 42 L.Ed. 568. Although this view has found approval in other cases, Burdeau v. McDowell, 256 U.S. 465, 475, 41 S.Ct. 574, 576, 65 L.Ed. 1048; Powers v. United States, 223 U.S. 303, 313, 32 S.Ct. 281, 283, 56 L.Ed. 448; Shotwell Mfg. Co. v. United States, 371 U.S. 341, 347, 83 S.Ct. 448, 453, 9 L.Ed.2d 357, it has also been questioned, see Brown v. State of Mississippi, 297 U.S. 278, 285, 56 S.Ct. 461, 464, 80 L.Ed. 682; United States v. Carignan, 342 U.S. 36, 41, 72 S.Ct. 97, 100, 96 L.Ed. 48; Stein v. People of State of New York, 346 U.S. 156, 191, n. 35, 73 S.Ct. 1077, 1095, 97 L.Ed. 1522, and finds scant support in either the English or American authorities, see generally Regina v. Scott,

Dears. & Bell 47; 3 Wigmore, Evidence § 823 (3d ed. 1940), at 249 ("a confession is not rejected because of any connection with the *privilege against self-incrimination*"), and 250, n. 5 (particularly criticizing *Bram*) ; 8 Wigmore, Evidence § 2266, at 400–401 (McNaughton rev. 1961). Whatever the source of the rule excluding coerced confessions, it is clear that prior to the application of the privilege itself to state courts, Malloy v. Hogan, 378 U.S. 1, 84 S.Ct. 1489, 12 L.Ed.2d 653, the admissibility of a confession in a state criminal prosecution was tested by the same standards as were applied in federal prosecutions. Id., at 6–7, 10, 84 S.Ct., at 1492–1493, 1494.

Bram, however, itself rejected the proposition which the Court now espouses. The question in *Bram* was whether a confession, obtained during custodial interrogation, had been compelled, and if such interrogation was to be deemed inherently vulnerable the Court's inquiry could have ended there. After examining the English and American authorities, however, the Court declared that: "In this court also it has been settled that the mere fact that the confession is made to a police officer, while the accused was under arrest in or out of prison, or was drawn out by his questions, does not necessarily render the confession involuntary, but, as one of the circumstances, such imprisonment or interrogation may be taken into account in determining whether or not the statements of the prisoner were voluntary." 168 U.S., at 558, 18 S.Ct., at 192.

In this respect the Court was wholly consistent with prior and subsequent pronouncements in this Court.

Thus prior to *Bram* the Court, in Hopt v. People of Territory of Utah, 110 U.S. 574, 583–587, 4 S.Ct. 202, 206, 28 L.Ed. 262, had upheld the admissibility of a confession made to police officers following arrest, the record being silent concerning what conversation had occurred between the officers and the defendant in the short period preceding the confession. Relying on *Hopt*, the Court rules squarely on the issue in Sparf and Hansen v. United States, 156 U.S. 51, 55, 15 S.Ct. 273, 275, 39 L.Ed. 343:

"Counsel for the accused insist that there cannot be a voluntary statement, a free open confession, while a defendant is confined and in irons under an accusation of having committed a capital offence. We have not been referred to any authority in support of that position. It is true that the fact of a prisoner being in custody at the time he makes a confession is a circumstance not to be overlooked, because it bears upon the inquiry whether the confession was voluntarily made or was extorted by threats or violence or made under the influence of fear. But confinement or imprison-

98

ment is not in itself sufficient to justify the exclusion of a confession, if it appears to have been voluntary, and was not obtained by putting the prisoner in fear or by promises. Wharton's Cr.Ev. 9th Ed. §§ 661, 663, and authorities cited."

Accord, Pierce v. United States, 160 U.S. 355, 357, 16 S.Ct. 321, 322, 40 L.Ed. 454.

And in Wilson v. United States, 162 U.S. 613, 623, 16 S.Ct. 895, 899, 40 L.Ed. 1090, the Court had considered the significance of custodial interrogation without any antecedent warnings regarding the right to remain silent or the right to counsel. There the defendant had answered questions posed by a Commissioner, who had failed to advise him of his rights, and his answers were held admissible over his claim of involuntariness. "The fact that [a defendant] is in custody and manacled does not necessarily render his statement involuntary, nor is that necessarily the effect of popular excitement shortly preceding. * * * And it is laid down that it is not essential to the admissibility of a confession that it should appear that the person was warned that what he said would be used against him, but on the contrary, if the confession was voluntary, it is sufficient though it appear that he was not so warned."

Since *Bram*, the admissibility of statements made during custodial interrogation has been frequently reiterated. Powers v. United States, 223 U.S. 303, 32 S.Ct. 281, cited *Wilson* approvingly and held admissible as voluntary statements the accused's testimony at a preliminary hearing even though he was not warned that what he said might be used against him. Without any discussion of the presence or absence of warnings, presumably because such discussion was deemed unnecessary, numerous other cases have declared that "[t]he mere fact that a confession was made while in the custody of the police does not render it inadmissible," McNabb v. United States, 318 U.S. 332, 346, 63 S.Ct. 608, 615, 87 L.Ed. 819; accord, United States v. Mitchell, 322 U.S. 65, 64 S.Ct. 896, 88 L.Ed. 1140, despite its having been elicited by police examination, Ziang Sung Wan v. United States, 266 U.S. 1, 14, 45 S.Ct. 3; United States v. Carignan, 342 U.S. 36, 39, 72 S.Ct. 97, 99. Likewise, in Crooker v. State of California, 357 U.S. 433, 437, 78 S.Ct. 1287, 1290, 2 L.Ed.2d 1448, the Court said that "the bare fact of police 'detention and police examination in private of one in official state custody' does not render involuntary a confession by the one so detained." And finally, in Cicenia v. La Gay, 357 U.S. 504, 78 S.Ct. 1297, 2 L.Ed.2d 1523, a confession obtained by police interrogation after arrest was held voluntary even though the authorities refused to permit the defendant to consult with his attorney. See generally Culombe v. Connecticut, 367 U.S. 568, 587–602, 81 S.Ct.

1860, 1870, 6 L.Ed.2d 1037 (opinion of Frankfurter, J.) ; 3 Wigmore, Evidence § 851, at 313 (3d ed. 1940) ; see also Joy, Admissibility of Confessions 38, 46 (1842).

Only a tiny minority of our judges who have dealt with the question, including today's majority, have considered in-custody interrogation, without more, to be a violation of the Fifth Amendment. And this Court, as every member knows, has left standing literally thousands of criminal convictions that rested at least in part on confessions taken in the course of interrogation by the police after arrest.

II.

That the Court's holding today is neither compelled nor even strongly suggested by the language of the Fifth Amendment, is at odds with American and English legal history, and involves a departure from a long line of precedent does not prove either that the Court has exceeded its powers or that the Court is wrong or unwise in its present reinterpretation of the Fifth Amendment. It does, however, underscore the obvious—that the Court has not discovered or found the law in making today's decision, nor has it derived it from some irrefutable sources; what it has done is to make new law and new public policy in much the same way that it has in the course of interpreting other great clauses of the Constitution.[1] This is what the Court historically has done. Indeed, it is what it must do and will continue to do until and unless there is some fundamental change in the constitutional distribution of governmental powers.

But if the Court is here and now to announce new and fundamental policy to govern certain aspects of our affairs, it is wholly legitimate to examine the mode of this or any other constitutional decision in this Court and to inquire into the advisability of its end product in terms of the long-range interest of the country. At the very least, the Court's text and reasoning should withstand analysis and be a fair exposition of the constitutional provision which its opinion interprets. Decisions like these cannot rest alone on syllogism, metaphysics or some ill-defined notions of natural justice, although each will perhaps play its part. In proceeding to such constructions as it now announces, the Court should also duly consider all the factors and interests bearing upon the cases, at least insofar as the relevant materials are available; and if the

---

[1] Of course the Court does not deny that it is departing from prior precedent; it expressly overrules *Crooker* and *Cicenia*, ante, n. 48, and it acknowledges that in the instant "cases we might not find the defendants' statements to have been involuntary in traditional terms," ante.

necessary considerations are not treated in the record or obtainable from some other reliable source, the Court should not proceed to formulate fundamental policies based on speculation alone.

III.

First, we may inquire what are the textual and factual bases of this new fundamental rule. To reach the result announced on the grounds it does, the Court must stay within the confines of the Fifth Amendment, which forbids self-incrimination only if *compelled*. Hence the core of the Court's opinion is that because of the "compulsion inherent in custodial surroundings, no statement obtained from [a] defendant [in custody] can truly be the product of his free choice," ante, at 458, absent the use of adequate protective devices as described by the Court. However, the Court does not point to any sudden inrush of new knowledge requiring the rejection of 70 years' experience. Nor does it assert that its novel conclusion reflects a changing consensus among state courts, see Mapp v. Ohio, 367 U.S. 643, 81 S.Ct. 1684, 6 L.Ed.2d 1081, or that a succession of cases had steadily eroded the old rule and proved it unworkable, see Gideon v. Wainwright, 372 U.S. 335, 83 S.Ct. 792, 9 L.Ed.2d 799. Rather than asserting new knowledge, the Court concedes that it cannot truly know what occurs during custodial questioning, because of the innate secrecy of such proceedings. It extrapolates a picture of what it conceives to be the norm from police investigatorial manuals, published in 1959 and 1962 or earlier, without any attempt to allow for adjustments in police practices that may have occurred in the wake of more recent decisions of state appellate tribunals or this Court. But even if the relentless application of the described procedures could lead to involuntary confessions, it most assuredly does not follow that each and every case will disclose this kind of interrogation or this kind of consequence.[2] Insofar as appears from the Court's opinion, it has not examined a single transcript of any police interrogation, let alone the interrogation that took place in any one

---

[2] In fact, the type of sustained interrogation described by the Court appears to be the exception rather than the rule. A survey of 399 cases in one city found that in almost half of the cases the interrogation lasted less than 30 minutes. Barrett, Police Practices and the Law—From Arrest to Release or Charge, 50 Calif.L.Rev. 11, 41–45 (1962). Questioning tends to be confused and sporadic and is usually concentrated on confrontations with witnesses or new items of evidence, as these are obtained by officers conducting the investigation. See generally LaFave, Arrest: The Decision to Take a Suspect into Custody 386 (1965); ALI, A Model Code of Pre-Arraignment Procedure, Commentary § 5.01, at 170, n. 4 (Tent.Draft No. 1, 1966).

of these cases which it decides today. Judged by any of the standards for empirical investigation utilized in the social sciences the factual basis for the Court's premise is patently inadequate.

Although in the Court's view in-custody interrogation is inherently coercive, the Court says that the spontaneous product of the coercion of arrest and detention is still to be deemed voluntary. An accused, arrested on probable cause, may blurt out a confession which will be admissible despite the fact that he is alone and in custody, without any showing that he had any notion of his right to remain silent or of the consequences of his admission. Yet, under the Court's rule, if the police ask him a single question such as "Do you have anything to say?" or "Did you kill your wife?" his response, if there is one, has somehow been compelled, even if the accused has been clearly warned of his right to remain silent. Common sense informs us to the contrary. While one may say that the response was "involuntary" in the sense the question provoked or was the occasion for the response and thus the defendant was induced to speak out when he might have remained silent if not arrested and not questioned, it is patently unsound to say the response is compelled.

Today's result would not follow even if it were agreed that to some extent custodial interrogation is inherently coercive. See Ashcraft v. State of Tennessee, 322 U.S. 143, 161, 64 S.Ct. 921, 929, 88 L.Ed. 1192 (Jackson, J., dissenting). The test has been whether the totality of circumstances deprived the defendant of a "free choice to admit, to deny, or to refuse to answer," Lisenba v. People of State of California, 314 U.S. 219, 241, 62 S.Ct. 280, 292, 86 L.Ed. 166, and whether physical or psychological coercion was of such a degree that "the defendant's will was overborne at the time he confessed," Haynes v. State of Washington, 373 U.S. 503, 513, 83 S.Ct. 1336, 1343, 10 L.Ed.2d 513; Lynumn v. State of Illinois, 372 U.S. 528, 534, 83 S.Ct. 917, 920, 9 L.Ed.2d 922. The duration and nature of incommunicado custody, the presence or absence of advice concerning the defendant's constitutional rights, and the granting or refusal of requests to communicate with lawyers, relatives or friends have all been rightly regarded as important data bearing on the basic inquiry. See, e.g., Ashcraft v. State of Tennessee, 322 U.S. 143, 64 S.Ct. 921; Haynes v. State of Washington, 373 U.S. 503, 83 S.Ct. 1336.[3] But it has never been suggested, until

---

[3] By contrast, the Court indicates that in applying this new rule it "will not pause to inquire in individual cases whether the defendant was aware of his rights without a warning being given." Ante, at 468. The reason given is that assessment of the knowledge of the defendant based on information as to age, education, intelligence, or prior contact with authorities can never be more than speculation,

today, that such questioning was so coercive and accused persons so lacking in hardihood that the very first response to the very first question following the commencement of custody must be conclusively presumed to be the product of an overborne will.

If the rule announced today were truly based on a conclusion that all confessions resulting from custodial interrogation are coerced, then it would simply have no rational foundation. Compare Tot v. United States, 319 U.S. 463, 466, 63 S.Ct. 1241, 1244, 87 L.Ed. 1519; United States v. Romano, 382 U.S. 136, 86 S.Ct. 279, 15 L.Ed.2d 210. *A fortiori* that would be true of the extension of the rule to exculpatory statements, which the Court effects after a brief discussion of why, in the Court's view, they must be deemed incriminatory but without any discussion of why they must be deemed coerced. See Wilson v. United States, 162 U.S. 613, 624, 16 S.Ct. 895, 900, 40 L.Ed. 1090. Even if one were to postulate that the Court's concern is not that all confessions induced by police interrogation are coerced but rather that some such confessions are coerced and present judicial procedures are believed to be inadequate to identify the confessions that are coerced and those that are not, it would still not be essential to impose the rule that the Court has now fashioned. Transcripts or observers could be required, specific time limits, tailored to fit the cause, could be imposed, or other devices could be utilized to reduce the chances that otherwise indiscernible coercion will produce an inadmissible confession.

On the other hand, even if one assumed that there was an adequate factual basis for the conclusion that all confessions obtained during in-custody interrogation are the product of compulsion, the rule propounded by the Court would still be irrational, for, apparently, it is only if the accused is also warned of his right to counsel and waives both that right and the right against self-incrimination that the inherent compulsiveness of interrogation disappears. But if the defendant may not answer without a warning a question such as "Where were you last night?" without having his answer be a compelled one, how can the Court ever accept his negative answer to the question of whether he wants to consult his retained counsel or counsel whom the court will appoint? And

---

while a warning is a clear-cut fact. But the officers' claim that they gave the requisite warnings may be disputed, and facts respecting the defendant's prior experience may be undisputed and be of such a nature as to virtually preclude any doubt that the defendant knew of his rights. See United States v. Bolden, 355 F.2d 453 (C.A.7th Cir. 1965), petition for cert. pending No. 1146, O. T. 1965 (Secret Service agent); People v. Du Bont, 235 Cal. App.2d 844, 45 Cal.Rptr. 717, pet. for cert. pending No. 1053, Misc., O. T. 1965 (former police officer).

why if counsel is present and the accused nevertheless confesses, or counsel tells the accused to tell the truth, and that is what the accused does, is the situation any less coercive insofar as the accused is concerned? The Court apparently realizes its dilemma of foreclosing questioning without the necessary warnings but at the same time permitting the accused, sitting in the same chair in front of the same policemen, to waive his right to consult an attorney. It expects, however, that the accused will not often waive the right; and if it is claimed that he has, the State faces a severe, if not impossible burden of proof.

All of this makes very little sense in terms of the compulsion which the Fifth Amendment proscribes. That amendment deals with compelling the accused himself. It is his free will that is involved. Confessions and incriminating admissions, as such, are not forbidden evidence; only those which are compelled are banned. I doubt that the Court observes these distinctions today. By considering any answers to any interrogation to be compelled regardless of the content and course of examination and by escalating the requirements to prove waiver, the Court not only prevents the use of compelled confessions but for all practical purposes forbids interrogation except in the presence of counsel. That is, instead of confining itself to protection of the right against compelled self-incrimination the Court has created a limited Fifth Amendment right to counsel—or, as the Court expresses it, a "need for counsel to protect the Fifth Amendment privilege * * *." Ante, at 470. The focus then is not on the will of the accused but on the will of counsel and how much influence he can have on the accused. Obviously there is no warrant in the Fifth Amendment for thus installing counsel as the arbiter of the privilege.

In sum, for all the Court's expounding on the menacing atmosphere of police interrogation procedures, it has failed to supply any foundation for the conclusions it draws or the measures it adopts.

IV.

Criticism of the Court's opinion, however, cannot stop with a demonstration that the factual and textual bases for the rule it propounds are, at best, less than compelling. Equally relevant is an assessment of the rule's consequences measured against community values. The Court's duty to assess the consequences of its action is not satisfied by the utterance of the truth that a value of our system of criminal justice is "to respect the inviolability of the human personality" and to require government to produce the evidence against the accused by its own independent labors. Ante, at 460. More than the human dignity of the accused is involved; the human personality of others in the society must also be preserved. Thus the values reflected by the privilege are not the sole desideratum; society's interest in the general security is of equal weight.

The obvious underpinning of the Court's decision is a deep-seated distrust of all confessions. As the Court declares that the accused may not be interrogated without counsel present, absent a waiver of the right to counsel, and as the Court all but admonishes the lawyer to advise the accused to remain silent, the result adds up to a judicial judgment that evidence from the accused should not be used against him in any way, whether compelled or not. This is the not so subtle overtone of the opinion—that it is inherently wrong for the police to gather evidence from the accused himself. And this is precisely the nub of this dissent. I see nothing wrong or immoral, and certainly nothing unconstitutional, in the police's asking a suspect whom they have reasonable cause to arrest whether or not he killed his wife or in confronting him with the evidence on which the arrest was based, at least where he has been plainly advised that he may remain completely silent, see Escobedo v. State of Illinois, 378 U.S. 478, 499, 84 S.Ct. 1758, 1769, 12 L.Ed.2d 977 (dissenting opinion). Until today, "the admissions or confessions of the prisoner, when voluntarily and freely made, have always ranked high in the scale of incriminating evidence." Brown v. Walker, 161 U.S. 591, 596, 16 S.Ct. 644, 646, 40 L.Ed. 819; see also Hopt v. People of Territory of Utah, 110 U.S. 574, 584–585, 4 S.Ct. 202, 207. Particularly when corroborated, as where the police have confirmed the accused's disclosure of the hiding place of implements or fruits of the crime, such confessions have the highest reliability and significantly contribute to the certitude with which we may believe the accused is guilty. Moreover, it is by no means certain that the process of confessing is injurious to the accused. To the contrary it may provide psychological relief and enhance the prospects for rehabilitation.

This is not to say that the value of respect for the inviolability of the accused's individual personality should be accorded no weight or that all confessions should be indiscriminately admitted. This Court has long read the Constitution to proscribe compelled confessions, a salutary rule from which there should be no retreat. But I see no sound basis, factual or otherwise, and the Court gives none, for concluding that the present rule against the receipt of coerced confessions is inadequate for the task of sorting out inadmissible evidence and must be replaced by the *per se* rule which is now imposed. Even if the new concept can be said to have advantages of some sort over the present law, they are far outweighed by its likely undesirable impact on other very relevant and important interests.

The most basic function of any government is to provide for the security of the individual and of his property. Lanzetta v. State of New Jersey, 306 U.S. 451, 455, 59 S.Ct. 618, 619, 83 L.Ed. 888. These ends of society are served by the criminal laws which for the most part are aimed at the prevention of crime. Without the reasonably effective performance of the task of preventing private violence and retaliation, it is idle to talk about human dignity and civilized values.

The modes by which the criminal laws serve the interest in general security are many. First the murderer who has taken the life of another is removed from the streets, deprived of his liberty and thereby prevented from repeating his offense. In view of the statistics on recidivism in this country[4] and of the number of instances

---

[4] Precise statistics on the extent of recidivism are unavailable, in part because not all crimes are solved and in part because criminal records of convictions in different jurisdictions are not brought together by a central data collection agency. Beginning in 1963, however, the Federal Bureau of Investigation began collating data on "Careers in Crime," which it publishes in its Uniform Crime Reports. Of 92,869 offenders processed in 1963 and 1964, 76% had a prior arrest record on some charge. Over a period of 10 years the group had accumulated 434,000 charges. FBI, Uniform Crime Reports—1964, 27–28. In 1963 and 1964 between 23% and 25% of all offenders sentenced in 88 federal district courts (excluding the District Court for the District of Columbia) whose criminal records were reported had previously been sentenced to a term of imprisonment of 13 months or more. Approximately an additional 40% had a prior record less than prison (juvenile record, probation record, etc.). Administrative Office of the United States Courts, Federal Offenders in the United States District Courts: 1964, x, 36 (hereinafter cited as Federal Offenders: 1964); Administrative Office of the United States Courts, Federal Offenders in the United States District Courts: 1963, 25–27 (hereinafter cited as Federal Offenders: 1963). During the same two years in the District Court for the District of Columbia between 28% and 35% of those sentenced had prior prison records and from 37% to 40% had a prior record less than prison. Federal Offenders: 1964, xii, 64, 66; Administrative Office of the United States Courts, Federal Offenders in the United States District Court for the District of Columbia: 1963, 8, 10 (hereinafter cited as District of Columbia Offenders: 1963).

A similar picture is obtained if one looks at the subsequent records of those released from confinement. In 1964, 12.3% of persons on federal probation had their probation revoked because of the commission of major violations (defined as one in which the probationer has been committed to imprisonment for a period of 90 days or more, been placed on probation for over one year on a new offense, or has absconded with felony charges outstanding). Twenty-three and two-tenths percent of parolees and 16.9% of those who had been mandatorily released after service of a portion of their sentence likewise committed major violations. Reports of the Proceedings of the Judicial Conference of the United States and Annual Report of the Director of the Administrative Office of the United States Courts: 1965, 138. See also Mandel et al., Recidivism Studied and Defined, 56 J. Crim.L., C. & P.S. 59 (1965) (within five years of release 62.33% of sample had committed offenses placing them in recidivist category).

in which apprehension occurs only after repeated offenses, no one can sensibly claim that this aspect of the criminal law does not prevent crime or contribute significantly to the personal security of the ordinary citizen.

Secondly, the swift and sure apprehension of those who refuse to respect the personal security and dignity of their neighbor unquestionably has its impact on others who might be similarly tempted. That the criminal law is wholly or partly ineffective with a segment of the population or with many of those who have been apprehended and convicted is a very faulty basis for concluding that it is not effective with respect to the great bulk of our citizens or for thinking that without the criminal laws, or in the absence of their enforcement, there would be no increase in crime. Arguments of this nature are not borne out by any kind of reliable evidence that I have seen to this date.

Thirdly, the law concerns itself with those whom it has confined. The hope and aim of modern penology, fortunately, is as soon as possible to return the convict to society a better and more law-abiding man than when he left. Sometimes there is success, sometimes failure. But at least the effort is made, and it should be made to the very maximum extent of our present and future capabilities.

The rule announced today will measurably weaken the ability of the criminal law to perform these tasks. It is a deliberate calculus to prevent interrogations, to reduce the incidence of confessions and pleas of guilty and to increase the number of trials.[5] Criminal trials, no matter how efficient the police are, are not sure

---

[5] Eighty-eight federal district courts (excluding the District Court for the District of Columbia) disposed of the cases of 33,381 criminal defendants in 1964. Only 12.5% of those cases were actually tried. Of the remaining cases, 89.9% were terminated by convictions upon pleas of guilty and 10.1% were dismissed. Stated differently, approximately 90% of all convictions resulted from guilty pleas. Federal Offenders: 1964, supra, note 4, 3–6. In the District Court for the District of Columbia a higher percentage, 27%, went to trial, and the defendant pleaded guilty in approximately 78% of the cases terminated prior to trial. Id., at 58–59. No reliable statistics are available concerning the percentage of cases in which guilty pleas are induced because of the existence of a confession or of physical evidence unearthed as a result of a confession. Undoubtedly the number of such cases is substantial.

Perhaps of equal significance is the number of instances of known crimes which are not solved. In 1964, only 388,946, or 23.9% of 1,626,574 serious known offenses were cleared. The clearance rate ranged from 89.8% for homicides to 18.7% for larceny. FBI, Uniform Crime Reports—1964, 20–22, 101. Those who would replace interrogation as an investigatorial tool by modern scientific investigation techniques significantly overestimate the effectiveness of present procedures, even when interrogation is included.

bets for the prosecution, nor should they be if the evidence is not forthcoming. Under the present law, the prosecution fails to prove its case in about 30% of the criminal cases actually tried in the federal courts. See Federal Offenders: 1964, supra, note 4, at 6 (Table 4), 59 (Table 1) ; Federal Offenders: 1963, supra, note 4, at 5 (Table 3) ; District of Columbia Offenders: 1963, supra, note 4, at 2 (Table 1). But it is something else again to remove from the ordinary criminal case all those confessions which heretofore have been held to be free and voluntary acts of the accused and to thus establish a new constitutional barrier to the ascertainment of truth by the judicial process. There is, in my view, every reason to believe that a good many criminal defendants who otherwise would have been convicted on what this Court has previously thought to be the most satisfactory kind of evidence will now, under this new version of the Fifth Amendment, either not be tried at all or will be acquitted if the State's evidence, minus the confession, is put to the test of litigation.

I have no desire whatsoever to share the responsibility for any such impact on the present criminal process.

In some unknown number of cases the Court's rule will return a killer, a rapist or other criminal to the streets and to the environment which produced him, to repeat his crime whenever it pleases him. As a consequence, there will not be a gain, but a loss, in human dignity. The real concern is not the unfortunate consequences of this new decision on the criminal law as an abstract, disembodied series of authoritative proscriptions, but the impact on those who rely on the public authority for protection and who without it can only engage in violent self-help with guns, knives and the help of their neighbors similarly inclined. There is, of course, a saving factor: the next victims are uncertain, unnamed and unrepresented in this case.

Nor can this decision do other than have a corrosive effect on the criminal laws as an effective device to prevent crime. A major component in its effectiveness in this regard is its swift and sure enforcement. The easier it is to get away with rape and murder, the less the deterrent effect on those who are inclined to attempt it. This is still good common sense. If it were not, we should posthaste liquidate the whole law enforcement establishment as a useless, misguided effort to control human conduct.

And what about the accused who has confessed or would confess in response to simple, noncoercive questioning and whose guilt could not otherwise be proved? Is it so clear that release is the best thing for him in every case? Has it so unquestionably been resolved that in each and every case it would be better for him not to confess and

108

to return to his environment with no attempt whatsoever to help him? I think not. It may well be that in many cases it will be no less than a callous disregard for his own welfare as well as for the interests of his next victim.

There is another aspect to the effect of the Court's rule on the person whom the police have arrested on probable cause. The fact is that he may not be guilty at all and may be able to extricate himself quickly and simply if he were told the circumstances of his arrest and were asked to explain. This effort, and his release, must now await the hiring of a lawyer or his appointment by the court, consultation with counsel and then a session with the police or the prosecutor. Similarly, where probable cause exists to arrest several suspects, as where the body of the victim is discovered in a house having several residents, compare Johnson v. State, 238 Md. 140, 207 A.2d 643 (1965), cert. denied, 382 U.S. 1013, 86 S.Ct. 623, 15 L.Ed.2d 528, it will often be true that a suspect may be cleared only through the results of interrogation of other suspects. Here too the release of the innocent may be delayed by the Court's rule.

Much of the trouble with the Court's new rule is that it will operate indiscriminately in all criminal cases, regardless of the severity of the crime or the circumstances involved. It applies to every defendant, whether the professional criminal or one committing a crime of momentary passion who is not part and parcel of organized crime. It will slow down the investigation and the apprehension of confederates in those cases where time is of the essence, such as kidnapping, see Brinegar v. United States, 338 U.S. 160, 183, 69 S.Ct. 1302, 1314, 93 L.Ed. 1879 (Jackson, J., dissenting); People v. Modesto, 62 Cal.2d 436, 446, 42 Cal.Rptr. 417, 423, 398 P.2d 753, 759 (1965), those involving the national security, see United States v. Drummond, 354 F.2d 132, 147 (C.A.2d Cir. 1965) (*en banc*) (espionage case), pet. for cert. pending, No. 1203, Misc., O.T. 1965; cf. Gessner v. United States, 354 F.2d 726, 730, n. 10 (C.A.10th Cir. 1965) (upholding, in espionage case, trial ruling that Government need not submit classified portions of interrogation transcript), and some of those involving organized crime. In the latter context the lawyer who arrives may also be the lawyer for the defendant's colleagues and can be relied upon to insure that no breach of the organization's security takes place even though the accused may feel that the best thing he can do is to cooperate.

At the same time, the Court's *per se* approach may not be justified on the ground that it provides a "bright line" permitting the authorities to judge in advance whether interrogation may safely be pursued without jeopardizing the admissibility of any information obtained as a consequence. Nor can it be claimed that judicial time and effort, assuming that is a relevant consideration, will be conserved because of the ease of application of the new rule. Today's decision leaves open such questions as whether the accused was in custody, whether his statements were spontaneous or the product of interrogation, whether the accused has effectively waived his rights, and whether nontestimonial evidence introduced at trial is the fruit of statements made during a prohibited interrogation, all of which are certain to prove productive of uncertainty during investigation and litigation during prosecution. For all these reasons, if further restrictions on police interrogation are desirable at this time, a more flexible approach makes much more sense than the Court's constitutional straitjacket which forecloses more discriminating treatment by legislative or rule-making pronouncements.

Applying the traditional standards to the cases before the Court, I would hold these confessions voluntary. I would therefore affirm in Nos. 759, 760, and 761, and reverse in No. 584.

United States v. Wade*

The police lineup comes under judicial scrutiny in this case. Wade was forced to participate in a police lineup, by dressing in attire resembling that of a felon and repeating words used by him, at the scene of the crime. All this took place without the presence of counsel. Wade contended that such tactics compelled him to be a witness against himself in violation of the Fifth Amendment, and deprived him of the assistance of counsel in violation of the Sixth Amendment.

Justice Douglas, Black, Fortas and Warren conclude that Wade's participation in the lineup violated his Fifth Amendment rights. The majority, relying on a prior Supreme Court decision, *Schmerber v California*,[1] held that it did not. In *Schmerber* the Court held that compelling a suspect to submit to a withdrawal of a sample of blood for analysis of alcoholic content and the admission of the report into evidence did not violate the suspect's Fifth Amendment rights.

But on the question of right to counsel, the Court ruled in Wade's favor, holding that counsel should be present at any lineup proceed-

---

* 388 U.S. 218, 87 S.Ct. 1926 (June 12, 1962)
[1] Schmerber v. California, 384 U.S. 757, 86 S.Ct. 1826 (1966).

ing as it is a critical stage of the prosecution. The concept of right to counsel is expanded again as it had been in *Escobedo*[2] and *Miranda*.[3]

Justices White, Harlan and Stewart dissented from the Court's holding on the right to counsel issue. The *Escobedo* and *Miranda* cases were five to four decisions with Justices White, Harlan, Stewart and Clark dissenting. It is interesting to note that Mr. Justice Clark has sided with the liberal view in *Wade*. This shift is probably no more than a reflection of the considerable factual differences between the *Wade* case and the other two decisions. Had Mr. Justice Clark been faced with additional *Escobedos* and *Mirandas*, it is likely that he would have reaffirmed the conservative view on the scope of an accused's right to counsel. But Mr. Justice Clark never participated in such additional decisions as his retirement became effective on the day the *Wade* decision was rendered.

After Wade's conviction was reversed, the Federal Government declined to prosecute him again. But Wade's freedom was short lived. He soon found himself in trouble with the State of Arizona. On October 14, 1968, he pleaded guilty in Arizona to a local offense, having committed armed robbery,[4] and he is presently serving a sentence of from twenty years to life on that conviction.

Text of Case

Several weeks after respondent's indictment for robbery of a federally insured bank and for conspiracy, respondent, without notice to his appointed counsel, was placed in a lineup in which each person wore strips of tape on his face, as the robber allegedly had done, and on direction repeated words like those the robber allegedly had used. Two bank employees identified respondent as the robber. At the trial when asked if the robber was in the courtroom, they identified respondent. The prior lineup identifications were elicited on cross-examination. Urging that the conduct of the line-up violated his Fifth Amendment privilege against self-incrimination and his Sixth Amendment right to counsel, respondent filed a motion for judgment of acquittal or, alternatively, to strike the courtroom identifications. The trial court denied the motions and respondent was convicted. The Court of Appeals reversed, holding that though there was no Fifth Amendment deprivation the absence of counsel at the lineup denied respondent

---

[2] Escobedo v. Illinois, 378 U.S. 478, 84 S.Ct. 1758 (1964).

[3] Miranda v. Arizona, 384 U.S. 436, 86 S.Ct. 1602 (1966).

[4] Federal Buereau of Investigation records, Dallas, Texas office.

his right to counsel under the Sixth Amendment and required the grant of a new trial at which the in-court identifications of those who had made lineup identifications would be excluded.

Beatrice Rosenberg argued the cause for the United States. With her on the brief were *Acting Solicitor General Spritzer, Assistant Attorney General Vinson, Nathan Lewin* and *Ronald L. Gainer.*

Weldon Holcomb argued the cause and filed a brief for respondent.

Mr. Justice BRENNAN delivered the opinion of the Court.

The question here is whether courtroom identifications of an accused at trial are to be excluded from evidence because the accused was exhibited to the witnesses before trial at a post-indictment lineup conducted for identification purposes without notice to and in the absence of the accused's appointed counsel.

The federally insured bank in Eustace, Texas, was robbed on September 21, 1964. A man with a small strip of tape on each side of his face entered the bank, pointed a pistol at the female cashier and the vice president, the only persons in the bank at the time, and forced them to fill a pillowcase with the bank's money. The man then drove away with an accomplice who had been waiting in a stolen car outside the bank. On March 23, 1965, an indictment was returned against respondent, Wade, and two others for conspiring to rob the bank, and against Wade and the accomplice for the robbery itself. Wade was arrested on April 2, and counsel was appointed to represent him on April 26. Fifteen days later an FBI agent, without notice to Wade's lawyer, arranged to have the two bank employees observe a lineup made up of Wade and five or six other prisoners and conducted in a courtroom of the local county courthouse. Each person in the line wore strips of tape such as allegedly worn by the robber and upon direction each said something like "put the money in the bag," the words allegedly uttered by the robber. Both bank employees indentified Wade in the lineup as the bank robber.

At trial, the two employees, when asked on direct examination if the robber was in the courtroom, pointed to Wade. The prior lineup identification was then elicited from both employees on cross-examination. At the close of testimony, Wade's counsel moved for a judgment of acquittal or, alternatively, to strike the bank officials' courtroom identifications on the ground that conduct of the lineup, without notice to and in the absence of his appointed counsel, violated his Fifth Amendment privilege against self-incrimination and his Sixth Amendment right to the assistance of counsel. The motion

112

was denied, and Wade was convicted. The Court of Appeals for the Fifth Circuit reversed the conviction and ordered a new trial at which the in-court identification evidence was to be excluded, holding that, though the lineup did not violate Wade's Fifth Amendment rights, "the lineup, held as it was, in the absence of counsel, already chosen to represent appellant, was a violation of his Sixth Amendment rights * * *." 358 F.2d 557, 560. We granted certiorari, 385 U.S. 811, 87 S.Ct. 81, 17 L.Ed.2d 53, and set the case for oral argument with No. 223, Gilbert v. State of California, post, p. 263, 388 U.S. 263, 87 S.Ct. 1951, 18 L.Ed.2d 1178, and No. 254, Stovall v. Denno, post, p. 263, 386 U.S. 293, 87 S.Ct. 1967, 18 L.Ed.2d 1199, which present similar questions. We reverse the judgment of the Court of Appeals and remand to that court with direction to enter a new judgment vacating the conviction and remanding the case to the District Court for further proceedings consistent with this opinion.

I.

Neither the lineup itself nor anything shown by this record that Wade was required to do in the lineup violated his privilege against self-incrimination. We have only recently reaffirmed that the privilege "protects an accused only from being compelled to testify against himself, or otherwise provide the State with evidence of a testimonial or communicative nature * * *." Schmerber v. State of California, 384 U.S. 757, 761, 86 S.Ct. 1826, 1830, 16 L.Ed.2d 908. We there held that compelling a suspect to submit to a withdrawal of a sample of his blood for analysis for alcohol content and the admission in evidence of the analysis report were not compulsion to those ends. That holding was supported by the opinion in Holt v. United States, 218 U.S. 245, 31 S.Ct. 2, 54 L.Ed. 1021, in which case a question arose as to whether a blouse belonged to the defendant. A witness testified at trial that the defendant put on the blouse and it had fit him. The defendant argued that the admission of the testimony was error because compelling him to put on the blouse was a violation of his privilege. The Court rejected the claim as "an extravagent extension of the Fifth Amendment," Mr. Justice Holmes saying for the Court:

"[T]he prohibition of compelling a man in a criminal court to be witness against himself is a prohibition of the use of physical or moral compulsion to extort communications from him, not an exclusion of his body as evidence when it may be material." 218 U.S., at 252–253, 31 S.Ct. at 6.

The Court in Holt, however, put aside any constitutional questions which might be involved in compelling an accused, as here, to exhibit himself before victims of or witnesses to an alleged crime;

the Court stated, "we need not consider how far a court would go in compelling a man to exhibit himself." Id., at 253, 31 S.Ct. at 6.[1]

We have no doubt that compelling the accused merely to exhibit his person for observation by a prosecution witness prior to trial involves no compulsion of the accused to give evidence having testimonial significance. It is compulsion of the accused to exhibit his physical characteristics, not compulsion to disclose any knowledge he might have. It is no different from compelling Schmerber to provide a blood sample or Holt to wear the blouse, and, as in those instances, is not within the cover of the privilege. Similarly, compelling Wade to speak within hearing distance of the witnesses, even to utter words purportedly uttered by the robber, was not compulsion to utter statements of a "testimonial" nature; he was required to use his voice as an identifying physical characteristic, not to speak his guilt. We held in *Schmerber,* supra, 384 U.S. at 761, 86 S.Ct. at 1830, that the distinction to be drawn under the Fifth Amendment privilege against self-incrimination is one between an accused's "communications" in whatever form, vocal or physical, and "compulsion which makes a suspect or accused the source of 'real or physical evidence,' " *Schmerber,* supra, at 764, 86 S.Ct. at 1832. We recognized that "both federal and state courts have usually held that * * * [the privilege] offers no protection against compulsion to submit to fingerprinting, photography, or measurements, to write or speak for identification, to appear in court, to stand, to assume a stance, to walk, or to make a particular gesture." Id., at 764, 86 S.Ct. at 1832. None of these activities becomes testimonial within the scope of the privilege because required of the accused in a pretrial lineup.

Moreover, it deserves emphasis that this case presents no question of the admissibility in evidence of anything Wade said or did at the lineup which implicates his privilege. The Government offered no such evidence as part of its case, and what came out about the lineup proceedings on Wade's cross-examination of the bank employees involved no violation of Wade's privilege.

---

[1] *Holt* was decided before Weeks v. United States, 232 U.S. 383, 34 S. Ct. 341, 58 L.Ed. 652, fashioned the rule excluding illegally obtained evidence in a federal prosecution. The Court therefore followed Adams v. People of State of New York, 192 U.S. 585, 24 S.Ct. 372, 48 L. Ed. 575, in holding that, in any event, "when he is exhibited, whether voluntarily or by order, and even if the order goes too far, the evidence, if material, is competent." 218 U.S., at 253, 31 S.Ct. at 6.

II.

The fact that the lineup involved no violation of Wade's privilege against self-incrimination does not, however, dispose of his contention that the courtroom identifications should have been excluded because the lineup was conducted without notice to and in the absence of his counsel. Our rejection of the right to counsel claim in *Schmerber* rested on our conclusion in that case that "[n]o issue of counsel's ability to assist petitioner in respect of any rights he did possess is presented." 384 U.S., at 766, 86 S.Ct. at 1833. In contrast, in this case it is urged that the assistance of counsel at the lineup was indispensable to protect Wade's most basic right as a criminal defendant—his right to a fair trial at which the witnesses against him might be meaningfully cross-examined.

The Framers of the Bill of Rights envisaged a broader role for counsel than under the practice then prevailing in England of merely advising his client in "matters of law," and eschewing any responsibility for "matters of fact."[2] The constitutions in at least 11 of the 13 States expressly or impliedly abolished this distinction. Powell v. State of Alabama, 287 U.S. 45, 60–65, 53 S.Ct. 55, 60–62, 77 L.Ed. 158; Note, 73 Yale L.J. 1000, 1030–1033 (1964). "Though the colonial provisions about counsel were in accord on few things, they agreed on the necessity of abolishing the facts-law distinction; the colonists appreciated that if a defendant were forced to stand alone against the state, his case was foredoomed." 73 Yale L.J., supra, at 1033–1034. This background is reflected in the scope given by our decisions to the Sixth Amendment's guarantee to an accused of the assistance of counsel for his defense. When the Bill of Rights was adopted, there were no organized police forces as we know them today.[3] The accused confronted the prosecutor and the witnesses against him, and the evidence was marshalled, largely at the trial itself. In contrast, today's law enforcement machinery involves critical confrontations of the accused by the prosecution at pretrial proceedings where the results might well settle the accused's fate and reduce the trial itself to a mere formality. In recognition of these realities of modern criminal prosecution, our cases have construed the Sixth Amendment guarantee to apply to "critical" stages of the proceedings. The guarantee reads: "In all criminal prosecutions, the accused shall enjoy the right * * * to have the Assistance of Counsel *for his defence.*" (Emphasis supplied.) The plain wording of this guarantee thus encompasses coun-

---

[2] See Powell v. State of Alabama, 287 U.S. 45, 60–65, 53 S.Ct. 55, 60–62, 77 L.Ed. 158; Beaney, Right to Counsel in American Courts 8–26.

[3] See Note, 73 Yale L.J. 1000, 1040–1042 (1964); Comment, 53 Calif. L.Rev. 337, 347–348 (1965).

sel's assistance whenever necessary to assure a meaningful "defence."

As early as Powell v. State of Alabama, supra, we recognized that the period from arraignment to trial was "perhaps the most critical period of the proceedings * * *," id., at 57, 53 S.Ct. at 59, during which the accused "requires the guiding hand of counsel * * *," id., at 69, 53 S.Ct. at 64 if the guarantee is not to prove an empty right. That principle has since been applied to require the assistance of counsel at the type of arraignment—for example, that provided by Alabama—where certain rights might be sacrificed or lost: "What happens there may affect the whole trial. Available defenses may be irretrievably lost, if not then and there asserted * * *." Hamilton v. State of Alabama, 368 U.S. 52, 54, 82 S.Ct. 157, 159, 7 L.Ed.2d 114. See White v. State of Maryland, 373 U.S. 59, 83 S.Ct. 1050, 10 L.Ed.2d 193. The principle was also applied in Massiah v. United States, 377 U.S. 201, 84 S.Ct. 1199, 12 L.Ed.2d 246, where we held that incriminating statements of the defendant should have been excluded from evidence when it appeared that they were overheard by federal agents who, without notice to the defendant's lawyer, arranged a meeting between the defendant and an accomplice turned informant. We said, quoting a concurring opinion in Spano v. People of State of New York, 360 U.S. 315, 326, 79 S.Ct. 1202, 1209, 3 L.Ed.2d 1265, that "[a]nything less * * * might deny a defendant 'effective representation by counsel at the only stage when legal aid and advice would help him.' " 377 U.S., at 204, 84 S.Ct. at 1202.

In Escobedo v. State of Illinois, 378 U.S. 478, 84 S.Ct. 1758, 12 L.Ed.2d 977, we drew upon the rationale of *Hamilton* and *Massiah* in holding that the right to counsel was guaranteed at the point where the accused, prior to arraignment, was subject to secret interrogation despite repeated requests to see his lawyer. We again noted the necessity of counsel's presence if the accused was to have a fair opportunity to present a defense at the trial itself:
"The rule sought by the State here, however, would make the trial no more than an appeal from the interrogation; and the 'right to use counsel at the formal trial [would be] a very hollow thing [if], for all practical purposes, the conviction is already assured by pretrial examination'. * * * 'One can imagine a cynical prosecutor saying: "Let them have the most illustrious counsel, now. They can't escape the noose. There is nothing that counsel can do for them at the trial." ' " 378 U.S., at 487–488, 84 S.Ct. at 1763.
Finally in Miranda v. State of Arizona, 384 U.S. 436, 86 S.Ct. 1602, 16 L.Ed.2d 694, the rules established for custodial interrogation included the right to the presence of counsel. The result was rested

on our finding that this and the other rules were necessary to safeguard the privilege against self-incrimination from being jeopardized by such interrogation.

Of course, nothing decided or said in the opinions in the cited cases links the right to counsel only to protection of Fifth Amendment rights. Rather those decisions "no more than reflect a constitutional principle established as long ago as Powell v. Alabama * * *." Massiah v. United States, supra, 377 U.S. at 205, 84 S.Ct. at 1202. It is central to that principle that in addition to counsel's presence at trial,[4] the accused is guaranteed that he need not stand alone against the State at any stage of the prosecution, formal or informal, in court or out, where counsel's absence might derogate from the accused's right to a fair trial.[5] The security of that right is as much the aim of the right to counsel as it is of the other guarantees of the Sixth Amendment—the right of the accused to a speedy and public trial by an impartial jury, his right to be informed of the nature and cause of the accusation, and his right to be confronted with the witnesses against him and to have compulsory process for obtaining witnesses in his favor. The presence of counsel at such critical confrontations, as at the trial itself, operates to assure that the accused's interests will be protected consistently with our adversary theory of criminal prosecution. Cf. Pointer v. State of Texas, 380 U.S. 400, 85 S.Ct. 1065, 13 L.Ed.2d 923.

In sum, the principle of Powell v. Alabama and succeeding cases requires that we scrutinize *any* pretrial confrontation of the accused to determine whether the presence of his counsel is necessary to preserve the defendant's basic right to a fair trial as affected by his right meaningfully to cross-examine the witnesses against him and to have effective assistance of counsel at the trial itself. It calls upon us to analyze whether potential substantial prejudice to defendant's rights inheres in the particular confrontation and the ability of counsel to help avoid that prejudice.

III.

The Government characterizes the lineup as a mere preparatory step in the gathering of the prosecution's evidence, not different— for Sixth Amendment purposes—from various other preparatory steps, such as systematized or scientific analyzing of the accused's

---

[4] See, e. g., Powell v. State of Alabama, 287 U.S. 45, 53 S.Ct. 55, 77 L.Ed. 158; Hamilton v. State of Alabama, 368 U.S. 52, 82 S.Ct. 157, 7 L.Ed.2d 114; White v. State of Maryland, 373 U.S. 59, 83 S.Ct. 1050, 10 L.Ed.2d 193; Escobedo v. State of Illinois, 378 U.S. 478, 84 S.Ct. 1758, 12 L.Ed.2d 977; Massiah v. United States, 377 U.S. 201, 84 S.Ct. 1199, 12 L.Ed.2d 246.

[5] See cases cited n. 4, supra; Avery v. State of Alabama, 308 U.S. 444, 446, 60 S.Ct. 321, 322, 84 L.Ed. 377.

fingerprints, blood sample, clothing, hair, and the like. We think there are differences which preclude such stages being characterized as critical stages at which the accused has the right to the presence of his counsel. Knowledge of the techniques of science and technology is sufficiently available, and the variables in techniques few enough, that the accused has the opportunity for a meaningful confrontation of the Government's case at trial through the ordinary processes of cross-examination of the Government's expert witnesses and the presentation of the evidence of his own experts. The denial of a right to have his counsel present at such analyses does not therefore violate the Sixth Amendment; they are not critical stages since there is minimal risk that his counsel's absence at such stages might derogate from his right to a fair trial.

IV.

But the confrontation compelled by the State between the accused and the victim or witnesses to a crime to elicit identification evidence is peculiarly riddled with innumerable dangers and variable factors which might seriously, even crucially, derogate from a fair trial. The vagaries of eyewitness identification are well-known; the annals of criminal law are rife with instances of mistaken identification.[6] Mr. Justice Frankfurter once said: "What is the worth of identification testimony even when uncontradicted? The identification of strangers is proverbially untrustworthy. The hazards of such testimony are established by a formidable number of instances in the records of English and American trials. These instances are recent—not due to the brutalities of ancient criminal procedure." The Case of Sacco and Vanzetti 30 (1927). A major factor contributing to the high incidence of miscarriage of justice from mistaken identification has been the degree of suggestion inherent in the manner in which the prosecution presents the suspect to witnesses for pretrial identification. A commentator has observed that "[t]he influence of improper suggestion upon identifying witnesses probably accounts for more miscarriages of justice than any other single factor—perhaps it is responsible for more such errors than all other factors combined." Wall, Eye-Witness Identification in Criminal Cases 26. Suggestion can be created intentionally or unintentionally

---

[6] Borchard, Convicting the Innocent; Frank & Frank, Not Guilty; Wall, Eye-Witness Identification in Criminal Cases; 3 Wigmore, Evidence § 786a (3d ed. 1940); Rolph, Personal Identity; Gross, Criminal Investigation 47–54 (Jackson ed. 1962); Williams, Proof of Guilt 83–98 (1955); Wills, Circumstantial Evidence 192–205 (7th ed. 1937); Wigmore, The Science of Judicial Proof §§ 250–253 (3d ed. 1937).

in many subtle ways.[7] And the dangers for the suspect are particularly grave when the witness' opportunity for observation was insubstantial, and thus his susceptibility to suggestion the greatest.

Moreover, "[i]t is a matter of common experience that, once a witness has picked out the accused at the line-up, he is not likely to go back on his word later on, so that in practice the issue of identity may (in the absence of other relevant evidence) for all practical purposes be determined there and then, before the trial."[8]

The pretrial confrontation for purpose of identification may take the form of a lineup, also known as an "identification parade" or "showup," as in the present case, or presentation of the suspect alone to the witness, as in Stovall v. Denno, supra. It is obvious that risks of suggestion attend either form of confrontation and increase the dangers inhering in eye-witness identification.[9] But as is the case with secret interrogations, there is serious difficulty in depicting what transpires at lineups and other forms of identification confrontations. "Privacy results in secrecy and this in turn results in a gap in our knowledge as to what in fact goes on * * *." Miranda v. State of Arizona, supra, 384 U.S. at 448, 86 S.Ct. at 1614. For the same reasons, the defense can seldom reconstruct the manner and mode of lineup identification for judge or jury at trial. Those participating in a lineup with the accused may often be police officers;[10] in any event, the participants' names are rarely recorded or divulged at trial.[11] The impediments to an objective observation are increased when the victim is the witness. Lineups are prevalent in rape and robbery prosecutions and present a particular hazard that a victim's understandable outrage may excite vengeful or spiteful motives.[12] In any

---

[7] See Wall, supra, n. 6, at 26–65; Murray, The Criminal Lineup at Home and Abroad, 1966 UtahL. Rev. 610; Napley. Problems of Effecting the Presentation of the Case for a Defendant, 66 Col.L.Rev. 94, 98–99 (1966); Williams, Identification Parades, [1955] Crim.L.Rev. (Eng.) 525; Paul, Identification of Accused Persons, 12 Austl.L.J. 42 (1938); Houts, From Evidence to Proof 25; Williams & Hammelmann, Identification Parades, Parts I & II, [1963] Crim.L.Rev. 479–490, 545–555; Gorphe, Showing Prisoners to Witnesses for Identification, 1 Am.J.Police Sci. 79 (1930); Wigmore, The Science of Judicial Proof, supra, n. 6, at § 253; Devlin, The Criminal Prosecution in England 70; Williams, Proof of Guilt 95–97.

[8] Williams & Hammelmann, Identification Parades, Part 1, [1963] Crim.L.Rev. 479, 482.

[9] Williams & Hammelmann, Identification Parades, Part I, supra, n. 7.

[10] See Wall, supra, n. 6, at 57–59; see, e. g., People v. Boney, 28 Ill.2d 505, 192 N.E.2d 920 (1963); People v. James, 218 Cal.App.2d 166, 32 Cal.Rptr. 283 (1963).

[11] See Rolph, Personal Identity 50: "The bright burden of identity, at these parades, is lifted from the innocent participants to hover about the suspect. leaving the rest featureless and unknown and without interest."

[12] See Williams & Hammelmann, Identification Parades, Part II, [1963] Crim.L.Rev. 545, 546; Borchard, Convicting the Innocent 367.

event, neither witnesses nor lineup participants are apt to be alert for conditions prejudicial to the suspect. And if they were, it would likely be of scant benefit to the suspect since neither witnesses nor lineup participants are likely to be schooled in the detection of suggestive influences.[13] Improper influences may go undetected by a suspect, guilty or not, who experiences the emotional tension which we might expect in one being confronted with potential accusers.[14] Even when he does observe abuse, if he has a criminal record he may be reluctant to take the stand and open up the admission of prior convictions. Moreover, any protestations by the suspect of the fairness of the lineup made at trial are likely to be in vain;[15] the jury's choice is between the accused's unsupported version and that of the police officers present.[16] In short, the accused's inability

---

[13] An additional impediment to the detection of such influences by participants, including the suspect, is the physical conditions often surrounding the conduct of the lineup. In many, lights shine on the stage in such a way that the suspect cannot see the witness. See Gilbert v. United States, 366 F.2d 923 (C. A.9th Cir. 1966). In some a one-way mirror is used and what is said on the witness' side cannot be heard. See Rigney v. Hendrick, 355 F.2d 710, 711, n. 2 (C.A.3d Cir. 1965); Aaron v. State, 273 Ala. 337, 139 So.2d 309 (1961).

[14] Williams & Hammelmann, Part I, supra, n. 7, at 489; Napley, supra, n. 7, at 99.

[15] See In re Groban, 352 U.S. 330, 340, 77 S.Ct. 510, 516, 1 L.Ed.2d 376 (Black, J., dissenting). The difficult position of defendants in attempting to protest the manner of pretrial identification is illustrated by the many state court cases in which contentions of blatant abuse rested on their unsupportable allegations, usually controverted by the police officers present. See, e. g., People v. Shields, 70 Cal.App.2d 628, 634-635, 161 P.2d 475, 478-479 (1945); People v. Hicks, 22 Ill. 2d 364, 176 N.E.2d 810 (1961); State v. Hill, 193 Kan. 512, 394 P.2d 106 (1964); Redmon v. Commonwealth, 321 S.W.2d 397 (Ky.Ct. App. 1959); Lubinski v. State, 180 Md. 1, 8, 22 A.2d 455, 459 (1941). For a striking case in which hardly anyone agreed upon what occurred at the lineup, including who

identified whom, see Johnson v. State, 237 Md. 283, 206 A.2d 138 (1965).

[16] An instructive example of the defendant's predicament may be found in Proctor v. State, 223 Md. 394, 164 A.2d 708 (1960). A prior identification is admissible in Maryland only under the salutary rule that it cannot have been made "under conditions of unfairness or unreliability." Id., at 401, 164 A.2d, at 712. Against the defendant's contention that these conditions had not been met, the Court stated:

"In the instant case, there are no such facts as, in our judgment, would call for a finding that the identification * * * was made under conditions of unfairness or unreliability. The relatively large number of persons put into the room together for [the victim] to look at is one circumstance indicating fairness, and the fact that the police officer was unable to remember the appearances of the others and could not recall if they had physical characteristics similar to [the defendant's] or not is at least suggestive that they were not of any one type or that they all differed markedly in looks from the defendant. There is no evidence that the Police Sergeant gave the complaining witness any indication as to which of the thirteen men was the defendant; the Sergeant's testimony is simply that he asked [the victim] if he could identify [the defendant] after having put the thirteen men in the courtroom."

120

effectively to reconstruct at trial any unfairness that occurred at the lineup may deprive him of his only opportunity meaningfully to attack the credibility of the witness' courtroom identification.

What facts have been disclosed in specific cases about the conduct of pretrial confrontations for identification illustrate both the potential for substantial prejudice to the accused at that stage and the need for its revelation at trial. A commentator provides some striking examples:

"In a Canadian case * * * the defendant had been picked out of a line-up of six men, of which he was the only Oriental. In other cases, a black-haired suspect was placed among a group of light-haired persons, tall suspects have been made to stand with short non-suspects, and, in a case where the perpetrator of the crime was known to be a youth, a suspect under twenty was placed in a line-up with five other persons, all of whom were forty or over."[17]

Similarly state reports, in the course of describing prior identifications admitted as evidence of guilt, reveal numerous instances of suggestive procedures, for example, that all in the lineup but the suspect were known to the identifying witness,[18] that the other participants in a lineup were grossly dissimilar in appearance to the suspect,[19] that only the suspect was required to wear distinctive clothing which the culprit allegedly wore,[20] that the witness is told by the police that they have caught the culprit after which the defendant is brought before the witness alone or is viewed in jail,[21] that the suspect is pointed out before or during a lineup,[22] and that

---

[17] Wall, Eye-Witness Identification in Criminal Cases 53. For other such examples see Houts, From Evidence to Proof 25; Frankfurter, The Case of Sacco and Vanzetti 12–14, 30–32; 3 Wigmore, Evidence § 786a, at 164, n. 2 (3d ed. 1940); Paul, Identification of Accused Persons, 12 Austl.L.J. 42, 44 (1938); Rolph, Personal Identity 34–43.

[18] See People v. James, 218 Cal. App. 2d 166, 170–171, 32 Cal.Rptr. 283, 286 (1963); People v. Boney, 28 Ill.2d 505, 192 N.E.2d 920 (1963).

[19] See Fredricksen v. United States, 105 U.S.App.D.C. 262, 266 F.2d 463 (1959); People v. Adell, 75 Ill.App. 2d 385, 221 N.E.2d 72 (1966); State v. Hill, 193 Kan. 512, 394 P.2d 106 (1964); People v. Seppi, 221 N.Y. 62, 116 N.E. 793 (197); State v. Duggan, 215 Or. 151, 162, 333 P.2d 907, 912 (1958).

[20] See People v. Crenshaw, 15 Ill.2d 458, 460, 155 N.E.2d 599, 602 (1959); Presley v. State, 224 Md. 550, 168 A.2d 510 (1961); State v. Ramirez, 76 N.M. 72, 412 P.2d 246 (1966); State v. Bazemore, 193 N.C. 336, 137 S.E. 172 (1927); Barrett v. State, 190 Tenn. 366, 229 S.W.2d 516, 18 A.L.R.2d 789 (1950).

[21] See Aaron v. State, 273 Ala. 337, 139 So.2d 309 (1961); Bishop v. State, 236 Ark. 12, 364 S.W.2d 676 (1963); People v. Thompson, 406 Ill. 555, 94 N.E.2d 349 (1950); People v. Berne, 384 Ill. 334, 51 N.E.2d 578 (1943); People v. Martin, 304 Ill. 494, 136 N.E. 711 (1922); Barrett v. State, 190 Tenn. 366, 229 S.W.2d 516, 18 A.L.R.2d 789 (1950).

[22] See People v. Clark, 28 Ill.2d 423, 192 N.E.2d 851 (1963); Gillespie v. State, 355 P.2d 451, 454 (Okl.Cr. 1960).

the participants in the lineup are asked to try on an article of clothing which fits only the suspect.[23]

The potential for improper influence is illustrated by the circumstances, insofar as they appear, surrounding the prior identifications in the three cases we decide today. In the present case, the testimony of the identifying witnesses elicited on cross-examination revealed that those witnesses were taken to the courthouse and seated in the courtroom to await assembly of the lineup. The courtroom faced on a hallway observable to the witnesses through an open door. The cashier testified that she saw Wade "standing in the hall" within sight of an FBI agent. Five or six other prisoners later appeared in the hall. The vice president testified that he saw a person in the hall in the custody of the agent who "resembled the person that we identified as the one that had entered the bank."[24]

The lineup in *Gilbert,* supra, was conducted in an auditorium in which some 100 witnesses to several alleged state and federal robberies charged to Gilbert made wholesale identifications of Gilbert as the robber in each other's presence, a procedure said to be fraught with dangers of suggestion.[25] And the vice of suggestion created by the identification in *Stovall,* supra, was the presentation to the witness of the suspect alone handcuffed to police officers. It is hard to imagine a situation more clearly conveying the suggestion to the witness that the one presented is believed guilty by the police. See Frankfurter, The Case of Sacco and Vanzetti 31–32.

The few cases that have surfaced therefore reveal the existence of a process attended with hazards of serious unfairness to the criminal accused and strongly suggest the plight of the more numerous defendants who are unable to ferret out suggestive influences in the secrecy of the confrontation. We do not assume that these risks are the result of police procedures intentionally designed to prejudice an accused. Rather we assume they derive from the dangers inherent in eyewitness identification and the suggestibility inherent in the context of the pretrial identification. Williams & Hammelmann, in one of the most comprehensive studies of such forms of identification, said, "[T]he fact that the police themselves have, in a given case, little or no doubt that the man put up for

---

[23] See People v. Parham, 60 Cal.2d 378, 33 Cal.Rptr. 497, 384 P.2d 1001 (1963).

[24] See Wall, supra, n. 6, at 48; Napley, supra, n. 7, at 99: "[W]hile many identification parades are conducted by the police with scrupulous regard for fairness, it is not unknown for the identifying witness to be placed in a position where he can see the suspect before the parade forms * * *."

[25] Williams & Hammelmann, Part I, supra, n. 7, at 486; Burtt, Applied Psychology 254–255.

identification has committed the offense, and that their chief preoccupation is with the problem of getting sufficient proof, because he has not 'come clean,' involves a danger that this persuasion may communicate itself even in a doubtful case to the witness in some way * * *." Identification Parades, Part I, [1963] Crim.L.Rev. 479, 483.

Insofar as the accused's conviction may rest on a courtroom identification in fact the fruit of a suspect pretrial identification which the accused is helpless to subject to effective scrutiny at trial, the accused is deprived of that right of cross-examination which is an essential safeguard to his right to confront the witnesses against him. Pointer v. State of Texas, 380 U.S. 400, 85 S.Ct. 1065, 13 L.Ed.2d 923. And even though cross-examination is a precious safeguard to a fair trial, it cannot be viewed as an absolute assurance of accuracy and reliability. Thus in the present context, where so many variables and pitfalls exist, the first line of defense must be the prevention of unfairness and the lessening of the hazards of eyewitness identification at the lineup itself. The trial which might determine the accused's fate may well not be that in the courtroom but that at the pretrial confrontation, with the State aligned against the accused, the witness the sole jury, and the accused unprotected against the overreaching, intentional or unintentional, and with little or no effective appeal from the judgment there rendered by the witness—"that's the man."

Since it appears that there is grave potential for prejudice, intentional or not, in the pretrial lineup, which may not be capable of reconstruction at trial, and since presence of counsel itself can often avert prejudice and assure a meaningful confrontation at trial,[26] there can be little doubt that for Wade the post-indictment

---

[26] One commentator proposes a model statute providing not only for counsel, but other safeguards as well:
"Most, if not all, of the attacks on the lineup process could be averted by a uniform statute modeled upon the best features of the civilian codes. Any proposed statute should provide for the right to counsel during any lineup or during any confrontation. Provision should be made that any person, whether a victim or a witness, must give a description of the suspect before he views any arrested person. A written record of this description should be required, and the witness should be made to sign it.

This written record would be available for inspection by defense counsel for copying before the trial and for use at the trial in testing the accuracy of the identification made during the lineup and during the trial.
"This ideal statute would require at least six persons in addition to the accused in a lineup, and these persons would have to be of approximately the same height, weight, coloration of hair and skin, and bodily types as the suspect. In addition, all of these men should, as nearly as possible, be dressed alike. If distinctive garb was used during the crime, the suspect should

lineup was a critical stage of the prosecution at which he was "as much entitled to such aid [of counsel] * * * as at the trial itself." Powell v. State of Alabama, 287 U.S. 45, at 57, 53 S.Ct. 55, at 60, 77 L.Ed. 158. Thus both Wade and his counsel should have been notified of the impending lineup, and counsel's presence should have been a requisite to conduct of the lineup, absent an "intelligent waiver." See Carnley v. Cochran, 369 U.S. 506, 82 S.Ct. 884, 8 L.Ed.2d 70. No substantial countervailing policy considerations have been advanced against the requirement of the presence of counsel. Concern is expressed that the requirement will forestall prompt identifications and result in obstruction of the confrontations. As for the first, we note that in the two cases in which the right to counsel is today held to apply, counsel had already been appointed and no argument is made in either case that notice to counsel would have prejudicially delayed the confrontations. Moreover, we leave open the question whether the presence of substitute counsel might not suffice where notification and presence of the suspect's own counsel would result in prejudicial delay.[27] And to refuse to recognize the right to counsel for fear that counsel will obstruct the course of justice is contrary to the basic assumptions upon which this Court has operated in Sixth Amendment cases. We rejected similar logic in Miranda v. State of Arizona, concerning presence of counsel during custodial interrogation, 384 U.S. at 480–481, 86 S. Ct. at 1631, 16 L.Ed.2d 694:

not be forced to wear similar clothing in the lineup unless all of the other persons are similarly garbed. A complete written report of the names, addresses, descriptive details of the other persons in the lineup, and of everything which transpired during the identification would be mandatory. This report would include everything stated by the identifying witness during this step, including any reasons given by him as to what features, etc., have sparked his recognition.

"This statute should permit voice identification tests by having each person in the lineup repeat identical innocuous phrases, and it would be impermissible to force the use of words allegedly used during a criminal act.

"The statute would enjoin the police from suggesting to any viewer that one or more persons in the lineup had been arrested as a suspect. If more than one witness is to make an identification, each witness should be required to do so separately and should be forbidden to speak to another witness until all of them have completed the process.

"The statute could require the use of movie cameras and tape recorders to record the lineup process in those states which are financially able to afford these devices. Finally, the statute should provide that any evidence obtained as the result of a violation of this statute would be inadmissible." Murray, The Criminal Lineup at Home and Abroad, 1966 Utah L.Rev. 610, 627–628.

27 Although the right to counsel usually means a right to the suspect's own counsel, provision for substitute counsel may be justified on the ground that the substitute counsel's presence may eliminate the hazards which render the lineup a critical stage for the presence of the suspect's *own* counsel.

"[A]n attorney is merely exercising the good professional judgment he has been taught. This is not cause for considering the attorney a menace to law enforcement. He is merely carrying out what he is sworn to do under his oath—to protect to the extent of his ability the rights of his client. In fulfilling this responsibility the attorney plays a vital role in the administration of criminal justice under our Constitution."

In our view counsel can hardly impede legitimate law enforcement; on the contrary, for the reasons expressed, law enforcement may be assisted by preventing the infiltration of taint in the prosecution's identification evidence.[28] That result cannot help the guilty avoid conviction but can only help assure that the right man has been brought to justice.[29]

Legislative or other regulations, such as those of local police departments, which eliminate the risks of abuse and unintentional suggestion at lineup preceedings and the impediments to meaningful confrontation at trial may also remove the basis for regarding the stage as "critical."[30] But neither Congress nor the federal au-

---

[28] Concern is also expressed that the presence of counsel will force divulgence of the identity of government witnesses whose identity the Government may want to conceal. To the extent that this is a valid or significant state interest there are police practices commonly used to effect concealment, for example, masking the face.

[29] Many other nations surround the lineup with safeguards against prejudice to the suspect. In England the suspect must be allowed the presence of his solicitor or a friend, Napley, supra, n. 7, at 98–99; Germany requires the presence of retained counsel; France forbids the confrontation of the suspect in the absence of his counsel; Spain, Mexico, and Italy provide detailed procedures prescribing the conditions under which confrontation must occur under the supervision of a judicial officer who sees to it that the proceedings are officially recorded to assure adequate scrutiny at trial. Murray, The Criminal Lineup at Home and Abroad, 1966 Utah L.Rev. 610, 621–627.

[30] Thirty years ago Wigmore suggested a "scientific method" of pretrial identification "to reduce the risk of error hitherto inherent in such pro-ceedings." Wigmore, The Science of Judicial Proof 541 (3 ed. 1937). Under this approach, at least 100 talking films would be prepared of men from various occupations, races, etc. Each would be photographed in a number of stock movements, with and without hat and coat, and would read aloud a standard passage. The suspect would be filmed in the same manner. Some 25 of the films would be shown in succession in a special projection room in which each witness would be provided an electric button which would activate a board backstage when pressed to indicate that the witness had identified a given person. Provision would be made for the degree of hesitancy in the identification to be indicated by the number of presses. Id., at 540–541. Of course, the more systematic and scientific a process or proceeding, including one for purposes of identification, the less the impediment to reconstruction of the conditions bearing upon the reliability of that process or proceeding at trial. See discussion of fingerprint and like tests, Part III, supra, and of handwriting exemplars in Gilbert v. California, supra.

thorities have seen fit to provide a solution. What we hold today "in no way creates a constitutional straitjacket which will handicap sound efforts at reform, nor is it intended to have this effect." Miranda v. State of Arizona, supra, at 467, 86 S.Ct. at 1624.

V.

We come now to the question whether the denial of Wade's motion to strike the courtroom identification by the bank witnesses at trial because of the absence of his counsel at the lineup required, as the Court of Appeals held, the grant of a new trial at which such evidence is to be excluded. We do not think this disposition can be justified without first giving the Government the opportunity to establish by clear and convincing evidence that the in-court identifications were based upon observations of the suspect other than the lineup identification. See Murphy v. Waterfront Commission, 378 U.S. 52, 79, n. 18, 84 S.Ct. 1594, 1609, 12 L.Ed.2d 678.[31] Where, as here, the admissibility of evidence of the lineup identification itself is not involved, a *per se* rule of exclusion of courtroom identification would be unjustified.[32] See Nardone v. United States, 308 U.S. 338, 341, 60 S.Ct. 266, 267 84 L.Ed. 307. A rule limited solely to the exclusion of testimony concerning identification at the lineup itself, without regard to admissibility of the courtroom identification, would render the right to counsel an empty one. The lineup is most often used, as in the present case, to crystallize the witnesses' identification of the defendant for future reference. We have already noted that the lineup identification will have that effect. The State may then rest upon the witnesses' unequivocal courtroom identification, and not mention the pretrial identification as part of the State's case at trial. Counsel is then in the predicament in which Wade's counsel found himself—realizing that possible unfairness at the lineup may be the sole means of attack upon the unequivocal courtroom identification, and having to probe in the dark in an attempt to discover and reveal unfairness, while bolstering the government witness' courtroom identification by bringing out and dwelling upon his prior

---

[31] See Goldstein v. United States, 316 U.S. 114, 124, n. 1, 62 S.Ct. 1000, 1005, 86 L.Ed. 1312 (Murphy, J., dissenting). "[A]fter an accused sustains the initial burden, imposed by Nardone v. United States, 308 U.S. 338, 60 S.Ct. 266, 84 L.Ed. 307, of proving to the satisfaction of the trial judge in the preliminary hearing that wire-tapping was unlawfully employed, as petitioners did here, it is only fair that the burden should then shift to the Government to convince the trial judge that its proof had an independent origin."

[32] We reach a contrary conclusion in Gilbert v. California, supra, as to the admissibility of the witness' testimony that the also identified the accused at the lineup.

identification. Since counsel's presence at the lineup would equip him to attack not only the lineup identification but the courtroom identification as well, limiting the impact of violation of the right to counsel to exclusion of evidence only of identification at the lineup itself disregards a critical element of that right.

We think it follows that the proper test to be applied in these situations is that quoted in Wong Sun v. United States, 371 U.S. 471, 488, 83 S.Ct. 407, 417, 9 L.Ed.2d 441, " '[W]hether, granting establishment of the primary illegality, the evidence to which instant objection is made has been come at by exploitation of that illegality or instead by means sufficiently distinguishable to be purged of the primary taint.' Maguire, Evidence of Guilt, 221 (1959)." See also Hoffa v. United States, 385 U.S. 293, 309, 87 S.Ct. 408, 17 L.Ed.2d 374. Application of this test in the present context requires consideration of various factors; for example, the prior opportunity to observe the alleged criminal act, the existence of any discrepancy between any pre-lineup description and the defendant's actual description, any identification prior to lineup of another person, the identification by picture of the defendant prior to the lineup, failure to identify the defendant on a prior occasion, and the lapse of time between the alleged act and the lineup identification. It is also relevant to consider those facts which, despite the absence of counsel, are disclosed concerning the conduct of the lineup.[33]

We doubt that the Court of Appeals applied the proper test for exclusion of the in-court identification of the two witnesses. The court stated that "it cannot be said with any certainty that they would have recognized appellant at the time of trial if this intervening lineup had not occurred," and that the testimony of the two witnesses "may well have been colored by the illegal procedure [and] was prejudicial." 358 F.2d, at 560. Moreover, the court was persuaded, in part, by the "compulsory verbal responses made by Wade at the instance of the Special Agent." Ibid. This implies the erroneous holding that Wade's privilege against self-incrimination

---

[33] Thus it is not the case that "[i]t matters not how well the witness knows the suspect, whether the witness is the suspect's mother, brother, or long-time associate, and no matter how long or well the witness observed the perpetrator at the scene of the crime." Such factors will have an important bearing upon the true basis of the witness' in-court identification. Moreover, the State's inability to bolster the witness' courtroom identification by introduction of the lineup identification itself, see Gilbert v. California, supra, will become less significant the more the evidence of other opportunities of the witness to observe the defendant. Thus where the witness is a "kidnap victim who has lived for days with his abductor" the value to the State of admission of the lineup identification is indeed marginal, and such identification would be a mere formality.

was violated so that the denial of counsel required exclusion.

On the record now before us we cannot make the determination whether the in-court identifications had an independent origin. This was not an issue at trial, although there is some evidence relevant to a determination. That inquiry is most properly made in the District Court. We therefore think the appropriate procedure to be followed is to vacate the conviction pending a hearing to determine whether the in-court identifications had an independent source, or whether, in any event, the introduction of the evidence was harmless error, Chapman v. State of California, 386 U.S. 18, 87 S.Ct. 824, 17 L.Ed.2d 705, and for the District Court to reinstate the conviction or order a new trial, as may be proper. See United States v. Shotwell Mfg. Co., 355 U.S. 233, 245–246, 78 S.Ct. 245, 253, 2 L.Ed. 2d 234.

The judgment of the Court of Appeals is vacated and the case is remanded to that court with direction to enter a new judgment vacating the conviction and remanding the case to the District Court for further proceedings consistent with this opinion.

It is so ordered.

THE CHIEF JUSTICE joins the opinion of the Court except for Part I, from which he dissents for the reasons expressed in the opinion of Mr. Justice FORTAS.

Mr. Justice DOUGLAS joins the opinion of the Court except for Part I. On that phase of the case he adheres to the dissenting views in Schmerber v. State of California, 384 U.S. 757, 772–779, 86 S.Ct. 1826, 16 L.Ed.2d 908, since he believes that compulsory lineup violates the privilege against self-incrimination contained in the Fifth Amendment.

Mr. Justice CLARK, concurring.

With reference to the lineup point involved in this case I cannot, for the life of me, see why a lineup is not a critical stage of the prosecution. Identification of the suspect—a prerequisite to establishment of guilt—occurs at this stage, and with Miranda v. State of Arizona, 384 U.S. 436, 86 S.Ct. 1602, 16 L.Ed.2d 694 (1966), on the books, the requirement of the presence of counsel arises, unless waived by the suspect. I dissented in *Miranda* but I am bound by it now, as we all are. Schmerber v. State of California, 384 U.S. 757, 86 S.Ct. 1826, 16 L.Ed.2d 908 (1966), precludes petitioner's claim of self-incrimination. I therefore join the opinion of the Court.

Mr. Justice BLACK, dissenting in part and concurring in part.

On March 23, 1965, respondent Wade was indicted for robbing a bank; on April 2, he was arrested; and on April 26, the court appointed a lawyer to represent him. Fifteen days later while Wade was still in custody, an FBI agent took him and several other prisoners into a room at the courthouse, directed each to participate in a lineup wearing strips of tape on his face and to speak the words used by the robber at the bank. This was all done in order to let the bank employee witnesses look at Wade for identification purposes. Wade's lawyer was not notified of or present at the lineup to protect his client's interests. At Wade's trial, two bank employees identified him in the courtroom. Wade objected to this testimony, when, on cross-examination, his counsel elicited from these witnesses the fact that they had seen Wade in the lineup. He contended that by forcing him to participate in the lineup, wear strips of tape on his face, and repeat the words used by the robber, all without counsel, the Government had (1) compelled him to be a witness against himself in violation of the Fifth Amendment, and (2) deprived him of the assistance of counsel for his defense in violation of the Sixth Amendment.

The Court in Part I of its opinion rejects Wade's Fifth Amendment contention. From that I dissent. In Parts II–IV of its opinion, the Court sustains Wade's claim of denial of right to counsel in the out-of-court lineup, and in that I concur. In Part V, the Court remands the case to the District Court to consider whether the courtroom identification of Wade was the fruit of the illegal lineup, and, if it was, to grant him a new trial unless the court concludes that the courtroom identification was harmless error. I would reverse the Court of Appeals' reversal of Wade's conviction, but I would not remand for further proceedings. Since the prosecution did not use the out-of-court lineup identification against Wade at his trial, I believe the conviction should be affirmed.

I.

In rejecting Wade's claim that his privilege against self-incrimination was violated by compelling him to appear in the lineup wearing the tape and uttering the words given him by the police, the Court relies on the recent holding in Schmerber v. State of California, 384 U.S. 757, 86 S.Ct. 1826, 16 L.Ed.2d 908. In that case the Court held that taking blood from a man's body against his will in order to convict him of a crime did not compel him to be a witness against himself. I dissented from that holding, 384 U.S., at 773, 86 S.Ct., at 1837, and still dissent. The Court's reason for its holding was that the sample of Schmerber's blood taken in order to convict him of crime was neither "testimonial" nor "communicative" evidence. I think it was both. It seems quite plain to me that the Fifth Amendment's Self-incrimination Clause was designed to bar the Government from forcing any person to supply proof of his own crime, precisely what Schmerber was forced to do when he was forced to supply his blood. The Government simply took his blood against his will and over his counsel's protest for the purpose of convicting him of crime. So here, having Wade in its custody awaiting trial to see if he could or would be convicted of crime, the Government forced him to stand in a lineup, wear strips on his face, and speak certain words, in order to make it possible for government witnesses to identify him as a criminal. Had Wade been compelled to utter these or any other words in open court, it is plain that he would have been entitled to a new trial because of having been compelled to be a witness against himself. Being forced by the Government to help convict himself and to supply evidence against himself by talking outside the courtroom is equally violative of his constitutional right not to be compelled to be a witness against himself. Consequently, because of this violation of the Fifth Amendment, and not because of my own personal view that the Government's conduct was "unfair," "prejudicial," or "improper," I would prohibit the prosecution's use of lineup identification at trial.

II.

I agree with the Court, in large part because of the reasons it gives, that failure to notify Wade's counsel that Wade was to be put in a lineup by government officers and to be forced to talk and wear tape on his face denied Wade the right to counsel in violation of the Sixth Amendment. Once again, my reason for this conclusion is solely the Sixth Amendment's guarantee that "the accused shall enjoy the right * * * to have the Assistance of Counsel for his defence." As this Court's opinion points out, "[t]he plain wording of this guarantee thus encompasses counsel's assistance whenever necessary to assure a meaningful 'defence.'" And I agree with the Court that a lineup is a "critical stage" of the criminal proceedings against an accused, because it is a stage at which the Government makes use of his custody to obtain crucial evidence against him. Besides counsel's presence at the lineup being necessary to protect the defendant's specific constitutional rights to confrontation and the assistance of counsel at the trial itself, the assistance of counsel at the lineup is also necessary to protect the defendant's in-custody assertion of his privilege against self-incrimination, Miranda v. State of Arizona, 384 U.S. 436, 86 S.Ct. 1602, 16 L.Ed.2d 694, for, contrary to the Court, I believe that counsel may advise the defendant not to participate in the lineup or to participate only under certain conditions.

I agree with the Court that counsel's presence at the lineup is necessary to protect the accused's right to a "fair trial," only if by "fair trial" the Court means a trial in accordance with the "Law of the Land" as specifically set out in the Constitution. But there are implications in the Court's opinion that by a "fair trial" the Court means a trial which a majority of this Court deems to be "fair" and that a lineup is a "critical stage" only because the Court, now assessing the "innumerable dangers" which inhere in it, thinks it is such. That these implications are justified is evidenced by the Court's suggestion that "[l]egislative or other regulations * * * which eliminate the risks of abuse * * * at lineup proceedings * * * may also remove the basis for regarding the stage as 'critical.' " And it is clear from the Court's opinion in Gilbert v. California, post, p. 263, 87 S.Ct. 1951, 18 L.Ed.2d 1178, that it is willing to make the Sixth Amendment's guarantee of right to counsel dependent on the Court's own view of whether a particular stage of the proceedings—though "critical" in the sense of the prosecution's gathering of evidence—is "critical" to the Court's own view of a "fair trial." I am wholly unwilling to make the specific constitutional right of counsel dependent on judges' vague and transitory notions of fairness and their equally transitory, though thought to be empirical, assessment of the "risk that * * * counsel's absence * * * might derogate from * * * [a defendant's] right to a fair trial." Ante, at 228. See Pointer v. State of Texas, 380 U.S. 400, 412, 85 S.Ct. 1065, 1072, 13 L.Ed.2d 923 (concurring opinion of Goldberg, J.).

III.

I would reverse Wade's conviction without further ado had the prosecution at trial made use of his lineup identification either in place of courtroom identification or to bolster in a harmful manner crucial courtroom identification. But the prosecution here did neither of these things. After prosecution witnesses under oath identified Wade in the courtroom, it was the defense, and not the prosecution, which brought out the prior lineup identification. While stating that "a *per se* rule of exclusion of courtroom identification would be unjustified," the Court, nevertheless remands this case for "a hearing to determine whether the in-court identifications had an independent source," or were the tainted fruits of the invalidly conducted lineup. From this holding I dissent.

In the first place, even if this Court has power to establish such a rule of evidence, I think the rule fashioned by the Court is unsound. The "tainted fruit" determination required by the Court involves more than considerable difficulty. I think it is practically impossible. How is a witness capable of probing the recesses of his mind to draw a sharp line between a courtroom identification due exclusively to an earlier lineup and a courtroom identification due to memory not based on the lineup? What kind of "clear and convincing evidence" can the prosecution offer to prove upon what particular events memories resulting in an in-court identification rest? How long will trials be delayed while judges turn psychologists to probe the subconscious minds of witnesses? All these questions are posed but not answered by the Court's opinion. In my view, the Fifth and Sixth Amendments are satisfied if the prosecution is precluded from using lineup identification as either an alternative to or corroboration of courtroom identification. If the prosecution does neither and its witnesses under oath identify the defendant in the courtroom, then I can find no justification for stopping the trial in midstream to hold a lengthy "tainted fruit" hearing. The fact of and circumstances surrounding a prior lineup identification might be used by the defense to impeach the credibility of the in-court identifications, but not to exclude them completely.

But more important, there is no constitutional provision upon which I can rely that directly or by implication gives this Court power to establish what amounts to a constitutional rule of evidence to govern, not only the Federal Government, but the States in their trial of state crimes under state laws in state courts. See Gilbert v. California, supra. The Constitution deliberately reposed in the States very broad power to create and to try crimes according to their own rules and policies. Spencer v. State of Texas, 385 U.S. 554, 87 S.Ct. 648, 17 L.Ed.2d 606. Before being deprived of this power, the least that they can ask is that we should be able to point to a federal constitutional provision that either by express language or by necessary implication grants us the power to fashion this novel rule of evidence to govern their criminal trials. Cf. Berger v. New York, ante, p. 70, 87 S.Ct. 1889, 18 L.Ed.2d 1040 (Black, J., dissenting). Neither Nardone v. United States, 308 U.S. 338, 60 S.Ct. 266, 84 L.Ed. 307, nor Wong Sun v. United States, 371 U.S. 471, 83 S.Ct. 407, 9 L.Ed.2d 441, both federal cases and both decided "in other contexts," supports what the Court demands of the States today.

Perhaps the Court presumes to write this constitutional rule of evidence on the basis of the Fourteenth Amendment's Due Process Clause. This is not the time or place to consider that claim. Suffice it for me to say briefly that I find no such authority in the Due

Process Clause. It undoubtedly provides that a person must be tried in accordance with the "Law of the Land." Consequently, it violates due process to try a person in a way prohibited by the Fourth, Fifth, or Sixth Amendments of our written Constitution. But I have never been able to subscribe to the dogma that the Due Process Clause empowers this Court to declare any law, including a rule of evidence, unconstitutional which it believes is contrary to tradition, decency, fundamental justice, or any of the other wide-meaning words used by judges to claim power under the Due Process Clause. See, e. g., Rochin v. People of State of California, 342 U.S. 165, 72 S.Ct. 205, 96 L.Ed. 183. I have an abiding idea that if the Framers had wanted to let judges write the Constitution on any such day-to-day beliefs of theirs, they would have said so instead of so carefully defining their grants and prohibitions in a written constitution. With no more authority than the Due Process Clause I am wholly unwilling to tell the state or federal courts that the United States Constitution forbids them to allow courtroom identification without the prosecution's first proving that the identification does not rest in whole or in part on an illegal lineup. Should I do so, I would feel that we are deciding what the Constitution is, not from what it says, but from what we think it would have been wise for the Framers to put in it. That to me would be "judicial activism" at its worst. I would leave the States and Federal Government free to decide their own rules of evidence. That, I believe, is their constitutional prerogative.

I would affirm Wade's conviction.

Mr. Justice WHITE, whom Mr. Justice HARLAN and Mr. Justice STEWART join, dissenting in part and concurring in part.

The Court has again propounded a broad constitutional rule barring use of a wide spectrum of relevant and probative evidence, solely because a step in its ascertainment or discovery occurs outside the presence of defense counsel. This was the approach of the Court in Miranda v. State of Arizona, 384 U.S. 436, 86 S.Ct. 1602, 16 L.Ed.2d 694. I objected then to what I thought was an uncritical and doctrinaire approach without satisfactory factual foundation. I have much the same view of the present ruling and therefore dissent from the judgment and from Parts II, IV, and V of the Court's opinion.

The Court's opinion is far-reaching. It proceeds first by creating a new *per se* rule of constitutional law: a criminal suspect cannot be subjected to a pretrial identification process in the absence of his counsel without violating the Sixth Amendment. If he is, the State may not buttress a later courtroom identification of the witness

133

by any reference to the previous identification. Furthermore, the courtroom identification is not admissible at all unless the State can establish by clear and convincing proof that the testimony is not the fruit of the earlier identification made in the absence of defendant's counsel—admittedly a heavy burden for the State and probably an impossible one. To all intents and purposes, courtroom identifications are barred if pretrial identifications have occurred without counsel being present.

The rule applies to any lineup, to any other techniques employed to produce an identification and *a fortiori* to a face-to-face encounter between the witness and the suspect alone, regardless of when the identification occurs, in time or place, and whether before or after indictment or information. It matters not how well the witness knows the suspect, whether the witness is the suspect's mother, brother, or long-time associate, and no matter how long or well the witness observed the perpetrator at the scene of the crime. The kidnap victim who has lived for days with his abductor is in the same category as the witness who has had only a fleeting glimpse of the criminal. Neither may identify the suspect without defendant's counsel being present. The same strictures apply regardless of the number of other witnesses who positively identify the defendant and regardless of the corroborative evidence showing that it was the defendant who had committed the crime.

The premise for the Court's rule is not the general unreliability of eyewitness identifications nor the difficulties inherent in observation, recall, and recognition. The Court assumes a narrower evil as the basis for its rule—improper police suggestion which contributes to erroneous identifications. The Court apparently believes that improper police procedures are so widespread that a broad prophylactic rule must be laid down, requiring the presence of counsel at all pretrial identifications, in order to detect recurring instances of police misconduct.[1] I do not share this pervasive distrust of all official investigations. None of the materials the Court relies upon supports it.[2] Certainly, I would bow to solid fact,

---

[1] Yet in Stovall v. Denno, 388 U.S. 293, 87 S.Ct. 1967, 18 L.Ed.2d 1199, the Court recognizes that improper police conduct in the identification process has not been so widespread as to justify full retroactivity for its new rule.

[2] In Miranda v. State of Arizona, 384 U.S. 436, 449, 86 S.Ct. 1602, 1614, 16 L.Ed.2d 694, the Court noted that O'Hara, Fundamentals of Criminal Investigation (1956) is a text that has enjoyed extensive use among law enforcement agencies and among students of police science. The quality of the work was said to rest on the author's long service as observer, lecturer in police science, and work as a federal crime investigator. O'Hara does not suggest that the police should or do use identification machinery improperly; instead he argues for techniques that would increase the reliability of eyewitness identifications, and there is no reason to sug-

but the Court quite obviously does not have before it any reliable, comprehesive survey of current police practices on which to base its new rule. Until it does, the Court should avoid excluding relevant evidence from state criminal trials. Cf. Washington v. Texas, ante, p. 14, 87 S.Ct. 1920, 18 L.Ed.2d 1019.

The Court goes beyond assuming that a great majority of the country's police departments are following improper practices at pretrial identifications. To find the lineup a "critical" stage of the proceeding and to exclude identifications made in the absence of counsel, the Court must also assume that police "suggestion," if it occurs at all, leads to erroneous rather than accurate identifications and that reprehensible police conduct will have an unavoidable and largely undiscoverable impact on the trial. This in turn assumes that there is now no adequate source from which defense counsel can learn about the circumstances of the pretrial identification in order to place before the jury all of the considerations which should enter into an appraisal of courtroom identification evidence. But these are treacherous and unsupported assumptions,[3] resting as they do on the notion that the defendant will not be aware, that the police and the witnesses will forget or prevaricate, that defense counsel will be unable to bring out the truth and that neither jury, judge, nor appellate court is a sufficient safeguard against unacceptable police conduct occurring at a pretrial identification procedure. I am unable to share the Court's view of the willingness of the police and the ordinary citizen-witness to dissemble, either with respect to the identification of the defendant or with respect to the circumstances surrounding a pretrial identification.

There are several striking aspects to the Court's holding. First, the rule does not bar courtroom identifications where there have been no previous identifications in the presence of the police, al-

gest that O'Hara's views are not shared and practiced by the majority of police departments throughout the land.

[3] The instant case and its companions, Gilbert v. California, 388 U.S. 263, 87 S.Ct. 1951, 18 L.Ed.2d 1178, and Stovall v. Denno, 388 U.S. 293, 87 S.Ct. 1967, 18 L.Ed.2d 199, certainly lend no support to the Court's assumptions. The police conduct deemed improper by the Court in the three cases seems to have come to light at trial in the ordinary course of events. One can ask what more counsel would have learned at the pretrial identifications that would have been relevant for truth determination at trial. When the Court premises its constitutional rule on police conduct so subtle as to defy description and subsequent disclosure it deals in pure speculation. If police conduct is intentionally veiled, the police will know about it, and I am unwilling to speculate that defense counsel at trial will be unable to reconstruct the known circumstances of the pretrial identification. And if the "unknown" influence on identifications is "innocent," the Court's general premise evaporates and the problem is simply that of the inherent shortcomings of eyewitness testimony.

though when identified in the courtroom, the defendant is known to be in custody and charged with the commission of a crime. Second, the Court seems to say that if suitable legislative standards were adopted for the conduct of pretrial identifications, thereby lessening the hazards in such confrontations, it would not insist on the presence of counsel. But if this is true, why does not the Court simply fashion what it deems to be constitutionally acceptable procedures for the authorities to follow? Certainly the Court is correct in suggesting that the new rule will be wholly inapplicable where police departments themselves have established suitable safeguards.

Third, courtroom identification may be barred, absent counsel at a prior identification, regardless of the extent of counsel's information concerning the circumstances of the previous confrontation between witness and defendant—apparently even if there were recordings or sound-movies of the events as they occurred. But if the rule is premised on the defendant's right to have his counsel know, there seems little basis for not accepting other means to inform. A disinterested observer, recordings, photographs—any one of them would seem adequate to furnish the basis for a meaningful cross-examination of the eyewitness who identifies the defendant in the courtroom.

I share the Court's view that the criminal trial, at the very least, should aim at truthful factfinding, including accurate eyewitness identifications. I doubt, however, on the basis of our present information, that the tragic mistakes which have occurred in criminal trials are as much the product of improper police conduct as they are the consequence of the difficulties inherent in eyewitness testimony and in resolving evidentiary conflicts by court or jury. I doubt that the Court's new rule will obviate these difficulties, or that the situation will be measurably improved by inserting defense counsel into the investigative processes of police departments everywhere.

But, it may be asked, what possible state interest militates against requiring the presence of defense counsel at lineups? After all, the argument goes, he *may* do some good, he *may* upgrade the quality of identification evidence in state courts and he can scarcely do any harm. Even if true, this is a feeble foundation for fastening an ironclad constitutional rule upon state criminal procedures. Absent some reliably established constitutional violation, the processes by which the States enforce their criminal laws are their own prerogative. The States *do* have an interest in conducting their own affairs, an interest which cannot be displaced simply by saying that there are no valid arguments with respect to the merits of a federal rule emanating from this Court.

Beyond this, however, requiring counsel at pretrial identifications as an invariable rule trenches on other valid state interests. One of them is its concern with the prompt and efficient enforcement of its criminal laws. Identifications frequently take place after arrest but before an indictment is returned or an information is filed. The police may have arrested a suspect on probable cause but may still have the wrong man. Both the suspect and the State have every interest in a prompt identification at that stage, the suspect in order to secure his immediate release and the State because prompt and early identification enhances *accurate* identification and because it must know whether it is on the right investigative track. Unavoidably, however, the absolute rule requiring the presence of counsel will cause significant delay and it may very well result in no pretrial identification at all. Counsel must be appointed and a time arranged convenient for him and the witnesses. Meanwhile, it may be necessary to file charges against the suspect who may then be released on bail, in the federal system very often on his own recognizance, with neither the State nor the defendant having the benefit of a properly conducted identification procedure.

Nor do I think the witnesses themselves can be ignored. They will now be required to be present at the convenience of counsel rather than their own. Many may be much less willing to participate if the identification stage is transformed into an adversary proceeding not under the control of a judge. Others may fear for their own safety if their identity is known at an early date, especially when there is no way of knowing until the lineup occurs whether or not the police really have the right man.[4]

Finally, I think the Court's new rule is vulnerable in terms of its own unimpeachable purpose of increasing the reliability of identification testimony.

Law enforcement officers have the obligation to convict the guilty and to make sure they do not convict the innocent. They must be dedicated to making the criminal trial a procedure for the ascertainment of the true facts surrounding the commission of the crime.[5] To this extent, our so-called adversary system is not ad-

---

[4] I would not have thought that the State's interest regarding its sources of identification is any less than its interest in protecting informants, especially those who may aid in identification but who will not be used as witnesses. See McCray v. Illinois, 386 U.S. 300, 87 S.Ct. 1056, 18 L.Ed.2d 62.

[5] "The United States Attorney is the representative not of an ordinary party to a controversy, but of a sovereignty whose obligation to govern impartially is as compelling as

versary at all; nor should it be. But defense counsel has no comparable obligation to ascertain or present the truth. Our system assigns him a different mission. He must be and is interested in preventing the conviction of the innocent, but, absent a voluntary plea of guilty, we also insist that he defend his client whether he is innocent or guilty. The State has the obligation to present the evidence. Defense counsel need present nothing, even if he knows what the truth is. He need not furnish any witnesses to the police, or reveal any confidences of his client, or furnish any other information to help the prosecution's case. If he can confuse a witness, even a truthful one, or make him appear at a disadvantage, unsure or indecisive, that will be his normal course.[6] Our interest in not

---

its obligation to govern at all; and whose interest, therefore, in a criminal prosecution is not that it shall win a case, but that justice shall be done. As such, he is in a peculiar and very definite sense the servant of the law, the two-fold aim of which is that guilt shall not escape or innocence suffer. He may prosecute with earnestness and vigor—indeed, he should do so. But, while he may strike hard blows, he is not at liberty to strike foul ones. It is as much his duty to refrain from improper methods calculated to produce a wrongful conviction as it is to use every legitimate means to bring about a just one." Berger v. United States, 295 U.S. 78, 88, 55 S.Ct. 629, 633, 79 L.Ed. 1314. See also Mooney v. Holohan, 294 U.S. 103, 55 S.Ct. 340, 79 L. Ed. 791; Pyle v. State of Kansas, 317 U.S. 213, 63 S.Ct. 177, 87 L.Ed. 214; Alcorta v. State of Texas, 355 U.S. 28, 78 S.Ct. 103, 2 L.Ed.2d 9; Napue v. Illinois, 360 U.S. 264, 79 S.Ct. 1173, 3 L.Ed.2d 1217; Brady v. Maryland, 373 U.S. 83, 83 S.Ct. 1194, 10 L.Ed.2d 215; Giles v. Maryland, 386 U.S. 66, 87 S.Ct. 793, 17 L.Ed.2d 737; Miller v. Pate, 386 U.S. 1, 87 S.Ct. 785, 17 L.Ed.2d 690.

[6] One point of view about the role of the courtroom lawyer appears in [Frank, Courts on Trial 82–83. "What is the role of the lawyers in bringing the evidence before the trial court—As you may learn by reading any one of a dozen or more

handbooks on how to try a law-suit, an experienced lawyer uses all sorts of stratagems to minimize the effects on the judge or jury of testimony disadvantageous to his client, even when the lawyer has no doubt of the accuracy and honesty of that testimony. * * * If such a witness happens to be timid, frightened by the unfamiliarity of courtroom ways, the lawyer in his cross-examination, plays on that weakness, in order to confuse the witness and make it appear that he is concealing significant facts. Longenecker, in his book Hints On the Trial of a Law Suit (a book endorsed by the great Wigmore in writing of the 'truthful, honest, over-cautious' witness, tells how 'a skillful advocate by a rapid cross-examination may ruin the testimony of such a witness.' The author does not even hint any disapproval of that accomplishment. Longenecker's and other similar books recommended that a lawyer try to prod an irritable but honest 'adverse' witness into displaying his undesirable characteristics in their most unpleasant form, in order to discredit him with the judge or jury. 'You may,' writes Harris, 'sometimes destroy the effect of an adverse witness by making him appear more hostile than he really is. You may make him exaggerate or unsay something and say it again.' Taft says that a clever cross-examiner, dealing with an honest but egotistic witness, will 'deftly tempt the witness to indulge in his propen-

convicting the innocent permits counsel to put the State to its proof, to put the State's case in the worst possible light, regardless of what he thinks or knows to be the truth. Undoubtedly there are some limits which defense counsel must observe[7] but more often than not, defense counsel will cross-examine a prosecution witness, and impeach him if he can, even if he thinks the witness is telling the truth, just as he will attempt to destroy a witness who he thinks is lying. In this respect, as part of our modified adversary system and as part of the duty imposed on the most honorable defense counsel, we countenance or require conduct which in many instances has little, if any, relation to the search for truth.

I would not extend this system, at least as it presently operates, to police investigations and would not require counsel's presence at pretrial identification procedures. Counsel's interest is in not having his client placed at the scene of the crime, regardless of his whereabouts. Some counsel may advise their clients to refuse to make any movements or to speak any words in a lineup or even to appear in one. To that extent the impact on truthful factfinding is quite obvious. Others will not only observe what occurs and develop possibilities for later cross-examination but will hover over witnesses and begin their cross-examination then, menacing truthful factfinding as thoroughly as the Court fears the police now do. Certainly there is an implicit invitation to counsel to suggest rules for the lineup and to manage and produce it as best he can. I therefore doubt that the Court's new rule, at least absent some clearly defined limits on counsel's role, will measurably contribute to more reliable pretrial identifications. My fears are that it will have precisely the opposite result. It may well produce fewer con-

---

sity for exaggeration, so as to make him "hang himself." 'And thus,' adds Taft, 'it may happen that not only is the value of his testimony lost, but the side which produces him suffers for seeking aid from such a source'—although, I would add, that may be the only source of evidence of a fact on which the decision will turn.

" 'An intimidating manner in putting questions,' writes Wigmore, 'may so coerce or disconcert the witness that his answers do not represent his actual knowledge on the subject. So also, questions which in form or subject cause embarrassment, shame or anger in the witness may unfairly lead him to such demeanor or utterances that the impression produced by his statements does not do justice to its real testimonial value.' "

[7] See the materials collected in c. 3 of Countryman & Finman. The Lawyer in Modern Society; Joint Committee on Continuing Legal Education of American Law Institute and the American Bar Association, The Problem of a Criminal Defense 1–46 (1961); Stovall, Aspects of the Advocate's Dual Responsibility, 22 The Alabama Lawyer 66; Gold, Split Loyalty: An Ethical Problem for the Criminal Defense Lawyer, 14 Clev.-Mar.L.Rev. 65; Symposium on Professional Ethics, 64 Mich.L.Rev. 1469–1498.

victions, but that is hardly a proper measure of its long-run acceptability. In my view, the State is entitled to investigate and develop its case outside the presence of defense counsel. This includes the right to have private conversations with identification witnesses, just as defense counsel may have his own consultations with these and other witnesses without having the prosecutor present.

Whether today's judgment would be an acceptable exercise of supervisory power over federal courts is another question. But as a constitutional matter, the judgment in this case is erroneous and although I concur in Parts I and III of the Court's opinion I respectfully register this dissent.

Mr. Justice FORTAS, with whom THE CHIEF JUSTICE and Mr. Justice DOUGLAS join, concurring in part and dissenting in part.

1. I agree with the Court that the exhibition of the person of the accused at a lineup is not itself a violation of the privilege against self-incrimination. In itself, it is no more subject to constitutional objection than the exhibition of the person of the accused in the courtroom for identification purposes. It is an incident of the State's power to arrest, and a reasonable and justifiable aspect of the State's custody resulting from arrest. It does not require that the accused take affirmative, volitional action, but only that, having been duly arrested he may be seen for identification purposes. It is, however, a "critical stage" in the prosecution, and I agree with the Court that the opportunity to have counsel present must be made available.

2. In my view, however, the accused may not be compelled in a lineup to speak the words uttered by the person who committed the crime. I am confident that it could not be compelled in court. It cannot be compelled in a lineup. It is more than passive, mute assistance to the eyes of the victim or of witnesses. It is the kind of volitional act—the kind of forced cooperation by the accused— which is within the historical perimeter of the privilege against compelled self-incrimination.

Our history and tradition teach and command that an accused may stand mute. The privilege means just that; not less than that. According to the Court, an accused may be jailed—indefinitely— until he is willing to say, for an identifying audience, whatever was said in the course of the commission of the crime. Presumably this would include, "Your money or your life"—or perhaps, words of assault in a rape case. This is intolerable under our constitutional system.

I completely agree that the accused must be advised of and given the right to counsel before a lineup—and I join in that part of the Court's opinion; but this is an empty right unless we mean to insist upon the accused's fundamental constitutional immunities. One of these is that the accused may not be compelled to speak. To compel him to speak would violate the privilege against self-incrimination, which is incorporated in the Fifth Amendment.

This great privilege is not merely a shield for the accused. It is also a prescription of technique designed to guide the State's investigation. History teaches us that self-accusation is an unreliable instrument of detection, apt to inculpate the innocent-but-weak and to enable the guilty to escape. But this is not the end of the story. The privilege historically goes to the roots of democratic and religious principle. It prevents the debasement of the citizen which would result from compelling him to "accuse" himself before the power of the state. The roots of the privilege are deeper than the rack and the screw used to extort confessions. They go to the nature of a free man and to his relationship to the state.

An accused cannot be compelled to utter the words spoken by the criminal in the course of the crime. I thoroughly disagree with the Court's statement that such compulsion does not violate the Fifth Amendment. The Court relies upon Schmerber v. State of California, 384 U.S. 757, 86 S.Ct. 1826, 16 L.Ed.2d 908 (1966), to support this. I dissented in *Schmerber*, but if it were controlling here, I should, of course, acknowledge its binding effect unless we were prepared to overrule it. But *Schmerber*, which authorized the forced extraction of blood from the veins of an unwilling human being, did not compel the person actively to cooperate—to accuse himself by a volitional act which differs only in degree from compelling him to act out the crime, which, I assume, would be rebuffed by the Court. It is the latter feature which places the compelled utterance by the accused squarely within the history and noble purpose of the Fifth Amendment's commandment.

To permit *Schmerber* to apply in any respect beyond its holding is, in my opinion, indefensible. To permit its insidious doctrine to extend beyond the invasion of the body, which it permits, to compulsion of the will of a man, is to deny and defy a precious part of our historical faith and to discard one of the most profoundly cherished instruments by which we have established the freedom and dignity of the individual. We should not so alter the balance between the rights of the individual and of the state, achieved over centuries of conflict.

3. While the Court holds that the accused must be advised of and given the right to counsel at the lineup, it makes the privilege

meaningless in this important respect. Unless counsel has been waived or, being present, has not objected to the accused's utterance of words used in the course of committing the crime, to compel such an utterance is constitutional error.*

Accordingly, while I join the Court in requiring vacating of the judgment below for a determination as to whether the identification of respondent was based upon factors independent of the lineup, I would do so not only because of the failure to offer counsel before the lineup but also because of the violation of respondent's Fifth Amendment rights.

In Re Gault†

In this "juvenile delinquency case" the Supreme Court considers the extent to which a youth charged with being a delinquent is to be afforded procedural safeguards equivalent to those enjoyed by an adult facing a criminal charge. The Court considers four specific constitutional guarantees and the extent to which they apply in juvenile proceedings: the right to notice, the right to counsel, the right to remain silent and the right of confrontation.

A next door neighbor complained that Gault, a fifteen-year-old male, had made "indecent" remarks to her over the telephone. Without being advised that he had a right to remain silent and a right to counsel, Gault was questioned by the authorities and made damaging statements which later were used against him at a juvenile proceeding. Neither he nor his parents received notice of the charges which were to be presented against him at this proceeding. At the hearing, Gault was not apprized of his right to counsel nor extended the right of confrontation. Indeed, the complaining neighbor didn't even appear at the proceeding.

Gault was adjudicated a delinquent and committed to a state industrial school until the age of twenty-one. Had he been an adult at the time of the alleged misconduct the maximum penalty he could have received would have been a fine of fifty dollars or two months in jail. Thus, Gault's commitment of almost six years amounted to a loss of freedom for a period far in excess of that which an adult could have received for the same offense. In addition, as an adult Gault would have been afforded numerous procedural safeguards

---

* While it is conceivable that legislation might provide a meticulous lineup procedure which would *satisfy* constitutional requirements, I do not agree with the Court that this would "remove the basis for regarding the [lineup] stage as 'critical.' "

† 387 U.S. 1, 87 S.Ct. 1428 (May 15, 1967)

which the constitution guarantees to one accused of a crime. As a juvenile he received none of these safeguards.

The Supreme Court, with only Mr. Justice Stewart dissenting, reversed Gault's commitment. But notwithstanding this near unanimity the *Gault Case* represents a complete turnabout in the legal attributes of juvenile court proceedings. Prior to this decision the prevailing attitude in most all jurisdictions was that juvenile proceedings were civil in nature, with the State merely acting in the role of a parent, purportedly in the best interests of the youth in question. Since any commitment which resulted was not viewed as a criminal penalty, commitments were to "training schools", "rehabilitation homes" etc., for the "protection and benefit" of the minor rather than to jails or prisons. In this case, the Supreme Court holds that such an attitude is of little significance as far as the child is concerned. Although a training school might not be so labeled, in effect it is a place of criminal confinement. The labels placed on both the proceedings and the actions taken thereunder are not important. It is the substantive nature of these things which is of consequence. Substantively, juvenile commitments are similar enough to criminal confinements that they should be treated in a similar manner. Henceforth juveniles accused of being delinquent are to enjoy many of the constitutional guarantees heretofore applicable only to the accused criminal.

This decision has had a profound effect on the juvenile court system in most states. The administrative procedures of the juvenile courts in these states had to be modified considerably to make them conform to this decision.

A reading of the full text of the opinion provides the reader with a general survey of the old philosophies which are explicitly rejected plus an introduction to the new concepts which are to be utilized in the application of the United States Constitution to juvenile court proceedings.

Text of Case

Appellants' 15-year-old son, Gerald Gault, was taken into custody as the result of a complaint that he made lewd telephone calls. After hearings before a juvenile court judge, Gerald was ordered committed to the State Industrial School as a juvenile delinquent until he should reach majority. Appellants brought a habeas corpus action in the state courts to challenge the constitutionality of the Arizona Juvenile Code and the procedure actually used in Gerald's case, on the ground of denial of various procedural due process rights. The State Supreme Court affirmed dismissal of the writ. Agreeing that the constitutional guarantee of due process applies to proceedings in which juveniles are charged as delinquents, the court held that the Arizona Juvenile Code impliedly includes the requirements of due process in delinquency proceedings, and that such due process requirements were not offended by the procedure leading to Gerald's commitment.

Norman Dorsen argued the cause for appellants. With him on the brief were *Melvin L. Wulf, Amelia D. Lewis* and *Daniel A. Rezneck.*

Frank A. Parks, Assistant Attorney General of Arizona, argued the cause for appellee, *pro hac vice,* by special leave of Court. With him on the brief was *Darrell F. Smith,* Attorney General.

Merritt W. Green argued the cause for the Ohio Association of Juvenile Court Judges, as *amicus curiae,* urging affirmance. With him on the brief was *Leo G. Chimo.*

The Kansas Association of Probate and Juvenile Judges joined the appellee's brief and the brief of the Ohio Association of Juvenile Court Judges.

Briefs of *amici curiae,* urging reversal, were filed by *L. Michael Getty, James J. Doherty* and *Marshall J. Hartman* for the National Legal Aid and Defender Association, and by *Edward Q. Carr, Jr.,* and *Nanette Dembitz* for the Legal Aid Society and Citizens' Committee for Children of New York, Inc.

Nicholas N. Kittrie filed a brief for the American Parents Committee, as *amicus curiae.*

Mr. Justice FORTAS delivered the opinion of the Court.

This is an appeal under 28 U.S.C. § 1257 (2) from a judgment of the Supreme Court of Arizona affirming the dismissal of a petition for a writ of habeas corpus. 99 Ariz. 181, 407 P.2d 760 (1965). The petition sought the release of Gerald Francis Gault, appellants' 15-year-old son, who had been committed as a juvenile delinquent to the State Industrial School by the Juvenile Court of Gila County, Arizona. The Supreme Court of Arizona affirmed dismissal of the writ against various arguments which included an attack upon the constitutionality of the Arizona Juvenile Code because of its alleged denial of procedural due process rights to juveniles charged with being "delinquents." The court agreed that the constitutional guarantee of due process of law is applicable in such proceedings. It held that Arizona's Juvenile Code is to be read as "impliedly" implementing the "due process concept." It then proceeded to identify and describe "the particular elements which constitute due process in a juvenile hearing." It concluded that the proceedings ending in commitment of Gerald Gault did not offend those requirements. We do not agree, and we reverse. We begin with a statement of the facts.

I.

On Monday, June 8, 1964, at about 10 a. m., Gerald Francis Gault and a friend, Ronald Lewis, were taken into custody by the Sheriff of Gila County. Gerald was then still subject to a six months' probation order which had been entered on February 25, 1964, as a result of his having been in the company of another boy who had stolen a wallet from a lady's purse. The police action on June 8 was taken as the result of a verbal complaint by a neighbor of the boys, Mrs. Cook, about a telephone call made to her in which the caller or callers made lewd or indecent remarks. It will suffice for purposes of this opinion to say that the remarks or questions put to her were of the irritatingly offensive, adolescent, sex variety.

At the time Gerald was picked up, his mother and father were both at work. No notice that Gerald was being taken into custody was left at the home. No other steps were taken to advise them that their son had, in effect, been arrested. Gerald was taken to the Children's Detention Home. When his mother arrived home at about 6 o'clock, Gerald was not there. Gerald's older brother was sent to look for him at the trailer home of the Lewis family. He apparently learned then that Gerald was in custody. He so informed his mother. The two of them went to the Detention Home. The deputy probation officer, Flagg, who was also superintendent of the Detention Home, told Mrs. Gault "why Jerry was there" and said that a hearing would be held in Juvenile Court at 3 o'clock the following day, June 9.

Officer Flagg filed a petition with the court on the hearing day, June 9, 1964. It was not served on the Gaults. Indeed, none of them saw this petition until the habeas corpus hearing on August 17, 1964. The petition was entirely formal. It made no reference to any factual basis for the judicial action which it initiated. It recited only that "said minor is under the age of eighteen years, and is in need of the protection of this Honorable Court; [and that] said minor is a delinquent minor." It prayed for a hearing and an order regarding "the care and custody of said minor." Officer Flagg executed a formal affidavit in support of the petition.

On June 9, Gerald, his mother, his older brother, and Probation Officers Flagg and Henderson appeared before the Juvenile Judge in chambers. Gerald's father was not there. He was at work out of the city. Mrs. Cook, the complainant, was not there. No one was sworn at this hearing. No transcript or recording was made. No memorandum or record of the substance of the proceedings was prepared. Our information about the proceedings and the subsequent hearing on June 15, derives entirely from the testi-

145

mony of the Juvenile Court Judge,[1] Mr. and Mrs. Gault and Officer Flagg at the habeas corpus proceeding conducted two months later. From this, it appears that at the June 9 hearing Gerald was questioned by the judge about the telephone call. There was conflict as to what he said. His mother recalled that Gerald said he only dialed Mrs. Cook's number and handed the telephone to his friend, Ronald. Officer Flagg recalled that Gerald had admitted making the lewd remarks. Judge McGhee testified that Gerald "admitted making one of these [lewd] statements." At the conclusion of the hearing, the judge said he would "think about it." Gerald was taken back to the Detention Home. He was not sent to his own home with his parents. On June 11 or 12, after having been detained since June 8, Gerald was released and driven home.[2] There is no explanation in the record as to why he was kept in the Detention Home or why he was released. At 5 p. m. on the day of Gerald's release, Mrs. Gault received a note signed by Officer Flagg. It was on plain paper, not letterhead. Its entire text was as follows:

"Mrs. Gault:

"Judge McGHEE has set Monday June 15, 1964 at 11:00 A. M. as the date and time for further Hearings on Gerald's delinquency

"/s/Flagg"

At the appointed time on Monday, June 15, Gerald, his father and mother, Ronald Lewis and his father, and Officers Flagg and Henderson were present before Judge McGhee. Witnesses at the habeas corpus proceeding differed in their recollections of Gerald's testimony at the June 15 hearing. Mr. and Mrs. Gault recalled that Gerald again testified that he had only dialed the number and that the other boy had made the remarks. Officer Flagg agreed that at this hearing Gerald did not admit making the lewd remarks.[3] But Judge McGhee recalled that "there was some admission again of some of the lewd statements. He—he didn't ad-

---

[1] Under Arizona law, juvenile hearings are conducted by a judge of the Superior Court, designated by his colleagues on the Superior Court to serve as Juvenile Court Judge. Arizona Const., Art. 6, § 15, A.R.S.; Arizona Revised Statutes (hereinafter ARS) §§ 8–201, 8–202.

[2] There is a conflict between the recollection of Mrs. Gault and that of Officer Flagg. Mrs. Gault testified that Gerald was released on Friday, June 12, Officer Flagg that it had been on Thursday, June

11. This was from memory; he had no record, and the note hereafter referred to was undated.

[3] Officer Flagg also testified that Gerald had not, when questioned at the Detention Home, admitted having made any of the lewd statements, but that each boy had sought to put the blame on the other. There was conflicting testimony as to whether Ronald had accused Gerald of making the lewd statements during the June 15 hearing.

mit any of the more serious lewd statements."[4] Again, the complainant, Mrs. Cook, was not present. Mrs. Gault asked that Mrs. Cook be present "so she could see which boy that done the talking, the dirty talking over the phone." The Juvenile Judge said "she didn't have to be present at that hearing." The judge did not speak to Mrs. Cook or communicate with her at any time. Probation Officer Flagg had talked to her once—over the telephone on June 9.

At this June 15 hearing a "referral report" made by the probation officers was filed with the court, although not disclosed to Gerald or his parents. This listed the charge as "Lewd Phone Calls." At the conclusion of the hearing, the judge committed Gerald as a juvenile delinquent to the State Industrial School "for the period of his minority [that is, until 21], unless sooner discharged by due process of law." An order to that effect was entered. It recites that "after a full hearing and due deliberation the Court finds that said minor is a delinquent child, and that said minor is of the age of 15 years."

No appeal is permitted by Arizona law in juvenile cases. On August 3, 1964, a petition for a writ of habeas corpus was filed with the Supreme Court of Arizona and referred by it to the Superior Court for hearing.

At the habeas corpus hearing on August 17, Judge McGhee was vigorously cross-examined as to the basis for his actions. He testified that he had taken into account the fact that Gerald was on probation. He was asked "under what section of * * * the code you found the boy delinquent?"

His answer is set forth in the margin.[5] In substance, he concluded that Gerald came within ARS § 8–201–6(a), which specifies that a "delinquent child" includes one "who has violated a law of the state or an ordinance or regulation of a political subdivision thereof." The law which Gerald was found to have violated is ARS § 13–377. This section of the Arizona Criminal Code provides that a person who "in the presence or hearing of any

[4] Judge McGhee also testified that Gerald had not denied "certain statements" made to him at the hearing by Officer Henderson.

[5] "Q. All right. Now, Judge, would you tell me under what section of the law or tell me under what section of—of the code you found the boy delinquent?

"A. Well, there is a—I think it amounts to disturbing the peace. I can't give you the section, but I can tell you the law, that when one person uses lewd language in the presence of another person, that it can amount to—and I consider that when a person makes it over the phone, that it is considered in the presence, I might be wrong, that is one section. The other section upon which I consider the boy delinquent is Section 8–201, Subsection (d), habitually involved in immoral matters."

woman or child * * * uses vulgar, abusive or obscene language, is guilty of a misdemeanor * * *." The penalty specified in the Criminal Code, which would apply to an adult, is $5 to $50, or imprisonment for not more than two months. The judge also testified that he acted under ARS § 8–201–6(d) which includes in the definition of a "delinquent child" one who, as the judge phrased it, is "habitually involved in immoral matters."[6]

Asked about the basis for his conclusion that Gerald was "habitually involved in immoral matters," the judge testified, somewhat vaguely, that two years earlier, on July 2, 1962, a "referral" was made concerning Gerald, "where the boy had stolen a baseball glove from another boy and lied to the Police Department about it." The judge said there was "no hearing," and "no accusation" relating to this incident, "because of lack of material foundation." But it seems to have remained in his mind as a relevant factor. The judge also testified that Gerald had admitted making other nuisance phone calls in the past which, as the judge recalled the boy's testimony, were "silly calls, or funny calls, or something like that."

The Superior Court dismissed the writ, and appellants sought review in the Arizona Supreme Court. That court stated that it considered appellants' assignments of error as urging (1) that the Juvenile Code, ARS § 8–201 to § 8–239, is unconstitutional because it does not require that parents and children be apprised of the specific charges, does not require proper notice of a hearing, and does not provide for an appeal; and (2) that the proceedings and order relating to Gerald constituted a denial of due process of law because of the absence of adequate notice of the charge and the hearing; failure to notify appellants of certain constitutional rights including the rights to counsel and to confrontation, and the privilege against self-incrimination; the use of unsworn hearsay testimony; and the failure to make a record of the proceedings. Appellants further asserted that it was error for the Juvenile Court to remove Gerald from the custody of his parents without a showing and finding of their unsuitability, and alleged a miscellany of other errors under state law.

---

[6] ARS § 8–201, subsec. 6, the section of the Arizona Juvenile Code which defines a delinquent child, reads:

" 'Delinquent child' includes:

"(a) A child who has violated a law of the state or an ordinance or regulation of a political subdivision thereof.

"(b) A child who, by reason of being incorrigible, wayward or habitually disobedient, is uncontrolled by his parent, guardian or custodian.

"(c) A child who is habitually truant from school or home.

"(d) A child who habitually so deports himself as to injure or endanger the morals or health of himself or others."

The Supreme Court handed down an elaborate and wide-ranging opinion affirming dismissal of the writ and stating the court's conclusions as to the issues raised by appellants and other aspects of the juvenile process. In their jurisdictional statement and brief in this Court, appellants do not urge upon us all of the points passed upon by the Supreme Court of Arizona. They urge that we hold the Juvenile Code of Arizona invalid on its face or as applied in this case because, contrary to the Due Process Clause of the Fourteenth Amendment, the juvenile is taken from the custody of his parents and committed to a state institution pursuant to proceedings in which the Juvenile Court has virtually unlimited discretion, and in which the following basic rights are denied:

1. Notice of the charges;
2. Right to counsel;
3. Right to confrontation and cross-examination;
4. Privilege against self-incrimination;
5. Right to a transcript of the proceedings; and
6. Right to appellate review.

We shall not consider other issues which were passed upon by the Supreme Court of Arizona. We emphasize that we indicate no opinion as to whether the decision of that court with respect to such other issues does or does not conflict with requirements of the Federal Constitution.[7]

---

[7] For example, the laws of Arizona allow arrest for a misdemeanor only if a warrant is obtained or if it is committed in the presence of the officer. ARS § 13–1403. The Supreme Court of Arizona held that this is inapplicable in the case of juveniles. See ARS § 8–221 which relates specifically to juveniles. But compare Two Brothers and a Case of Liquor, Juv.Ct.D.C., Nos. 66–2652–J, 66–2653–J, December 28, 1966 (opinion of Judge Ketcham); Standards for Juvenile and Family Courts, Children's Bureau Pub. No. 437–1966, p. 47 (hereinafter cited as Standards); New York Family Court Act § 721 (1963) (hereinafter cited as N.Y.Family Court Act).

The court also held that the judge may consider hearsay if it is "of a kind on which reasonable men are accustomed to rely in serious affairs." But compare Note, Juvenile Delinquents: The Police, State Courts, and Individualized Justice,

79 Harv.L.Rev. 775, 794–795 (1966) (hereinafter cited as Harvard Law Review Note):

"The informality of juvenile court hearings frequently leads to the admission of hearsay and unsworn testimony. It is said that 'close adherence to the strict rules of evidence might prevent the court from obtaining important facts as to the child's character and condition which could only be to the child's detriment.' The assumption is that the judge will give normally inadmissible evidence only its proper weight. It is also declared in support of these evidentiary practices that the juvenile court is not a criminal court, that the importance of the hearsay rule has been overestimated, and that allowing an attorney to make 'technical objections' would disrupt the desired informality of the proceedings. But to the extent that the rules of evidence are not merely technical or historical, but like the

II.

The Supreme Court of Arizona held that due process of law is requisite to the constitutional validity of proceedings in which a court reaches the conclusion that a juvenile has been at fault, has engaged in conduct prohibited by law, or has otherwise misbehaved with the consequence that he is committed to an institution in which his freedom is curtailed. This conclusion is in accord with the decisions of a number of courts under both federal and state constitutions.[8]

This Court has not heretofore decided the precise question. In Kent v. United States, 383 U.S. 541, 86 S.Ct. 1045, 16 L.Ed.2d 84 (1966), we considered the requirements for a valid waiver of the "exclusive" jurisdiction of the Juvenile Court of the District of Columbia so that a juvenile could be tried in the adult criminal court of the District. Although our decision turned upon the language of the statute, we emphasized the necessity that "the basic requirements of due process and fairness" be satisfied in such proceedings.[9] Haley v. State of Ohio, 332 U.S. 596, 68 S.Ct. 302, 92 L.Ed. 224 (1948), involved the admissibility, in a state criminal court of general jurisdiction, of a confession by a 15-year-old boy. The Court held that the Fourteenth Amendment applied to prohibit the use of the coerced confession. Mr. Justice Douglas said, "Neither man nor child can be allowed to stand condemned by methods which flout constitutional requirements of due process of law."[10] To the same effect is Gallegos v. State of Colorado, 370 U.S. 49, 82 S.Ct. 1209, 8 L.Ed.2d 325 (1962). Accordingly, while these cases relate only to restricted aspects of the subject, they unmistakably indicate that, whatever may be their precise impact,

---

hearsay rule have a sound basis in human experience, they should not be rejected in any judicial inquiry. Juvenile court judges in Los Angeles, Tucson, and Wisconsin Rapids, Wisconsin report that they are satisfied with the operation of their courts despite application of unrelaxed rules of evidence." (Footnotes omitted.)

It ruled that the correct burden of proof is that "the juvenile judge must be persuaded by clear and convincing evidence that the infant has committed the alleged delinquent act." Compare the "preponderance of the evidence" test, N.Y. Family Court Act § 744 (where maximum commitment is three years, §§ 753, 758). Cf. Harvard Law Review Note, p. 795.

[8] See, e. g., In Matters of W. and S., 19 N.Y.2d 55, 277 N.Y.S.2d 675, 224 N.E.2d 102 (1966); In Interests of Carlo and Stasilowicz, 48 N.J. 224, 225 A.2d 110 (1966); People v. Dotson, 46 Cal.2d 891, 299 P.2d 875 (1956); Pee v. United States, 107 U.S.App. D.C. 47, 274 F.2d. 556 (1959); Wissenburg v. Bradley, 209 Iowa 813, 229 N.W.205, 67 A.L. R. 1075 (1930); Bryant v. Brown, 151 Miss. 398, 118 So. 184, 60 A.L. R. 1325 (1928); Dendy v. Wilson, 142 Tex. 460, 179 S.W.2d 269, 151 A.L.R. 1217 (1944); Application of Johnson, 178 F.Supp. 155 (D.C. N.J. 1957).

[9] 383 U.S., at 553, 86 S.Ct., at 105.

[10] 332 U.S., at 601, 68 S.Ct., at 304 (opinion for four Justices).

neither the Fourteenth Amendment nor the Bill of Rights is for adults alone.

We do not in this opinion consider the impact of these constitutional provisions upon the totality of the relationship of the juvenile and the state. We do not even consider the entire process relating to juvenile "delinquents." For example, we are not here concerned with the procedures or constitutional rights applicable to the pre-judicial stages of the juvenile process, nor do we direct our attention to the post-adjudicative or dispositional process. See note 48, infra. We consider only the problems presented to us by this case. These relate to the proceedings by which a determination is made as to whether a juvenile is a "delinquent" as a result of alleged misconduct on his part, with the consequence that he may be committed to a state institution. As to these proceedings, there appears to be little current dissent from the proposition that the Due Process Clause has a role to play.[11] The problem is to ascertain the precise impact of the due process requirement upon such proceedings.

From the inception of the juvenile court system, wide differences have been tolerated—indeed insisted upon—between the procedural rights accorded to adults and those of juveniles. In practically all jurisdictions, there are rights granted to adults which are withheld from juveniles. In addition to the specific problems involved in the present case, for example, it has been held that the juvenile is not entitled to bail, to indictment by grand jury, to a public trial or to trial by jury.[12] It is frequent practice that rules governing the arrest and interrogation of adults by the police are not observed in the case of juveniles.[13]

The history and theory underlying this development are well-known, but a recapitulation is necessary for purposes of this opinion. The Juvenile Court movement began in this country at the end of the last century. From the juvenile court statute adopted in Illinois in 1899, the system has spread to every State in the

---

[11] See Report by the President's Commission on Law Enforcement and Administration of Justice, "The Challenge of Crime in a Free Society" (1967) (hereinafter cited as Nat'l Crime Comm'n Report), pp. 81, 85–86; Standards, p. 71; Gardner, The Kent Case and the Juvenile Court: A Challenge to Lawyers, 52 A.B.A.J. 923 (1966); Paulsen, Fairness to the Juvenile Offender, 41 Minn.L.Rev. 547 (1957); Ketcham, The Legal Renaissance in the Juvenile Court, 60 Nw.U.L.Rev. 585 (1965); Allen, The Borderland of Criminal Justice (1964), pp. 19–23; Harvard Law Review Note, p. 791; Note, Rights and Rehabilitation in the Juvenile Courts, 67 Col. L.Rev. 281 (1967); Comment, Criminal Offenders in the Juvenile Court: More Brickbats and Another Proposal, 114 U.Pa.L.Rev. 1171 (1966).

[12] See Kent v. United States, 383 U.S. 541, 555, 86 S.Ct. 1045, 1054 and n. 22 (1966).

[13] See n. 7, supra.

Union, the District of Columbia, and Puerto Rico.[14] The constitutionality of juvenile court laws has been sustained in over 40 jurisdictions against a variety of attacks.[15]

The early reformers were appalled by adult procedures and penalties, and by the fact that children could be given long prison sentences and mixed in jails with hardened criminals. They were profoundly convinced that society's duty to the child could not be confined by the concept of justice alone. They believed that society's role was not to ascertain whether the child was "guilty" or "innocent," but "What is he, how has he become what he is, and what had best be done in his interest and in the interest of the state to save him from a downward career."[16] The child—essentially good, as they saw it—was to be made "to feel that he is the object of [the state's] care and solicitude,"[17] not that he was under arrest or on trial. The rules of criminal procedure were therefore altogether inapplicable. The apparent rigidities, technicalities, and harshness which they observed in both substantive and procedural criminal law were therefore to be discarded. The idea of crime and punishment was to be abandoned. The child was to be "treated" and "rehabilitated" and the procedures, from apprehension through institutionalization, were to be "clinical" rather than punitive.

These results were to be achieved, without coming to conceptual and constitutional grief, by insisting that the proceedings were not adversary, but that the state was proceeding as *parens pat-*

---

[14] See National Council of Juvenile Court Judges, Directory and Manual (1964), p. 1. The number of Juvenile Judges as of 1964 is listed as 2,987, of whom 213 are full-time Juvenile Court Judges. Id., at 305. The Nat'l Crime Comm'n Report indicates that half of these judges have no undergraduate degree, a fifth have no college education at all, a fifth are not members of the bar, and three-quarters devote less than one-quarter of their time to juvenile matters. See also McCune, Profile of the Nation's Juvenile Court Judges (monograph, George Washington University, Center for the Behavioral Sciences, 1965), which is a detailed statistical study of Juvenile Court Judges, and indicates additionally that about a quarter of these judges have no law school training at all. About one-third of all judges have no probation and social work staff available to them; between eighty and ninety percent have no available psychologist or psychiatrist. Ibid. It has been observed that while "good will, compassion, and similar virtues are * * * admirably prevalent throughout the system * * * expertise, the keystone of the whole venture, is lacking." Harvard Law Review Note, p. 809. In 1965, over 697,00 delinquency cases (excluding traffic) were disposed of in these courts, involving some 601,000 children, or 2% of all children between 10 and 17. Juvenile Court Statistics—1965, Children's Bureau Statistical Series No. 85 (1966), p. 2.

[15] See Paulsen, Kent v. United States: The Constitutional Context of Juvenile Cases, 1966 Sup.Ct.Review 167, 174.

[16] Julian Mack, The Juvenile Court, 23 Harv.L.Rev. 104, 119–120 (1909).

[17] Id., at 120.

riae.[18] The Latin phrase proved to be a great help to those who sought to rationalize the exclusion of juveniles from the constitutional scheme; but its meaning is murky and its historic credentials are of dubious relevance. The phrase was taken from chancery practice, where, however, it was used to describe the power of the state to act *in loco parentis* for the purpose of protecting the property interests and the person of the child.[19] But there is no trace of the doctrine in the history of criminal jurisprudence. At common law, children under seven were considered incapable of possessing criminal intent. Beyond that age, they were subjected to arrest, trial, and in theory to punishment like adult offenders.[20] In these old days, the state was not deemed to have authority to accord them fewer procedural rights than adults.

The right of the state, as *parens patriae*, to deny to the child procedural rights available to his elders was elaborated by the assertion that a child, unlike an adult, has a right "not to liberty but to custody." He can be made to attorn to his parents, to go to school, etc. If his parents default in effectively performing their custodial functions—that is, if the child is "delinquent"—the state may intervene. In doing so, it does not deprive the child of any rights, because he has none. It merely provides the "custody" to which the child is entitled.[21] On this basis, proceedings involving juveniles were described as "civil" not "criminal" and therefore not subject to the requirements which restrict the state when it seeks to deprive a person of his liberty.[22]

---

[18] Id., at 109; Paulsen, op. cit. supra, n. 15, at 173–174. There seems to have been little early constitutional objection to the special procedures of juvenile courts. But see Waite, How Far Can Court Procedure Be Socialized Without Impairing Individual Rights, 12 J.Crim.L. & Criminology 339, 340 (1922): "The court which must direct its procedure even apparently to do something *to* a child because of what he *has done,* is parted from the court which is avowedly concerned only with doing something *for* a child because of what he *is* and *needs,* by a gulf too wide to be bridged by any humanity which the judge may introduce into his hearings, or by the habitual use of corrective rather than punitive methods after conviction."

[19] Paulsen, op. cit. supra, n. 15, at 173; Hurley, Origin of the Illinois Juvenile Court Law, in The Child, The Clinic, and the Court (1925), pp. 320, 328.

[20] Julian Mack, The Chancery Procedure in the Juvenile Court, in The Child, The Clinic, and the Court (1925), p. 310.

[21] See, e.g., Shears, Legal Problems Peculiar to Children's Courts, 48 A.B.A.J. 719, 720 (1962) ("The basic right of a juvenile is not to liberty but to custody. He has the right to have someone take care of him, and if his parents do not afford him this custodial privilege, the law must do so."); Ex parte Crouse, 4 Whart. 9, 11 (Sup.Ct.Pa. 1839); Petition of Ferrier, 103 Ill. 367, 371–373 (1882).

[22] The Appendix to the opinion of Judge Prettyman in Pee v. United States, 107 U.S.App.D.C. 47, 274 F.2d 556 (1959), lists authority in 51 jurisdictions to this effect. Even rules required by due process in

Accordingly, the highest motives and most enlightened impulses led to a peculiar system for juveniles, unknown to our law in any comparable context. The constitutional and theoretical basis for this peculiar system is—to say the least—debatable. And in practice, as we remarked in the *Kent* case, supra, the results have not been entirely satisfactory.[23] Juvenile Court history has again demonstrated that unbridled discretion, however benevolently motivated, is frequently a poor substitute for principle and procedure. In 1937, Dean Pound wrote: "The powers of the Star Chamber were a trifle in comparison with those of our juvenile courts * * *."[24] The absence of substantive standards has not necessarily meant that children receive careful, compassionate, individualized treatment. The absence of procedural rules based upon constitutional principle has not always produced fair, efficient, and effective procedures. Departures from established principles of due process have frequently resulted not in enlightened procedure, but in arbitrariness. The Chairman of the Pennsylvania Council of Juvenile Court Judges has recently observed: "Unfortunately, loose procedures, high-handed methods and crowded court calendars, either singly or in combination, all too often, have resulted in de-

---

civil proceedings, however, have not generally been deemed compulsory as to proceedings affecting juveniles. For example, constitutional requirements as to notice of issues, which would commonly apply in civil cases, are commonly disregarded in juvenile proceedings, as this case illustrates.

[23] "There is evidence * * * that there may be grounds for concern that the child receives the worst of both worlds; that he gets neither the protections accorded to adults nor the solicitous care and regenerative treatment postulated for children." 383 U.S., at 556, 86 S.Ct., at 1054, citing Handler, The Juvenile Court and the Adversary system: Problems of Function and Forum, 1965 Wis.L.Rev. 7; Harvard Law Review Note; and various congressional materials set forth in 383 U.S., at 546, 86 S.Ct., at 1050, n. 5.

On the other hand, while this opinion and much recent writing concentrate upon the failures of the Juvenile Court system to live up to the expectations of its founders, the observation of the Nat'l Crime Comm'n Report should be kept in mind: "Although its shortcomings are many and its results too often disappointing, the juvenile justice system in many cities is operated by people who are better educated and more highly skilled, can call on more and better facilities and services, and has more ancillary agencies to which to refer its clientele than its adult counterpart." Id., at 78.

[24] Foreword to Young, Social Treatment in Probation and Delinquency (1937), p. xxvii. The 1965 Report of the United States Commission on Civil Rights, "Law Enforcement —A Report on Equal Protection in the South," pp. 80–83, documents numerous instances in which "local authorities used the broad discretion afforded them by the absence of safeguards [in the juvenile process]" to punish, intimidate, and obstruct youthful participants in civil rights demonstrations. See also Paulsen, Juvenile Courts, Family Courts, and the Poor Man, 54 Calif.L.Rev. 694, 707–709 (1966).

priving some juveniles of fundamental rights that have resulted in a denial of due process."[25]

Failure to observe the fundamental requirements of due process has resulted in instances, which might have been avoided, of unfairness to individuals and inadequate or inaccurate findings of fact and unfortunate prescriptions of remedy. Due process of law is the primary and indispensable foundation of individual freedom. It is the basic and essential term in the social compact which defines the rights of the individual and delimits the powers which the state may exercise.[26] As Mr. Justice Frankfurter has

[25] Lehman, A Juvenile's Right to Counsel in a Delinquency Hearing, 17 Juvenile Court Judges Journal 53, 54 (1966).

Compare the observation of the late Arthur T. Vanderbilt, Chief Justice of the Supreme Court of New Jersey, in a foreword to Virtue, Basic Structure for Children's Services in Michigan (1953), p. x:

"In their zeal to care for children neither juvenile judges nor welfare workers can be permitted to violate the Constitution, especially the constitutional provisions as to due process that are involved in moving a child from its home. The indispensable elements of due process are: first, a tribunal with jurisdiction; second, notice of a hearing to the proper parties; and finally, a fair hearing. All three must be present if we are to treat the child as an individual human being and not to revert, in spite of good intentions, to the more primitive days when he was treated as a chattel."

We are warned that the system must not "degenerate into a star chamber proceeding with the judge imposing his own particular brand of culture and morals on indigent people * * *." Judge Marion G. Woodward, letter reproduced in 18 Social Service Review 366, 368 (1944). Doctor Bovet, the Swiss psychiatrist, in his monograph for the World Health Organization, Psychiatric Aspects of Juvenile Delinquency (1951), p. 79, stated that: "One of the most definite conclusions of this investigation is that few fields exist in which more serious coercive measures are applied, on such flimsy objective evidence,

than in that of juvenile delinquency." We are told that "The judge as amateur psychologist, experimenting upon the unfortunate children who must appear before him, is neither an attractive nor a convincing figure." Harvard Law Review Note, at 808.

[26] The impact of denying fundamental procedural due process to juveniles involved in "delinquency" charges is dramatized by the following considerations: (1) In 1965, persons under 18 accounted for about one-fifth of all arrests for serious crimes (Nat'l Crime Comm'n, Report, p. 55) and over half of all arrests for serious property offenses (id., at 56), and in the same year some 601,000 children under 18, or 2% of all children between 10 and 17, came before juvenile courts (Juvenile Court Statistics—1965, Children's Bureau Statistical Series No. 85 (1966) p. 2). About one out of nine youths will be referred to juvenile court in connection with a delinquent act (excluding traffic offenses) before he is 18 (Nat'l Crime Comm'n Report, p. 55). Cf. also Wheeler & Cottrell, Juvenile Delinquency—Its Prevention and Control (Russell Sage Foundation, 1965), p. 2; Report of the President's Commission on Crime in the District of Columbia (1966) (hereinafter cited as D.C.Crime Comm'n Report), p. 773. Furthermore, most juvenile crime apparently goes undetected or not formally punished. Wheeler & Cottrell, supra, observe that "[A]lmost all youngsters have committed at least one of the petty forms of theft and vandalism in the course of their adolescence."

said: "The history of American freedom is, in no small measure, the history of procedure."[27] But, in addition, the procedural rules which have been fashioned from the generality of due process are our best instruments for the distillation and evaluation of essential facts from the conflicting welter of data that life and our adversary methods present. It is these instruments of due process which enhance the possibility that truth will emerge from the confrontation of opposing versions and conflicting data. "Procedure is to law what 'scientific method' is to science."[28]

It is claimed that juveniles obtain benefits from the special procedures applicable to them which more than offset the disadvantages of denial of the substance of normal due process. As we shall discuss, the observance of due process standards, intelligently and not ruthlessly administered, will not compel the States to abandon or displace any of the substantive benefits of the juvenile process.[29] But it is important, we think, that the claimed benefits of the juvenile process should be candidly appraised. Neither sentiment nor folklore should cause us to shut our eyes, for example, to such startling findings as that reported in an exceptionally reliable study of repeaters or recidivism conducted by the Stanford Research Institute for the President's Commission on Crime in the District of Columbia. This Commission's Report states:

Id., at 28–29. See also Nat'l Crime Comm'n Report, p. 55, where it is stated that "self-report studies reveal that perhaps 90 percent of all young people have committed at least one act for which they could have been brought to juvenile court." It seems that the rate of juvenile delinquency is also steadily rising. See Nat'l Crime Comm'n report, p. 56; Juvenile Court Statistics, supra, pp. 2–3. (2) In New York, where most juveniles are represented by counsel (see n. 69, infra) and substantial procedural rights are afforded (see, e. g., nn. 80, 81, 99, infra), out of a fiscal year 1965–1966 total of 10,755 juvenile proceedings involving boys, 2,242 were dismissed for failure of proof at the fact-finding hearing; for girls, the figures were 306 out of a total of 1,051. New York Judicial Conference, Twelfth Annual Report, pp. 314, 316 (1967). (3) In about one-half of the States, a juvenile may be transferred to an adult penal institution after a juvenile court has found him "delin-

quent" (Delinquent Children in Penal Institutions, Children's Bureau Pub. No. 415–1964, p. 1). (4) In some jurisdictions a juvenile may be subjected to criminal prosecution for the same offense for which he has served under a juvenile court commitment. However, the Texas procedure to this effect has recently been held unconstitutional by a federal district court judge, in a habeas corpus action. Sawyer v. Hauck, 245 F.Supp. 55 (D.C.W.D. Tex. 1965). (5) In most of the States the juvenile may end in criminal court through wavier (Harvard Law Review Note, p. 793).

[27] Malinski v. People of State of New York, 324 U.S. 401, 414, 65 S.Ct. 781, 787, 89 L.Ed. 1029 (1945) (separate opinion).

[28] Foster, Social Work, the Law, and Social Action, in Social Casework, July 1964, pp. 383, 386.

[29] See Note, Rights and Rehabilitation in the Juvenile Courts, 67 Col.L. Rev. 281, 321 and *passim* (1967).

"In fiscal 1966 approximately 66 percent of the 16- and 17-year-old juveniles referred to the court by the Youth Aid Division had been before the court previously. In 1965, 56 percent of those in the Receiving Home were repeaters. The SRI study revealed that 61 percent of the sample Juvenile Court referrals in 1965 had been previously referred at least once and that 42 percent had been referred at least twice before." Id., at 773.

Certainly, these figures and the high crime rates among juveniles to which we have referred (supra, n. 26), could not lead us to conclude that the absence of constitutional protections reduces crime, or that the juvenile system, functioning free of constitutional inhibitions as it has largely done, is effective to reduce crime or rehabilitate offenders. We do not mean by this to denigrate the juvenile court process or to suggest that there are not aspects of the juvenile system relating to offenders which are valuable. But the features of the juvenile system which its proponents have asserted are of unique benefit will not be impaired by constitutional domestication. For example, the commendable principles relating to the processing and treatment of juveniles separately from adults are in no way involved or affected by the procedural issues under discussion.[30] Further, we are told that one of the important benefits

---

[30] Here again, however, there is substantial question as to whether fact and pretension, with respect to the separate handling and treatment of children, coincide. See generally infra.

While we are concerned only with procedure before the juvenile court in this case, it should be noted that to the extent that the special procedures for juveniles are thought to be justified by the special consideration and treatment afforded them, there is reason to doubt that juveniles always receive the benefits of such a id pro quo. As to the problem and importance of special care at the adjudicatory stage, cf. nn. 14 and 26, supra. As to treatment, see Nat'l Crime Comm'n Report, pp. 80, 87; D.C. Crime Comm'n Report, pp. 665-676, 686-687 (at p. 687 the Report refers to the District's "bankruptcy of dispositional resources"), 692-695, 700-718 (at p. 701 the Report observes that "The Department of Public Welfare currently lacks even the rudiments of essential diagnostic and clinical services"); Wheeler & Cottrell, Juvenile Delinquency—

Its Prevention and Control (Russell Sage Foundation, 1965), pp. 32 -35; Harvard Law Review Note, p. 809; Paulsen, Juvenile Courts, Family Courts, and the Poor Man, 54 Calif.L.Rev. 694, 709-712 (1966); Polier, A View From the Bench (1964). Cf. also, In the Matter of the Youth House, Inc., Report of the July 1966 "A" Term of the Bronx County Grand Jury, Supreme Court of New York, County of Bronx, Trial Term, Part XII, March 21, 1967 (cf. New York Times, March 23, 1967, p. 1, col. 8). The high rate of juvenile recidivism casts some doubt upon the adequacy of treatment afforded juveniles. See D.C.Crime Comm'n Report, p. 773; Nat'l Crime Comm'n Report, pp. 55, 78.

In fact, some courts have recently indicated that appropriate treatment is essential to the validity of juvenile custody, and therefore that a juvenile may challenge the validity of his custody on the ground that he is not in fact receiving any special treatment. See Creek v. Stone, 379 F.2d 106 (D.C. Cir. 1967); Kautter v. Reid, 183

of the special juvenile court procedures is that they avoid classifying the juvenile as a "criminal." The juvenile offender is now classed as a "delinquent." There is, of course, no reason why this should not continue. It is disconcerting, however, that this term has come to involve only slightly less stigma than the term "criminal" applied to adults.[31] It is also emphasized that in practically all jurisdictions, statutes provide that an adjudication of the child as a delinquent shall not operate as a civil disability or disqualify him for civil service appointment.[32] There is no reason why the application of due process requirements should interfere with such provisions.

Beyond this, it is frequently said that juveniles are protected by the process from disclosure of their deviational behavior. As the Supreme Court of Arizona phrased it in the present case, the summary procedures of Juvenile Courts are sometimes defended by a statement that it is the law's policy "to hide youthful errors from the full gaze of the public and bury them in the graveyard of the forgotten past." This claim of secrecy, however, is more rhetoric then reality. Disclosure of court records is discretionary with the judge in most jurisdictions. Statutory restrictions almost invariably apply only to the court records, and even as to those the evidence is that many courts routinely furnish information to the FBI and the military, and on request to government agencies and even to private employers.[33] Of more importance are police records. In most States the police keep a complete file of juvenile "police contacts" and have complete discretion as to disclosure of juvenile records. Police departments receive requests for information from the FBI and other law-enforcement agencies, the Armed Forces, and social service agencies, and most of them generally comply.[34]

F.Supp. 352 (D.C.D.C.1960); White v. Reid, 125 F.Supp. 647 (D.C.D.C. 1954). See also Elmore v. Stone, 122 U.S.App.D.C. 416, 355 F.2d 841 (1966) (separate statement of Bazelon, C. J.); Clayton v. Stone, 123 U.S.App.D.C. 181, 358 F.2d 548 (1966) (separate statement of Bazelon, C.J.). Cf. Wheeler & Cottrell, supra, pp. 32, 35; In re Rich, 125 Vt. 373. 216 A.2d 266 (1966). Cf. also Rouse v. Cameron, 125 U.S.App.D.C. 366, 373 F.2d 451 (1966); Millard v. Cameron, 125 U.S.App.D.C. 383, 373 F.2d 468 (1966).

[31] "[T]he word 'delinquent' has today developed such invidious connotations that the terminology is in the process of being altered; the new descriptive phrase is 'persons in need of supervision,' usually shortened to 'pins.' " Harvard Law Review Note, p. 799, n. 140. The N.Y. Family Court Act § 712 distinguishes between "delinquents" and "persons in need of supervision."

[32] See, e. g., the Arizona provision, ARS § 8–228.

[33] Harvard Law Review Note, pp. 784 –785, 800. Cf. Nat'l Crime Comm'n Report, pp. 87–88; Ketcham, The Unfulfilled Promise of the Juvenile Court, 7 Crime & Delin. 97, 102–103 (1961).

[34] Harvard Law Review Note, pp. 785 –787.

Private employers word their application forms to produce information concerning juvenile arrests and court proceedings, and in some jurisdictions information concerning juvenile police contacts is furnished private employers as well as government agencies.[35]

In any event, there is no reason why, consistently with due process, a State cannot continue, if it deems it appropriate, to provide and to improve provision for the confidentiality of records of police contacts and court action relating to juveniles. It is interesting to note, however, that the Arizona Supreme Court used the confidentiality argument as a justification for the type of notice which is here attacked as inadequate for due process purposes. The parents were given merely general notice that their child was charged with "delinquency." No facts were specified. The Arizona court held, however, as we shall discuss, that in addition to this general "notice," the child and his parents must be advised "of the facts involved in the case" no later than the initial hearing by the judge. Obviously, this does not "bury" the word about the child's transgressions. It merely defers the time of disclosure to a point when it is of limited use to the child or his parents in preparing his defense or explanation.

Further, it is urged that the juvenile benefits from informal proceedings in the court. The early conception of the Juvenile Court proceeding was one in which a fatherly judge touched the heart and conscience of the erring youth by talking over his problems, by paternal advice and admonition, and in which, in extreme situations, benevolent and wise institutions of the State provided guidance and help "to save him from a downward career."[36] Then, as now, goodwill and compassion were admirably prevalent. But recent studies have, with surprising unanimity, entered sharp dissent as to the validity of this gentle conception. They suggest that the appearance as well as the actuality of fairness, impartiality and orderliness—in short, the essentials of due process—may be a more impressive and more therapeutic attitude so far as the juvenile is concerned. For example, in a recent study, the sociologists Wheeler and Cottrell observe that when the procedural laxness of the *"parens patriae"* attitude is followed by stern disciplining, the contrast may have an adverse effect upon the child, who feels that he has been deceived or enticed. They conclude as follows: "Unless appropriate due process of law is followed, even the

[35] Id., at 785, 800. See also, with respect to the problem of confidentiality of records, Note, Rights and Rehabilitation in the Juvenile Courts, 67 Col.L.Rev. 281, 286–289 (1967). Even the privacy of the juvenile hearing itself is not always adequately protected. Id., at 285–286.

[36] Mack, the Juvenile Court, 23 Harv. L.Rev. 104, 120 (1909).

juvenile who has violated the law may not feel that he is being fairly treated and may therefore resist the rehabilitative efforts of court personnel."[37] Of course, it is not suggested that juvenile court judges should fail appropriately to take account, in their demeanor and conduct, of the emotional and psychological attitude of the juveniles with whom they are confronted. While due process requirements will, in some instances, introduce a degree of order and regularity to Juvenile Court proceedings to determine delinquency, and in contested cases will introduce some elements of the adversary system, nothing will require that the conception of the kindly juvenile judge be replaced by its opposite, nor do we here rule upon the question whether ordinary due process requirements must be observed with respect to hearings to determine the disposition of the delinquent child.

Ultimately, however, we confront the reality of that portion of the Juvenile Court process with which we deal in this case. A boy is charged with misconduct. The boy is committed to an institution where he may be restrained of liberty for years. It is of no constitutional consequence—and of limited practical meaning—that the institution to which he is committed is called an Industrial School. The fact of the matter is that, however euphemistic the title, a "receiving home" or an "industrial school" for juveniles is an institution of confinement in which the child is incarcerated for a greater or lesser time. His world becomes "a building with whitewashed walls, regimented routine and institutional hours * * *."[38] Instead of mother and father and sisters and brothers and friends and classmates, his world is peopled by guards, custodians, state employees, and "delinquents" confined with him for anything from waywardness[39] to rape and homicide.

In view of this, it would be extraordinary if our Constitution did not require the procedural regularity and the exercise of care implied in the phrase "due process." Under our Constitution, the

[37] Juvenile Delinquency—Its Prevention and Control (Russell Sage Foundation, 1966), p. 33. The conclusion of the Nat'l Crime Comm'n Report is similar: "[T]here is increasing evidence that the informal procedures, contrary to the original expectation, may themselves constitute a further obstacle to effective treatment of the delinquent to the extent that they engender in the child a sense of injustice provoked by seemingly all-powerful and challengeless exercise of authority by judges and probation officers." Id., at 85. See also Allen, The Borderland of Criminal Justice (1964), p. 19.

[38] Holmes' Appeal, 379 Pa. 599, 616, 109 A.2d 523, 530 (1954) (Musmanno, J., dissenting). See also The State (Sheerin) v. Governor, [1966] I.R. 379 (Supreme Court of Ireland); Trimble v. Stone, 187 F.Supp. 483, 485–486 (D.C.D.C. 1960); Allen, The Borderland of Criminal Justice (1964), pp. 18, 52–56.

[39] Cf. the Juvenile Code of Arizona, ARS § 8–201, subsec. 6.

condition of being a boy does not justify a kangaroo court. The traditional ideas of Juvenile Court procedure, indeed, contemplated that time would be available and care would be used to establish precisely what the juvenile did and why he did it—was it a prank of adolescence or a brutal act threatening serious consequences to himself or society unless corrected?[40] Under traditional notions, one would assume that in a case like that of Gerald Gault, where the juvenile appears to have a home, a working mother and father, and an older brother, the Juvenile Judge would have made a careful inquiry and judgment as to the possibility that the boy could be disciplined and dealt with at home, despite his previous transgressions.[41] Indeed, so far as appears in the record before us, except for some conversation with Gerald about his school work and his "wanting to go to * * * Grand Canyon with his father," the points to which the judge directed his attention were little different from those that would be involved in determining any charge of violation of a penal statute.[42] The essential difference between Gerald's case and a normal criminal case is that safeguards available to adults were discarded in Gerald's case. The summary procedure as well as the long commitment was possible because Gerald was 15 years of age instead of over 18.

If Gerald had been over 18, he would not have been subject to Juvenile Court proceedings.[43] For the particular offense immediately involved, the maximum punishment would have been a fine of $5 to $50, or imprisonment in jail for not more than two months. Instead, he was committed to custody for a maximum of six years. If he had been over 18 and had committed an offense to which such a sentence might apply, he would have been entitled to substantial rights under the Constitution of the United States

---

[40] Cf., however, the conclusions of the D.C. Crime Comm'n Report, pp. 692 –693, concerning the inadequacy of the "social study records" upon which the Juvenile Court Judge must make this determination and decide on appropriate treatment.

[41] The Juvenile Judge's testimony at the habeas corpus proceeding is devoid of any meaningful discussion of this. He appears to have centered his attention upon whether Gerald made the phone call and used lewd words. He was impressed by the fact that Gerald was on six months' probation because he was with another boy who allegedly stole a purse—a different sort of offense, sharing the feature that Gerald was "along." And he even referred to a report which he said was not investigated because "there was no accusation" "because of lack of material foundation."

With respect to the possible duty of a trial court to explore alternatives to involuntary commitment in a civil proceeding, cf. Lake v. Cameron, 124 U.S.App.D.C. 264, 364 F.2d 657 (1966), which arose under statutes relating to treatment of the mentally ill.

[42] While appellee's brief suggests that the probation officer made some investigation of Gerald's home life, etc., there is not even a claim that the judge went beyond the point stated in the text.

[43] ARS §§ 8–201, 8–202.

161

as well as under Arizona's laws and constitution. The United States Constitution would guarantee him rights and protections with respect to arrest, search and seizure, and pretrial interrogation. It would assure him of specific notice of the charges and adequate time to decide his course of action and to prepare his defense. He would be entitled to clear advice that he could be represented by counsel, and, at least if a felony were involved, the State would be required to provide counsel if his parents were unable to afford it. If the court acted on the basis of his confession, careful procedures would be required to assure its voluntariness. If the case went to trial, confrontation and opportunity for cross-examination would be guaranteed. So wide a gulf between the State's treatment of the adult and of the child requires a bridge sturdier than mere verbiage, and reasons more persuasive than cliché can provide. As Wheeler and Cottrell have put it, "The rhetoric of the juvenile court movement has developed without any necessarily close correspondence to the realities of court and institutional routines."[44]

In Kent v. United States, supra, we stated that the Juvenile Court Judge's exercise of the power of the state as *parens patriae* was not unlimited. We said that "the admonition to function in a 'parental' relationship is not an invitation to procedural arbitrariness."[45] With respect to the waiver by the Juvenile Court to the adult court of jurisdiction over an offense committed by a youth, we said that "there is no place in our system of law for reaching a result of such tremendous consequences without ceremony—without hearing, without effective assistance of counsel, without a statement of reasons."[46] We announced with respect to such waiver proceedings that while "We do not mean * * * to indicate that the hearing to be held must conform with all of the requirements of a criminal trial or even of the usual administrative hearing; but we do hold that the hearing must measure up to the essentials of due process and fair treatment."[47] We reiterate this view, here in connection with a juvenile court adjudication of "delinquency," as

---

[44] Juvenile Delinquency—Its Prevention and Control (Russell Sage Foundation, 1966), p. 35. The gap between rhetoric and reality is also emphasized in the Nat'l Crime Comm'n Report, pp. 80–81.

[45] 383 U.S., at 555, 86 S.Ct., at 1054.

[46] 383 U.S., at 554, 86 S.Ct., at 1053. The Chief Justice stated in a recent speech to a conference of the National Council of Juvenile Court Judges, that a juvenile court "must function within the framework of law and * * * in the attainment of its objectives it cannot act with unbridled caprice." Equal Justice for Juveniles, 15 Juvenile Court Judges Journal, No. 3, pp. 14, 15 (1964).

[47] 383 U.S., at 562, 86 S.Ct., at 1057.

a requirement which is part of the Due Process Clause of the Fourteenth Amendment of our Constitution.[48]

We now turn to the specific issues which are presented to us in the present case.

III.

NOTICE OF CHARGES.

Appellants allege that the Arizona Juvenile Code is unconstitutional or alternatively that the proceedings before the Juvenile Court were constitutionally defective because of failure to provide adequate notice of the hearings. No notice was given to Gerald's parents when he was taken into custody on Monday, June 8. On that night, when Mrs. Gault went to the Detention Home, she was orally informed that there would be a hearing the next afternoon and was told the reason why Gerald was in custody. The only written notice Gerald's parents received at any time was a note on plain paper from Officer Flagg delivered on Thursday or Friday, June 11 or 12, to the effect that the judge had set Monday, June 15, "for further Hearings on Gerald's delinquency."

A "petition" was filed with the court on June 9 by Officer Flagg, reciting only that he was informed and believed that "said minor is a delinquent minor and that it is necessary that some order be made by the Honorable Court for said minor's welfare." The applicable Arizona statute provides for a petition to be filed in Juvenile Court, alleging in general terms that the child is "neglected, dependent or delinquent." The statute explicitly states that such a general allegation is sufficient, "without alleging the facts."[49] There is no requirement that the petition be served and it was not served upon, given to, or shown to Gerald or his parents.[50]

---

[48] The Nat'l Crime Comm'n Report recommends that "Juvenile courts should make fullest feasible use of preliminary conferences to dispose of cases short of adjudication." Id., at 84. See also D.C. Crime Comm'n Report, pp. 662–665. Since this "consent decree" procedure would involve neither adjudication of delinquency nor institutionalization, nothing we say in this opinion should be construed as expressing any views with respect to such procedure. The problems of pre-adjudication treatment of juveniles, and of post-adjudication disposition, are unique to the juvenile process; hence what we hold in this opinion with regard to the procedural requirements at the adjudicatory stage has no necessary applicability to other steps of the juvenile process.

[49] ARS § 8–222, (B).

[50] Arizona's Juvenile Code does not provide for notice of any sort to be given at the commencement of the proceedings to the child or his parents. Its only notice provision is to the effect that if a person other than the parent or guardian is cited to appear, the parent or guardian shall be notified "by personal service" of the time and place of hearing. ARS § 8–224. The procedure for initiating a proceeding, as specified by the statute, seems to

The Supreme Court of Arizona rejected appellants' claim that due process was denied because of inadequate notice. It stated that "Mrs. Gault knew the exact nature of the charge against Gerald from the day he was taken to the detention home." The court also pointed out that the Gaults appeared at the two hearings "without objection." The court held that because "the policy of the juvenile law is to hide youthful errors from the full gaze of the public and bury them in the graveyard of the forgotten past," advance notice of the specific charges or basis for taking the juvenile into custody and for the hearing is not necessary. It held that the appropriate rule is that "the infant and his parent or guardian will receive a petition only reciting a conclusion of delinquency.[51] But no later than the initial hearing by the judge, they must be advised of the facts involved in the case. If the charges are denied, they must be given a reasonable period of time to prepare."

We cannot agree with the court's conclusion that adequate notice was given in this case. Notice, to comply with due process requirements, must be given sufficiently in advance of scheduled court proceedings so that reasonable opportunity to prepare will be afforded, and it must "set forth the alleged misconduct with particularity."[52] It is obvious, as we have discussed above, that no purpose of shielding the child from the public stigma of knowledge of his having been taken into custody and scheduled for hearing is served by the procedure approved by the court below. The "initial hearing" in the present case was a hearing on the merits. Notice at that time is not timely; and even if there were a conceivable purpose served by the deferral proposed by the court below, it would have to yield to the requirements that the child and his parents or guardian be notified, in writing, of the specific charge or factual allegations to be considered at the hearing, and that such written notice be given at the earliest practicable time, and in any event sufficiently in advance of the hearing to permit preparation. Due process of law requires notice of the sort we have described —that is, notice which would be deemed constitutionally adequate in a civil or criminal proceeding.[53] It does not allow a hearing to

require that after a preliminary inquiry by the court, a determination may be made "that formal jurisdiction should be acquired." Thereupon the court may authorize a petition to be filed. ARS § 8–222. It does not appear that this procedure was followed in the present case.

51 No such petition was served or supplied in the present case.

52 Nat'l Crime Comm'n Report, p. 87. The Commission observed that "The unfairness of too much informality is * * * reflected in the inadequacy of notice to parents and juveniles about charges and hearings." Ibid.

53 For application of the due process requirement of adequate notice in a criminal context, see, e. g., Cole v. State of Arkansas, 333 U.S. 196, 68 S.Ct. 514, 92 L.Ed. 644 (1948);

be held in which a youth's freedom and his parents' right to his custody are at stake without giving them timely notice, in advance of the hearing, of the specific issues that they must meet. Nor, in the circumstances of this case, can it reasonably be said that the requirement of notice was waived.[54]

IV.

RIGHT TO COUNSEL.

Appellants charge that the Juvenile Court proceedings were fatally defective because the court did not advise Gerald or his parents of their right to counsel, and proceeded with the hearing, the adjudication of delinquency and the order of commitment in the absence of counsel for the child and his parents or an express waiver of the right thereto. The Supreme Court of Arizona pointed out that "[t] here is disagreement [among the various jurisdictions] as to whether the court must advise the infant that he has a right to counsel."[55] It noted its own decision in Arizona State

---

In re Oliver, 333 U.S. 257, 273–278, 68 S.Ct. 499, 507–510, 92 L.Ed. 682 (1948). For application in a civil context, see, e. g., Armstrong v. Manzo, 380 U.S. 545, 85 S.Ct. 1187, 14 L.Ed.2d 62 (1965); Mullane v. Central Hanover Bank & Tr. Co., 339 U.S. 306, 70 S.Ct. 652, 94 L.Ed. 865 (1950). Cf. also Chaloner v. Sherman, 242 U.S. 455, 37 S.Ct. 136, 61 L.Ed. 427 (1917). The Court's discussion in these cases of the right to timely and adequate notice forecloses any contention that the notice approved by the Arizona Supreme Court, or the notice actually given the Gaults, was constitutionally adequate. See also Antieau, Constitutional Rights in Juvenile Courts, 46 Cornell L.Q. 387, 395 (1961); Paulsen, Fairness to the Juvenile Offender, 41 Minn.L.Rev. 547, 557 (1957). Cf. Standards, pp. 63–65; Procedures and Evidence in the Juvenile Court, A Guidebook for Judges, prepared by the Advisory Council of Judges of the National Council on Crime and Delinquency (1962), pp. 9–23 (and see cases discussed therein).

[54] Mrs. Gault's "knowledge" of the charge against Gerald, and/or the asserted failure to object, does not excuse the lack of adequate notice. Indeed, one of the purposes of no-

tice is to clarify the issues to be considered, and as our discussion of the facts, supra, shows, even the Juvenile Court Judge was uncertain as to the precise issues determined at the two "hearings." Since the Gaults had no counsel and were not told of their right to counsel, we cannot consider their failure to object to the lack of constitutionally adequate notice as a waiver of their rights. Because of our conclusion that notice given only at the first hearing is inadequate, we need not reach the question whether the Gaults ever received adequately specific notice even at the June 9 hearing, in light of the fact they were never apprised of the charge of being habitually involved in immoral matters.

[55] For recent cases in the District of Columbia holding that there must be advice of the right to counsel, and to have counsel appointed if necessary, see, e. g., Shioutakon v. District of Columbia, 98 U.S.App. D.C. 371, 236 F.2d 666, 60 A.L.R.2d 686 (1956); Black v. United States, 122 U.S.App.D.C. 393, 355 F.2d 104 (1965); In re Poff, 135 F.Supp. 224 (D.C.D.C.1955). Cf. also In re Long, 184 So.2d 861, 862 (Sup.Ct.Miss., 1966); People v. Dotson, 46 Cal.2d 891, 299 P.2d 875 (1956).

COLOR ME JUSTICE

Dept. of Public Welfare v. Barlow, 80 Ariz. 249, 296 P.2d 298
(1956), to the effect "that *the parents* of an infant in a juvenile
proceeding cannot be denied representation by counsel of their
choosing." (Emphasis added.) It referred to a provision of the
Juvenile Code which it characterized as requiring "that the probation officer shall look after the interests of neglected, delinquent
and dependent children," including representing their interests in
court.[56] The court argued that "The parent and the probation officer
may be relied upon to protect the infant's interests." Accordingly
it rejected the proposition that "due process requires that an infant have a right to counsel." It said that juvenile courts have the
discretion, but not the duty, to allow such representation; it referred specifically to the situation in which the Juvenile Court dis-
cerns conflict between the child and his parents as an instance
in which this discretion might be exercised. We do not agree. Probation officers, in the Arizona scheme, are also arresting officers.
They initiate proceedings and file petitions which they verify, as
here, alleging the delinquency of the child; and they testify, as
here, against the child. And here the probation officer was also
superintendent of the Detention Home. The probation officer cannot
act as counsel for the child. His role in the adjudicatory hearing,
by statute and in fact, is as arresting officer and witness against
the child. Nor can the judge represent the child. There is no material difference in this respect between adult and juvenile proceedings of the sort here involved. In adult proceedings, this contention has been foreclosed by decisions of this Court.[57] A proceeding
where the issue is whether the child will be found to be "delinquent" and subjected to the loss of his liberty for years is comparable in seriousness to a felony prosecution. The juvenile needs
the assistance of counsel to cope with problems of law,[58] to make

---

[56] The section cited by the court, ARS
§ 8–204–C, reads as follows:
"The probation officer shall have
the authority of a peace officer. He
shall:
"1. Look after the interests of
neglected, delinquent and dependent
children of the county.
"2. Make investigations and file
petitions.
"3. Be present in court when cases
are heard concerning children
and represent their interests.
"4. Furnish the court information and assistance as it may require.
"5. Assist in the collection of

sums ordered paid for the support
of children.
"6. Perform other acts ordered
by the court."
[57] Powell v. State of Alabama, 287
U.S. 45, 61, 53 S.Ct. 55, 61, 77 L.Ed.
158 (1932); Gideon v. Wainwright,
372 U.S. 335, 83 S.Ct. 792, 9 L.Ed.2d
799 (1963).
[58] In the present proceeding, for example, although the Juvenile Judge
believed that Gerald's telephone
conversation was within the condemnation of ARS § 13–377, he suggested some uncertainty because
the statute prohibits the use of vulgar language "in the presence or
hearing of" a woman or child.

166

skilled inquiry into the facts, to insist upon regularity of the proceedings, and to ascertain whether he has a defense and to prepare and submit it. The child "requires the guiding hand of counsel at every step in the proceedings against him."[59] Just as in Kent v. United States, supra, at 561–562, 86 S.Ct., at 1057–1058, we indicated our agreement with the United States Court of Appeals for the District of Columbia Circuit that the assistance of counsel is essential for purposes of waiver proceedings, so we hold now that it is equally essential for the determination of delinquency, carrying with it the awesome prospect of incarceration in a state institution until the juvenile reaches the age of 21.[60]

During the last decade, court decisions,[61] experts,[62] and legislatures[63] have demonstrated increasing recognition of this view. In at least one-third of the States, statutes now provide for the right of representation by retained counsel in juvenile delinquency proceedings, notice of the right, or assignment of counsel, or a

[59] Powell v. State of Alabama, 287 U.S. 45, 69, 53 S.Ct. 55, 64 (1932).

[60] This means that the commitment, in virtually all cases, is for a minimum of three years since jurisdiction of juvenile courts is usually limited to age 18 and under.

[61] See cases cited in n. 55, supra.

[62] See, e. g., Schinitsky, 17 The Record 10 (N.Y. City Bar Assn. 1962); Paulsen, Fairness to the Juvenile Offender, 41 Minn.L.Rev. 547, 568–573 (1957); Antieau, Constitutional Rights in Juvenile Courts, 46 Cornell L.Q. 387, 404–407 (1961); Paulsen, Kent v. United States: The Constitutional Context of Juvenile Cases, 1966 Sup.Ct.Rev. 167, 187–189; Ketcham, The Legal Renaissance in the Juvenile Court, 60 Nw. U.L.Rev. 585 (1965); Elson, Juvenile Courts & Due Process, in Justice for the Child (Rosenheim ed.) 95, 103–105 (1962); Note, Rights and Rehabilitation in the Juvenile Courts, 67 Col.L.Rev. 281, 321–327 (1967). See also Nat'l Probation and Parole Assn., Standard Family Court Act (1959) § 19, and Standard Juvenile Court Act (1959) § 19, in 5 NPPA Journal 99, 137, 323, 367 (1959) (hereinafter cited as Standard Family Court Act and Standard Juvenile Court Act, respectively).

[63] Only a few state statutes require advice of the right to counsel and to have counsel appointed. See N. Y. Family Court Act §§ 241, 249, 728, 741; Calif.Welf. & Inst'ns Code §§ 633, 634, 659, 700 (1966) (appointment is mandatory only if conduct would be a felony in the case of an adult); Minn.Stat.Ann. § 260.155(2) (1966 Supp.) (see Comment of Legislative Commission accompanying this section); District of Columbia Legal Aid Act, D.C. Code Ann. § 2–2202 (1961) (Legal Aid Agency "shall make attorneys available to represent indigents * * * in proceedings before the juvenile court * * *." See Black v. United States, 122 U.S.App.D.C. 393, 395–396, 355 F.2d 104, 106–107 (1965), construing this Act as providing a right to appointed counsel and to be informed of that right). Other state statutes allow appointment on request, or in some classes of cases, or in the discretion of the court, etc. The state statutes are collected and classified in Riederer, The Role of Counsel in the Juvenile Court, 2 J.Fam.Law 16, 19–20 (1962), which, however, does not treat the statutes cited above. See also Note, Rights and Rehabilitation in the Juvenile Courts, 67 Col.L.Rev. 281, 321–322 (1967).

combination of these. In other States, court rules have similar provisions.[64]

The President's Crime Commission has recently recommended that in order to assure "procedural justice for the child," it is necessary that "Counsel * * * be appointed as a matter of course wherever coercive action is a possibility, without requiring any affirmative choice by child or parent."[65] As stated by the author-

---

[64] Skoler & Tenney, Attorney Representation in Juvenile Court, 4 J. Fam.Law 77, 95–96 (1964); Riederer, The Role of Counsel in the Juvenile Court, 2 J.Fam.Law 16 (1962).

Recognition of the right to counsel involves no necessary interference with the special purposes of juvenile court procedures; indeed, it seems that counsel can play an important role in the process of rehabilitation. See Note, Rights and Rehabilitation in the Juvenile Courts, 67 Col.L.Rev. 281, 324–327 (1967).

[65] Nat'l Crime Comm'n Report, pp. 86–87. The Commission's statement of its position is very forceful:

"The Commission believes that no single action holds more potential for achieving procedural justice for the child in the juvenile court than provision of counsel. The presence of an independent legal representative of the child, or of his parent, is the keystone of the whole structure of guarantees that a minimum system of procedural justice requires. The rights to confront one's accusers, to cross-examine witnesses, to present evidence and testimony of one's own, to be unaffected by prejudicial and unreliable evidence, to participate meaningfully in the dispositional decision, to take an appeal have substantial meaning for the overwhelming majority of persons brought before the juvenile court only if they are provided with competent lawyers who can invoke those rights effectively. The most informal and well-intentioned of judicial proceedings are technical; few adults without legal training can influence or even understand them; certainly children cannot. Papers are drawn and charges expressed in legal language. Events

follow one another in a manner that appears arbitrary and confusing to the uninitiated. Decisions, unexplained, appear too official to challenge. But with lawyers come records of proceedings; records make possible appeals which, even if they do not occur, impart by their possibility a healthy atmosphere of accountability.

"Fears have been expressed that lawyers would make juvenile court proceedings adversary. No doubt this is partly true, but it is partly desirable. Informality is often abused. The juvenile courts deal with cases in which facts are disputed and in which, therefore, rules of evidence, confrontation of witnesses, and other adversary procedures are called for. They deal with many cases involving conduct that can lead to incarceration or close supervision for long periods, and therefore juveniles often need the same safeguards that are granted to adults. And in all cases children need advocates to speak for them and guard their interests, particularly when disposition decisions are made. It is the disposition stage at which the opportunity arises to offer individualized treatment plans and in which the danger inheres that the court's coercive power will be applied without adequate knowledge of the circumstances.

"Fears also have been expressed that the formality lawyers would bring into juvenile court would defeat the therapeutic aims of the court. But informality has no necessary connection with therapy; it is a device that has been used to approach therapy, and it is not the only possible device. It is quite possible that in many instances lawyers, for all their commitment to formality, could do more to further therapy for their clients than can

itative "Standards for Juvenile and Family Courts," published by the Children's Bureau of the United States Department of Health, Education, and Welfare:

"As a component part of a fair hearing required by due process guaranteed under the 14th amendment, notice of the right to counsel should be required at all hearings and counsel provided upon request when the family is financially unable to employ counsel." Standards, p. 57.

This statement was "reviewed" by the National Council of Juvenile Court Judges at its 1965 Convention and they "found no fault" with it.[66] The New York Family Court Act contains the following statement:

"This act declares that minors have a right to the assistance of counsel of their own choosing or of law guardians[[67]] in neglect proceedings under article three and in proceedings to determine juvenile delinquency and whether a person is in need of supervision under article seven. This declaration is based on a finding that counsel is often indispensable to a practical realization of due process of law and may be helpful in making reasoned determinations of fact and proper orders of disposition."[68]

The Act provides that "At the commencement of any hearing" under the delinquency article of the statute, the juvenile and his parent shall be advised of the juvenile's "right to be represented by counsel chosen by him or his parent * * * or by a law guardian

---

the small, overworked social staffs of the courts. * * *

"The Commission believes it is essential that counsel be appointed by the juvenile court for those who are unable to provide their own. Experience under the prevailing systems in which children are free to seek counsel of their choice reveals how empty of meaning the right is for those typically the subjects of juvenile court proceedings. Moreover, providing counsel only when the child is sophisticated enough to be aware of his need and to ask for one or when he fails to waive his announced right [is] not enough, as experience in numerous jurisdictions reveals.

The Commission recommends

"COUNSEL SHOULD BE APPOINTED AS A MATTER OF COURSE WHEREVER COERCIVE ACTION IS A POSSIBILITY, WITHOUT REQUIRING ANY AFFIRMA-CHOICE BY CHILD OR PARENT."

[66] Lehman, A Juvenile's Right to Counsel in A Delinquency Hearing, 17 Juvenile Court Judge's Journal 53 (1966). In an interesting review of the 1966 edition of the Children's Bureau's "Standards," Rosenheim, Standards for Juvenile and Family Courts: Old Wine in a New Bottle, 1 Fam.L.Q. 25, 29 (1967), the author observes that "The 'Standards' of 1966, just like the 'Standards' of 1954, are valuable precisely because they represent a diligent and thoughtful search for an accommodation between the aspirations of the founders of the juvenile court and the grim realities of life against which, in part, the due process of criminal and civil law offers us protection."

[67] These are lawyers designated, as provided by the statute, to represent minors. N.Y.Family Court Act § 242.

[68] N.Y.Family Court Act § 241.

assigned by the court * * *."[69] The California Act (1961) also requires appointment of counsel.[70]

We conclude that the Due Process Clause of the Fourteenth Amendment requires that in respect of proceedings to determine delinquency which may result in commitment to an institution in which the juvenile's freedom is curtailed, the child and his parents must be notified of the child's right to be represented by counsel retained by them, or if they are unable to afford counsel, that counsel will be appointed to represent the child.

At the habeas corpus proceeding, Mrs. Gault testified that she knew that she could have appeared with counsel at the juvenile hearing. This knowledge is not a waiver of the right to counsel which she and her juvenile son had, as we have defined it. They had a right expressly to be advised that they might retain counsel and to be confronted with the need for specific consideration of whether they did or did not choose to waive the right. If they were unable to afford to employ counsel, they were entitled in view of the seriousness of the charge in the potential commitment, to appointed counsel, unless they chose waiver. Mrs. Gault's knowledge that she could employ counsel was not an "intentional relinquishment or abandonment" of a fully known right.[71]

---

[69] N.Y.Family Court Act § 741. For accounts of New York practice under the new procedures, see Isaacs, The Role of the Lawyer in Representing Minors in the New Family Court, 12 Buffalo L.Rev. 501 (1963); Dembitz, Ferment and Experiment in New York: Juvenile Cases in the New Family Court, 48 Cornell L.Q. 499, 508–512 (1963). Since introduction of the law guardian system in September of 1962, it is stated that attorneys are present in the great majority of cases. Harvard Law Review Note, p. 796. See New York Judicial Conference, Twelfth Annual Report, pp. 288–291 (1967), for detailed statistics on representation of juveniles in New York. For the situation before 1962, see Schinitsky, The Role of the Lawyer in Children's Court, 17 The Record 10 (N.Y.City Bar Assn. 1962). In the District of Columbia, where statute and court decisions require that a lawyer be appointed if the family is unable to retain counsel, see n. 63, supra, and where the juvenile and his parents are so informed at the initial hearing, about 85% to 90% do not choose to be represented and sign a written waiver form. D.C. Crime Comm'n Report, p. 646. The Commission recommends adoption in the District of Columbia of a "law guardian" system similar to that of New York, with more effective notification of the right to appointed counsel, in order to eliminate the problems of procedural fairness, accuracy of fact-finding, and appropriateness of disposition which the absence of counsel in so many juvenile court proceedings involves. Id., at 681–685.

[70] See n. 63, supra.

[71] Johnson v. Zerbst, 304 U.S. 458, 464 58 S.Ct. 1019, 1023, 82 L.Ed. 1461 (1938); Carnley v. Cochran, 369 U.S. 506, 82 S.Ct. 884, 8 L.Ed.2d 70 (1962); United States ex rel. Brown v. Fay, 242 F.Supp. 273 (D.C.S.D.N.Y.1965).

V.

CONFRONTATION, SELF-INCRIMINATION, CROSS-EXAMINATION.

Appellants urge that the writ of habeas corpus should have been granted because of the denial of the rights of confrontation and cross-examination in the Juvenile Court hearings, and because the privilege against self-incrimination was not observed. The Juvenile Court Judge testified at the habeas corpus hearing that he had proceeded on the basis of Gerald's admissions at the two hearings. Appellants attack this on the ground that the admissions were obtained in disregard of the privilege against self-incrimination.[72] If the confession is disregarded, appellants argue that the delinquency conclusion, since it was fundamentally based on a finding that Gerald had made lewd remarks during the phone call to Mrs. Cook, is fatally defective for failure to accord the rights of confrontation and cross-examination which the Due Process Clause of the Fourteenth Amendment of the Federal Constitution guarantees in state proceedings generally.[73]

Our first question, then, is whether Gerald's admission was improperly obtained and relied on as the basis of decision, in conflict with the Federal Constitution. For this purpose, it is necessary briefly to recall the relevant facts.

Mrs. Cook, the complainant, and the recipient of the alleged telephone call, was not called as a witness. Gerald's mother asked the Juvenile Court Judge why Mrs. Cook was not present and the judge replied that "she didn't have to be present." So far as appears, Mrs. Cook was spoken to only once, by Officer Flagg, and this was by telephone. The judge did not speak with her on any occasion. Gerald had been questioned by the probation officer after having been taken into custody. The exact circumstances of this questioning do not appear but any admissions Gerald may have made at this time do not appear in the record.[74] Gerald was also questioned by the Juvenile Court Judge at each of the two hearings. The judge testified in the habeas corpus proceeding that Gerald admitted making "some of the lewd statements * * * [but not]

---

[72] The privilege is applicable to state proceedings. Malloy v. Hogan, 378 U.S. 1, 84 S.Ct. 1489, 12 L.Ed.2d 653 (1964).

[73] Pointer v. State of Texas, 380 U.S. 400, 85 S.Ct. 1065, 13 L.Ed.2d 923 (1965); Douglas v. State of Alabama, 380 U.S. 415, 85 S.Ct. 1074, 13 L.Ed.2d 934 (1965).

[74] For this reason, we cannot consider the status of Gerald's alleged admissions to the probation officers. Cf., however, Comment, Miranda Guarantees in the California Juvenile Court, 7 Santa Clara Lawyer 114 (1966).

any of the more serious lewd statements." There was conflict and uncertainty among the witnesses at the habeas corpus proceeding—the Juvenile Court Judge, Mr. and Mrs. Gault, and the probation officer—as to what Gerald did or did not admit.

We shall assume that Gerald made admissions of the sort described by the Juvenile Court Judge, as quoted above. Neither Gerald nor his parents were advised that he did not have to testify or make a statement, or that an incriminating statement might result in his commitment as a "delinquent."

The Arizona Supreme Court rejected appellants' contention that Gerald had a right to be advised that he need not incriminate himself. It said: "We think the necessary flexibility for individualized treatment will be enhanced by a rule which does not require the judge to advise the infant of a privilege against self-incrimination."

In reviewing this conclusion of Arizona's Supreme Court, we emphasize again that we are here concerned only with a proceeding to determine whether a minor is a "delinquent" and which may result in commitment to a state institution. Specifically, the question is whether, in such a proceeding, an admission by the juvenile may be used against him in the absence of clear and unequivocal evidence that the admission was made with knowledge that he was not obliged to speak and would not be penalized for remaining silent. In light of Miranda v. State of Arizona, 384 U.S. 436, 86 S.Ct. 1602, 16 L.Ed.2d 694 (1966), we must also consider whether, if the privilege against self-incrimination is available, it can effectively be waived unless counsel is present or the right to counsel has been waived.

It has long been recognized that the eliciting and use of confessions or admissions require careful scrutiny. Dean Wigmore states:

"The ground of distrust of confessions made in certain situations is, in a rough and indefinite way, judicial experience. There has been no careful collection of statistics of untrue confessions, nor has any great number of instances been even loosely reported * * * but enough have been verified to fortify the conclusion, based on ordinary observation of human conduct, that under certain stresses a person, especially one of defective mentality or peculiar temperament, may falsely acknowledge guilt. This possibility arises wherever the innocent person is placed in such a situation that the untrue acknowledgment of guilt is at the time the more promising of two alternatives between which he is obliged to choose; that is, he chooses any risk that may be in falsely acknowledging guilt, in preference to some worse alternative associated with silence.

* * * * *

"The principle, then, upon which a confession may be excluded is that it is, under certain conditions, *testimonially untrustworthy* * * *. [T]he essential feature is that the principle of exclusion is a testimonial one, analogous to the other principles which exclude narrations as untrustworthy * * *."[75]

This Court has emphasized that admissions and confessions of juveniles require special caution. In Haley v. State of Ohio, 332 U.S. 596, 68 S.Ct. 302, 92 L.Ed. 224, where this Court reversed the conviction of a 15-year-old boy for murder, Mr. Justice Douglas said:

"What transpired would make us pause for careful inquiry if a mature man were involved. And when, as here, a mere child—an easy victim of the law—is before us, special care in scrutinizing the record must be used. Age 15 is a tender and difficult age for a boy of any race. He cannot be judged by the more exacting standards of maturity. That which would leave a man cold and unimpressed can overawe and overwhelm a lad in his early teens. This is the period of great instability which the crisis of adolescence produces. A 15-year-old lad, questioned through the dead of night by relays of police, is a ready victim of the inquisition. Mature men possibly might stand the ordeal from midnight to 5 a. m. But we cannot believe that a lad of tender years is a match for the police in such a contest. He needs counsel and support if he is not to become the victim first of fear, then of panic. He needs someone on whom to lean lest the overpowering presence of the law, as he knows it, crush him. No friend stood at the side of this 15-year-old boy as the police, working in relays, questioned him hour after hour, from midnight until dawn. No lawyer stood guard to make sure that the police went so far and no farther, to see to it that they stopped short of the point where he became the victim of coercion. No counsel or friend was called during the critical hours of questioning."[76]

In *Haley*, as we have discussed, the boy was convicted in an adult court, and not a juvenile court. In notable decisions, the New York Court of Appeals and the Supreme Court of New Jersey have recently considered decisions of Juvenile Courts in which boys have been adjudged "delinquent" on the basis of confessions obtained in circumstances comparable to those in *Haley*. In both in-

[75] 3 Wigmore, Evidence § 822 (3d ed. 1940).

[76] 332 U.S., at 599–600, 68 S.Ct., at 303 (opinion of Mr. Justice Douglas, joined by Justices Black, Murphy and Rutledge; Justice Frankfurter concurred in a separate opinion).

stances, the State contended before its highest tribunal that constitutional requirements governing inculpatory statements applicable in adult courts do not apply to juvenile proceedings. In each case, the State's contention was rejected, and the juvenile court's determination of delinquency was set aside on the grounds of inadmissibility of the confession. In the Matters of Gregory W. and Gerald S., 19 N.Y. 2d 55, 277 N.Y.S.2d 675, 224 N.E.2d 102 (1966) (opinion by Keating, J.), and In the Interests of Carlo and Stasilowicz, 48 N.J. 224, 225 A.2d 110 (1966) (opinion by Proctor, J.).

The privilege against self-incrimination is, of course, related to the question of the safeguards necessary to assure that admissions or confessions are reasonably trustworthy, that they are not the mere fruits of fear or coercion, but are reliable expressions of the truth. The roots of the privilege are, however, far deeper. They tap the basic stream of religious and political principle because the privilege reflects the limits of the individual's attornment to the state and—in a philosophical sense—insists upon the equality of the individual and the state.[77] In other words, the privilege has a broader and deeper thrust than the rule which prevents the use of confessions which are the product of coercion because coercion is thought to carry with it the danger of unreliability. One of its purposes is to prevent the state, whether by force or by psychological domination, from overcoming the mind and will of the person under investigation and depriving him of the freedom to decide whether to assist the state in securing his conviction.[78]

It would indeed be surprising if the privilege against self-incrimination were available to hardened criminals but not to children. The language of the Fifth Amendment, applicable to the States by operation of the Fourteenth Amendment, is unequivocal and without exception. And the scope of the privilege is comprehensive. As Mr. Justice White, concurring, stated in Murphy v. Waterfront Commission, 378 U.S. 52, 94, 84 S.Ct. 1594, 1611, 12 L.Ed.2d 678 (1964):

"The privilege can be claimed in *any proceeding,* be it criminal or civil, administrative or judicial, investigatory or adjudicatory * * * it protects *any disclosures* which the witness may reasonably apprehend *could be used in a criminal prosecution or which could lead to other evidence that might be so used."*[79] (Emphasis added.)

[77] See Fortas, The Fifth Amendment, 25 Cleveland Bar Assn. Journal 91 (1954).

[78] See Rogers v. Richmond, 365 U.S. 534, 81 S.Ct. 735, 5 L.Ed.2d 760 (1961); Culombe v. Connecticut, 367 U.S. 568, 81 S.Ct. 1860, 6 L.Ed. 2d 1037 (1961) (opinion of Mr. Justice Frankfurter, joined by Mr. Justice Stewart); Miranda v. State of Arizona, 384 U.S. 436, 86 S.Ct. 1602, 16 L.Ed.2d 694 (1966).

[79] See also Malloy v. Hogan, 378 U.S. 1, 84 S.Ct. 1489, 12 L.Ed.2d 653 (1964); McCarthy v. Arndstein, 266 U.S. 34, 40, 45 S.Ct. 16, 17, 69 L.Ed. 158 (1924).

With respect to juveniles, both common observation and expert opinion emphasize that the "distrust of confessions made in certain situations" to which Dean Wigmore referred in the passage quoted supra, at 44–45, is imperative in the case of children from an early age through adolescence. In New York, for example, the recently enacted Family Court Act provides that the juvenile and his parents must be advised at the start of the hearing of his right to remain silent.[80] The New York statute also provides that the police must attempt to communicate with the juvenile's parents before questioning him,[81] and that absent "special circumstances" a confession may not be obtained from a child prior to notifying his parents or relatives and releasing the child either to them or to the Family Court.[82] In In the Matters of Gregory W. and Gerald S., referred to above, the New York Court of Appeals held that the privilege against self-incrimination applies in juvenile delinquency cases and requires the exclusion of involuntary confessions, and that People v. Lewis, 260 N.Y. 171, 183 N.E. 353, 86 A.L.R. 1001 (1932), holding the contrary, had been specifically overruled by statute.

The authoritative "Standards for Juvenile and Family Courts" concludes that, "Whether or not transfer to the criminal court is a possibility, certain procedures should always be followed. Before being interviewed [by the police], the child and his parents should be informed of his right to have legal counsel present and to refuse to answer questions or be fingerprinted[83] if he should so decide."[84]

Against the application to juveniles of the right to silence, it is argued that juvenile proceedings are "civil" and not "criminal," and therefore the privilege should not apply. It is true that the statement of the privilege in the Fifth Amendment, which is applicable to the States by reason of the Fourteenth Amendment, is that no person "shall be compelled in any *criminal case* to be a witness against himself." However, it is also clear that the availability of the privilege does not turn upon the type of proceeding in which its protection is invoked, but upon the nature of the state-

---

[80] N.Y.Family Court Act § 741.

[81] N.Y.Family Court Act § 724(a). In In Matter of Williams, 49 Misc.2d 154, 267 N.Y.S.2d 91 (1966), the New York Family Court held that "The failure of the police to notify this child's parents that he had been taken into custody, if not alone sufficient to render his confession inadmissible, is germane on the issue of its voluntary character * * *." Id., at 165, 267 N.Y.S.2d, at

106. The confession was held involuntary and therefore inadmissible.

[82] N.Y.Family Court Act § 724 (as amended 1963, see Supp.1966). See In the Matter of Addison, 20 A.D.2d 90, 245 N.Y.S.2d 243 (1963).

[83] The issues relating to fingerprinting of juveniles are not presented here, and we express no opinion concerning them.

[84] Standards, p. 49.

ment or admission and the exposure which it invites. The privilege may, for example, be claimed in a civil or administrative proceeding, if the statement is or may be inculpatory.[85]

It would be entirely unrealistic to carve out of the Fifth Amendment all statements by juveniles on the ground that these cannot lead to "criminal" involvement. In the first place, juvenile proceedings to determine "delinquency," which may lead to commitment to a state institution, must be regarded as "criminal" for purposes of the privilege against self-incrimination. To hold otherwise would be to disregard substance because of the feeble enticement of the "civil" label-of-convenience which has been attached to juvenile proceedings. Indeed, in over half of the States, there is not even assurance that the juvenile will be kept in separate institutions, apart from adult "criminals." In those States juveniles may be placed in or transferred to adult penal institutions[86] after having been found "delinquent" by a juvenile court. For this purpose, at least, commitment is a deprivation of liberty. It is incarceration against one's will, whether it is called "criminal" or "civil." And our Constitution guarantees that no person shall be "compelled" to be a witness against himself when he is threatened with deprivation of his liberty—a command which this Court has broadly applied and generously implemented in accordance with the teaching of the history of the privilege and its great office in mankind's battle for freedom.[87]

In addition, apart from the equivalence for this purpose of exposure to commitment as a juvenile delinquent and exposure to imprisonment as an adult offender, the fact of the matter is that there is little or no assurance in Arizona, as in most if not all of the States, that a juvenile apprehended and interrogated by the police or even by the Juvenile Court itself will remain outside of the reach of adult courts as a consequence of the offense for which he has been taken into custody. In Arizona, as in other States, provision is made for Juvenile Courts to relinquish or waive jurisdiction to

---

[85] See n. 79, supra, and accompanying text.

[86] Delinquent Children in Penal Institutions, Children's Bureau Pub. No. 415—1964, p. 1.

[87] See, e. g., Miranda v. State of Arizona, 384 U.S. 436, S.Ct. 1602, 16 L.Ed.2d 694 (1966); Garrity v. State of New Jersey, 385 U.S. 493, 87 S.Ct. 616, 17 L.Ed.2d 562 (1967); Spevack v. Klein, 385 U.S. 511, 87 S.Ct. 625, 636, 17 L.Ed2d 574 (1967); Haynes v. State of Washington, 373 U.S. 503, 83 S.Ct. 1336, 10 L.Ed.2d 513 (1963); Culombe v. State of Connecticut, 367 U.S. 568, 81 S.Ct. 1860, 6 L.Ed.2d 1037 (1961); Rogers v. Richmond, 365 U.S. 534, 81 S.Ct. 735, 5 L.Ed.2d 760 (1961); Malloy v. Hogan, 378 U.S. 1, 84 S.Ct. 1489, 12 L.Ed.2d 653 (1964); Griffin v. State of California, 380 U.S. 609, 85 S.Ct. 1229, 14 L.Ed.2d 106 (1965).

the ordinary criminal courts.[88] In the present case, when Gerald Gault was interrogated concerning violation of a section of the Arizona Criminal Code, it could not be certain that the Juvenile Court Judge would decide to "suspend" criminal prosecution in court for adults by proceeding to an adjudication in Juvenile Court.[89]

It is also urged, as the Supreme Court of Arizona here asserted, that the juvenile and presumably his parents should not be advised of the juvenile's right to silence because confession is good for the child as the commencement of the assumed therapy of the juvenile court process, and he should be encouraged to assume an attitude of trust and confidence toward the officials of the juvenile process. This proposition has been subjected to widespread challenge on the basis of current reappraisals of the rhetoric and realities of the handling of juvenile offenders.

In fact, evidence is accumulating that confessions by juveniles do not aid in "individualized treatment," as the court below put it, and that compelling the child to answer questions, without warning or advice as to his right to remain silent, does not serve this or any other good purpose. In light of the observations of Wheeler and Cottrell,[90] and others, it seems probable that where children are induced to confess by "paternal" urgings on the part of officials and the confession is then followed by disciplinary action, the child's reaction is likely to be hostile and adverse—the child may well feel that he has been led or tricked into confession and that despite his confession, he is being punished.[91]

Further, authoritative opinion has cast formidable doubt upon the reliability and trustworthiness of "confessions" by children. This Court's observations in Haley v. State of Ohio are set forth above. The recent decision of the New York Court of Appeals referred to above, In the Matters of Gregory W. and Gerald S., deals with a dramatic and, it is to be hoped, extreme example. Two 12-year-old Negro boys were taken into custody for the brutal assault and rape of two aged domestics, one of whom died as the result of the attack. One of the boys was schizophrenic and had been locked in the security ward of a mental institution at the time of the attacks. By a process that may best be described as bizarre, his confession was

---

[88] Arizona Constitution, Art. 6, § 15 (as amended 1960); ARS §§ 8–223, 8–228, subsec. A; Harvard Law Review Note, p. 793. Because of this possibility that criminal jurisdiction may attach it is urged that "* * * all of the procedural safeguards in the criminal law should be followed." Standards, p. 49. Cf.

Harling v. United States, 111 U.S. App.D.C. 174, 295 F.2d 161 (1961).

[89] ARS § 8–228, subsec. A.

[90] Juvenile Delinquency—Its Prevention and Control (Russell Sage Foundation, 1966).

[91] Id., at 33. See also the other materials cited in n. 37, supra.

obtained by the police. A psychiatrist testified that the boy would admit "whatever he thought was expected so that he could get out of the immediate situation." The other 12-year-old also "confessed." Both confessions were in specific detail, albeit they contained various inconsistencies. The Court of Appeals, in an opinion by Keating, J., concluded that the confessions were products of the will of the police instead of the boys. The confessions were therefore held involuntary and the order of the Appellate Division affirming the order of the Family Court adjudging the defendants to be juvenile delinquents was reversed.

A similar and equally instructive case has recently been decided by the Supreme Court of New Jersey. In the Interests of Carlo and Stasilowicz, supra. The body of a 10-year-old girl was found. She had been strangled. Neighborhood boys who knew the girl were questioned. The two appellants, aged 13 and 15, confessed to the police, with vivid detail and some inconsistencies. At the Juvenile Court hearing, both denied any complicity in the killing. They testified that their confessions were the product of fear and fatigue due to extensive police grilling. The Juvenile Court Judge found that the confessions were voluntary and admissible. On appeal, in an extensive opinion by Proctor, J., the Supreme Court of New Jersey reversed. It rejected the State's argument that the constitutional safeguard of voluntariness governing the use of confessions does not apply in proceedings before the Juvenile Court. It pointed out that under New Jersey court rules, juveniles under the age of 16 accused of committing a homicide are tried in a proceeding which "has all of the appurtenances of a criminal trial," including participation by the county prosecutor, and requirements that the juvenile be provided with counsel, that a stenographic record be made, etc. It also pointed out that under New Jersey law, the confinement of the boys after reaching age 21 could be extended until they had served the maximum sentence which could have been imposed on an adult for such a homicide, here found to be second-degree murder carrying up to 30 years' imprisonment.[92] The court concluded that the confessions were involuntary, stressing that the boys, contrary to statute, were placed in the police station and there interrogated;[93] that the parents of both boys were not allowed to see them while they were being interrogated;[94] that inconsistencies ap-

---

[92] N.J.Rev.Stat. § 2A:4–37(b) (2), N.J.S.A. (Supp. 1966); N.J.Rev. Stat. 2 A: 113–4, N.J.S.A.

[93] N.J.Rev.Stat. § 2A: 4–32, 33, N.J. S.A. The court emphasized that the "frightening atmosphere" of a police station is likely to have "harm-

ful effects on the mind and will of the boy," citing In Matter of Rutane, 37 Misc.2d 234, 234 N.Y.S.2d 777 (Fam.Ct.Kings County, 1962).

[94] The court held that this alone might be enough to show that the confessions were involuntary "even

peared among the various statements of the boys and with the objective evidence of the crime; and that there were protracted periods of questioning. The court noted the State's contention that both boys were advised of their constitutional rights before they made their statements, but it held that this should not be given "significant weight in our determination of voluntariness."[95] Accordingly, the judgment of the Juvenile Court was reversed.

In a recent case before the Juvenile Court of the District of Columbia, Judge Ketcham rejected the proffer of evidence as to oral statements made at police headquarters by four juveniles who had been taken into custody for alleged involvement in an assault and attempted robbery. In the Matter of Four Youths, Nos. 28–776–J, 28–778–J, 28–783–J, 28–859–J, Juvenile Court of the District of Columbia, April 7, 1961. The court explicitly stated that it did not rest its decision on a showing that the statements were involuntary, but because they were untrustworthy. Judge Ketcham said:

"Simply stated, the Court's decision in this case rests upon the considered opinion—after nearly four busy years on the Juvenile Court bench during which the testimony of thousands of such juveniles has been heard—that the statements of adolescents under 18 years of age who are arrested and charged with violations of law are frequently untrustworthy and often distort the truth."

We conclude that the constitutional privilege against self-incrimination is applicable in the case of juveniles as it is with respect to adults. We appreciate that special problems may arise with respect to waiver of the privilege by or on behalf of children, and that there may well be some differences in technique—but not in principle—depending upon the age of the child and the presence and competence of parents. The participation of counsel will, of course, assist the police, Juvenile Courts and appellate tribunals in administering the privilege. If counsel was not present for some permissible reason

---

though, as the police testified, the boys did not wish to see their parents" (citing Gallegos v. State of Colorado, 370 U.S. 49, 82 S.Ct. 1209, 8 L.Ed.2d 325 (1962)).

[95] The court quoted the following passage from Haley v. State of Ohio, supra, 332 U.S., at 601, 68 S.Ct. at 304:

"But we are told that this boy was advised of his constitutional rights before he signed the confession and that, knowing them, he nevertheless confessed. That assumes, however, that a boy of fifteen, without aid of counsel, would have a full appreciation of that advice and that on the facts of this record he had a freedom of choice. We cannot indulge those assumptions. Moreover, we cannot give any weight to recitals which merely formalize constitutional requirements. Formulas of respect for constitutional safeguards cannot prevail over the facts of life which contradict them. They may not become a cloak for inquisitorial practices and make an empty form of the due process of law for which free men fought and died to obtain."

when an admission was obtained, the greatest care must be taken to assure that the admission was voluntary, in the sense not only that it was not coerced or suggested, but also that it was not the product of ignorance of rights or of adolescent fantasy, fright or despair.[96]

The "confession" of Gerald Gault was first obtained by Officer Flagg, out of the presence of Gerald's parents, without counsel and without advising him of his right to silence, as far as appears. The judgment of the Juvenile Court was stated by the judge to be based on Gerald's admissions in court. Neither "admission" was reduced to writing, and, to say the least, the process by which the "admissions" were obtained and received must be characterized as lacking the certainty and order which are required of proceedings of such formidable consequences.[97] Apart from the "admissions," there was nothing upon which a judgment or finding might be based. There was no sworn testimony. Mrs. Cook, the complainant, was not present. The Arizona Supreme Court held that "sworn testimony must be required of all witnesses including police officers, probation officers and others who are part of or officially related to the juvenile court structure." We hold that this is not enough. No reason is suggested or appears for a different rule in respect of sworn testimony in juvenile courts than in adult tribunals. Absent a valid confession adequate to support the determination of the Juvenile Court, confrontation and sworn testimony by witnesses available for cross-examination were essential for a finding of "delinquency" and an order committing Gerald to a state institution for a maximum of six years.

The recommendations in the Children's Bureau's "Standards for Juvenile and Family Courts" are in general accord with our conclusions. They state that testimony should be under oath and that only competent, material and relevant evidence under rules applicable to civil cases should be admitted in evidence.[98] The New York

---

[96] The N.Y.Family Court Act § 744(b) provides that "an uncorroborated confession made out of court by a respondent is not sufficient" to constitute the required "preponderance of the evidence."

See United States v. Morales, 233 F.Supp. 160 (D.C.Mont.1964), holding a confession inadmissible in proceedings under the Federal Juvenile Delinquency Act (18 U.S.C. § 5031 et seq.) because, in the circumstances in which it was made, the District Court could not conclude that it "was freely made while Morales was afforded all of the re-

quisites of due process required in the case of a sixteen year old boy of his experience." Id., at 170.

[97] Cf. Jackson v. Denno, 378 U.S. 368, 84 S.Ct. 1774, 12 L.Ed.2d 908 (1964); Miranda v. State of Arizona, 384 U.S. 436, 86 S.Ct. 1602, 16 L.Ed.2d 694 (1966).

[98] Standards, pp. 72–73. The Nat'l Crime Comm'n Report concludes that "the evidence admissible at the adjudicatory hearing should be so limited that findings are not dependent upon or unduly influenced by hearsay, gossip, rumor, and

Family Court Act contains a similar provision.[99]

As we said in Kent v. United States, 383 U.S. 541, 554, 86 S.Ct. 1045, 1053, 16 L.Ed.2d 84 (1966), with respect to waiver proceedings, "there is no place in our system of law for reaching a result of such tremendous consequences without ceremony * * *." We now hold that, absent a valid confession, a determination of delinquency and an order of commitment to a state institution cannot be sustained in the absence of sworn testimony subjected to the opportunity for cross-examination in accordance with our law and constitutional requirements.

VI.

APPELLATE REVIEW AND TRANSCRIPT OF PROCEEDINGS.

Appellants urge that the Arizona statute is unconstitutional under the Due Process Clause because, as construed by its Supreme Court, "there is no right of appeal from a juvenile court order * * *." The court held that there is no right to a transcript because there is no right to appeal and because the proceedings are confidential and any record must be destroyed after a prescribed period of time.[100] Whether a transcript or other recording is made, it held, is a matter for the discretion of the juvenile court.

This Court has not held that a State is required by the Federal Constitution "to provide appellate courts or a right to appellate review at all."[101] In view of the fact that we must reverse the Supreme Court of Arizona's affirmance of the dismissal of the writ of habeas corpus for other reasons, we need not rule on this question in the present case or upon the failure to provide a transcript or recording of the hearings—or, indeed, the failure of the Juvenile Judge to state the grounds for his conclusion. Cf. Kent v. United

other unreliable types of information. To minimize the danger that adjudication will be affected by inappropriate considerations, social investigation reports should not be made known to the judge in advance of adjudication." Id., at 87 (bold face eliminated). See also Note, Rights and Rehabilitation in the Juvenile Courts, 67 Col.L.Rev. 281, 336 (1967): "At the adjudication stage, the use of clearly incompetent evidence in order to prove the youth's involvement in the alleged misconduct * * * is not justifiable. Particularly in delinquency cases, where the issue of fact is the commission of a crime, the introduction of hearsay—such as the report of a policeman who did not witness the events—contravenes the purposes underlying the sixth amendment right of confrontation." (Footnote omitted.)

[99] N.Y. Family Court Act § 744(a). See also Harvard Law Review Note, p. 795. Cf. Willner v. Committee on Character, 373 U.S. 96, 83 S.Ct. 1175, 10 L.Ed.2d 224 (1963).

[100] ARS § 8–238.

[101] Griffin v. People of State of Illinois, 351 U.S. 12, 18, 76 S.Ct. 585, 590, 100 L.Ed. 891 (1956).

States, supra, at 561, 86 S.Ct., at 1057, where we said, in the context of a decision of the juvenile court waiving jurisdiction to the adult court, which by local law, was permissible: "* * * it is incumbent upon the Juvenile Court to accompany its waiver order with a statement of the reasons or considerations therefore." As the present case illustrates, the consequences of failure to provide an appeal, to record the proceedings, or to make findings or state the grounds for the juvenile court's conclusion may be to throw a burden upon the machinery for habeas corpus, to saddle the reviewing process with the burden of attempting to reconstruct a record, and to impose upon the Juvenile Judge the unseemly duty of testifying under cross-examination as to the events that transpired in the hearings before him.[102]

For the reasons stated, the judgment of the Supreme Court of Arizona is reversed and the cause remanded for further proceedings not inconsistent with this opinion.

It is so ordered.

Mr. Justice BLACK, concurring.

The juvenile court laws of Arizona and other States, as the Court points out, are the result of plans promoted by humane and forward-looking people to provide a system of courts, procedures, and sanctions deemed to be less harmful and more lenient to children than to adults. For this reason such state laws generally provide less formal and less public methods for the trial of children. In line with this policy, both courts and legislators have shrunk back from labeling these laws as "criminal" and have preferred to call them "civil." This, in part, was to prevent the full application to juvenile court cases of the Bill of Rights safeguards, including notice as provided in the Sixth Amendment,[1] the right to counsel guaranteed

---

[102] "Standards for Juvenile and Family Courts" recommends "written findings of fact, some form of record of the hearing" "and the right to appeal." Standards, p. 8. It recommends verbatim recording of the hearing by stenotypist or mechanical recording (p. 76) and urges that the judge make clear to the child and family their right to appeal (p. 78). See also, Standard Family Court Act §§ 19, 24, 28; Standard Juvenile Court Act §§ 19, 24, 28. The Harvard Law Review Note. p. 799, states that "The result [of the infrequency of appeals due to absence of record, indigency, etc.] is that juvenile court proceedings are largely unsupervised." The Nat'l Crime Comm'n Report observes, p. 86, that "records make possible appeals which, even if they do not occur, impart by their possibility a healthy atmosphere of accountability."

[1] "In all criminal prosecutions, the accused shall enjoy the right * * * to be informed of the nature and cause of the accusation * * *." Also requiring notice is the Fifth Amendment's provision that "No person shall be held to answer for a capital, or otherwise infamous crime, unless on a presentment or indictment of a Grand Jury * * *."

by the Sixth,[2] the right against self-incrimination guaranteed by the Fifth,[3] and the right to confrontation guaranteed by the Sixth.[4] The Court here holds, however, that these four Bill of Rights safeguards apply to protect a juvenile accused in a juvenile court on a charge under which he can be imprisoned for a term of years. This holding strikes a well-nigh fatal blow to much that is unique about the juvenile courts in the Nation. For this reason, there is much to be said for the position of my Brother STEWART that we should not pass on all these issues until they are more squarely presented. But since the majority of the Court chooses to decide all of these questions, I must either do the same or leave my views unexpressed on the important issues determined. In these circumstances, I feel impelled to express my views.

The juvenile court planners envisaged a system that would practically immunize juveniles from "punishment" for "crimes" in an effort to save them from youthful indiscretions and stigmas due to criminal charges or convictions. I agree with the Court, however, that this exalted ideal has failed of achievement since the beginning of the system. Indeed, the state laws from the first one on contained provisions, written in emphatic terms, for arresting and charging juveniles with violations of state criminal laws, as well as for taking juveniles by force of law away from their parents and turning them over to different individuals or groups or for confinement within some state school or institution for a number of years. The latter occurred in this case. Young Gault was arrested and detained on a charge of violating an Arizona penal law by using vile and offensive language to a lady on the telephone. If an adult, he could only have been fined or imprisoned for two months for his conduct. As a juvenile, however, he was put through a more or less secret, informal hearing by the court, after which he was ordered, or, more realistically, "sentenced," to confinement in Arizona's Industrial School until he reaches 21 years of age. Thus, in a juvenile system designed to lighten or avoid punishment for criminality, he was ordered by the State to six years' confinement in what is in all but name a penitentiary or jail.

Where a person, infant or adult, can be seized by the State, charged, and convicted for violating a state criminal law, and then ordered by the State to be confined for six years, I think the Constitution requires that he be tried in accordance with the guarantees

---

[2] "In all criminal prosecutions, the accused shall * * * have the Assistance of Counsel in his defence."

[3] "No person * * * shall be compelled in any criminal case to be a witness against himself * * *."

[4] "In all criminal prosecutions, the accused shall enjoy the right * * * to be confronted with the witnesses against him * * *."

of all the provisions of the Bill of Rights made applicable to the States by the Fourteenth Amendment. Undoubtedly this would be true of an adult defendant, and it would be a plain denial of equal protection of the laws—an invidious discrimination—to hold that others subject to heavier punishments could, because they are children, be denied these same constitutional safeguards. I consequently agree with the Court that the Arizona law as applied here denied to the parents and their son the right of notice, right to counsel, right against self-incrimination, and right to confront the witnesses against young Gault. Appellants are entitled to these rights, not because "fairness, impartiality and orderliness—in short, the essentials of due process"—require them and not because they are "the procedural rules which have been fashioned from the generality of due process," but because they are specifically and unequivocally granted by provisions of the Fifth and Sixth Amendments which the Fourteenth Amendment makes applicable to the States.

A few words should be added because of the opinion of my Brother HARLAN who rests his concurrence and dissent on the Due Process Clause alone. He reads that clause alone as allowing this Court "to determine what forms of procedural protection are necessary to guarantee the fundamental fairness of juvenile proceedings" "in a fashion consistent with the 'traditions and conscience of our people.'" Cf. Rochin v. People of California, 342 U.S. 165, 72 S.Ct. 205, 96 L.Ed. 183. He believes that the Due Process Clause gives this Court the power, upon weighing a "compelling public interest," to impose on the States only those specific constitutional rights which the Court deems "imperative" and "necessary" to comport with the Court's notions of "fundamental fairness."

I cannot subscribe to any such interpretation of the Due Process Clause. Nothing in its words or its history permits it, and "fair distillations of relevant judicial history" are no substitute for the words and history of the clause itself. The phrase "due process of law" has through the years evolved as the successor in purpose and meaning to the words "law of the land" in Magna Charta which more plainly intended to call for a trial according to the existing law of the land in effect at the time an alleged offense had been committed. That provision in Magna Charta was designed to prevent defendants from being tried according to criminal laws or proclamations specifically promulgated to fit particular cases or to attach new consequences to old conduct. Nothing done since Magna Charta can be pointed to as intimating that the Due Process Clause gives courts power to fashion laws in order to meet new conditions, to fit the "decencies" of changed conditions, or to keep their consciences from being shocked by legislation, state or federal.

And, of course, the existence of such awesome judicial power cannot be buttressed or created by relying on the word "procedural." Whether labeled as "procedural" or "substantive," the Bill of Rights safeguards, far from being mere "tools with which" other unspecified "rights could be fully vindicated," are the very vitals of a sound constitutional legal system designed to protect and safeguard the most cherished liberties of a free people. These safeguards were written into our Constitution not by judges but by Constitution makers. Freedom in this Nation will be far less secure the very moment that it is decided that judges can determine which of these safeguards "should" or "should not be imposed" according to their notions of what constitutional provisions are consistent with the "traditions and conscience of our people." Judges with such power, even though they profess to "proceed with restraint," will be above the Constitution, with power to write it, not merely to interpret it, which I believe to be the only power constitutionally committed to judges.

There is one ominous sentence, if not more, in my Brother HARLAN's opinion which bodes ill, in my judgment, both for legislative programs and constitutional commands. Speaking of procedural safeguards in the Bill of Rights, he says:
"These factors in combination suggest that legislatures may properly expect only a cautious deference for their procedural judgments, but that, conversely, courts must exercise their special responsibility for procedural guarantees with care to permit ample scope for achieving the purposes of legislative programs. * * * [T]he court should necessarily proceed with restraint."

It is to be noted here that this case concerns Bill of Rights Amendments; that the "procedure" power my Brother HARLAN claims for the Court here relates solely to Bill of Rights safeguards; and that he is here claiming for the Court a supreme power to fashion new Bill of Rights safeguards according to the Court's notions of what fits tradition and conscience. I do not believe that the Constitution vests any such power in judges, either in the Due Process Clause or anywhere else. Consequently, I do not vote to invalidate this Arizona law on the ground that it is "unfair" but solely on the ground that it violates the Fifth and Sixth Amendments made obligatory on the States by the Fourteenth Amendment. Cf. Pointer v. State of Texas, 380 U.S. 400, 412, 85 S.Ct. 1065, 1072, 13 L.Ed.2d 923 (Goldberg, J., concurring). It is enough for me that the Arizona law as here applied collides head-on with the Fifth and Sixth Amendments in the four respects mentioned. The only relevance to me of the Due Process Clause is that it would, of course, violate due process or the "law of the land" to enforce a law that collides with the Bill of Rights.

Mr. Justice WHITE, concurring.

I join the Court's opinion except for Part V. I also agree that the privilege against compelled self-incrimination applies at the adjudicatory stage of juvenile court proceedings. I do not, however, find an adequate basis in the record for determining whether that privilege was violated in this case. The Fifth Amendment protects a person from being "compelled" in any criminal proceeding to be a witness against himself. Compulsion is essential to a violation. It may be that when a judge, armed with the authority he has or which people think he has, asks questions of a party or a witness in an adjudicatory hearing, that person, especially if a minor, would feel compelled to answer, absent a warning to the contrary or similar information from some other source. The difficulty is that the record made at the habeas corpus hearing, which is the only information we have concerning the proceedings in the juvenile court, does not directly inform us whether Gerald Gault or his parents were told of Gerald's right to remain silent; nor does it reveal whether the parties were aware of the privilege from some other source, just as they were already aware that they had the right to have the help of counsel and to have witnesses on their behalf. The petition for habeas corpus did not raise the Fifth Amendment issue nor did any of the witnesses focus on it.

I have previously recorded my views with respect to what I have deemed unsound applications of the Fifth Amendment. See, for example, Miranda v. State of Arizona, 384 U.S. 436, 526, 86 S.Ct. 1602, 1654, 16 L.Ed.2d 694, and Malloy v. Hogan, 378 U.S. 1, 33, 84 S.Ct. 1489, 1506, 12 L.Ed.2d 653, dissenting opinions. These views, of course, have not prevailed. But I do hope that the Court will proceed with some care in extending the privilege, with all its vigor, to proceedings in juvenile court, particularly the nonadjudicatory stages of those proceedings.

In any event, I would not reach the Fifth Amendment issue here. I think the Court is clearly ill-advised to review this case on the basis of Miranda v. State of Arizona, since the adjudication of delinquency took place in 1964, long before the Miranda decision. See Johnson v. State of New Jersey, 384 U.S. 719, 86 S.Ct. 1772, 16 L.Ed.2d 882. Under these circumstances, this case is a poor vehicle for resolving a difficult problem. Moreover, no prejudice to appellants is at stake in this regard. The judgment below must be reversed on other grounds and in the event further proceedings are to be had, Gerald Gault will have counsel available to advise him.

For somewhat similar reasons, I would not reach the questions of confrontation and cross-examination which are also dealt with in Part V of the opinion.

Mr. Justice HARLAN, concurring in part and dissenting in part.

Each of the 50 States has created a system of juvenile or family courts, in which distinctive rules are employed and special consequences imposed. The jurisdiction of these courts commonly extends both to cases which the States have withdrawn from the ordinary processes of criminal justice, and to cases which involve acts that, if performed by an adult, would not be penalized as criminal. Such courts are denominated civil, not criminal, and are characteristically said not to administer criminal penalties. One consequence of these systems, at least as Arizona construes its own, is that certain of the rights guaranteed to criminal defendants by the Constitution are withheld from juveniles. This case brings before this Court for the first time the question of what limitations the Constitution places upon the operation of such tribunals.[1] For reasons which follow, I have concluded that the Court has gone too far in some respects, and fallen short in others, in assessing the procedural requirements demanded by the Fourteenth Amendment.

I.

I must first acknowledge that I am unable to determine with any certainty by what standards the Court decides that Arizona's juvenile courts do not satisfy the obligations of due process. The Court's premise, itself the product of reasoning which is not described, is that the "constitutional and theoretical basis" of state systems of juvenile and family courts is "debatable"; it buttresses these doubts by marshaling a body of opinion which suggests that the accomplishments of these courts have often fallen short of expectations.[2] The Court does not indicate at what points or for what purposes such views, held either by it or by other observers, might be pertinent to the present issues. Its failure to provide any discernible standard for the measurement of due process in relation

---

[1] Kent v. United States, 383 U.S. 541, 86 S.Ct. 1045, 16 L.Ed.2d 84, decided at the 1965 Term, did not purport to rest on constitutional grounds.

[2] It is appropriate to observe that, whatever the relevance the Court may suppose that this criticism has to present issues, many of the critics have asserted that the deficiencies of juvenile courts have stemmed chiefly from the inadequacy of the personnel and resources available to those courts. See, e. g., Paulsen, Kent v. United States: The Constitutional Context of Juvenile Cases, 1966 Sup.Ct.Rev. 167, 191–192; Handler, The Juvenile Court and the Adversary System: Problems of Function and Form, 1965 Wis.L.Rev. 7, 46.

to juvenile proceedings unfortunately might be understood to mean that the Court is concerned principally with the wisdom of having such courts at all.

If this is the source of the Court's dissatisfaction, I cannot share it. I should have supposed that the constitutionality of juvenile courts was beyond proper question under the standards now employed to assess the substantive validity of state legislation under the Due Process Clause of the Fourteenth Amendment. It can scarcely be doubted that it is within the State's competence to adopt measures reasonably calculated to meet more effectively the persistent problems of juvenile delinquency; as the opinion for the Court makes abundantly plain, these are among the most vexing and ominous of the concerns which now face communities throughout the country.

The proper issue here is, however, not whether the State may constitutionally treat juvenile offenders through a system of specialized courts, but whether the proceedings in Arizona's juvenile courts include procedural guarantees which satisfy the requirements of the Fourteenth Amendment. Among the first premises of our constitutional system is the obligation to conduct any proceeding in which an individual may be deprived of liberty or property in a fashion consistent with the "traditions and conscience of our people." Snyder v. Commonwealth of Massachusetts, 291 U.S. 97, 105, 54 S.Ct. 330, 332, 78 L.Ed. 674. The importance of these procedural guarantees is doubly intensified here. First, many of the problems with which Arizona is concerned are among those traditionally confined to the processes of criminal justice; their disposition necessarily affects in the most direct and substantial manner the liberty of individual citizens. Quite obviously, systems of specialized penal justice might permit erosion, or even evasion, of the limitations placed by the Constitution upon state criminal proceedings. Second, we must recognize that the character and consequences of many juvenile court proceedings have in fact closely resembled those of ordinary criminal trials. Nothing before us suggests that juvenile courts were intended as a device to escape constitutional constraints, but I entirely agree with the Court that we are nonetheless obliged to examine with circumspection the procedural guarantees the State has provided.

The central issue here, and the principal one upon which I am divided from the Court, is the method by which the procedural requirements of due process should be measured. It must at the outset be emphasized that the protections necessary here cannot be determined by resort to any classification of juvenile proceedings either as criminal or as civil, whether made by the State or by this

Court. Both formulae are simply too imprecise to permit reasoned analysis of these difficult constitutional issues. The Court should instead measure the requirements of due process by reference both to the problems which confront the State and to the actual character of the procedural system which the State has created. The Court has for such purposes chiefly examined three connected sources: first, the "settled usages and modes of proceeding," Den ex dem. Murray's Lessee v. Hoboken Land & Improvement Co., 18 How. 272, 277, 15 L.Ed. 372; second, the "fundamental principles of liberty and justice which lie at the base of all our civil and political institutions," Hebert v. State of Louisiana, 272 U.S. 312, 316, 47 S.Ct. 103, 104, 71 L.Ed. 270 and third, the character and requirements of the circumstances presented in each situation. FCC v. WJR, The Goodwill Station, 337 U.S. 265, 277, 69 S.Ct. 1097, 1104, 93 L.Ed. 1353; Yakus v. United States, 321 U.S. 414, 64 S.Ct. 660, 88 L.Ed. 834. See, further, my dissenting opinion in Poe v. Ullman, 367 U.S. 497, 522, 81 S.Ct. 1752, 1765, 6 L.Ed.2d 989, and compare my opinion concurring in the result in Pointer v. State of Texas, 380 U.S. 400, 408, 85 S.Ct. 1065, 1070. Each of these factors is relevant to the issues here, but it is the last which demands particular examination.

The Court has repeatedly emphasized that determination of the constitutionally required procedural safeguards in any situation requires recognition both of the "interests affected" and of the "circumstances involved." FCC v. WJR, The Goodwill Station, supra, at 277, 69 S.Ct. at 1104. In particular, a "compelling public interest" must, under our cases, be taken fully into account in assessing the validity under the due process clauses of state or federal legislation and its application. See, e. g., Yakus v. United States, supra, at 442, 64 S.Ct. at 675; Bowles v. Willingham, 321 U.S. 503, 520, 64 S.Ct. 641, 650, 88 L.Ed. 892; Miller v. Schoene, 276 U.S. 272, 279, 48 S.Ct. 246, 247, 72 L.Ed. 568. Such interests would never warrant arbitrariness or the diminution of any specifically assured constitutional right, Home Bldg. & Loan Assn. v. Blaisdell, 290 U.S. 398, 426, 54 S.Ct. 231, 235, 78 L.Ed. 413, but they are an essential element of the context through which the legislation and proceedings under it must be read and evaluated.

No more evidence of the importance of the public interests at stake here is required than that furnished by the opinion of the Court; it indicates that "some 601,000 children under 18, or 2% of all children between 10 and 17, came before juvenile courts" in 1965, and that "about one-fifth of all arrests for serious crimes" in 1965 were of juveniles. The Court adds that the rate of juvenile crime is steadily rising. All this, as the Court suggests, indicates

189

the importance of these due process issues, but it mirrors no less vividly that state authorities are confronted by formidable and immediate problems involving the most fundamental social values. The state legislatures have determined that the most hopeful solution for these problems is to be found in specialized courts, organized under their own rules and imposing distinctive consequences. The terms and limitations of these systems are not identical, nor are the procedural arrangements which they include, but the States are uniform in their insistence that the ordinary processes of criminal justice are inappropriate, and that relatively informal proceedings, dedicated to premises and purposes only imperfectly reflected in the criminal law, are instead necessary.

It is well settled that the Court must give the widest deference to legislative judgments that concern the character and urgency of the problems with which the State is confronted. Legislatures are, as this Court has often acknowledged, the "main guardian" of the public interest, and, within their constitutional competence, their understanding of that interest must be accepted as "well-nigh" conclusive. Berman v. Parker, 348 U.S. 26, 32, 75 S.Ct. 98, 102, 99 L.Ed. 27. This principle does not, however, reach all the questions essential to the resolution of this case. The legislative judgments at issue here embrace assessments of the necessity and wisdom of procedural guarantee; these are questions which the Constitution has entrusted at least in part to courts, and upon which courts have been understood to possess particular competence. The fundamental issue here is, therefore, in what measure and fashion the Court must defer to legislative determinations which encompass constitutional issues of procedural protection.

It suffices for present purposes to summarize the factors which I believe to be pertinent. It must first be emphasized that the deference given to legislators upon substantive issues must realistically extend in part to ancillary procedural questions. Procedure at once reflects and creates substantive rights, and every effort of courts since the beginnings of the common law to separate the two has proved essentially futile. The distinction between them is particularly inadequate here, where the legislature's substantive preferences directly and unavoidably require judgments about procedural issues. The procedural framework is here a principal element of the substantive legislative system; meaningful deference to the latter must include a portion of deference to the former. The substantive-procedural dichotomy is, nonetheless, an indispensable tool of analysis, for it stems from fundamental limitations upon judicial authority under the Constitution. Its premise is ultimately that courts may not substitute for the judgments of legislators their own understanding of the public welfare, but must instead concern themselves with the validity under the Constitution of the methods which the legislature has selected. See, e. g., McLean v. State of Arkansas, 211 U.S. 539, 547, 29 S.Ct. 206, 208, 53 L.Ed. 315; Olsen v. State of Nebraska, 313 U.S. 236, 246–247, 61 S.Ct. 862, 865, 85 L.Ed. 1305. The Constitution has in this manner created for courts and legislators areas of primary responsibility which are essentially congruent to their areas of special competence. Courts are thus obliged both by constitutional command and by their distinctive functions to bear particular responsibility for the measurement of procedural due process. These factors in combination suggest that legislatures may properly expect only a cautious deference for their procedural judgments, but that, conversely, courts must exercise their special responsibility for procedural guarantees with care to permit ample scope for achieving the purposes of legislative programs. Plainly, courts can exercise such care only if they have in each case first studied thoroughly the objectives and implementation of the program at stake; if, upon completion of those studies, the effect of extensive procedural restrictions upon valid legislative purposes cannot be assessed with reasonable certainty, the court should necessarily proceed with restraint.

The foregoing considerations, which I believe to be fair distillations of relevant judicial history, suggest three criteria by which the procedural requirements of due process should be measured here: first, no more restrictions should be imposed than are imperative to assure the proceedings' fundamental fairness; second, the restrictions which are imposed should be those which preserve, so far as possible, the essential elements of the State's purpose; and finally, restrictions should be chosen which will later permit the orderly selection of any additional protections which may ultimately prove necessary. In this way, the Court may guarantee the fundamental fairness of the proceeding, and yet permit the State to continue development of an effective response to the problems of juvenile crime.

II.

Measured by these criteria, only three procedural requirements should, in my opinion, now be deemed required of state juvenile courts by the Due Process Clause of the Fourteenth Amendment: first, timely notice must be provided to parents and children of the nature and terms of any juvenile court proceedings in which a determination affecting their rights or interests may be made; second, unequivocal and timely notice must be given that counsel may appear in any such proceeding in behalf of the child and its parents, and that in cases in which the child may be confined in an

191

institution, counsel may, in circumstances of indigency, be appointed for them; and third, the court must maintain a written record, or its equivalent, adequate to permit effective review on appeal or in collateral proceedings. These requirements would guarantee to juveniles the tools with which their rights could be fully vindicated, and yet permit the States to pursue without unnecessary hindrance the purposes which they believe imperative in this field. Further, their imposition now would later permit more intelligent assessment of the necessity under the Fourteenth Amendment of additional requirements, by creating suitable records from which the character and deficiencies of juvenile proceedings could be accurately judged. I turn to consider each of these three requirements.

The Court has consistently made plain that adequate and timely notice is the fulcrum of due process, whatever the purposes of the proceeding. See, e. g., Roller v. Holly, 176 U.S. 398, 409, 20 S.Ct. 410, 413, 44 L.Ed. 520; Coe v. Armour Fertilizer Works, 237 U.S. 413, 424, 35 S.Ct. 625, 628, 59 L.Ed. 1027. Notice is ordinarily the prerequisite to effective assertion of any constitutional or other rights; without it, vindication of those rights must be essentially fortuitous. So fundamental a protection can neither be spared here nor left to the "favor or grace" of state authorities. Central of Georgia Ry. v. Wright, 207 U.S. 127, 138, 28 S.Ct. 47, 51, 52 L.Ed. 134; Coe v. Armour Fertilizer Works, supra, at 425, 35 S.Ct. at 628.

Provision of counsel and of a record, like adequate notice, would permit the juvenile to assert very much more effectively his rights and defenses, both in the juvenile proceedings and upon direct or collateral review. The Court has frequently emphasized their importance in proceedings in which an individual may be deprived of his liberty, see Gideon v. Wainwright, 372 U.S. 335, 83 S.Ct. 792, 9 L.Ed.2d 799, and Griffin v. People of State of Illinois, 351 U.S. 12, 76 S.Ct. 585, 100 L.Ed. 891; this reasoning must include with special force those who are commonly inexperienced and immature. See Powell v. State of Alabama, 287 U.S. 45, 53 S.Ct. 55, 77 L.Ed. 158. The facts of this case illustrate poignantly the difficulties of review without either an adequate record or the participation of counsel in the proceeding's initial stages. At the same time, these requirements should not cause any substantial modification in the character of juvenile court proceedings: counsel, although now present in only a small percentage of juvenile cases, have apparently already appeared without incident in virtually all juvenile courts;[3]

---

[3] The statistical evidence here is incomplete, but see generally Skoler & Tenney, Attorney Representation in Juvenile Court, 4 J. Fam.Law 77. They indicate that some 91% of the juvenile court judges whom they

and the maintenance of a record should not appreciably alter the conduct of these proceedings.

The question remains whether certain additional requirements, among them the privilege against self-incrimination, confrontation, and cross-examination, must now, as the Court holds, also be imposed. I share in part the views expressed in my Brother WHITE's concurring opinion, but believe that there are other, and more deep-seated, reasons to defer, at least for the present, the imposition of such requirements.

Initially, I must vouchsafe that I cannot determine with certainty the reasoning by which the Court concludes that these further requirements are now imperative. The Court begins from the premise, to which it gives force at several points, that juvenile courts need not satisfy "all of the requirements of a criminal trial." It therefore scarcely suffices to explain the selection of these particular procedural requirements for the Court to declare that juvenile court proceedings are essentially criminal, and thereupon to recall that these are requisites for a criminal trial. Nor does the Court's voucher of "authoritative opinion," which consists of four extraordinary juvenile cases, contribute materially to the solution of these issues. The Court has, even under its own premises, asked the wrong questions: the problem here is to determine what forms of procedural protection are necessary to guarantee the fundamental fairness of juvenile proceedings, and not which of the procedures now employed in criminal trials should be transplanted intact to proceedings in these specialized courts.

In my view, the Court should approach this question in terms of the criteria, described above, which emerge from the history of due process adjudication. Measured by them, there are compelling reasons at least to defer imposition of these additional requirements. First, quite unlike notice, counsel, and a record, these requirements might radically alter the character of juvenile court proceedings. The evidence from which the Court reasons that they would not is inconclusive,[4] and other available evidence suggests that they very likely would.[5] At the least, it is plain that these

---

polled favored representation by counsel in their courts. Id., at 88.

[4] Indeed, my Brother BLACK candidly recognizes that such is apt to be the effect of today's decision, ante. The Court itself is content merely to rely upon inapposite language from the recommendations of the Children's Bureau, plus the terms of a single statute.

[5] The most cogent evidence of course consists of the steady rejection of these requirements by state legislatures and courts. The wide disagreement and uncertainty upon this question are also reflected in Paulsen, Kent v. United States: The Constitutional Context of Juvenile Cases, 1966 Sup.Ct.Rev. 167, 186, 191. See also Paulsen, Fairness to

additional requirements would contribute materially to the creation in these proceedings of the atmosphere of an ordinary criminal trial, and would, even if they do no more, thereby largely frustrate a central purpose of these specialized courts. Further, these are restrictions intended to conform to the demands of an intensely adversary system of criminal justice; the broad purposes which they represent might be served in juvenile courts with equal effectiveness by procedural devices more consistent with the premises of proceedings in those courts. As the Court apparently acknowledges, the hazards of self-accusation, for example, might be avoided in juvenile proceedings without the imposition of all the requirements and limitations which surround the privilege against self-incrimination. The guarantee of adequate notice, counsel, and a record would create conditions in which suitable alternative procedures could be devised; but, unfortunately, the Court's haste to impose restrictions taken intact from criminal procedure may well seriously hamper the development of such alternatives. Surely this illustrates that prudence and the principles of the Fourteenth Amendment alike require that the Court should now impose no more procedural restrictions than are imperative to assure fundamental fairness, and that the States should instead be permitted additional opportunities to develop without unnecessary hindrance their systems of juvenile courts.

I find confirmation for these views in two ancillary considerations. First, it is clear that an uncertain, but very substantial number of the cases brought to juvenile courts involve children who are not in any sense guilty of criminal misconduct. Many of these children have simply the misfortune to be in some manner distressed; others have engaged in conduct, such as truancy, which is plainly not criminal.[6] Efforts are now being made to develop effective, and entirely noncriminal, methods of treatment for these children.[7] In such cases, the state authorities are in the most literal sense act-

the Juvenile Offender, 41 Minn.L. Rev. 547, 561–562; McLean, An Answer to the Challenge of Kent, 53 A.B.A.J. 456, 457; Alexander, Constitutional Rights in Juvenile Court, 46 A.B.A.J. 1206; Shears, Legal Problems Peculiar to Children's Courts, 48 A.B.A.J. 719; Siler, The Need for Defense Counsel in the Juvenile Court, 11 Crime & Delin. 45, 57–58. Compare Handler, The Juvenile Court and the Adversary System: Problems of Function and Form, 1965 Wis.L.Rev. 7, 32.

[6] Estimates of the number of children in this situation brought before ju-

venile courts range from 26% to some 48%; variation seems chiefly a product both of the inadequacy of records and of the difficulty of categorizing precisely the conduct with which juveniles are charged. See generally Sheridan, Juveniles Who Commit Noncriminal Acts: Why Treat in a Correctional System? 31 Fed. Probation 26, 27. By any standard, the number of juveniles involved is "considerable." Ibid.

[7] Id., at 28–30.

ing *in loco parentis*; they are, by any standard, concerned with the child's protection, and not with his punishment. I do not question that the methods employed in such cases must be consistent with the constitutional obligation to act in accordance with due process, but certainly the Fourteenth Amendment does not demand that they be constricted by the procedural guarantees devised for ordinary criminal prosecutions. Cf. State of Minnesota ex rel. Pearson v. Probate Court, 309 U.S. 270, 60 S.Ct. 523, 84 L.Ed. 744. It must be remembered that the various classifications of juvenile court proceedings are, as the vagaries of the available statistics illustrate, often arbitrary or ambiguous; it would therefore be imprudent, at the least, to build upon these classifications rigid systems of procedural requirements which would be applicable, or not, in accordance with the descriptive label given to the particular proceeding. It is better, it seems to me, to begin by now requiring the essential elements of fundamental fairness in juvenile courts, whatever the label given by the State to the proceeding; in this way the Court could avoid imposing unnecessarily rigid restrictions, and yet escape dependence upon classifications which may often prove to be illusory. Further, the provision of notice, counsel, and a record would permit orderly efforts to determine later whether more satisfactory classifications can be devised, and if they can, whether additional procedural requirements are necessary for them under the Fourteenth Amendment.

Second, it should not be forgotten that juvenile crime and juvenile courts are both now under earnest study throughout the country. I very much fear that this Court, by imposing these rigid procedural requirements, may inadvertently have served to discourage these efforts to find more satisfactory solutions for the problems of juvenile crime, and may thus now hamper enlightened development of the systems of juvenile courts. It is appropriate to recall that the Fourteenth Amendment does not compel the law to remain passive in the midst of change; to demand otherwise denies "every quality of the law but its age." Hurtado v. People of State of California, 110 U.S. 516, 529, 4 S.Ct. 111, 117, 28 L.Ed. 232.

III.

Finally, I turn to assess the validity of this juvenile court proceeding under the criteria discussed in this opinion. Measured by them, the judgment below must, in my opinion, fall. Gerald Gault and his parents were not provided adequate notice of the terms and purposes of the proceedings in which he was adjudged delinquent; they were not advised of their rights to be represented by counsel; and no record in any form was maintained of the proceedings. It follows, for the reasons given in this opinion, that Gerald Gault was deprived of his liberty without due process of law, and I therefore concur in the judgment of the Court.

Mr. Justice STEWART, dissenting.

The Court today uses an obscure Arizona case as a vehicle to impose upon thousands of juvenile courts throughout the Nation restrictions that the Constitution made applicable to adversary criminal trials.[1] I believe the Court's decision is wholly unsound as a matter of constitutional law, and sadly unwise as a matter of judicial policy.

Juvenile proceedings are not criminal trials. They are not civil trials. They are simply not adversary proceedings. Whether treating with a delinquent child, a neglected child, a defective child, or a dependent child, a juvenile proceeding's whole purpose and mission is the very opposite of the mission and purpose of a prosecution in a criminal court. The object of the one is correction of a condition. The object of the other is conviction and punishment for a criminal act.

In the last 70 years many dedicated men and women have devoted their professional lives to the enlightened task of bringing us out of the dark world of Charles Dickens in meeting our responsibilities to the child in our society. The result has been the creation in this century of a system of juvenile and family courts in each of the 50 States. There can be no denying that in many areas the performance of these agencies has fallen disappointingly short of the hopes and dreams of the courageous pioneers who first conceived them. For a variety of reasons, the reality has sometimes not even approached the ideal, and much remains to be accomplished in the administration of public juvenile and family agencies—in personnel, in planning, in financing, perhaps in the formulation of wholly new approaches.

I possess neither the specialized experience nor the expert knowledge to predict with any certainty where may lie the brightest hope for progress in dealing with the serious problems of juvenile delinquency. But I am certain that the answer does not lie in the

---

[1] I find it strange that a Court so intent upon fastening an absolute right to counsel upon nonadversary juvenile proceedings has not been willing even to consider whether the Constitution requires a lawyer's help in a criminal prosecution upon a misdemeanor charge. See Winters v. Beck, 385 U.S. 907, 87 S.Ct. 207, 17 L.Ed.2d 137; DeJoseph v. Connecticut, 385 U.S. 982, 87 S.Ct. 526, 17 L.Ed.2d 443.

Court's opinion in this case, which serves to convert a juvenile proceeding into a criminal prosecution.

The inflexible restrictions that the Constitution so wisely made applicable to adversary criminal trials have no inevitable place in the proceedings of those public social agencies known as juvenile or family courts. And to impose the Court's long catalog of requirements upon juvenile proceedings in every area of the country is to invite a long step backwards into the nineteenth century. In that era there were no juvenile proceedings, and a child was tried in a conventional criminal court with all the trappings of a conventional criminal trial. So it was that a 12-year-old boy named James Guild was tried in New Jersey for killing Catharine Beakes. A jury found him guilty of murder, and he was sentenced to death by hanging. The sentence was executed. It was all very constitutional.[2]

A State in all its dealings must, of course, accord every person due process of law. And due process may require that some of the same restrictions which the Constitution has placed upon criminal trials must be imposed upon juvenile proceedings. For example, I suppose that all would agree that a brutally coerced confession could not constitutionally be considered in a juvenile court hearing. But it surely does not follow that the testimonial privilege against self-incrimination is applicable in all juvenile proceedings.[3] Similarly, due process clearly requires timely notice of the purpose and scope

---

[2] State v. Guild, 5 Halst. 163, 10 N.J.L. 163, 18 Am.Dec. 404.

"Thus, also, in very modern times, a boy of ten years old was convicted on his own confession of murdering his bedfellow, there appearing in his whole behavior plain tokens of a mischievous discretion; and as the sparing this boy merely on account of his tender years might be of dangerous consequence to the public, by propagating a notion that children might commit such atrocious crimes with impunity, it was unanimously agreed by all the judges that he was a proper subject of capital punishment." 4 Blackstone, Commentaries 23 (Wendell ed. 1847).

[3] Until June 13, 1966, it was clear that the Fourteenth Amendment's ban upon the use of a coerced confession is constitutionally quite a different thing from the Fifth Amendment's testimonial privilege against self-incrimination. See, for example, the Court's unanimous opinion in *Brown* v. *Mississippi*, 297 U. S. 278, at 285–286, written by Chief Justice Hughes and joined by such distinguished members of this Court as Mr. Justice Brandeis, Mr. Justice Stone, and Mr. Justice Cardozo. See also *Tehan* v. *Shott*, 382 U. S. 406, decided January 19, 1966, where the Court emphasized the "contrast" between "the wrongful use of a coerced confession" and "the Fifth Amendment's privilege against self-incrimination." 382 U. S., at 416. The complete confusion of these separate constitutional doctrines in Part V of the Court's opinion today stems, no doubt, from *Miranda* v. *Arizona*, 384 U. S. 436, a decision which I continue to believe was constitutionally erroneous.

of any proceedings affecting the relationship of parent and child. Armstrong v. Manzo, 380 U.S. 545, 85 S.Ct. 1187, 14 L.Ed.2d 62. But it certainly does not follow that notice of a juvenile hearing must be framed with all the technical niceties of a criminal indictment. See Russell v. United States, 369 U.S. 749, 82 S.Ct. 1038, 8 L.Ed.2d 240.

In any event, there is no reason to deal with issues such as these in the present case. The Supreme Court of Arizona found that the parents of Gerald Gault "knew of their right to counsel, to subpoena and cross examine witnesses, of the right to confront the witnesses against Gerald and the possible consequences of a finding of delinquency." 99 Ariz. 181, 185, 407 P.2d 760, 763. It further found that "Mrs. Gault knew the exact nature of the charge against Gerald from the day he was taken to the detention home." 99 Ariz., at 193, 407 P.2d, at 768. And, as Mr. Justice WHITE correctly points out, pp. 64–65, ante, no issue of compulsory self-incrimination is presented by this case.

I would dismiss the appeal.

Rights of A Witness

Malloy v. Hogan*

In *Twining v New Jersey*,[1] a 1908 case, the Supreme Court held that the constitution does not make it mandatory that the privilege against self-incrimination be extended to a witness in a state proceeding. in the *Malloy case* the Supreme Court reverses this long standing precedent.

Malloy, who had served a jail sentence in Connecticut for violating its gaming laws, was called upon to testify before a State Judicial investigating body. When asked any questions concerning the events surrounding his arrest and conviction, Malloy repeatedly refused to respond stating ". . . it may tend to incriminate me".[2] He was adjudged in contempt and imprisoned until he would answer.

In a five to four decision written by Mr. Justice Brennan the Court ordered Malloy's release holding that the due process of laws clause of the Fourteenth Amendment provides a witness in a state proceeding with a constitutional privilege against self-incrimination. This privilege, which had always been available against the Federal Government under the Fifth Amendment, was now equally applicable to state action via the Fourteenth Amendment.

The alignment of the justices is worth noting in this case. Justices Warren, Brennan, Black, Goldberg and Douglas constituted the majority. They held the liberal view on the accused's right to remain silent. Justices Harlan, Clark, White and Stewart dissented arguing that constitutionally this right does not extend to state action.

This five to four alignment of the justices was to continue in some of the future noteworthy Supreme Court decisions involving the rights of the accused. In *Escobedo*[3] it was identical and in *Miranda*,[4] also a five to four decision, it was nearly identical. Jus-

---

* 378 U.S. 1, 84 S.Ct. 1489 (June 15, 1964)
[1] 211 U.S. 78 (1908)   [3] 378 U.S. 478, 84 S.Ct. 1758 (1964)
[2] Henry J. Abraham, *Freedom And*   [4] 384 U.S. 436, 86 S.Ct. 1602 (1966)
    The Court, page 63.

tice Goldberg had resigned prior to the *Miranda* case. His replacement, Justice Fortas, sided with the liberal majority. Had Goldberg's replacement been of a more conservative persuasion, the whole tenor of recent Supreme Court decisions in this area might have been different.

The philosophical and sociological persuasions of the men who comprise the bench of the Supreme Court should not be underestimated. These persuasions have a profound effect on the evolution of the law in our country. It is true that it is not the function of the Supreme Court to make laws, but to interpret them. But the justices of the Supreme Court are only human. They cannot completely detach themselves from their personal bias and prejudices in their efforts at interpretation.

Text of Case

Petitioner, who was on probation after pleading guilty to a gambling misdemeanor, was ordered to testify before a referee appointed by a state court to investigate gambling and other criminal activities. He refused to answer questions about the circumstances of his arrest and conviction on the ground that the answers might incriminate him. Adjudged in contempt and committed to prison until he answered, he filed an application for writ of habeas corpus, which the highest state court denied. It ruled that petitioner was protected against prosecution growing out of his replies to all but one question, and that as to that question his failure to explain how his answer would incriminate him negated his claim to the protection of the privilege under state law.

Harold Strauch argued the cause and filed a brief for petitioner.

John D. LaBelle, State's Attorney for Connecticut, argued the cause for respondent. With him on the brief were *George D. Stoughton* and *Harry W. Hultgren, Jr.,* Assistant State's Attorneys.

Melvin L. Wulf filed a brief for the American Civil Liberties Union, as *amicus curiae,* urging reversal.

Briefs of *amici curiae,* urging affirmance, were filed by *Stanley Mosk,* Attorney General of California, *William E. James,* Assistant Attorney General, and *Gordon Ringer,* Deputy Attorney General, for the State of California; and by *Frank S. Hogan, Edward S. Silver, H. Richard Uviller, Michael R. Juviler, Aaron E. Koota* and *Irving P. Seidman* for the National District Attorneys' Association.

Mr. Justice BRENNAN delivered the opinion of the Court.

In this case we are asked to reconsider prior decisions holding that the privilege against self-incrimination is not safeguarded against state action by the Fourteenth Amendment. Twining v.

New Jersey, 211 U.S. 78, 29 S.Ct. 14, 53 L.Ed. 97; Adamson v. California, 332 U.S. 46, 67 S.Ct. 1672, 91 L.Ed. 1903.[1]

The petitioner was arrested during a gambling raid in 1959 by Hartford, Connecticut, police. He pleaded guilty to the crime of pool selling, a misdemeanor, and was sentenced to one year in jail and fined $500. The sentence was ordered to be suspended after 90 days, at which time he was to be placed on probation for two years. About 16 months after his guilty plea, petitioner was ordered to testify before a referee appointed by the Superior Court of Hartford County to conduct an inquiry into alleged gambling and other criminal activities in the county. The petitioner was asked a number of questions related to events surrounding his arrest and conviction. He refused to answer any question "on the grounds it may tend to incriminate me." The Superior Court adjudged him in contempt, and committed him to prison until he was willing to answer the questions. Petitioner's application for a writ of habeas corpus was denied by the Superior Court, and the Connecticut Supreme Court of Errors affirmed. 150 Conn. 220, 187 A.2d 744. The latter court held that the Fifth Amendment's privilege against self-incrimination was not available to a witness in a state proceeding, that the Fourteenth Amendment extended no privilege to him, and that the petitioner had not properly invoked the privilege available under the Connecticut Constitution. We granted certiorari. 373 U.S. 948, 83 S.Ct. 1680, 10 L.Ed.2d 704. We reverse. We hold that the Fourteenth Amendment guaranteed the petitioner the protection of the Fifth Amendment's privilege against self-incrimination, and that under the applicable federal standard, the Connecticut Supreme Court of Errors erred in holding that the privilege was not properly invoked.

The extent to which the Fourteenth Amendment prevents state invasion of rights enumerated in the first eight Amendments has been considered in numerous cases in this Court since the Amendment's adoption in 1868. Although many Justices have deemed the Amendment to incorporate all eight of the Amendments,[2] the

[1] In both cases the question was whether comment upon the failure of an accused to take the stand in his own defense in a state prosecution violated the privilege. It was assumed, but not decided, in both cases that such comment in a federal prosecution for a federal offense would infringe the provision of the Fifth Amendment that "no person * * * shall be compelled in any criminal case to be a witness against himself." For other

statements by the Court that the Fourteenth Amendment does not apply the federal privilege in state proceedings, see Cohen v. Hurley, 366 U.S. 117, 127–129, 81 S.Ct. 954, 960–961, 6 L.Ed.2d 156; Snyder v. Commonwealth of Massachusetts, 291 U.S. 97, 105, 54 S.Ct. 330, 332, 78 L.Ed. 674.

[2] Ten Justices have supported this view. See Gideon v. Wainwright, 372 U.S. 335, 346, 83 S.Ct. 792, 797, 9 L.Ed.2d 799, (opinion of MR. JUS-

view which has thus far prevailed dates from the decision in 1897 in Chicago, B. & Q. R. Co. v. Chicago, 166 U.S. 226, 17 S.Ct. 581, 41 L.Ed. 979, which held that the Due Process Clause requires the States to pay just compensation for private property taken for public use.[3] It was on the authority of that decision that the Court said in 1908 in Twining v. New Jersey, supra, that "it is possible that some of the personal rights safeguarded by the first eight Amendments against national action may also be safeguarded against state action, because a denial of them would be a denial of due process of law." 211 U.S., at 99, 29 S.Ct., at 19.

The Court has not hesitated to re-examine past decisions according the Fourteenth Amendment a less central role in the preservation of basic liberties than that which was contemplated by its Framers when they added the Amendment to our constitutional scheme. Thus, although the Court as late as 1922 said that "neither the Fourteenth Amendment nor any other provision of the Constitution of the United States imposes upon the States any restrictions about 'freedom of speech' * * *," Prudential Ins. Co. of America v. Cheek, 259 U.S. 530, 543, 42 S.Ct. 516, 522, 66 L.Ed. 1044, three years later Gitlow v. New York, 268 U.S. 652, 45 S.Ct. 625, 69 L.Ed. 1138, initiated a series of decisions which today hold immune from state invasion every First Amendment protection for

---

TICE DOUGLAS). The Court expressed itself as unpersuaded to this view in In re Kemmler, 136 U.S. 436, 448–449, 10 S.Ct. 930, 934, 34 L.Ed. 519; McElvaine v. Brush, 142 U.S. 155, 158–159, 12 S.Ct. 156, 157, 35 L.Ed. 971; Maxwell v. Dow, 176 U.S. 581, 597–598, 20 S.Ct. 448, 454–455, 44 L.Ed. 597; Twining v. New Jersey, supra, 211 U.S. p. 96, 29 S.Ct. p. 18. See Spies v. Illinois, 123 U.S. 131, 8 S.Ct. 21, 22, 31 L. Ed. 80. Decisions that particular guarantees were not safeguarded against state action by the Privileges and Immunities Clause or other provision of the Fourteenth Amendment are: United States v. Cruikshank, 92 U.S. 542, 551, 23 L.Ed. 588; Prudential Ins. Co. of America v. Cheek, 259 U.S. 530, 543, 42 S.Ct. 516, 522 (First Amendment); Presser v. Illinois, 116 U.S. 252, 265, 6 S.Ct. 580, 584, 29 L.Ed. 615 (Second Amendment); Weeks v. United States, 232 U.S. 383, 398, 34 S.Ct. 341, 348, 58 L.Ed. 652 (Fourth Amendment); Hurtado v. California, 110 U.S. 516, 538, 4 S.Ct. 111, 122, 28 L.Ed. 232 (Fifth Amendment requirement of grand jury indictments); Palko v. Connecticut, 302 U.S. 319, 328, 58 S.Ct. 149, 153, 82 L.Ed. 288 (Fifth Amendment double jeopardy); Maxwell v. Dow supra, at 595, 20 S.Ct., at 454 (Sixth Amendment jury trial); Walker v. Sauvinet, 92 U.S. 90, 92, 23 L.Ed. 678 (Seventh Amendment jury trial); In re Kemmler, supra; McElvaine v. Brush, supra; O'Neil v. Vermont, 144 U.S. 323, 332, 12 S.Ct. 693, 697, 36 L.Ed. 450 (Eighth Amendment prohibition against cruel and unusual punishment).

[3] In Barron, for Use of Tiernan v. Mayor and City Council of City of Baltimore, 7 Pet. 243, 8 L.Ed. 672, decided before the adoption of the Fourteenth Amendment, Chief Justice Marshall, speaking for the Court, held that this right was not secured against state action by the Fifth Amendment's provision: "Nor shall private property be taken for public use, without just compensation."

the cherished rights of mind and spirit—the freedoms of speech, press, religion, assembly, association, and petition for redress of grievances.[4]

Similarly, Palko v. Connecticut, 302 U.S. 319, 58 S.Ct. 149, decided in 1937, suggested that the rights secured by the Fourth Amendment were not protected against state action, citing, 302 U.S., at 324, 58 S.Ct., at 151, the statement of the Court in 1914 in Weeks v. United States, 232 U.S. 383, 398, 34 S.Ct. 341, 346, that "the Fourth Amendment is not directed to individual misconduct of [state] officials." In 1961, however, the Court held that in the light of later decisions,[5] it was taken as settled that "* * * the Fourth Amendment's right of privacy has been declared enforceable against the States through the Due Process Clause of the Fourteenth * * *." Mapp v. Ohio, 367 U.S. 643, 655, 81 S.Ct. 1684, 1691, 6 L.Ed.2d 1081. Again, although the Court held in 1942 that in a state prosecution for a noncapital offense, "appointment of counsel is not a fundamental right," Betts v. Brady, 316 U.S. 455, 471, 62 S.Ct. 1252, 1261, 86 L.Ed. 1595; cf. Powell v. Alabama, 287 U.S. 45, 53 S.Ct. 55, 77 L.Ed. 158, only last Term this decision was re-examined and it was held that provision of counsel in all criminal cases was "a fundamental right, essential to a fair trial," and thus was made obligatory on the States by the Fourteenth Amendment. Gideon v. Wainwright, 372 U.S. 335, 343–344, 83 S.Ct. 792, 796.[6]

We hold today that the Fifth Amendment's exception from compulsory self-incrimination is also protected by the Fourteenth

---

[4] E. g., Gitlow v. New York, 268 U.S. 652, 666, 45 S.Ct. 625, 629 (speech and press); Lovell v. City of Griffin, 303 U.S. 444, 450, 58 S.Ct. 666, 668, 82 L.Ed. 949 (speech and press); New York Times Co. v. Sullivan, 376 U.S. 254, 84 S.Ct. 110, 11 L.Ed.2d 686 (speech and press); Staub v. City of Baxley, 355 U.S. 313, 321, 78 S.Ct. 277, 281, 2 L.Ed.2d 302 (speech); Grosjean v. American Press Co., 297 U.S. 233, 244, 56 S.Ct. 444, 446, 80 L.Ed. 660 (press); Cantwell v. Connecticut, 310 U.S. 296, 303, 60 S.Ct. 900, 903, 84 L.Ed. 1213 (religion); De Jonge v. Oregon, 299 U.S. 353, 364, 57 S.Ct. 255, 259, 81 L.Ed. 278 (assembly); Shelton v. Tucker, 364 U.S. 479, 486, 81 S.Ct. 247, 251, 5 L.Ed.2d 231 (association); Louisiana ex rel. Gremillion v. N.A.A.C.P., 366, U.S. 293, 296, 81 S.Ct. 1333, 1335, 6 L.Ed.2d 301 (association); N.A.A.C.P. v. Button, 371 U.S. 415, 83 S.Ct. 328, 9 L.Ed.2d 405 (association and speech); Brotherhood of Railroad Trainmen v. Virginia ex rel. Virginia State Bar, 377 U.S. 1, 84 S.Ct. 1113, 12 L.Ed. 2d 89 (association).

[5] See Wolf v. Colorado, 338 U.S. 25, 27–28, 69 S.Ct. 1359, 1361, 93 L.Ed. 1782; Elkins v. United States, 364 U.S. 206, 213, 80 S.Ct. 1437, 1441, 4 L.Ed.2d 1669.

[6] See also Robinson v. California, 370 U.S. 660, 666, 82 S.Ct. 1417, which, despite In re Kemmler, supra; McElvaine v. Brush, supra; O'Neil v. Vermont, supra, made applicable to the States the Eighth Amendment's ban on cruel and unusual punishments.

Amendment against abridgment by the States. Decisions of the Court since Twining and Adamson have departed from the contrary view expressed in those cases. We discuss first the decisions which forbid the use of coerced confessions in state criminal prosecutions.

Brown v. Mississippi, 297 U.S. 278, 56 S.Ct. 461, 80 L.Ed. 682, was the first case in which the Court held that the Due Process Clause prohibited the States from using the accused's coerced confessions against him. The Court in Brown felt impelled, in light of Twining, to say that its conclusion did not involve the privilege against self-incrimination. "Compulsion by torture to extort a confession is a different matter." 297 U.S., at 285, 56 S.Ct., at 464. But this distinction was soon abandoned, and today the admissibility of a confession in a state criminal prosecution is tested by the same standard applied in federal prosecutions since 1897, when, in Bram v. United States, 168 U.S. 532, 18 S.Ct. 183, 42 L.Ed. 568, the Court held that "[i]n criminal trials, in the courts of the United States, wherever a question arises whether a confession is incompetent because not voluntary, the issue is controlled by that portion of the Fifth Amendment to the Constitution of the United States, commanding that no person 'shall be compelled in any criminal case to be a witness against himself.' " Id., 168 U.S. at 542, 18 S.Ct. at 187. Under this test, the constitutional inquiry is not whether the conduct of state officers in obtaining the confession was shocking, but whether the confession was "free and voluntary: that is, [it] must not be extracted by any sort of threats or violence, nor obtained by any direct or implied promises, however slight, nor by the exertion of any improper influence. * * *" Id., 168 U.S. at 542–543, 18 S.Ct. at 186–187; see also Hardy v. United States, 186 U.S. 224, 229, 22 S.Ct. 889, 891, 46 L.Ed. 1137; Ziang Sun Wan v. United States, 266 U.S. 1, 14, 45 S.Ct. 1, 3, 69 L.Ed. 131; Smith v. United States, 348 U.S. 147, 150, 75 S.Ct. 194, 196, 99 L.Ed. 192. In other words the person must not have been compelled to incriminate himself. We have held inadmissible even a confession secured by so mild a whip as the refusal, under certain circumstances, to allow a suspect to call his wife until he confessed. Haynes v. Washington, 373 U.S. 503, 83 S.Ct. 1336, 10 L.Ed. 2d 513.

The marked shift to the federal standard in state cases began with Lisenba v. California, 314 U.S. 219, 62 S.Ct. 280, 86 L.Ed. 166, where the Court spoke of the accused's "free choice to admit, to deny, or to refuse to answer." Id., 314 U.S. at 241, 62 S.Ct. at 292. See Ashcraft v. Tennessee, 322 U.S. 143, 64 S.Ct. 921, 88 L.Ed. 1192; Malinski v. New York, 324 U.S. 401, 65 S.Ct. 781, 89 L.Ed.

1029; Spano v. New York, 360 U.S. 315, 79 S.Ct. 1202, 3 L.Ed.2d 1265; Lynumn v. Illinois, 372 U.S. 528, 83 S.Ct. 917, 9 L.Ed.2d 922; Haynes v. Washington, 373 U.S. 503. The shift reflects recognition that the American system of criminal prosecution is accusatorial, not inquisitorial, and that the Fifth Amendment privilege is its essential mainstay. Rogers v. Richmond, 365 U.S. 534, 541, 81 S.Ct. 735, 739, 5 L.Ed.2d 760. Governments, state and federal, are thus constitutionally compelled to establish guilt by evidence independently and freely secured, and may not by coercion prove a charge against an accused out of his own mouth. Since the Fourteenth Amendment prohibits the States from inducing a person to confess through "sympathy falsely aroused," Spano v. New York, supra, at 323, 79 S.Ct., at 1207, or other like inducement far short of "compulsion by torture," Haynes v. Washington, supra, it follows *a fortiori* that it also forbids the States to resort to imprisonment, as here, to compel him to answer questions that might incriminate him. The Fourteenth Amendment secures against state invasion the same privilege that the Fifth Amendment guarantees against federal infringement—the right of a person to remain silent unless he chooses to speak in the unfettered exercise of his own will, and to suffer no penalty, as held in Twining, for such silence.

This conclusion is fortified by our recent decision in Mapp v. Ohio, 367 U.S. 643, 81 S.Ct. 1684, overruling Wolf v. Colorado, 338 U.S. 25, 69 S.Ct. 1359, 93 L.Ed. 1782, which had held "that in a prosecution in a State court for a State crime the Fourteenth Amendment does not forbid the admission of evidence obtained by an unreasonable search and seizure," 338 U.S., at 33, 69 S.Ct., at 1364. Mapp held that the Fifth Amendment privilege against self-incrimination implemented the Fourth Amendment in such cases, and that the two guarantees of personal security conjoined in the Fourteenth Amendment to make the exclusionary rule obligatory upon the States. We relied upon the great Case of Boyd v. United States, 116 U.S. 616, 6 S.Ct. 524, 29 L.Ed. 746, decided in 1886, which, considering the Fourth and Fifth Amendments as running "almost into each other," id., 116 U.S., at 630, 6 S.Ct., at 532, held that "Breaking into a house and opening boxes and drawers are circumstances of aggravation; but any forcible and compulsory extortion of a man's own testimony, or of his private papers to be used as evidence to convict him of crime, or to forfeit his goods, is within the condemnation of [those Amendments] * * *." 116 U.S., at 630, 6 S.Ct., at 532. We said in Mapp:

"We find that, as to the Federal Government, the Fourth and Fifth Amendments and, as to the States, the freedom from unconscion-

205

able invasions of privacy and the freedom from convictions based upon coerced confessions do enjoy an 'intimate relation' in their perpetuation of 'principles of humanity and civil liberty [secured] * * * only after years of struggle,' Bram v. United States, 1897, 168 U.S. 532, 543–544, 18 S.Ct. 183 * * *. The philosophy of each Amendment and of each freedom is complementary to, although not dependent upon, that of the other in its sphere of influence— the very least that together they assure in either sphere is that no man is to be convicted on unconstitutional evidence." 367 U.S., at 656–657, 81 S.Ct., at 1692.

In thus returning to the Boyd view that the privilege is one of the "principles of a free government," 116 U.S., at 632, 6 S.Ct., at 533,[7] Mapp necessarily repudiated the Twining concept of the privilege as a mere rule of evidence "best defended not as an unchangeable principle of nuiversal justice, but as a law proved by experience to be expedient." 211 U.S., at 113, 29 S.Ct., at 25.

The respondent Sheriff concedes in his brief that under our decisions, particularly those involving coerced confessions, "the accusatorial system has become a fundamental part of the fabric of our society and, hence, is enforceable against the States."[8] The State urges, however, that the availability of the federal privilege to a witness in a state inquiry is to be determined according to a less stringent standard than is applicable in a federal proceeding. We disagree. We have held that the guarantees of the First Amendment, Gitlow v. New York, supra; Cantwell v. Connecticut,

[7] Boyd had said of the privilege, "* * * any compulsory discovery by extorting the party's oath * * * to convict him of crime * * * is contrary to the principles of a free government. It is abhorrent to the instincts of an Englishman; it is abhorrent to the instincts of an American. It may suit the purposes of despotic power; but it cannot abide the pure atmosphere of political liberty and personal freedom." 116 U.S., at 631–632, 6 S.Ct., at 533.

Dean Griswold has said: "I believe the Fifth Amendment is, and has been through this period of crisis, an expression of the moral striving of the community. It has been a reflection of our common conscience, a symbol of the America which stirs our hearts." The Fifth Amendment Today 73 (1955).

[8] The brief states further: "Underlying the decisions excluding coerced confessions is the implicit assumption that an accused is privileged against incriminating himself, either in the jail house, the grand jury room, or on the witness stand in a public trial. * * *

"* * * It is fundamentally inconsistent to suggest, as the Court's opinions now suggest, that the State is entirely free to compel an accused to incriminate himself before a grand jury, or at the trial, but cannot do so in the police station. Frank recognition of the fact that the Due Process Clause prohibits the States from enforcing their laws by compelling the accused to confess, regardless of where such compulsion occurs, would not only clarify the principles involved in confession cases, but would assist the States significantly in their efforts to comply with the limitations placed upon them by the Fourteenth Amendment."

310 U.S. 296, 60 S.Ct. 900, 84 L.Ed. 1213; Louisiana ex rel. Gremillion v. N.A.A.C.P., 366 U.S. 293, 81 S.Ct. 1333, 6 L.Ed.2d 301, the prohibition of unreasonable searches and seizures of the Fourth Amendment, Ker v. California, 374 U.S. 23, 83 S.Ct. 1623, 10 L.Ed. 726, and the right to counsel guaranteed by the Sixth Amendment, Gideon v. Wainwright, supra, are all to be enforced against the States under the Fourteenth Amendment according to the same standards that protect those personal rights against federal encroachment. In the coerced confession cases, involving the policies of the privilege itself, there has been no suggestion that a confession might be considered coerced if used in a federal but not a state tribunal. The Court thus has rejected the notion that the Fourteenth Amendment applies to the States only a "watered-down, subjective version of the individual guarantees of the Bill of Rights," Ohio ex rel. Eaton v. Price, 364 U.S. 263, 275, 80 S.Ct. 1463, 1470, 4 L.Ed.2d 1708 (dissenting opinion). If Cohen v. Hurley, 366 U.S. 117, 81 S.Ct. 954, and Adamson v. California, supra, suggest such an application of the privilege against self-incrimination, that suggestion cannot survive recognition of the degree to which the Twining view of the privilege has been eroded. What is accorded is a privilege of refusing to incriminate one's self, and the feared prosecution may be by either federal or state authorities. Murphy v. Waterfront Comm'n, post, p. 52, 84 S.Ct. 1594. It would be incongruous to have different standards determine the validity of a claim of privilege based on the same feared prosecution, depending on whether the claim was asserted in a state or federal court. Therefore, the same standards must determine whether an accused's silence in either a federal or state proceeding is justified.

We turn to the petitioner's claim that the State of Connecticut denied him the protection of his federal privilege. It must be considered irrelevant that the petitioner was a witness in a statutory inquiry and not a defendant in a criminal prosecution, for it has long been settled that the privilege protects witnesses in similar federal inquiries. Counselman v. Hitchcock, 142 U.S. 547, 12 S.Ct. 195, 35 L.Ed. 1110; McCarthy v. Arndstein, 266 U.S. 34, 45 S.Ct. 16, 69 L.Ed. 158; Hoffman v. United States, 341 U.S. 479, 71 S.Ct. 814, 95 L.Ed. 1118. We recently elaborated the content of the federal standard in Hoffman:

"The privilege afforded not only extends to answers that would in themselves support a conviction* * * but likewise embraces those which would furnish a link in the chain of evidence needed to prosecute. * * * [I]f the witness, upon interposing his claim, were required to prove the hazard * * * he would be compelled to surrender the very protection which the privilege is designed to guarantee. To sustain the privilege, it need only be evident from the implications of the question, in the setting in which it is asked, that a responsive answer to the question or an explanation of why it cannot be answered might be dangerous because injurious disclosure could result." 341 U.S., at 486–487, 71 S.Ct. at 818.

We also said that, in applying that test, the judge must be " *'perfectly clear,* from a careful consideration of all the circumstances in the case, that the witness is mistaken, and that the answer[s] *cannot possibly* have such tendency' to incriminate." 341 U.S., at 488, 71 S.Ct., at 819.

The State of Connecticut argues that the Connecticut courts properly applied the federal standards to the facts of this case. We disagree.

The investigation in the course of which petitioner was questioned began when the Superior Court in Hartford County appointed the Honorable Ernest A. Inglis, formerly Chief Justice of Connecticut, to conduct an inquiry into whether there was reasonable cause to believe that crimes, including gambling, were being committed in Hartford County. Petitioner appeared on January 16 and 25, 1961, and in both instances he was asked substantially the same questions about the circumstances surrounding his arrest and conviction for pool selling in late 1959. The questions which petitioner refused to answer may be summarized as follows: (1) for whom did he work on September 11, 1959; (2) who selected and paid his counsel in connection with his arrest on that date and subsequent conviction; (3) who selected and paid his bondsman; (4) who paid his fine; (5) what was the name of the tenant of the apartment in which he was arrested; and (6) did he know John Bergoti. The Connecticut Supreme Court of Errors ruled that the answers to these questions could not tend to incriminate him because the defenses of double jeopardy and the running of the one-year statute of limitations on misdemeanors would defeat any prosecution growing out of his answers to the first five questions. As for the sixth question, the court held that petitioner's failure to explain how a revelation of his relationship with Bergoti would incriminate him vitiated his claim to the protection of the privilege afforded by state law.

The conclusions of the Court of Errors, tested by the federal standard, fail to take sufficient account of the setting in which the questions were asked. The interrogation was part of a wide-ranging inquiry into crime, including gambling, in Hartford. It was admitted on behalf of the State at oral argument—and indeed it is obvious from the questions themselves—that the State desired to elicit from the petitioner the identity of the person who ran the pool-selling operation in connection with which he had been arrested in 1959. It was apparent that petitioner might apprehend that if this person were still engaged in unlawful activity, disclosure of his name might furnish a link in a chain of evidence sufficient to connect the petitioner with a more recent crime for which he might still be prosecuted.[9]

Analysis of the sixth question, concerning whether petitioner knew John Bergoti, yields a similar conclusion. In the context of the inquiry, it should have been apparent to the referee that Bergoti was suspected by the State to be involved in some way in the subject matter of the investigation. An affirmative answer to the question might well have either connected petitioner with a more recent crime, or at least have operated as a waiver of his privilege with reference to his relationship with a possible criminal. See Rogers v. United States, 340 U.S. 367, 71 S.Ct. 438, 95 L.Ed. 344. We conclude, therefore, that as to each of the questions, it was "evident from the implications of the question, in the setting in which it [was] asked, that a responsive answer to the question or an explanation of why it [could not] be answered might be dangerous because injurious disclosure could result," Hoffman v. United States, 341 U.S., at 486–487, 71 S.Ct. 818; see Singleton v. United States, 343 U.S. 944, 72 S.Ct. 1041.

Reversed.

While Mr. Justice DOUGLAS joins the opinion of the Court, he also adheres to his concurrence in Gideon v. Wainwright, 372 U.S. 335, 345, 83 S.Ct. 792, 797.

Mr. Justice HARLAN, whom Mr. Justice CLARK joins, dissenting.

Connecticut has adjudged this petitioner in contempt for refusing to answer questions in a state inquiry. The courts of the State, whose laws embody a privilege against self-incrimination, refused to recognize the petitioner's claim of privilege, finding that the questions asked him were not incriminatory. This Court now

---

[9] See Greenberg v. United States, 343 U.S. 918, 72 S.Ct. 674, 96 L.Ed. 1332, reversing per curiam, 3 Cir., 192 F.2d 201; Singleton v. United States, 343 U.S. 944, 72 S.Ct. 1041, 96 L. Ed. 1349, reversing per curiam, 3 Cir., 193 F.2d 464. In United States v. Coffey, 198 F.2d 438 (C. A.3d Cir.), cited with approval in Emspak v. United States, 349 U.S. 190, 75 S.Ct. 687, 99 L.Ed. 997, the Court of Appeals for the Third Circuit stated: "in determining whether the witness really apprehends danger in answering a question, the judge cannot permit himself to be skeptical; rather must he be acutely aware that in the deviousness of crime and its detection incrimination may be approached and achieved by obscure and unlikely lines of inquiry." 198 F.2d, at 440–441.

holds the contempt adjudication unconstitutional because, it is decided: (1) the Fourteenth Amendment makes the Fifth Amendment privilege against self-incrimination applicable to the States; (2) the federal standard justifying a claim of this privilege likewise applies to the States; and (3) judged by that standard the petitioner's claim of privilege should have been upheld.

Believing that the reasoning behind the Court's decision carries extremely mischievous, if not dangerous, consequences for our federal system in the realm of criminal law enforcement, I must dissent. The importance of the issue presented and the serious incursion which the Court makes on time-honored, basic constitutional principles justify a full exposition of my reasons.

I.

I can only read the Court's opinion as accepting in fact what it rejects in theory: the application to the States, via the Fourteenth Amendment, of the forms of federal criminal procedure embodied within the first eight Amendments to the Constitution. While it is true that the Court deals today with only one aspect of state criminal procedure, and rejects the wholesale "incorporation" of such federal constitutional requirements, the logical gap between the Court's premises and its novel constitutional conclusion can, I submit, be bridged only by the additional premise that the Due Process Clause of the Fourteenth Amendment is a shorthand directive to this Court to pick and choose among the provisions of the first eight Amendments and apply those chosen, freighted with their entire accompanying body of federal doctrine, to law enforcement in the States.

I accept and agree with the proposition that continuing re-examination of the constitutional conception of Fourteenth Amendment "due process" of law is required, and that development of the community's sense of justice may in time lead to expansion of the protection which due process affords. In particular in this case, I agree that principles of justice to which due process gives expression, as reflected in decisions of this Court, prohibit a State, as the Fifth Amendment prohibits the Federal Government, from imprisoning a person *solely* because he refuses to give evidence which may incriminate him under the laws of the State.[1] I do not under-

---

[1] That precise question has not heretofore been decided by this Court. Twining v. New Jersey, 211 U.S. 78, 29 S.Ct. 14, and the cases which followed it, see infra, p. 17, all involved issues not precisely similar. Although the Court has stated broadly that an individual could "be required to incriminate himself in * * * state proceedings," Cohen v. Hurley, 366 U.S. 117, 127, 81 S.Ct. 954, 960, the context in which such statements were made was that the State had in each case

stand, however, how this process of re-examination, which must refer always to the guiding standard of due process of law, including, of course, reference to the particular guarantees of the Bill of Rights, can be short-circuited by the simple device of incorporating into due process, without critical examination, the whole body of law which surrounds a specific prohibition directed against the Federal Government. The consequence of such an approach to due process as it pertains to the States is inevitably disregard of all relevant differences which may exist between state and federal criminal law and its enforcement. The ultimate result is compelled uniformity, which is inconsistent with the purpose of our federal system and which is achieved either by encroachment on the States' sovereign powers or by dilution in federal law enforcement of the specific protections found in the Bill of Rights.

II.

As recently as 1961, this Court reaffirmed that "the Fifth Amendment's privilege against self-incrimination," ante, p. 3, was not applicable against the States. Cohen v. Hurley, 366 U.S. 117, 81 S.Ct. 954. The question had been most fully explored in Twining v. New Jersey, 211 U.S. 78, 29 S.Ct. 14. Since 1908, when Twining was decided, this Court has adhered to the view there expressed that "the exemption from compulsory self-incrimination in the courts of the States is not secured by any part of the Federal Constitution," 211 U.S., at 114, 29 S.Ct., at 26. Snyder v. Commonwealth of Massachusetts, 291 U.S. 97, 105, 54 S.Ct. 330; Brown v. Mississippi, 297 U.S. 278, 285, 56 S.Ct. 461, 464; Palko v. Connecticut, 302 U.S. 319, 324, 58 S.Ct. 149, 151; Adamson v. California, 332 U.S. 46, 67 S.Ct. 1672, 91 L.Ed. 1903; Knapp v. Schweitzer, 357 U.S. 371, 374, 78 S.Ct. 1302, 1304, 2 L.Ed.2d 1393; Cohen, supra. Although none of

recognized the right to remain silent. In Twining, supra, until now the primary authority, the Court noted that "all the states of the Union have, from time to time, with varying form, but uniform meaning, included the privilege in their Constitutions, except the states of New Jersey and Iowa, and in those states it is held to be part of the existing law." 211 U.S., at 92, 29 S.Ct., at 16.

While I do not believe that the coerced confession cases furnish any basis for incorporating the Fifth Amendment into the Fourteenth, see infra, pp. 17–20, they do, it seems to me, carry an impli-

cation that coercion to incriminate oneself, even when under the forms of law, cf. Brown v. Mississippi, 297 U.S. 278, 285, 56 S.Ct. 461, 464, discussed infra, pp. 17–18, is inconsistent with due process. Since every State already recognizes a privilege against self-incrimination so defined, see VIII Wigmore, Evidence (McNaughton rev. 1961), § 2252, the effect of including such a privilege in due process is only to create the possibility that a federal question, to be decided under the Due Process Clause, would be raised by a State's refusal to accept a claim of the privilege.

these cases involved a commitment to prison for refusing to incriminate oneself under state law, and they are relevantly distinguishable from this case on that narrow ground,[2] it is perfectly clear from them that until today it has been regarded as settled law that the *Fifth Amendment* privilege did not, by any process of reasoning, apply *as such* to the States.

The Court suggests that this consistent line of authority has been undermined by the concurrent development of constitutional doctrine in the areas of coerced confessions and search and seizure. This is *post facto* reasoning at best. Certainly there has been no intimation until now that Twining has been tacitly overruled.

It was in Brown v. Mississippi, supra, that this Court first prohibited the use of a coerced confession in a state criminal trial. The petitioners in Brown had been tortured until they confessed. The Court was hardly making an artificial distinction when it said: "* * * [T]he question of the right of the State to withdraw the privilege against self-incrimination is not here involved. The compulsion to which the quoted statements [from Twining and Snyder, supra,] refer is that of the *processes of justice* by which the accused may be called as a witness and required to testify. *Compulsion by torture* to extort a confession is a different matter."[3] 297 U.S., at 285, 56 S.Ct. at 464. (Emphasis supplied.)

The majority is simply wrong when it asserts that this perfectly understandable distinction "was soon abandoned," ante, pp. 6–7. In none of the cases cited, ante, pp. 7–8, in which was developed the full sweep of the constitutional prohibition against the use of coerced confessions at state trials, was there anything to suggest that the Fifth Amendment was being made applicable to state proceedings. In Lisenba v. California, 314 U.S. 219, 62 S.Ct. 280, the privilege against self-incrimination is not mentioned. The relevant question before the Court was whether "the evidence [of coercion] requires that we set aside the finding of two courts and a jury, and adjudge the admission of the confessions so fundamentally unfair, so contrary to the common concept of ordered liberty, as to amount to a taking of life without due process of law." Id., 314 U.S. at 238, 62 S.Ct. at 291. The question was the same in Ashcraft v. Tennessee, 322 U.S. 143, 64 S.Ct. 921, 88 L.Ed. 1192; the Court there adverted to the "third degree," e. g., id., 322

---

[2] See note 1, supra.

[3] Nothing in the opinion in Brown supports the Court's intimation here, ante, p. 6, that if Twining had not been on the books, reversal of the convictions would have been based on the Fifth Amendment. The Court made it plain in Brown that it regarded the trial use of a confession extracted by torture as on a par with domination of a trial by a mob, see, e. g., Moore v. Dempsey, 261 U.S. 86, 43 S.Ct. 265, 67 L.Ed. 543, where the trial "is a mere pretense," 297 U.S., at 286, 56 S.Ct., at 465.

212

U.S. at 150, note 5, 64 S.Ct. at 924, and "secret inquisitorial practices," id., 322 U.S. at 152, 64 S.Ct. at 925. Malinski v. New York, 324 U.S. 401, 65 S.Ct. 781, is the same; the privilege against self-incrimination is not mentioned.[4] So too in Spano v. New York, 360 U.S. 315, 79 S.Ct. 1202; Lynumn v. Illinois, 372 U.S. 528, 83 U.S. 503, 83 S.Ct. 1336; and Haynes v. Washington, 373 U.S. 503. Finally, in Rogers v. Richmond, 365 U.S. 534, 81 S.Ct. 735, although the Court did recognize that "ours is an accusatorial and not an inquisitorial system," id., 365 U.S. at 541, 81 S.Ct. at 739, it is clear that the Court was concerned only with the problem of coerced confessions, see ibid.; the opinion includes nothing to support the Court's assertion here, ante, p. 7, that "the Fifth Amendment privilege is * * * [the] essential mainstay" of our system.

In Adamson, supra, the Court made it explicit that it did not regard the increasingly strict standard for determining the admissibility at trial of an out-of-court confession as undermining the holding of Twining. After stating that "the due process clause does not protect, by virtue of its mere existence, the accused's freedom from giving testimony by compulsion in state trials that is secured to him against federal interference by the Fifth Amendment," the Court said: "The due process clause forbids compulsion to testify by fear of hurt, torture or exhaustion. It forbids any other type of coercion that falls within the scope of due process." 332 U.S., at 54, 67 S.Ct. at 1676 (footnotes omitted). Plainly, the Court regarded these two lines of cases as distinct. See also Palko v. Connecticut, supra, 302 U.S., at 326, 58 S.Ct. at 152, to the same effect.[5] Cohen supra, which adhered to Twining, was decided after all but a few of the confession cases which the Court mentions.

The coerced confession cases are relevant to the problem of this case not because they overruled Twining sub silentio, but rather because they applied the same standard of fundamental fairness

---

[4] "And so, when a conviction in a state court is properly here for review, under a claim that a right protected by the Fourteenth Amendment has been denied, the question is not whether the record can be found to disclose an infraction of one of the specific provisions of the first eight amendments. To come concretely to the present case, the question is not whether the record permits a finding, by a tenuous process of psychological assumptions and reasoning, that Malinski by means of a confession was forced to self-incrimination in defiance of the Fifth Amendment. The ex-

act question is whether the criminal proceedings which resulted in his conviction deprived him of the due process of law by which he was constitutionally entitled to have his guilt determined." Malinski, supra. 324 U.S. at 416, 65 S.Ct. at 788 (opinion of Frankfurter, J.).

[5] In Adamson and Palko, supra, which adhered to the rule announced in Twining, supra, the Court cited some of the very cases now relied on by the majority to show that Twining was gradually being eroded. 332 U.S., at 54, notes 12, 13, 67 S.Ct., at 1676; 302 U.S., at 325, 326, 58 S.Ct., at 151, 152.

which is applicable here. The recognition in them that federal supervision of state criminal procedures must be directly based on the requirements of due process is entirely inconsistent with the theory here espoused by the majority. The parallel treatment of federal and state cases involving coerced confessions resulted from the fact that the same demand of due process was applicable in both; it was not the consequence of the automatic engrafting of federal law construing constitutional provisions inapplicable to the States onto the Fourteenth Amendment.

The decision in Mapp v. Ohio, 367 U.S. 643, 81 S.Ct. 1684, that evidence unconstitutionally seized, see Wolf v. Colorado, 338 U.S. 25, 28, 69 S.Ct. 1359, 1361, may not be used in a state criminal trial furnishes no "fortification," see ante, p. 8, for today's decision. The very passage from the Mapp opinion which the Court quotes, ante, p. 9, makes explicit the distinct bases of the exclusionary rule as applied in federal and state courts:

"We find that, as to the Federal Government, the Fourth and Fifth Amendments and, as to the States, the freedom from unconscionable invasions of privacy and the freedom from convictions based upon coerced confessions do enjoy an 'intimate relation' in their perpetuation of 'principles of humanity and civil liberty [secured] * * * only after years of struggle.' Bram v. United States, 168 U.S. 532, 543–544 (1897)." 367 U.S., at 656–657 (footnote omitted). See also id., at 655.

Although the Court discussed Boyd v. United States, 116 U.S. 616, 6 S.Ct. 524, a federal case involving both the Fourth and Fifth Amendments, nothing in Mapp supports the statement, ante, p. 8, that the Fifth Amendment was part of the basis for extending the exclusionary rule to the States. The elaboration of Mapp in Ker v. California, 374 U.S. 23, 83 S.Ct. 1623, 10 L.Ed.2d 726, did in my view make the Fourth Amendment applicable to the States through the Fourteenth; but there is nothing in it to suggest that the Fifth Amendment went along as baggage.

III.

The previous discussion shows that this Court's decisions do not dictate the "incorporation" of the Fifth Amendment's privilege against self-incrimination into the Fourteenth Amendment. Approaching the question more broadly, it is equally plain that the line of cases exemplified by Palko v. Connecticut, supra, in which this Court has reconsidered the requirements which the Due Process Clause imposes on the States in the light of current standards, furnishes no general theoretical framework for what the Court does today.

The view of the Due Process Clause of the Fourteenth Amendment which this Court has consistently accepted and which has "thus far prevailed," ante, p. 4, is that its requirements are as "old as a principle of civilized government," Munn v. Illinois, 94 U.S. 113, 123, 24 L.Ed. 77, the specific applications of which must be ascertained "by the gradual process of judicial inclusion and exclusion * * *," Davidson v. New Orleans, 96 U.S. 97, 104, 24 L.Ed. 616. Due process requires "observance of those general rules established in our system of jurisprudence for the security of private rights." Hagar v. Reclamation District No. 108, 111 U.S. 701, 708, 4 S.Ct. 663, 667, 28 L.Ed. 569. See Hurtado v. California, 110 U.S. 516, 537, 4 S.Ct. 111, 121.

"This court has never attempted to define with precision the words 'due process of law' * * *. It is sufficient to say that there are certain immutable principles of justice, which inhere in the very idea of free government which no member of the Union may disregard * * *." Holden v. Hardy, 169 U.S. 366, 389, 18 S.Ct. 383, 387, 42 L.Ed. 780.

It followed from this recognition that due process encompassed the fundamental safeguards of the individual against the abusive exercise of governmental power that some of the restraints on the Federal Government which were specifically enumerated in the Bill of Rights applied also against the States. But, while inclusion of a particular provision in the Bill of Rights might provide historical evidence that the right involved was traditionally regarded as fundamental, inclusion of the right in due process was otherwise entirely independent of the first eight Amendments:

"* * * [I]t is possible that some of the personal rights safeguarded by the first eight Amendments against National action may also be safeguarded against state action, because a denial of them would be a denial of due process of law. * * * *If this is so, it is not because those rights are enumerated in the first eight Amendments, but because they are of such a nature that they are included in the conception of due process of law.*" Twining, supra, 211 U.S. at 99, 29 S.Ct. at 19. (Emphasis supplied.)

Relying heavily on Twining, Mr. Justice Cardozo provided what may be regarded as a classic expression of this approach in Palko v. Connecticut, supra. After considering a number of individual rights (including the right not to incriminate oneself) which were "not of the very essence of a scheme of ordered liberty," id., 302 U.S. at 325, 58 S.Ct. at 152, he said:

"We reach a different plane of social and moral values when we pass to the privileges and immunities that have been taken over from the earlier articles of the federal bill of rights and brought

215

within the Fourteenth Amendment by a process of absorption. These in their origin were effective against the federal government alone. If the Fourteenth Amendment has absorbed them, the process of absorption has had its source in the belief that neither liberty nor justice would exist if they were sacrificed." Id., 302 U.S. at 326, 58 S.Ct. at 152.

Further on, Mr. Justice Cardozo made the independence of the Due Process Clause from the provisions of the first eight Amendments explicit:

"Fundamental * * * in the concept of due process, and so in that of liberty, is the thought that condemnation shall be rendered only after trial. Scott v. McNeal, 154 U.S. 34, 14 S.Ct. 1108, 38 L.Ed. 896; Blackmer v. United States, 284 U.S. 421, 52 S.Ct. 252, 76 L.Ed. 375. The hearing, moreover, must be a real one, not a sham or a pretense. Moore v. Dempsey, 261 U.S. 86, 43 S.Ct. 265, 67 L.Ed. 543; Mooney v. Holohan, 294 U.S. 103, 55 S.Ct. 340, 79 L.Ed. 791. For that reason, ignorant defendants in a capital case were held to have been condemned unlawfully when in truth, though not in form, they were refused the aid of counsel. Powell v. Alabama, supra, 287 U.S. 45, at pages 67, 68, 53 S.Ct. 55, 63, 77 L.Ed. 158, 84 A.L.R. 527. The decision did not turn upon the fact that the benefit of counsel would have been guaranteed to the defendants by the provisions of the Sixth Amendment if they had been prosecuted in a federal court. The decision turned upon the fact that in the particular situation laid before us in the evidence the benefit of counsel was essential to the substance of a hearing." Id., 302 U.S. at 327, 58 S.Ct. at 153.

It is apparent that Mr. Justice Cardozo's metaphor of "absorption" was *not* intended to suggest the transplantation of case law surrounding the specifics of the first eight Amendments to the very different soil of the Fourteenth Amendment's Due Process Clause. For, as he made perfectly plain, what the Fourteenth Amendment requires of the States does not basically depend on what the first eight Amendments require of the Federal Government.

Seen in proper perspective, therefore, the fact that First Amendment protections have generally been given equal scope in the federal and state domains or that in some areas of criminal procedure the Due Process Clause demands as much of the States as the Bill of Rights demands of the Federal Government, is only tangentially relevant to the question now before us. It is toying with constitutional principles to assert that the Court has "rejected the notion that the Fourteenth Amendment applies to the states only a 'watered-down, subjective version of the individual guarantees

216

of the Bill of Rights,' " ante, pp. 10–11. What the Court has, with the single exception of the Ker case, supra, p. 21; see infra, consistently rejected is p. 26, the notion that the Bill of Rights, as such, applies to the States in any aspect at all.

If one attends to those areas to which Court points, ante, p. 10, in which the prohibitions against the state and federal governments have moved in parallel tracks, the cases in fact reveal again that the Court's usual approach has been to ground the prohibitions against state action squarely on due process, without intermediate reliance on any of the first eight Amendments. Although more recently the Court has referred to the First Amendment to describe the protection of free expression against state infringement, earlier cases leave no doubt that such references are "shorthand" for doctrines developed by another route. In Gitlow v. New York, 268 U.S. 652, 666, 45 S.Ct. 625, 630, for example, the Court said:

"For present purposes we may and do assume that freedom of speech and of the press—which are protected by the First Amendment from abridgment by Congress—are among the fundamental personal rights and 'liberties' protected by the due process clause of the Fourteenth Amendment from impairment by the States." The Court went on to consider the extent of those freedoms in the context of state interests. Mr. Justice Holmes, in dissent, said: "The general principle of free speech, it seems to me, must be taken to be included in the Fourteenth Amendment, in view of the scope that has been given to the word 'liberty' as there used, although perhaps it may be accepted with a somewhat larger latitude of interpretation than is allowed to Congress by the sweeping language that governs or ought to govern the laws of the United States." Id., 268 U.S. at 672, 45 S.Ct. at 632.

Chief Justice Hughes, in De Jonge v. Oregon, 299 U.S. 353, 364, 57 S.Ct. 255, 260, gave a similar analysis:

"Freedom of speech and of the press are fundamental rights which are safeguarded by the due process clause of the Fourteenth Amendment of the Federal Constitution. * * * The right of peaceable assembly is a right cognate to those of free speech and free press and is equally fundamental. As this Court said in United States v. Cruikshank, 92 U.S. 542, 552, 23 L.Ed. 588: 'The very idea of a government, republican in form, implies a right on the part of its citizens to meet peaceably for consultation in respect to public affairs and to petition for a redress of grievances.' The First Amendment of the Federal Constitution expressly guarantees that right against abridgment by Congress. But explicit mention there does not argue exclusion elsewhere. For the right is one that cannot be denied without violating those fundamental principles of

217

liberty and justice which lie at the base of all civil and political institutions,—principles which the Fourteenth Amendment embodies in the general terms of its due process clause."

The coerced confession and search and seizure cases have already been considered. The former, decided always directly on grounds of fundamental fairness, furnish no support for the Court's present views. Ker v. California, supra, did indeed incorporate the Fourth Amendment's protection against invasions of privacy into the Due Process Clause. But that case should be regarded as the exception which proves the rule.[6] The right to counsel in state criminal proceedings, which this Court assured in Gideon v. Wainwright, 372 U.S. 335, 83 S.Ct. 792, does not depend on the Sixth Amendment. In Betts v. Brady, 316 U.S. 455, 462, 62 S.Ct. 1252, 1256, this Court had said:

"Due process of law is secured against invasion by the federal Government by the Fifth Amendment, and is safeguarded against state action in identical words by the Fourteenth. The phrase formulates a concept less rigid and more fluid than those envisaged in other specific and particular provisions of the Bill of Rights. Its application is less a matter of rule. Asserted denial is to be tested by an appraisal of the totality of facts in a given case. That which may, in one setting, constitute a denial of fundamental fairness, shocking to the universal sense of justice, may, in other circumstances, and in the light of other considerations, fall short of such denial." (Footnote omitted.)

Although Gideon overruled Betts, the constitutional approach in both cases was the same. Gideon was based on the Court's conclusion, contrary to that reached in Betts, that the appointment of counsel for an indigent criminal defendant *was* essential to the conduct of a fair trial, and was therefore part of due process. 372 U.S., at 342–345, 83 S.Ct. at 795–797.

The Court's approach in the present case is in fact nothing more or less than "incorporation" in snatches. If, however, the Due Process Clause *is* something more than a reference to the Bill of Rights and protects only those rights which derive from fundamental principles, as the majority purports to believe, it is just as contrary to precedent and just as illogical to incorporate the provisions of the Bill of Rights one at a time as it is to incorporate them all at once.

---

[6] Cf. the majority and dissenting opinions in Aguilar v. Texas, 378 U.S. 108, 84 S.Ct. 1509.

IV.

The Court's undiscriminating approach to the Due Process Clause carries serious implications for the sound working of our federal system in the field of criminal law.

The Court concludes, almost without discussion, that "the same standards must determine whether an accused's silence in either a federal or state proceeding is justified," ante, p. 11. About all that the Court offers in explanation of this conclusion is the observation that it would be "incongruous" if different standards governed the assertion of a privilege to remain silent in state and federal tribunals. Such "incongruity," however, is at the heart of our federal system. The powers and responsibilities of the state and federal governments are not congruent; under our Constitution, they are not intended to be. Why should it be thought, as an *a priori* matter, that limitations on the investigative power of the States are in all respects identical with limitations on the investigative power of the Federal Government? This certainly does not follow from the fact that we deal here with constitutional requirements; for the provisions of the Constitution which are construed are different.

As the Court pointed out in Abbate v. United States, 359 U.S. 187, 195, 79 S.Ct. 666, 671, 3 L.Ed.2d 729, "the States under our federal system have the principal responsibility for defining and prosecuting crimes." The Court endangers this allocation of responsibility for the prevention of crime when it applies to the States doctrines developed in the context of federal law enforcement, without any attention to the special problems which the States as a group or particular States may face. If the power of the States to deal with local crime is unduly restricted, the likely consequence is a shift of responsibility in this area to the Federal Government, with its vastly greater resources. Such a shift, if it occurs, may in the end serve to weaken the very liberties which the Fourteenth Amendment safeguards by bringing us closer to the monolithic society which our federalism rejects. Equally dangerous to our liberties is the alternative of watering down protections against the Federal Government embodied in the Bill of Rights so as not unduly to restrict the powers of the States. The dissenting opinion in Aguilar v. Texas, 378 U.S., post, p. 116, 84 S.Ct., p. 1515, evidences that this danger is not imaginary. See my concurring opinion in Aguilar, ibid.

Rather than insisting, almost by rote, that the Connecticut court, in considering the petitioner's claim of privilege, was required to apply the "federal standard," the Court should have fulfilled its responsibility under the Due Process Clause by inquiring whether the proceedings below met the demands of fundamental fairness which due process embodies. Such an approach may not satisfy those who see in the Fourteenth Amendment a set of easily applied "absolutes" which can afford a haven from unsettling doubt. It is, however, truer to the spirit which requires this Court constantly to re-examine fundamental principles and at the same time enjoins it from reading its own preferences into the Constitution.

The Connecticut Supreme Court of Errors gave full and careful consideration to the petitioner's claim that he would incriminate himself if he answered the questions put to him. It noted that its decisions "from a time antedating the adoption of * * * [the Connecticut] constitution in 1818" had upheld a privilege to refuse to answer incriminating questions. 150 Conn. 220, 223, 187 A.2d 744, 746. Stating that federal cases treating the Fifth Amendment privilege had "persuasive force" in interpreting its own constitutional provision, and citing Hoffman v. United States, 341 U.S. 479, 71 S.Ct. 814, in particular, the Supreme Court of Errors described the requirements for assertion of the privilege by quoting from one of its own cases, id., 150 Conn., at 225, 187 A.2d, at 747:

"[A] witness * * * has the right to refuse to answer any question which would tend to incriminate him. But a mere claim on his part that the evidence will tend to incriminate him is not sufficient. * * * [He having] made his claim, it is then * * * [necessary for the judge] to determine in the exercise of a legal discretion whether, from the circumstances of the case and the nature of the evidence which the witness is called upon to give, there is reasonable ground to apprehend danger of criminal liability from his being compelled to answer. That danger 'must be real and appreciable, with reference to the ordinary operation of law in the ordinary course of things—not a danger of an imaginary and unsubstantial character, having reference to some extraordinary and barely possible contingency, so improbable that no reasonable man would suffer it to influence his conduct. We think that a merely remote and naked possibility, out of the ordinary course of law and such as no reasonable man would be affected by, should not be suffered to obstruct the administration of justice. The object of the law is to afford to a party, called upon to give evidence in a proceeding *inter alios*, protection against being brought by means of his own evidence within the penalties of the law. But it would be to convert a salutary protection into a means of abuse if it were to be held that a mere imaginary possibility of danger, however remote and improbable, was sufficient to justify the withholding of evidence essential to the ends of justice.' Cockburn, C. J., in Regina v. Boyes, 1 B. & S. 311, 330 * * *." McCarthy v. Clancy, 110 Conn. 482, 488–489, 148 A. 551, 555.

The court carefully applied the above standard to each question which the petitioner was asked. It dealt first with the question whether he knew John Bergoti. The court said:

"Bergoti is nowhere described or in any way identified, either as to his occupation, actual or reputed, or as to any criminal record he may have had. * * * Malloy made no attempt even to suggest to the court how an answer to the question whether he knew Bergoti could possibly incriminate him. * * * On this state of the record the question was proper, and Malloy's claim of privilege, made without explanation, was correctly overruled. Malloy 'chose to keep the door tightly closed and to deny the court the smallest glimpse of the danger he apprehended. He cannot then complain that we see none.' In re Pillo, 11 N.J. 8, 22, 93 A.2d 176, 183 * * *." 150 Conn., at 226–227, 187 A.2d, at 748.

The remaining questions are summarized in the majority's opinion, ante, p. 12. All of them deal with the circumstances surrounding the petitioner's conviction on a gambling charge in 1959. The court declined to decide "whether, on their face and apart from any consideration of Malloy's immunity from prosecution, the questions should or should not have been answered in the light of his failure to give any hint of explanation as to how answers to them could incriminate him." 150 Conn., at 227, 187 A.2d, at 748. The court considered the State's claim that the petitioner's prior conviction was sufficient to clothe him with immunity from prosecution for other crimes to which the questions might pertain, but declined to rest its decision on that basis. Id., 150 Conn., at 227–229, 187 A.2d, at 748–749. The court concluded, however, that the running of the statute of limitations on misdemeanors committed in 1959 and the absence of any indication that Malloy had engaged in any crime other than a misdemeanor removed all appearance of danger of incrimination from the questions propounded concerning the petitioner's activities in 1959. The court summarized this conclusion as follows:

"In all this, Malloy confounds vague and improbable possiblities of prosecution with reasonably appreciable ones. Under claims like his, it would always be possible to work out some finespun and improbable theory from which an outside chance of prosecution could be envisioned. Such claims are not enough to support a claim of privilege, at least where, as here, a witness suggests no rational explanation of his fears of incrimination, and the questions themselves, under all the circumstances, suggest none." Id., 150 Conn., at 230–231, 187 A.2d, at 750.

Peremptorily rejecting all of the careful analysis of the Connecticut court, this Court creates its own "finespun and improbable theory" about how these questions might have incriminated the petitioner. With respect to his acquaintance with Bergoti, this Court says only:

"In the context of the inquiry, it should have been apparent to the referee that Bergoti was suspected by the State to be involved in some way in the subject matter of the investigation. An affirmative answer to the question might well have either connected petitioner with a more recent crime, or at least have operated as a waiver of his privilege with reference to his relationship with a possible criminal." Ante, pp. 13–14.

The other five questions, treated at length in the Connecticut court's opinion, get equally short shrift from this Court; it takes the majority, unfamiliar with Connecticut law and far removed from the proceedings below, only a dozen lines to consider the questions and conclude that they were incriminating:

"The interrogation was a part of a wide-ranging inquiry into crime, including gambling, in Hartford. It was admitted on behalf of the State at oral argument—and indeed it is obvious from the questions themselves—that the State desired to elicit from the petitioner the identity of the person who ran the pool-selling operation in connection with which he had been arrested in 1959. It was apparent that petitioner might apprehend that if this person were still engaged in unlawful activity, disclosure of his name might furnish a link in a chain of evidence sufficient to connect the petitioner with a more recent crime for which he might still be prosecuted." (Footnote omitted.) Ante, p. 13.

I do not understand how anyone could read the opinion of the Connecticut court and conclude that the state law which was the basis of its decision or the decision itself was lacking in fundamental fairness. The truth of the matter is that under any standard —state or federal—the commitment for contempt was proper. Indeed, as indicated above, there is every reason to believe that the Connecticut court did apply the Hoffman standard quoted approvingly in the majority's opinion. I entirely agree with my Brother WHITE, post, pp. 36–38, that if the matter is viewed only from the standpoint of the federal standard, such standard was fully satisfied. The Court's reference to a federal standard is, to put it bluntly, simply an excuse for the Court to substitute its own superficial assessment of the facts and state law for the careful and better informed conclusions of the state court. No one who scans the two opinions with an objective eye will, I think, reach any other conclusion.

I would affirm.

Mr. Justice WHITE, with whom Mr. Justice STEWART joins, dissenting.

I.

The Fifth Amendment safeguards an important complex of values, but it is difficult for me to preceive how these values are served by the Court's holding that the privilege was properly invoked in this case. While purporting to apply the prevailing federal standard of incrimination—the same standard of incrimination that the Connecticut courts applied—the Court has all but stated that a witness' invocation of the privilege to any question is to be automatically, and without more, accepted. With deference, I prefer the rule permitting the judge rather than the witness to determine when an answer sought is incriminating.

The established rule has been that the witness' claim of the privilege is not final, for the privilege qualifies a citizen's general duty of disclosure only when his answers would subject him to danger from the criminal law. The privilege against self-incrimination or any other evidentiary privilege does not protect silence which is solely an expression of political protest, a desire not to inform, a fear of social obloquy or economic disadvantage or fear of prosecution for future crimes. Smith v. United States, 337 U.S. 137, 147, 69 S.Ct. 1000, 1005, 93 L.Ed. 1264; Brown v. Walker, 161 U.S. 591, 605, 16 S.Ct. 644, 650, 40 L.Ed. 819. If the general duty to testify when subpoenaed is to remain and the privilege is to be retained as a protection against compelled incriminating answers, the trial judge must be permitted to make a meaningful determination of when answers tend to incriminate. See The Queen v. Boyes, 1 B. & S. 311, 329–330 (1861); Mason v. United States, 244 U.S. 362, 37 S.Ct. 621, 61 L.Ed. 1198. I do not think today's decision permits such a determination.

Answers which would furnish a lead to other evidence needed to prosecute or convict a claimant of a crime—clue evidence—cannot be compelled, but "this protection must be confined to instances where the witness has reasonable cause to apprehend danger from a direct answer." Hoffman v. United States, 341 U.S. 479, at 486, 71 S.Ct. 814, at 818; Mason v. United States, 244 U.S. 362, 37 S.Ct. 621. Of course the witness is not required to disclose so much of the danger as to render his privilege nugatory. But that does not justify a flat rule of no inquiry and automatic acceptance of the claim of privilege. In determining whether the witness has a reasonable apprehension, the test in the federal courts has been that the judge is to decide from the circumstances of the case, his knowledge of matters surrounding the inquiry and the nature of the evidence which is demanded from the witness. Hoffman v. United

223

States, 341 U.S. 479, 71 S.Ct. 814; Mason v. United States, 244 U.S. 362, 37 S.Ct. 621. Cf. Rogers v. United States, 340 U.S. 367, 71 S.Ct. 438. This rule seeks and achieves a workable accommodation between what are obviously important competing interests. As Mr. Chief Justice Marshall said: "The principle which entitles the United States to the testimony of every citizen, and the principle by which every witness is privileged not to accuse himself, can neither of them be entirely disregarded. * * * When a question is propounded, it belongs to the court to consider and to decide whether any direct answer to it can implicate the witness." In re Willie, 25 Fed. Cas. No. 14,692e, at 39–40. I would not only retain this rule but apply it in its present form. Under this test, Malloy's refusals to answer some, if not all, of the questions put to him were clearly not privileged.

II.

In November 1959, Malloy was arrested in a gambling raid in Hartford and was convicted of pool selling, an offense defined as occupying and keeping a building containing gambling apparatus. After a 90-day jail term, his one-year sentence was suspended and Malloy was placed on probation for two years. In early 1961, Malloy was summoned to appear in an investigation into whether crimes, including gambling, had been committed in Hartford County, and was asked various questions obviously and solely designed to ascertain who Malloy's associates were in connection with his pool-selling activities in Hartford in 1959. Malloy initially refused to answer virtually all the questions put to him, including such innocuous ones as whether he was the William Malloy arrested and convicted of pool selling in 1959. After he was advised to consult with counsel and did so, he declined to answer each one of the following questions on the ground that it would tend to incriminate him:

"Q. Now, on September 11, 1959, when you were arrested at 600 Asylum Street, and the same arrest for which you were convicted in the Superior Court on November 5, 1959, for whom were you working?

*　　*　　*　　*　　*　　*　　*　　*　　*

"Q. On September 11, 1959, when you were arrested, and the same arrest for which you were convicted in the Superior Court on November 5, 1959, who furnished the money to pay your fine when you were convicted in the Superior Court?

*　　*　　*　　*　　*　　*　　*　　*　　*

"Q. After your arrest on September 11, 1959, and the same arrest for which you were convicted on November 5, 1959, who selected your bondsman?

* * * * * * * * * *

"Q. As a result of your arrest on September 11, 1959, and the same arrest for which you were convicted on November 5, 1959, who furnished the money to pay your fine?

* * * * * * * * *

"Q. Do you know whose apartment it was [that you were arrested in on September 11, 1959]?

* * * * * * * * *

"Q. Do you know John Bergoti?

* * * * * * * * *

"Q. I ask you again, Mr. Malloy, now, so there will be no misunderstanding of what I want to know. When you were arrested on September 11, 1959, at 600 Asylum Street in Hartford, and the same arrest for which you were convicted in Superior Court on November 5, 1959, for whom were you working?"
It was for refusing to answer these questions that Malloy was cited for contempt, the Connecticut courts noting that the privilege does not protect one against informing on friends or associates.

These were not wholly innocuous questions on their face, but they clearly were in light of the finding, of which Malloy was told, that he was immune from prosecution for any pool-selling activities in 1959. As the Connecticut Supreme Court of Errors found, the State bore its burden of proving that the statute of limitations barred any prosecution for any type of violation of the state pool-selling statute in 1959. Malloy advanced the claim before the Connecticut courts, and again before this Court, that he could perhaps be prosecuted for a conspiracy and that the statute of limitations on a felony was five years. But the Connecticut courts were unable to find any state statute which Malloy's gambling activities in 1959 in Hartford, the subject of the inquiry, could have violated and Malloy has not yet pointed to one. Beyond this Malloy declined to offer any explanation or hint at how the answers sought could have incriminated him. In these circumstances it is wholly speculative to find that the questions about others, not Malloy, posed a substantial hazard of criminal prosecution to Malloy. Theoretically, under some unknown but perhaps possible conditions any fact is potentially incriminating. But if this be the rule, there obviously is no reason for the judge, rather than the witness, to pass on the claim of privilege. The privilege becomes a general one against answering distasteful questions.

The Court finds that the questions were incriminating because petitioner "might apprehend that if [his associates in 1959] were still engaged in unlawful activity, disclosure of [their names] might furnish a link in a chain of evidence sufficient to connect the petitioner with a more recent crime for which he might still be prosecuted." Ante, p. 13. The assumption necessary to the above reasoning is that all persons, or all who have committed a misdemeanor, are continuously engaged in crime. This is but another way of making the claim of privilege automatic. It is not only unrealistic generally but peculiarly inappropriate in this case. Unlike cases relied on by the Court, like Hoffman v. United States, supra, where the claimant was known to be involved in rackets in the area, which were the subject of the inquiry, and had a "broadly published police record," Malloy had no record as a felon. He had engaged once in an unlawful activity—pool selling—a misdemeanor and was given a suspended sentence. He had been on probation since that time and was on probation at the time of the inquiry. Again, unlike Hoffman, nothing in these questions indicates petitioner was called because he was suspected of criminal activities after 1959. There is no support at all in this record for the cynical assumption that he had committed criminal acts after his release in 1960.

Even on the Court's assumption that persons convicted of a misdemeanor are necessarily suspect criminals, sustaining the privilege in these circumstances is unwarranted, for Malloy placed no reliance on this theory in the courts below or in this Court. In order to allow the judge passing on the claim to understand how the answers sought are incriminating, I would at least require the claimant to state his grounds for asserting the privilege to questions seemingly irrelevant to any incriminating matters.

Adherence to the federal standard of incrimination stated in Mason and Hoffman, supra, in form only, while its content is eroded in application, is hardly an auspicious beginning for application of the privilege to the States. As was well stated in a closely analogous situation, "[t]o continue a rule which is honored by this Court only with lip service is not a healthy thing and in the long run will do disservice to the federal system." Gideon v. Wainwright, 372 U.S. 335, at 351, 83 S.Ct. 792, at 800 (HARLAN, J., concurring).

I would affirm.

Right of Privacy

This chapter involves one of the most sensitive subjects presently confronting the courts—the scope and extent of the right to privacy. Six cases and one act of Congress have been selected for inclusion in this part of the text because of their significance to a proper understanding of this important area. The factual matter of these cases varies greatly but they all contain one dominant theme —an alleged violation of the defendant's rights which violation involves an invasion of his right to privacy.

Mapp v. Ohio*

This "search warrant case" easily ranks as one of the most significant decisions handed down by the Warren Court. It overruled a long standing precedent and caused a considerable alteration to be made in law enforcement methods throughout the United States.

Acting on an alleged "tip" that Miss Mapp was hiding a fugitive and a considerable amount of "policy paraphernalia" in her home, the police forced their way into her home without a warrant. The forceable entry was to find the fugitive and/or evidence that Miss Mapp was engaged in gaming activities. Although they found no fugitive or gambling materials they did find certain pictures which they felt were "obscene." Miss Mapp was prosecuted and convicted under an Ohio statute prohibiting the possession of "obscene" materials.

In the appeal before the United States Supreme Court, counsel for Miss Mapp argued that the materials in question should not have been admitted at her trial because they were the product of an illegal search and seizure. This argument was in direct conflict with the 1949 Supreme Court decision in *Wolf v Colorado*,[1] which

* 367 U.S. 643, 81 S.Ct. 1684 June 19, 1961.
[1] 338 U.S. 25, 69 S.Ct. 1359 (1949).

sanctioned the admissibility of evidence so obtained. Counsel for Miss Mapp contended that the federal standard enunciated in the 1914 case of *Weeks v United States*,[2] that illegally obtained evidence was inadmissible in federal proceedings, should be made applicable to state proceedings.

Speaking for a six to three majority, Mr. Justice Clark overruled the long standing *Wolf* precedent, ruling that "all evidence obtained by searches and seizures in violation of the Constitution is, by that same authority, inadmissible in a state Court . . . ."[3]

The Fourth Amendment's requirement that a warrant be obtained prior to a search had been declared enforceable against the States through the Fourteenth Amendment long before the *Mapp Case*.[4] But the individual states were permitted to develop their own methods of enforcing this right of privacy. Heretofore evidence, no matter how obtained, was admissible in most state courts. The means which these states had chosen to enforce this right, was to permit a defendant, in those cases where it was violated, to sue the officers who conducted the warrantless search. Such a suit would be for money damages and would be brought in a civil, rather than a criminal, court. Needless to say, this amounted to virtually no redress to the defendant who was the victim of an illegal search. In this decision the United States Supreme Court determined that the constitutional guarantee must be enforced by the states in the same manner as it is enforced on the federal level. Illegally obtained evidence is inadmissible evidence in any court, federal or state.

Justices Harlan, Frankfurter, and Whittaker participated in a dissent in which they argued that the Court should never have considered the exclusionary problem, i. e. ruling as inadmissible evidence obtained by an illegal search, claiming the emphasis should have been on the constitutionality of the Ohio Statute under which defendant was convicted. Their reasoning is in effect an attack on the majority for judicial lawmaking.

The result of the majority opinion was to force the State of Ohio to either retry Miss Mapp without the benefit of the illegally obtained evidence or to drop all charges against her. Understandably, Ohio declined to prosecute Miss Mapp a second time for they had no evidence against her other than the illegally seized pictures.

The *Mapp* holding enjoys a prominent place in the history of Supreme Court decisions. It is important, in and of itself, because of the far-reaching impact it produced on state law enforcement

---

[2] 232 U.S. 383, 34 S.Ct. 341 (1914).
[3] Mapp v. Ohio, 367 U.S. 643, 655, 81 S.Ct. 1684, 1691 (1961).
[4] Wolf v. People of State of Colorado, 338 U.S. 25, 69 S.Ct. 1359 (1949); People v. Cahan, 44 Cal.2d 434, 282 P.2d 905 (1955).

procedures. Local authorities throughout the country greeted the decision with outcrys of indignation. And it also has importance in that it is one of the first, in a long line of recent Supreme Court cases, expanding the rights of the accused. This line of cases has not been without controversy. It has led many officials, and a substantial segment of the public as a whole, to question the wisdom of the Warren Court. These individuals argue that the rights of society have been trampled in expanding the rights of the accused. Whether this be true or not, the impact of these cases on our criminal jurisprudence cannot be questioned.

Text of Case

All evidence obtained by searches and seizures in violation of the Federal Constitution is inadmissible in a criminal trial in a state court. *Wolf* v. *Colorado*, 338 U.S. 25, overruled insofar as it holds to the contrary. Pp. 643–660.

A. L. Kearns argued the cause for appellant. With him on the brief was *Walter L. Greene.*

Gertrude Bauer Mahon argued the cause for appellee. With her on the brief was *John T. Corrigan.*

Bernard A. Berkman argued the cause for the American Civil Liberties Union et al., as *amici curiae*, urging reversal. With him on the brief was *Rowland Watts.*

Mr. Justice CLARK delivered the opinion of the Court.

Appellant stands convicted of knowingly having had in her possession and under her control certain lewd and lascivious books, pictures, and photographs in violation of § 2905.34 of Ohio's Revised Code.[1] As officially stated in the syllabus to its opinion, the Supreme Court of Ohio found that her conviction was valid though "based primarily upon the introduction in evidence of lewd and lascivious books and pictures unlawfully seized during an unlawful search of defendant's home * * *." 170 Ohio St. 427–428, 166 N.E. 2d 387, 388.

On May 23, 1957, three Cleveland police officers arrived at appellant's residence in that city pursuant to information that "a person [was] hiding out in the home, who was wanted for questioning in connection with a recent bombing, and that there was a large amount of policy paraphernalia being hidden in the home."

---

[1] The statute provides in pertinent part that

"No person shall knowingly * * * have in his possession or under his control an obscene, lewd, or lascivious book [or] * * * picture * * *.

"Whoever violates this section shall be fined not less than two hundred nor more than two thousand dollars or imprisoned not less than one nor more than seven years, or both."

Miss Mapp and her daughter by a former marriage lived on the top floor of the two-family dwelling. Upon their arrival at that house, the officers knocked on the door and demanded entrance but appellant, after telephoning her attorney, refused to admit them without a search warrant. They advised their headquarters of the situation and undertook a surveillance of the house.

The officers again sought entrance some three hours later when four or more additional officers arrived on the scene. When Miss Mapp did not come to the door immediately, at least one of the several doors to the house was forcibly opened[2] and the policemen gained admittance. Meanwhile Miss Mapp's attorney arrived, but the officers, having secured their own entry, and continuing in their defiance of the law, would permit him neither to see Miss Mapp nor to enter the house. It appears that Miss Mapp was halfway down the stairs from the upper floor to the front door when the officers, in this highhanded manner, broke into the hall. She demanded to see the search warrant. A paper, claimed to be a warrant, was held up by one of the officers. She grabbed the "warrant" and placed it in her bosom. A struggle ensued in which the officers recovered the piece of paper and as a result of which they handcuffed appellant because she had been "belligerent" in resisting their official rescue of the "warrant" from her person. Running roughshod over appellant, a policeman "grabbed" her, "twisted [her] hand," and she "yelled [and] pleaded with him" because "it was hurting." Appellant, in handcuffs, was then forcibly taken upstairs to her bedroom where the officers searched a dresser, a chest of drawers, a closet and some suitcases. They also looked into a photo album and through personal papers belonging to the appellant. The search spread to the rest of the second floor including the child's bedroom, the living room, the kitchen and a dinette. The basement of the building and a trunk found therein were also searched. The obscene materials for possession of which she was ultimately convicted were discovered in the course of that widespread search.

At the trial no search warrant was produced by the prosecution, nor was the failure to produce one explained or accounted for. At best, "There is, in the record, considerable doubt as to whether there ever was any warrant for the search of defendant's home." 170 Ohio St., at page 430, 166 N.E.2d, at page 389. The Ohio Supreme Court believed a "reasonable argument" could be made that

---

[2] A police officer testified that "we did pry the screen door to gain entrance"; the attorney on the scene testified that a policeman "tried * * * to kick in the door" and then "broke the glass in the door and somebody reached in and opened the door and let them in"; the appellant testified that "The back door was broken."

the conviction should be reversed "because the 'methods' employed to obtain the [evidence] * * * were such as to 'offend "a sense of justice," ' " but the court found determinative the fact that the evidence had not been taken "from defendant's person by the use of brutal or offensive physical force against defendant." 170 Ohio St., at page 431, 166 N.E.2d, at pages 389–390.

The State says that even if the search were made without authority, or otherwise unreasonably, it is not prevented from using the unconstitutionally seized evidence at trial, citing Wolf v. People of State of Colorado, 1949, 338 U.S. 25, at page 33, 69 S.Ct. 1359, at page 1364, 93 L.Ed. 1782, in which this Court did indeed hold "that in a prosecution in a State court for a State crime the Fourteenth Amendment does not forbid the admission of evidence obtained by an unreasonable search and seizure." On this appeal, of which we have noted probable jurisdiction, 364 U.S. 868, 81 S.Ct. 111, 5 L.Ed.2d 90, it is urged once again that we review that holding.[3]

I.

Seventy-five years ago, in Boyd v. United States, 1886, 116 U.S. 616, 630, 6 S.Ct. 524, 532, 29 L.Ed. 746, considering the Fourth[4] and Fifth Amendments as running "almost into each other"[5] on the facts before it, this Court held that the doctrines of those Amendments
"apply to all invasions on the part of the government and its employés of the sanctity of a man's home and the privacies of life. It is not the breaking of his doors, and the rummaging of his drawers, that constitutes the essence of the offence; but it is

---

[3]Other issues have been raised on this appeal but, in the view we have taken of the case, they need not be decided. Although appellant chose to urge what may have appeared to be the surer ground for favorable disposition and did not insist that Wolf be overruled, the *amicus curiae*, who was also permitted to participate in the oral argument, did urge the Court to overrule Wolf.

[4]"The right of the people to be secure in their persons, houses, papers, and effects, against unreasonable searches and seizures, shall not be violated, and no Warrants shall issue, but upon probable cause, supported by Oath or affirmation, and particularly describing the place to be searched and the persons or things to be seized."

[5]The close connection between the concepts later embodied in these two Amendments had been noted at least as early as 1765 by Lord Camden, on whose opinion in Ent'ck v. Carrington, 19 Howell's State Trials 1029, the Boyd court drew heavily. Lord Camden had noted, at 1073:
"It is very certain, that the law obligeth no man to accuse himself; because the necessary means of compelling self-accusation, falling upon the innocent as well as the guilty, would be both cruel and unjust; and it should seem, that search for evidence is disallowed upon the same principle. There too the innocent would be confounded with the guilty."

the invasion of his indefeasible right of personal security, personal liberty and private property * * *. Breaking into a house and opening boxes and drawers are circumstances of aggravation; but any forcible and compulsory extortion of a man's own testimony or of his private papers to be used as evidence to convict him of crime or to forfeit his goods, is within the condemnation * * * [of those Amendments]."

The Court noted that

"constitutional provisions for the security of person and property should be liberally construed. * * * It is the duty of courts to be watchful for the constitutional rights of the citizen, and against any stealthy encroachments thereon." At page 635 of 116 U.S., at page 535 of 6 S.Ct.

In this jealous regard for maintaining the integrity of individual rights, the Court gave life to Madison's prediction that "independent tribunals of justice * * * will be naturally led to resist every encroachment upon rights expressly stipulated for in the Constitution by the declaration of rights." I Annals of Cong. 439 (1789). Concluding, the Court specifically referred to the use of the evidence there seized as "unconstitutional." At page 638 of 116 U.S., at page 536 of 6 S.Ct.

Less than 30 years after Boyd, this Court, in Weeks v. United States, 1914, 232 U.S. 383, at pages 391–392, 34 S.Ct. 341, at page 344, 58 L.Ed. 652, stated that

"the Fourth Amendment * * * put the courts of the United States and Federal officials, in the exercise of their power and authority, under limitations and restraints [and] * * * forever secure[d] the people, their persons, houses, papers and effects against all unreasonable searches and seizures under the guise of law * * * and the duty of giving to it force and effect is obligatory upon all entrusted under our Federal system with the enforcement of the laws." At pp. 319–392.

Specifically dealing with the use of the evidence unconstitutionally seized, the Court concluded:

"If letters and private documents can thus be seized and held and used in evidence against a citizen accused of an offense, the protection of the Fourth Amendment declaring his right to be secure against such searches and seizures is of no value, and, so far as those thus placed are concerned, might as well be stricken from the Constitution. The efforts of the courts and their officials to bring the guilty to punishment, praiseworthy as they are, are not to be aided by the sacrifice of those great principles established by years of endeavor and suffering which have resulted in their embodiment in the fundamental law of the land." At page 393 of 232 U.S., at page 344 of 34 S.Ct.

Finally, the Court in that case clearly stated that use of the seized evidence involved "a denial of the constitutional rights of the accused." At page 398 of 232 U.S., at page 346 of 34 S.Ct. Thus, in the year 1914, in the Weeks case, this Court "for the first time" held that "in a federal prosecution the Fourth Amendment barred the use of evidence secured through an illegal search and seizure." Wolf v. People of State of Colorado, supra, 338 U.S. at page 28, 69 S.Ct. at page 1361. This Court has ever since required of federal law officers a strict adherence to that command which this Court has held to be a clear, specific, and constitutionally required— even if judicially implied—deterrent safeguard without insistence upon which the Fourth Amendment would have been reduced to "a form of words." Holmes, J., Silverthorne Lumber Co. v. United States, 1920, 251 U.S. 385, 392, 40 S.Ct. 182, 183, 64 L.Ed. 319. It meant, quite simply, that "conviction by means of unlawful seizures and enforced confessions * * * should find no sanction in the judgments of the courts * * *," Weeks v. United States, supra, 232 U.S. at page 392, 34 S.Ct. at page 344, and that such evidence "shall not be used at all." Silverthorne Lumber Co. v. United States, supra, 251 U.S. at page 392, 40 S.Ct. at page 183.

There are in the cases of this Court some passing references to the Weeks rule as being one of evidence. But the plain and unequivocal language of Weeks—and its later paraphrase in Wolf—to the effect that the Weeks rule is of constitutional origin, remains entirely undisturbed. In Byars v. United States, 1927, 273 U.S. 28, at pages 29–30, 47 S.Ct. 248, at pages 248–249, 71 L.Ed. 520, a unanimous Court declared that "the doctrine [cannot] * * * be tolerated *under our constitutional system*, that evidences of crime discovered by a federal officer in making a search without lawful warrant may be used against the victim of the unlawful search where a timely challenge has been interposed." At pp. 29–30 (emphasis added). The Court, in Olmstead v. United States, 1928, 277 U.S. 438, at page 462, 48 S.Ct. 564, 567, 72 L.Ed. 944, in unmistakable language restated the Weeks rule:

"The striking outcome of the Weeks case and those which followed it was the sweeping declaration that the Fourth Amendment, although not referring to or limiting the use of evidence in court, really forbade its introduction if obtained by government officers through a violation of the amendment." At p. 462.

In McNabb v. United States, 1943, 318 U.S. 332, at pages 339–340, 63 S.Ct. 608, at page 612, 87 L.Ed. 819, we note this statement:

"[A] conviction in the federal courts, the foundation of which is evidence obtained in disregard of liberties deemed fundamental

233

by the Constitution, cannot stand. Boyd v. United States * * * Weeks v. United States * * *. And this Court has, on Constitutional grounds, set aside convictions, both in the federal and state courts, which were based upon confessions 'secured by protracted and repeated questioning of ignorant and untutored persons, in whose minds the power of officers was greatly magnified' or 'who have been unlawfully held incommunicado without advice of friends or counsel' * * *." At pp. 339–340.

Significantly, in McNabb, the Court did then pass on to formulate a rule of evidence, saying, "[i]n the view we take of the case, however, it becomes unnecessary to reach the Constitutional issue [for] * * * [t]he principles governing the admissibility of evidence in federal criminal trials have not been restricted * * * to those derived solely from the Constitution." At pages 340–341 of 318 U.S., at page 613 of 63 S.Ct.

II.

In 1949, 35 years after Weeks was announced, this Court, in Wolf v. People of State of Colorado, supra, again for the first time,[6] discussed the effect of the Fourth Amendment upon the States through the operation of the Due Process Clause of the Fourteenth Amendment. It said:

"[W]e have no hesitation in saying that were a State affirmatively to sanction such police incursion into privacy it would run counter to the guaranty of the Fourteenth Amendment." At page 28 of 338 U.S., at page 1361 of 69 S.Ct.

Nevertheless, after declaring that the "security of one's privacy against arbitrary intrusion by the police" is "implicit in 'the concept of ordered liberty' and as such enforceable against the States through the Due Process Clause," cf. Palko v. State of Connecticut, 1937, 302 U.S. 319, 58 S.Ct. 149, 82 L.Ed. 288, and announcing that it "stoutly adhere[d]" to the Weeks decision, the Court decided that the Weeks exclusionary rule would not then be imposed upon the States as "an essential ingredient of the right." 338 U.S. at pages 27–29, 69 S.Ct. at page 1362. The Court's reasons for not considering essential to the right to privacy, as a curb imposed upon the States by the Due Process Clause, that which decades before had been posited as part and parcel of the Fourth Amendment's limitation upon federal encroachment of individual privacy, were bottomed on factual considerations.

---

[6] See, however, National Safe Deposit Co. v. Stead, 1914, 232 U.S. 58, 34 S.Ct. 209, 58 L.Ed. 504, and Adams v. People of State of New York, 1904, 192 U.S. 585, 24 S.Ct. 372, 48 L.Ed. 575.

While they are not basically relevant to a decision that the exclusionary rule is an essential ingredient of the Fourth Amendment as the right it embodies is vouchsafed against the States by the Due Process Clause, we will consider the current validity of the factual grounds upon which Wolf was based.

The Court in Wolf first stated that "[t]he contrariety of views of the States" on the adoption of the exclusionary rule of Weeks was "particularly impressive" (338 U.S. at page 29, 69 S.Ct. at page 1362) ; and, in this connection, that it could not "brush aside the experience of States which deem the incidence of such conduct by the police too slight to call for a deterrent remedy * * * by overriding the [States'] relevant rules of evidence." At pages 31–32 of 338 U.S., at page 1363 of 69 S.Ct. While in 1949, prior to the Wolf case, almost two-thirds of the States were opposed to the use of the exclusionary rule, now, despite the Wolf case, more than half of those since passing upon it, by their own legislative or judicial decision, have wholly or partly adopted or adhered to the Weeks rule. See Elkins v. United States, 1960, 364 U.S. 206, Appendix, at pages 224–232, 80 S.Ct. 1437, at pages 1448–1453, 4 L.Ed.2d 1669. Significantly, among those now following the rule is California, which, according to its highest court, was "compelled to reach that conclusion because other remedies have completely failed to secure compliance with the constitutional provisions * * *." People v. Cahan, 1955, 44 Cal.2d 434, 445, 282 P.2d 905, 911, 50 A.L.R.2d 513. In connection with this California case, we note that the second basis elaborated in Wolf in support of its failure to enforce the exclusionary doctrine against the States was that "other means of protection" have been afforded "the right to privacy."[7] 338 U.S. at page 30, 69 S.Ct. at page 1362. The ex-

---

[7] Less than half of the States have any criminal provisions relating directly to unreasonable searches and seizures. The punitive sanctions of the 23 States attempting to control such invasions of the right of privacy may be classified as follows:
Criminal Liability of Affiant for Malicious Procurement of Search Warrant.—Ala. Code, 1958, Tit. 15, § 99; Alaska Comp.Laws Ann. 1949, § 66–7–15; Ariz.Rev.Stat.Ann. 1956, § 13–1454; Cal.Pen.Code § 170; Fla. Stat.1959, § 933.16, F.S.A. Ga.Code Ann.1953, § 27–301; Idaho Code Ann.1948, § 18–709; Iowa Code Ann., 1950, § 751.38; Minn.Stat. Ann.1947, § 613.54; Mont.Rev. Codes Ann.1947, § 94–35–122; Nev. Rev.Stat. §§ 199.130, 199.140; N.J. Stat.Ann.1940, § 33:1–64; N.Y. Penn.Law, § 1786, N.Y. Code Crim. Proc. § 811; N.C.Gen.Stat. 1953, § 15–27 (applies to "officers" only) ; N.D.Century Code Ann. 1960, §§ 12–17–08, 29–29–18; Okla.Stat., 1951, Tit. 21, § 585, Tit. 22, § 1239; Ore. Rev.Stat. § 141.990; S.D.Code, 1939 (Supp.1960) § 34.9904; Utah Code Ann.1953, § 77–54–21.
Criminal Liability of Magistrate Issuing Warrant Without Supporting Affidavit.—N.C.Gen.Stat.1953, § 15–27; Va.Code Ann., 1960 Replacement Volume, § 19.1–89.
Criminal Liability of Officer Willfully Exceeding Authority of Search Warrant.—Fla.Stat.Ann. 1944, § 933.17; Iowa Code Ann., 1950, § 751.39; Minn.Stat.Ann.1947,

perience of California that such other remedies have been worthless and futile is buttressed by the experience of other States. The obvious futility of relegating the Fourth Amendment to the protection of other remedies has, moreover, been recognized by this Court since Wolf. See Irvine v. People of State of California, 1954, 347 U.S. 128, 137, 74 S.Ct. 381, 385, 98 L.Ed. 561.

Likewise, time has set its face against what Wolf called the "weighty testimony" of People v. Defore, 1926, 242 N.Y. 13, 150 N.E. 585. There Justice (then Judge) Cardozo, rejecting adoption of the Weeks exclusionary rule in New York, had said that "[t]he Federal rule as it stands is either too strict or too lax." 242 N.Y. at page 22, 150 N.E. at page 588. However, the force of that reasoning has been largely vitiated by later decisions of this Court. These include the recent discarding of the "silver platter" doctrine which allowed federal judicial use of evidence seized in violation of the Constitution by state agents, Elkins v. United States, supra; the relaxation of the formerly strict requirements as to standing to challenge the use of evidence thus seized, so that now the procedure of exclusion, "ultimately referrable to constitutional safeguards," is available to anyone even "legitimately on [the] premises" unlawfully searched, Jones v. United States, 1960, 362 U.S. 257, 266–267, 80 S.Ct. 725, 734, 4 L.Ed.2d 697; and, finally, the formulation of a method to prevent state use of evidence unconstitutionally seized by federal agents, Rea v. United States, 1956, 350 U.S. 214, 76 S.Ct. 292, 100 L.Ed. 233. Because there can be no fixed formula, we are admittedly met with "recurring questions of the reasonableness of searches," but less is not to be expected when dealing with a Constitution, and, at any rate, "[r]easonableness is in the first instance for the [trial court] * * * to determine." United States v. Rabinowitz, 1950, 339 U.S. 56, 63, 70 S.Ct. 430, 434, 94 L.Ed. 653.

It, therefore, plainly appears that the factual considerations supporting the failure of the Wolf Court to include the Weeks exclusionary rule when it recognized the enforceability of the right to privacy against the States in 1949, while not basically relevant to

---

§ 613.54; Nev.Rev.Stat. § 199.450; N.Y.Pen.Law. § 1847, N.Y.Code Crim.Proc. § 812; N.D.Century Code Ann.1960, §§ 12–17–07, 29–29–19; Okla.Stat.1951, Tit. 21, § 536, Tit. 22, § 1240; S.D.Code, 1939 (Supp.1960) § 34.9905; Tenn.Code Ann.1955, § 40–510; Utah Code Ann.1953, § 77–54–22.

Criminal Liability of Officer for Search with Invalid Warrant or no Warrant.—Idaho Code Ann.1948, § 18–703; Minn.Stat.Ann. 1947, §§ 613.53, 621.17; Mo.Ann. Stat.1953, § 558.190; Mont.Rev. Codes Ann.1947, § 94–3506; N.J. Stat.Ann.1940, § 33:1–65; N.Y.Pen. Law, § 1846; N.D.Century Code Ann. 1960, § 12–17–06; Okla.Stat. Ann. 1958, Tit. 21, § 535; Utah Code Ann. 1953, § 76–28–53; Va. Code Ann. 1960 Replacement Volume, § 19.1–88; Wash.Rev.Code §§ 10.79.040, 10.79.045.

the constitutional consideration, could not, in any analysis, now be deemed controlling.

III.

Some five years after Wolf, in answer to a plea made here Term after Term that we overturn its doctrine on applicability of the Weeks exclusionary rule, this Court indicated that such should not be done until the States had "adequate opportunity to adopt or reject the [Weeks] rule." Irvine v. People of State of California, supra, 347 U.S. at page 134, 74 S.Ct. at page 384. There again it was said:

"Never until June of 1949 did this Court hold the basic search-and-seizure prohibition in any way applicable to the states under the Fourteenth Amendment." Ibid.

And only last Term, after again carefully re-examining the Wolf doctrine in Elkins v. United States, supra, the Court pointed out that "the controlling principles" as to search and seizure and the problem of admissibility "seemed clear" (364 U.S. at page 212, 1441 of 80 S.Ct.) until the announcement in Wolf "that the Due Process Clause of the Fourteenth Amendment does not itself require state courts to adopt the exclusionary rule" of the Weeks case. At page 213 of 364 U.S., at page 1442 of 80 S.Ct. at the same time, the Court pointed out, "the underlying constitutional doctrine which Wolf established * * * that the Federal Constitution * * * prohibits unreasonable searches and seizures by state officers" had undermined the "foundation upon which the admissibility of state-seized evidence in a federal trial originally rested * * *." Ibid. The Court concluded that it was therefore obliged to hold, although it chose the narrower ground on which to do so, that all evidence obtained by an unconstitutional search and seizure was inadmissible in a federal court regardless of its source. Today we once again examine Wolf's constitutional documentation of the right to privacy free from unreasonable state intrusion, and, after its dozen years on our books, are led by it to close the only courtroom door remaining open to evidence secured by official lawlessness in flagrant abuse of that basic right, reserved to all persons as a specific guarantee against that very same unlawful conduct. We hold that all evidence obtained by searches and seizures in violation of the Constitution is, by that same authority, inadmissible in a state court.

IV.

Since the Fourth Amendment's right of privacy has been declared enforceable against the States through the Due Process Clause of the Fourteenth, it is enforceable against them by the same sanction of exclusion as is used against the Federal Government. Were it otherwise, then just as without the Weeks rule the assurance against unreasonable federal searches and seizures would be "a form of words", valueless and undeserving of mention in a perpetual charter of inestimable human liberties, so too, without that rule the freedom from state invasions of privacy would be so ephemeral and so neatly severed from its conceptual nexus with the freedom from all brutish means of coercing evidence as not to merit this Court's high regard as a freedom "implicit in the concept of ordered liberty." At the time that the Court held in Wolf that the Amendment was applicable to the States through the Due Process Clause, the cases of this Court, as we have seen, had steadfastly held that as to federal officers the Fourth Amendment included the exclusion of the evidence seized in violation of its provisions. Even Wolf "stoutly adhered" to that proposition. The right to privacy, when conceded operatively enforceable against the States, was not susceptible of destruction by avulsion of the sanction upon which its protection and enjoyment had always been deemed dependent under the Boyd, Weeks and Silverthorne cases. Therefore, in extending the substantive protections of due process to all constitutionally unreasonable searches—state or federal—it was logically and constitutionally necessary that the exclusion doctrine—an essential part of the right to privacy—be also insisted upon as an essential ingredient of the right newly recognized by the Wolf case. In short, the admission of the new constitutional right by Wolf could not consistently tolerate denial of its most important constitutional privilege, namely, the exclusion of the evidence which an accused had been forced to give by reason of the unlawful seizure. To hold otherwise is to grant the right but in reality to withhold its privilege and enjoyment. Only last year the Court itself recognized that the purpose of the exclusionary rule "is to deter—to compel respect for the constitutional guaranty in the only effectively available way—by removing the incentive to disregard it." Elkins v. United States, supra, 364 U.S. at page 217, 80 S.Ct. at page 1444.

Indeed, we are aware of no restraint, similar to that rejected today, conditioning the enforcement of any other basic constitutional right. The right to privacy, no less important than any other right carefully and particularly reserved to the people, would stand in marked contrast to all other rights declared as "basic to a free society." Wolf v. People of State of Colorado, supra, 338 U.S. at page 27, 69 S.Ct. at page 1361. This Court has not hestitated to enforce as strictly against the States as it does against the Federal Government the rights of free speech and of a free press, the rights to notice and to a fair, public trial, including, as it does, the right not to be convicted by use of a coerced confession, however logically relevant it be, and without regard to its reliability. Rogers v. Richmond, 1961, 365 U.S. 534, 81 S.Ct. 735, 5 L.Ed.2d 760. And nothing could be more certain that that when a coerced confession is involved, "the relevant rules of evidence" are overridden without regard to "the incidence of such conduct by the police," slight or frequent. Why should not the same rule apply to what is tantamount to coerced testimony by way of unconstitutional seizure of goods, papers, effects, documents, etc.? We find that, as to the Federal Government, the Fourth and Fifth Amendments and, as to the States, the freedom from unconscionable invasions of privacy and the freedom from convictions based upon coerced confessions do enjoy an "intimate relation"[8] in their perpetuation of "principles of humanity and civil liberty [secured] * * * only after years of struggle." Bram v. United States, 1897, 168 U.S. 532, 543–544, 18 S.Ct. 183, 187, 42 L.Ed. 568. They express "supplementing phases of the same constitutional purpose—to maintain inviolate large areas of personal privacy." Feldman v. United States, 1944, 322 U.S. 487, 489–490, 64 S.Ct. 1082, 1083, 88 L.Ed. 1408. The philosophy of each Amendment and of each freedom is complementary to, although not dependent upon, that of the other in its sphere of influence the very least that together they assure in either sphere is that no man is to be convicted on unconstitutional evidence. Cf. Rochin v. People of State of California, 1952, 342 U.S. 165, 173, 72 S.Ct. 205, 210, 96 L.Ed. 183.

V.

Moreover, our holding that the exclusionary rule is an essential part of both the Fourth and Fourteenth Amendments is not only the logical dictate of prior cases, but it also makes very good sense. There is no war between the Constitution and common sense. Presently, a federal prosecutor may make no use of evidence illegally seized, but a State's attorney across the street may, although he supposedly is operating under the enforceable prohibitions of the same Amendment. Thus the State, by admitting evidence unlawfully seized, serves to encourage disobedience to the Federal Constitution which it is bound to uphold. Moreover, as was said in Elkins, "[t]he very essence of a healthy federalism de-

---

8 But compare Waley v. Johnston, 316 U.S. 101, 104, 62 S.Ct. 964, 965, 86 L.Ed. 1302, and Chambers v. State of Florida, 309 U.S. 227, 236, 60 S.Ct. 472, 477, 84 L.Ed. 716, with Weeks v. United States, 232 U.S. 383, 34 S.Ct. 341, 58 L.Ed. 652, and Wolf v. People of State of Colorado, 338 U.S. 25, 69 S.Ct. 1359, 93 L.Ed. 1782.

pends upon the avoidance of needless conflict between state and federal courts." 364 U.S. at page 221, 80 S.Ct. at page 1446. Such a conflict, hereafter needless, arose this very Term, in Wilson v. Schnettler, 1961, 365 U.S. 381, 81 S.Ct. 632, 5 L.Ed.2d 620, in which, and in spite of the promise made by Rea, we gave full recognition to our practice in this regard by refusing to restrain a federal officer from testifying in a state court as to evidence unconstitutionally seized by him in the performance of his duties. Yet the double standard recognized until today hardly put such a thesis into practice. In non-exclusionary States, federal officers, being human, were by it invited to and did, as our cases indicate, step across the street to the State's attorney with their unconstitutionally seized evidence. Prosecution on the basis of that evidence was then had in a state court in utter disregard of the enforceable Fourth Amendment. If the fruits of an unconstitutional search had been inadmissible in both state and federal courts, this inducement to evasion would have been sooner eliminated. There would be no need to reconcile such cases as Rea and Schnettler, each pointing up the hazardous uncertainties of our heretofore ambivalent approach.

Federal-state cooperation in the solution of crime under constitutional standards will be promoted, if only by recognition of their now mutual obligation to respect the same fundamental criteria in their approaches. "However much in a particular case insistence upon such rules may appear as a technicality that inures to the benefit of a guilty person, the history of the criminal law proves that tolerence of shortcut methods in law enforcement impairs its enduring effectiveness." Miller v. United States, 1958, 357 U.S. 301, 313, 78 S.Ct. 1190, 1197, 2 L.Ed.2d 1332. Denying shortcuts to only one of two cooperating law enforcement agencies tends naturally to breed legitimate suspicion of "working arrangements" whose results are equally tainted. Byars v. United States, 1927, 273 U.S. 28, 47 S.Ct. 248, 71 L.Ed. 520; Lustig v. United States, 1949, 338 U.S. 74, 69 S.Ct. 1372, 93 L.Ed. 1819.

There are those who say, as did Justice (then Judge) Cardozo, that under our constitutional exclusionary doctrine "[t]he criminal is to go free because the constable has blundered." People v. Defore, 242 N.Y. at page 21, 150 N.E. at page 587. In some cases this will undoubtedly be the result.[9] But, as was said in Elkins,

---

[9] As is always the case, however, state procedural requirements governing assertion and pursuance of direct and collateral constitutional challenges to criminal prosecutions must be respected. We note, moreover, that the class of state convictions possibly affected by this decision is of relatively narrow compass when compared with Burns v. State of Ohio, 360 U.S. 252, 79 S.Ct. 1164, 3 L.Ed.2d 1209; Griffin v. People of State of Illinois, 351 U.S. 12, 76 S.Ct. 585, 100 L.Ed. 891 and Commonwealth of Pennsylvania ex rel. Herman v. Claudy,

"there is another consideration—the imperative of judicial integrity." 364 U.S. at page 222, 80 S.Ct. at page 1447. The criminal goes free, if he must, but it is the law that sets him free. Nothing can destroy a government more quickly than its failure to observe its own laws, or worse, its disregard of the charter of its own existence. As Mr. Justice Brandeis, dissenting, said in Olmstead v. United States, 1928, 277 U.S. 438, 485, 48 S.Ct. 564, 575, 72 L.Ed. 944: "Our Government is the potent, the omnipresent teacher. For good or for ill, it teaches the whole people by its example. * * * If the Government becomes a lawbreaker, it breeds contempt for law; it invites every man to become a law unto himself; it invites anarchy." Nor can it lightly be assumed that, as a practical matter, adoption of the exclusionary rule fetters law enforcement. Only last year this Court expressly considered that contention and found that "pragmatic evidence of a sort" to the contrary was not wanting. Elkins v. United States, supra, 364 U.S. at page 218, 80 S.Ct. at page 1444. The Court noted that

"The federal courts themselves have operated under the exclusionary rule of Weeks for almost half a century; yet it has not been suggested either that the Federal Bureau of Investigation[10] has thereby been rendered ineffective, or that the administration of criminal justice in the federal courts has thereby been disrupted. Moreover, the experience of the states is impressive * * *. The movement towards the rule of exclusion has been halting but seemingly inexorable." Id., 364 U.S. at pages 218–219, 80 S.Ct. at pages 1444–1445.

The ignoble shortcut to conviction left open to the State tends to destroy the entire system of constitutional restraints on which the liberties of the people rest.[11] Having once recognized that the right to privacy embodied in the Fourth Amendment is enforceable against the States, and that the right to be secure against rude invasions of privacy by state officers is, therefore, constitutional in origin, we can no longer permit that right to remain an empty promise. Because it is enforceable in the same manner and to like effect as other basic rights secured by the Due Process Clause, we can no longer permit it to be revocable at the whim of any police officer who, in the name of law enforcement itself, chooses to suspend

350 U.S. 116, 76 S.Ct. 223, 100 L.Ed. 126. In those cases the same contention was urged and later proved unfounded. In any case, further delay in reaching the present result could have no effect other than to compound the difficulties.

[10] See the remarks of Mr. Hoover, Director of the Federal Bureau of Investigation, FBI Law Enforcement Bulletin, September, 1952, pp. 1–2, quoted in Elkins v. United States, 364 U.S. 206, 218–219, 80 S.Ct. 1437, 1444–1445, note 8.

[11] Cf. Marcus v. Search Warrant, post, p. 717.

its enjoyment. Our decision, founded on reason and truth, gives to the individual no more than that which the Constitution guarantees him, to the police officer no less than that to which honest law enforcement is entitled, and, to the courts, that judicial integrity so necessary in the true administration of justice.

The judgment of the Supreme Court of Ohio is reversed and the cause remanded for further proceedings not inconsistent with this opinion.

Reversed and remanded.

Mr. Justice BLACK, concurring.

For nearly fifty years, since the decision of this Court in Weeks v. United States,[1] federal courts have refused to permit the introduction into evidence against an accused of his papers and effects obtained by "unreasonable searches and seizures" in violation of the Fourth Amendment. In Wolf v. People of State of Colorado, decided in 1948, however, this Court held that "in a prosecution in a State court for a State crime the Fourteenth Amendment does not forbid the admission of evidence obtained by an unreasonable search and seizure."[2] I concurred in that holding on these grounds:

"For reasons stated in my dissenting opinion in Adamson v. [People of State of] California, 332 U.S. 46, 68 [67 S.Ct. 1672, 1683, 91 L.Ed. 1903], I agree with the conclusion of the Court that the Fourth Amendment's prohibition of 'unreasonable searches and seizures' is enforceable against the states. Consequently, I should be for reversal of this case if I thought the Fourth Amendment not only prohibited 'unreasonable searches and seizures,' but also, of itself, barred the use of evidence so unlawfully obtained. But I agree with what appears to be a plain implication of the Court's opinion that the federal exclusionary rule is not a command of the Fourth Amendment but is a judicially created rule of evidence which Congress might negate."[3]

I am still not persuaded that the Fourth Amendment, standing alone, would be enough to bar the introduction into evidence against an accused of papers and effects seized from him in violation of its commands. For the Fourth Amendment does not itself contain any provision expressly precluding the use of such evidence, and I am extremely doubtful that such a provision could properly be inferred from nothing more than the basic command against unreasonable

---

[1] 232 U.S. 383, 34 S.Ct. 341, 58 L.Ed. 652, decided in 1914.

[2] 338 U.S. 25, 33, 69 S.Ct. 1359, 1364, 93 L.Ed. 1782.

[3] Id., 338 U.S. at pages 39–40, 69 S.Ct. at page 1367.

searches and seizures. Reflection on the problem, however, in the light of cases coming before the Court since Wolf, has led me to conclude that when the Fourth Amendment's ban against unreasonable searches and seizures is considered together with the Fifth Amendment's ban against compelled self-incrimination, a constitutional basis emerges which not only justifies but actually requires the exclusionary rule.

The close interrelationship between the Fourth and Fifth Amendments, as they apply to this problem,[4] has long been recognized and, indeed, was expressly made the ground for this Court's holding in Boyd v. United States.[5] There the Court fully discussed this relationship and declared itself "unable to perceive that the seizure of a man's private books and papers to be used in evidence against him is substantially different from compelling him to be a witness against himself."[6] It was upon this ground that Mr. Justice Rutledge largely relied in his dissenting opinion in the Wolf case.[7] And, although I rejected the argument at that time, its force has, for me at least, become compelling with the more thorough understanding of the problem brought on by recent cases. In the final analysis, it seems to me that the Boyd doctrine, though perhaps not required by the express language of the Constitution strictly construed, is amply justified from an historical standpoint, soundly based in reason, and entirely consistent with what I regard to be the proper approach to interpretation of our Bill of Rights—an approach well set out by Mr. Justice Bradley in the Boyd case:

"[C]onstitutional provisions for the security of person and property should be liberally construed. A close and literal construction deprives them of half their efficacy, and leads to gradual depreciation of the right, as if it consisted more in sound than in substance. It is the duty of the courts to be watchful for the constitutional rights of the citizen, and against any stealthy encroachments thereon."[8]

---

[4] The interrelationship between the Fourth and the Fifth Amendments in this area does not, of course, justify a narrowing in the interpretation of either of these Amendments with respect to areas in which they operate separately. See Feldman v. United States, 322 U.S. 487, 502–503, 64 S.Ct. 1082, 1089, 88 L.Ed. 1408 (dissenting opinion); Frank v. State of Maryland, 359 U.S. 360, 374–384, 79 S.Ct. 804, 812–818, 3 L.Ed.2d 877 (dissenting opinion).

[5] 116 U.S. 616, 6 S.Ct. 524, 29 L.Ed. 746.

[6] Id., 116 U.S. at page 633, 6 S.Ct. at page 534.

[7] 338 U.S. at pages 47–48, 69 S.Ct. at pages 1368–1369.

[8] 116 U.S. at page 635, 6 S.Ct. at page 535. As the Court points out, Mr. Justice Bradley's approach to interpretation of the Bill of Rights stemmed directly from the spirit in which that great charter of liberty was offered for adoption on the floor of House of Representatives by its framer, James Madison: "If they [the first ten Amendments] are incorporated into the Constitution, independent tribunals of jus-

The case of Rochin v. People of California,[9] which we decided three years after the Wolf case, authenticated, I think, the soundness of Mr. Justice Bradley's and Mr. Justice Rutledge's reliance upon the interrelationship between the Fourth and Fifth Amendments as requiring the exclusion of unconstitutionally seized evidence. In the Rochin case, three police officers, acting with neither a judicial warrant nor probable cause, entered Rochin's home for the purpose of conducting a search and broke down the door to a bedroom occupied by Rochin and his wife. Upon their entry into the room, the officers saw Rochin pick up and swallow two small capsules. They immediately seized him and took him in handcuffs to a hospital where the capsules were recovered by use of a stomach pump. Investigation showed that the capsules contained morphine and evidence of that fact was made the basis of his conviction of a crime in a state court.

When the question of the validity of that conviction was brought here, we were presented with an almost perfect example of the interrelationship between the Fourth and Fifth Amendments. Indeed, every member of this Court who participated in the decision of that case recognized this interrelationship and relied on it, to some extent at least, as justifying reversal of Rochin's conviction. The majority, though careful not to mention the Fifth Amendment's provision that "[n]o person * * * shall be compelled in any criminal case to be a witness against himself," showed at least that it was not unaware that such a provision exists, stating: "Coerced confessions offend the community's sense of fair play and decency. * * * It would be a stultification of the responsibility which the course of constitutional history has cast upon this Court to hold that in order to convict a man the police cannot extract by force what is in his mind but can extract what is in his stomach."[10] The methods used by the police thus were, according to the majority, "too close to the rack and the screw to permit of constitutional differentiation,"[11] and the case was reversed on the ground that these methods had violated the due Process Clause of the Fourteenth Amendment in that the treatment accorded Rochin was of a kind that "shocks

---

tice will consider themselves in a peculiar manner the guardians of those rights; they will be an impenetrable bulwark against every assumption of power in the Legislative or Executive; they will be naturally led to resist every encroachment upon rights expressly stipulated for in the Constitution by the declaration of rights." I Annals of Congress 439 (1789).

[9] 342 U.S. 165, 72 S.Ct. 205, 96 L.Ed. 183.

[10] Id., 342 U.S. at page 173, 72 S.Ct. at page 210.

[11] Id., 342 U.S. at page 172, 72 S.Ct. at page 210.

the conscience," "offend[s] 'a sense of justice' " and fails to "respect certain decencies of civilized conduct."[12]

I concurred in the reversal of the Rochin case, but on the ground that the Fourteenth Amendment made the Fifth Amendment's provision against self-incrimination applicable to the States and that, given a broad rather than a narrow construction, that provision barred the introduction of this "capsule" evidence just as much as it would have forbidden the use of words Rochin might have been coerced to speak.[13] In reaching this conclusion I cited and relied on the Boyd case, the constitutional doctrine of which was, of course, necessary to my disposition of the case. At that time, however, these views were very definitely in the minority for only Mr. Justice DOUGLAS and I rejected the flexible and uncertain standards of the "shock-the-conscience test" used in the majority opinion.[14]

Two years after Rochin, in Irvine v. People of State of California,[15] we were again called upon to consider the validity of a conviction based on evidence which had been obtained in a manner clearly unconstitutional and arguably shocking to the conscience. The five opinions written by this Court in that case demonstrate the utter confusion and uncertainty that had been brought about by the Wolf and Rochin decisions. In concurring, Mr. Justice CLARK emphasized the unsatisfactory nature of the Court's "shock-the-conscience test," saying that this "test" "makes for such uncertainty and unpredictability that it would be impossible to foretell—other than by guesswork—just how brazen the invasion of the intimate privacies of one's home must be in order to shock itself into the protective arms of the Constitution. In truth, the practical result of this *ad hoc* approach is simply that when five Justices are sufficiently revolted by local police action, a conviction is overturned and a guilty man may go free."[16]

Only one thing emerged with complete clarity from the Irvine case—that is that seven Justices rejected the "shock-the-conscience" constitutional standard enunciated in the Wolf and Rochin cases. But even this did not lessen the confusion in this area of the law because the continued existence of mutually inconsistent precedents together with the Court's inability to settle upon a majority opinion in the Irvine case left the situation at least as uncertain

---

12 Id., 342 U.S. at pages 172, 173, 72 S.Ct. at pages 209–210.

13 Id., 342 U.S. at pages 174–177, 72 S.Ct. at pages 210–212.

14 For the concurring opinion of Mr. Justice Douglas see id., 342 U.S. at pages 177–179, 72 S.Ct. at pages 212, 213.

15 347 U.S. 128, 74 S.Ct. 381, 98 L.Ed. 561.

16 Id., 347 U.S. at page 138, 74 S.Ct. at page 386.

as it had been before.[17] Finally, today, we clear up that uncertainty. As I understand the Court's opinion in this case, we again reject the confusing "shock-the-conscience" standard of the Wolf and Rochin cases and, instead, set aside this state conviction in reliance upon the precise, intelligible and more predictable constitutional doctrine enunciated in the Boyd case. I fully agree with Mr. Justice Bradley's opinion that the two Amendments upon which the Boyd doctrine rests are of vital importance in our constitutional scheme of liberty and that both are entitled to a liberal rather than a niggardly interpretation. The courts of the country are entitled to know with as much certainty as possible what scope they cover. The Court's opinion, in my judgment, dissipates the doubt and uncertainty in this field of constitutional law and I am persuaded, for this and other reasons stated, to depart from my prior views, to accept the Boyd doctrine as controlling in this state case and to join the Court's judgment and opinion which are in accordance with that constitutional doctrine.

Mr. Justice DOUGLAS, concurring.

Though I have joined the opinion of the Court, I add a few words. This criminal proceeding started with a lawless search and seizure. The police entered a home forcefully, and seized documents that were later used to convict the occupant of a crime.

She lived alone with her fifteen-year-old daughter in the second-floor flat of a duplex in Cleveland. At about 1:30 in the afternoon of May 23, 1957, three policemen arrived at this house. They rang the bell, and the appellant, appearing at her window, asked them what they wanted. According to their later testimony, the policemen had come to the house on information from "a confidential source that there was a person hiding out in the home, who was wanted for questioning in connection with a recent bombing."[1] To the appellant's question, however, they replied only that they wanted to question her and would not state the subject about which they wanted to talk.

The appellant, who had retained an attorney in connection with a pending civil matter, told the police she would call him to ask if she should let them in. On her attorney's advice, she told them she would let them in only when they produced a valid search warrant. For the next two and a half hours, the police laid siege

---

[17] See also United States v. Rabinowitz, 339 U.S. 56, 66–68, 70 S.Ct. 430, 444–445, 94 L.Ed. 653 (dissenting opinion).

[1] This "confidential source" told the police, in the same breath, that "there was a large amount of policy paraphernalia being hidden in the home."

to the house. At four o'clock, their number was increased to at least seven. Appellant's lawyer appeared on the scene; and one of the policemen told him that they now had a search warrant, but the officer refused to show it. Instead, going to the back door, the officer first tried to kick it in and, when that proved unsuccessful, he broke the glass in the door and opened it from the inside.

The appellant, who was on the steps going up to her flat, demanded to see the search warrant; but the officer refused to let her see it although he waved a paper in front of her face. She grabbed it and thrust it down the front of her dress. The policemen seized her, took the paper from her, and had her handcuffed to another officer. She was taken upstairs, thus bound, and into the larger of the two bedrooms in the apartment; there she was forced to sit on the bed. Meanwhile, the officers entered the house and made a complete search of the four rooms of her flat and of the basement of the house.

The testimony concerning the search is largely nonconflicting. The approach of the officers; their long wait outside the home, watching all its doors; the arrival of reinforcements armed with a paper;[2] breaking into the house; putting their hands on appellant and handcuffing her; numerous officers ran-sacking through every room and piece of furniture, while the appellant sat, a prisoner in her own bedroom. There is direct conflict in the testimony, however, as to where the evidence which is the basis of this case was found. To understand the meaning of that conflict, one must understand that this case is based on the knowing possession[3] of four little pamphlets, a couple of photographs and a little pencil doodle—all of which are alleged to be pornographic.

According to the police officers who participated in the search, these articles were found, some in appellant's dressers and some in a suitcase found by her bed. According to appellant, most of the articles were found in a cardboard box in the basement; one in the

---

[2] The purported warrant has disappeared from the case. The State made no attempt to prove its existence, issuance or contents, either at the trial or on the hearing of a preliminary motion to suppress. The Supreme Court of Ohio said: "There is, in the record, considerable doubt as to whether there ever was *any* warrant for the search of defendant's home. * * * Admittedly * * * there was no warrant authorizing a search * * * for any 'lewd, or lascivious book * * * print, [or] picture.' " 170 Ohio St.

427, 430, 166 N.E.2d 387, 389. (Emphasis added.)

[3] Ohio Rev.Code, § 2905.34: "No person shall knowingly * * * have in his possession or under his control an obscene, lewd, or lascivious book, magazine, pamphlet, paper, writing, advertisement, circular, print, picture * * * or drawing * * * of an indecent or immoral nature * * *. Whoever violates this section shall be fined not less than two hundred nor more than two thousand dollars or imprisoned not less than one nor more than seven years, or both."

suitcase beside her bed. All of this material, appellant—and a friend of hers—said were odds and ends belonging to a recent boarder, a man who had left suddenly for New York and had been detained there. As the Supreme Court of Ohio read the statute under which appellant is charged, she is guilty of the crime whichever story is true.

The Ohio Supreme Court sustained the conviction even though it was based on the documents obtained in the lawless search. For in Ohio evidence obtained by an unlawful search and seizure is admissible in a criminal prosecution at least where it was not taken from the "defendant's person by the use of brutal or offensive force against defendant." State v. Mapp, 170 Ohio St. 427, 166 N.E.2d 387, at page 388, syllabus 2; State v. Lindway, 131 Ohio St. 166, 2 N.E.2d 490. This evidence would have been inadmissible in a federal prosecution. Weeks v. United States, 232 U.S. 383, 34 S.Ct. 341, 58 L.Ed. 652; Elkins v. United States, 364 U.S. 206, 80 S.Ct. 1437, 4 L.Ed.2d 1669. For, as stated in the former decision, "The effect of the Fourth Amendment is to put the courts of the United States and Federal officials, in the exercise of their power and authority, under limitations and restraints * * *." Id., 232 U.S. at pages 391–392, 34 S.Ct. at page 344. It was therefore held that evidence obtained (which in that case was documents and correspondence) from a home without any warrant was not admissible in a federal prosecution.

We held in Wolf v. People of State of Colorado, 338 U.S. 25, 69 S.Ct. 1359, 93 L.Ed. 1782, that the Fourth Amendment was applicable to the States by reason of the Due Process Clause of the Fourteenth Amendment. But a majority held that the exclusionary rule of the Weeks case was not required of the States, that they could apply such sanctions as they chose. That position had the necessary votes to carry the day. But with all respect it was not the voice of reason or principle.

As stated in the Weeks case, if evidence seized in violation of the Fourth Amendment can be used against an accused, "his right to be secure against such searches and seizures is of no value, and * * * might as well be stricken from the Constitution." 232 U.S. at page 393, 34 S.Ct. at page 344.

When we allowed States to give constitutional sanction to the "shabby business" of unlawful entry into a home (to use an expression of Mr. Justice Murphy, Wolf v. People of State of Colorado, 338 U.S. at page 46, 69 S.Ct. at page 1371), we did indeed rob the Fourth Amendment of much meaningful force. There are, of course, other theoretical remedies. One is disciplinary action within the hierarchy of the police system, including prosecution of the police officer for a crime. Yet as Mr. Justice Murphy said in Wolf v. People of State of Colorado, 338 U.S. at page 42, 69 S.Ct. at page 1369, "Self-scrutiny is a lofty ideal, but its exaltation reaches new heights if we expect a District Attorney to prosecute himself or his associates for well-meaning violations of the search and seizure clause during a raid the District Attorney or his associates have ordered."

The only remaining remedy, if exclusion of the evidence is not required, is an action of trespass by the homeowner against the offending officer. Mr. Justice Murphy showed how onerous and difficult it would be for the citizen to maintain that action and how meagre the relief even if the citizen prevails. 338 U.S. 42–44, 69 S.Ct. 1369–1370. The truth is that trespass actions against officers who make unlawful searches and seizures are mainly illusory remedies.

Without judicial action making the exclusionary rule applicable to the States, Wolf v. People of State of Colorado in practical effect reduced the guarantee against unreasonable searches and seizures to "a dead letter," as Mr. Justice Rutledge said in his dissent. See 338 U.S. at page 47, 69 S.Ct. at page 1368.

Wolf v. People of State of Colorado, supra, was decided in 1949. The immediate result was a storm of constitutional controversy which only today finds its end. I believe that this is an appropriate case in which to put an end to the asymmetry which Wolf imported into the law. See Stefanelli v. Minard, 342 U.S. 117, 72 S.Ct. 118, 96 L.Ed. 138; Rea v. United States, 350 U.S. 214, 76 S.Ct. 292, 100 L.Ed. 233; Elkins v. United States, supra; Monroe v. Pape, 365 U.S. 167, 81 S.Ct. 473, 5 L.Ed.2d 492. It is an appropriate case because the facts it presents show—as would few other cases—the casual arrogance of those who have the untrammelled power to invade one's home and to seize one's person.

It is also an appropriate case in the narrower and more technical sense. The issues of the illegality of the search and the admissibility of the evidence have been presented to the state court and were duly raised here in accordance with the applicable Rule of Practice.[4] The question was raised in the notice of appeal, the jurisdictional statement and in appellant's brief on the merits.[5] It is true that argument was mostly directed to another issue in the case, but that is often the fact. See Rogers v. Richmond, 365 U.S. 534–540,

---

[4] "The notice of appeal * * * shall set forth the questions presented by the appeal * * *. Only the questions set forth in the notice of appeal or fairly comprised therein will be considered by the court." Rule 10, subd. 2(c), Rules of the Supreme Court of the United States, 28 U.S.C.

[5] "Did the conduct of the police in procuring the books, papers and pictures placed in evidence by the Prosecution violate Amendment IV, and Amendment XIV Section 1 of the United States Constitution * * *?"

81 S.Ct. 735, 736–739, 5 L.Ed.2d 760. Of course, an earnest advocate of a position always believes that, had he only an additional opportunity for argument, his side would win. But, subject to the sound discretion of a court, all argument must at last come to a halt. This is especially so as to an issue about which this Court said last year that "The arguments of its antagonists and of its proponents have been so many times marshalled as to require no lengthy elaboration here." Elkins v. United States, supra, 364 U.S. 216, 80 S.Ct. 1443.

Moreover, continuance of Wolf v. People of State of Colorado in its full vigor breeds the unseemly shopping around of the kind revealed in Wilson v. Schnettler, 365 U.S. 381, 81 S.Ct. 632, 5 L.Ed.2d 620. Once evidence, inadmissible in a federal court, is admissible in a state court a "double standard" exists which, as the Court points out, leads to "working arrangements" that undercut federal policy and reduce some aspects of law enforcement to shabby business. The rule that supports that practice does not have the force of reason behind it.

Memorandum of Mr. Justice STEWART.

Agreeing fully with Part I of Mr. Justice HARLAN's dissenting opinion, I express no view as to the merits of the constitutional issue which the Court today decides. I would, however, reverse the judgment in this case, because I am persuaded that the provision of § 2905.34 of the Ohio Revised Code, upon which the petitioner's conviction was based, is, in the words of Mr. Justice HARLAN, not "consistent with the rights of free thought and expression assured against state action by the Fourteenth Amendment."

Mr. Justice HARLAN, whom Mr. Justice FRANKFURTER and Mr. Justice WHITTAKER join, dissenting.

In overruling the Wolf case the Court, in my opinion, has forgotten the sense of judicial restraint which, with due regard for *stare decisis,* is one element that should enter into deciding whether a past decision of this Court should be overruled. Apart from that I also believe that the Wolf rule represents sounder Constitutional doctrine than the new rule which now replaces it.

I.

From the Court's statement of the case one would gather that the central, if not controlling, issue on this appeal is whether illegally state-seized evidence is Constitutionally admissible in a state prosecution, an issue which would of course face us with the need for re-examining Wolf. However, such is not the situation. For, although that question was indeed raised here and below among appellant's subordinate points, the new and pivotal issue brought to the Court by this appeal is whether § 2905.34 of the Ohio Revised Code making criminal the *mere* knowing the possession or control of obscene material,[1] and under which appellant has been convicted, is consistent with the rights of free thought and expression assured against state action by the Fourteenth Amendment.[2] That was the principal issue which was decided by the Ohio Supreme Court,[3] which was tendered by appellant's Jurisdictional Statement,[4] and which was briefed[5] and argued[6] in this Court.

---

[1] The material parts of that law are quoted in note 1 of the Court's opinion, 367 U.S. at page 643, 81 S.Ct. at page 1685.

[2] In its note 3, 367 U.S. at page 646, 81 S.Ct. at page 1686, the Court, it seems to me, has turned upside down the relative importance of appellant's reliance on the various points made by him on this appeal.

[3] See 170 Ohio St. 427, 166 N.E.2d 387. Because of the unusual provision of the Ohio Constitution requiring "the concurrence of at least all but one of the judges" of the Ohio Supreme Court before a state law is held unconstitutional (except in the case of affirmance of a holding of unconstitutionality by the Ohio Court of Appeals). Ohio Const. Art. IV, § 2, the State Supreme Court was compelled to uphold the constitutionality of § 2905.34, despite the fact that four of its seven judges thought the statute offensive to the Fourteenth Amendment.

[4] Respecting the "substantiality" of the federal questions tendered by this appeal, appellant's Jurisdictional Statement contained the following:
"The Federal questions raised by this appeal are substantial for the following reasons:
"The Ohio Statute under which the defendant was convicted violates one's sacred right to own and hold property, which has been held inviolate by the Federal Constitution. The right of the individual 'to read, to believe or disbelieve, and to think without governmental supervision is one of our basic liberties, but to dictate to the mature adult what books he may have in his own private library seems to be a clear infringement of the constitutional rights of the individual' (Justice Herbert's dissenting Opinion, Appendix 'A'). Many convictions have followed that of the defendant in the State Courts of Ohio based upon this very same statute. Unless this Honorable Court hears this matter and determines once and for all that the Statute is unconstitutional as defendant contends, there will be many such appeals. When Sections 2905.34, 2905.37 and 3767.01 of the Ohio Revised Code [the latter two Sections providing exceptions to the coverage of § 2905.34 and related provisions of Ohio's obscenity statutes] are read together, * * * they obviously contravene the Federal and State constitutional provisions; by being convicted under the statute involved herein, and in the manner in which she was convicted, Defendant-Appellant has been denied due process of law; a sentence of from one (1) to seven (7) years in a penal institution for alleged violation of this unconstitutional section of the Ohio Revised Code deprives the defendant of her right to liberty and the pursuit of happiness, contrary to the Federal and State constitutional provisions, for circumstances which she herself did not put in motion, and is a cruel and unusual punishment inflicted upon her contrary to the State and Federal Constitutions."

[5] The appellant's brief did not urge the overruling of Wolf. Indeed it did not even cite the case. The brief of the appellee merely relied on Wolf in support of the State's contention that appellant's conviction was not vitiated by the admission in evidence of the fruits of the al-

In this posture of things, I think it fair to say that five members of this Court have simply "reached out" to overrule Wolf. With all respect for the views of the majority, and recognizing that *stare decisis* carries different weight in Constitutional adjudication than it does in nonconstitutional decision, I can perceive no justification for regarding this case as an appropriate occasion for re-examining Wolf.

The action of the Court finds no support in the rule that decision of Constitutional issues should be avoided wherever possible. For in overruling Wolf the Court, instead of passing upon the validity of Ohio's § 2905.34, has simply chosen between two Constitutional questions. Moreover, I submit that it has chosen the more difficult and less appropriate of the two questions. The Ohio statute which, as construed by the State Supreme Court, punishes knowing possession or control of obscene material, irrespective of the purposes of such possession or control (with exceptions not here applicable)[7] and irrespective of whether the accused had any reasonable opportunity to rid himself of the material after discovering

leged unlawful search and seizure by the police. The brief of the American and Ohio Civil Liberties Unions, as *amici*, did in one short concluding paragraph of its argument "request" the Court to re-examine and overrule Wolf, but without argumentation. I quote in full this part of their brief:

"This case presents the issue of whether evidence obtained in an illegal search and seizure can constitutionally be used in a State criminal proceeding. We are aware of the view that this Court has taken on this issue in Wolf v. People of State of Colorado, 338 U.S. 25, 69 S.Ct. 1359, 93 L.Ed. 1782. It is our purpose by this paragraph to respectfully request that this Court re-examine this issue and conclude that the ordered liberty concept guaranteed to persons by the due process clause of the Fourteenth Amendment necessarily requires that evidence illegally obtained in violation thereof, not be admissible in state criminal proceedings."

[6] Counsel for appellant on oral argument, as in his brief, did not urge that Wolf be overruled. Indeed, when pressed by questioning from the bench whether he was not in fact urging us to overrule Wolf,

counsel expressly disavowed any such purpose.

[7] "2905.37 Legitimate publications not obscene.

"Sections 2905.33 to 2905.36, inclusive, of the Revised Code do not affect teaching in regularly chartered medical colleges, the publication of standard medical books, or regular practitioners of medicine or druggists in their legitimate business, nor do they affect the publication and distribution of bona fide works of art. No articles specified in sections 2905.33, 2905.34, and 2905.36 of the Revised Code shall be considered a work of art unless such article is made, published, and distributed by a bona fide association of artists or an association for the advancement of art whose demonstrated purpose does not contravene sections 2905.06 to 2905.44, inclusive, of the Revised Code, and which is not organized for profit."
§ 3767.01(C)
"This section and sections 2905.34, * * * 2905.37 * * * of the Revised Code shall not affect * * * any newspaper, magazine, or other publication entered as second class matter by the post-office department."

that it was obscene,[8] surely presents a Constitutional question which is both simpler and less far-reaching than the question which the Court decides today. It seems to me that justice might well have been done in this case without overturning a decision on which the administration of criminal law in many of the States has long justifiably relied.

Since the demands of the case before us do not require us to reach the question of the validity of Wolf, I think this case furnishes a singularly inappropriate occasion for reconsideration of that decision, if reconsideration is indeed warranted. Even the most cursory examination will reveal that the doctrine of the Wolf case has been of continuing importance in the administration of state criminal law. Indeed, certainly as regards its "nonexclusionary" aspect, Wolf did no more than articulate the then existing assumption among the States that the federal cases enforcing the exclusionary rule "do not bind [the States], for they construe provisions of the Federal Constitution, the Fourth and Fifth Amendments, not applicable to the States." People v. Defore, 242 N.Y. 13, 20, 150 N.E. 585, 587. Though, of course, not reflecting the full measure of this continuing reliance, I find that during the last three Terms, for instance, the issue of the inadmissibility of illegally state-obtained evidence appears on an average of about fifteen times per Term just in the *in forma pauperis* cases summarily disposed of by us. This would indicate both that the issue which is now being decided may well have untoward practical ramifications respecting state cases long since disposed of in reliance on Wolf, and that were we determined to re-examine that doctrine we would not lack future opportunity.

The occasion which the Court has taken here is in the context of a case where the question was briefed not at all and argued only extremely tangentially. The unwisdom of overruling Wolf without full-dress argument is aggravated by the circumstance that that decision is a comparatively recent one (1949) to which three members of the present majority have at one time or other expressly subscribed, one to be sure with explicit misgivings.[9] I would think

---

[8] The Ohio Supreme Court, in its construction of § 2905.34, controlling upon us here, refused to import into it any other exceptions than those expressly provided by the the statute. See note 7, supra. Instead it held that "If anyone looks at a book and finds it lewd, he is forthwith, under this legislation, guilty * * *." [170 Ohio St. 427, 166 N.E.2d 391.]

[9] See Wolf v. People of State of Col-

orado, 338 U.S. at pages 39–40, 69 S.Ct. at pages 1367–1368; Irvine v. People of State of California, 347 U.S. 128, 133–134, and at pages 138–139, 74 S.Ct. 381, 383–384, and at pages 386–387, 98 L.Ed. 561. In the latter case, decided in 1954, Mr. Justice Jackson, writing for the majority, said (347 U.S. at page 134, 74 S.Ct. at page 384): "We think that the Wolf decision should not be overruled, for the reasons so

that our obligation to the States, on whom we impose this new rule, as well as the obligation of orderly adherence to our own processes would demand that we seek that aid which adequate briefing and argument lends to the determination of an important issue. It certainly has never been a postulate of judicial power that mere altered disposition, or subsequent membership on the Court, is sufficient warrant for overturning a deliberately decided rule of Constitutional law.

Thus, if the Court were bent on reconsidering Wolf, I think that there would soon have presented itself an appropriate opportunity in which we could have had the benefit of full briefing and argument. In any event, at the very least, the present cast should have been set down for reargument, in view of the inadequate briefing and argument we have received on the Wolf point. To all intents and purposes the Court's present action amounts to a summary reversal of Wolf, without argument.

I am bound to say that what has been done is not likely to promote respect either for the Court's adjudicatory process or for the stability of its decisions. Having been unable, however, to persuade any of the majority to a different procedural course, I now turn to the merits of the present decision.

II.

Essential to the majority's argument against Wolf is the proposition that the rule of Weeks v. United States, 232 U.S. 383, 34 S.Ct. 341, 58 L.Ed. 632, excluding in federal criminal trials the use of evidence obtained in violation of the Fourth Amendment, derives not from the "supervisory power" of this Court over the federal judicial system, but from Constitutional requirement. This is so because no one, I suppose, would suggest that this Court possesses any general supervisory power over the state courts. Although I entertain considerable doubt as to the soundness of this foundational proposition of the majority, cf. Wolf v. People of State of Colorado, 338 U.S. at pages 39–40, 69 S.Ct. at pages 1367–1368 (concurring opinion), I shall assume, for present purposes, that the Weeks rule "is of constitutional origin."

At the heart of the majority's opinion in this case is the following syllogism: (1) the rule excluding in federal criminal trials evidence which is the product of an illegal search and seizure is "part and parcel" of the Fourth Amendment; (2) Wolf held that the pri-

---

persuasively stated therein." Compare Schwartz v. Texas, 344 U.S. 199, 73 S.Ct. 232, 97 L.Ed. 231, and Stefanelli v. Minard, 342 U.S. 117, 72 S.Ct. 188, 96 L.Ed. 138, in which the Wolf case was discussed and in no way disapproved. And see Pugach v. Dollinger, 365 U.S. 458, 81 S.Ct. 650, 5 L.Ed.2d 678, which relied on Schwartz.

vacy" assured against federal action by the Fourth Amendment is also protected against state action by the Fourteenth Amendment; and (3) it is therefore "logically and constitutionally necessary" that the Weeks exclusionary rule should also be enforced against the States.[10]

This reasoning ultimately rests on the unsound premise that because Wolf carried into the States, as part of "the concept of ordered liberty" embodied in the Fourteenth Amendment, the principle of "privacy" underlying the Fourth Amendment (338 U.S. at page 27, 69 S.Ct. at page 1361), it must follow that whatever configurations of the Fourth Amendment have been developed in the particularizing federal precedents are likewise to be deemed a part of "ordered liberty," and as such are enforceable against the States. For me, this does not follow at all.

It cannot be too much emphasized that what was recognized in Wolf was not that the Fourth Amendment *as such* is enforceable against the States as a facet of due process, a view of the Fourteenth Amendment which, as Wolf itself pointed out (338 U.S. at page 26, 69 S.Ct. at page 1360), has long since been discredited, but the principle of privacy "which is at the core of the Fourth Amendment." Id., 338 U.S. at page 27, 69 S.Ct. at page 1361. It would not be proper to expect or impose any precise equivalence, either as regards the scope of the right or the means of its implementation, between the requirements of the Fourth and Fourteenth Amendments. For the Fourth, unlike what was said in Wolf of the Fourteenth, does not state a general principle only; it is a particular command, having its setting in a pre-existing legal context on which both interpreting decisions and enabling statutes must at least build.

Thus, even in a case which presented simply the question of whether a particular search and seizure was constitutionally "unreasonable"—say in a tort action against state officers—we would not be true to the Fourteenth Amendment were we merely to stretch the general principle of individual privacy on a Procrustean bed of federal precedents under the Fourth Amendment. But in this instance more than that is involved, for here we are reviewing not a determination that what the state police did was Constitutionally permissible (since the state court quite evidently assumed that it was not), but a determination that appellant was properly found guilty of conduct which, for present purposes, it is to be assumed the State could Constitutionally punish. Since there is not the slightest suggestion that Ohio's policy is "affirmatively to sanction

---

[10] Actually, only four members of the majority support this reasoning. See, 367 U.S. at pages 685–686, 81 S.Ct. at page 1708.

* * * police incursion into privacy" (338 U.S. at page 28, 69 S.Ct. at page 1361), compare Marcus v. Search Warrants, etc., 367 U.S. 717, 81 S.Ct. 1708, 6 L.Ed.2d 1127, what the Court is now doing is to impose upon the States not only federal substantive standards of "search and seizure" but also the basic federal remedy for violation of those standards. For I think it entirely clear that the Weeks excusionary rule is but a remedy which, by penalizing past official misconduct, is aimed at deterring such conduct in the future.

I would not impose upon the States this federal exclusionary remedy. The reasons given by the majority for now suddenly turning its back on Wolf seem to me notably unconvincing.

First, it is said that "the factual grounds upon which Wolf was based" have since changed, in that more States now follow the Weeks exclusionary rule than was so at the time Wolf was decided. While that is true, a recent survey indicates that at present one-half of the States still adhere to the common-law non-exclusionary rule, and one, Maryland, retains the rule as to felonies. Berman and Oberst, Admissibility of Evidence Obtained by an Unconstitutional Search and Seizure, 55 N.W.L.Rev. 525, 532–533. But in any case surely all this is beside the point, as the majority itself indeed seems to recognize. Our concern here, as it was in Wolf, is not with the desirability of that rule but only with the question whether the States are Constitutionally free to follow it or not as they may themselves determine, and the relevance of the disparity of views among the States on this point lies simply in the fact that the judgment involved is a debatable one. Moreover, the very fact on which the majority relies, instead of lending support to what is now being done, points away from the need of replacing voluntary state action with federal compulsion.

The preservation of a proper balance between state and federal responsibility in the administration of criminal justice demands patience on the part of those who might like to see things move faster among the States in this respect. Problems of criminal law enforcement vary widely from State to State. One State, in considering the totality of its legal picture, may conclude that the need for embracing the Weeks rule is pressing because other remedies are are unavailable or inadequate to secure compliance with the substantive Constitutional principle involved. Another, though equally solicitous of Constitutional rights, may choose to pursue one purpose at at time, allowing all evidence relevant to guilt to be brought into a criminal trial, and dealing with Constitutional infractions by other means. Still another may consider the exclusionary rule too rough-and-ready a remedy, in that it reaches only unconstitutional intrusions which eventuate in criminal prosecution of the victims.

256

Further, a State after experimenting with the Weeks rule for a time may, because of unsatisfactory experience with it, decide to revert to a non-exclusionary rule. And so on. From the standpoint of Constitutional permissibility in pointing a State in one direction or another, I do not see at all why "time has set its face against" the considerations which led Mr. Justice Cardozo, then chief judge of the New York Court of Appeals, to reject for New York in People v. Defore, 242 N.Y. 13, 150 N.E. 585, the Weeks exclusionary rule. For us the question remains, as it has always been, one of state power, not one of passing judgment on the wisdom of one state course or another. In my view this Court should continue to forbear from fettering the States with an adamant rule which may embarrass them in coping with their own peculiar problems in criminal law enforcement.

Further, we are told that imposition of the Weeks rule on the States makes "very good sense," in that it will promote recognition by state and federal officials of their "mutual obligation to respect the same fundamental criteria" in their approach to law enforcement, and will avoid " 'needless conflict between state and federal courts.' " Indeed the majority now finds an incongruity in Wolf's discriminating perception between the demands of "ordered liberty" as respects the basic right of "privacy" and the means of securing it among the States. That perception, resting both on a sensitive regard for our federal system and a sound recognition of this Court's remoteness from particular state problems, is for me the strength of that decision.

An approach which regards the issue as one of achieving procedural symmetry or of serving administrative convenience surely disfigures the boundaries of this Court's functions in relation to the state and federal courts. Our role in promulgating the Weeks rule and its extensions in such cases as Rea, Elkins, and Rios[11] was quite a different one than it is here. There, in implementing the Fourth Amendment, we occupied the position of a tribunal having the ultimate responsibility for developing the standards and procedures of judicial administration within the judicial system over which it presides. Here we review state procedures whose measure is to be taken not against the specific substantive commands of the Fourth Amendment but under the flexible contours of the Due Process Clause. I do not believe that the Fourteenth Amendment empowers this Court to mould state remedies effectuating the right to freedom from "arbitrary intrusion by the police" to suit its own notions of how things should be done, as, for instance, the California

---

[11] Rea v. United States, 350 U.S. 214; Elkins v. United States, 364 U.S. 206; Rios v. United States, 364 U.S. 253.

Supreme Court did in People v. Cahan, 44 Cal.2d 434, 282 P.2d 905, with reference to procedures in the California courts or as this Court did in Weeks for the lower federal courts.

A state conviction comes to us as the complete product of a sovereign judicial system. Typically a case will have been tried in a trial court, tested in some final appellate court, and will go no further. In the comparatively rare instance when a conviction is reviewed by us on due process grounds we deal then with a finished product in the creation of which we are allowed no hand, and our task, far from being one of over-all supervision, is, speaking generally, restricted to a determination of whether the prosecution was Constitutionally fair. The specifics of trial procedure, which in every mature legal system will vary greatly in detail, are within the sole competence of the States. I do not see how it can be said that a trial becomes unfair simply because a State determines that evidence may be considered by the trier of fact, regardless of how it was obtained, if it is relevant to the one issue with which the trial is concerned, the guilt or innocence of the accused. Of course, a court may use its procedures as an incidental means of pursuing other ends than the correct resolution of the controversies before it. Such indeed is the Weeks rule, but if a State does not choose to use its courts in this way, I do not believe that this Court is empowered to impose this much-debated procedure on local courts, however efficacious we may consider the Weeks rule to be as a means of securing Constitutional rights.

Finally, it is said that the overruling of Wolf is supported by the established doctrine that the admission in evidence of an involuntary confession renders a state conviction Constitutionally invalid. Since such a confession may often be entirely reliable, and therefore of the greatest relevance to the issue of the trial, the argument continues, this doctrine is ample warrant in precedent that the way evidence was obtained, and not just its relevance, is Constitutionally significant to the fairness of a trial. I believe this analogy is not a true one. The "coerced confession" rule is certainly not a rule that any illegally obtained statements may not be used in evidence. I would suppose that a statement which is procured during a period of illegal detention, McNabb v. United States, 318 U.S. 332, 63 S.Ct. 608, 87 L.Ed. 819, is, as much as unlawfully seized evidence, illegally obtained, but this Court has consistently refused to reverse state convictions resting on the use of such statements. Indeed it would seem the Court laid at rest the very argument now made by the majority when in Lisenba v. People of State of California, 314 U.S. 219, at page 235, 62 S.Ct. 280, at page 289, 86 L.Ed. 166, a state-coerced confession case, it said:

"It may be assumed [that the] treatment of the petitioner [by the police] * * * deprived him of his liberty without due process and that the petitioner would have been afforded preventive relief if he could have gained access to a court to seek it.

"But illegal acts, as such, committed in the course of obtaining a confession * * * do not furnish an answer to the constitutional question we must decide. * * * The gravamen of his complaint is the unfairness of the *use* of his confessions, and what occurred in their procurement is relevant only as it bears on that issue." (emphasis supplied.)

The point, then, must be that in requiring exclusion of an involuntary statement of an accused, we are concerned not with an appropriate remedy for what the police have done, but with something which is regarded as going to the heart of our concepts of fairness and judicial procedure. The operative assumption of our procedural system is that "Ours is the accusatorial as opposed to the inquisitorial system. Such has been the characteristic of Anglo-American criminal justice since it freed itself from practices borrowed by the Star Chamber from the Continent whereby an accused was interrogated in secret for hours on end." Watts v. State of Indiana, 338 U.S. 49, 54, 69 S.Ct. 1347, 1350, 93 L.Ed. 1801. See Rogers v. Richmond, 365 U.S. 534, 541, 81 S.Ct. 735, 740, 5 L.Ed.2d 760. The pressures brought to bear against an accused leading to a confession, unlike an unconstitutional violation of privacy, do not, apart from the use of the confession at trial, necessarily involve independent Constitutional violations. What is crucial is that the trial defense to which an accused is entitled should not be rendered an empty formality by reason of statements wrung from him, for then "a prisoner * * * [has been] made the deluded instrument of his own conviction." 2 Hawkins, Pleas of the Crown (8th ed., 1824), c. 46, § 34. That this is a *procedural right,* and that its violation occurs at the time his improperly obtained statement is admitted at trial, is manifest. For without this right all the careful safeguards erected around the giving of testimony, whether by an accused or any other witness, would become empty formalities in a procedure where the most compelling possible evidence of guilt, a confession, would have already been obtained at the unsupervised pleasure of the police.

This, and not the disciplining of the police, as with illegally seized evidence, is surely the true basis for excluding a statement of the accused which was unconstitutionally obtained. In sum, I think the coerced confession analogy works strongly *against* what the Court does today.

In conclusion, it should be noted that the majority opinion in this case is in fact an opinion only for the *judgment* overruling Wolf, and not for the basic rationale by which four members of the majority have reached that result. For my Brother BLACK is unwilling to subscribe to their view that the Weeks exclusionary rule derives from the Fourth Amendment itself (see 367 U.S. at page 661, 81 S.Ct. at page 1694), but joins the majority opinion on the premise that its end result can be achieved by bringing the Fifth Amendment to the aid of the Fourth (see 367 U.S. at pages 662–665, 81 S.Ct. at pages 1695–1697).[12] On that score I need only say that whatever the validity of the "Fourth-Fifth Amendment" correlation which the Boyd case (116 U.S. 616, 6 S.Ct. 524, 29 L.Ed. 746) found, see 8 Wigmore, Evidence (3d ed. 1940), § 2184, we have only very recently again reiterated the long-established doctrine of this Court that the Fifth Amendment privilege against self-incrimination is not applicable to the States. See Cohen v. Hurley, 366 U.S. 117, 81 S.Ct. 954, 6 L.Ed.2d 156.

I regret that I find so unwise in principle and so inexpedient in policy a decision motivated by the high purpose of increasing respect for Constitutional rights. But in the last analysis I think this Court can increase respect for the Constitution only if it rigidly respects the limitations which the Constitution places upon it, and respects as well the principles inherent in its own processes. In the present case I think we exceed both, and that our voice becomes only a voice of power, not of reason.

Terry v. Ohio*

The extent to which the police may "stop and frisk" suspicious persons is considered by the Supreme Court in the *Terry Case*. Establishing the boundaries within which such law enforcement practices are tolerable is one of the most sensitive judgments the Supreme Court has been called on to make. The reason for this lies in the sanctity which our society attributes to the individual's person. Any permissible governmental intrusion in this area is not to be granted lightly. At best it is barely tolerable.

Terry and a companion were kept under observation by a plain-clothes policeman after their actions had aroused his curiosity. Continued observation turned curiosity into suspicion, suspicion that Terry and his companion might be about to commit an armed

---

[12] My Brother STEWART concurs in the Court's judgment on grounds which have nothing to do with Wolf.

*392 U.S. 1, 88 S.Ct. 1868 (June 10, 1968)

robbery. Acting solely on this suspicion, the officer stopped the men and conducted a "frisk" to see if they were armed. Should he not have done so he feared the answer to his inquiries might be a bullet. As a result of this search, concealed weapons were confiscated and Terry was convicted of possessing a concealed weapon.

The Supreme Court now had to pass on the admissibility of the evidence so acquired. In an eight to one decision, the Supreme Court ruled that the evidence was properly admitted and Terry's conviction was affirmed.

The Court made it clear that a "stop and frisk" is a "search and seizure". Accordingly, the power of the public to stop and frisk is subject to Fourth Amendment limitations which prohibit unreasonable searches and seizures. That Amendment provides:

> The right of the people to be secure in their persons, homes, papers and effects, against unreasonable searches and seizures, shall not be violated, and no warrants shall issue, but upon probable cause, supported by Oath or affirmation, and particularly describing the place to be searched, and the persons or things to be seized.

In prior decisions the Supreme Court has held that under certain circumstances and conditions, i.e., a search incident to a valid arrest, a warrantless search and seizure is constitutionally valid. A stop and frisk by definition amounts to a search and seizure without a warrant. In this case the Supreme Court had to face the issue of whether a stop and frisk could ever be made under such circumstances and conditions that the warrantless search, which it amounts to, would be valid. The Court answered this issue in the affirmative.

What are those circumstances and conditions? The Court indicated that each case would have to be decided on its own merits, on the facts presented therein. What were the factual conditions of the *Terry Case* which lead to a determination that the warrantless search was valid. First, the officer had reasonable suspicion that the defendant had engaged in or was engaging in a crime. The concept of "reasonable suspicion" encompasses less than what is required to establish "probable cause." Probable cause (facts which would justify the officer's arresting of Terry) did not exist in this case. However, the reasonable suspicion must be based on more than a mere hunch. It must be based on facts which the officer is able to articulate. And these facts must permit a reasonable inference that the subject has engaged in or is engaging in a crime.

The second factual condition of importance in this case is that the officer had reason to believe that the defendant might be

261

armed. "Reason to believe" contemplates facts which the officer can articulate and which permit the inference that the subject might be armed. The third and last important factor was that the search was designed solely for the purpose of determining if the subject did in fact possess any weapons. The *Terry Case* decides that when these three factors are present a stop and frisk is valid.

The Warren Court, noted for its decisions expanding the rights of the accused, has taken the opposite course in this case. The Court concludes that at least in limited circumstances the right of society to be protected from lawlessness must be given more weight than an individual's right to be secure in his person.

In reading this decision its sociological implications should be kept in mind. At this time in our history, the relationship between the police and urban minority groups is somewhat strained. Misunderstandings between the two are frequent. Misunderstanding could lead to suspicion which in turn could lead to a stop and frisk. The broader the police power to search and seize the greater the tendency for such a confrontation between these two groups. Of course, confrontations are not necessarily bad. The confrontation between police and criminal is desirable. But what about a confrontation between the police and an innocent member of a minority group? The indignity suffered by such an individual is not likely to promote respect for the law.

Text of Case

A Cleveland detective (McFadden), on a downtown beat which he had been patrolling for many years, observed two strangers (petitioner and another man, Chilton) on a street corner. He saw them proceed alternately back and forth along an identical route, pausing to stare in the same store window, which they did for a total of about 24 times. Each completion of the route was followed by a conference between the two on a corner, at one of which they were joined by a third man (Katz) who left swiftly. Suspecting the two men of "casing a job, a stick-up," the officer followed them and saw them rejoin the third man a couple of blocks away in front of a store. The officer approached the three, identified himself as a policeman, and asked their names. The men "mumbled something," whereupon McFadden spun petitioner around, patted down his outside clothing, and found in his overcoat pocket, but was unable to remove, a pistol. The officer ordered the three into the store. He removed petitioner's overcoat, took out a revolver, and ordered the three to face the wall with their hands raised. He patted down the outer clothing of Chilton and Katz and seized a revolver from Chilton's outside overcoat pocket. He did not put his hands under the

262

outer garments of Katz (since he discovered nothing in his pat-down which might have been a weapon), or under petitioner's or Chilton's outer garments until he felt the guns. The three were taken to the police station. Petitioner and Chilton were charged with carrying concealed weapons. The defense moved to suppress the weapons. Though the trial court rejected the prosecution theory that the guns had been seized during a search incident to a lawful arrest, the court denied the motion to suppress and admitted the weapons into evidence on the ground that the officer had cause to believe that petitioner and Chilton were acting suspiciously, that their interrogation was warranted, and that the officer for his own protection had the right to pat down their outer clothing having reasonable cause to believe that they might be armed. The court distinguished between an investigatory "stop" and an arrest, and between a "frisk" of the outer clothing for weapons and a full-blown search for evidence of crime. Petitioner and Chilton were found guilty, an intermediate appellate court affirmed, and the State Supreme Court dismissed the appeal on the ground that "no substantial constitutional question" was involved.

Louis Stokes argued the cause for petitioner. With him on the brief was *Jack G. Day.*

Reuben M. Payne argued the cause for respondent. With him on the brief was *John T. Corrigan.*

Briefs of *amici curiae,* urging reversal, were filed by *Jack Greenberg, James M. Nabrit III, Michael Meltsner, Melvyn Zarr,* and *Anthony G. Amsterdam* for the NAACP Legal Defense and Educational Fund, Inc., and by *Bernard A. Berkman, Melvin L. Wulf,* and *Alan H. Levine* for the American Civil Liberties Union et al.

Briefs of *amici curiae,* urging affirmance, were filed by *Solicitor General Griswold, Assistant Attorney General Vinson, Ralph S. Spritzer, Beatrice Rosenberg,* and *Mervyn Hamburg* for the United States; by *Louis J. Lefkowitz, pro se, Samuel A. Hirshowitz,* First Assistant Attorney General, and *Maria L. Marcus* and *Brenda Soloff,* Assistant Attorneys General, for the Attorney General of New York; by *Charles Moylan, Jr., Evelle J. Younger,* and *Harry Wood* for the National District Attorneys' Assn., and by *James R. Thompson* for Americans for Effective Law Enforcement.

Mr. Chief Justice WARREN delivered the opinion of the Court.

This case presents serious questions concerning the role of the Fourth Amendment in the confrontation on the street between the citizen and the policeman investigating suspicious circumstances.

Petitioner Terry was convicted of carrying a concealed weapon and sentenced to the statutorily prescribed term of one to three years in the penitentiary.[1] Following the denial of a pretrial motion to suppress, the prosecution introduced in evidence two revolvers and a number of bullets seized from Terry and a codefendant, Richard Chilton,[2] by Cleveland Police Detective Martin McFadden. At the hearing on the motion to suppress this evidence, Officer McFadden testified that while he was patrolling in plain clothes in downtown Cleveland at approximately 2:30 in the afternoon of October 31, 1963, his attention was attracted by two men, Chilton and Terry, standing on the corner of Huron Road and Euclid Avenue. He had never seen the two men before, and he was unable to say precisely what first drew his eye to them. However, he testified that he had been a policeman for 39 years and a detective for 35 and that he had been assigned to patrol this vicinity of downtown Cleveland for shoplifters and pickpockets for 30 years. He explained that he had developed routine habits of observation over the years and that he would "stand and watch people or walk and watch people at many intervals of the day." He added: "Now, in this case when I looked over they didn't look right to me at the time."

His interest aroused, Officer McFadden took up a post of observation in the entrance to a store 300 to 400 feet away from the two men. "I get more purpose to watch them when I seen their movements," he testified. He saw one of the men leave the other one and walk southwest on Huron Road, past some stores. The man paused for a moment and looked in a store window, then walked on a short distance, turned around and walked back toward the corner, pausing once again to look in the same store window. He rejoined his companion at the corner, and the two conferred briefly. Then the second man went through the same series of motions, strolling down Huron Road, looking in the same window, walk-

---

[1] Ohio Rev. Code § 2923.01 (1953) provides in part that "[n]o person shall carry a pistol, bowie knife, dirk, or other dangerous weapon concealed on or about his person." An exception is made for properly authorized law enforcement officers.

[2] Terry and Chilton were arrested, indicted, tried, and convicted together. They were represented by the same attorney, and they made a joint motion to suppress the guns. After the motion was denied, evidence was taken in the case against Chilton. This evidence consisted of the testimony of the arresting offi-

cer and of Chilton. It was then stipulated that this testimony would be applied to the case against Terry, and no further evidence was introduced in that case. The trial judge considered the two cases together, rendered the decisions at the same time and sentenced the two men at the same time. They prosecuted their state court appeals together through the same attorney, and they petitioned this Court for certiorari together. Following the grant of the writ upon this joint petition, Chilton died. Thus, only Terry's conviction is here for review.

ing on a short distance, turning back, peering in the store window again, and returning to confer with the first man at the corner. The two men repeated this ritual alternately between five and six times apiece—in all, roughly a dozen trips. At one point, while the two were standing together on the corner, a third man approached them and engaged them briefly in conversation. This man then left the two others and walked west on Euclid Avenue. Chilton and Terry resumed their measured pacing, peering, and conferring. After this had gone on for 10 to 12 minutes, the two men walked off together, heading west on Euclid Avenue, following the path taken earlier by the third man.

By this time Officer McFadden had become thoroughly suspicious. He testified that after observing their elaborately casual and oft-repeated reconnaissance of the store window on Huron Road, he suspected the two men of "casing a job, a stick-up," and that he considered it his duty as a police officer to investigate further. He added that he feared "they may have a gun." Thus, Officer McFadden followed Chilton and Terry and saw them stop in front of Zucker's store to talk to the same man who had conferred with them earlier on the street corner. Deciding that the situation was ripe for direct action, Officer McFadden approached the three men, identified himself as a police officer and asked for their names. At this point his knowledge was confined to what he had observed. He was not acquainted with any of the three men by name or by sight, and he had received no information concerning them from any other source. When the men "mumbled something" in response to his inquiries, Officer McFadden grabbed petitioner Terry, spun him around so that they were facing the other two, with Terry between McFadden and the others, and patted down the outside of his clothing. In the left breast pocket of Terry's overcoat Officer McFadden felt a pistol. He reached inside the overcoat pocket, but was unable to remove the gun. At this point, keeping Terry between himself and the others, the officer ordered all three men to enter Zucker's store. As they went in, he removed Terry's overcoat completely, removed a .38-caliber revolver from the pocket and ordered all three men to face the wall with their hands raised. Officer McFadden proceeded to pat down the outer clothing of Chilton and the third man, Katz. He discovered another revolver in the outer pocket of Chilton's overcoat, but no weapons were found on Katz. The officer testified that he only patted the men down to see whether they had weapons, and that he did not put his hands beneath the outer garments of either Terry or Chilton until he felt their guns. So far as appears from the record, he never placed his hands beneath Katz' outer garments. Officer McFadden seized Chilton's gun, asked the pro-

265

prietor of the store to call a police wagon, and took all three men to the station, where Chilton and Terry were formally charged with carrying concealed weapons.

On the motion to suppress the guns the prosecution took the position that they had been seized following a search incident to a lawful arrest. The trial court rejected this theory, stating that it "would be stretching the facts beyond reasonable comprehension" to find that Officer McFadden had had probable cause to arrest the men before he patted them down for weapons. However, the court denied the defendants' motion on the ground that Officer McFadden, on the basis of his experience, "had reasonable cause to believe * * * that the defendants were conducting themselves suspiciously, and some interrogation should be made of their action." Purely for his own protection, the court held, the officer had the right to pat down the outer clothing of these men, who he had reasonable cause to believe might be armed. The court distinguished between an investigatory "stop" and an arrest, and between a "frisk" of the outer clothing for weapons and a full-blown search for evidence of crime. The frisk, it held, was essential to the proper performance of the officer's investigatory duties, for without it "the answer to the police officer may be a bullet, and a loaded pistol discovered during the frisk is admissible."

After the court denied their motion to suppress, Chilton and Terry waived jury trial and pleaded not guilty. The court adjudged them guilty, and the Court of Appeals for the Eighth Judicial District, Cuyahoga County, affirmed. State v. Terry, 5 Ohio App.2d 122, 214 N.E.2d 114 (1966). The Supreme Court of Ohio dismissed their appeal on the ground that no "substantial constitutional question" was involved. We granted certiorari, 387 U.S. 929, 87 S.Ct. 2050, 18 L.Ed.2d 989 (1967), to determine whether the admission of the revolvers in evidence violated petitioner's rights under the Fourth Amendment, made applicable to the States by the Fourteenth. Mapp v. Ohio, 367 U.S. 643, 81 S.Ct. 1684, 6 L.Ed.2d 1081 (1961). We affirm the conviction.

I.

The Fourth Amendment provides that "the right of the people to be secure in their persons, houses, papers, and effects, against unreasonable searches and seizures, shall not be violated * * *." This inestimable right of personal security belongs as much to the citizen on the streets of our cities as to the homeowner closeted in his study to dispose of his secret affairs. For, as this Court has always recognized,

"No right is held more sacred, or is more carefully guarded, by the common law, than the right of every individual to the possession and control of his own person, free from all restraint or interference of others, unless by clear and unquestionable authority of law." Union Pac. R. Co. v. Botsford, 141 U.S. 250, 251, 11 S.Ct. 1000, 1001, 35 L.Ed. 734 (1891).
We have recently held that "the Fourth Amendment protects people, not places," Katz v. United States, 389 U.S. 347, 351, 88 S.Ct. 507, 511, 19 L.Ed.2d 576 (1967), and wherever an individual may harbor a reasonable "expectation of privacy," id., at 361, 88 S.Ct. at 507 (Mr. Justice Harlan, concurring), he is entitled to be free from unreasonable governmental intrusion. Of course, the specific content and incidents of this right must be shaped by the context in which it is asserted. For "what the Constitution forbids is not all searches and seizures, but unreasonable searches and seizures." Elkins v. United States, 364 U.S. 206, 222, 80 S.Ct. 1437, 1446, 4 L.Ed.2d 1669 (1960). Unquestionably petitioner was entitled to the protection of the Fourth Amendment as he walked down the street in Cleveland. Beck v. State of Ohio, 379 U.S. 89, 85 S.Ct. 223, 13 L.Ed.2d 142 (1964); Rios v. United States, 364 U.S. 253, 80 S.Ct. 1431, 4 L.Ed.2d 1688 (1960); Henry v. United States, 361 U.S. 98, 80 S.Ct. 168, 4 L.Ed.2d 134 (1959); United States v. Di Re, 332 U.S. 581, 68 S.Ct. 222, 92 L.Ed. 210 (1948); Carroll v. United States, 267 U.S. 132, 45 S.Ct. 280, 69 L.Ed. 543 (1925). The question is whether in all the circumstances of this on-the-street encounter, his right to personal security was violated by an unreasonable search and seizure.
We would be less than candid if we did not acknowledge that this question thrusts to the fore difficult and troublesome issues regarding a sensitive area of police activity—issues which have never before been squarely presented to this Court. Reflective of the tensions involved are the practical and constitutional arguments pressed with great vigor on both sides of the public debate over the power of the police to "stop and frisk"—as it is sometimes euphemistically termed—suspicious persons.
On the one hand, it is frequently argued that in dealing with the rapidly unfolding and often dangerous situations on city streets the police are in need of an escalating set of flexible responses, graduated in relation to the amount of information they possess. For this purpose it is urged that distinctions should be made between a "stop" and an "arrest" (or a "seizure" of a person), and between a "frisk" and a "search."[3] Thus, it is argued, the police

---

[3] Both the trial court and the Ohio Court of Appeals in this case re-

lied upon such a distinction. State v. Terry, 5 Ohio App.2d 122, 125–

should be allowed to "stop" a person and detain him briefly for questioning upon suspicion that he may be connected with crimi- nal activity. Upon suspicion that the person may be armed, the police should have the power to "frisk" him for weapons. If the "stop" and the "frisk" give rise to probable cause to believe that the suspect has committed a crime, then the police should be em- powered to make a formal "arrest," and a full incident "search" of the person. This scheme is justified in part upon the notion that a "stop" and a "frisk" amount to a mere "minor inconven- ience and petty indignity,"[4] which can properly be imposed upon the citizen in the interest of effective law enforcement on the basis of a police officer's suspicion.[5]

On the other side the argument is made that the authority of the police must be strictly circumscribed by the law of arrest and search as it has developed to date in the traditional jurisprudence of the Fourth Amendment.[6] It is contended with some force that there is not—and cannot be—a variety of police activity which does not depend solely upon the voluntary cooperation of the citizen and yet which stops short of an arrest based upon probable cause to make such an arrest. The heart of the Fourth Amendment, the ar- gument runs, is a severe requirement of specific justification for any intrusion upon protected personal security, coupled with a highly developed system of judicial controls to enforce upon the agents

---

130, 214 N.E.2d 114, 117–120 (1966). See also, e. g., People v. Rivera, 14 N.Y.2d 441, 252 N.Y.S.2d 458, 201 N.E.2d 32 (1964), cert. denied, 379 U.S. 978, 85 S.Ct. 679, 13 L.Ed. 2d 568 (1965); Aspen, Arrest and Arrest Alternatives: Recent Trends, 1966 U.Ill.L.F. 241, 249–254; War- ner, The Uniform Arrest Act, 28 Va.L.Rev. 315 (1942); Note, Stop and Frisk in California, 18 Hast- ings L.J. 623, 629–632 (1967).

[4] People v. Rivera, supra, n. 3, at 447, 252 N.Y.S.2d, at 464, 201 N.E.2d, at 36.

[5] The theory is well laid out in the *Rivera* opinion:
"[T]he evidence needed to make the inquiry is not of the same de- gree of conclusiveness as that re- quired for an arrest. The stopping of the individual to inquire is not an arrest and the ground upon which the police may make the in- quiry may be less incriminating than the ground for an arrest for a crime known to have been com- mitted. * * *

*   *   *   *   *

"And as the right to stop and inquire is to be justified for a cause less conclusive than that which would sustain an arrest, so the right to frisk may be justified as an incident to inquiry upon grounds of elemental safety and precaution which might not initially sustain a search. Ultimately the validity of the frisk narrows down to whether there is or is not a right by the police to touch the person ques- tioned. The sense of exterior touch here involved is not very far dif- ferent from the sense of sight or hearing—senses upon which police customarily act." People v. Rivera, 14 N.Y.2d 441, 445, 447, 252 N.Y. S.2d 458, 461, 463, 201 N.E.2d 32, 34, 35 (1964), cert. denied, 379 U.S. 978, 85 S.Ct. 679, 13 L.Ed.2d 568 (1965).

[6] See, e. g., Foote, The Fourth Amendment: Obstacle or Necessity in the Law of Arrest?, 51 J. Crim.L.C. & P.S. 402 (1960).

of the State the commands of the Constitution. Acquiescence by the courts in the compulsion inherent in the field interrogation practices at issue here, it is urged, would constitute an abdication of judicial control over, and indeed an encouragement of, substantial interference with liberty and personal security by police officers whose judgment is necessarily colored by their primary involvement in "the often competitive enterprise of ferreting out crime." Johnson v. United States, 333 U.S. 10, 14, 68 S.Ct. 367, 369, 92 L.Ed. 436 (1948). This, it is argued, can only serve to exacerbate police-community tensions in the crowded centers of our Nation's cities.[7]

In this context we approach the issues in this case mindful of the limitations of the judicial function in controlling the myriad daily situations in which policemen and citizens confront each other on the street. The State has characterized the issue here as "the right of a police officer * * * to make an on-the-street stop, interrogate and pat down for weapons (known in street vernacular as 'stop and frisk')."[8] But this is only partly accurate. For the issue is not the abstract propriety of the police conduct, but the admissibility against petitioner of the evidence uncovered by the search and seizure. Ever since its inception, the rule excluding evidence seized in violation of the Fourth Amendment has been recognized as a principal mode of discouraging lawless police conduct. See Weeks v. United States, 232 U.S. 383, 391–393, 34 S.Ct. 341, 344, 58 L.Ed. 652 (1914). Thus its major thrust is a deterrent one, see Linkletter v. Walker, 381 U.S. 618, 629–635, 85 S.Ct. 1731, 1741, 14 L.Ed.2d 601 (1965), and experience has taught that it is the only effective deterrent to police misconduct in the criminal context, and that without it the constitutional guarantee against unreasonable searches and seizures would be a mere "form of words." Mapp v. Ohio, 367 U.S. 643, 655, 81 S.Ct. 1684, 1692, 6 L.Ed.2d 1081 (1961). The rule also serves another vital function—"the imperative of judicial integrity." Elkins v. United States, 364 U.S. 206, 222, 80 S.Ct. 1437, 1447, 4 L.Ed.2d 1669 (1960). Courts which sit under our Constitution cannot and will not be made party to lawless invasions of the constitutional rights of citizens by permitting unhindered governmental use of the fruits of such invasions. Thus in our system evidentiary rulings provide the context in which the judicial process of inclusion and exclusion approves some conduct as comporting with constitutional guarantees and disapproves other actions by state agents. A ruling admitting evidence in a criminal trial, we recognize, has the necessary effect of legitimizing the con-

---

[7] See n. 11, infra.
[8] Brief for Respondent 2.

duct which produced the evidence, while an application of the exclusionary rule withholds the constitutional imprimatur.

The exclusionary rule has its limitations, however, as a tool of judicial control. It cannot properly be invoked to exclude the products of legitimate police investigative techniques on the ground that much conduct which is closely similar involves unwarranted intrusions upon constitutional protections. Moreover, in some contexts the rule is ineffective as a deterrent. Street encounters between citizens and police officers are incredibly rich in diversity. They range from wholly friendly exchanges of pleasantries or mutually useful information to hostile confrontations of armed men involving arrests, or injuries, or loss of life. Moreover, hostile confrontations are not all of a piece. Some of them begin in a friendly enough manner, only to take a different turn upon the injection of some unexpected element into the conversation. Encounters are initiated by the police for a wide variety of purposes, some of which are wholly unrelated to a desire to prosecute for crime.[9] Doubtless some police "field interrogation" conduct violates the Fourth Amendment. But a stern refusal by this Court to condone such activity does not necessarily render it responsive to the exclusionary rule. Regardless of how effective the rule may be where obtaining convictions is an important objective of the police,[10] it is powerless to deter invasions of constitutionally guaranteed rights where the police either have no interest in prosecuting or are willing to forgo successful prosecution in the interest of serving some other goal.

Proper adjudication of cases in which the exclusionary rule is invoked demands a constant awareness of these limitations. The wholesale harrassment by certain elements of the police community, of which minority groups, particularly Negroes, frequently complain,[11] will not be stopped by the exclusion of any evidence from

---

[9] See L. Tiffany, D. McIntyre & D. Rotenberg, Detection of Crime: Stopping and Questioning, Search and Seizure, Encouragement and Entrapment 18–56 (1967). This sort of police conduct may, for example, be designed simply to help an intoxicated person find his way home, with no intention of arresting him unless be becomes obstreperous. Or the police may be seeking to mediate a domestic quarrel which threatens to erupt into violence. They may accost a woman in an area known for prostitution as part of a harassment campaign designed to drive prostitutes away without the considerable difficulty involved in prosecuting them. Or they may be conducting a dragnet search of all teenagers in a particular section of the city for weapons because they have heard rumors of an impending gang fight.

[10] See Tiffany, McIntyre & Rotenberg, supra, n. 9, at 100–101; Comment, 47 Nw.U.L.Rev. 493, 497–499 (1952).

[11] The President's Commission on Law Enforcement and Administration of Justice found that "[i]n many communities, field interrogations are a major source of friction between the police and minority groups." President's Commission on Law Enforcement and Administration of Justice, Task Force Report: The Police 183

any criminal trial. Yet a rigid and unthinking application of the exclusionary rule, in futile protest against practices which it can never be used effectively to control, may exact a high toll in human injury and frustration of efforts to prevent crime. No judicial opinion can comprehend the protean variety of the street encounter, and we can only judge the facts of the case before us. Nothing we say today is to be taken as indicating approval of police conduct outside the legitimate investigative sphere. Under our decision, courts still retain their traditional responsibility to guard against police conduct which is overbearing or harassing, or which trenches upon personal security without the objective evidentiary justification which the Constitution requires. When such conduct is identified, it must be condemned by the judiciary and its fruits must be excluded from evidence in criminal trials. And, of course, our approval of legitimate and restrained investigative conduct undertaken on the basis of ample factual justification should in no way discourage the employment of other remedies than the exclusionary rule to curtail abuses for which that sanction may prove inappropriate.

Having thus roughly sketched the perimeters of the constitutional debate over the limits on police investigative conduct in general and the background against which this case presents itself, we turn our attention to the quite narrow question posed by the facts before us: whether it is always unreasonable for a policeman to seize a person and subject him to a limited search for weapons unless there is probable cause for an arrest. Given the narrowness of this question, we have no occasion to canvass in detail the constitutional limitations upon the scope of a policeman's power when he confronts a citizen without probable cause to arrest him.

II.

Our first task is to establish at what point in this encounter the Fourth Amendment becomes relevant. That is, we must de-

---

(1967). It was reported that the friction caused by "[m]isuse of field interrogations" increases "as more police departments adopt 'aggressive patrol' in which officers are encouraged routinely to stop and question persons on the street who are unknown to them, who are suspicious, or whose purpose for being abroad is not readily evident." Id., at 184. While the frequency with which "frisking" forms a part of field interrogation practice varies tremendously with the locale, the objective of the in-

terrogation, and the particular officer, see Tiffany, McIntyre & Rotenberg, supra, n. 9, at 47–48, it cannot help but be a severely exacerbating factor in police-community tensions. This is particularly true in situations where the "stop and frisk" of youths or minority group members is "motivated by the officers' perceived need to maintain the power image of the beat officer, an aim sometimes accomplished by humiliating anyone who attempts to undermine police control of the streets." Ibid.

cide whether and when Officer McFadden "seized" Terry and whether and when he conducted a "search." There is some suggestion in the use of such terms as "stop" and "frisk" that such police conduct is outside the purview of the Fourth Amendment because neither action rises to the level of a "search" or "seizure" within the meaning of the Constitution.[12] We emphatically reject this notion. It is quite plain that the Fourth Amendment governs "seizures" of the person which do not eventuate in a trip to the station house and prosecution for crime—"arrests" in traditional terminology. It must be recognized that whenever a police officer accosts an individual and restrains his freedom to walk away, he has "seized" that person. And it is nothing less than sheer torture of the English language to suggest that a careful exploration of the outer surfaces of a person's clothing all over his or her body in an attempt to find weapons is not a "search." Moreover, it is simply fantastic to urge that such a procedure performed in public by a policeman while the citizen stands helpless, perhaps facing a wall with his hands raised, is a "petty indignity."[13] It is a serious intrusion upon the sanctity of the person, which may inflict great indignity and arouse strong resentment, and it is not to be undertaken lightly.[14]

The danger in the logic which proceeds upon distinctions between a "stop" and an "arrest," or "seizure" of the person, and between a "frisk" and a "search" is twofold. It seeks to isolate from constitutional scrutiny the initial stages of the contact between the

---

[12] In this case, for example, the Ohio Court of Appeals stated that "we must be careful to distinguish that the 'frisk' authorized herein includes only a 'frisk' for a dangerous weapon. It by no means authorizes a search for contraband, evidentiary material, or anything else in the absence of reasonable grounds to arrest. Such a search is controlled by the requirements of the Fourth Amendment, and probable cause is essential." State v. Terry, 5 Ohio App.2d 122, 130, 214 N.E.2d 114, 120 (1966). See also, e. g., Ellis v. United States, 105 U.S.App.D.C. 86, 88, 264 F.2d 372, 374 (1959); Comment, 65 Col. L.Rev. 848, 860, and n. 81 (1965).

[13] Consider the following apt description:
"[T]he officer must feel with sensitive fingers every portion of the prisoner's body. A thorough search must be made of the prisoner's arms and armpits, waistline and back, the groin and area about the testicles, and entire surface of the legs down to the feet." Priar & Martin, Searching and Disarming Criminals, 45 J.Crim.L.C. & P.S. 481 (1954).

[14] See n. 11, supra, and accompanying text.
We have noted that the abusive practices which play a major, though by no means exclusive, role in creating this friction are not susceptible of control by means of the exclusionary rule, and cannot properly dictate our decision with respect to the powers of the police in genuine investigative and preventive situations. However, the degree of community resentment aroused by particular practices is clearly relevant to an assessment of the quality of the intrusion upon reasonable expectations of personal security caused by those practices.

policeman and the citizen. And by suggesting a rigid all-or-nothing model of justification and regulation under the Amendment, it obscures the utility of limitations upon the scope, as well as the initiation, of police action as a means of constitutional regulation.[15] This Court has held in the past that a search which is reasonable at its inception may violate the Fourth Amendment by virtue of its intolerable intensity and scope. Kremen v. United States, 353 U.S. 346, 77 S.Ct. 828, 1 L.Ed.2d 876 (1957); Go-Bart Importing Co. v. United States, 282 U.S. 344, 356–358, 51 S.Ct. 153, 158, 75 L.Ed. 374, (1931); see United States v. Di Re, 332 U.S. 581, 586–587, 68 S.Ct. 222, 225, 92 L.Ed. 210 (1948). The scope of the search

---

[15]These dangers are illustrated in part by the course of adjudication in the Court of Appeals of New York. Although its first decision in this area, People v. Rivera, 14 N.Y. 2d 441, 252 N.Y.S.2d 458, 201 N.E. 2d 32 (1964), cert. denied, 379 U.S. 978, 85 S.Ct. 679, 13 L.Ed.2d 568 (1965), rested squarely on the notion that a "frisk" was not a "search," see nn. 3–5, supra, it was compelled to recognize in People v. Taggart, 20 N.Y.2d 335, 342, 283 N.Y.S.2d 1, 8, 229 N.E.2d 581, 586 (1967), that what it had actually authorized in *Rivera* and subsequent decisions, see, e. g., People v. Pugach, 15 N.Y.2d 65, 255 N.Y.S.2d 833, 204 N.E.2d 176 (1964), cert. denied, 380 U.S. 936, 85 S.Ct. 946, 13 L.Ed.2d 823 (1965), was a "search" upon less than probable cause. However, in acknowledging that no valid distinction could be maintained on the basis of its cases, the Court of Appeals continued to distinguish between the two in theory. It still defined "search" as it had in *Rivera*—as an essentially unlimited examination of the person for any and all seizable items —and merely noted that the cases had upheld police intrusions which went far beyond the original limited conception of a "frisk." Thus, principally because it failed to consider limitations upon the scope of searches in individual cases as a potential mode of regulation, the Court of Appeals in three short years arrived at the position that the Constitution must, in the name of necessity, be held to permit unrestrained rummaging about a person and his effects upon mere suspicion. It did apparently limit its holding to "cases involving serious personal injury or grave irreparable property damage," thus excluding those involving "the enforcement of sumptuary laws, such as gambling, and laws of limited public consequence, such as narcotics violations, prostitution, larcenies of the ordinary kind, and the like." People v. Taggart, supra, at 340, 283 N.Y.S. 2d, at 6, 214 N.E.2d, at 584.

In our view the sounder course is to recognize that the Fourth Amendment governs all intrusions by agents of the public upon personal security, and to make the scope of the particular intrusion, in light of all the exigencies of the case, a central element in the analysis of reasonableness. Cf. Brinegar v. United States, 338 U.S. 160, 183, 69 S.Ct. 1302, 1314, 93 L.Ed. 1879 (1949) (Mr. Justice Jackson, dissenting). Compare Camara v. Municipal Court, 387 U.S. 523, 537, 87 S.Ct. 1727, 1735, 18 L.Ed.2d 930 (1967). This seems preferable to an approach which attributes too much significance to an overly technical definition of "search," and which turns in part upon a judge-made hierarchy of legislative enactments in the criminal sphere. Focusing the inquiry squarely on the dangers and demands of the particular situation also seems more likely to produce rules which are intelligible to the police and the public alike than requiring the officer in the heat of an unfolding encounter on the street to make a judgment as to which laws are "of limited public consequence."

must be "strictly tied to and justified by" the circumstances which rendered its initiation permissible. Warden v. Hayden, 387 U.S. 294, 310, 87 S.Ct. 1642, 1652 (1967) (Mr. Justice Fortas, concurring) ; see, e. g., Preston v. United States, 376 U.S. 364, 367–368, 84 S.Ct. 881, 884, 11 L.Ed.2d 777 (1964) ; Agnello v. United States, 269 U.S. 20, 30–31, 46 S.Ct. 4, 6, 70 L.Ed. 145 (1925).

The distinctions of classical "stop-and-frisk" theory thus serve to divert attention from the central inquiry under the Fourth Amendment—the reasonableness in all the circumstances of the particular governmental invasion of a citizen's personal security. "Search" and "seizure" are not talismans. We therefore reject the notions that the Fourth Amendment does not come into play at all as a limitation upon police conduct if the officers stop short of something called a "technical arrest" or a "full-blown search."

In this case there can be no question, then, that Officer McFadden "seized" petitioner and subjected him to a "search" when he took hold of him and patted down the outer surfaces of his clothing. We must decide whether at that point it was reasonable for Officer McFadden to have interfered with petitioner's personal security as he did.[16] And in determining whether the seizure and search were "unreasonable" our inquiry is a dual one—whether the officer's action was justified at its inception, and whether it was reasonably related in scope to the circumstances which justified the interference in the first place.

III.

If this case involved police conduct subject to the Warrant Clause of the Fourth Amendment, we would have to ascertain whether "probable cause" existed to justify the search and seizure which took place. However, that is not the case. We do not retreat from our holdings that the police must, whenever practicable, obtain advance judicial approval of searches and seizures through the warrant procedure, see, e. g., Katz v. United States, 389 U.S. 347, 88 S.Ct. 507, 19 L.Ed.2d 576 (1967) ; Beck v. State of Ohio, 379

---

[16] We thus decide nothing today concerning the constitutional propriety of an investigative "seizure" upon less than probable cause for purposes of "detention" and/or interrogation. Obviously, not all personal intercourse between policemen and citizens involves "seizures" of persons. Only when the officer, by means of physical force or show of authority, has in some way restrained the liberty of a citizen may we conclude that a "seizure" has occurred. We cannot tell with any certainty upon this record whether any such "seizure" took place here prior to Officer McFadden's initiation of physical contact for purposes of searching Terry for weapons, and we thus may assume that up to that point no intrusion upon constitutionally protected rights had occurred.

U.S. 89, 96, 85 S.Ct. 223, 228, 13 L.Ed.2d 142 (1964) ; Chapman v. United States, 365 U.S. 610, 81 S.Ct. 776, 5 L.Ed.2d 828 (1961), or that in most instances failure to comply with the warrant requirement can only be excused by exigent circumstances, see, e. g., Warden v. Hayden, 387 U.S. 294, 87 S.Ct. 1642, 18 L.Ed.2d 782 (1967) (hot pursuit) ; cf. Preston v. United States, 376 U.S. 364, 367–368, 84 S.Ct. 881, 884, 11 L.Ed.2d 777 (1964). But we deal here with an entire rubric of police conduct—necessarily swift action predicated upon the on-the-spot observations of the officer on the beat—which historically has not been, and as a practical matter could not be, subjected to the warrant procedure. Instead, the conduct involved in this case must be tested by the Fourth Amendment's general proscription against unreasonable searches and seizures.[17]

Nonetheless, the notions which underlie both the warrant procedure and the requirement of probable cause remain fully relevant in this context. In order to assess the reasonableness of Officer McFadden's conduct as a general proposition, it is necessary "first to focus upon the governmental interest which allegedly justifies official intrusion upon the constitutionally protected interests of the private citizen," for there is "no ready test for determining reasonableness other than by balancing the need to search [or seize] against the invasion which the search [or seizure] entails." Camara v. Municipal Court, 387 U.S. 523, 534–535, 536–537, 87 S.Ct. 1727, 1735, 18 L.Ed.2d 930 (1967). And in justifying the particular intrusion the police officer must be able to point to specific and articulable facts which, taken together with rational inferences from those facts, reasonably warrant that intrusion.[18] The scheme of the

---

[17] See generally Leagre, The Fourth Amendment and the Law of Arrest, 54 J.Crim.L.C. & P.S. 393, 396–403 (1963).

[18] This demand for specificity in the information upon which police action is predicated is the central teaching of this Court's Fourth Amendment jurisprudence. See Beck v. State of Ohio, 379 U.S. 89, 96–97, 85 S.Ct. 223, 229, 13 L.Ed. 2d 142 (1964); Ker v. State of California, 374 U.S. 23, 34–37, 83 S.Ct. 1623, 1632, 10 L.Ed.2d 726 (1963); Wong Sun v. United States, 371 U.S. 471, 479–484, 83 S.Ct. 407, 416, 9 L.Ed.2d 441 (1963); Rios v. United States, 364 U.S. 253, 261–262, 80 S.Ct. 1431, 1437, 4 L.Ed.2d 1688 (1960); Henry v. United States, 361 U.S. 98, 100–102, 80 S. Ct. 168, 171, 4 L.Ed.2d 134 (1959); Draper v. United States, 358 U.S. 307, 312–314, 79 S.Ct. 329, 333, 3 L.Ed.2d 327 (1959); Brinegar v. United States, 338 U.S. 160, 175–178, 69 S.Ct. 1302, 1312, 93 L.Ed. 1879 (1949); Johnson v. United States, 333 U.S. 10, 15–17, 68 S.Ct. 367, 371, 92 L.Ed. 436 (1948); United States v. Di Re, 332 U.S. 581, 593–595, 68 S.Ct. 222, 229, 92 L.Ed. 210 (1948); Husty v. United States, 282 U.S. 694, 700–701, 51 S.Ct. 240, 242, 75 L.Ed. 629 (1931); Dunbra v. United States, 268 U.S. 435, 441, 45 S.Ct. 546, 549, 69 L.Ed. 1032 (1925); Carroll v. United States, 267 U.S. 132, 159–162, 45 S.Ct. 280, 288, 69 L.Ed. 543 (1925); Stacey v. Emery, 97 U.S. 642, 645, 24 L.Ed. 1035 (1878).

Fourth Amendment becomes meaningful only when it is assured that at some point the conduct of those charged with enforcing the laws can be subjected to the more detached, neutral scrutiny of a judge who must evaluate the reasonableness of a particular search or seizure in light of the particular circumstances.[19] And in making that assessment it is imperative that the facts be judged against an objective standard: would the facts available to the officer at the moment of the seizure or the search "warrant a man of reasonable caution in the belief" that the action taken was appropriate? Cf. Carroll v. United States, 267 U.S. 132, 45 S.Ct. 280, 69 L.Ed. 543 (1925); Beck v. State of Ohio, 379 U.S. 89, 96–97, 85 S.Ct. 223, 229, 13 L.Ed.2d 142 (1964).[20] Anything less would invite intrusions upon constitutionally guaranteed rights based on nothing more substantial than inarticulate hunches, a result this Court has consistently refused to sanction. See, e. g., Beck v. Ohio, supra; Rios v. United States, 364 U.S. 253, 80 S.Ct. 1431, 4 L.Ed.2d 1688 (1960); Henry v. United States, 361 U.S. 98, 80 S.Ct. 168, 4 L.Ed.2d 134 (1959). And simple " 'Good faith on the part of the arresting officer is not enough.' * * * If subjective good faith alone were the test, the protections of the Fourth Amendment would evaporate, and the people would be 'secure in their persons, houses, papers, and effects,' only in the discretion of the police." Beck v. Ohio, supra, at 97, 85 S.Ct. at 229.

Applying these principles to this case, we consider first the nature and extent of the governmental interests involved. One general interest is of course that of effective crime prevention and detection; it is this interest which underlies the recognition that a police officer may in appropriate circumstances and in an appropriate manner approach a person for purposes of investigating possibly criminal behavior even though there is no probable cause to make an arrest. It was this legitimate investigative function Officer McFadden was discharging when he decided to approach petitioner and his companions. He had observed Terry, Chilton, and Katz go through a series of acts, each of them perhaps innocent in itself, but which taken together warranted further investigation. There is nothing unusual in two men standing together on a street corner, perhaps waiting for someone. Nor is there anything suspicious

---

[19] See, e. g., Katz v. United States, 389 U.S. 347, 354–357, 88 S.Ct. 507, 514, 19 L.Ed.2d 576 (1967); Berger v. State of New York, 388 U.S. 41, 54–60, 87 S.Ct. 1873, 1884, 18 L.Ed. 2d 1040 (1967); Johnson v. United States, 333 U.S. 10, 13–15, 68 S.Ct. 367, 369, 92 L.Ed. 436 (1948); cf. Wong Sun v. United States, 371 U.S. 471, 479–480, 83 S.Ct. 407, 413, 9 L.Ed.2d 441 (1963). See also Aguilar v. State of Texas, 378 U.S. 108, 110–115, 84 S.Ct. 1509, 1514, 12 L.Ed.2d 723 (1964).

[20] See also cases cited in n. 18, supra.

about people in such circumstances strolling up and down the street, singly or in pairs. Store windows, moreover, are made to be looked in. But the story is quite different where, as here, two men hover about a street corner for an extended period of time, at the end of which it becomes apparent that they are not waiting for anyone or anything; where these men pace alternately along an identical route, pausing to stare in the same store window roughly 24 times; where each completion of this route is followed immediately by a conference between the two men on the corner; where they are joined in one of these conferences by a third man who leaves swiftly; and where the two men finally follow the third and rejoin him a couple of blocks away. It would have been poor police work indeed for an officer of 30 years' experience in the detection of thievery from stores in this same neighborhood to have failed to investigate this behavior further.

The crux of this case, however, is not the propriety of Officer McFadden's taking steps to investigate petitioner's suspicious behavior, but rather, whether there was justification for McFadden's invasion of Terry's personal security by searching him for weapons in the course of that investigation. We are now concerned with more than the governmental interest in investigating crime; in addition, there is the more immediate interest of the police officer in taking steps to assure himself that the person with whom he is dealing is not armed with a weapon that could unexpectedly and fatally be used against him. Certainly it would be unreasonable to require that police officers take unnecessary risks in the performance of their duties. American criminals have a long tradition of armed violence, and every year in this country many law enforcement officers are killed in the line of duty, and thousands more are wounded. Virtually all of these deaths and a substantial portion of the injuries are inflicted with guns and knives.[21]

---

[21]Fifty-seven law enforcement officers were killed in the line of duty in this country in 1966, bringing the total to 335 for the seven-year period beginning with 1960. Also in 1966, there were 23,851 assaults on police officers, 9,113 of which resulted in injuries to the policemen. Fifty-five of the 57 officers killed in 1966 died from gunshot wounds, 41 of them inflicted by handguns easily secreted about the person. The remaining two murders were perpetrated by knives. See Federal Bureau of Investigation, Uniform Crime Reports for the United States—1966, at 45–48, 152 and Table 51.

The easy availability of firearms to potential criminals in this country is well known and has provoked much debate. See, e. g., President's Commission on Law Enforcement and Administration of Justice, The Challenge of Crime in a Free Society 239–243 (1967). Whatever the merits of gun-control proposals, this fact is relevant to an assessment of the need for some form of self-protective search power.

In view of these facts, we cannot blind ourselves to the need for law enforcement officers to protect themselves and other prospective victims of violence in situations where they may lack probable cause for an arrest. When an officer is justified in believing that the individual whose suspicious behavior he is investigating at close range is armed and presently dangerous to the officer or to others, it would appear to be clearly unreasonable to deny the officer the power to take necessary measures to determine whether the person is in fact carrying a weapon and to neutralize the threat of physical harm.

We must still consider, however, the nature and quality of the intrusion on individual rights which must be accepted if police officers are to be conceded the right to search for weapons in situations where probable cause to arrest for crime is lacking. Even a limited search of the outer clothing for weapons constitutes a severe, though brief, intrusion upon cherished personal security, and it must surely be an annoying, frightening, and perhaps humiliating experience. Petitioner contends that such an intrusion is permissible only incident to a lawful arrest, either for a crime involving the possession of weapons or for a crime the commission of which led the officer to investigate in the first place. However, this argument must be closely examined.

Petitioner does not argue that a police officer should refrain from making any investigation of suspicious circumstances until such time as he has probable cause to make an arrest; nor does he deny that police officers in properly discharging their investigative function may find themselves confronting persons who might well be armed and dangerous. Moreover, he does not say that an officer is always unjustified in searching a suspect to discover weapons. Rather, he says it is unreasonable for the policeman to take that step until such time as the situation evolves to a point where there is probable cause to make an arrest. When that point has been reached, petitioner would concede the officer's right to conduct a search of the suspect for weapons, fruits or instrumentalities of the crime, or "mere" evidence, incident to the arrest.

There are two weaknesses in this line of reasoning, however. First, it fails to take account of traditional limitations upon the scope of searches, and thus recognizes no distinction in purpose, character, and extent between a search incident to an arrest and a limited search for weapons. The former, although justified in part by the acknowledged necessity to protect the arresting officer from assault with a concealed weapon, Preston v. United States, 376 U.S. 364, 367, 84 S.Ct. 881, 883, 11 L.Ed.2d 777 (1964), is also justified on other grounds, ibid., and can therefore involve a relatively extensive exploration of the person. A search for weapons in the absence of probable cause to arrest, however, must, like any other search, be strictly circumscribed by the exigencies which justify its initiation. Warden v. Hayden, 387 U.S. 294, 310, 87 S.Ct. 1642, 1652, 18 L.Ed.2d 782 (1967) (Mr. Justice Fortas, concurring). Thus it must be limited to that which is necessary for the discovery of weapons which might be used to harm the officer or others nearby, and may realistically be characterized as something less than a "full" search, even though it remains a serious intrusion.

A second, and related, objection to petitioner's argument is that it assumes that the law of arrest has already worked out the balance between the particular interests involved here—the neutralization of danger to the policeman in the investigative circumstance and the sanctity of the individual. But this is not so. An arrest is a wholly different kind of intrusion upon individual freedom from a limited search for weapons, and the interests each is designed to serve are likewise quite different. An arrest is the initial stage of a criminal prosecution. It is intended to vindicate society's interest in having its laws obeyed, and it is inevitably accompanied by future interference with the individual's freedom of movement, whether or not trial or conviction ultimately follows.[22] The protective search for weapons, on the other hand, constitutes a brief, though far from inconsiderable, intrusion upon the sanctity of the person. It does not follow that because an officer may lawfully arrest a person only when he is apprised of facts sufficient to warrant a belief that the person has committed or is committing a crime, the officer is equally unjustified, absent that kind of evidence, in making any intrusions short of an arrest. Moreover, a perfectly reasonable apprehension of danger may arise long before the officer is possessed of adequate information to justify taking a person into custody for the purpose of prosecuting him for a crime. Petitioner's reliance on cases which have worked out standards of reasonableness with regard to "seizures" constituting arrests and searches incident thereto is thus misplaced. It assumes that the interests sought to be vindicated and the invasions of personal security may be equated in the two cases, and thereby ignores a vital aspect of the analysis of the reasonableness of particular types of conduct under the Fourth Amendment. See Camara v. Municipal Court, supra.

Our evaluation of the proper balance that has to be struck in this type of case leads us to conclude that there must be a narrowly

---

[22] See generally W. LaFave, Arrest—
The Decision to Take a Suspect into
Custody 1–13 (1965).

drawn authority to permit a reasonable search for weapons for the protection of the police officer, where he has reason to believe that he is dealing with an armed and dangerous individual, regardless of whether he has probable cause to arrest the individual for a crime. The officer need not be absolutely certain that the individual is armed; the issue is whether a reasonably prudent man in the circumstances would be warranted in the belief that his safety or that of others was in danger. Cf. Beck v. State of Ohio, 379 U.S. 89, 91, 85 S.Ct. 223, 226, 13 L.Ed.2d 142 (1964); Brinegar v. United States, 338 U.S. 160, 174–176, 69 S.Ct. 1302, 1311, 93 L.Ed. 1879 (1949); Stacey v. Emery, 97 U.S. 642, 645, 24 L.Ed. 1035 (1878).[23] And in determining whether the officer acted reasonably in such circumstances, due weight must be given, not to his inchoate and unparticularized suspicion or "hunch," but to the specific reasonable inferences which he is entitled to draw from the facts in light of his experience. Cf. Brinegar v. United States, supra.

IV.

We must now examine the conduct of Officer McFadden in this case to determine whether his search and seizure of petitioner were reasonable, both at their inception and as conducted. He had observed Terry, together with Chilton and another man, acting in a manner he took to be preface to a "stick-up." We think on the facts and circumstances Officer McFadden detailed before the trial judge a reasonably prudent man would have been warranted in believing petitioner was armed and thus presented a threat to the officer's safety while he was investigating his suspicious behavior. The actions of Terry and Chilton were consistent with McFadden's hypothesis that these men were contemplating a daylight robbery—which, it is reasonable to assume, would be likely to involve the use of weapons—and nothing in their conduct from the time he first noticed them until the time he confronted them and identified himself as a police officer gave him sufficient reason to negate that hypothesis. Although the trio had departed the original scene, there was nothing to indicate abandonment of an intent to commit a robbery at some point. Thus, when Officer McFadden approached the three men gathered before the display window at Zucker's store he had observed enough to make it quite reasonable to fear that they were armed; and nothing in their response to his hailing them, identifying himself as a police officer, and asking their names served to dispel that reasonable belief. We cannot say his decision at that point to seize Terry and pat his clothing for weapons was the

---

[23] See also cases cited in n. 18, supra.

product of a volatile or inventive imagination, or was undertaken simply as an act of harassment; the record evidences the tempered act of a policeman who in the course of an investigation had to make a quick decision as to how to protect himself and others from possible danger, and took limited steps to do so.

The manner in which the seizure and search were conducted is, of course, as vital a part of the inquiry as whether they were warranted at all. The Fourth Amendment proceeds as much by limitations upon the scope of governmental action as by imposing preconditions upon its initiation. Compare Katz v. United States, 389 U.S. 347, 354–356, 88 S.Ct. 507, 514, 19 L.Ed.2d 576 (1967). The entire deterrent purpose of the rule excluding evidence seized in violation of the Fourth Amendment rests on the assumption that "limitations upon the fruit to be gathered tend to limit the quest itself." United States v. Poller, 43 F.2d 911, 914, 74 A.L.R. 1382 (C.A.2d Cir. 1930); see, e. g., Linkletter v. Walker, 381 U.S. 618, 629–635, 85 S.Ct. 1731, 1741, 14 L.Ed.2d 601 (1965); Mapp v. Ohio, 367 U.S. 643, 81 S.Ct. 1684, 6 L.Ed.2d 1081 (1961); Elkins v. United States, 364 U.S. 206, 216–221, 80 S.Ct. 1437, 1446, 4 L.Ed.2d 1669 (1960). Thus, evidence may not be introduced if it was discovered by means of a seizure and search which were not reasonably related in scope to the justification for their initiation. Warden v. Hayden, 387 U.S. 294, 310, 87 S.Ct. 1642, 1652, 18 L.Ed.2d 782 (1967) (Mr. Justice Fortas, concurring).

We need not develop at length in this case, however, the limitations which the Fourth Amendment places upon a protective seizure and search for weapons. These limitations will have to be developed in the concrete factual circumstances of individual cases. See Sibron v. New York, post, 392 U.S. 40, 88 S.Ct. 1889, 1912, 20 L.Ed. 2d 917, decided today. Suffice it to note that such a search, unlike a search without a warrant incident to a lawful arrest, is not justified by any need to prevent the disappearance or destruction of evidence of crime. See Preston v. United States, 376 U.S. 364, 367, 84 S.Ct. 1642, 1652, 18 L.Ed.2d 782 (1964). The sole justification of the search in the present situation is the protection of the police officer and others nearby, and it must therefore be confined in scope to an intrusion reasonably designed to discover guns, knives, clubs, or other hidden instruments for the assault of the police officer.

The scope of the search in this case presents no serious problem in light of these standards. Officer McFadden patted down the outer clothing of petitioner and his two companions. He did not place his hands in their pockets or under the outer surface of their garments until he had felt weapons, and then he merely reached for and removed the guns. He never did invade Katz' person beyond the outer surfaces of his clothes, since he discovered nothing in his pat-down which might have been a weapon. Officer McFadden confined his search strictly to what was minimally necessary to learn whether the men were armed and to disarm them once he discovered the weapons. He did not conduct a general exploratory search for whatever evidence of criminal activity he might find.

V.

We conclude that the revolver seized from Terry was properly admitted in evidence against him. At the time he seized petitioner and searched him for weapons, Officer McFadden had reasonable grounds to believe that petitioner was armed and dangerous, and it was necessary for the protection of himself and others to take swift measures to discover the true facts and neutralize the threat of harm if it materialized. The policeman carefully restricted his search to what was appropriate to the discovery of the particular items which he sought. Each case of this sort will, of course, have to be decided on its own facts. We merely hold today that where a police officer observes unusual conduct which leads him reasonably to conclude in light of his experience that criminal activity may be afoot and that the persons with whom he is dealing may be armed and presently dangerous, where in the course of investigating this behavior he identifies himself as a policeman and makes reasonable inquiries, and where nothing in the initial stages of the encounter serves to dispel his reasonable fear for his own or others' safety, he is entitled for the protection of himself and others in the area to conduct a carefully limited search of the outer clothing of such persons in an attempt to discover weapons which might be used to assault him. Such a search is a reasonable search under the Fourth Amendment, and any weapons seized may properly be introduced in evidence against the person from whom they were taken.

Affirmed.

Mr. Justice BLACK concurs in the judgment and the opinion except where the opinion quotes from and relies upon this Court's opinion in Katz v. United States and the concurring opinion in Warden v. Hayden.

Mr. Justice HARLAN, concurring.

While I unreservedly agree with the Court's ultimate holding in this case, I am constrained to fill in a few gaps, as I see them, in its opinion. I do this because what is said by this Court today will serve as initial guidelines for law enforcement authorities and courts throughout the land as this important new field of law develops.

A police officer's right to make an on-the-street "stop" and an accompanying "frisk" for weapons is of course bounded by the protections afforded by the Fourth and Fourteenth Amendments. The Court holds, and I agree, that while the right does not depend upon possession by the officer of a valid warrant, nor upon the existence of probable cause, such activities must be reasonable under the circumstances as the officer credibly relates them in court. Since the question in this and most cases is whether evidence produced by a frisk is admissible, the problem is to determine what makes a frisk reasonable.

If the State of Ohio were to provide that police officers could, on articulable suspicion less than probable cause, forcibly frisk and disarm persons thought to be carrying concealed weapons, I would have little doubt that action taken pursuant to such authority could be constitutionally reasonable. Concealed weapons create an immediate and severe danger to the public, and though that danger might not warrant routine general weapons checks, it could well warrant action on less than a "probability." I mention this line of analysis because I think it vital to point out that it cannot be applied in this case. On the record before us Ohio has not clothed its policemen with routine authority to frisk and disarm on suspicion; in the absence of state authority, policemen have no more right to "pat down" the outer clothing of passers-by, or of persons to whom they address casual questions, than does any other citizen. Consequently, the Ohio courts did not rest the constitutionality of this frisk upon any general authority in Officer McFadden to take reasonable steps to protect the citizenry, including himself, from dangerous weapons.

The state courts held, instead, that when an officer is lawfully confronting a possibly hostile person in the line of duty he has a right, springing only from the necessity of the situation and not from any broader right to disarm, to frisk for his own protection. This holding, with which I agree and with which I think the Court agrees, offers the only satisfactory basis I can think of for affirming this conviction. The holding has, however, two logical corollaries that I do not think the Court has fully expressed.

In the first place, if the frisk is justified in order to protect the officer during an encounter with a citizen, the officer must first have constitutional grounds to insist on an encounter, to make a *forcible* stop. Any person, including a policeman, is at liberty to avoid a person he considers dangerous. If and when a policeman has a right

283

instead to disarm such a person for his own protection, he must first have a right not to avoid him but to be in his presence. That right must be more than the liberty (again, possessed by every citizen) to address questions to other persons, for ordinarily the person addressed has an equal right to ignore his interrogator and walk away; he certainly need not submit to a frisk for the questioner's protection. I would make it perfectly clear that the right to frisk in this case depends upon the reasonableness of a forcible stop to investigate a suspected crime.

Where such a stop is reasonable, however, the right to frisk must be immediate and automatic if the reason for the stop is, as here, an articulable suspicion of a crime of violence. Just as a full search incident to a lawful arrest requires no additional justification, a limited frisk incident to a lawful stop must often be rapid and routine. There is no reason why an officer, rightfully but forcibly confronting a person suspected of a serious crime, should have to ask one question and take the risk that the answer might be a bullet.

The facts of this case are illustrative of a proper stop and an incident frisk. Officer McFadden had no probable cause to arrest Terry for anything, but he had observed circumstances that would reasonably lead an experienced, prudent policeman to suspect that Terry was about to engage in burglary or robbery. His justifiable suspicion afforded a proper constitutional basis for accosting Terry, restraining his liberty of movement briefly, and addressing questions to him, and Officer McFadden did so. When he did, he had no reason whatever to suppose that Terry might be armed, apart from the fact that he suspected him of planning a violent crime. McFadden asked Terry his name, to which Terry "mumbled something." Whereupon McFadden, without asking Terry to speak louder and without giving him any chance to explain his presence or his actions, forcibly frisked him.

I would affirm this conviction for what I believe to be the same reasons the Court relies on. I would, however, make explicit what I think is implicit in affirmance on the present facts. Officer McFadden's right to interrupt Terry's freedom of movement and invade his privacy arose only because circumstances warranted forcing an encounter with Terry in an effort to prevent or investigate a crime. Once that forced encounter was justified, however, the officer's right to take suitable measures for his own safety followed automatically.

Upon the foregoing premises, I join the opinion of the Court.

Mr. Justice WHITE, concurring.

I join the opinion of the Court, reserving judgment, however, on some of the Court's general remarks about the scope and purpose of the exclusionary rule which the Court has fashioned in the process of enforcing the Fourth Amendment.

Also, although the Court puts the matter aside in the context of this case, I think an additional word is in order concerning the matter of interrogation during an investigative stop. There is nothing in the Constitution which prevents a policeman from addressing questions to anyone on the streets. Absent special circumstances, the person approached may not be detained or frisked but may refuse to cooperate and go on his way. However, given the proper circumstances, such as those in this case, it seems to me the person may be briefly detained against his will while pertinent questions are directed to him. Of course, the person stopped is not obliged to answer, answers may not be compelled, and refusal to answer furnishes no basis for an arrest, although it may alert the officer to the need for continued observation. In my view, it is temporary detention, warranted by the circumstances, which chiefly justifies the protective frisk for weapons. Perhaps the frisk itself, where proper, will have beneficial results whether questions are asked or not. If weapons are found, an arrest will follow. If none are found, the frisk may nevertheless serve preventive ends because of its unmistakable message that suspicion has been aroused. But if the investigative stop is sustainable at all, constitutional rights are not necessarily violated if pertinent questions are asked and the person is restrained briefly in the process.

Mr. Justice DOUGLAS, dissenting.

I agree that petitioner was "seized" within the meaning of the Fourth Amendment. I also agree that frisking petitioner and his companions for guns was a "search." But it is a mystery how that "search" and that "seizure" can be constitutional by Fourth Amendment standards, unless there was "probable cause"[1] to believe that

---

[1] The meaning of "probable cause" has been developed in cases where an officer has reasonable grounds to believe that a crime has been or is being committed. See, e. g., The Thompson, 3 Wall. 155, 18 L.Ed. 55; Stacey v. Emery, 97 U.S. 642, 24 L.Ed. 1035; Director General v. Kastenbaum, 263 U.S. 25, 44 S.Ct. 52, 68 L.Ed. 146; Carroll v. United States, 267 U.S. 132, 45 S.Ct. 280, 69 L.Ed.2d 543; United States v. Di Re, 332 U.S. 581, 68 S.Ct. 222, 92 L.Ed. 210; Brinegar v. United States, 338 U.S. 160, 69 S.Ct. 1302, 93 L.Ed. 1879; Draper v. United States, 358 U.S. 307, 79 S.Ct. 329, 3 L.Ed.2d 327; Henry v. United States, 361 U.S. 98, 80 S.Ct. 168, 4 L.Ed.2d 134. In such cases, of course, the officer may make an "arrest" which results in charging the individual with commission of a crime. But while arresting persons who have already committed crimes is an important task of law enforcement, an equally if not more important function is crime prevention and deterrence of would-be criminals. "[T]here is no war between the Constitution and common sense," Mapp v. Ohio, 367 U.S. 643, 657, 81 S.Ct. 1684, 1693. Police officers need not wait until they see

(1) a crime had been committed or (2) a crime was in the process of being committed or (3) a crime was about to be committed. The opinion of the Court disclaims the existence of "probable cause." If loitering were in issue and that was the offense charged, there would be "probable cause" shown. But the crime here is carrying concealed weapons;[2] and there is no basis for concluding that the officer had "probable cause" for believing that that crime was being committed. Had a warrant been sought, a magistrate would, therefore, have been unauthorized to issue one, for he can act only if there is a showing of "probable cause." We hold today that the police have greater authority to make a "seizure" and conduct a "search" than a judge has to authorize such action. We have said precisely the opposite over and over again.[3]

In other words, police officers up to today have been permitted to effect arrests or searches without warrants only when the facts

---

a person actually commit a crime before they are able to "seize" that person. Respect for our constitutional system and personal liberty demands in return, however, that such a "seizure" be made only upon "probable cause."

[2] Ohio Rev. Code § 2923.01.

[3] This Court has always used the language of "probable cause" in determining the constitutionality of an arrest without a warrant. See, e. g., Carroll v. United States, 267 U.S. 132, 156, 161–162, 45 S.Ct. 280, 288, 69 L.Ed. 543; Johnson v. United States, 333 U.S. 10, 13–15; McDonald v. United States, 335 U.S. 451, 455–456, 69 S.Ct. 191, 194, 93 L.Ed. 153; Henry v. United States, 361 U.S. 98, 80 S.Ct. 168, 4 L.Ed.2d 134; Wong Sun v. United States, 371 U.S. 471, 479–484, 83 S.Ct. 407, 416, 9 L.Ed.2d 441. To give power to the police to seize a person on some grounds different from or less than "probable cause" would be handing them *more* authority than could be exercised by a magistrate in issuing a warrant to seize a person. As we stated in Wong Sun v. United States, 371 U.S. 471, 83 S.Ct. 407, with respect to requirements for arrests without warrants: "Whether or not the requirements of reliability and particularity of the information on which an officer may act are more stringent where an arrest warrant is absent, they surely cannot be less

stringent than where an arrest warrant is obtained." Id., at 479, 83 S.Ct. at 413. And we said in Brinegar v. United States, 338 U.S. 160, 176, 69 S.Ct. 1302, 1311, 93 L.Ed. 1879:

"These long-prevailing standards [for probable cause] seek to safeguard citizens from rash and unreasonable interferences with privacy and from unfounded charges of crime. They also seek to give fair leeway for enforcing the law in the community's protection. Because many situations which confront officers in the course of executing their duties are more or less ambiguous, room must be allowed for some mistakes on their part. But the mistakes must be those of reasonable men, acting on facts leading sensibly to their conclusions of probability. The rule of probable cause is a practical, nontechnical conception affording the best compromise that has been found for accommodating these often opposing interests. Requiring more would unduly hamper law enforcement. To allow less would be to leave law-abiding citizens at the mercy of the officers' whim or caprice." And see Johnson v. United States, 333 U.S. 10, 14–15, 68 S.Ct. 367, 369, 92 L.Ed. 436; Wrightson v. United States, 95 U.S.App.D.C. 390, 393–394, 222 F.2d 556, 559–560 (1955).

within their personal knowledge would satisfy the constitutional standard of *probable cause*. At the time of their "seizure" without a warrant they must possess facts concerning the person arrested that would have satisfied a magistrate that "probable cause" was indeed present. The term "probable cause" rings a bell of certainty that is not sounded by phrases such as "reasonable suspicion." Moreover, the meaning of "probable cause" is deeply imbedded in our constitutional history. As we stated in Henry v. United States, 361 U.S. 98, 100–102, 80 S.Ct. 168, 170:

"The requirement of probable cause has roots that are deep in our history. The general warrant, in which the name of the person to be arrested was left blank, and the writs of assistance, against which James Otis inveighed, both perpetuated the oppressive practice of allowing the police to arrest and search on suspicion. Police control took the place of judicial control, since no showing of 'probable cause' before a magistrate was required.

*   *   *   *   *   *   *   *   *   *

"That philosophy [rebelling against these practices] later was reflected in the Fourth Amendment. And as the early American decisions both before and immediately after its adoption show, common rumor or report, suspicion, or even 'strong reason to suspect' was not adequate to support a warrant for arrest. And that principle has survived to this day. * * *

"* * * It is important, we think, that this requirement [of probable cause] be strictly enforced, for the standard set by the Constitution protects both the officer and the citizen. If the officer acts with probable cause, he is protected even though it turns out that the citizen is innocent. * * * And while a search without a warrant is, within limits, permissible if incident to a lawful arrest, if an arrest without a warrant is to support an incidental search, it must be made with probable cause. * * * This immunity of officers cannot fairly be enlarged without jeopardizing the privacy or security of the citizen."

The infringement on personal liberty of any "seizure" of a person can only be "reasonable" under the Fourth Amendment if we require the police to possess "probable cause" before they seize him. Only that line draws a meaningful distinction between an officer's mere inkling and the presence of facts within the officer's personal knowledge which would convince a reasonable man that the person seized has committed, is committing, or is about to commit a particular crime. "In dealing with probable cause, * * * as the very name implies, we deal with probabilities. These are not technical; they are the factual and practical considerations of everyday life on which reasonable and prudent men, not legal techni-

287

cians, act." Brinegar v. United States, 338 U.S. 160, 175, 69 S.Ct. 1302, 1310.

To give the police greater power than a magistrate is to take a long step down the totalitarian path. Perhaps such a step is desirable to cope with modern forms of lawlessness. But if it is taken, it should be the deliberate choice of the people through a constitutional amendment. Until the Fourth Amendment, which is closely allied with the Fifth,[4] is rewritten, the person and the effects of the individual are beyond the reach of all government agencies until there are reasonable grounds to believe (probable cause) that a criminal venture has been launched or is about to be launched.

There have been powerful hydraulic pressures throughout our history that bear heavily on the Court to water down constitutional guarantees and give the police the upper hand. That hydraulic pressure has probably never been greater than it is today.

Yet if the individual is no longer to be sovereign, if the police can pick him up whenever they do not like the cut of his jib, if they can "seize" and "search" him in their discretion, we enter a new regime. The decision to enter it should be made only after a full debate by the people of this country.

Sibron v. New York*

This "search and seizure case" was decided the same day as the *Terry decision*,[1] in which the Supreme Court established boundaries within which the police may properly conduct a stop and frisk. *Sibron* further clarifies those boundaries.

The opinion involves two separate cases which the Court considers together because of the similarity of issues raised in each. As in the *Terry decision* the Court had to determine the propriety of a policeman's stop and frisk.

In the first of these two cases the conviction of one Sibron was overturned. He had been observed over a period of several hours

---

[4] See Boyd v. United States, 116 U.S. 616, 633, 6 S.Ct. 524, 534, 29 L.Ed. 746:

"For the 'unreasonable searches and seizures' condemned in the Fourth Amendment are almost always made for the purpose of compelling a man to give evidence against himself, which in criminal cases is condemned in the Fifth Amendment; and compelling a man 'in a criminal case to be a witness against himself,' which is condemned in the Fifth Amendment, throws light on the question as to what is an 'unreasonable search and seizure' within the meaning of the Fourth Amendment."

* 392 U.S. 40, 88 S.Ct. 1889 (June 10, 1969)

[1] Terry v. State of Ohio, 88 S.Ct. 1868 (1969)

having conversations with several known narcotic addicts. For this reason he was seized and a search of one of his pockets revealed his possession of heroin. Emphasizing the fact that it did not appear that the officer was looking for a weapon when he conducted the search, the Supreme Court reversed his conviction by a margin of eight to one. Even the dissent, written by Mr. Justice Black, agreed with the majority on the law of the case. Black predicated his dissent on a disagreement with a majority relative to the facts of the case. Black felt that the evidence was such that the officer may have been looking for a weapon when the search was made.

The second case involved a defendant, named Peters. An off-duty officer observed him acting in a suspicious manner, a manner which would lead a reasonable person to believe he was about to commit a theft. Although a search and seizure revealed defendant's possession of burglar tools, it appeared that the search was conducted solely for the purpose of determining if defendant possessed a weapon. Emphasizing the fact that the search was conducted solely for the purpose of ascertaining if Peters was armed, the Supreme Court unanimously affirmed his convictions.

The *Terry* and *Sibron* cases combined with prior Supreme Court decisions, have developed standards to determine the validity of a warrantless stop and frisk. In examining those standards keep in mind that a stop and frisk is a search and seizure. Therefore, the constitutional guarantees of the Fourth and Fourteenth Amendments—prohibiting unreasonable searches and seizures—have equal applicability to a stop and frisk.

These standards developed by the Supreme Court may be summarized in the following manner. If probable cause for an arrest exists (facts which would justify an arrest) the warrantless stop and frisk would be proper. This standard has been clear for some time. Many Supreme Court decisions[2] have held that a search incident to a valid arrest is proper notwithstanding the lack of a warrant. Absent probable cause for an arrest a warrantless stop and frisk is valid provided two conditions are met. First, there must be reasonable suspicion that the subject is engaging in an unlawful enterprise. Second, the search must be limited to a frisk for weapons. This normally—though not necessarily—would consist of a patting down of the subject's outer garments. If such a patting down reveals the possible presence of a weapon the article in question may be removed from his person.

There is an additional point worth noting in this case. It has oftentimes been said that "justice delayed, is justice denied." No-

---

[2] Harris v. United States, 331 U.S. 145, 67 S.Ct. 1098 (1946); United States v. Rabinowitz, 339 U.S. 56, 70 S.Ct. 430 (1949).

where is the import of that quote more applicable than in the *Sibron case*. By the time the case reached the Supreme Court Sibron had already served his entire sentence. Thus, to Sibron, the victory may have had a hollow ring.

Text of Case*

In No. 63, a New York police officer on patrol observed during an eight-hour period a man (appellant Sibron), whom he did not know and had no information about, in conversation with six or eight persons whom the officer knew as narcotics addicts. Later the officer saw Sibron in a restaurant with three more known addicts. The officer on none of these occasions overheard any conversation or saw anything pass between Sibron and the others. Later the officer ordered Sibron outside the restaurant, where the officer said, "You know what I am after." When Sibron reached into his pocket the officer reached into the same pocket and found some envelopes containing heroin. Sibron was charged with the unlawful possession of the heroin. The trial court rejected Sibron's motion to suppress the heroin as illegally seized, holding that the officer had probable cause to make the arrest and to seize the heroin. Thereafter Sibron pleaded guilty, preserving his right to appeal the evidentiary ruling. Sibron, who was precluded from obtaining bail pending appeal, completed service of his six-month sentence roughly two months before it was physically possible for him to present his case on appeal. His conviction was affirmed by the intermediate state appellate court and then by the New York Court of Appeals. In this Court the State initially sought to justify the search on the basis of New York's "stop-and-frisk" law, N.Y. Code Crim. Proc. § 180–a, which the New York Court of Appeals apparently viewed as authorizing the search. That law provides that a "police officer may stop any person abroad in a public place whom he reasonably suspects is committing . . ." certain crimes "and may demand . . . his name, address and an explanation of his actions," and when the officer "suspects that he is in danger . . . he may search such person for a dangerous weapon." After this Court noted probable jurisdiction the county District Attorney confessed error. In No. 74, an officer, at home in the apartment where he had lived for 12 years, heard a noise at the door. Through the peephole he saw two strangers (appellant Peters and another) tiptoeing furtively about the hallway. He called the police, dressed, and armed himself with his service revolver. He observed the two still engaged in suspicious maneuvers and, believing that they were attempting a burg-

---

* Together with No. 74, *Peters* v. *New York*, argued on December 12, 1967, also on appeal from the same court.

lary, the officer pursued them, catching Peters by the collar in the apartment hallway. Peters said that he had been visiting a girl friend, whom he declined to identify. The officer patted Peters down for weapons and discovered a hard object which he thought might be a knife but which turned out to be a container with burglar's tools, for the possession of which Peters was later charged. The trial court denied Peters' motion to suppress that evidence, refusing to credit Peters' testimony that he had been visiting a girl friend and finding that the officer had the requisite "reasonable suspicion" under § 180 a to stop and question Peters and to "frisk" him for a dangerous weapon in the apartment hallway, which the court found was a "public place," within the meaning of the statute. Peters then pleaded guilty, preserving his right to appeal the rejection of his motion to suppress. The intermediate appellate court affirmed, as did the New York Court of Appeals, which held the search justified under § 180–a. The parties on both sides contend that the principal issue in both cases is the constitutionality of § 180–a "on its face."

Kalman Finkel and *Gretchen White Oberman* argued the cause and filed briefs for appellant in No. 63. *Robert Stuart Friedman* argued the cause and filed a brief for appellant in No. 74.

William I. Siegel argued the cause for appellee in No. 63. With him on the brief was *Aaron E. Koota. James J. Duggan* argued the cause for appellee in No. 74. With him on the briefs was *Leonard Rubenfeld.*

Michael Juviler argued the cause for the District Attorney of New York County, as *amicus curiae,* in No. 63. With him on the brief filed in both cases were *Frank S. Hogan* and *H. Richard Uviller. Mr. Siegel* argued the cause for the District Attorney of Kings County, as *amicus curiae,* in No. 74.

Briefs of *amici curiae,* urging reversal in both cases, were filed by *Jack Greenberg, James M. Nabrit III, Michael Meltsner, Melvyn Zarr,* and *Anthony G. Amsterdam* for the NAACP Legal Defense and Educational Fund, Inc., and by *Bernard A. Berkman, Melvin L. Wulf,* and *Alan H. Levine* for the American Civil Liberties Union et al.

Louis J. Lefkowitz, pro se, Samuel A. Hirshowitz, First Assistant Attorney General, and *Maria L. Marcus* and *Brenda Soloff,* Assistant Attorneys General, filed a brief for the Attorney General of New York, as *amicus curiae,* urging affirmance in both cases.

MR. CHIEF JUSTICE WARREN delivered the opinion of the Court.

These are companion cases to No. 67, *Terry* v. *Ohio, ante,* p. 1, decided today. They present related questions under the Fourth and Fourteenth Amendments, but the cases arise in the context of

291

New York's "stop-and-frisk" law, N.Y. Code Crim. Proc. § 180–a. This statute provides:

"1. A police officer may stop any person abroad in a public place whom he reasonably suspects is committing, has committed or is about to commit a felony or any of the offenses specified in section five hundred fifty-two of this chapter, and may demand of him his name, address and an explanation of his actions.

"2. When a police officer has stopped a person for questioning pursuant to this section and reasonably suspects that he is in danger of life or limb, he may search such person for a dangerous weapon. If the police officer finds such a weapon or any other thing the possession of which may constitute a crime, he may take and keep it until the completion of the questioning, at which time he shall either return it, if lawfully possessed, or arrest such person."

The appellants, Sibron and Peters, were both convicted of crimes in New York state courts on the basis of evidence seized from their persons by police officers. The Court of Appeals of New York held that the evidence was properly admitted, on the ground that the searches which uncovered it were authorized by the statute. *People* v. *Sibron*, 18 N.Y.2d 603, 219 N.E.2d 196, 272 N.Y.S.2d 374 (1966) (memorandum); *People* v. *Peters*, 18 N.Y.2d 238, 219 N.E.2d 595, 273 N.Y.S.2d 217 (1966). Sibron and Peters have appealed their convictions to this Court, claiming that § 180–a is unconstitutional on its face and as construed and applied, because the searches and seizures which it was held to have authorized violated their rights under the Fourth Amendment, made applicable to the States by the Fourteenth. *Mapp* v. *Ohio*, 367 U.S. 643 (1961). We noted probable jurisdiction, 386 U.S. 954 (1967); 386 U.S. 980 (1967), and consolidated the two cases for argument with No. 67.

The facts in these cases may be stated briefly. Sibron, the appellant in No. 63, was convicted of the unlawful possession of heroin.[1] He moved before trial to suppress the heroin seized from his person by the arresting officer, Brooklyn Patrolman Anthony Martin. After the trial court denied his motion, Sibron pleaded guilty to the charge, preserving his right to appeal the evidentiary

---

[1] N. Y. Pub. Health Law § 3305 makes the unauthorized possession of any narcotic drug unlawful, and §§ 1751 and 1751-a of the N.Y. Penal Law of 1909, then in effect, made the grade of the offense depend upon the amount of the drugs found in the possession of the defendant. The complaint in this case origi-nally charged a felony, but the trial court granted the prosecutor's motion to reduce the charge on the ground that "the Laboratory report will indicate a misdemeanor charge." Sibron was convicted of a misdemeanor and sentenced to six months in jail.

ruling.[2] At the hearing on the motion to suppress, Officer Martin testified that while he was patrolling his beat in uniform on March 9, 1965, he observed Sibron "continually from the hours of 4:00 P. M. to 12:00, midnight . . . in the vicinity of 742 Broadway." He stated that during this period of time he saw Sibron in conversation with six or eight persons whom he (Patrolman Martin) knew from past experience to be narcotics addicts. The officer testified that he did not overhear any of these conversations, and that he did not see anything pass between Sibron and any of the others. Late in the evening Sibron entered a restaurant. Patrolman Martin saw Sibron speak with three more known addicts inside the restaurant. Once again, nothing was overheard and nothing was seen to pass between Sibron and the addicts. Sibron sat down and ordered pie and coffee, and, as he was eating, Patrolman Martin approached him and told him to come outside. Once outside, the officer said to Sibron, "You know what I am after." According to the officer, Sibron "mumbled something and reached into his pocket." Simultaneously, Patrolman Martin thrust his hand into the same pocket, discovering several glassine envelopes, which, it turned out, contained heroin.

The State has had some difficulty in settling upon a theory for the admissibility of these envelopes of heroin. In his sworn complaint Patrolman Martin stated:

"As the officer approached the defendant, the latter being in the direction of the officer and seeing him, he did put his hand in his left jacket pocket and pulled out a tinfoil envelope and did attempt to throw same to the ground. The officer never losing sight of the said envelope seized it from the def[endan]t's left hand, examined it and found it to contain ten glascine [*sic*] envelopes with a white substance alleged to be Heroin."

This version of the encounter, however, bears very little resemblance to Patrolman Martin's testimony at the hearing on the motion to suppress. In fact, he discarded the abandonment theory at the hearing.[3] Nor did the officer ever seriously suggest that he

---

2 N. Y. Code Crim. Proc. § 813-c provides that an order denying a motion to suppress evidence in a criminal case "may be reviewed on appeal from a judgment of conviction notwithstanding the fact that such judgment of conviction is predicated upon a plea of guilty."

3 Patrolman Martin stated several times that he put his hand into Sibron's pocket and seized the heroin before Sibron had any opportunity to remove his own hand from the pocket. The trial court questioned him on this point:

"Q. Would you say at that time that he reached into his pocket and handed the packets to you? Is that what he did or did he drop the packets?

"A. He did not drop them. *I do not know what his intentions were.* He pushed his hand into his pocket.

"MR. JOSEPH [Prosecutor]: You intercepted it; didn't you, Officer?

was in fear of bodily harm and that he searched Sibron in self-protection to find weapons.[4]

The prosecutor's theory at the hearing was that Patrolman Martin had probable cause to believe that Sibron was in possession of narcotics because he had seen him conversing with a number of known addicts over an eight-hour period. In the absence of any knowledge on Patrolman Martin's part concerning the nature of the intercourse between Sibron and the addicts, however, the trial court was inclined to grant the motion to suppress. As the judge stated, "All he knows about the unknown men: They are narcotics addicts. They might have been talking about the World Series. They might have been talking about prize fights." The prosecutor, however, reminded the judge that Sibron had admitted on the stand, in Patrolman Martin's absence, that he had been talking to the addicts about narcotics. Thereupon, the trial judge changed his mind and ruled that the officer had probable cause for an arrest.

Section 180–a, the "stop-and-frisk" statute, was not mentioned at any point in the trial court. The Appellate Term of the Supreme Court affirmed the conviction without opinion. In the Court of Appeals of New York, Sibron's case was consolidated with the *Peters* case, No. 74. The Court of Appeals held that the search in *Peters* was justified under the statute, but it wrote no opinion in Sibron's case. The dissents of Judges Fuld and Van Voorhis, however, indicate that the court rested its holding on § 180–a. At any rate, in its Brief in Opposition to the Jurisdictional Statement in this Court, the State sought to justify the search on the basis of the statute. After we noted probable jurisdiction, the District Attorney for Kings County confessed error.

Peters, the appellant in No. 74, was convicted of possessing burglary tools under circumstances evincing an intent to employ

---

"THE WITNESS: Yes." (Emphasis added.)

It is of course highly unlikely that Sibron, facing the officer at such close quarters, would have tried to remove the heroin from his pocket and throw it to the ground in the hope that he could escape responsibility for it.

[4] The possibility that Sibron, who never, so far as appears from the record, offered any resistance, might have posed a danger to Patrolman Martin's safety was never even discussed as a potential justification for the search. The only mention of weapons by the officer in his entire testimony came in response to a leading question by Sibron's counsel, when Martin stated that he "thought he [Sibron] might have been" reaching for a gun. Even so, Patrolman Martin did not accept this suggestion by the opposition regarding the reason for his action; the discussion continued upon the plain premise that he had been looking for narcotics all the time.

them in the commission of a crime.[5] The tools were seized from his person at the time of his arrest, and like Sibron he made a pretrial motion to suppress them. When the trial court denied the motion, he too pleaded guilty, preserving his right to appeal. Officer Samuel Lasky of the New York City Police Department testified at the hearing on the motion that he was at home in his apartment in Mount Vernon, New York, at about 1 p. m. on July 10, 1964. He had just finished taking a shower and was drying himself when he heard a noise at his door. His attempt to investigate was interrupted by a telephone call, but when he returned and looked through the peephole into the hall, Officer Lasky saw "two men tiptoeing out of the alcove toward the stairway." He immediately called the police, put on some civilian clothes and armed himself with his service revolver. Returning to the peephole, he saw "a tall man tiptoeing away from the alcove and followed by this shorter man, Mr. Peters, toward the stairway." Officer Lasky testified that he had lived in the 120-unit building for 12 years and that he did not recognize either of the men as tenants. Believing that he had happened upon the two men in the course of an attempted burglary,[6] Officer Lasky opened his door, entered the hallway and slammed the door loudly behind him. This precipitated a flight down the stairs on the part of the two men,[7] and Officer Lasky gave chase. His apartment was located on the sixth floor, and he apprehended Peters between the fourth and fifth floors. Grabbing Peters by the collar, he continued down another flight in unsuccessful pursuit of the other man. Peters explained his presence in the building to Officer Lasky by saying that he was visiting a girl friend. However, he declined to reveal the girl friend's name, on the ground that she was a married woman. Officer Lasky

---

[5] N. Y. Pen. Law of 1909, § 408, made the possession of such tools under such circumstances a misdemeanor for first offenders and a felony for all those who have "been previously convicted of any crime." Peters was convicted of a felony under this section.

[6] Officer Lasky testified that when he called the police immediately before leaving his apartment, he "told the Sergeant at the desk that two burglars were on my floor."

[7] Officer Lasky testified that when he emerged from his apartment, "I slammed the door, I had my gun and I ran down the stairs after them." A sworn affidavit of the Assistant District Attorney, which

was before the trial court when it ruled on the motion to suppress, stated that when apprehended Peters was "fleeing down the steps of the building." The trial court explicitly took note of the flight of Peters and his companion as a factor contributing to Officer Lasky's "reasonable suspicion" of them:
"We think the testimony at the hearing does not require further laboring of this aspect of the matter, unless one is to believe that it is legitimately normal for a man to tip-toe about in the public hall of an apartment house while on a visit to his unidentified girl-friend, and, when observed by another tenant, to rapidly descend by stairway in the presence of elevators."

patted Peters down for weapons, and discovered a hard object in his pocket. He stated at the hearing that the object did not feel like a gun, but that it might have been a knife. He removed the object from Peters' pocket. It was an opaque plastic envelope, containing burglar's tools.

The trial court explicitly refused to credit Peters' testimony that he was merely in the building to visit his girl friend. It found that Officer Lasky had the requisite "reasonable suspicion" of Peters under § 180–a to stop him and question him. It also found that Peters' response was "clearly unsatisfactory," and that "under the circumstances Lasky's action in frisking Peters for a dangerous weapon was reasonable, even though Lasky was himself armed." It held that the hallway of the apartment building was a "public place" within the meaning of the statute. The Appellate Division of the Supreme Court affirmed without opinion. The Court of Appeals also affirmed, essentially adopting the reasoning of the trial judge, with Judges Fuld and Van Voorhis dissenting separately.

I.

At the outset we must deal with the question whether we have jurisdiction in No. 63. It is asserted that because Sibron has completed service of the six-month sentence imposed upon him as a result of his conviction, the case has become moot under *St. Pierre* v. *United States,* 319 U.S. 41 (1943).[8] We have concluded that the case is not moot.

In the first place, it is clear that the broad dictum with which the Court commenced its discussion in *St. Pierre*—that "the case is moot because, after petitioner's service of his sentence and its

---

[8] The first suggestion of mootness in this case came upon oral argument, when it was revealed for the first time that appellant had been released. This fact did not appear in the record, despite the fact that the release occurred well over two years before the case was argued here. Nor was mootness hinted at by the State in its Brief in Opposition to the Jurisdictional Statement in this Court—where it took the position that the decision below was so clearly right that it did not merit further review—or in its brief on the merits—in which it conceded that the decision below clearly violated Sibron's constitutional rights and urged that it was an aberrant interpretation which should not impair the constitutionality of the New York statute. Following the suggestion of mootness on oral argument, moreover, the State filed a brief in which it amplified its views as to why the case should be held moot, but added the extraordinary suggestion that this Court should ignore the problem and pronounce upon the constitutionality of a statute in a case which has become moot. Normally in these circumstances we would consider ourselves fully justified in foreclosing a party upon an issue; however, since the question goes to the very existence of a controversy for us to adjudicate, we have undertaken to review it.

expiration, there was no longer a subject matter on which the judgment of this Court could operate" (319 U.S., at 42)—fails to take account of significant qualifications recognized in *St. Pierre* and developed in later cases. Only a few days ago we held unanimously that the writ of habeas corpus was available to test the constitutionality of a state conviction where the petitioner had been in custody when he applied for the writ, but had been released before this Court could adjudicate his claims. *Carafas* v. *LaVallee*, 391 U.S. 234 (1968). On numerous occasions in the past this Court has proceeded to adjudicate the merits of criminal cases in which the sentence had been fully served or the probationary period during which a suspended sentence could be reimposed had terminated. *Ginsberg* v. *New York*, 390 U.S. 629 (1968); *Pollard* v. *United States*, 352 U.S. 354 (1957); *United States* v. *Morgan*, 346 U.S. 502 (1954); *Fiswick* v. *United States*, 329 U.S. 211 (1946).

Thus mere release of the prisoner does not mechanically foreclose consideration of the merits by this Court.

St. Pierre itself recognized two possible exceptions to its "doctrine" of mootness, and both of them appear to us to be applicable here. The Court stated that "[i]t does not appear that petitioner could not have brought his case to this Court for review before the expiration of his sentence," noting also that because the petitioner's conviction was for contempt and because his controversy with the Government was a continuing one, there was a good chance that there would be "ample opportunity to review" the important question presented on the merits in a future proceeding. 319 U.S., at 43. This was a plain recognition of the vital importance of keeping open avenues of judicial review of deprivations of constitutional right.[9] There was no way for Sibron to bring his case here before his six-month sentence expired. By statute he was precluded from obtaining bail pending appeal,[10] and by virtue of the inevitable delays of the New York court system, he was released less than a month after his newly appointed appellate counsel had been supplied with a copy of the transcript and roughly two months before it was physically possible to present his case to the first tier in the state appellate court system.[11] This was true despite the fact

[9] Cf. *Fay* v. *Noia*, 372 U.S. 391, 424 (1963):
"[C]onventional notions of finality in criminal litigation cannot be permitted to defeat the manifest federal policy that federal constitutional rights of personal liberty shall not be denied without the fullest opportunity for plenary federal judicial review."

[10] See N. Y. Code Crim. Proc. § 555 subd. 2.

[11] Sibron was arrested on March 9, 1965, and was unable to make bail before trial because of his indigency. He thus remained in jail from that time until the expiration of his sentence (with good time credit) on July 10, 1965. He was

that he took all steps to perfect his appeal in a prompt, diligent, and timely manner.

Many deep and abiding constitutional problems are encountered primarily at a level of "low visibility" in the criminal process—in the context of prosecutions for "minor" offenses which carry only short sentences.[12] We do not believe that the Constitution contemplates that people deprived of constitutional rights at this level should be left utterly remediless and defenseless against repetitions of unconstitutional conduct. A State may not cut off federal review of whole classes of such cases by the simple expedient of a blanket denial of bail pending appeal. As *St. Pierre* clearly recognized, a State may not effectively deny a convict access to its appellate courts until he has been released and then argue that his case has been mooted by his failure to do what it alone prevented him from doing.[13]

The second exception recognized in *St. Pierre* permits adjudication of the merits of a criminal case where "under either state or federal law further penalties or disabilities can be imposed . . . as a result of the judgment which has . . . been satisfied." 319 U.S., at 43. Subsequent cases have expanded this exception to the

---

convicted on April 23. His application for leave to proceed *in forma pauperis* was not granted until May 14, and his assigned appellate counsel was not provided with a transcript until June 11. The Appellate Term of the Supreme Court recessed on June 7 until September. Thus Sibron was released well before there had been any opportunity even to argue his case in the intermediate state appellate court. A decision by the Court of Appeals of New York was not had until July 10, 1966, the anniversary of Sibron's release.

[12] Cf., *e.g.*, *Thompson* v. *City of Louisville*, 362 U.S. 199 (1960).

[13] In *St. Pierre* the Court noted that the petitioner could have taken steps to preserve his case, but that "he did not apply to this Court for a stay or a supersedeas." 319 U.S., at 43. Here however, it is abundantly clear that there is no procedure of which Sibron could have availed himself to prevent the expiration of his sentence long before this Court could hear his case. A supersedeas from this Court is a purely ancillary writ, and may issue only in connection with an appeal actually taken. *Ex parte Ralston*. 119 U.S. 613 (1887); Sup. Ct. Rule 18; see R. Robertson & F. Kirkham, Jurisdiction of the Supreme Court of the United States § 435, at 883 (R. Wolfson & P. Kurland ed., 1951). At the time Sibron completed service of his sentence, the only judgment outstanding was the conviction itself, rendered by the Criminal Court of the City of New York, County of Kings. This Court had no jurisdiction to hear an appeal from that judgment, since it was not rendered by the "highest court of a State in which a decision could be had." 28 U. S. C. § 1257, and there could be no warrant for interference with the orderly appellate processes of the state courts. Thus no supersedeas could have issued. Nor could this Court have ordered Sibron admitted to bail before the expiration of his sentence, since the offense was not bailable, 18 U. S. C. § 3144; see n. 10, *supra*. Thus this case is distinguishable from *St. Pierre* in that Sibron "could not have brought his case to this Court for review before the expiration of his sentence." 319 U. S., at 43.

point where it may realistically be said that inroads have been made upon the principle itself. *St. Pierre* implied that the burden was upon the convict to show the existence of collateral legal consequences. Three years later in *Fiswick* v. *United States*, 329 U.S. 211 (1946), however, the Court held that a criminal case had not become moot upon release of the prisoner, noting that the convict, an alien, might be subject to deportation for having committed a crime of "moral turpitude"—even though it had never been held (and the Court refused to hold) that the crime of which he was convicted fell into this category. The Court also pointed to the fact that if the petitioner should in the future decide he wanted to become an American citizen, he might have difficulty proving that he was of "good moral character." *Id.*, at 222.[14]

The next case which dealt with the problem of collateral consequences was *United States* v. *Morgan*, 346 U.S. 502 (1954). There the convict had probably been subjected to a higher sentence as a recidivist by a state court on account of the old federal conviction which he sought to attack. But as the dissent pointed out, there was no indication that the recidivist increment would be removed from his state sentence upon invalidation of the federal conviction, *id.*, at 516, n. 4, and the Court chose to rest its holding that the case was not moot upon a broader view of the matter. Without canvassing the possible disabilities which might be imposed upon Morgan or alluding specifically to the recidivist sentence, the Court stated:

"Although the term has been served, the results of the conviction may persist. Subsequent convictions may carry heavier penalties, civil rights may be affected. As the power to remedy an invalid sentence exists, we think, respondent is entitled to an opportunity to attempt to show that this conviction was invalid." *Id.*, at 512–513.

Three years later, in *Pollard* v. *United States*, 352 U.S. 354 (1957), the Court abandoned all inquiry into the actual existence of specific collateral consequences and in effect presumed that they existed. With nothing more than citations to *Morgan* and *Fiswick*, and a statement that "convictions may entail collateral legal disadvantages in the future," *id.*, at 358, the Court concluded that "[t]he possibility of consequences collateral to the imposition of

---

14 Compare *Ginsberg* v. *New York*, 390 U. S. 629, 633, n. 2 (1968), where this Court held that the mere possibility that the Commissioner of Buildings of the Town of Hempstead, New York, might "in his discretion" attempt in the future to revoke a license to run a luncheonette because of a single conviction for selling relatively inoffensive "girlie" magazines to a 16-year-old boy was sufficient to preserve a criminal case from mootness.

sentence is sufficiently substantial to justify our dealing with the merits." *Ibid.* The Court thus acknowledged the obvious fact of life that most criminal convictions do in fact entail adverse collateral legal consequences.[15] The mere "possibility" that this will be the case is enough to preserve a criminal case from ending "ignominiously in the limbo of mootness." *Parker* v. *Ellis*, 362 U.S. 574, 577 (1960) (dissenting opinion).

This case certainly meets that test for survival. Without pausing to canvass the possibilities in detail, we note that New York expressly provides by statute that Sibron's conviction may be used to impeach his character should he choose to put it in issue at any future criminal trial, N.Y. Code Crim. Proc. § 393–c, and that it must be submitted to a trial judge for his consideration in sentencing should Sibron again be convicted of a crime, N.Y. Code Crim. Proc. § 482. There are doubtless other collateral consequences. Moreover, we see no relevance in the fact that Sibron is a multiple offender. Morgan was a multiple offender, see 346 U.S. at 503–504, and so was Pollard, see 352 U.S., at 355–357. A judge or jury faced with a question of character, like a sentencing judge, may be inclined to forgive or at least discount a limited number of minor transgressions, particularly if they occurred at some time in the relatively distant past.[16] It is impossible for this Court to say at what point the number of convictions on a man's record renders his reputation irredeemable.[17] And even if we believed that an individual had reached that point, it would be impossible for us to say that he had no interest in beginning the process of redemption with the particular case sought to be adjudicated. We cannot foretell what opportunities might present themselves in the future for the removal of other convictions from an individual's record. The question of the validity of a criminal conviction can arise in many contexts, compare *Burgett* v. *Texas*, 389 U.S. 109 (1967), and the sooner the issue is fully litigated the better for all concerned. It is always preferable to litigate a matter when it is directly and principally in dispute, rather than in a proceeding where it is col-

---

[15] See generally Note, 53 Va. L. Rev. 403 (1967).

[16] We do not know from the record how many convictions Sibron had, for what crimes, or when they were rendered. At the hearing he admitted to a 1955 conviction for burglary and a 1957 misdemeanor conviction for possession of narcotics. He also admitted that he had other convictions, but none were specifically alluded to.

[17] We note that there is a clear distinction between a general impairment of credibility, to which the Court referred in *St. Pierre*, see 319 U.S., at 43, and New York's specific statutory authorization for use of the conviction to impeach the "character" of a defendant in a criminal proceeding. The latter is a clear legal disability deliberately and specifically imposed by the legislature.

300

lateral to the central controversy. Moreover, litigation is better conducted when the dispute is fresh and additional facts may, if necessary, be taken without a substantial risk that witnesses will die or memories fade. And it is far better to eliminate the source of a potential legal disability than to require the citizen to suffer the possibly unjustified consequences of the disability itself for an indefinite period of time before he can secure adjudication of the State's right to impose it on the basis of some past action. Cf. *Peyton* v. *Rowe,* 391 U.S. 54, 64 (1968).[18]

None of the concededly imperative policies behind the constitutional rule against entertaining moot controversies would be served by a dismissal in this case. There is nothing abstract, feigned, or hypothetical about Sibron's appeal. Nor is there any suggestion that either Sibron or the State has been wanting in diligence or fervor in the litigation. We have before us a fully developed record of testimony about contested historical facts, which reflects the "impact of actuality"[19] to a far greater degree than many controversies accepted for adjudication as a matter of course under the Federal Declaratory Judgment Act, 28 U.S.C. § 2201.

St. Pierre v. *United States, supra,* must be read in light of later cases to mean that a criminal case is moot only if it is shown that there is no possibility that any collateral legal consequences will be imposed on the basis of the challenged conviction. That certainly is not the case here. Sibron "has a substantial stake in the judgment of conviction which survives the satisfaction of the sentence imposed on him." *Fiswick* v. *United States, supra,* at 222. The case is not moot.

II.

We deal next with the confession of error by the District Attorney for Kings County in No. 63. Confessions of error are, of course, entitled to and given great weight, but they do not "relieve this Court of the performance of the judicial function." *Young* v. *United States,* 315 U.S. 257, 258 (1942). It is the uniform practice of this Court to conduct its own examination of the record in all cases where the Federal Government or a State confesses that a conviction has been erroneously obtained. For one thing, as we noted in *Young,* "our judgments are precedents, and the proper administration of the criminal law cannot be left merely to the

---

[18] This factor has clearly been considered relevant by the Court in the past in determining the issue of mootness. See *Fiswick* v. *United States,* 329 U. S. 211, 221–222 (1946).

[19] Frankfurter, A Note on Advisory Opinions, 37 Harv. L. Rev. 1002, 1006 (1924). See also *Parker* v. *Ellis,* 362 U. S. 574, 592–593 (1960) (dissenting opinion).

stipulation of parties." 315 U.S., at 259. See also *Marino* v. *Ragen*, 332 U.S. 561 (1947). This consideration is entitled to special weight where, as in this case, we deal with a judgment of a State's highest court interpreting a state statute which is challenged on constitutional grounds. The need for such authoritative declarations of state law in sensitive constitutional contexts has been the very reason for the development of the abstention doctrine by this Court. See, *e. g., Railroad Comm'n* v. *Pullman Co.*, 312 U.S. 496 (1941). Such a judgment is the final product of a sovereign judicial system, and is deserving of respectful treatment by this Court. Moreover, in this case the confession of error on behalf of the entire state executive and judicial branches is made, not by a state official, but by the elected legal officer of one political subdivision within the State. The District Attorney for Kings County seems to have come late to the opinion that this conviction violated Sibron's constitutional rights. For us to accept his view blindly in the circumstances, when a majority of the Court of Appeals of New York has expressed the contrary view, would be a disservice to the State of New York and an abdication of our obligation to lower courts to decide cases upon proper constitutional grounds in a manner which permits them to conform their future behavior to the demands of the Constitution. We turn to the merits.

III.

The parties on both sides of these two cases have urged that the principle issue before us is the constitutionality of § 180–a "on its face." We decline, however, to be drawn into what we view as the abstract and unproductive exercise of laying the extraordinarily elastic categories of § 180–a next to the categories of the Fourth Amendment in an effort to determine whether the two are in some sense compatible. The constitutional validity of a warrantless search is pre-eminently the sort of question which can only be decided in the concrete factual context of the individual case. In this respect it is quite different from the question of the adequacy of the procedural safeguards written into a statute which purports to authorize the issuance of search warrants in certain circumstances. See *Berger* v. *New York*, 388 U.S. 41 (1967). No search required to be made under a warrant is valid if the procedure for the issuance of the warrant is inadequate to ensure the sort of neutral contemplation by a magistrate of the grounds for the search and its proposed scope, which lies at the heart of the Fourth Amendment. *E. g., Aguilar* v. *Texas*, 378 U.S. 108 (1964); *Giordenello* v. *United States*, 357 U.S. 480 (1958). This Court held last Term in *Berger* v. *New York, supra,* that N.Y. Code Crim. Proc. § 813–a, which established a procedure for the issuance of search warrants to permit electronic eavesdropping, failed to embody the safeguards demanded by the Fourth and Fourteenth Amendments.

Section 180–a, unlike § 813–a, deals with the substantive validity of certain types of seizures and searches without warrants. It purports to authorize police officers to "stop" people, "demand" explanations of them and "search [them] for dangerous weapon[s]" in certain circumstances upon "reasonable suspicion" that they are engaged in criminal activity and that they represent a danger to the policeman. The operative categories of § 180–a are not the categories of the Fourth Amendment, and they are susceptible of a wide variety of interpretations.[20] New York is, of

---

[20] It is not apparent, for example, whether the power to "stop" granted by the statute entails a power to "detain" for investigation or interrogation upon less than probable cause, or if so what sort of durational limitations upon such detention are contemplated. And while the statute's apparent grant of a power of compulsion indicates that many "stops" will constitute "seizures," it is not clear that all conduct analyzed under the rubric of the statute will either rise to the level of a "seizure" or be based upon less than probable cause. In No. 74, the *Peters* case, for example, the New York courts justified the seizure of appellant under § 180–a, but we have concluded that there was in fact probable cause for an arrest when Officer Lasky seized Peters on the stairway. See *infra,* at 66. In any event, a pronouncement by this Court upon the abstract validity of § 180–a's "stop" category would be most inappropriate in these cases, since we have concluded that neither of them presents the question of the validity of a seizure of the person for purposes of interrogation upon less than probable cause.

The statute's other categories are equally elastic, and it was passed too recently for the State's highest court to have ruled upon many of the questions involving potential intersections with federal constitutional guarantees. We cannot tell, for example, whether the officer's power to "demand" of a person an "explanation of his actions" contemplates either an obligation on the part of the citizen to answer or some additional power on the part of the officer in the event of a refusal to answer, or even whether the interrogation following the "stop" is "custodial." Compare *Miranda* v. *Arizona,* 384 U. S. 436 (1966). There are, moreover, substantial indications that the statutory category of a "search for a dangerous weapon" may encompass conduct considerably broader in scope than that which we approved in *Terry* v. *Ohio, ante,* p. 1. See *infra,* at 65–66. See also *People* v. *Taggart,* 20 N.Y.2d 335, 229 N.E.2d 581, 283 N.Y.S. 2d 1 (1967). At least some of the activity apparently permitted under the rubric of searching for dangerous weapons may thus be permissible under the Constitution only if the "reasonable suspicion" of criminal activity rises to the level of probable cause. Finally, it is impossible to tell whether the standard of "reasonable suspicion" connotes the same sort of specificity, reliability, and objectivity which is the touchstone of permissible governmental action under the Fourth Amendment. Compare *Terry* v. *Ohio, supra,* with *People* v. *Taggart, supra.* In this connection we note that the searches and seizures in both *Sibron* and *Peters* were upheld by the Court of Appeals of New York as predicated upon "reasonable suspicion," whereas we have concluded that the officer in

course, free to develop its own law of search and seizure to meet the needs of local law enforcement, see *Ker* v. *California,* 374 U.S. 23, 34 (1963), and in the process it may call the standards it employs by any names it may choose. It may not, however, authorize police conduct which trenches upon Fourth Amendment rights, regardless of the labels which it attaches to such conduct. The question in this Court upon review of a state-approved search or seizure "is not whether the search [or seizure] was authorized by state law. The question is rather whether the search was reasonable under the Fourth Amendment. Just as a search authorized by state law may be an unreasonable one under that amendment, so may a search not expressly authorized by state law be justified as a constitutionally reasonable one." *Cooper* v. *California,* 386 U.S. 58, 61 (1967).

Accordingly, we make no pronouncement on the facial constitutionality of § 180–a. The constitutional point with respect to a statute of this peculiar sort, as the Court of Appeals of New York recognized, is "not so much . . . the language employed as . . . the conduct it authorizes." *People* v. *Peters,* 18 N.Y.2d 238, 245, 219 N.E.2d 595, 599, 273 N.Y.S.2d 217, 222 (1966). We have held today in *Terry* v. *Ohio, ante,* p. 1, that police conduct of the sort with which § 180–a deals must be judged under the Reasonable Search and Seizure Clause of the Fourth Amendment. The inquiry under that clause may differ sharply from the inquiry set up by the categories of § 180–a. Our constitutional inquiry would not be furthered here by an attempt to pronounce judgment on the words of the statute. We must confine our review instead to the reasonableness of the searches and seizures which underlie these two convictions.

IV.

Turning to the facts of Sibron's case, it is clear that the heroin was inadmissible in evidence against him. The prosecution has quite properly abandoned the notion that there was probable cause to arrest Sibron for any crime at the time Patrolman Martin accosted him in the restaurant, took him outside and searched him. The officer was not acquainted with Sibron and had no information concerning him. He merely saw Sibron talking to a number of known narcotics addicts over a period of eight hours. It must be emphasized that Patrolman Martin was completely ignorant regarding the content of these conversations, and that he saw nothing pass between Sibron and the addicts. So far as he knew, they might

---

Peters had probable cause for an arrest, while the policeman in *Sibron* was not possessed of any information which would justify an intrusion upon rights protected by the Fourth Amendment.

indeed "have been talking about the World Series." The inference that persons who talk to narcotics addicts are engaged in the criminal traffic in narcotics is simply not the sort of reasonable inference required to support an intrusion by the police upon an individual's personal security. Nothing resembling probable cause existed until after the search had turned up the envelopes of heroin. It is axiomatic that an incident search may not precede an arrest and serve as part of its justification. *E. g., Henry* v. *United States*, 361 U.S. 98 (1959) ; *Johnson* v. *United States*, 333 U.S. 10, 16–17 (1948). Thus the search cannot be justified as incident to a lawful arrest.

If Patrolman Martin lacked probable cause for an arrest, however, his seizure and search of Sibron might still have been justified at the outset if he had reasonable grounds to believe that Sibron was armed and dangerous. *Terry* v. *Ohio, ante,* p. 1. We are not called upon to decide in this case whether there was a "seizure" of Sibron inside the restaurant antecedent to the physical seizure which accompanied the search. The record is unclear with respect to what transpired between Sibron and the officer inside the restaurant. It is totally barren of any indication whether Sibron accompanied Patrolman Martin outside in submission to a show of force or authority which left him no choice, or whether he went voluntarily in a spirit of apparent cooperation with the officer's investigation. In any event, this deficiency in the record is immaterial, since Patrolman Martin obtained no new information in the interval between his initiation of the encounter in the restaurant and his physical seizure and search of Sibron outside.

Although the Court of Appeals of New York wrote no opinion in this case, it seems to have viewed the search here as a self-protective search for weapons and to have affirmed on the basis of § 180–a, which authorizes such a search when the officer "reasonably suspects that he is in danger of life or limb." The Court of Appeals has, at any rate, justified searches during field interrogation on the ground that "[t]he answer to the question propounded by the policeman may be a bullet; in any case the exposure to danger could be very great." *People* v. *Rivera,* 14 N.Y.2d 441, 446, 201 N.E.2d 32, 35, 252 N.Y.S.2d 458, 463 (1964), cert. denied, 379 U.S. 978 (1965). But the application of this reasoning to the facts of this case proves too much. The police officer is not entitled to seize and search every person whom he sees on the street or of whom he makes inquiries. Before he places a hand on the person of a citizen in search of anything, he must have constitutionally adequate, reasonable grounds for doing so. In the case of the self-protective search for weapons, he must be able to point

305

to particular facts from which he reasonably inferred that the individual was armed and dangerous. *Terry* v. *Ohio, supra*. Patrolman Martin's testimony reveals no such facts. The suspect's mere act of talking with a number of known narcotics addicts over an eight-hour period no more gives rise to reasonable fear of life or limb on the part of the police officer than it justifies an arrest for committing a crime. Nor did Patrolman Martin urge that when Sibron put his hand in his pocket, he feared that he was going for a weapon and acted in self-defense. His opening statement to Sibron—"You know what I am after"—made it abundantly clear that he sought narcotics, and his testimony at the hearing left no doubt that he thought there were narcotics in Sibron's pocket.[21]

Even assuming *arguendo* that there were adequate grounds to search Sibron for weapons, the nature and scope of the search conducted by Patrolman Martin were so clearly unrelated to that justification as to render the heroin inadmissible. The search for weapons approved in *Terry* consisted solely of a limited patting of the outer clothing of the suspect for concealed objects which might be used as instruments of assault. Only when he discovered such objects did the officer in *Terry* place his hands in the pockets of the men he searched. In this case, with no attempt at an initial limited exploration for arms, Patrolman Martin thrust his hand into Sibron's pocket and took from him envelopes of heroin. His testi-

---

[21] It is argued in dissent that this Court has in effect overturned factual findings by the two courts below that the search in this case was a self-protective measure on the part of Patrolman Martin, who thought that Sibron might have been reaching for a gun. It is true, as we have noted, that the Court of Appeals of New York apparently rested its approval of the search on this view. The trial court, however, made no such finding of fact. The trial judge adopted the theory of the prosecution at the hearing on the motion to suppress. This theory was that there was probable cause to arrest Sibron for some crime having to do with narcotics. The fact which tipped the scales for the trial court had nothing to do with danger to the policeman. The judge expressly changed his original view and held the heroin admissible upon being reminded that Sibron had admitted on the stand that he spoke to the addicts about narcotics. This admission was not relevant on the issue of probable cause, and we do not understand the dissent to take the position that prior to the discovery of heroin, there was probable cause for an arrest.

Moreover, Patrolman Martin himself never at any time put forth the notion that he acted to protect himself. As we have noted, this subject never came up, until on re-direct examination defense counsel raised the question whether Patrolman Martin thought Sibron was going for a gun. See n. 4, *supra*. This was the only reference to weapons at any point in the hearing, and the subject was swiftly dropped. In the circumstances an unarticulated "finding" by an appellate court which wrote no opinion, apparently to the effect that the officer's invasion of Sibron's person comported with the Constitution because of the need to protect himself, is not deserving of controlling deference.

mony shows that he was looking for narcotics, and he found them. The search was not reasonably limited in scope to the accomplishment of the only goal which might conceivably have justified its inception—the protection of the officer by disarming a potentially dangerous man. Such a search violates the guarantee of the Fourth Amendment, which protects the sanctity of the person against unreasonable intrusions on the part of all government agents.

V.

We think it is equally clear that the search in Peters' case was wholly reasonable under the Constitution. The Court of Appeals of New York held that the search was made legal by § 180-a, since Peters was "abroad in a public place," and since Officer Lasky was reasonably suspicious of his activities and, once he had stopped Peters, reasonably suspected that he was in danger of life or limb, even though he held Peters at gun point. This may be the justification for the search under state law. We think, however, that for purposes of the Fourth Amendment the search was properly incident to a lawful arrest. By the time Officer Lasky caught up with Peters on the stairway between the fourth and fifth floors of the apartment building, he had probable cause to arrest him for attempted burglary. The officer heard strange noises at his door which apparently led him to believe that someone sought to force entry. When he investigated these noises he saw two men, whom he had never seen before in his 12 years in the building, tiptoeing furtively about the hallway. They were still engaged in these maneuvers after he called the police and dressed hurriedly. And when Officer Lasky entered the hallway, the men fled down the stairs. It is difficult to conceive of stronger grounds for an arrest, short of actual eyewitness observation of criminal activity. As the trial court explicitly recognized,[22] deliberately furtive actions and flight at the approach of strangers or law officers are strong indicia of *mens rea,* and when coupled with specific knowledge on the part of the officer relating the suspect to the evidence of crime, they are proper factors to be considered in the decision to make an arrest. *Brinegar* v. *United States,* 338 U.S. 160 (1949) ; *Husty* v. *United States,* 282 U.S. 694 (1931) ; see *Henry* v. *United States,* 361 U.S. 98, 103 (1959).

As we noted in Sibron's case, a search incident to a lawful arrest may not precede the arrest and serve as part of its justification. It is a question of fact precisely when, in each case, the arrest took place. *Rios* v. *United States,* 364 U.S. 253, 261–262 (1960).

---

[22] See n. 7, *supra.*

And while there was some inconclusive discussion in the trial court concerning when Officer Lasky "arrested" Peters, it is clear that the arrest had, for purposes of constitutional justification, already taken place before the search commenced. When the policeman grabbed Peters by the collar, he abruptly "seized" him and curtailed his freedom of movement on the basis of probable cause to believe that he was engaged in criminal activity. See *Henry* v. *United States, supra,* at 103. At that point he had the authority to search Peters, and the incident search was obviously justified "by the need to seize weapons and other things which might be used to assault an officer or effect an escape, as well as by the need to prevent the destruction of evidence of the crime." *Preston* v. *United States,* 376 U.S. 364, 367 (1964). Moreover, it was reasonably limited in scope by these purposes. Officer Lasky did not engage in an unrestrained and thorough-going examination of Peters and his personal effects. He seized him to cut short his flight, and he searched him primarily for weapons. While patting down his outer clothing, Officer Lasky discovered an object in his pocket which might have been used as a weapon. He seized it and discovered it to be a potential instrument of the crime of burglary.

We have concluded that Peters' conviction fully comports with the commands of the Fourth and Fourteenth Amendments, and must be affirmed. The conviction in No. 63, however, must be reversed, on the ground that the heroin was unconstitutionally admitted in evidence against the appellant.

It is so ordered.

MR. JUSTICE DOUGLAS, concurring in No. 63.

Officer Martin testified that on the night in question he observed appellant Sibron continually from 4 p. m. to 12 midnight and that during that eight-hour period, Sibron conversed with different persons each personally known to Martin as narcotics addicts. When Sibron entered a restaurant, Martin followed him inside where he observed Sibron talking to three other persons also personally known to Martin as narcotics addicts. At that point he approached Sibron and asked him to come outside. When Sibron stepped out, Martin said, "You know what I am after." Sibron then reached inside his pocket, and at the same time Martin reached into the same pocket and discovered several glassine envelopes which were found to contain heroin. Sibron was subsequently convicted of unlawful possession of heroin.

Consorting with criminals may in a particular factual setting be a basis for believing that a criminal project is underway. Yet talking with addicts without more rises no higher than suspicion. That is all we have here; and if it is sufficient for a "seizure" and a "search," then there is no such thing as privacy for this vast group of "sick" people.

MR. JUSTICE DOUGLAS, concurring in No. 74.

Officer Lasky testified that he resided in a multiple-dwelling apartment house in Mount Vernon, New York. His apartment was on the sixth floor. At about 1 in the afternoon, he had just stepped out of the shower and was drying himself when he heard a noise at his door. Just then his phone rang and he answered the call. After hanging up, he looked through the peephole of his door and saw two men, one of whom was appellant, tiptoeing out of an alcove toward the stairway. He phoned his headquarters to report this occurrence, and then put on some clothes and proceeded back to the door. This time he saw a tall man tiptoeing away from the alcove, followed by appellant, toward the stairway. Lasky came out of his apartment, slammed the door behind him, and then gave chase, gun in hand, as the two men began to run down the stairs. He apprehended appellant on the stairway between the fourth and fifth floors, and asked what he was doing in the building. Appellant replied that he was looking for a girl friend, but refused to give her name, saying that she was a married woman. Lasky then "frisked" appellant for a weapon, and discovered in his right pants pocket a plastic envelope. The envelope contained a tension bar, 6 picks and 2 Allen wrenches with the short leg filed down to a screwdriver edge. Appellant was subsequently convicted for possession of burglary tools.

I would hold that at the time Lasky seized appellant, he had probable cause to believe that appellant was on some kind of burglary or housebreaking mission.* In my view he had probable cause to seize appellant and accordingly to conduct a limited search of his person for weapons.

MR. JUSTICE WHITE, concurring.

I join Parts I–IV of the Court's opinion. With respect to appellant Peters, I join the affirmance of his conviction, not because there was probable cause to arrest, a question I do not reach, but because there was probable cause to stop Peters for questioning and thus to frisk him for dangerous weapons. See my concurring opinion in *Terry* v. *Ohio, ante,* p. 34. While patting down Peters' clothing the officer "discovered an object in his pocket which might have been used as a weapon." *Ante,* at 67. That object turned out

---

* See N.Y.Pen. Code §§ 140.20, 140.25 (1967).

to be a package of burglar's tools. In my view those tools were properly admitted into evidence.

MR. JUSTICE FORTAS, concurring.

1. I would construe *St. Pierre* v. *United States*, 319 U.S. 41 (1943), in light of later cases, to mean that a criminal case is moot *if it appears* that no collateral legal consequences will be imposed on the basis of the challenged conviction. (Cf. majority opinion, *ante*, at 57–58.)

2. I join without qualification in the Court's judgment and opinion concerning the standards to be used in determining whether § 180–a as applied to particular situations is constitutional. But I would explicitly reserve the possibility that a statute purporting to authorize a warrantless search might be so extreme as to justify our concluding that it is unconstitutional "on its face," regardless of the facts of the particular case. To the extent that the Court's opinion may indicate the contrary, I disagree. (Cf. majority opinion, *ante*, at 59–62.)

3. In Sibron's case (No. 63), I would conclude that we find nothing in the record of this case or pertinent principles of law to cause us to disregard the confession of error by counsel for Kings County. I would not discourage confessions of error nor would I disregard them. (Cf. majority opinion, pt. II, *ante*, at 58–59.)

MR. JUSTICE HARLAN, concurring in the result.

I fully agree with the results the Court has reached in these cases. They are, I think, consonant with and dictated by the decision in *Terry* v. *Ohio, ante*, p. 1. For reasons I do not understand, however, the Court has declined to rest the judgments here upon the principles of *Terry*. In doing so it has, in at least one particular, made serious inroads upon the protection afforded by the Fourth and Fourteenth Amendments.

The Court is of course entirely correct in concluding that we should not pass upon the constitutionality of the New York stop-and-frisk law "on its face." The statute is certainly not unconstitutional on its face: that is, it does not plainly purport to authorize unconstitutional activities by policemen. Nor is it "constitutional on its face" if that expression means that any action now or later thought to fall within the terms of the statute is, *ipso facto*, within constitutional limits as well. No statute, state or federal, receives any such *imprimatur* from this Court.

This does not mean, however, that the statute should be ignored here. The State of New York has made a deliberate effort to deal with the complex problem of on-the-street policework. Without giving *carte blanche* to any particular verbal formulation, we should, I think, where relevant, indicate the extent to which that effort has been constitutionally successful. The core of the New York statute is the permission to stop any person reasonably suspected of crime. Under the decision in *Terry* a right to stop may indeed be premised on reasonable suspicion and does not require probable cause, and hence the New York formulation is to that extent constitutional. This does not mean that suspicion need not be "reasonable" in the constitutional as well as the statutory sense. Nor does it mean that this Court has approved more than a momentary stop or has indicated what questioning may constitutionally occur during a stop, for the cases before us do not raise these questions.[1]

Turning to the individual cases, I agree that the conviction in No. 63, *Sibron*, should be reversed, and would do so upon the premises of *Terry*. At the outset, I agree that sufficient collateral legal consequences of Sibron's conviction have been shown to prevent this case from being moot, and I agree that the case should not be reversed simply on the State's confession of error.

The considerable confusion that has surrounded the "search" or "frisk" of Sibron that led to the actual recovery of the heroin seems to me irrelevant for our purposes. Officer Martin repudiated his first statement, which might conceivably have indicated a theory of "abandonment," see *ante*, at 45–46. No matter which of the other theories is adopted, it is clear that there was at least a forcible frisk, comparable to that which occurred in *Terry*, which requires constitutional justification.

Since carrying heroin is a crime in New York, probable cause to believe Sibron was carrying heroin would also have been probable cause to arrest him. As the Court says, Officer Martin clearly had neither. Although Sibron had had conversations with several known addicts, he had done nothing, during the several hours he was under surveillance, that made it "probable" that he was either carrying heroin himself or engaging in transactions with these acquaintances.

Nor were there here reasonable grounds for a *Terry*-type "stop" short of an arrest. I would accept, as an adequate general formula, the New York requirement that the officer must "reasonably suspect" that the person he stops "is committing, has committed or is about to commit a felony." N.Y. Code Crim. Proc. § 180–a. "On its face," this requirement is, if anything, more stringent than the

---

[1] For a thoughtful study of many of these points, see ALI Model Code of Pre-Arraignment Procedure, Tentative Draft No. 1, §§ 2.01, 2.02, and the commentary on these sections appearing at 87–105.

requirement stated by the Court in *Terry*: "where a police officer observes unusual conduct which leads him reasonably to conclude in light of his experience that criminal activity may be afoot . . . ." *Ante*, at 30. The interpretation of the New York statute is of course a matter for the New York courts, but any particular stop must meet the *Terry* standard as well.

The forcible encounter between Officer Martin and Sibron did not meet the *Terry* reasonableness standard. In the first place, although association with known criminals may, I think, properly be a factor contributing to the suspiciousness of circumstances, it does not, entirely by itself, create suspicion adequate to support a stop. There must be something at least in the activities of the person being observed or in his surroundings that affirmatively suggests particular criminal activity, completed, current, or intended. That was the case in *Terry*, but it palpably was not the case here. For eight continuous hours, up to the point when he interrupted Sibron eating a piece of pie, Officer Martin apparently observed not a single suspicious action and heard not a single suspicious word on the part of Sibron himself or any person with whom he associated. If anything, that period of surveillance pointed away from suspicion.

Furthermore, in *Terry*, the police officer judged that his suspect was about to commit a violent crime and that he had to assert himself in order to prevent it. Here there was no reason for Officer Martin to think that an incipient crime, or flight, or the destruction of evidence would occur if he stayed his hand; indeed, there was no more reason for him to intrude upon Sibron at the moment when he did than there had been four hours earlier, and no reason to think the situation would have changed four hours later. While no hard-and-fast rule can be drawn, I would suggest that one important factor, missing here, that should be taken into account in determining whether there are reasonable grounds for a forcible intrusion is whether there is any need for immediate action.

For these reasons I would hold that Officer Martin lacked reasonable grounds to intrude forcibly upon Sibron. In consequence, the essential premise for the right to conduct a self-protective frisk was lacking. See my concurring opinion in *Terry, ante,* p. 31. I therefore find it unnecessary to reach two further troublesome questions. First, although I think that, as in *Terry*, the right to frisk is automatic when an officer lawfully stops a person suspected of a crime whose nature creates a substantial likelihood that he is armed, it is not clear that suspected possession of narcotics falls into this category. If the nature of the suspected offense creates no reasonable apprehension for the officer's safety, I would not permit him to frisk unless other circumstances did so. Second, I agree with the Court that even where a self-protective frisk is proper, its scope should be limited to what is adequate for its purposes. I see no need here to resolve the question whether this frisk exceeded those bounds.

Turning now to No. 74, *Peters*, I agree that the conviction should be upheld, but here I would differ strongly and fundamentally with the Court's approach. The Court holds that the burglar's tools were recovered from Peters in a search incident to a lawful arrest. I do not think that Officer Lasky had anything close to probable cause to arrest Peters before he recovered the burglar's tools. Indeed, if probable cause existed here, I find it difficult to see why a different rationale was necessary to support the stop and frisk in *Terry* and why States such as New York have had to devote so much thought to the constitutional problems of field interrogation. This case will be the latest in an exceedingly small number of cases in this Court indicating what suffices for probable cause. While, as the Court noted in *Terry*, the influence of this Court on police tactics "in the field" is necessarily limited, the influence of a decision here on hundreds of courts and magistrates who have to decide whether there is probable cause for a real arrest or a full search will be large.

Officer Lasky testified that at 1 o'clock in the afternoon he heard a noise at the door to his apartment. He did not testify, nor did any state court conclude, that this "led him to believe that someone sought to force entry." *Ante*, at 66. He looked out into the public hallway and saw two men whom he did not recognize, surely not a strange occurrence in a large apartment building. One of them appeared to be tip-toeing. Lasky did not testify that the other man was tiptoeing or that either of them was behaving "furtively." *Ibid*. Lasky left his apartment and ran to them, gun in hand. He did not testify that there was any "flight," *ante*, at 66,[2] though flight at the approach of a gun-carrying stranger (Lasky was apparently not in uniform) is hardly indicative of *mens rea*.

Probable cause to arrest means evidence that would warrant a prudent and reasonable man (such as a magistrate, actual or hypothetical) in believing that a particular person has committed or is committing a crime.[3] Officer Lasky had no extrinsic reason to

---

[2] It is true, as the Court states, that the New York courts attributed such a statement to him. The attribution seems to me unwarranted by the record.

[3] *E. g., Beck* v. *Ohio*, 379 U.S. 89; *Rios* v. *United States*, 364 U.S. 253; *Henry* v. *United States*, 361 U.S. 98. In *Henry, supra*, at 100, the Court said that 18 U.S.C. § 3052

think that a crime had been or was being committed, so whether it would have been proper to issue a warrant depends entirely on his statements of his observations of the men. Apart from his conclusory statement that he thought the men were burglars, he offered very little specific evidence. I find it hard to believe that if Peters had made good his escape and there were no report of a burglary in the neighborhood, this Court would hold it proper for a prudent neutral magistrate to issue a warrant for his arrest.[4]

In the course of upholding Peters' conviction, the Court makes two other points that may lead to future confusion. The first concerns the "moment of arrest." If there is an escalating encounter between a policeman and a citizen, beginning perhaps with a friendly conversation but ending in imprisonment, and if evidence is developing during that encounter, it may be important to identify the moment of arrest, *i. e.*, the moment when the policeman was not permitted to proceed further unless he by then had probable cause. This moment-of-arrest problem is not, on the Court's premises, in any way involved in this case: the Court holds that Officer Lasky had probable cause to arrest at the moment he caught Peters, and hence probable cause clearly preceded anything that might be thought an arrest. The Court implies, however, that although there is no problem about whether the arrest of Peters occurred *late* enough, *i. e.*, after probable cause developed, there might be a problem about whether it occurred *early* enough, *i. e.*, before Peters was searched. This seems to me a false problem. Of course, the fruits of a search may not be used to justify an arrest to which it is incident, but this means only that probable cause to arrest must precede the search. If the prosecution shows probable cause to arrest prior to a search of a man's person, it has met its total burden. There is *no* case in which a defendant may validly say, "Although the officer had a right to arrest me at the moment

---

"states the constitutional standard" for felony arrests by FBI agents without warrant. That section authorized agents to "make arrests without warrant for any offense against the United States committed in their presence, or for any felony cognizable under the laws of the United States if they have reasonable grounds to believe that the person to be arrested has committed or is committing such felony." Under *Ker* v. *California*, 374 U.S. 23, a parallel standard is applicable to warrantless arrests by state and local police.

[4] Compare *Henry* v. *United States*, 361 U.S. 98, in which the Court said there was "far from enough evidence . . . to justify a magistrate in issuing a warrant." *Id.*, at 103. Agents knew that a federal crime, theft of whisky from an interstate shipment, had been committed "in the neighborhood." Petitioner was observed driving into an alley, picking up packages, and driving away. I agree that these facts did not constitute probable cause, but find it hard to see that the evidence here was more impressive.

when he seized me and searched my person, the search is invalid
because he did not in fact arrest me until afterwards."

This fact is important because, as demonstrated by *Terry*, not
every curtailment of freedom of movement is an "arrest" requiring antecedent probable cause. At the same time, an officer who
does have probable cause may of course seize and search immediately. Hence while certain police actions will undoubtedly turn an
encounter into an arrest requiring antecedent probable cause, the
prosecution must be able to date the arrest as *early* as it chooses
following the development of probable cause.

The second possible source of confusion is the Court's statement
that "Officer Lasky did not engage in an unrestrained and thorough-
going examination of Peters and his personal effects." *Ante*, at
67. Since the Court found probable cause to arrest Peters, and since
an officer arresting on probable cause is entitled to make a very
full incident search,[5] I assume that this is merely a factual observation. As a factual matter, I agree with it.

Although the articulable circumstances are somewhat less suspicious here than they were in *Terry*, I would affirm on the *Terry*
ground that Officer Lasky had reasonable cause to make a forced
stop. Unlike probable cause to arrest, reasonable grounds to stop
do not depend on any degree of likelihood that a crime *has* been
committed. An officer may forcibly intrude upon an incipient crime
even where he could not make an arrest for the simple reason
that there is nothing to arrest anyone for. Hence although Officer
Lasky had small reason to believe that a crime had been committed,
his right to stop Peters can be justified if he had a reasonable
suspicion that Peters was about to attempt burglary.

It was clear that the officer had to act quickly if he was going
to act at all, and, as stated above, it seems to me that where
immediate action is obviously required, a police officer is justified
in acting on rather less objectively articulable evidence than when
there is more time for consideration of alternative courses of action. Perhaps more important, the Court's opinion in *Terry* emphasized the special qualifications of an experienced police officer. While
"probable cause" to arrest or search has always depended on the
existence of hard evidence that would persuade a "reasonable
man," in judging on-the-street encounters it seems to me proper
to take into account a police officer's trained instinctive judgment
operating on a multitude of small gestures and actions impossible
to reconstruct. Thus the statement by an officer that "he looked like
a burglar to me" adds little to an affidavit filed with a magistrate

---

[5] The leading case is *United States
v. Rabinowitz*, 339 U.S. 56.

in an effort to obtain a warrant. When the question is whether it was reasonable to take limited but forcible steps in a situation requiring immediate action, however, such a statement looms larger. A court is of course entitled to disbelieve the officer (who is subject to cross-examination), but when it believes him and when there are some articulable supporting facts, it is entitled to find action taken under fire to be reasonable.

Given Officer Lasky's statement of the circumstances, and crediting his experienced judgment as he watched the two men, the state courts were entitled to conclude, as they did, that Lasky forcibly stopped Peters on "reasonable suspicion." The frisk made incident to that stop was a limited one, which turned up burglar's tools. Although the frisk is constitutionally permitted only in order to protect the officer, if it is lawful the State is of course entitled to the use of any other contraband that appears.

For the foregoing reasons I concur in the result in these cases.

MR. JUSTICE BLACK, concurring in No. 74 and dissenting in No. 63.

I concur in the affirmance of the judgment against Peters but dissent from the reversal of No. 63, *Sibron* v. *New York,* and would affirm that conviction. Sibron was convicted of violating New York's anti-narcotics law on the basis of evidence seized from him by the police. The Court reverses on the ground that the narcotics were seized as the result of an unreasonable search in violation of the Fourth Amendment. The Court has decided today in *Terry* v. *Ohio* and in No. 74, *Peters* v. *New York,* that a policeman does not violate the Fourth Amendment when he makes a limited search for weapons on the person of a man who the policeman has probable cause to believe has a dangerous weapon on him with which he might injure the policeman or others or both, unless he is searched and the weapon is taken away from him. And, of course, under established principles it is not a violation of the Fourth Amendment for a policeman to search a person who he has probable cause to believe is committing a felony at the time. For both these reasons I think the seizure of the narcotics from Sibron was not unreasonable under the Fourth Amendment. Because of a different emphasis on the facts, I find it necessary to restate them.

About 4 p. m. Patrolman Martin saw appellant Sibron in the vicinity of 742 Broadway. From then until 12 o'clock midnight Sibron remained there. During that time the policeman saw Sibron talking with six or eight persons whom the policeman knew from past experience to be narcotics addicts. Later, at about 12 o'clock, Sibron went into a restaurant and there the patrolman saw Sibron speak with three more known addicts. While Sibron was eating in the restaurant the policeman went to him and asked him to come out. Sibron came out. There the officer said to Sibron, "You know what I am after." Sibron mumbled something and reached into his left coat pocket. The officer also moved his hand to the pocket and seized what was in it, which turned out to be heroin. The patrolman testified at the hearing to suppress use of the heroin as evidence that he "thought he [Sibron] might have been" reaching for a gun.

Counsel for New York for some reason that I have not been able to understand, has attempted to confess error—that is, that for some reason the search or seizure here violated the Fourth Amendment. I agree with the Court that we need not and should not accept this confession of error. But, unlike the Court, I think, for two reasons, that the seizure did not violate the Fourth Amendment and that the heroin was properly admitted in evidence.

First. I think there was probable cause for the policeman to believe that when Sibron reached his hand to his coat pocket, Sibron had a dangerous weapon which he might use if it were not taken away from him. This, according to the Court's own opinion, seems to have been the ground on which the Court of Appeals of New York justified the search, since it "affirmed on the basis of § 180-a, which authorizes such a search when the officer 'reasonably suspects that he is in danger of life or limb.' " Ante, at 63. And it seems to me to be a reasonable inference that when Sibron, who had been approaching and talking to addicts for eight hours, reached his hand quickly to his left coat pocket, he might well be reaching for a gun. And as the Court has emphasized today in its opinions in the other stop-and-frisk cases, a policeman under such circumstances has to act in a split second; delay may mean death for him. No one can know when an addict may be moved to shoot or stab, and particularly when he moves his hand hurriedly to a pocket where weapons are known to be habitually carried, it behooves an officer who wants to live to act at once as this officer did. It is true that the officer might also have thought Sibron was about to get heroin instead of a weapon. But the law enforcement officers all over the Nation have gained little protection from the courts through opinions here if they are now left helpless to act in self defense when a man associating intimately and continuously with addicts, upon meeting an officer, shifts his hand immediately to a pocket where weapons are constantly carried.

In appraising the facts as I have I realize that the Court has chosen to draw inferences different from mine and those drawn by the courts below. The Court for illustration draws inferences that the officer's testimony at the hearing continued upon the "plain

317

premise that he had been looking for narcotics all the time." *Ante*, at 47, n. 4. But this Court is hardly, at this distance from the place and atmosphere of the trial, in a position to overturn the trial and appellate courts on its own independent finding of an unspoken "premise" of the officer's inner thoughts.

In acting upon its own findings and rejecting those of the lower state courts, this Court, sitting in the marble halls of the Supreme Court Building in Washington, D. C., should be most cautious. Due to our holding in *Mapp* v. *Ohio*, 367 U.S. 643, we are due to get for review literally thousands of cases raising questions like those before us here. If we are setting ourselves meticulously to review all such findings our task will be endless and many will rue the day when *Mapp* was decided. It is not only wise but imperative that where findings of the facts of reasonableness and probable cause are involved in such state cases, we should not overturn state court findings unless in the most extravagant and egregious errors. It seems fantastic to me even to suggest that this is such a case. I would leave these state court holdings alone.

Second, I think also that there was sufficient evidence here on which to base findings that after recovery of the heroin, in particular, an officer could reasonably believe there was probable cause to charge Sibron with violating New York's narcotics laws. As I have previously argued, there was, I think, ample evidence to give the officer probable cause to believe Sibron had a dangerous weapon and that he might use it. Under such circumstances the officer had a right to search him in the very limited fashion he did here. Since, therefore, this was a reasonable and justified search, the use of the heroin discovered by it was admissible in evidence.

I would affirm.

*Spinelli v. United States**

In this "search warrant case" the United States Supreme Court sets up strict guidelines which are to be followed in the obtaining of a search warrant based on an informant's tip. Failure to comply will result in an illegal search. Those who attack the Warren Court on the basis of its decisions pertaining to law enforcement, have an additional irritant in this case.

Suspected by the Federal Bureau of Investigation (F.B.I.) of participating in gaming activities, Spinelli's movements were followed for several days. His observed actions coupled with a "tip"

* 393 U.S. 410, 89 S.Ct. 584 (January 27, 1969)

from a "reliable informant" formed the basis of an F.B.I. affidavit seeking a search warrant. The magistrate, to whom it was presented, issued the warrant which authorized the F.B.I. to search an apartment which Spinelli had frequented while being observed. Evidence obtained while making such a search led to Spinelli's conviction of interstate travel in aid of racketeering.

In a six to three decision the Supreme Court overturned his conviction holding that probable cause to issue the warrant did not exist. The F.B.I. affidavit lacked sufficient detail to permit the magistrate to find probable cause. Specifically it lacked a) information relative to the underlying circumstances from which the informant concluded that defendant was engaged in gaming activities; and b) information relative to the F.B.I.'s conclusion that the informer was reliable. The Supreme Court ruled that if one of the elements used in an effort to establish probable cause for the issuance of a search warrant is an informer's tip, the affidavit must contain information on the above two points. It is in the enunciation of this rule that the significance of this case lies.

Justices Black, Fortas, and Stewart each wrote separate dissents. Mr. Justice Black was most vociferous in his dissent. He declared that this holding goes a long way toward requiring a full evidentiary hearing as a prerequisite to obtaining a search warrant. Speaking with tongue in cheek, he stated that the majority's reasoning almost requires the magistrate to be satisfied of guilt beyond a reasonable doubt before issuance of a warrant.

Although the Court hasn't gone nearly that far the strict guidelines delineated in this opinion, with which a search warrant affidavit must comply in a case involving communications from an informer, have made the law enforcement task a more difficult one. But this is not necessarily bad. Security of one's privacy against arbitrary intrusion by the police—which is at the very core of the Fourth Amendment—is basic to a free society. Whether the guidelines set forth in this opinion are necessary to insure that privacy is up to the reader to decide. Certainly the Court felt they were.

Text of Case

Petitioner was convicted of illegal interstate gambling activities despite his claim that the Commissioner's warrant authorizing the FBI search that uncovered evidence used at his trial violated the Fourth Amendment. He argued that the FBI agent's supporting affidavit did not afford probable cause for issuance of the warrant. The affidavit alleged that: the FBI had followed petitioner on five days, on four of which he had been seen crossing one of two

319

bridges leading from Illinois to St. Louis, Missouri, and had been seen parking his car at a St. Louis apartment house parking lot; he was seen one day to enter a particular apartment; the apartment contained two telephones with specified numbers; petitioner was known to affiant as a gambler and associate of gamblers; and the FBI had "been informed by a confidential reliable informant" that petitioner was "operating a handbook and accepting wagers and disseminating wagering information by means of the telephones" which had been assigned the specified numbers. Viewing the information in the affidavit in its totality the Court of Appeals deemed the principles of *Aguilar* v. *Texas*, 378 U.S. 108, satisfied and upheld the conviction.

Irl B. Baris argued the cause and filed a brief for petitioner.

Joseph J. Connolly argued the cause for the United States, *pro hac vice*. With him on the brief were *Soliciter General Griswold, Assistant Attorney General Vinson, Beatrice Rosenberg,* and *Sidney M. Glazer.*

Mr. Justice HARLAN delivered the opinion of the Court.

William Spinelli was convicted under 18 U.S.C. § 1952[1] of traveling to St. Louis, Missouri, from a nearby Illinois suburb with the intention of conducting gambling activities proscribed by Missouri law. See Mo.Rev.Stat. § 563.360 (1959), V.A.M.S. At every appropriate stage in the proceedings in the lower courts, the petitioner challenged the constitutionality of the warrant which authorized the FBI search that uncovered the evidence necessary for his conviction. At each stage, Spinelli's challenge was treated in a different way. At a pretrial suppression hearing, the United States District Court for the Eastern District of Missouri held that Spinelli lacked standing to raise a Fourth Amendment objection. A unanimous panel of the Court of Appeals for the Eighth Circuit rejected the District Court's ground, a majority holding further that the warrant was issued without probable cause. After an *en banc*

---

[1] The relevant portion of the statute reads:

"(a) Whoever travels in interstate or foreign commerce or uses any facility in interstate * * * commerce * * * with intent to—

* * * * *

"(3) otherwise promote, manage, establish, carry on * * * any unlawful activity, and thereafter performs or attempts to perform any of the acts specified in subparagraphs (1), (2), and (3), shall be fined not more than $10,000 or imprisoned for not more than five years, or both.

"(b) As used in the section 'unlawful activity' means (1) any business enterprise involving gambling * * * in violation of the laws of the State in which they are committed or of the United States * * *."

rehearing, the Court of Appeals sustained the warrant and affirmed the conviction by a vote of six to two. 382 F.2d 871. Both the majority and dissenting *en banc* opinions reflect a most conscientious effort to apply the principles we announced in Aguilar v. Texas, 378 U.S. 108, 84 S.Ct. 1509, 12 L.Ed.2d 723 (1964), to a factual situation whose basic characteristics have not been at all uncommon in recent search warrant cases. Believing it desirable that the principles of *Aguilar* should be further explicated, we granted certiorari, 390 U.S. 942, 88 S.Ct. 1025, 19 L.Ed.2d 1130, our writ being later limited to the question of the constitutional validity of the search and seizure.[2] 391 U.S. 933, 88 S.Ct. 1834, 20 L.Ed.2d 853. For reasons that follow we reverse.

In *Aguilar*, a search warrant had issued upon an affidavit of police officers who swore only that they had "received reliable information from a credible person and do believe" that narcotics were being illegally stored on the described premises. While recognizing that the constitutional requirement of probable cause can be satisfied by hearsay information, this Court held the affidavit inadequate for two reasons. First, the application failed to set forth any of the "underlying circumstances" necessary to enable the magistrate independently to judge of the validity of the informant's conclusion that the narcotics were where he said they were. Second, the affiant-officers did not attempt to support their claim that their informant was " 'credible' or his information 'reliable.' " The Government is, however, quite right in saying that the FBI affidavit in the present case is more ample than that in *Aguilar*. Not only does it contain a report from an anonymous informant, but it also contains a report of an independent FBI investigation which is said to corroborate the informant's tip. We are, then, required to delineate the manner in which *Aguilar*'s two-pronged test should be applied in these circumstances.

---

[2] We agree with the Court of Appeals that Spinelli has standing to raise his Fourth Amendment claim. The issue arises because at the time the FBI searched the apartment in which Spinelli was alleged to be conducting his bookmaking operation, the petitioner was not on the premises. Instead, the agents did not execute their search warrant until Spinelli was seen to leave the apartment, lock the door, and enter the hallway. At that point, petitioner was arrested, the key to the apartment was demanded of him, and the search commenced. Since petitioner would plainly have standing if he had been arrested inside the apartment, Jones v. United States, 362 U.S. 257, 267, 80 S.Ct. 725, 734, 4 L.Ed.2d 697 (1960), it cannot matter that the agents preferred to delay the arrest until petitioner stepped into the hallway— especially when the FBI only managed to gain entry into the apartment by requiring petitioner to surrender his key.

In essence, the affidavit, reproduced in full in the Appendix to this opinion, contained the following allegations:[3]

1. The FBI had kept track of Spinelli's movements on five days during the month of August 1965. On four of these occasions, Spinelli was seen crossing one of two bridges leading from Illinois into St. Louis, Missouri, between 11 a. m. and 12:15 p. m. On four of the five days, Spinelli was also seen parking his car in a lot used by residents of an apartment house at 1108 Indian Circle Drive in St. Louis, between 3:30 p. m. and 4:45 p. m.[4] On one day, Spinelli was followed further and seen to enter a particular apartment in the building.

2. An FBI check with the telephone company revealed that this apartment contained two telephones listed under the name of Grace P. Hagen, and carrying the numbers WYdown 4-0029 and WYdown 4-0136.

3. The application stated that "William Spinelli is known to this affiant and to federal law enforcement agents and local law enforcement agents as a bookmaker, an associate of bookmakers, a gambler, and an associate of gamblers."

4. Finally, it was stated that the FBI "has been informed by a confidential reliable informant the William Spinelli is operating a handbook and accepting wagers and disseminating wagering information by means of the telephones which have been assigned the numbers WYdown 4-0029 and WYdown 4-0136."

There can be no question that the last item mentioned, detailing the informant's tip, has a fundamental place in this warrant application. Without it, probable cause could not be established. The first two items reflect only innocent-seeming activity and data. Spinelli's travels to and from the apartment building and his entry into a particular apartment on one occasion could hardly be taken as bespeaking gambling activity; and there is surely nothing unusual about an apartment containing two separate telephones. Many a householder indulges himself in this petty luxury. Finally, the alle-

---

[3] It is, of course, of no consequence that the agents might have had additional information which could have been given to the Commissioner. "It is elementary that in passing on the validity of a warrant, the reviewing court may consider *only* information brought to the magistrate's attention." Aguilar v. Texas, 378 U.S. 108, 109, n. 1, 84 S.Ct. 1509, 1511 (emphasis in original). Since the Government does not argue that whatever additional information the agents may have possessed was sufficient to provide probable cause for the arrest, thereby justifying the resultant search as well, we need not consider that question.

[4] No report was made as to Spinelli's movements during the period between his arrival in St. Louis at noon and his arrival at the parking lot in the late afternoon. In fact, the evidence at trial indicated that Spinelli frequented the offices of his stockbroker during this period.

gation that Spinelli was "known" to the affiant and to other federal and local law enforcement officers as a gambler and an associate of gamblers is but a bald and unilluminating assertion of suspicion that is entitled to no weight in appraising the magistrate's decision. Nathanson v. United States, 290 U.S. 41, 46, 54 S.Ct. 11, 12, 78 L.Ed. 159 (1933).

So much indeed the Government does not deny. Rather, following the reasoning of the Court of Appeals, the Government claims that the informant's tip gives a suspicious color to the FBI's reports detailing Spinelli's innocent-seeming conduct and that, conversely, the FBI's surveillance corroborates the informant's tip, thereby entitling it to more weight. It is true, of course, that the magistrate is obligated to render a judgment based upon a common-sense reading of the entire affidavit. United States v. Ventresca, 380 U.S. 102, 108, 85 S.Ct. 741, 745, 13 L.Ed.2d 684 (1965). We believe, however, that the "totality of circumstances" approach taken by the Court of Appeals paints with too broad a brush. Where, as here, the informer's tip is a necessary element in a finding of probable cause, its proper weight must be determined by a more precise anlysis.

The informer's report must first be measured against *Aguilar*'s standards so that its probative value can be assessed. If the tip is found inadequate under *Aguilar*, the other allegations which corroborate the information contained in the hearsay report should then be considered. At this stage as well, however, the standards enunciated in *Aguilar* must inform the magistrate's decision. He must ask: Can it fairly be said that the tip, even when certain parts of it have been corroborated by independent sources, is as trustworthy as a tip which would pass *Aguilar*'s tests without independent corroboration? *Aguilar* is relevant at this stage of the inquiry as well because the tests it establishes were designed to implement the long-standing principle that probable cause must be determined by a "neutral and detached magistrate," and not by "the officer engaged in the often competitive enterprise of ferreting out crime." Johnson v. United States, 333 U.S. 10, 14, 68 S.Ct. 367, 369, 92 L.Ed. 436 (1948). A magistrate cannot be said to have properly discharged his constitutional duty if he relies on an informer's tip which—even when partially corroborated—is not as reliable as one which passes *Aguilar*'s requirements when standing alone.

Applying these principles to the present case, we first consider the weight to be given the informer's tip when it is considered apart from the rest of the affidavit. It is clear that a Commissioner could not credit it without abdicating his constitutional function. Though the affiant swore that his confidant was "reliable," he offered the magistrate no reason in support of this conclusion. Perhaps even more important is the fact that *Aguilar*'s other test has not been satisfied. The tip does not contain a sufficient statement of the underlying circumstances from which the informer concluded that Spinelli was running a bookmaking operation. We are not told how the FBI's source received his information—it is not alleged that the informant personally observed Spinelli at work or that he had ever placed a bet with him. Moreover, if the informant came by the information indirectly, he did not explain why his sources were reliable. Compare Jaben v. United States, 381 U.S. 214, 85 S.Ct. 1365, 14 L.Ed.2d 345 (1965). In the absence of a statement detailing the manner in which the information was gathered, it is especially important that the tip describe the accused's criminal activity in sufficient detail so that the magistrate may know that he is relying on something more substantial than a casual rumor circulating in the underworld or an accusation based merely on an individual's general reputation.

The detail provided by the informant in Draper v. United States, 358 U.S. 307, 79 S.Ct. 329, 3 L.Ed.2d 327 (1959), provides a suitable benchmark. While Hereford, the Government's informer in that case, did not state the way in which he had obtained his information, he reported that Draper had gone to Chicago the day before by train and that he would return to Denver by train with three ounces of heroin on one of two specified mornings. Moreover, Hereford went on to describe, with minute particularity, the clothes that Draper would be wearing upon his arrival at the Denver station. A magistrate, when confronted with such detail, could reasonably infer that the informant had gained his information in a reliable way.[5] Such an inference cannot be made in the present case. Here, the only facts supplied were that Spinelli was using two specified telephones and that these phones were being used in gambling operations. This meager report could easily have been obtained from an offhand remark heard at a neighborhood bar.

Nor do we believe that the patent doubts *Aguilar* raises as to the report's reliability are adquately resolved by a consideration of the allegations detailing the FBI's independent investigative efforts. At most, these allegations indicated that Spinelli could have used the telephones specified by the informant for some purpose. This cannot by itself be said to support both the inference that the informer was generally trustworthy and that he had made his

---

[5]While *Draper* involved the question whether the police had probable cause for an arrest without a warrant, the analysis required for an answer to this question is basically similar to that demanded of a magistrate when he considers whether a search warrant should issue.

charge against Spinelli on the basis of information obtained in a reliable way. Once again, *Draper* provides a relevant comparison. Independent police work in that case corroborated much more than one small detail that had been provided by the informant. There, the police, upon greeting the inbound Denver train on the second morning specified by informer Hereford, saw a man whose dress corresponded precisely to Hereford's detailed description. It was then apparent that the informant had not been fabricating his report out of whole cloth; since the report was of the sort which in common experience may be recognized as having been obtained in a reliable way, it was perfectly clear that probable cause had been established.

We conclude, then, that in the present case the informant's tip — even when corroborated to the extent indicated—was not sufficient to provide the basis for a finding of probable cause. This is not to say that the tip was so insubstantial that it could not properly have counted in the magistrate's determination. Rather, it needed some further support. When we look to the other parts of the application, however, we find nothing alleged which would permit the suspicions engendered by the informant's report to ripen into a judgment that a crime was probably being committed. As we have already seen, the allegations detailing the FBI's surveillance of Spinelli and its investigation of the telephone company records contain no suggestion of criminal conduct when taken by themselves—and they are not endowed with an aura of suspicion by virtue of the informer's tip. Nor do we find that the FBI's reports take on a sinister color when read in light of common knowledge that bookmaking is often carried on over the telephone and from premises ostensibly used by others for perfectly normal purposes. Such an argument would carry weight in a situation in which the premises contain an unusual number of telephones or abnormal activity is observed, cf. McCray v. Illinois, 386 U.S. 300, 302, 87 S.Ct. 1056, 1057, 18 L.Ed.2d 62 (1967), but it does not fit this case where neither of these factors is present.[6] All that remains to be considered is the flat statement that Spinelli was "known" to the FBI and others as a gambler. But just as a simple assertion of police suspicion is not itself a sufficient basis for a magistrate's finding of probable cause, we do not believe it may be used to give additional weight to allegations that would otherwise be insufficient.

The affidavit, then, falls short of the standards set forth in *Aguilar, Draper,* and our other decisions that give content to the notion

---

[6]A box containing three uninstalled telephones was found in the apartment, but only after execution of the search warrant.

of probable cause.[7] In holding as we have done, we do not retreat from the established propositions that only the probability, and not a prima facie showing, of criminal activity is the standard of probable cause, Beck v. Ohio, 379 U.S. 89, 96, 85 S.Ct. 223, 228, 13 L.Ed.2d 142 (1964); that affidavits of probable cause are tested by much less rigorous standards than those governing the admissibility of evidence at trial, McCray v. Illinois, 386 U.S. 300, 311, 87 S.Ct. 1056, 1062 (1967); that in judging probable cause issuing magistrates are not to be confined by niggardly limitations or by restrictions on the use of their common sense, United States v. Ventresca, 380 U.S. 102, 108, 85 S.Ct. 741, 745 (1965); and that their determination of probable cause should be paid great deference by reviewing courts, Jones v. United States, 362 U.S. 257, 270–271, 80 S.Ct. 725, 735–736 (1960). But we cannot sustain this warrant without diluting important safeguards that assure that the judgment of a disinterested judicial officer will interpose itself between the police and the citizenry.[8]

The judgment of the Court of Appeals is reversed and the case is remanded to that court for further proceedings consistent with this opinion.

It is so ordered.

Mr. Justice MARSHALL took no part in the consideration or decision of this case.

APPENDIX TO OPINION OF THE COURT.
AFFIDIVIT IN SUPPORT OF SEARCH WARRANT.

I, Robert L. Bender, being duly sworn, depose and say that I am a Special Agent of the Federal Bureau of Investigation, and as such am authorized to make searches and seizures.

---

[7] In those cases in which this Court has found probable cause established, the showing made was much more substantial than the one made here. Thus, in United States v. Ventresca, 380 U.S. 102, 104, 85 S.Ct. 741, 743 (1965), FBI agents observed repeated deliveries of loads of sugar in 60-pound bags, smelled the odor of fermenting mash, and heard " 'sounds similar to that of a motor or a pump coming from the direction of' Ventresca's house." Again, in McCray v. Illinois, 386 U.S. 300, 303–304, 87 S.Ct. 1056, 1058 (1967), the informant reported that McCray " 'was selling narcotics and had narcotics on his person now in the vicinity of 47th and Calumet.' " When the police arrived at the intersection, they observed McCray engaging in various suspicious activities. 386 U.S., at 302, 87 S.Ct., at 1058.

[8] In the view we have taken of this case, it becomes unnecessary to decide whether the search warrant was properly executed, or whether it sufficiently described the things that were seized.

That on August 6, 1965, at approximately 11:44 a. m., William Spinelli was observed by an Agent of the Federal Bureau of Investigation driving a 1964 Ford convertible, Missouri license HC3-649, onto the Eastern approach of the Veterans Bridge leading from East St. Louis, Illinois, to St. Louis, Missouri.

That on August 11, 1965, at approximately 11:16 a. m., William Spinelli was observed by an Agent of the Federal Bureau of Investigation driving a 1964 Ford convertible, Missouri license HC3-649, onto the Eastern approach of the Eads Bridge leading from East St. Louis, Illinois, to St. Louis, Missouri.

Further, at approximately 11:18 a. m. on August 11, 1965, I observed William Spinelli driving the aforesaid Ford convertible from the Western approach of the Eads Bridge into St. Louis, Missouri.

Further, at approximately 4:40 p. m. on August 11, 1965, I observed the aforesaid Ford convertible, bearing Missouri license HC3-649, parked in a parking lot used by residents of The Chieftain Manor Apartments, approximately one block east of 1108 Indian Circle Drive.

On August 12, 1965, at approximately 12:07 p. m., William Spinelli was observed by an Agent of the Federal Bureau of Investigation driving the aforesaid 1964 Ford convertible onto the Eastern approach of the Veterans Bridge from East St. Louis, Illinois, in the direction of St. Louis, Missouri.

Further, on August 12, 1965, at approximately 3:46 p. m., I observed William Spinelli driving the aforesaid 1964 Ford convertible onto the parking lot used by the residents of The Chieftain Manor Apartments approximately one block east of 1108 Indian Circle Drive.

Further, on August 12, 1965, at approximately 3:49 p. m., William Spinelli was observed by an Agent of the Federal Bureau of Investigation entering the front entrance of the two-story apartment building located at 1108 Indian Circle Drive, this building being one of the Chieftain Manor Apartments.

On August 13, 1965, at approximately 11:08 a. m., William Spinelli was observed by an Agent of the Federal Bureau of Investigation driving the aforesaid Ford convertible onto the Eastern approach of the Eads Bridge from East St. Louis, Illinois, heading towards St. Louis, Missouri.

Further, on August 13, 1965, at approximately 11:11 a. m., I observed William Spinelli driving the aforesaid Ford convertible from the Western approach of the Eads Bridge into St. Louis, Missouri.

Further, on August 13, 1965, at approximately 3:45 p. m., I observed William Spinelli driving the aforesaid 1964 Ford convertible onto the parking area used by residents of The Chieftain Manor Apartments, said parking area being approximately one block from 1108 Indian Circle Drive.

Further, on August 13, 1965, at approximately 3:55 p. m., William Spinelli was observed by an Agent of the Federal Bureau of Investigation entering the corner apartment located on the second floor in the southwest corner, known as Apartment F, of the two-story apartment building known and numbered as 1108 Indian Circle Drive.

On August 16, 1965, at approximately 3:22 p. m., I observed William Spinelli driving the aforesaid Ford convertible onto the parking lot used by the residents of The Chieftain Manor Apartments approximately one block east of 1108 Indian Circle Drive.

Further, an Agent of the F. B. I. observed William Spinelli alight from the aforesaid Ford convertible and walk toward the apartment building located at 1108 Indian Circle Drive.

The records of the Southwestern Bell Telephone Company reflect that there are two telephones located in the southwest corner apartment on the second floor of the apartment building located at 1108 Indian Circle Drive under the name of Grace P. Hagen. The numbers listed in the Southwestern Bell Telephone Company records for the aforesaid telephones are WYdown 4-0029 and WYdown 4-0136.

William Spinelli is known to this affiant and to federal law enforcement agents and local law enforcement agents as a bookmaker, an associate of bookmakers, a gambler, and an associate of gamblers.

The Federal Bureau of Investigation has been informed by a confidential reliable informant that William Spinelli is operating a handbook and accepting wagers and disseminating wagering information by means of the telephones which have been assigned the numbers WYdown 4-0029 and WYdown 4-0136.

/s/ Robert L. Bender,
Robert L. Bender,
Special Agent Federal Bureau
of Investigation.

Subscribed and sworn to before me this 18th day of August, 1965, at St. Louis, Missouri.

/s/ William R. O'Toole.

328

Mr. Justice WHITE, concurring.

An investigator's affidavit that he has seen gambling equipment being moved into a house at a specified address will support the issuance of a search warrant. The oath affirms the honesty of the statement and negatives the lie or imagination. Personal observation attests to the facts asserted—that there is gambling equipment on the premises at the named address.

But if the officer simply avers, without more, that there is gambling paraphernalia on certain premises, the warrant should not issue, even though the belief of the officer is an honest one, as evidenced by his oath, and even though the magistrate knows him to be an experienced, intelligent officer who has been reliable in the past. This much was settled in Nathanson v. United States, 290 U.S. 41, 54 S.Ct. 11, 78 L.Ed. 159 (1933), where the Court held insufficient an officer's affidavit swearing he had cause to believe that there was illegal liquor on the premises for which the warrant was sought. The unsupported assertion or belief of the officer does not satisfy the requirement of probable cause. Jones v. United States, 362 U.S. 257, 269, 80 S.Ct. 725, 735, 4 L.Ed.2d 697 (1960); Grau v. United States, 287 U.S. 124, 53 S.Ct. 38, 77 L.Ed. 212 (1932); Byars v. United States, 273 U.S. 28, 29, 47 S.Ct. 248, 71 L.Ed. 520 (1927).

What is missing in *Nathanson* and like cases is a statement of the basis for the affiant's believing the facts contained in the affidavit—the good "cause" which the officer in *Nathanson* said he had. If an officer swears that there is gambling equipment at a certain address, the possibilities are (1) that he has seen the equipment; (2) that he has observed or perceived facts from which the presence of the equipment may reasonably be inferred; and (3) that he has obtained the information from someone else. If (1) is true, the affidavit is good. But in (2), the affidavit is insufficient unless the perceived facts are given, for it is the magistrate, not the officer, who is to judge the existence of probable cause. Aguilar v. Texas, 378 U.S. 108, 84 S.Ct. 1509, 12 L.Ed.2d 723 (1964); Giordenello v. United States, 357 U.S. 480, 486, 78 S.Ct. 1245, 1250, 2 L.Ed.2d 1503 (1958); Johnson v. United States, 333 U.S. 10, 14, 68 S.Ct. 367, 369, 92 L.Ed. 436 (1948). With respect to (3), where the officer's information is hearsay, no warrant should issue absent good cause for crediting that hearsay. Because an affidavit asserting, without more, the location of gambling equipment at a particular address does not claim personal observation of any of the facts by the officer, and because of the likelihood that the information came from an unidentified third party, affidavits of this type are unacceptable.

329

Neither should the warrant issue if the officer states that there is gambling equipment in a particular apartment and that his information comes from an informant, named or unnamed, since the honesty of the informant and the basis for his report are unknown. Nor would the missing elements be completely supplied by the officer's oath that the informant has often furnished reliable information in the past. This attests to the honesty of the informant, but Aguilar v. Texas, supra, requires something more—did the information come from observation, or did the informant in turn receive it from another? Absent additional facts for believing the informant's report, his assertion stands no better than the oath of the officer to the same effect. Indeed, if the affidavit of an officer, known by the magistrate to be honest and experienced, stating that gambling equipment is located in a certain building is unacceptable, it would be quixotic if a similar statement from an honest informant were found to furnish probable cause. A strong argument can be made that both should be acceptable under the Fourth Amendment, but under our cases neither is. The past reliability of the informant can no more furnish probable cause for believing his current report than can previous experience with the officer himself.

If the affidavit rests on hearsay—an informant's report—what is necessary under *Aguilar* is one of two things: the informant must declare either (1) that he has himself seen or perceived the fact or facts asserted; or (2) that his information is hearsay, but there is good reason for believing it—perhaps one of the usual grounds for crediting hearsay information. The first presents few problems: since the report, although hearsay, purports to be first-hand observation, remaining doubt centers on the honesty of the informant, and that worry is dissipated by the officer's previous experience with the informant. The other basis for accepting the informant's report is more complicated. But if, for example, the informer's hearsay comes from one of the actors in the crime in the nature of admission against interest, the affidavit giving this information should be held sufficient.

I am inclined to agree with the majority that there are limited special circumstances in which an "honest" informant's report, if sufficiently detailed, will in effect verify itself—that is, the magistrate when confronted with such detail could reasonably infer that the informant had gained his information in a reliable way. See ante, at 417. Detailed information may sometimes imply that the informant himself has observed the facts. Suppose an informant with whom an officer has had satisfactory experience states that there is gambling equipment in the living room of a specified apart-

ment and describes in detail not only the equipment itself but the
appointments and furnishings in the apartment. Detail like this,
if true at all, must rest on personal observation either of the informant or of someone else. If the latter, we know nothing of the
third person's honesty or sources; he may be fabricating a wholly
false report. But it is arguable that on these facts it was the informant himself who has perceived the facts, for the information
reported is not usually the subject of casual, day-to-day conversation. Because the informant is honest and it is probable that he
has viewed the facts, there is probable cause for the issuance of
a warrant.

So too in the special circumstances of Draper v. United States,
358 U.S. 307, 79 S.Ct. 329, 3 L.Ed.2d 327 (1959), the kind of information related by the informant is not generally sent ahead of
a person's arrival in a city except to those who are intimately connected with making careful arrangements for meeting him. The informant, posited as honest, somehow had the reported facts, very
likely from one of the actors in the plan, or as one of them himself.
The majority's suggestion is that a warrant could have been obtained based only on the informer's report. I am inclined to agree,
although it seems quite plain that if it may be so easily inferred
from the affidavit that the informant has himself observed the facts
or has them from an actor in the event, no possible harm could come
from requiring a statement to that effect, thereby removing the
difficult and recurring questions which arise in such situations.

Of course, *Draper* itself did not proceed on this basis. Instead, the
Court pointed out that when the officer saw a person getting off
the train at the specified time, dressed and conducting himself precisely as the informant had predicted, all but the critical fact with
respect to possessing narcotics had then been verified and for that
reason the officer had "reasonable grounds" to believe also that
Draper was carrying narcotics. Unquestionably, verification of arrival time, dress and gait reenforced the honesty of the informant
—he had not reported a made-up story. But if what *Draper* stands
for is that the existence of the tenth and critical fact is made sufficiently probable to justify the issuance of a warrant by verifying
nine other facts coming from the same source, I have my doubts
about that case.

In the first place, the proposition is not that the tenth fact may
be logically inferred from the other nine or that the tenth fact is
usually found in conjunction with the other nine. No one would
suggest that just anyone getting off the 10:30 train dressed as
Draper was, with a brisk walk and carrying a zipper bag, should
be arrested for carrying narcotics. The thrust of *Draper* is not that

the verified facts have independent significance with respect to proof of the tenth. The argument instead relates to the reliability of the source: because an informant is right about some things, he is more probably right about other facts, usually the critical, unverified facts.

But the Court's cases have already rejected for Fourth Amendment purposes the notion that the past reliability of an officer is sufficient reason for believing his current assertions. Nor would it suffice, I suppose, if a reliable informant states there is gambling equipment in Apartment 607 and then proceeds to describe in detail Apartment 201, a description which is verified before applying for the warrant. He was right about 201, but that hardly makes him more believable about the equipment in 607. But what if he states that there are narcotics locked in a safe in Apartment 300, which is described in detail, and the apartment manager verifies everything but the contents of the safe? I doubt that the report about the narcotics is made appreciably more believable by the verification. The informant could still have gotten his information concerning the safe from others about whom nothing is known or could have inferred the presence of narcotics from circumstances which a magistrate would find unacceptable.

The tension between *Draper* and the *Nathanson-Aguilar* line of cases is evident from the course followed by the majority opinion. First, it is held that the report from a reliable informant that Spinelli is using two telephones with specified numbers to conduct a gambling business plus Spinelli's reputation in police circles as a gambler does not add up to probable cause. This is wholly consistent with *Aguilar* and *Nathanson*: the informant did not reveal whether he had personally observed the facts or heard them from another and, if the latter, no basis for crediting the hearsay was presented. Nor were the facts, as Mr. Justice HARLAN says, of such a nature that they normally would be obtainable only by the personal observation of the informant himself. The police, however, did not stop with the informant's report. Independently, they established the existence of two phones having the given numbers and located them in an apartment house which Spinelli was regularly frequenting away from his home. There remained little question but that Spinelli was using the phones, and it was a fair inference that the use was not for domestic but for business purposes. The informant had claimed the business involved gambling. Since his specific information about Spinelli using two phones with particular numbers had been verified, did not his allegation about gambling thereby become sufficiently more believable if the *Draper* principle is to be given any scope at all? I would think so, particularly since

332

the information from the informant which was verified was not neutral, irrelevant information but was material to proving the gambling allegation: two phones with different numbers in an apartment used away from home indicates a business use in an operation, like bookmaking, where multiple phones are needed. The *Draper* approach would reasonably justify the issuance of a warrant in this case, particularly since the police had some awareness of Spinelli's past activities. The majority, however, while seemingly embracing *Draper*, confines that case to its own facts. Pending full-scale reconsideration of that case, on the one hand, or of the *Nathanson-Aguilar* cases on the other, I join the opinion of the Court and the judgment of reversal, especially since a vote to affirm would produce an equally divided Court.

Mr. Justice BLACK, dissenting.

In my view, this Court's decision in Aguilar v. Texas, 378 U.S. 108, 84 S.Ct. 1509, 12 L.Ed.2d 723 (1964), was bad enough. That decision went very far toward elevating the magistrate's hearing for issuance of a search warrant to a full-fledged trial, where witnesses must be brought forward to attest personally to all the facts alleged. But not content with this, the Court today expands *Aguilar* to almost unbelievable proportions. Of course, it would strengthen the probable cause presentation if eyewitnesses could testify that they saw the defendant commit the crime. It would be stronger still if these witnesses could explain in detail the nature of the sensual perceptions on which they based their "conclusion" that the person they had seen was the defendant and that he was responsible for the events they observed. Nothing in our Constitution, however, requires that the facts be established with that degree of certainty and with such elaborate specificity before a policeman can be authorized by a disinterested magistrate to conduct a carefully limited search.

The Fourth Amendment provides that "no Warrants shall issue, but upon probable cause, supported by Oath or affirmation, and particularly describing the place to be searched, and the persons or things to be seized." In this case a search warrant was issued supported by an oath and particularly describing the place to be searched and the things to be seized. The supporting oath was three printed pages and the full text of it is included in an Appendix to the Court's opinion. The magistrate, I think properly, held the information set forth sufficient facts to show "probable cause" that the defendant was violating the law. Six members of the Court of Appeals also agreed that the affidavit was sufficient to show probable cause. A majority of this Court today holds, however, that the magistrate and all of these judges were wrong. In doing so, they substitute their own opinion for that of the local magistrate and the circuit judges, and reject the *en banc* factual conclusion of the Eighth Circuit and reverse the judgment based upon that factual conclusion. I cannot join in any such disposition of an issue so vital to the administration of justice, and dissent as vigorously as I can.

I repeat my belief that the affidavit given the magistrate was more than ample to show probable cause of the petitioner's guilt. The affidavit meticulously set out facts sufficient to show the following:

1. The petitioner had been shown going to and coming from a room in an apartment which contained two telephones listed under the name of another person. Nothing in the record indicates that the apartment was of that large and luxurious type which could only be occupied by a person to whom it would be a "petty luxury" to have two separate telephones, with different numbers, both listed under the name of a person who did not live there.

2. The petitioner's car had been observed parked in the apartment's parking lot. This fact was, of course, highly relevant in showing that the petitioner was extremely interested in some enterprise which was located in the apartment.

3. The FBI had been informed by a reliable informant that the petitioner was accepting wagering information by telephones—the particular telephones located in the apartment the defendant had been repeatedly visiting. Unless the Court, going beyond the requirements of the Fourth Amendment, wishes to require magistrates to hold trials before issuing warrants, it is not necessary—as the Court holds—to have the affiant explain "the underlying circumstances from which the informer concluded that Spinelli was running a bookmaking operation." Ante, at 416.

4. The petitioner was known by federal and local law enforcement agents as a bookmaker and an associate of gamblers. I cannot agree with the Court that this knowledge was only a "bald and unilluminating assertion of suspicion that is entitled to no weight in appraising the magistrate's decision." Ante, at 414. Although the statement is hearsay that might not be admissible in a regular trial, everyone knows, unless he shuts his eyes to the realities of life, that this is a relevant fact which, together with other circumstances, might indicate a factual probability that gambling is taking place.

The foregoing facts should be enough to constitute probable cause for anyone who does not believe that the only way to obtain a search warrant is to prove beyond a reasonable doubt that a defendant is guilty. Even *Aguilar*, on which the Court relies, cannot support the contrary result, at least as that decision was written before today's massive escalation of it. In *Aguilar* the Court dealt with an affidavit that stated only:

"Affiants have received reliable information from a credible person and do believe that heroin * * * and other narcotics and narcotic paraphernalia are being kept at the above described premises for the purpose of sale and use contrary to the provisions of the law." 378 U.S., at 109, 84 S.Ct., at 1511.

The Court held, over the dissent of Mr. Justice Clark, Mr. Justice Stewart, and myself, that this unsupported conclusion of an unidentified informant provided no basis for the magistrate to make an independent judgment as to the persuasiveness of the facts re lied upon to show probable cause. Here, of course, we have much more, and the Court in *Aguilar* was careful to point out that additional information of the kind presented in the affidavit before us now would be highly relevant:

"If the fact and results of such a surveillance had been appropriately presented to the magistrate, this would, of course, present an entirely different case." 378 U.S. 109, n. 1, 84 S.Ct. 1511.

In the present case even the two-judge minority of the court below recognized, as this Court seems to recognize today, that this additional information took the case beyond the rule of *Aguilar*. Six of the other circuit judges disagreed with the two dissenting judges, finding that all the circumstances considered together could support a reasonable judgment that gambling probably was taking place. I fully agree with this carefully considered opinion of the court below. 382 F.2d 871.

I regret to say I consider today's decision an indefensible departure from the principles of our former cases. Less than four years ago we reaffirmed these principles in United States v. Ventresca, 380 U.S. 102, 108, 85 S.Ct. 741, 746, 13 L.Ed.2d 684 (1965):

"If the teachings of the Court's cases are to be followed and the constitutional policy served, affidavits for search warrants * * * must be tested and interpreted by magistrates and courts in a common-sense and realistic fashion. * * * Technical requirements of elaborate specificity once exacted under common law pleadings have no proper place in this area."

See also Husty v. United States, 282 U.S. 694, 700–701, 51 S.Ct. 240, 241–242, 74 L.Ed. 629 (1931).

Departures of this kind are responsible for considerable uneasiness in our lower courts, and I must say I am deeply troubled by the statements of Judge Gibson in the court below:

"I am, indeed, disturbed by decision after decision of our courts which place increasingly technical burdens upon law enforcement officials. I am disturbed by these decisions that appear to relent-

335

lessly chip away at the ever narrowing area of effective police operation. I believe the holdings in *Aguilar*, and Rugendorf v. United States, 376 U.S. 528 [84 S.Ct. 825, 11 L.Ed.2d 887] (1964) are sufficient to protect the privacy of individuals from hastily conceived intrusions, and I do not think the limitations and requirements on the issuance of search warrants should be expanded by setting up over-technical requirements approaching the now discarded pitfalls of common law proceedings. Moreover, if we become increasingly technical and rigid in our demands upon police officers, I fear we make it increasingly easy for criminals to operate, detected but unpunished. I feel the significant movement of the law beyond its present state is unwarranted, unneeded, and dangerous to law enforcement efficiency." (Dissenting from panel opinion.)

The Court of Appeals in this case took a sensible view of the Fourth Amendment, and I would wholeheartedly affirm its decision.

Mapp v. Ohio, 367 U.S. 643, 81 S.Ct. 1684, 6 L.Ed.2d 1081 decided in 1961 held for the first time that the Fourth Amendment and the exclusionary rule of Weeks v. United States, 232 U.S. 383, 34 S.Ct. 341, 58 L.Ed. 652 (1914) are now applicable to the States. That Amendment provides that search warrants shall not be issued without probable cause. The existence of probable cause is a factual matter that calls for the determination of a factual question. While no statistics are immediately available, questions of probable cause to issue search warrants and to make arrests are doubtless involved in many thousands of cases in state courts. All of those probable cause state cases are now potentially reviewable by this Court. It is, of course, physically impossible for this Court to review the evidence in all or even a substantial percentage of those cases. Consequently, whether desirable or not, we must inevitably accept most of the fact findings of the state courts, particularly when, as here in a federal case, both the trial and appellate courts have decided the facts the same way. It cannot be said that the trial judge and six members of the Court of Appeals committed flagrant error in finding from evidence that the magistrate had probable cause to issue the search warrant here. It seems to me that this Court would best serve itself and the administration of justice by accepting the judgment of the two courts below. After all, they too are lawyers and judges, and much closer to the practical, everyday affairs of life than we are.

Notwithstanding the Court's belief to the contrary, I think that in holding as it does, the Court does:

"retreat from the established propositions that only the probability, and not a prima facie showing, of criminal activity is the standard of probable cause, Beck v. Ohio, 379 U.S. 89, 96, 85 S.Ct. 223,

228, 13 L.Ed.2d 142 (1964) ; that affidavits of probable cause are
tested by much less rigorous standards than those governing the
admissibility of evidence at trial, McCray v. Illinois, 386 U.S. 300,
311, 87 S.Ct. 1056, 1062 (1967) ; that in judging probable cause issuing magistrates are not to be confined by niggardly limitations or by restrictions on the use of their common sense, United
States v. Ventresca, 380 U.S. 102, 108, 85 S.Ct. 741, 745 (1965) ;
and that their determination of probable cause should be paid
great deference by reviewing courts, Jones v. United States, 362
U.S. 257, 270–271, 80 S.Ct. 725, 735–736 (1960)." Ante, p. 419.
In fact, I believe the Court is moving rapidly, through complex
analysis and obfuscatory language, toward the holding that no
magistrate can issue a warrant unless according to some unknown
standard of proof he can be persuaded that the suspect defendant
is actually guilty of a crime. I would affirm this conviction.

Mr. Justice FORTAS, dissenting.

My Brother HARLAN's opinion for the Court is animated by a
conviction which I share that "[t]he security of one's privacy
against arbitrary intrusion by the police—which is at the core of
the Fourth Amendment— is basic to a free society." Wolf v. Colorado, 338 U.S. 25, 27, 69 S.Ct. 1359, 1361, 93 L.Ed. 1782 (1949).

We may well insist upon a sympathetic and even an indulgent
view of the latitude which must be accorded to the police for performance of their vital task; but only a foolish or careless people
will deduce from this that the public welfare requires or permits
the police to disregard the restraints on their actions which historic
struggles for freedom have developed for the protection of liberty
and dignity of citizens against arbitrary state power.

As Justice Jackson (dissenting) stated in Brinegar v. United
States, 338 U.S. 160, 180–181 (1949):

"[The provisions of the Fourth Amendment] are not mere
second-class rights but belong in the catalog of indispensible freedoms. Among deprivations of rights, none is so effective in cowing a
population, crushing the spirit of the individual and putting terror
in every heart. Uncontrolled search and seizure is one of the first
and most effective weapons in the arsenal of every arbitrary government. And one need only briefly to have dwelt and worked among
a people possessed of many admirable qualities but deprived of these
rights to know that the human personality deteriorates and dignity
and self-reliance disappear where homes, persons and possessions
are subject at any hour to unheralded search and seizure by the
police."

History[1] teaches us that this protection requires that the judgment of a judicial officer be interposed between the police, hot in pursuit of their appointed target, and the citizen;[2] that the judicial officer must judge and not merely rubber-stamp; and that his judgment must be based upon judicially reliable facts adequate to demonstrate that the search is justified by the probability that it will yield the fruits or instruments of crime—or, as this Court has only recently ruled, tangible evidence of its commission.[3] The exceptions to the requirement of a search warrant have always been narrowly restricted[4] because of this Court's long-standing awareness of the fundamental role of the magistrate's judgment in the preservation of a proper balance between individual freedom and state power. See Trupiano v. United States, 334 U.S. 699, 700, 68 S.Ct. 1229, 1230, 92 L.Ed. 1663 (1948).

Today's decision deals, not with the necessity of obtaining a warrant prior to search, but with the difficult problem of the nature of the showing that must be made before the magistrate to justify his issuance of a search warrant. While I do not subscribe to the criticism of the majority expressed by my Brother BLACK in dissent, I believe—with all respect—that the majority is in error in holding that the affidavit supporting the warrant in this case is constitutionally inadequate.

The affidavit is unusually long and detailed. In fact, it recites so many minute and detailed facts developed in the course of the investigation of Spinelli that its substance is somewhat obscured. It is paradoxical that this very fullness of the affidavit may be the source of the constitutional infirmity that the majority finds. Stated in language more direct and less circumstantial than that used by the FBI agent who executed the affidavit, it sets forth that the FBI has been informed that Spinelli is accepting wagers by means of telephones numbered WY 4–0029 and WY 4–0136; that Spinelli

---

[1] "The knock at the door, whether by day or by night, as a prelude to a search, without authority of law but solely on the authority of the police, did not need the commentary of recent history to be condemned as inconsistent with the conception of human rights enshrined in the history and the basic constitutional documents of English-speaking peoples." Wolf v. Colorado, 338 U.S. 25, 28, 69 S.Ct. 1359, 1361 (1949). See United States v. Rabinowitz, 339 U.S. 56, 69–70, 70 S.Ct. 430, 436–437, 94 L.Ed. 653 (1950) (Frankfurter, J., dissenting). See generally with respect to the history of the Fourth Amendment N. Lasson, The History and Development of the Fourth Amendment to the United States Constitution.

[2] See Johnson v. United States, 333 U.S. 10, 13–14, 68 S.Ct. 367, 368–369, 92 L.Ed. 436 (1948).

[3] Warden, Md. Penitentiary v. Hayden, 387 U.S. 294, 87 S.Ct. 1642, 18 L.Ed.2d 782 (1967).

[4] See Jones v. United States, 357 U.S. 493, 499, 78 S.Ct. 1253, 1257, 2 L.Ed.2d 1514 (1958); Warden, Md. Penitentiary v. Hayden, 387 U.S. 294, 311, 87 S.Ct. 1642, 1652 (1967) (concurring opinion).

is known to the affiant agent and to law enforcement agencies as a bookmaker; that telephones numbered WY 4–0029 and WY 4–0136 are located in a certain apartment; that Spinelli was placed under surveillance and his observed movements were such as to show his use of that apartment and to indicate that he frequented the apartment on a regular basis.

Aguilar v. Texas, 378 U.S. 108, 84 S.Ct. 1509, 12 L.Ed.2d 723 (1964), holds that the reference in an affidavit to information described only as received from "a confidential reliable informant," standing alone, is not an adequate basis for issuance of a search warrant. The majority agrees that the "FBI affidavit in the present case is more ample than that in *Aguilar*," but concludes that it is nevertheless constitutionally inadequate. The majority states that the present affidavit fails to meet the "two-pronged test" of *Aguilar* because (a) it does not set forth the basis for the assertion that the informer is "reliable" and (b) it fails to state the "underlying circumstances" upon which the informant based his conclusion that Spinelli was engaged in bookmaking.

The majority acknowledges, however, that its reference to a "two-pronged test" should not be understood as meaning that an affidavit deficient in these respects is necessarily inadequate to support a search warrant. Other facts and circumstances may be attested which will supply the evidence of probable cause needed to support the search warrant. On this general statement we are agreed. Our difference is that I believe such facts and circumstances are present in this case, and the majority arrives at the opposite conclusion.

Aguilar expressly recognized that if, in that case, the affidavit's conclusory report of the informant's story had been supplemented by "the fact and results of * * * a surveillance * * * this would, of course, present an entirely different case." 378 U.S., at 109, n. 1, 84 S.Ct., at 1511. In the present case, as I view it, the affidavit showed not only relevant surveillance, entitled to some probative weight for purposes of the issuance of a search warrant, but also additional, specific facts of significance and adequate reliability: that Spinelli was using two telephone numbers, identified by an "informant" as being used for bookmaking, in his illegal operations; that these telephones were in an identified apartment; and that Spinelli, a known bookmaker,[5] frequented the apartment. Certainly, this is enough.

---

[5] Although Spinelli's reputation standing alone would not, of course, justify the search, this Court has held that such a reputation may make the informer's report "much less subject to scepticism than would be such a charge against one without such a history." Jones v. United States, 362 U.S. 257, 271, 80 S.Ct. 725, 736, 4 L.Ed.2d 697 (1960).

A policeman's affidavit should not be judged as an entry in an essay contest. It is not "abracadabra."[6] As the majority recognizes, a policeman's affidavit is entitled to common-sense evaluation. So viewed, I conclude that the judgment of the Court of Appeals for the Eighth Circuit should be affirmed.

Mr. Justice STEWART, dissenting.

For substantially the reasons stated by my Brothers BLACK and FORTAS, I believe the warrant in this case was supported by a sufficient showing of probable cause. I would therefore affirm the judgment.

Berger v. New York*

This case concerns electronic eavesdropping under a warrant issued in accordance with a permissive eavesdrop statute. The statute is declared unconstitutional. The Court rules that the statute is offensive to the Fourteenth Amendment in that it is too broad in its sweep, resulting in the trepassory intrusion into a constitutionally protected area—privacy. Specifically, the statute did not require the law enforcement officer seeking the warrant to provide information relative to the alleged crime locus, the place to be searched and the conversations sought.

Scientific advances in the eavesdropping field and the failure of the Courts to keep pace, together with a historical outline of the evolution of eavesdropping and an analysis of the holdings in the previously decided cases included in the opinion makes this case a very significant one.

Text of Case

Petitioner was indicted and convicted of conspiracy to bribe the Chairman of the New York State Liquor Authority based upon evidence obtained by eavesdropping. An order pursuant to § 813-a of the N. Y. Code of Crim. Proc. permitting the installation of a recording device in an attorney's office for a period of 60 days was issued by a justice of the State Supreme Court, after he was advised of recorded interviews between a complainant and first an Authority employee and later the attorney in question. Section 813-a authorizes the issuance of an "ex parte order for eavesdropping" upon "oath or affirmation of a district attorney, or of

---

[c] See Time, Inc. v. Hill. 385 U.S. 374, 418. 87 S.Ct. 534, 557, 17 L.Ed.2d 456 (1967) (dissent) (relating to jury instructions).

* 388 U.S. 41 87 S.Ct. 1873, (June 12, 1967)

the attorney general or of an officer above the rank of sergeant of any police department." The oath must state "that there is reasonable ground to believe that evidence of a crime may be thus obtained, and particularly describing the person or persons whose communications . . . are to be overheard or recorded and the purpose thereof." The order must specify the duration of the eavesdrop, which may not exceed two months, unless extended. On the basis of leads obtained from this eavesdrop, a second order, also for a 60-day period, permitting an installation elsewhere was issued. After two weeks of eavesdropping a conspiracy, in which petitioner was a "go-between," was uncovered. The New York courts sustained the statute against constitutional challenge.

Joseph E. Brill argued the cause for petitioner. With him on the brief was *Abraham Glasser*.

H. Richard Uviller argued the cause for respondent. With him on the brief were *Frank S. Hogan* and *Alan F. Scribner*.

Briefs of *amici curiae*, urging reversal, were filed by *Jack Grant Day* and *Gerald Zuckerman* for the National Association of Defense Lawyers in Criminal Cases; by *John J. McAvoy* for the New York Civil Liberties Union, and by *Raymond W. Bergan* for the International Brotherhood of Teamsters, Chauffeurs, Warehousemen & Helpers of America.

Briefs of *amici curiae*, urging affirmance, were filed by *Louis J. Lefkowitz*, Attorney General, *pro se*, *Samuel A. Hirshowitz*, First Assistant Attorney General, and *Amy Juviler*, Assistant Attorney General, for the Attorney General of the State of New York, and by *G. Robert Blakey* for Elliot L. Richardson, Attorney General of Massachusetts, *Robert Y. Thornton*, Attorney General of Oregon, and the National District Attorneys' Association.

MR. JUSTICE CLARK delivered the opinion of the Court.

This writ tests the validity of New York's permissive eavesdrop statute, N. Y. Code Crim. Proc. § 813–a,[1] under the Fourth, Fifth,

---

[1] "§ 813-a. Ex parte order for eavesdropping

"An ex parte order for eavesdropping as defined in subdivisions one and two of section seven hundred thirty-eight of the penal law may be issued by any justice of the supreme court or judge of a county court or of the court of general sessions of the county of New York upon oath or affirmation of a district attorney, or of the attorney-general or of an officer above the rank of sergeant of any police department of the state or of any political subdivision thereof, that there is reasonable ground to believe that evidence of crime may be thus obtained, and particularly describing the person or persons whose communications, conversations or discussions are to be overheard or recorded and the purpose thereof, and, in the case of a telegraphic or telephonic communication, identifying the particular telephone number or telegraph line involved. In connection with the issuance of such

Ninth, and Fourteenth Amendments. The claim is that the statute sets up a system of surveillance which involves trespassory intrusions into private, constitutionally protected premises, authorizes "general searches" for "mere evidence,"[2] and is an invasion of the privilege against self-incrimination. The trial court upheld the statute, the Appellate Division affirmed without opinion, 25 App. Div. 2d 718, 269 N.Y.S.2d 368, and the Court of Appeals did likewise by a divided vote. 18 N.Y.2d 638, 219 N.E.2d 295. We granted certiorari, 385 U.S. 967 (1966). We have concluded that the language of New York's statute is too broad in its sweep resulting in a trespassory intrusion into a constitutionally protected area and is, therefore, violative of the Fourth and Fourteenth Amendments. This disposition obviates the necessity for any discussion of the other points raised.

I.

Berger, the petitioner, was convicted on two counts of conspiracy to bribe the Chairman of the New York State Liquor Authority. The case arose out of the complaint of one Ralph Pansini to the District Attorney's office that agents of the State Liquor Authority had entered his bar and grill and without cause seized his books and records. Pansini asserted that the raid was in reprisal for his failure to pay a bribe for a liquor license. Numerous complaints had been filed with the District Attorney's office charging the payment of bribes by applicants for liquor licenses. On the direction of that office, Pansini while equipped with a "minifon" recording device, interviewed an employee of the Authority. The employee advised Pansini that the price for a license was $10,000 and suggested that he contact attorney Harry Neyer. Neyer subsequently told Pansini that

---

an order the justice or judge may examine on oath the applicant and any other witness he may produce and shall satisfy himself of the existence of reasonable grounds for the granting of such application. Any such order shall be effective for the time specified therein but not for a period of more than two months unless extended or renewed by the justice or judge who signed and issued the original order upon satisfying himself that such extension or renewal is in the public interest. Any such order together with the papers upon which the application was based, shall be delivered to and retained by the appli-

cant as authority for the eavesdropping authorized therein. A true copy of such order shall at all times be retained in his possession by the judge or justice issuing the same, and, in the event of the denial of an application for such an order, a true copy of the papers upon which the application was based shall in like manner be retained by the judge or justice denying the same. As amended L. 1958, c. 676, eff. July 1, 1958."

[2] This contention is disposed of in *Warden, Maryland Penitentiary* v. *Hayden,* 387 U. S. 294, adversely to petitioner's assertion here.

he worked with the Authority employee before and that the latter was aware of the going rate on liquor licenses downtown.

On the basis of this evidence an eavesdrop order was obtained from a Justice of the State Supreme Court, as provided by § 813–a. The order permitted the installation, for a period of 60 days, of a recording device in Neyer's office. On the basis of leads obtained from this eavesdrop a second order permitting the installation, for a like period, of a recording device in the office of one Harry Steinman was obtained. After some two weeks of eavesdropping a conspiracy was uncovered involving the issuance of liquor licenses for the Playboy and Tenement Clubs, both of New York City. Petitioner was indicted as "a go-between" for the principal conspirators, who though not named in the indictment were disclosed in a bill of particulars. Relevant portions of the recordings were received in evidence at the trial and were played to the jury, all over the objection of the petitioner. The parties have stipulated that the District Attorney "had no information upon which to proceed to present a case to the Grand Jury, or on the basis of which to prosecute" the petitioner except by the use of the eavesdrop evidence.

II.

Eavesdropping is an ancient practice which at common law was condemned as a nuisance. 4 Blackstone, Commentaries 168. At one time the eavesdropper listened by naked ear under the eaves of houses or their windows, or beyond their walls seeking out private discourse. The awkwardness and undignified manner of this method as well as its susceptibility to abuse was immediately recognized. Electricity, however, provided a better vehicle and with the advent of the telegraph surreptitious interception of messages began. As early as 1862 California found it necessary to prohibit the practice by statute. Statutes of California 1862, p. 288, CCLXII. During the Civil War General J. E. B. Stuart is reputed to have had his own eavesdropper along with him in the field whose job it was to intercept military communications of the opposing forces. Subsequently newspapers reportedly raided one another's news gathering lines to save energy, time, and money. Racing news was likewise intercepted and flashed to bettors before the official result arrived.

The telephone brought on a new and more modern eavesdropper known as the "wiretapper." Interception was made by a connection with a telephone line. This activity has been with us for three-quarters of a century. Like its cousins, wiretapping proved to be a commercial as well as a police technique. Illinois outlawed it in 1895 and in 1905 California extended its telegraph interception prohibition to the telephone. Some 50 years ago a New York legislative committee found that police, in cooperation with the telephone company, had been tapping telephone lines in New York despite an Act passed in 1895 prohibiting it. During prohibition days wiretaps were the principal source of information relied upon by the police as the basis for prosecutions. In 1934 the Congress outlawed the interception without authorization, and the divulging or publishing of the contents of wiretaps by passing § 605 of the Communications Act of 1934.[3] New York, in 1938, declared by constitutional amendment that "[t]he right of the people to be secure against unreasonable interception of telephone and telegraph communications shall not be violated," but permitted by *ex parte* order of the Supreme Court of the State the interception of communications on a showing of "reasonable ground to believe that evidence of crime" might be obtained. N.Y. Const. Art. I, § 12.

Sophisticated electronic devices have now been developed (commonly known as "bugs") which are capable of eavesdropping on anyone in almost any given situation. They are to be distinguished from "wiretaps" which are confined to the interception of telegraphic and telephonic communications. Miniature in size ($3/8''$ x $3/8''$ x $1/8''$)—no larger than a postage stamp—these gadgets pick up whispers within a room and broadcast them half a block away to a receiver. It is said that certain types of electronic rays beamed at walls of glass windows are capable of catching voice vibrations as they are bounced off the surfaces. Since 1940 eavesdropping has become a big business. Manufacturing concerns offer complete detection systems which automatically record voices under almost any conditions by remote control. A microphone concealed in a book, a lamp, or other unsuspected place in a room, or made into a fountain pen, tie clasp, lapel button, or cuff link increases the range of these powerful wireless transmitters to a half mile. Receivers pick up the transmission with interference-free reception on a special wave frequency. And, of late, a combination mirror transmitter has been developed which permits not only sight but voice transmission up to 300 feet. Likewise, parabolic microphones, which can overhear conversations without being placed within the premises monitored, have been developed. See Westin, Science, Privacy, and Freedom: Issues and Proposals for the 1970's, 66 Col. L. Rev. 1003, 1005–1010.

As science developed these detection techniques, lawmakers, sensing the resulting invasion of individual privacy, have provided some statutory protection for the public. Seven States, California, Illinois, Maryland, Massachusetts, Nevada, New York, and Oregon,

---

[3] 48 Stat. 1103, 47 U. S. C. § 605.

prohibit surreptitious eavesdropping by mechanical or electronic device.[4] However, all save Illinois permit official court-ordered eavesdropping. Some 36 States prohibit wiretapping.[5] But of these, 27 permit "authorized" interception of some type. Federal law, as we have seen, prohibits interception and divulging or publishing of the content of wiretaps without exception.[6] In sum, it is fair to say that wiretapping on the whole is outlawed, except for permissive use by law enforcement officials in some States; while electronic eavesdropping is—save for seven States—permitted both officially and privately. And, in six of the seven States electronic eavesdropping ("bugging") is permissible on court order.

III.

The law, though jealous of individual privacy, has not kept pace with these advances in scientific knowledge. This is not to say that individual privacy has been relegated to a second-class position for it has been held since Lord Camden's day that intrusions into it are "subversive of all the comforts of society." *Entick* v. *Carrington*, 19 How. St. Tr. 1029, 1066 (1765). And the Founders so de-

---

[4] Cal. Pen. Code §§ 653h–j; Ill. Rev. Stat., c. 38, §§ 14–1 to 14–7 (1965); Md. Ann. Code, Art. 27, § 125A (1957); Mass. Gen. Laws, c. 272, § 99 (Supp. 1966); Nev. Rev. Stat. § 200.650 (1963); N. Y. Pen. Law § 738 (Supp. 1966); Ore. Rev. Stat. § 165.540 (1)(c) (Supp. 1965).

[5] Ala. Code, Tit. 48, § 414 (1958); Alaska Stat. § 42.20.100 (1962); Ark. Stat. Ann. § 73–1810 (1957); Cal. Pen. Code § 640; Colo. Rev. Stat. Ann. § 40–4–17 (1963); Conn. Gen. Stat. Rev. § 53–140 (1958); Del. Code Ann., Tit. 11, § 757 (Supp. 1966); Fla. Stat. § 822.10 (1965); Hawaii Rev. Laws § 309 A–1 (Supp. 1963); Idaho Code Ann. §§ 18–6704, 6705 (1947); Ill. Rev. Stat., c. 134, § 16 (1965); Iowa Code § 716.8 (1962); Ky. Rev. Stat. § 433.430 (1962); La. Rev. Stat. § 14:322 (1950); Md. Ann. Code, Art. 35, §§ 92, 93 (1957); Mass. Gen. Laws, c. 272, § 99 (Supp. 1966); Mich. Stat. Ann. § 28.808 (1954); Mont. Rev. Codes Ann. § 94–3203 (Supp. 1965); Neb. Rev. Stat. § 86–328 (1966); Nev. Rev. Stat. §§ 200.620, 200.630 (1963); N. J. Rev. Stat. § 2A:146–1 (1953); N. M. Stat. Ann. § 40A–12–1 (1964);

N. Y. Pen. Law § 738 (Supp. 1966); N. C. Gen. Stat. § 14–155 (1953); N. D. Cent. Code § 8–10–07 (1959); Ohio Rev. Code Ann. § 4931.28 (1954); Okla. Stat., Tit. 21, § 1757 (1961); Ore. Rev. Stat. § 165.540 (1) (Supp. 1965); Pa. Stat. Ann., Tit. 15, § 2443 (1958); R. I. Gen. Laws Ann. § 11–35–12 (1956); S. D. Code § 13.4519 (1939); Tenn. Code Ann. § 65–2117 (1955); Utah Code Ann. § 76–48–11 (1953); Va. Code Ann. § 18.1–156 (1960 Repl. Vol.); Wis. Stat. § 134.39 (1963); Wyo. Stat. Ann. § 37–259 (1957).

[6] A recent Federal Communications Commission Regulation, 31 Fed. Reg. 3400, 47 CFR § 2.701, prohibits the use of "a device required to be licensed by section 301 of the Communications Act" for the purpose of eavesdropping. This regulation, however, exempts use under "lawful authority" by police officers and the sanctions are limited to loss of license and the imposition of a fine. The memorandum accompanying the regulation stated: "What constitutes a crime under State law reflecting State policy applicable to radio eavesdropping is, of course, unaffected by our rules." *Id.*, at 3399.

cided a quarter of a century later when they declared in the Fourth Amendment that the people had a right "to be secure in their persons, houses, papers, and effects, against unreasonable searches and seizures . . . ." Indeed, that right, they wrote, "shall not be violated, and no Warrants shall issue, but upon probable cause, supported by Oath or affirmation, and particularly describing the place to be searched, and the persons or things to be seized." Almost a century thereafter this Court took specific and lengthy notice of *Entick* v. *Carrington, supra,* finding that its holding was undoubtedly familiar to and "in the minds of those who framed the Fourth Amendment . . . ." *Boyd* v. *United States,* 116 U.S. 616, 626–627 (1886). And after quoting from Lord Camden's opinion at some length, Mr. Justice Bradley characterized it thus:

"The principles laid down in this opinion affect the very essence of constitutional liberty and security. They reach farther than the concrete form of the case . . . they apply to all invasions on the part of the government and its employés of the sanctity of a man's home and the privacies of life." At 630.

Boyd held unconstitutional an Act of the Congress authorizing a court of the United States to require a defendant in a revenue case to produce in court his private books, invoices, and papers or else the allegations of the Government were to be taken as confessed. The Court found that "the essence of the offense . . . [was] the invasion of this sacred right which underlies and constitutes the essence of Lord Camden's judgment." *Ibid.* The Act—the Court found—violated the Fourth Amendment in that it authorized a general search contrary to the Amendment's guarantee.

The Amendment, however, carried no criminal sanction, and the federal statutes not affording one, the Court in 1914 formulated and pronounced the federal exclusionary rule in *Weeks* v. *United States,* 232 U.S. 383. Prohibiting the use in federal courts of any evidence seized in violation of the Amendment, the Court held:

"The effect of the Fourth Amendment is to put the courts of the United States . . . under limitations and restraints as to the exercise of such power . . . and to forever secure the people . . . against all unreasonable searches and seizures under the guise of law. This protection reaches all alike, whether accused of crime or not, and the duty of giving to it force and effect is obligatory upon all . . . . The tendency of those who execute the criminal laws of the country to obtain conviction by means of unlawful seizures . . . should find no sanction in the judgments of the courts which are charged at all times with the support of the Constitution and to which people of all conditions have a right to appeal for the maintenance of such fundamental rights." At 391–392.

IV.

The Court was faced with its first wiretap case in 1928, *Olmstead* v. *United States*, 277 U.S. 438. There the interception of Olmstead's telephone line was accomplished without entry upon his premises and was, therefore, found not to be proscribed by the Fourth Amendment. The basis of the decision was that the Constitution did not forbid the obtaining of evidence by wiretapping unless it involved actual unlawful entry into the house. Statements in the opinion that a conversation passing over a telephone wire cannot be said to come within the Fourth Amendment's enumeration of "persons, houses, papers, and effects" have been negated by our subsequent cases as hereinafter noted. They found "conversation" was within the Fourth Amendment's protections, and that the use of electronic devices to capture it was a "search" within the meaning of the Amendment, and we so hold. In any event, Congress soon thereafter, and some say in answer to *Olmstead*, specifically prohibited the interception without authorization and the divulging or publishing of the contents of telephonic communications. And the *Nardone* cases, 302 U.S. 379 (1937) and 308 U.S. 338 (1939), extended the exclusionary rule to wiretap evidence offered in federal prosecutions.

The first "bugging" case reached the Court in 1942 in *Goldman* v. *United States*, 316 U.S. 129. There the Court found that the use of a detectaphone placed against an office wall in order to hear private conversations in the office next door did not violate the Fourth Amendment because there was no physical trespass in connection with the relevant interception. And in *On Lee* v. *United States*, 343 U.S. 747 (1952), we found that since "no trespass was committed" a conversation between Lee and a federal agent, occurring in the former's laundry and electronically recorded, was not condemned by the Fourth Amendment. Thereafter in *Silverman* v. *United States*, 365 U.S. 505 (1961), the Court found "that the eavesdropping was accomplished by means of an unauthorized physical penetration into the premises occupied by the petitioners." At 509. A spike a foot long with a microphone attached to it was inserted under a baseboard into a party wall until it made contact with the heating duct that ran through the entire house occupied by Silverman, making a perfect sounding board through which the conversations in question were overheard. Significantly, the Court held that its decision did "not turn upon the technicality of a trespass upon a party wall as a matter of local law. It is based upon the reality of an actual intrusion into a constitutionally protected area." At 512.

347

In *Wong Sun* v. *United States*, 371 U.S. 471 (1963), the Court for the first time specifically held that verbal evidence may be the fruit of official illegality under the Fourth Amendment along with the more common tangible fruits of unwarranted intrusion. It used these words:

"The exclusionary rule has traditionally barred from trial physical, tangible materials obtained either during or as a direct result of an unlawful invasion. It follows from our holding in *Silverman* v. *United States*, 365 U.S. 505, that the Fourth Amendment may protect against the overhearing of verbal statements as well as against the more traditional seizure of 'papers and effects.'" At 485.

And in *Lopez* v. *United States*, 373 U.S. 427 (1963), the Court confirmed that it had "in the past sustained instances of 'electronic eavesdropping' against constitutional challenge, when devices have been used to enable government agents to overhear conversations which would have been beyond the reach of the human ear . . . . It has been insisted only that the electronic device not be planted by an unlawful physical invasion of a constitutionally protected area." At 438–439. In this case a recording of a conversation between a federal agent and the petitioner in which the latter offered the agent a bribe was admitted in evidence. Rather than constituting "eavesdropping" the Court found that the recording "was used only to obtain the most reliable evidence possible of a conversation in which the Government's own agent was a participant and which that agent was fully entitled to disclose." At 439.

V.

It is now well settled that "the Fourth Amendment's right of privacy has been declared enforceable against the States through the Due Process Clause of the Fourteenth" Amendment. *Mapp* v. *Ohio*, 367 U.S. 643, 655 (1961). "The security of one's privacy against arbitrary intrusion by the police—which is at the core of the Fourth Amendment—is basic to a free society." *Wolf* v. *Colorado*, 338 U.S. 25, 27 (1949). And its "fundamental protections . . . are guaranteed . . . against invasion by the States." *Stanford* v. *Texas*, 379 U.S. 476, 481 (1965). This right has most recently received enunciation in *Camara* v. *Municipal Court*, 387 U.S. 523. "The basic purpose of this Amendment, as recognized in countless decisions of this Court, is to safeguard the privacy and security of individuals against arbitrary invasions by governmental officials." At 528. Likewise the Court has decided that while the "standards of reasonableness" required under the Fourth Amendment are the same under the Fourteenth, they "are not susceptible of Procrus-

tean application . . ." *Ker* v. *California,* 374 U.S. 23, 33 (1963).
We said there that "the reasonableness of a search is . . . [to be de-
termined] by the trial court from the facts and circumstances of
the case and in the light of the 'fundamental criteria' laid down
by the Fourth Amendment and in opinions of this Court applying
that Amendment." *Ibid.*

We, therefore, turn to New York's statute to determine the
basis of the search and seizure authorized by it upon the order
of a state supreme court justice, a county judge or general sessions
judge of New York County. Section 813-a authorizes the issuance of
an "ex parte order for eavesdropping" upon "oath or affirmation
of a district attorney, or of the attorney-general or of an officer
above the rank of sergeant of any police department of the state
or of any political subdivision thereof . . . ." The oath must state
"that there is reasonable ground to believe that evidence of crime
may be thus obtained, and particularly describing the person or
persons whose communications, conversations or discussions are to
be overheard or recorded and the purpose thereof, and . . . identifying the particular telephone number of telegraph line involved."
The judge "may examine on oath the applicant and any other witness he may produce and shall satisfy himself of the existence of
reasonable grounds for the granting of such application." The order must specify the duration of the eavesdrop—not exceeding two
months unless extended and "[a]ny such order together with
the papers upon which the application was based, shall be delivered
to and retained by the applicant as authority for the eavesdropping
authorized therein."

While New York's statute satisfies the Fourth Amendment's requirement that a neutral and detached authority be interposed between the police and the public, *Johnson* v. *United States,* 333 U.S.
10, 14 (1948), the broad sweep of the statute is immediately observable. It permits the issuance of the order, or warrant for
eavesdropping, upon the oath of the attorney general, the district
attorney or any police officer above the rank of sergeant stating
that "there is reasonable ground to believe that evidence of crime
may be thus obtained . . . ." Such a requirement raises a serious
probable-cause question under the Fourth Amendment. Under it
warrants may only issue "but upon probable cause, supported by
Oath or affirmation, and particularly describing the place to be
searched, and the persons or things to be seized." Probable cause
under the Fourth Amendment exists where the facts and circumstances within the affiant's knowledge, and of which he has reasonably trustworthy information, are sufficient unto themselves to
warrant a man of reasonable caution to believe that an offense

349

has been or is being committed. *Carroll* v. *United States*, 267 U.S. 132, 162 (1925); *Husty* v. *United States*, 282 U.S. 694, 700–701 (1931); *Brinegar* v. *United States*, 338 U.S. 160, 175–176 (1949).

It is said, however, by the petitioner, and the State agrees, that the "reasonable ground" requirement of § 813–a "is undisputedly equivalent to the probable cause requirement of the Fourth Amendment." This is indicated by *People* v. *Grossman*, 45 Misc. 2d 557, 257 N.Y.S.2d 266, reversed on other grounds, 27 App.Div. 2d 572, 276 N.Y.S.2d 168. Also see *People* v. *Beshany*, 43 Misc.2d 521, 252 N.Y.S.2d 110. While we have found no case on the point by New York's highest court, we need not pursue the question further because we have concluded that the statute is deficient on its face in other respects. Since petitioner clearly has standing to challenge the statute, being indisputably affected by it, we need not consider either the sufficiency of the affidavits upon which the eavesdrop orders were based, or the standing of petitioner to attack the search and seizure made thereunder.

The Fourth Amendment commands that a warrant issue not only upon probable cause supported by oath or affirmation, but also "particularly describing the place to be searched, and the persons or things to be seized." New York's statute lacks this particularization. It merely says that a warrant may issue on reasonable ground to believe that evidence of crime may be obtained by the eavesdrop. It lays down no requirement for particularity in the warrant as to what specific crime has been or is being committed, nor "the place to be searched," or "the persons or things to be seized" as specifically required by the Fourth Amendment. The need for particularity and evidence of reliability in the showing required when judicial authorization of a search is sought is especially great in the case of eavesdropping. By its very nature eavesdropping involves an intrusion on privacy that is broad in scope. As was said in *Osborn* v. *United States*, 385 U.S. 323 (1966), the "indiscriminate use of such devices in law enforcement raises grave constitutional questions under the Fourth and Fifth Amendments," and imposes "a heavier responsibility on this Court in its supervision of the fairness of procedures . . . ." At 329, n. 7. There, two judges acting jointly authorized the installation of a device on the person of a prospective witness to record conversations between him and an attorney for a defendant then on trial in the United States District Court. The judicial authorization was based on an affidavit of the witness setting out in detail previous conversations between the witness and the attorney concerning the bribery of jurors in the case. The recording device was, as the Court said, authorized "under the most precise and discriminate circumstances, circumstances

350

which fully met the 'requirement of particularity' " of the Fourth Amendment. The Court was asked to exclude the evidence of the recording of the conversations seized pursuant to the order on constitutional grounds, *Weeks* v. *United States,* supra, or in the exercise of supervisory power, *McNabb* v. *United States,* 318 U.S. 332 (1943). The Court refused to do so finding that the recording, although an invasion of the privacy protected by the Fourth Amendment, was admissible because of the authorization of the judges, based upon "a detailed factual affidavit alleging the commission of a specific criminal offense directly and immediately affecting the administration of justice . . . for the narrow and particularized purpose of ascertaining the truth of the affidavit's allegations." At 330. The invasion was lawful because there was sufficient proof to obtain a search warrant to make the search for the limited purpose outlined in the order of the judges. Through these "precise and discriminate" procedures the order authorizing the use of the electronic device afforded similar protections to those that are present in the use of conventional warrants authorizing the seizure of tangible evidence. Among other safeguards, the order described the type of conversation sought with particularity, thus indicating the specific objective of the Government in entering the constitutionally protected area and the limitations placed upon the officer executing the warrant. Under it the officer could not search unauthorized areas; likewise, once the property sought, and for which the order was issued, was found the officer could not use the order as a passkey to further search. In addition, the order authorized one limited intrusion rather than a series or a continuous surveillance. And, we note that a new order was issued when the officer sought to resume the search and probable cause was shown for the succeeding one. Moreover, the order was executed by the officer with dispatch, not over a prolonged and extended period. In this manner no greater invasion of privacy was permitted than was necessary under the circumstances. Finally the officer was required to and did make a return on the order showing how it was executed and what was seized. Through these strict precautions the danger of an unlawful search and seizure was minimized.

By contrast, New York's statute lays down no such "precise and discriminate" requirements. Indeed, it authorizes the "indiscriminate use" of electronic devices as specifically condemned in *Osborn.* "The proceeding by search warrant is a drastic one," *Sgro* v. *United States,* 287 U.S. 206, 210 (1932), and must be carefully circumscribed so as to prevent unauthorized invasions of "the sanctity of a man's home and the privacies of life." *Boyd* v. *United States,* 116 U.S. 616, 630. New York's broadside authorization rather than be-

351

ing "carefully circumscribed" so as to prevent unauthorized invasions of privacy actually permits general searches by electronic devices, the truly offensive character of which was first condemned in *Entick* v. *Carrington*, 19 How. St. Tr. 1029, and which were then known as "general warrants." The use of the latter was a motivating factor behind the Declaration of Independence. In view of the many cases commenting on the practice it is sufficient here to point out that under these "general warrants" customs officials were given blanket authority to conduct general searches for goods imported to the Colonies in violation of the tax laws of the Crown. The Fourth Amendment's requirement that a warrant "particularly describ[e] the place to be searched, and the persons or things to be seized," repudiated these general warrants and "makes general searches . . . impossible and prevents the seizure of one thing under a warrant describing another. As to what is to be taken, nothing is left to the discretion of the officer executing the warrant." *Marron* v. *United States*, 275 U.S. 192, 196 (1927) ; *Stanford* v. *Texas, supra.*

We believe the statute here is equally offensive. First, as we have mentioned, eavesdropping is authorized without requiring belief that any particular offense has been or is being committed; nor that the "property" sought, the conversations, be particularly described. The purpose of the probable-cause requirement of the Fourth Amendment, to keep the state out of constitutionally protected areas until it has reason to believe that a specific crime has been or is being committed, is thereby wholly aborted. Likewise the statute's failure to describe with particularity the conversations sought gives the officer a roving commission to "seize" any and all conversations. It is true that the statute requires the naming of "the person or persons whose communications, conversations or discussions are to be overheard or recorded . . . ." But this does no more than identify the person whose constitutionally protected area is to be invaded rather than "particularly describing" the communications, conversations, or discussions to be seized. As with general warrants this leaves too much to the discretion of the officer executing the order. Secondly, authorization of eavesdropping for a two-month period is the equivalent of a series of intrusions, searches, and seizures pursuant to a single showing of probable cause. Prompt execution is also avoided. During such a long and continuous (24 hours a day) period the conversations of any and all persons coming into the area covered by the device will be seized indiscriminately and without regard to their connection with the crime under investigation. Moreover, the statute permits, and there were authorized here, extensions of the original two-month period—presumably for two months each—on a mere showing that such extension is "in the public interest." Apparently the original grounds on which the eavesdrop order was initially issued also form the basis of the renewal. This we believe insufficient without a showing of present probable cause for the continuance of the eavesdrop. Third, the statute places no termination date on the eavesdrop once the conversation sought is seized. This is left entirely in the discretion of the officer. Finally, the statute's procedure, necessarily because its success depends on secrecy, has no requirement for notice as do conventional warrants, nor does it overcome this defect by requiring some showing of special facts. On the contrary, it permits unconsented entry without any showing of exigent circumstances. Such a showing of exigency, in order to avoid notice, would appear more important in eavesdropping, with its inherent dangers, than that required when conventional procedures of search and seizure are utilized. Nor does the statute provide for a return on the warrant thereby leaving full discretion in the officer as to the use of seized conversations of innocent as well as guilty parties. In short, the statute's blanket grant of permission to eavesdrop is without adequate judicial supervision or protective procedures.

VI.

It is said with fervor that electronic eavesdropping is a most important technique of law enforcement and that outlawing it will severely cripple crime detection. The monumental report of the President's Commission on Law Enforcement and Administration of Justice entitled "The Challenge of Crime in a Free Society" informs us that the majority of law enforcement officials say that this is especially true in the detection of organized crime. As the Commission reports, there can be no question about the serious proportions of professional criminal activity in this country. However, we have found no empirical statistics on the use of electronic devices (bugging) in the fight against organized crime. Indeed, there are even figures available in the wiretap category which indicate to the contrary. See District Attorney Silver's Poll of New York Prosecutors, in Dash, Schwartz & Knowlton, The Eavesdroppers 105, 117–119 (1959). Also see Semerjian, Proposals on Wiretapping in Light of Recent Senate Hearings, 45 B. U. L. Rev. 217, 229. As the Commission points out, "[w]iretapping was the mainstay of the New York attack against organized crime until Federal court decisions intervened. Recently chief reliance in some offices has been placed on bugging, where the information is to be used in court. Law enforcement officials believe that the successes achieved in some parts of the State are attributable primarily to a combination of dedicated and competent personnel and adequate legal tools;

and that the failure to do more in New York has resulted primarily from the failure to commit additional resources of time and men," rather than electronic devices. At 201–202. Moreover, Brooklyn's District Attorney Silver's poll of the State of New York indicates that during the 12-year period (1942–1954) duly authorized wiretaps in bribery and corruption cases constituted only a small percentage of the whole. It indicates that this category involved only 10% of the total wiretaps. The overwhelming majority were in the categories of larceny, extortion, coercion, and blackmail, accounting for almost 50%. Organized gambling was about 11%. Statistics are not available on subsequent years. Dash, Schwartz & Knowlton, *supra,* at 40.

An often repeated statement of District Attorney Hogan of New York County was made at a hearing before the Senate Judiciary Committee at which he advocated the amendment of the Communications Act of 1934, *supra,* so as to permit "telephonic interception" of conversations. As he testified, "Federal statutory law [the 1934 Act] has been interpreted in such a way as to bar us from divulging wiretap evidence, even in the courtroom in the course of criminal prosecution." Mr. Hogan then said that "[w]ithout it [wiretaps] my own office could not have convicted" "top figures in the underworld." He then named nine persons his office had convicted and one on whom he had furnished "leads" secured from wiretaps to the authorities of New Jersey. Evidence secured from wiretaps, as Mr. Hogan said, was not admissible in "criminal prosecutions." He was advocating that the Congress adopt a measure that would make it admissible; Hearings on S. 2813 and S. 1495, before the Senate Committee on the Judiciary, 87th Cong., 2d Sess., pp. 173, 174 (1962). The President's Commission also emphasizes in its report the need for wiretapping in the investigation of organized crime because of the telephone's "relatively free use" by those engaged in the business and the difficulty of infiltrating their organizations. P. 201. The Congress, though long importuned, has not amended the 1934 Act to permit it.

We are also advised by the Solicitor General of the United States that the Federal Government has abandoned the use of electronic eavesdropping for "prosecutorial purposes." See Supplemental Memorandum, *Schipani* v. *United States,* No. 504, October Term, 1966, 385 U.S. 372. See also *Black* v. *United States,* 385 U.S. 26 (1966); *O'Brien* v. *United States,* 386 U.S. 345 (1967); *Hoffa* v. *United States,* 387 U.S. 231 (1967); *Markis* v. *United States,* 387 U.S. 425; *Moretti* v. *United States,* 387 U.S. 425. Despite these actions of the Federal Government there has been no failure of law enforcement in that field.

As THE CHIEF JUSTICE said in concurring in the result in *Lopez* v. *United States,* 373 U.S. 427, "the fantastic advances in the field of electronic communication constitute a great danger to the privacy of the individual; . . . indiscriminate use of such devices in law enforcement raises grave constitutional questions under the Fourth and Fifth Amendments . . . ." At 441.

In any event we cannot forgive the requirements of the Fourth Amendment in the name of law enforcement. This is no formality that we require today but a fundamental rule that has long been recognized as basic to the privacy of every home in America. While "[t]he requirements of the Fourth Amendment are not inflexible, or obtusely unyielding to the legitimate needs of law enforcement," *Lopez* v. *United States, supra,* at 464 (dissenting opinion of BRENNAN, J.), it is not asking too much that officers be required to comply with the basic command of the Fourth Amendment before the innermost secrets of one's home or office are invaded. Few threats to liberty exist which are greater than that posed by the use of eavesdropping devices. Some may claim that without the use of such devices crime detection in certain areas may suffer some delays since eavesdropping is quicker, easier, and more certain. However, techniques and practices may well be developed that will operate just as speedily and certainly and—what is more important—without attending illegality.

It is said that neither a warrant nor a statute authorizing eavesdropping can be drawn so as to meet the Fourth Amendment's requirements. If that be true then the "fruits" of eavesdropping devices are barred under the Amendment. On the other hand this Court has in the past, under specific conditions and circumstances, sustained the use of eavesdropping devices. See *Goldman* v. *United States,* 316 U.S. 129; *On Lee* v. *United States,* 343 U.S. 747; *Lopez* v. *United States, supra;* and *Osborn* v. *United States, supra.* In the latter case the eavesdropping device was permitted where the "commission of a specific offense" was charged, its use was "under the most precise and discriminate circumstances" and the effective administration of justice in a federal court was at stake. The States are under no greater restrictions. The Fourth Amendment does not make the "precincts of the home or the office . . . sanctuaries where the law can never reach," DOUGLAS, J., dissenting in *Warden, Maryland Penitentiary* v. *Hayden,* 387 U.S. 294, 321, but it does prescribe a constitutional standard that must be met before official invasion is permissible. Our concern with the statute here is whether its language permits a trespassory invasion of the home or office, by general warrant, contrary to the command of the Fourth Amendment. As it is written, we believe that it does.

Reversed.

355

MR. JUSTICE DOUGLAS, concurring.

I join the opinion of the Court because at long last it overrules *Sub silentio Olmstead* v. *United States,* 277 U.S. 438, and its offspring and brings wiretapping and other electronic eavesdropping fully within the purview of the Fourth Amendment. I also join the opinion because it condemns electronic surveillance, for its similarity to the general warrants out of which our Revolution sprang and allows a discreet surveillance only on a showing of "probable cause." These safeguards are minimal if we are to live under a regime of wiretapping and other electronic surveillance.

Yet there persists my overriding objection to electronic surveillance, *viz.,* that it is a search for "mere evidence" which, as I have maintained on other occasions (*Osborn* v. *United States,* 385 U.S. 323, 349–354), is a violation of the Fourth and Fifth Amendments, no matter with what nicety and precision a warrant may be drawn, a proposition that I developed in detail in my dissent in *Warden* v. *Hayden,* 387 U.S. 294, 312, decided only the other day.

A discreet selective wiretap or electronic "bugging" is of course not rummaging around, collecting everything in the particular time and space zone. But even though it is limited in time, it is the greatest of all invasions of privacy. It places a government agent in the bedroom, in the business conference, in the social hour, in the lawyer's office—everywhere and anywhere a "bug" can be placed.

If a statute were to authorize placing a policeman in every home or office where it was shown that there was probable cause to believe that evidence of crime would be obtained, there is little doubt that it would be struck down as a bald invasion of privacy, far worse than the general warrants prohibited by the Fourth Amendment. I can see no difference between such a statute and one authorizing electronic surveillance, which, in effect, places an invisible policeman in the home. If anything, the latter is more offensive because the homeowner is completely unaware of the invasion of privacy.

The traditional wiretap or electronic eavesdropping device constitutes a dragnet, sweeping in all conversations within its scope—without regard to the participants or the nature of the conversations. It intrudes upon the privacy of those not even suspected of crime and intercepts the most intimate of conversations. Thus, in the *Coplon* case (*United States* v. *Coplon,* 91 F.Supp. 867, rev'd, 191 F.2d 749) wiretaps of the defendant's home and office telephones recorded conversations between the defendant and her mother, a quarrel between a husband and wife who had no connection with the case, and conferences between the defendant and her attorney concerning the preparation of briefs, testimony of government witnesses, selection of jurors and trial strategy. Westin, The Wire-Tapping Problem: An Analysis and a Legislative Proposal, 52 Col. L. Rev. 165, 170–171 (1952) ; Barth, The Loyalty of Free Men 173 (1951). It is also reported that the FBI incidentally learned about an affair, totally unrelated to espionage, between the defendant and a Justice Department attorney. Barth, *supra*, at 173. While tapping one telephone, police recorded conversations involving, at the other end, The Juilliard School of Music, Brooklyn Law School, Consolidated Radio Artists, Western Union, Mercantile Commercial Bank, several restaurants, a real estate company, a drug store, many attorneys, an importer, a dry cleaning establishment, a number of taverns, a garage, and the Prudential Insurance Company. Westin, *supra*, at 188, n. 112. These cases are but a few of many demonstrating the sweeping nature of electronic total surveillance as we know it today.

It is, of course, possible for a statute to provide that wiretap or electronic eavesdrop evidence is admissible only in a prosecution for the crime to which the showing of probable cause related. See Nev. Rev. Stat. § 200.680 (1963). But such a limitation would not alter the fact that the order authorizes a general search. Whether or not the evidence obtained is used at a trial for another crime, the privacy of the individual has been infringed by the interception of all of his conversations. And, even though the information is not introduced as evidence, it can and probably will be used as leads and background information. Again, a statute could provide that evidence developed from eavesdrop information could not be used at trial. Cf. *Silverthorne Lumber Co., Inc.* v. *United States*, 251 U.S. 385, 392; *Nardone* v. *United States*, 308 U.S. 338; *Silverman* v. *United States*, 365 U.S. 505. But, under a regime of total surveillance, where a multitude of conversations are recorded, it would be very difficult to show which aspects of the information had been used as investigative information.

As my Brother WHITE says in his dissent, this same vice inheres in any search for tangible evidence such as invoices, letters, diaries, and the like. "In searching for seizable matters, the police must necessarily see or hear, and comprehend, items which do not relate to the purpose of the search." That is precisely why the Fourth Amendment made any such rummaging around unconstitutional, even though supported by a formally adequate warrant. That underwrites my dissent in *Hayden*.

With all respect, my Brother BLACK misses the point of the Fourth Amendment. It does not make every search constitutional provided there is a warrant that is technically adequate. The history of the Fourth Amendment, as I have shown in my dissent in

357

the *Hayden* case, makes it plain that any search in the precincts of the home for personal items that are lawfully possessed and not articles of a crime is "unreasonable." That is the essence of the "mere evidence" rule that long obtained until overruled by *Hayden*.

The words that a man says consciously on a radio are public property. But I do not see how government using surreptitious methods can put a person on the radio and use his words to convict him. Under our regime a man stands mute if he chooses, or talks if he chooses. The test is whether he acts voluntarily. That is the essence of the face of privacy protected by the "mere evidence" rule. For the Fourth Amendment and the Fifth come into play when the accused is "the unwilling source of the evidence" (*Gouled* v. *United States*, 255 U.S. 298, 306), there being no difference whether he be obliged to supply evidence against himself or whether such evidence be obtained by an illegal search of his premises and seizure of his private papers." *Ibid.*

That is the essence of my dissent in *Hayden.* In short, I do not see how any electronic surveillance that collects evidence or provides leads to evidence is or can be constitutional under the Fourth and Fifth Amendments. We could amend the Constitution and so provide—a step that would take us closer to the ideological group we profess to despise. Until the amending process ushers us into that kind of totalitarian regime, I would adhere to the protection of privacy which the Fourth Amendment, fashioned in Congress and submitted to the people, was designed to afford the individual. And unlike my Brother BLACK, I would adhere to *Mapp* v. *Ohio,* 367 U.S. 643, and apply the exclusionary rule in state as well as federal trials—a rule fashioned out of the Fourth Amendment and constituting a high constitutional barricade against the intrusion of Big Brother into the lives of all of us.

MR. JUSTICE STEWART, concurring in the result.

I fully agree with MR. JUSTICE BLACK, MR. JUSTICE HARLAN, and MR. JUSTICE WHITE that this New York law is entirely constitutional. In short, I think that "electronic eavesdropping, *as such* or as it is permitted by this statute, is not an unreasonable search and seizure."[1] The statute contains many provisions more stringent than the Fourth Amendment generally requires, as MR. JUSTICE BLACK has so forcefully pointed out. And the petitioner himself has told us that the law's "reasonable grounds" requirement "is undisputedly equivalent to the probable cause requirement of the Fourth Amendment." This is confirmed by decisions

---

[1] Dissenting opinion of MR. JUSTICE HARLAN, *post,* p. 89, at 94.

358

of the New York courts. *People* v. *Cohen*, 42 Misc.2d 403, 248 N.Y. S.2d 339; *People* v. *Beshany*, 43 Misc.2d 521, 252 N.Y.S.2d 110; *People* v. *Grossman*, 45 Misc.2d 557, 257 N.Y.S.2d 266. Of course, a state court's construction of a state statute is binding upon us.

In order to hold this statute unconstitutional, therefore, we would have to either rewrite the statute or rewrite the Constitution. I can only conclude that the Court today seems to have rewritten both.

The issue before us, as MR. JUSTICE WHITE says, is "whether *this* search complied with Fourth Amendment standards." For me that issue is an extremely close one in the circumstances of this case. It certainly cannot be resolved by incantation of ritual phrases like "general warrant." Its resolution involves "the unavoidable task in any search and seizure case: was the particular search and seizure reasonable or not?"[2]

I would hold that the affidavits on which the judicial order issued in this case did not constitute a showing of probable cause adequate to justify the authorizing order. The need for particularity and evidence of reliability in the showing required when judicial authorization is sought for the kind of electronic eavesdropping involved in this case is especially great. The standard of reasonableness embodied in the Fourth Amendment demands that the showing of justification match the degree of intrusion. By its very nature electronic eavesdropping for a 60-day period, even of a specified office, involves a broad invasion of a constitutionally protected area. Only the most precise and rigorous standard of probable cause should justify an intrusion of this sort. I think the affidavits presented to the judge who authorized the electronic surveillance of the Steinman office failed to meet such a standard.

So far as the record shows, the only basis for the Steinman order consisted of two affidavits. One of them contained factual allegations supported only by bare, unexplained references to "evidence" in the district attorney's office and "evidence" obtained by the Neyer eavesdrop. No underlying facts were presented on the basis of which the judge could evaluate these general allegations. The second affidavit was no more than a statement of another assistant district attorney that he had read his associate's affidavit and was satisfied on that basis alone that proper grounds were presented for the issuance of an authorizing order.

This might be enough to satisfy the standards of the Fourth Amendment for a conventional search or arrest. Cf. *Aguilar* v. *Texas*, 378 U.S. 108, 116 (dissenting opinion). But I think it was

---

[2] See dissenting opinion of MR. JUSTICE BLACK, *post*, p. 70, at 83.

constitutionally insufficient to constitute probable cause to justify an intrusion of the scope and duration that was permitted in this case.

Accordingly, I would reverse the judgment.

MR. JUSTICE BLACK, dissenting.

New York has an eavesdropping statute which permits its judges to authorize state officers to place on other people's premises electronic devices that will overhear and record telephonic and other conversations for the purpose of detecting secret crimes and conspiracies and obtaining evidence to convict criminals in court. Judges cannot issue such eavesdropping permits except upon oath or affirmation of certain state officers that "there is reasonable ground to believe that evidence of crime may be thus obtained, and particularly describing the person or persons whose communications, conversations or discussions are to be overheard or recorded, and the purpose thereof . . . ." N.Y. Code Crim. Proc. § 813–a. Evidence obtained by such electronic eavesdropping was used to convict the petitioner here of conspiracy to bribe the chairman of the State Liquor Authority which controls the issuance of liquor licenses in New York. It is stipulated that without this evidence a conviction could not have been obtained, and it seems apparent that use of that evidence showed petitioner to be a briber beyond all reasonable doubt. Notwithstanding petitioner's obvious guilt, however, the Court now strikes down his conviction in a way that plainly makes it impossible ever to convict him again. This is true because the Court not only holds that the judicial orders which were the basis of the authority to eavesdrop were insufficient, but also holds that the New York eavesdropping statute is *on its face* violative of the Fourth Amendment. And while the Court faintly intimates to the contrary, it seems obvious to me that its holding, by creating obstacles that cannot be overcome, makes it completely impossible for the State or the Federal Government ever to have a valid eavesdropping statute. All of this is done, it seems to me, in part because of the Court's hostility to eavesdropping as "ignoble" and "dirty business"[1] and in part because of fear that rapidly advancing science and technology is making eavesdropping more and more effective. Cf. *Lopez* v. *United States*, 373 U.S. 427, 446 (dissenting opinion of BRENNAN, J.). Neither these, nor any other grounds that I can think of, are sufficient in my judgment to justify a holding that the use of evidence secured by eavesdropping is barred by the Constitution.

---

[1] Mr. Justice Holmes dissenting in *Olmstead* v. *United States*, 277 U. S. 438, 470.

I.

Perhaps as good a definition of eavesdropping as another is that it is listening secretly and sometimes "snoopily" to conversations and discussions believed to be private by those who engage in them. Needless to say, eavesdropping is not ranked as one of the most learned or most polite professions, nor perhaps would an eavesdropper be selected by many people as the most desirable and attractive associate. But the practice has undoubtedly gone on since the beginning of human society, and during that time it has developed a usefulness of its own, particularly in the detection and prosecution of crime.

Eavesdroppers have always been deemed competent witnesses in English and American courts. The main test of admissibility has been relevance and first-hand knowledge, not by whom or by what method proffered evidence was obtained. It is true that in England people who obtained evidence by unlawful means were held liable in damages as in *Entick* v. *Carrington*, 19 How. St. Tr. 1029. But even that famous civil liberties case made no departure from the traditional common-law rule that relevant evidence is admissible, even though obtained contrary to ethics, morals, or law. And, for reasons that follow, this evidentiary rule is well adapted to our Government, set up, as it was, to "insure domestic tranquility" under a system of laws.

Today this country is painfully realizing that evidence of crime is difficult for governments to secure. Criminals are shrewd and constantly seek, too often successfully, to conceal their tracks and their outlawry from law officers. But in carrying on their nefarious practices professional criminals usually talk considerably. Naturally, this talk is done, they hope, in a secret way that will keep it from being heard by law enforcement authorities or by others who might report to the authorities. In this situation "eavesdroppers," "informers," and "squealers," as they are variously called, are helpful, even though unpopular, agents of law enforcement. And it needs no empirical studies or statistics to establish that eavesdropping testimony plays an important role in exposing criminals and bands of criminals who but for such evidence would go along their criminal way with little possibility of exposure, prosecution, or punishment. Such, of course, is this particular case before us.

The eavesdrop evidence here shows this petitioner to be a briber, a corrupter of trusted public officials, a poisoner of the honest administration of government, upon which good people must depend to obtain the blessings of a decent orderly society. No man's privacy, property, liberty, or life is secure, if organized or even unorganized criminals can go their way unmolested, ever and ever further in

361

their unbounded lawlessness. However obnoxious eavesdroppers may be they are assuredly not engaged in a more "ignoble" or "dirty business" than are bribers, thieves, burglars, robbers, rapists, kidnapers, and murderers, not to speak of others. And it cannot be denied that to deal with such specimens of our society, eavesdroppers are not merely useful, they are frequently a necessity. I realize that some may say, "well, let the prosecuting officers use more scientific measures than eavesdropping." It is always easy to hint at mysterious means available just around the corner to catch outlaws. But crimes, unspeakably horrid crimes, are with us in this country, and we cannot afford to dispense with any known method of detecting and correcting them unless it is forbidden by the Constitution or deemed inadvisable by legislative policy—neither of which I believe to be true about eavesdropping.

II.

Since eavesdrop evidence obtained by individuals is admissible and helpful I can perceive no permissible reason for courts to reject it, even when obtained surreptitiously by machines, electronic or otherwise. Certainly evidence picked up and recorded on a machine is not less trustworthy. In both perception and retention a machine is more accurate than a human listener. The machine does not have to depend on a defective memory to repeat what was said in its presence for it repeats the very words uttered. I realize that there is complaint that sometimes the words are jumbled or indistinct. But machine evidence need not be done away with to correct such occasional defective recording. The trial judge has ample power to refuse to admit indistinct or garbled recordings.

The plain facts are, however, that there is no inherent danger to a defendant in using these electronic recordings except that which results from the use of testimony that is so unerringly accurate that it is practically bound to bring about a conviction. In other words, this kind of transcribed eavesdropping evidence is far more likely to lead a judge or jury to reach a correct judgment or verdict—the basic and always-present objective of a trial.

III.

The superior quality of evidence recorded and transcribed on an electronic device is, of course, no excuse for using it against a defendant, if, as the Court holds, its use violates the Fourth Amendment. If that is true, no amount of common-law tradition or anything else can justify admitting such evidence. But I do not believe the Fourth Amendment, or any other, bans the use of evidence obtained by eavesdropping.

362

There are constitutional amendments that speak in clear unambiguous prohibitions or commands. The First, for illustration, declares that "Congress shall make no law . . . abridging the freedom of speech, or of the press . . . ." The Fifth declares that a person shall not be held to answer for a capital or otherwise infamous crime except on a grand jury indictment; shall not twice be put in jeopardy of life or limb for the same offense; nor be compelled in any criminal case to be a witness against himself. These provisions of the First and Fifth Amendments, as well as others I need not mention at this time, are clear unconditional commands that something shall not be done. Particularly of interest in comparison with the Fourth Amendment is the Fifth Amendment's prohibition against compelling a person to be a witness against himself. The Fifth Amendment's language forbids a court to hear evidence against a person that he has been compelled to give, without regard to reasonableness or anything else. Unlike all of these just-named Fifth Amendment provisions, the Fourth Amendment relating to searches and seizures contains no such unequivocal commands. It provides:

"The right of the people to be secure in their persons, houses, papers, and effects, against unreasonable searches and seizures, shall not be violated, and no Warrants shall issue, but upon probable cause, supported by Oath or affirmation, and particularly describing the place to be searched, and the persons or things to be seized."

Obviously, those who wrote this Fourth Amendment knew from experience that searches and seizures were too valuable to law enforcement to prohibit them entirely, but also knew at the same time that while searches or seizures must not be stopped, they should be slowed down, and warrants should be issued only after studied caution. This accounts for use of the imprecise and flexible term, "unreasonable," the key word permeating this whole Amendment. Also it is noticeable that this Amendment contains no appropriate language, as does the Fifth, to forbid the use and introduction of search and seizure evidence even though secured "unreasonably." Nor does this Fourth Amendment attempt to describe with precision what was meant by its words, "probable cause"; nor by whom the "Oath or affirmation" should be taken; nor what it need contain. Although the Amendment does specifically say that the warrant should particularly describe "the place to be searched, and the persons or things to be seized," it does not impose any precise limits on the spatial or temporal extent of the search or the quantitative extent of the seizure. Thus this Amendment, aimed against only "unreasonable" searches and seizures, seeks to guard against them by providing, as the Court says, that a "neutral and detached authority be interposed between the police and the public, *Johnson* v. *United States,* 333 U.S. 10, 14." And, as the Court admits, the Amendment itself provides no sanctions to enforce its standards of searches, seizures, and warrants. This was left for Congress to carry out if it chose to do so.

Had the framers of this Amendment desired to prohibit the use in court of evidence secured by an unreasonable search or seizure, they would have used plain appropriate language to do so, just as they did in prohibiting the use of enforced self-incriminatory evidence in the Fifth Amendment. Since the Fourth Amendment contains no language forbidding the use of such evidence, I think there is no such constitutional rule. So I continue to believe that the exclusionary rule formulated to bar such evidence in the *Weeks*[2] case is not rooted in the Fourth Amendment but rests on the "supervisory power" of this Court over the other federal courts—the same judicial power invoked in *McNabb* v. *United States,* 318 U.S. 332. See my concurring opinions in *Wolf* v. *Colorado,* 338 U.S. 25, 39, and *Mapp* v. *Ohio,* 367 U.S. 643, 661.[3] For these reasons and others to be stated, I do not believe the Fourth Amendment standing alone, even if applicable to electronic eavesdropping, commands exclusion of the overheard evidence in this case.

In reaching my conclusion that the Fourth Amendment itself does not bar the use of eavesdropping evidence in courts, I do not overlook the fact that the Court at present is reading the Amendment as expressly and unqualifiedly barring invasions of "privacy" rather than merely forbidding "unreasonable searches and seizures." On this premise of the changed command of the Amendment, the Court's task in passing on the use of eavesdropping evidence becomes a simple one. Its syllogism is this:

The Fourth Amendment forbids invasion of privacy and excludes evidence obtained by such invasion;

To listen secretly to a man's conversations or to tap his telephone conversations invades his privacy;

Therefore, the Fourth Amendment bars use of evidence obtained by eavesdropping or by tapping telephone wires.

The foregoing syllogism is faulty for at least two reasons: (1) the Fourth Amendment itself contains no provision from which can be implied a purpose to bar evidence or anything else secured by an

---

[2] *Weeks* v. *United States,* 232 U. S. 383. Compare *Adams* v. *New York,* 192 U. S. 585.

[3] I concurred in *Mapp* because "[t]he close interrelationship between the Fourth and Fifth Amendments," 367 U. S., at 662, as they applied to the facts of that case required the exclusion there of the unconstitutionally seized evidence.

"unreasonable search or seizure"; (2) the Fourth Amendment's language, fairly construed, refers specifically to "unreasonable searches and seizures" and not to a broad undefined right to "privacy" in general. To attempt to transform the meaning of the Amendment, as the Court does here, is to play sleight-of-hand tricks with it. It is impossible for me to think that the wise Framers of the Fourth Amendment would ever have dreamed about drafting an amendment to protect the "right of privacy." That expression, like a chameleon, has a different color for every turning. In fact, use of "privacy" as the keyword in the Fourth Amendment simply gives this Court a useful new tool, as I see it, both to usurp the policy-making power of the Congress and to hold more state and federal laws unconstitutional when the Court entertains a sufficient hostility to them. I therefore cannot agree to hold New York's law unconstitutional on the premise that all laws that unreasonably invade privacy violate the Fourth Amendment.

IV.

While the electronic eavesdropping here bears some analogy to the problems with which the Fourth Amendment is concerned, I am by no means satisfied that the Amendment controls the constitutionality of such eavesdropping. As pointed out, the Amendment only bans searches and seizures of "persons, houses, papers, and effects." This literal language imports tangible things, and it would require an expansion of the language used by the framers, in the interest of "privacy" or some equally vague judge-made goal, to hold that it applies to the spoken word. It simply requires an imaginative transformation of the English language to say that conversations can be searched and words seized. Referring to wiretapping, this Court in *Olmstead* v. *United States*, 277 U.S. 438, 465, refused to make that transformation:

"Justice Bradley in the *Boyd* case, and Justice Clark[e] in the *Gouled* case, said that the Fifth Amendment and the Fourth Amendment were to be liberally construed . . . . But that can not justify enlargement of the language employed beyond the possible practical meaning of houses, persons, papers, and effects, or so to apply the words search and seizure as to forbid hearing or sight."
Though *Olmstead* has been severely criticized by various individual members of this Court. and though the Court stated an alternative ground for holding the Amendment inapplicable in that case, the *Olmstead* holding that the Fourth Amendment does not apply to efforts to hear and obtain oral conversations has never been overruled by this Court. The Court today, however, suggests that this holding has been "negated" by subsequent congressional action

and by four decisions of this Court. First, the Court intimates, though it does not exactly state, that Congress "in answer to *Olmstead*," passed an Act to prohibit "the interception without authorization and the divulging or publishing of the contents of telephonic communications." The Court cites no authority for this strange surmise, and I assert with confidence that none can be recited. And even if it could, Congress' action would not have the slightest relevance to the scope of the Fourth Amendment. Second, the Court cites *Goldman* v. *United States*, 316 U.S. 129, and *On Lee* v. *United States*, 343 U.S. 747, in an effort to explain away *Olmstead*. But neither of those cases purported to repudiate the *Olmstead* case or any part of it. In fact, in both of those cases the Court refused to exclude the challenged eavesdrop evidence. Finally, the Court relies on *Silverman* v. *United States*, 365 U.S. 505, and *Wong Sun* v. *United States*, 371 U.S. 471. In both of these cases the Court did imply that the "Fourth Amendment *may* protect against the overhearing of verbal statements as well as against the more traditional seizure of 'papers and effects,' " 371 U.S., at 485 (emphasis added), but in neither did the Court find it necessary to overrule *Olmstead*, an action that would have been required had the Court based its exclusion of the oral conversations solely on the ground of the Fourth Amendment. The fact is that both *Silverman* and *Wong Sun* were federal cases dealing with the use of verbal evidence in federal courts, and the Court held the evidence should be excluded by virtue of the exclusionary rule of the *Weeks* case. As I have previously pointed out, that rule rested on the Court's supervisory power over federal courts, not on the Fourth Amendment: it is not required by the Amendment, nor is a violation of the Amendment a prerequisite to its application. I would not have agreed with the Court's opinion in *Silverman*, which, by the way, cited *Olmstead* with approval, had I thought that the result depended on finding a violation of the Fourth Amendment or had I any inkling that the Court's general statements about the scope of the Amendment were intended to negate the clear holding of *Olmstead*. And again in *Wong Sun*, which did not even mention *Olmstead*, let alone overrule it, the Court clearly based its exclusion of oral statements made to federal agents during an illegal arrest on its supervisory power to deter lawless conduct by federal officers and on the alternative ground that the incriminating statements were made under compulsive circumstances and were not the product of a free will. It is impossible for me to read into that non-eavesdropping federal case an intent to overrule *Olmstead* implicitly. In short, the only way this Court can escape *Olmstead* here is to overrule it. Without expressly saying so, the Court's opinion, as my Brother DOUGLAS acknowledges, does just that. And that overruling is accomplished by the simple expedient of substituting for the Amendment's words, "The right of the people to be secure in their persons, houses, papers, and effects," the words "The right of the people to be secure in their privacy," words the Court believes the Framers should have used, but did not. I have frequently stated my opposition to such judicial substitution. Although here the Court uses it to expand the scope of the Fourth Amendment to include words, the Court has been applying the same process to contract the Fifth Amendment's privilege against self-incrimination so as to exclude all types of incriminating evidence but words, or what the Court prefers to call "testimonial evidence." See *United States* v. *Wade, post,* p. 218; *Gilbert* v. *California, post,* p. 263.

There is yet another reason why I would adhere to the holding of *Olmstead* that the Fourth Amendment does not apply to eavesdropping. Since the Framers in the first clause of the Amendment specified that only persons, houses, and things were to be protected, they obviously wrote the second clause, regulating search warrants, in reference only to such tangible things. To hold, as the Court does, that the first clause protects words, necessitates either a virtual re-writing of the particularity requirements of the Warrant Clause or a literal application of that clause's requirements and our cases construing them to situations they were never designed to cover. I am convinced that the Framers of the Amendment never intended this Court to do either, and yet it seems to me clear that the Court here does a little of both.

V.

Assuming, as the Court holds, that the Fourth Amendment applies to eavesdropping and that the evidence obtained by an eavesdrop which violates the Fourth Amendment must be excluded in state courts, I disagree with the Court's holding that the New York statute on its face fails to comport with the Amendment. I also agree with my Brother WHITE that the statute as here applied did not violate any of petitioner's Fourth Amendment rights—assuming again that he has some—and that he is not entitled to a reversal of his conviction merely because the statute might have been applied in some way that would not have accorded with the Amendment.

This case deals only with a trespassory eavesdrop, an eavesdrop accomplished by placing "bugging" devices in certain offices. Significantly, the Court does not purport to disturb the *Olmstead-Silverman-Goldman* distinction between eavesdrops which are accompanied by a physical invasion and those that are not. Neither does the Court purport to overrule the holdings of *On Lee* v. *United*

367

States, 343 U.S. 747, and *Lopez* v. *United States*, 373 U.S. 427, which exempt from the Amendment's requirements the use of an electronic device to record, and perhaps even transmit, a conversation to which the user is a party. It is thus clear that at least certain types of electronic eavesdropping, until today, were completely outside the scope of the Fourth Amendment. Nevertheless, New York has made it a crime to engage in almost any kind of electronic eavesdropping, N.Y. Pen. Law § 738, and the only way eavesdropping, even the kind this Court has held constitutional, can be accomplished with immunity from criminal punishment is pursuant to § 813–a of the Code of Criminal Procedure, N.Y. Pen. Law § 739. The Court now strikes down § 813–a in its entirety, and that may well have the result of making it impossible for state law enforcement officers merely to listen through a closed door by means of an inverted cone or some other crude amplifying device, eavesdropping which this Court has to date refused to hold violative of the Fourth Amendment. Certainly there is no justification for striking down completely New York's statute, covering all kinds of eavesdropping, merely because it fails to contain the "strict precautions" which the Court derives—or more accurately fabricates—as conditions to eavesdrops covered by the Fourth Amendment. In failing to distinguish between types of eavesdropping and in failing to make clear that the New York statute is invalid only as applied to certain kinds of eavesdropping, the Court's opinion leaves the definite impression that all eavesdropping is governed by the Fourth Amendment. Such a step would require overruling of almost every opinion this Court has ever written on the subject. Indeed, from the Court's eavesdropping catalogue of horrors—electronic rays beamed at walls, lapel and cuff-link microphones, and off-premise parabolic microphones—it does not take too much insight to see that the Court is about ready to do, if it has not today done, just that.

I agree with my Brother WHITE that instead of looking for technical defects in the language of the New York statute, the Court should examine the actual circumstances of its application in this case to determine whether petitioner's rights have here been violated. That to me seems to be the unavoidable task in any search and seizure case: was the particular search and seizure reasonable or not? We have just this Term held that a search and seizure without a warrant and even without authorization of state law, can nevertheless, under all the circumstances, be "reasonable" for Fourth Amendment purposes. *Cooper* v. *California*, 386 U.S. 58. I do not see why that could not be equally true in the case of a search and seizure with a warrant and pursuant to a state law, even though the state law is itself too broad to be valid. Certainly a search and seizure may comply with the Fourth Amendment even in the absence of an authorizing statute which embodies the Amendment's requirements. *Osborn* v. *United States*, 385 U.S. 323, upon which the Court so heavily relies, is a good example of a case where the Court sustained the tape recording of a conversation by examining the particular circumstances surrounding it, even though no federal statute prescribed the precautions taken by the district judges there. Here New York has gone much further than the Federal Government and most of the States to outlaw all eavesdropping except under the limited circumstances of § 813-a, a statute which, as I shall demonstrate, contains many more safeguards than the Fourth Amendment itself. But today New York fares far worse than those States which have done nothing to implement and supplement the Fourth Amendment: it must release a convicted criminal, not because it has deprived him of constitutional rights, but because it has inartfully (according to the Court) tried to guarantee him those rights. The New York statute aside, the affidavits in this case were sufficient to justify a finding of probable cause, and the *ex parte* eavesdrop orders identified the person whose conversations were to be overheard, the place where the eavesdropping was to take place, and, when read in reference to the supporting affidavits, the type of conversations sought, *i. e.*, those relating to extortion and bribery.

The Court concludes its analysis of § 813-a by asserting that "the statute's blanket grant of permission to eavesdrop is without adequate judicial supervision or protective procedures." Even if the Court's fear that "[f]ew threats to liberty exist which are greater than that posed by the use of eavesdropping devices" justifies it in rewriting the Fourth Amendment to impose on eavesdroppers "strict precautions" which are not imposed on other searchers, it is an undeserved criticism of New York to characterize its studied efforts to regulate eavesdropping as resulting in a statute "without adequate judicial supervision or protective procedures." Let us look at the New York statute. It provides:

(1) New York judges are to issue authorizations. (The Fourth Amendment does not command any such desirable judicial participation.)

(2) The judge must have an "oath" from New York officials. (The Fourth Amendment does not specify who must execute the oath it requires.)

(3) The oath must state "reasonably ground to believe that evidence of crime may be thus obtained," and the judge may examine the affiant and any other witnesses to make certain that this

369

is the case. (The Fourth Amendment requires a showing of "probable cause," but the Court does not dispute New York's assertion that "reasonable ground" and "probable cause" are the same. The Amendment does not specify, as the New York statute does, a procedure by which the judge may "satisfy himself" of the existence of probable cause.)

(4) The "person or persons whose communications, conversations or discussions are to be overheard or recorded and the purpose thereof" must be particularly described. (In the case of conversation it would seem impossible to require a more particular description than this. Tangible things in existence at the time a warrant for their seizure is issued could be more particularly described, but the only way to describe future conversations is by a description of the anticipated subject matter of the conversation. When the "purpose" of the eavesdropping is stated, the subject of the conversation sought to be seized is readily recognizable. Nothing more was required in *Osborn;* nothing more should be required here.)

(5) The eavesdrop order must be limited in time to no more than two months. (The Fourth Amendment merely requires that the place to be searched be described. It does not require the warrant to limit the time of a search, and it imposes no limit, other than that of reasonableness, on the dimensions of the place to be searched.)

Thus, it seems impossible for the Court to condemn this statute on the ground that it lacks "adequate judicial supervision or protective procedures." Rather, the only way the Court can invalidate it is to find it lacking in some of the safeguards which the Court today fashions without any reference to the language of the Fourth Amendment whatsoever. In fact, from the deficiencies the Court finds in the New York statute, it seems that the Court would be compelled to strike down a state statute which merely tracked verbatim the language of the Fourth Amendment itself. First, the Court thinks the affidavits or the orders must particularize the crime being committed. The Fourth Amendment's particularity requirement relates to the place searched and the thing seized, not to the crime being committed. Second, the Court holds that two months for an eavesdrop order to be outstanding is too long. There are, however, no time limits of any kind in the Fourth Amendment other than the notion that a search should not last longer than reasonably necessary to search the place described in the warrant, and the extent of that place may also be limited by the concept of reasonableness. The Court does not explain why two months, regardless of the circumstances, is *per se* an unreasonable length of time to accomplish a verbal search. Third, the Court finds the statute deficient in not providing for a termination of the eavesdrop once the object is obtained and in not providing for a return of the warrant at that time. Where in the Fourth Amendment does the Court think it possible to find these requirements? Finally, the Court makes the fantastic suggestion that the eavesdropper must give notice to the person whose conversation is to be overheard or that the eavesdropper must show "exigent circumstances" before he can perform his eavesdrop without consent. Now, if never before, the Court's purpose is clear: it is determined to ban all eavesdropping. As the Court recognizes, eavesdropping "necessarily . . . depends on secrecy." Since secrecy is an essential, indeed a definitional, element of eavesdropping, when the Court says there shall be no eavesdropping without notice, the Court means to inform the Nation there shall be no eavesdropping—period.

It should now be clear that in order to strike down the New York law the Court has been compelled to rewrite completely the Fourth Amendment. By substituting the word "privacy" for the language of the first clause of the Amendment, the Court expands the scope of the Amendment to include oral conversations; then by applying the literal particularity requirements of the second clause without adjustment for the Court's expansion of the Amendment's scope, the Court makes constitutional eavesdropping improbable; and finally, by inventing requirements found in neither clause—requirements with which neither New York nor any other State can possibly comply—the Court makes such eavesdropping impossible. If the Fourth Amendment does not ban all searches and seizures, I do not see how it can possibly ban all eavesdrops.

VI.

As I see it, the differences between the Court and me in this case rest on different basic beliefs as to our duty in interpreting the Constitution. This basic charter of our Government was written in few words to define governmental powers generally on the one hand and to define governmental limitations on the other. I believe it is the Court's duty to interpret these grants and limitations so as to carry out as nearly as possible the original intent of the Framers. But I do not believe that it is our duty to go further than the Framers did on the theory that the judges are charged with responsibility for keeping the Constitution "up to date." Of course, where the Constitution has stated a broad purpose to be accomplished under any circumstances, we must consider that modern science has made it necessary to use new means in accomplishing the Framers' goal. A good illustration of this is the Commerce Clause which gives Congress power to regulate commerce between the States however it may be carried on, whether by ox wagons or jet planes. But the Fourth Amendment gives no hint that it was designed to put an end to the age-old practice of using eavesdropping to combat crime. If changes in that Amendment are necessary, due to contemporary human reaction to technological advances, I think those changes should be accomplished by amendments, as the Constitution itself provides.

Then again, a constitution like ours is not designed to be a full code of laws as some of our States and some foreign countries have made theirs. And if constitutional provisions require new rules and sanctions to make them as fully effective as might be desired, my belief is that calls for action, not by us, but by Congress or state legislatures, vested with powers to choose between conflicting policies. Here, for illustration, there are widely diverging views about eavesdropping. Some would make it a crime, barring it absolutely and in all events; others would bar it except in searching for evidence in the field of "national security," whatever that means; still others would pass no law either authorizing or forbidding it, leaving it to follow its natural course. This is plainly the type of question that can and should be decided by legislative bodies, unless some constitutional provision *expressly* governs the matter, just as the Fifth Amendment *expressly* forbids enforced self-incrimination. There is no such express prohibition in the Fourth Amendment nor can one be implied. The Fourth Amendment can only be made to prohibit or to regulate eavesdropping by taking away some of its words and by adding others.

Both the States and the National Government are at present confronted with a crime problem that threatens the peace, order, and tranquility of the people. There are, as I have pointed out, some constitutional commands that leave no room for doubt—certain procedures must be followed by courts regardless of how much more difficult they make it to convict and punish for crime. These commands we should enforce firmly and to the letter. But my objection to what the Court does today is the picking out of a broad general provision against unreasonable searches and seizures and the erecting out of it a constitutional obstacle against electronic eavesdropping that makes it impossible for lawmakers to overcome. Honest men may rightly differ on the potential dangers or benefits inherent in electronic eavesdropping and wiretapping. See *Lopez* v. *United States, supra.* But that is the very reason that legislatures, like New York's, should be left free to pass laws about the subject, rather than be told that the Constitution forbids it on grounds no more forceful than the Court has been able to muster in this case.

Mr. Justice Harlan, dissenting.

The Court in recent years has more and more taken to itself sole responsibility for setting the pattern of criminal law enforcement throughout the country. Time-honored distinctions between the constitutional protections afforded against federal authority by the Bill of Rights and those provided against state action by the Fourteenth Amendment have been obliterated, thus increasingly subjecting state criminal law enforcement policies to oversight by this Court. See, e. g., *Mapp* v. *Ohio,* 367 U. S. 643; *Ker* v. *California,* 374 U. S. 23; *Malloy* v. *Hogan,* 378 U. S. 1; *Murphy* v. *Waterfront Commission,* 378 U. S. 52. Newly contrived constitutional rights have been established without any apparent concern for the empirical process that goes with legislative reform. See, e. g., *Miranda* v. *Arizona,* 384 U. S. 436. And overlying the particular decisions to which this course has given rise is the fact that, short of future action by this Court, their impact can only be undone or modified by the slow and uncertain process of constitutional amendment.

Today's decision is in this mold. Despite the fact that the use of electronic eavesdropping devices as instruments of criminal law enforcement is currently being comprehensively addressed by the Congress and various other bodies in the country, the Court has chosen, quite unnecessarily, to decide this case in a manner which will seriously restrict, if not entirely thwart, such efforts, and will freeze further progress in this field, except as the Court may itself act or a constitutional amendment may set things right.

In my opinion what the Court is doing is very wrong, and I must respectfully dissent.

I.

I am, at the outset, divided from the majority by the way in which it has determined to approach the case. Without pausing to explain or to justify its reasoning, it has undertaken both to circumvent rules which have hitherto governed the presentation of constitutional issues to this Court, and to disregard the construction consistently attributed to a state statute by the State's own courts. Each of these omissions is, in my opinion, most unfortunate.

The Court declares, without further explanation, that since petitioner was "affected" by § 813-a, he may challenge its validity on its face. Nothing in the cases of this Court supports this wholly ambiguous standard; the Court until now has, in recognition of the intense difficulties so wide a rule might create for the orderly adjudication of constitutional issues, limited the situations in which state statutes may be challenged on their face. There is no reason here, apart from the momentary conveniences of this case, to abandon those limitations: none of the circumstances which have before properly been thought to warrant challenges of statutes on their face is present, cf. *Thornhill* v. *Alabama*, 310 U.S. 88, 98, and no justification for additional exceptions has been offered. See generally *United States* v. *National Dairy Products Corp.*, 372 U. S. 29, 36; *Aptheker* v. *Secretary of State*, 378 U. S. 500, 521 (dissenting opinion). Petitioner's rights, and those of others similarly situated, can be fully vindicated through the adjudication of the consistency with the Fourteenth Amendment of each eavesdropping order.

If the statute is to be assessed on its face, the Court should at least adhere to the principle that, for purposes of assessing the validity under the Constitution of a state statute, the construction given the statute by the State's courts is conclusive of its scope and meaning. *Fox* v. *Washington*, 236 U. S. 273; *Winters* v. *New York*, 333 U. S. 507; *Poulos* v. *New Hampshire*, 345 U. S. 395. This principle is ultimately a consequence of the differences in function of the state and federal judicial systems. The strength with which it has hitherto been held may be estimated in part by the frequency with which the Court has in the past declined to adjudicate issues, often of great practical and constitutional importance, until the state courts "have been afforded a reasonable opportunity to pass upon them." *Harrison* v. *NAACP*, 360 U. S. 167, 176. See, *e. g.*, *Railroad Comm'n* v. *Pullman Co.*, 312 U.S. 496; *Spector Motor Service, Inc.* v. *McLaughlin*, 323 U. S. 101; *Shipman* v. *DuPre*, 339 U. S. 321; *Albertson* v. *Millard*, 345 U. S. 242; *Government Employees* v. *Windsor*, 353 U. S. 364.

The Court today entirely disregards this principle. In its haste to give force to its distaste for eavesdropping, it has apparently resolved that no attention need be given to the construction of § 813-a adopted by the state courts. Apart from a brief and partial acknowledgment, spurred by petitioner's concession, that the state cases might warrant exploration, the Court has been content simply to compare the terms of the statute with the provisions of the Fourth Amendment; upon discovery that their words differ, it has concluded that the statute is constitutionally impermissible. In sharp contrast, when confronted by Fourth Amendment issues under a federal statute which did not, and does not now, reproduce *ipsissimis verbis* the Fourth Amendment, 26 U. S. C. § 7607 (2), the Court readily concluded, upon the authority of cases in the courts of appeals, that the statute effectively embodied the Amendment's requirements. *Draper* v. *United States*, 358 U. S. 307, 310 n. And the Court, without the assistance even of state authorities, reached an identical conclusion as to a similar state statute in *Ker* v. *California*, 374 U. S. 23, 36 n. The circumstances of the present case do not come even within the narrow exceptions to the rule that the Court ordinarily awaits a state court's construction before adjudicating the validity of a state statute. Cf. *Dombrowski* v. *Pfister*, 380 U.S. 479; *Baggett* v. *Bullitt*, 377 U.S. 360. The Court has shown no justification for its disregard of existing and pertinent state authorities.

II.

The Court's precipitate neglect of the New York cases is the more obviously regrettable when their terms are examined, for they make quite plain that the state courts have fully recognized the applicability of the relevant federal constitutional requirements, and that they have construed § 813-a in conformity with those requirements. Opinions of the state courts repeatedly suggest that the "reasonable grounds" prescribed by the section are understood to be synonymous with the "probable cause" demanded by the Fourth and Fourteenth Amendments. *People* v. *Cohen*, 42 Misc. 2d 403, 404, 248 N. Y. S. 2d 339, 341; *People* v. *Grossman*, 45 Misc. 2d 557, 568, 257 N. Y. S. 2d 266, 277; *People* v. *Beshany*, 43 Misc. 2d 521, 525, 252 N. Y. S. 2d 110, 115. The terms are frequently employed interchangeably, without the least suggestion of any shadings of meaning. See, *e. g.*, *People* v. *Rogers*, 46 Misc. 2d 860, 863, 261 N. Y. S. 2d 152, 155; *People* v. *McDonough*, 51 Misc. 2d 1065, 1069, 275 N. Y. S. 2d 8, 12. Further, a lower state court has stated quite specifically that "the same standards, at the least, must be applied" to orders under § 813-a as to warrants for the search and seizure of tangible objects. *People* v. *Cohen, supra*, at 407–408, 248 N. Y. S. 2d, at 344. Indeed, the court went on to say that the standards "should be much more stringent than those applied to search warrants." *Id.*, at 408, 248 N. Y. S. 2d, at 344. Compare *Siegel* v. *People*, 16 N. Y. 2d 330, 332, 213 N. E. 2d 682, 683. The court in *Cohen* was concerned with a wiretap order, but the order had been issued under § 813-a, and there was no suggestion there or elsewhere that eavesdropping orders should be differently treated. New York's statutory requirements for search warrants, it must be emphasized, are virtually a literal reiteration of the terms of the Fourth Amendment. N. Y. Code Crim. Proc. § 793. If the Court wished a precise invocation of the terms of the Fourth Amendment, it had only to examine the pertinent state authorities.

There is still additional evidence that the State fully recognizes the applicability to eavesdropping orders of the Fourth Amendment's constraints. The Legislature of New York adopted in 1962 comprehensive restrictions upon the use of eavesdropped information obtained without a prior § 813-a order. N. Y. Civ. Prac. § 4506.

The restrictions were expected and intended to give full force to the mandate of the opinion for this Court in *Mapp* v. *Ohio,* 367 U. S. 643. See 2 McKinney's Session Laws of New York 3677 (1962); New York State Legislative Annual 16 (1962). If it was then supposed that information obtained without a prior § 813-a order must, as a consequence of *Mapp,* be excluded from evidence, but that evidence obtained with a § 813-a order need not be excluded, it can only have been assumed that the requirements applicable to the issuance of § 813-a orders were entirely consistent with the demands of the Fourth and Fourteenth Amendments. The legislature recognized the "hiatus" in its law created by *Mapp,* and wished to set its own "house . . . in order." New York State Legislative Annual, *supra,* at 18. It plainly understood that the Amendments were applicable, and intended to adhere fully to their requirements.

New York's permissive eavesdropping statute must, for purposes of assessing its constitutional validity on its face, be read "as though" this judicial gloss had been "written into" it. *Poulos* v. *New Hampshire, supra,* at 402. I can only conclude that, so read, the statute incorporates as limitations upon its employment the requirements of the Fourth Amendment.

III.

The Court has frequently observed that the Fourth Amendment's two clauses impose separate, although related, limitations upon searches and seizures; the first "is general and forbids every search that is unreasonable," *Go-Bart Co.* v. *United States,* 282 U. S. 344, 357; the second places a number of specific constraints upon the issuance and character of warrants. It would be inappropriate and fruitless to undertake now to set the perimeters of "reasonableness" with respect to eavesdropping orders in general; any limitations, for example, necessary upon the period over which eavesdropping may be conducted, or upon the use of intercepted information unconnected with the offenses for which the eavesdropping order was first issued, should properly be developed only through a case-by-case examination of the pertinent questions. It suffices here to emphasize that, in my view, electronic eavesdropping, *as such* or as it is permitted by this statute, is not an unreasonable search and seizure.

At the least, reasonableness surely implies that this Court must not constrain in any grudging fashion the development of procedures, consistent with the Amendment's essential purposes, by which methods of search and seizure unknown in 1789 may be appropriately controlled. It is instead obliged to permit, and indeed even to encourage, serious efforts to approach constructively the difficult problems created by electronic eavesdropping. In this situation, the Court should recognize and give weight to the State's careful efforts to restrict the excessive or unauthorized employment of these devices. New York has provided that no use may be made of eavesdropping devices without a prior court order, and that such an order is obtainable only upon the application of state prosecutorial authorities or of policemen of suitable seniority. N. Y. Code Crim. Proc. § 813-a. Eavesdropping conducted without an order is punishable by imprisonment for as much as two years. N. Y. Pen. Law §§ 738, 740. Information obtained through impermissible eavesdropping may not be employed for any purpose in any civil or criminal action, proceeding, or hearing, except in the criminal prosecution of the unauthorized eavesdropper himself. N. Y. Civ. Prac. § 4506. These restrictions are calculated to prevent the "unbridled,"[1] "unauthorized,"[2] and "indiscriminate"[3] electronic searches and seizures which members of this Court have frequently condemned. Surely the State's efforts warrant at least a careful, and even sympathetic, examination of the fashion in which the state courts have construed these provisions, and in which they have applied them to the situation before us. I cannot, in any event, agree that the Fourth Amendment can properly be taken as a roadblock to the use, within appropriate limits, of law enforcement techniques necessary to keep abreast of modern-day criminal activity. The importance of these devices as a tool of effective law enforcement is impressively attested by the data marshalled in my Brother WHITE's dissenting opinion. *Post*, p. 107.

IV.

I turn to what properly is the central issue in this case: the validity under the Warrants Clause of the Fourth Amendment of the eavesdropping order under which the recordings employed at petitioner's trial were obtained. It is essential first to set out certain of the pertinent facts.

The disputed recordings were made under the authority of a § 813-a order, dated June 12, 1962, permitting the installation of an eavesdropping device in the business office of one Harry Steinman; the order, in turn, was, so far as this record shows, issued solely upon the basis of information contained in affidavits submitted to the issuing judge by two assistant district attorneys. The first affidavit, signed by Assistant District Attorney Goldstein, indicated

---

[1] *Hoffa* v. *United States*, 385 U. S. 293, 317 (dissenting opinion).

[2] *Silverman* v. *United States*, 365 U.S. 505, 510.

[3] *Lopez* v. *United States*, 373 U.S. 427, 441 (opinion concurring in result).

that the Rackets Bureau of the District Attorney's Office of New York County was then conducting an investigation of alleged corruption in the State Liquor Authority, and that the Bureau had received information that persons desiring to obtain or retain liquor licenses were obliged to pay large sums to officials of the Authority. It described the methods by which the bribe money was transmitted through certain attorneys to the officials. The affidavit asserted that one Harry Neyer, a former employee of the Authority, served as a "conduit." It indicated that evidence had been obtained "over a duly authorized eavesdropping device installed in the office of the aforesaid Harry Neyer," that conferences "relative to the payment of unlawful fees" occurred in Steinman's office. The number and street address of the office were provided. The affidavit specified that the "evidence indicates that the said Harry Steinman has agreed to pay, through the aforesaid Harry Neyer, $30,000" in order to secure a license for the Palladium Ballroom, an establishment within New York City. The Palladium, it was noted, had been the subject of hearings before the Authority "because of narcotic arrests therein." On the basis of this information, the affidavit sought an order to install a recording device in Steinman's business office.

The second affidavit, signed by Assistant District Attorney Scotti, averred that Scotti, as the Chief of the Bureau to which Goldstein was assigned, had read Goldstein's affidavit, and had concluded that the order might properly issue under § 813–a.

The order as issued permitted the recording of "any and all conversations, communications and discussions" in Steinman's business office for a period of 60 days.

The central objections mounted to this order by petitioner, and repeated as to the statute itself by the Court, are three: first, that it fails to specify with adequate particularity the conversations to be seized; second, that it permits a general and indiscriminate search and seizure; and third, that the order was issued without a showing of probable cause.[4]

Each of the first two objections depends principally upon a problem of definition: the meaning in this context of the constitutional distinction between "search" and "seizure." If listening alone completes a "seizure," it would be virtually impossible for state author-

---

[4] Two of petitioner's other contentions are plainly foreclosed by recent opinions of this Court. His contention that eavesdropping unavoidably infringes the rule forbidding the seizure of "mere evidence" is precluded by *Warden* v. *Hayden*, 387 U.S. 294. His contention that eavesdropping violates his constitutional privilege against self-incrimination is answered by *Osborn* v. *United States*, 385 U. S. 323, and *Hoffa* v. *United States*, 385 U. S. 293.

ities at a probable cause hearing to describe with particularity
the seizures which would later be made during extended eavesdropping; correspondingly, seizures would unavoidably be made
which lacked any sufficient nexus with the offenses for which the
order was first issued. Cf. *Kremen* v. *United States,* 353 U.S. 346;
Warden v. *Hayden,* 387 U.S. 294. There is no need for present purposes to explore at length the question's subtleties; it suffices to
indicate that, in my view, conversations are not "seized" either by
eavesdropping alone, or by their recording so that they may later
be heard at the eavesdropper's convenience. Just as some exercise
of dominion, beyond mere perception, is necessary for the seizure
of tangibles, so some use of the conversation beyond the initial
listening process is required for the seizure of the spoken word.
Cf. *Lopez* v. *United States,* 373 U.S. 427, 459 (dissenting opinion) ;
United States v. *On Lee,* 193 F.2d 306, 313–314 (dissenting opinion) ; *District of Columbia* v. *Little,* 85 U.S. App. D. C. 242, 247,
178 F.2d 13, 18, affirmed on other grounds, 339 U.S. 1. With this
premise, I turn to these three objections.

The "particularity" demanded by the Fourth Amendment has
never been thought by this Court to be reducible "to formula";
Oklahoma Press Pub. Co. v. *Walling,* 327 U.S. 186, 209; it has instead been made plain that its measurement must take fully
into account the character both of the materials to be seized and
of the purposes of the seizures. Accordingly, where the materials
"are books, and the basis for their seizure is the ideas which they
contain," the most "scrupulous exactitude" is demanded in the warrant's description; *Stanford* v. *Texas,* 379 U.S. 476, 485; see also
Marcus v. *Search Warrant,* 367 U.S. 717; but where the special
problems associated with the First Amendment are not involved,
as they are not here, a more "reasonable particularity," *Brown* v.
United States, 276 U.S. 134, 143; *Consolidated Rendering Co.* v.
Vermont, 207 U.S. 541, 554, is permissible. The degree of particularity necessary is best measured by that requirement's purposes.
The central purpose of the particularity requirement is to leave
"nothing . . . to the discretion of the officer executing the warrant,"
Marron v. *United States,* 275 U.S. 192, 196, by describing the materials to be seized with precision sufficient to prevent "the seizure
of one thing under a warrant describing another." *Ibid.* The state
authorities are not compelled at the probable cause hearing to
wager, upon penalty of a subsequent reversal, that they can successfully predict each of the characteristics of the materials which
they will later seize, cf. *Consolidated Rendering Co.* v. *Vermont, supra,* at 554; such a demand would, by discouraging the use of the

judicial process, defeat the Amendment's central purpose. *United States* v. *Ventresca,* 380 U.S. 102, 108.

The materials to be seized are instead described with sufficient particularity if the warrant readily permits their identification both by those entrusted with the warrant's execution and by the court in any subsequent judicial proceeding. "It is," the Court has said with reference to the particularity of the place to be searched, "enough if the description is such that the officer . . . can with reasonable effort ascertain and identify" the warrant's objects. *Steele* v. *United States No. 1,* 267 U.S. 498, 503.

These standards must be equally applicable to the seizure of words, and, under them, this order did not lack the requisite particularity. The order here permitted the interception, or search, of any and all conversations occurring within the order's time limitations at the specified location; but this direction must be read in light of the terms of the affidavits, which, under § 813, form part of the authority for the eavesdropping. The affidavits make plain that, among the intercepted conversations, the police were authorized to seize only those "relative to the payment of unlawful fees necessary to obtain liquor licenses." These directions sufficed to provide a standard which left nothing in the choice of materials to be seized to the "whim," *Stanford* v. *Texas, supra,* at 485, of the state authorities. There could be no difficulty, either in the course of the search or in any subsequent judicial proceeding, in determining whether specific conversations were among those authorized for seizure by the order. The Fourth and Fourteenth Amendments do not demand more. Compare Kamisar, The Wiretapping-Eavesdropping Problem: A Professor's View, 44 Minn. L.Rev. 891, 913.

Nor was the order invalid because it permitted the search of any and all conversations occurring at the specified location; if the requisite papers have identified the materials to be seized with sufficient particularity, as they did here, and if the search was confined to an appropriate area, the order is not invalidated by the examination of all within that area reasonably necessary for discovery of the materials to be seized. I do not doubt that searches by eavesdrop must be confined in time precisely as the search for tangibles is confined in space, but the actual duration of the intrusion here, or for that matter the total period authorized by the order, was not, given the character of the offenses involved, excessive. All the disputed evidence was obtained within 13 days, scarcely unreasonable in light of an alleged conspiracy involving many individuals and a lengthy series of transactions.

The question therefore remains only whether, as petitioner suggests, the order was issued without an adequate showing of probable cause. The standards for the measurement of probable cause have often been explicated in the opinions of this Court; see, *e. g.*, *United States* v. *Ventresca,* 380 U.S. 102; its suffices now simply to emphasize that the information presented to the magistrate or commissioner must permit him to "judge for himself the persuasiveness of the facts relied on by a complaining officer." *Giordenello* v. *United States,* 357 U.S. 480, 486. The magistrate must "assess independently the probability" that the facts are as the complainant has alleged; *id.,* at 487; he may not "accept without question the complainant's mere conclusion." *Id.,* at 486.

As measured by the terms of the affidavits here, the issuing judge could properly have concluded that probable cause existed for the order. Unlike the situations in *Nathanson* v. *United States,* 290 U.S. 41, and *Giordenello* v. *United States, supra,* the judge was provided the evidence which supported the affiants' conclusions; he was not compelled to rely merely on their "affirmation of suspicion and belief," *Nathanson* v. *United States, supra,* at 46. Compare *Rugendorf* v. *United States,* 376 U.S. 528; *Aguilar* v. *Texas,* 378 U.S. 108. In my opinion, taking the Steinman affidavits on their face, the constitutional requirements of probable cause were fully satisfied.

V.

It is, however, plain that the Steinman order was issued principally upon the basis of evidence obtained under the authority of the Neyer order; absent the Neyer eavesdropped evidence, the Steinman affidavits consist entirely of conclusory assertions, and they would, in my judgment, be insufficient. It is, therefore, also necessary to examine the Neyer order.

The threshold issue is whether petitioner has standing to challenge the validity under the Constitution of the Neyer order. Standing to challenge the constitutional validity of a search and seizure has been an issue of some difficulty and uncertainty;[5] it has, nevertheless, hitherto been thought to hinge, not upon the use against the challenging party of evidence seized during the search, but instead upon whether the privacy of the challenging party's premises or person has been invaded. *Jones* v. *United States,* 362 U.S. 257; *Wong Sun* v. *United States,* 371 U.S. 471. These cases centered

---

[5] See, *e. g.,* Edwards, Standing to Suppress Unreasonably Seized Evidence, 47 Nw. U. L. Rev. 471; Comment, Standing to Object to an Unreasonable Search and Seizure, 34 U. Chi. L. Rev. 342; Recent Development, Search and Seizure: Admissibility of Illegally Acquired Evidence Against Third Parties, 66 Col. L. Rev. 400.

upon searches conducted by federal authorities and challenged under Fed. Rule Crim. Proc. 41(e), but there is no reason now to suppose that any different standard is required by the Fourteenth Amendment for searches conducted by state officials. See generally Maguire, Evidence of Guilt 215–216 (1959).

The record before us does not indicate with precision what information was obtained under the Neyer order, but it appears, and petitioner does not otherwise assert, that petitioner was never present in Neyer's office during the period in which eavesdropping was conducted. There is, moreover, no suggestion that petitioner had any property interest in the premises in which the eavesdropping device was installed. Apart from the use of evidence obtained under the Neyer order to justify issuance of the Steinman order, under which petitioner's privacy was assuredly invaded, petitioner is linked with activities under the Neyer order only by one fleeting and ambiguous reference in the record.

In a pretrial hearing conducted on a motion to suppress the Steinman recordings, counsel for the State briefly described the materials obtained under the Neyer order. Counsel indicated that "Mr. Neyer then has conversations with Mr. Steinman and other persons. In the course of some of these conversations, we have one-half of a telephone call, of several telephone calls between Mr. Neyer and a person he refers to on the telephone as Mr. Berger; and in the conversation with Mr. Berger, Mr. Neyer discusses also the obtaining of a liquor license for the Palladium and mentions the fact that this is going to be a big one."

Counsel for petitioner responded, shortly after, that "I take it . . . that none of the subject matter to which [counsel for the State] has just adverted is any part of this case . . . ." Counsel for the State responded:

"That's right, your Honor. I am not—I think evidence can be brought out during the trial that Berger, who Mr. Steinman, Mr. Neyer speaks to concerning the Palladium, is, in fact, the defendant Ralph Berger."

However oblique this invasion of petitioner's personal privacy might at first seem, it would entirely suffice, in my view, to afford petitioner standing to challenge the validity of the Neyer order. It is surely without significance in these circumstances that petitioner did not conduct the conversation from a position physically within the room in which the device was placed; the fortuitousness of his location can matter no more than if he had been present for a conference in Neyer's office, but had not spoken, or had been seated beyond the limits of the device's hearing. The central question should properly be whether his privacy has been violated by the search; it is enough for this purpose that he participated in a discussion into which the recording intruded. Standing should not, in any event, be made an insuperable barrier which unnecessarily deprives of an adequate remedy those whose rights have been abridged; to impose distinctions of excessive refinement upon the doctrine "would not comport with our justly proud claim of the procedural protections accorded to those charged with crime." *Jones v. United States, supra*, at 267. It would instead "permit a quibbling distinction to overturn a principle which was designed to protect a fundamental right." *United States v. Jeffers*, 342 U.S. 48, 52. I would conclude that, under the circumstances here, the recording of a portion of a telephone conversation to which petitioner was party would suffice to give him standing to challenge the validity under the Constitution of the Neyer order.[6]

Given petitioner's standing under federal law to challenge the validity of the Neyer order, I would conclude that such order was issued without an adequate showing of probable cause. It seems quite plain, from the facts described by the State, that at the moment the Neyer order was sought the Rackets Bureau indeed had ample information to justify the issuance of an eavesdropping order. Nonetheless, the affidavits presented at the Neyer hearing unaccountably contained only the most conclusory allegations of suspicion. The record before us is silent on whether additional information might have been orally presented to the issuing judge.[7] Under these circumstances, I am impelled to the view that the judge lacked sufficient information to permit him to assess the circumstances as a "neutral and detached magistrate," *Johnson v. United States*, 333 U.S. 10, 14, and accordingly that the Neyer order was impermissible.

VI.

It does not follow, however, that evidence obtained under the Neyer order could not properly have been employed to support issuance of the Steinman order. The basic question here is the scope of the exclusionary rule fashioned in *Weeks v. United States*, 232

---

[6] While on this record it cannot be said with entire assurance that the "Berger" mentioned in the Neyer eavesdropped conversation was this petitioner, I think it proper to proceed at this juncture on the basis that such is the case, leaving whatever questions of identity there may be to such state proceedings as, on the premises of this opinion, might subsequently eventuate in the state courts. See n. 8, *infra*.

[7] The only additional reference in the record possibly pertinent to the content of the Neyer hearing is a conclusory assertion by counsel for the State in argument on the motion to suppress that the State had shown its evidence to the issuing judge. The reference is obscure, but its context suggests strongly that counsel meant only that the Steinman affidavits were adequate for purposes of probable cause.

U.S. 383, and made applicable to state proceedings in *Mapp* v. *Ohio*, 367 U.S. 643. The Court determined in *Weeks* that the purposes of the Fourth Amendment could be fully vindicated only if materials seized in violation of its requirements were excluded from subsequent use against parties aggrieved by the seizure. Despite broader statements in certain of the cases, see, *e. g., Silverthorne Lumber Co.* v. *United States*, 251 U.S. 385, 392, the situations for which the *Weeks* rule was devised, and to which it has since been applied, have uniformly involved misconduct by police or prosecutorial authorities. The rule's purposes have thus been said to be both to discourage "disobedience to the Federal Constitution," *Mapp* v. *Ohio, supra,* at 657, and to avoid any possibility that the courts themselves might be "accomplices in the willful disobedience of a Constitution they are sworn to uphold." *Elkins* v. *United States,* 364 U.S. 206, 223. The Court has cautioned that the exclusionary rule was not intended to establish supervisory jurisdiction over the administration of state criminal justice, and that the States might still fashion "workable rules governing arrests, searches and seizures." *Ker* v. *California,* 374 U.S. 23, 34.

I find nothing in the terms or purposes of the rule which demands the invalidation, under the circumstances at issue here, of the Steinman order. The state authorities appeared, as the statute requires, before a judicial official, and held themselves ready to provide information to justify the issuance of an eavesdropping order. The necessary evidence was at hand, and there was apparently no reason for the State to have preferred that it not be given to the issuing judge. The Neyer order is thus invalid simply as a consequence of the judge's willingness to act upon substantially less information than the Fourteenth Amendment obliged him to demand; correspondingly, the only "misconduct" that could be charged against the prosecution consists entirely of its failure to press additional evidence upon him. If the exclusionary rule were to be applied in this and similar situations, praiseworthy efforts of law enforcement authorities would be seriously, and quite unnecessarily, hampered; the evidence lawfully obtained under a lengthy series of valid warrants might, for example, be lost by the haste of a single magistrate. The rule applied in that manner would not encourage police officers to adhere to the requirements of the Constitution; it would simply deprive the State of evidence it has sought in accordance with those requirements.

I would hold that where, as here, authorities have obtained a warrant in a judicial proceeding untainted by fraud, a second warrant issued on the authority of evidence gathered under the first is not invalidated by a subsequent finding that the first was issued without a showing of probable cause.

VII.

It follows that the Steinman order was, as a matter of constitutional requirement, validly issued, that the recordings obtained under it were properly admitted at petitioner's trial, and, accordingly, that his conviction must be affirmed.[8]

MR. JUSTICE WHITE, dissenting.

With all due respect, I dissent from the majority's decision which unjustifiably strikes down "on its face" a 1938 New York statute applied by state officials in securing petitioner's conviction. In addition, I find no violation of petitioner's constitutional rights and I would affirm.

I.

At petitioner's trial for conspiring to bribe the Chairman of the New York State Liquor Authority, the prosecution introduced tape recordings obtained through an eavesdrop of the office of Harry Steinman which had been authorized by court order pursuant to § 813-a, a N.Y. Code Crim. Proc. Since Berger was rightfully in Steinman's office when his conversations were recorded through the Steinman eavesdrop, he is entitled to have those recordings excluded at his trial if they were unconstitutionally obtained. *Jones* v. *United States,* 362 U.S. 257; *Silverman* v. *United States,* 365 U.S. 505. Petitioner vigorously argues that all judicially authorized eavesdropping violates Fourth Amendment rights, but his position is unsound.

Two of petitioner's theories are easily answered. First, surreptitious electronic recording of conversations among private persons, and introduction of the recording during a criminal trial, do not violate the Fifth Amendment's ban against compulsory self-incrimination because the conversations are not the product of any official compulsion. *Olmstead* v. *United States,* 277 U.S. 438; *Hoffa* v. *United States,* 385 U.S. 293; *Osborn* v. *United States,* 385 U.S. 323. Second, our decision in *Warden* v. *Hayden,* 387 U.S. 294, an-

---

[3] Whether N. Y. Civ. Prac. § 4506, as amended to take effect July 1, 1962, some 18 days after the issuance of the Steinman order, would be deemed, under the premises of this opinion, to render inadmissible at Berger's trial the evidence procured under it, is a matter for the state courts to decide. See *People* v. *Cohen,* 42 Misc. 2d 403, 408, 409, 248 N. Y. S. 2d 339, 344, 345; *People* v. *Beshany,* 43 Misc. 2d 521, 532, 252 N. Y. S. 2d 110, 121. Further state proceedings on that score would of course not be foreclosed under a disposition in accordance with this opinion.

swers petitioner's contention that eavesdropping under § 813–a constitutes an unlawful search for "mere evidence"; whatever the limits of the search and seizure power may be under the Fourth Amendment, the oral evidence of a furtive bribery conspiracy sought in the application for the Steinman eavesdrop order was within the scope of proper police investigation into suspected criminal activity.

Petitioner primarily argues that eavesdropping is invalid, even pursuant to court order or search warrant, because it constitutes a "general search" barred by the Fourth Amendment. Petitioner suggests that the search is inherently overbroad because the eavesdropper will overhear conversations which do not relate to criminal activity. But the same is true of almost all searches of private property which the Fourth Amendment permits. In searching for seizable matters, the police must necessarily see or hear, and comprehend, items which do not relate to the purpose of the search. That this occurs, however, does not render the search invalid, so long as it is authorized by a suitable search warrant and so long as the police, in executing that warrant, limit themselves to searching for items which may constitutionally be seized.[1] Thus, while I would agree with petitioner that individual searches of private property through surreptitious eavesdropping with a warrant must be carefully circumscribed to avoid excessive invasion of privacy and security, I cannot agree that all such intrusions are constitutionally impermissible general searches.

This case boils down, therefore, to the question of whether § 813–a was constitutionally applied in this case. At the outset, it is essential to note that the recordings of the Neyer office eavesdrop were not introduced at petitioner's trial, nor was petitioner present during this electronic surveillance, nor were any of petitioner's words recorded by that eavesdrop. The only links between the Neyer eavesdrop and petitioner's conviction are (a) that evidence secured from the Neyer recordings was used in the Steinman affidavits, which in turn led to the Steinman eavesdrop where petitioner's incriminating conversations were overheard; and (b) that the Neyer eavesdrop recorded what *may have been*[2] the Neyer

---

[1] Recording an innocent conversation is no more a "seizure" than occurs when the policeman personally overhears conversation while conducting a search with a warrant.

[2] Petitioner has not included a transcript of the Neyer recording in the record before this Court. In an oral statement during the hearing on petitioner's motion to suppress

eavesdrop evidence, the prosecutor stated:

"In the course of some of these conversations [recorded by the Neyer eavesdrop], we have one-half of a telephone call, of several telephone calls between Mr. Neyer and a person he refers to on the telephone as Mr. Berger; and in the conversation with Mr. Berger, Mr. Neyer

end of a telephone conversation between Neyer and Berger. In my opinion, it is clear that neither of these circumstances is enough to establish that Berger's Fourth Amendment interests were invaded by the eavesdrop in Neyer's office. *Wong Sun* v. *United States,* 371 U.S. 471; *Jones* v. *United States,* 362 U.S. 257. Thus, petitioner cannot secure reversal on the basis of the allegedly unconstitutional Neyer eavesdrop.

I turn to the circumstances surrounding the issuance of the one eavesdrop order which petitioner has "standing" to challenge. On June 11, 1962, Assistant District Attorney David Goldstein filed an affidavit before Judge Joseph Sarafit of the New York County Court of General Sessions requesting a court order under § 813-a authorizing the Steinman eavesdrop. Goldstein averred that the District Attorney's office was investigating alleged corruption in the State Liquor Authority, that the office had obtained evidence of a conspiracy between Authority officials and private attorneys to extort large illegal payments from liquor license applicants, that a "duly authorized eavesdropping device" had previously been installed in the office of Neyer who was suspected of acting as a conduit for the bribes, and that this device had obtained evidence "that conferences relative to the payment of unlawful fees necessary to obtain liquor licenses occur in the office of one Harry Steinman, located in Room 801 at 15 East 48th Street, in the County, City and State of New York." The affidavit went on to describe Steinman at length as a prospective liquor license applicant and to relate evidence of a specific payoff which Steinman was likely to make, through Neyer, in the immediate future. On the basis of these facts, the affidavit concluded that "there is reasonable ground to believe that evidence of crime may be obtained by overhearing and recording the conversations, communications and discussions that may take place in the office of Harry Steinman which is located in Room 801 at 15 East 48th Street," and requested an order authorizing an eavesdrop until August 11, 1962. An affidavit of Assistant District Attorney Alfred Scotti verified the information contained in the Goldstein affidavit. The record also indicates that the affidavits were supplemented by orally presenting to Judge Sarafite all of the evidence obtained from the Neyer eavesdrop. But assuming that the Steinman court order was issued on the af-

---

discusses also the obtaining of a liquor license for the Palladium and mentions the fact that this is going to be a big one." R., at 27. Petitioner made no argument, and offered no evidence, at the suppres-

sion hearing that the alleged Neyer-Berger phone conversation provided the State with evidence that was used to secure the Steinman eavesdrop order.

fidavits alone, I am confident that those affidavits are sufficient under the Fourth Amendment.

Goldstein's affidavit described with "particularity" what crime Goldstein believed was being committed; it requested authority to search one specific room; it described the principal object of the search—Steinman and his co-conspirators—and the specific conversations which the affiant hoped to seize; it gave a precise time limit to the search; and it told the judge the manner in which the affiant had acquired his information. Petitioner argues that the reliability of the Neyer eavesdrop information was not adequately verified in the Steinman affidavit. But the Neyer eavesdrop need not be explained in detail in an application to the very judge who had authorized it just two months previously. Judge Sarafite had every reason to conclude that the Neyer eavesdrop was a reliable basis for suspecting a criminal conspiracy (consisting as the recording did of admissions by Steinman and other co-conspirators) and that it was the source of the specific evidence recited in the Steinman affidavits. "[A]ffidavits for search warrants, such as the one involved here, must be tested and interpreted by magistrates and courts in a commonsense and realistic fashion," *United States* v. *Ventresca,* 380 U.S. 102, 108. I conclude that the Steinman affidavits fully satisfied the Fourth Amendment requirements of probable cause and particularity in the issuance of search warrants.

The Court, however, seems irresistibly determined to strike down the New York statute. The majority criticizes the *ex parte* nature of § 813–a court orders, the lack of a requirement that "exigent circumstances" be shown, and the fact that one court order authorizes "a series or a continuous surveillance." But where are such search warrant requirements to be found in the Fourth Amendment or in any prior case construing it? The Court appears intent upon creating out of whole cloth new constitutionally mandated warrant procedures carefully tailored to make eavesdrop warrants unobtainable. That is not a judicial function. The question here is whether *this* search complied with Fourth Amendment standards. There is no indication in this record that the District Attorney's office seized and used conversations not described in the Goldstein affidavit, nor that officials continued the search after the time when they had gathered the evidence which they sought. Given the constitutional adequacy of the Goldstein affidavit in terms of Fourth Amendment requirements of probable cause and particularity, I conclude that both the search and seizure in Steinman's office satisfied Fourth Amendment mandates. Regardless of how the Court would like eavesdropping legislation to read, our function ends in a state case with the determination of these questions.

II.

Unregulated use of electronic surveillance devices by law enforcement officials and by private parties poses a grave threat to the privacy and security of our citizens. As the majority recognizes, New York is one of a handful of States that have reacted to this threat by enacting legislation that limits official use of all such devices to situations where designated officers obtain judicial authorization to eavesdrop. Except in these States, there is a serious lack of comprehensive and sensible legislation in this field, a need that has been noted by many, including the President's prestigious Commission on Law Enforcement and Administration of Justice (the "Crime Commission") in its just-published reports.[3] Bills have been introduced at this session of Congress to fill this legislative gap, and extensive hearings are in progress before the Subcommittee on Administrative Practice and Procedure of the Senate Committee on the Judiciary, and before Subcommittee No. 5 of the House Committee on the Judiciary.

At least three positions have been presented at these hearings. Opponents of eavesdropping and wiretapping argue that they are so "odious" an invasion of privacy that they should never be tolerated. The Justice Department, in advocating the Administration's current position, asserts a more limited view; its bill would prohibit all wiretapping and eavesdropping by state and federal authorities except in cases involving the "national security," and in addition would ban judicial use of evidence gathered even in national security cases. S. 928 and H. R. 5386, 90th Cong., 1st Sess. Advocates of a third position, who include many New York law enforcement personnel and others, agree that official eavesdropping and wiretapping must be stringently controlled but argue that such methods are irreplaceable investigative tools which are needed for the enforcement of criminal laws and which can be adequately regulated through legislation such as New York's § 813–a.

The grant of certiorari in this case has been widely noted, and our decision can be expected to have a substantial impact on the current legislative consideration of these issues. Today's majority does not, in so many words, hold that all wiretapping and eaves-

---

[3] The portion of the Crime Commission's report dealing with wiretapping and eavesdropping is reproduced in Appendix A to this opinion. A more detailed explanation of why most Commission members favored legislation permitting controlled use of electronic surveillance for law enforcement purposes can be found in the Commission's Task Force Report on Organized Crime, cited *infra*.

dropping are constitutionally impermissible. But by transparent indirection it achieves practically the same result by striking down the New York statute and imposing a series of requirements for legalized electronic surveillance that will be almost impossible to satisfy.

In so doing, the Court ignores or discounts the need for wiretapping authority and incredibly suggests that there has been no breakdown of federal law enforcement despite the unavailability of a federal statute legalizing electronic surveillance. The Court thereby impliedly disagrees with the carefully documented reports of the Crime Commission which, contrary to the Court's intimations, underline the serious proportions of professional criminal activity in this country, the failure of current national and state efforts to eliminate it, and the need for a statute permitting carefully controlled official use of electronic surveillance, particularly in dealing with organized crime and official corruption. See Appendix A, *infra*; Report of the Crime Commission's Task Force on Organized Crime 17–19, 80, 91–113 (1967). How the Court can feel itself so much better qualified than the Commission, which spent months on its study, to assess the needs of law enforcement is beyond my comprehension. We have only just decided that reasonableness of a search under the Fourth Amendment must be determined by weighing the invasions of Fourth Amendment interests which wiretapping and eavesdropping entail against the public need justifying such invasions. *Camara* v. *Municipal Court*, 387 U.S. 523; *See* v. *City of Seattle*, 387 U.S. 541. In these terms, it would seem imperative that the Court at least deal with facts of the real world. This the Court utterly fails to do. In my view, its opinion is wholly unresponsive to the test of reasonableness under the Fourth Amendment.

The Court also seeks support in the fact that the Federal Government does not now condone electronic eavesdropping. But here the Court is treading on treacherous ground.[4] It is true that the Department of Justice has now disowned the relevant findings and recommendations of the Crime Commission, see Hearings on H. R. 5386 before Subcommittee No. 5 of the House Committee on the Judiciary, 90th Cong., 1st Sess., ser. 3, at 308 (1967) (hereafter cited as "House Hearings"), and that it has recommended to the Congress a bill which would impose broad prohibitions on wiretap-

---

[4] The Court should draw no support from the Solicitor General's confession of error in recent cases, for they involved surreptitious eavesdropping by federal officers without judicial authorization. Such searches are clearly invalid because they violate the Fourth Amendment's warrant requirements. *Silverman* v. *United States, supra.*

ping and eavesdropping. But although the Department's communication to the Congress speaks of "exercis[ing] the full reach of our constitutional powers to outlaw electronic eavesdropping on private conversations,"[5] the fact is, as I have already indicated, that the bill does nothing of the kind. Both H. R. 5386 and its counterpart in the Senate, S. 928, provide that the prohibitions in the bill shall not be deemed to apply to interceptions in national security cases. Apparently, under this legislation, the President without court order would be permitted to authorize wiretapping or eavesdropping "to protect the Nation against actual or potential attack or other hostile acts of a foreign power or any other serious threat to the security of the United States, or to protect national security information against foreign intelligence activities." H. R. 5386 and S. 928, § 3.

There are several interesting aspects to this proposed national security exemption in light of the Court's opinion. First, there is no limitation on the President's power to delegate his authority, and it seems likely that at least the Attorney General would exercise it. House Hearings, at 302. Second, the national security exception would reach cases like sabotage and investigations of organizations controlled by a foreign government. For example, wiretapping to prove an individual is a member of the Communist Party, it is said, would be permissible under the statute. House Hearings, at 292. Third, information from authorized surveillance in the national security area would not be admissible in evidence; to the contrary, the surveillance would apparently be for investigative and informational use only, not for use in a criminal prosecution and not authorized because of any belief or suspicion that a crime is being committed or is about to be committed. House Hearings, at 289. Fourth, the Department of Justice has recommended that the Congress not await this Court's decision in the case now before us because whether or not the Court upholds the New York statute the power of Congress to enact the proposed legislation would not be affected. House Hearings, at 308. But if electronic surveillance is a "general search," or if it must be circumscribed in the manner the Court now suggests, how can surreptitious electronic surveillance of a suspected Communist or a suspected saboteur escape the strictures of the Fourth Amendment? It seems obvious from the Department of Justice bill that the present Administration believes that there are some purposes and uses of electronic surveillance which do not involve violations of the Fourth

---

[5] Letter from the Acting Attorney General to the Speaker of the House of Representatives submitting the Administration's "Right of Privacy Act of 1967" (H. R. 5386), Feb. 8, 1967.

Amendment by the Executive Branch. Such being the case, even if the views of the Executive were to be the final answer in this case, the requirements imposed by the Court to constitutionalize wiretapping and eavesdropping are a far cry from the practice anticipated under the proposed federal legislation now before the Congress.

But I do not think the views of the Executive should be dispositive of the broader Fourth Amendment issues raised in this case. If the security of the National Government is a sufficient interest to render eavesdropping reasonable, on what tenable basis can a contrary conclusion be reached when a State asserts a purpose to prevent the corruption of its major officials, to protect the integrity of its fundamental processes, and to maintain itself as a viable institution? The serious threat which organized crime poses to our society has been frequently documented. The interrelation between organized crime and corruption of governmental officials is likewise well established,[6] and the enormous difficulty of eradicating both forms of social cancer is proved by the persistence of the problems if by nothing else. The Crime Commission has concluded that "only in New York have law enforcement officials been able to mount a relatively continuous and relatively successful attack on an organized crime problem," that "electronic surveillance techniques . . . have been *the* tools" making possible such an attack, and that practice under New York's § 813–a has achieved a proper balance between the interests of "privacy and justice." Task Force Report, at 95. And New York County District Attorney Frank S. Hogan, who has been on the job almost as long as any member of this Court, has said of the need for legislation similar to § 813–a:

"The judicially supervised system under which we operate has worked. It has served efficiently to protect the rights, liberties, property, and general welfare of the law-abiding members of our community. It has permitted us to undertake major investigations of organized crime. Without it, and I confine myself to top figures in the underworld, my own office would not have convicted Charles 'Lucky' Luciano, Jimmy Hines, Louis 'Lepke' Buchalter, Jacob 'Gurrah' Shapiro, Joseph 'Socks' Lanza, George Scalise, Frank Erick-

---

[6] "All available data indicate that organized crime flourishes only where it has corrupted local officials. As the scope and variety of organized crime's activities have expanded, its need to involve public officials at every level of local government has grown. And as government regulation expands into more and more areas of private and business activity, the power to corrupt likewise affords the corrupter more control over matters affecting the everyday life of each citizen." Task Force Report, at 6.

son, John 'Dio' Dioguardi, and Frank Carbo. Joseph 'Adonis' Doto, who was tried in New Jersey, was convicted and deported on evidence supplied by our office and obtained by assiduously following leads secured through wiretapping." Hearings on S. 2813 before the Senate Committee on the Judiciary, 87th Cong., 2d Sess., at 173 (1962).

To rebut such evidence of the reasonableness of regulated use of official eavesdropping, the Court presents only outdated statistics on the use of § 813–a in the organized crime and corruption arenas, the failure of the Congress thus far to enact similar legislation for federal law enforcement officials, and the blind hope that other "techniques and practices may well be developed that will operate just as speedily and certainly." None of this is even remotely responsive to the question whether the use of eavesdropping techniques to unveil the debilitating corruption involved in this case was reasonable under the Fourth Amendment. At best, the Court puts forth an apologetic and grossly inadequate justification for frustrating New York law enforcement by invalidating § 813–a.

In any event, I do not consider this case a proper vehicle for resolving all of these broad constitutional and legislative issues raised by the problem of official use of wiretapping and eavesdropping. I would hold only that electronic surveillance was a reasonable investigative tool to apply in uncovering corruption among high state officials, compare *Osborn* v. *United States*, 385 U.S. 323, that the § 813–a court procedure as used in this case satisfied the Fourth Amendment's search warrant requirements, and that New York officials limited themselves to a constitutionally permissible search and seizure of petitioner's private conversations in executing that court order. Therefore, I would affirm.

APPENDIX TO OPINION OF MR. JUSTICE WHITE.

Excerpt from "The Challenge of Crime in a Free Society," A Report by the President's Commission on Law Enforcement and Administration of Justice, at 200–203 (1967).

A NATIONAL STRATEGY AGAINST ORGANIZED CRIME

Law enforcement's way of fighting organized crime has been primitive compared to organized crime's way of operating. Law enforcement must use methods at least as efficient as organized crime's. The public and law enforcement must make a full-scale commitment to destroy the power of organized crime groups. The Commission's program indicates ways to implement that commitment.

PROOF OF CRIMINAL VIOLATION

The previous section has described the difficulties that law enforcement agencies meet in trying to prove the participation of organized crime family members in criminal acts. Although earlier studies indicated a need for new substantive criminal laws, the Commission believes that on the Federal level, and in most State jurisdictions where organized crime exists, the major problem relates to matters of proof rather than inadequacy of substantive criminal laws, as the latter—for the most part—are reasonably adequate to deal with organized crime activity. The laws of conspiracy have provided an effective substantive tool with which to confront the criminal groups. From a legal standpoint, organized crime continues to grow because of defects in the evidence-gathering process. Under present procedures, too few witnesses have been produced to prove the link between criminal group members and the illicit activities that they sponsor.

Grand Juries. A compulsory process is necessary to obtain essential testimony or material. This is most readily accomplished by an investigative grand jury or an alternate mechanism through which the attendance of witnesses and production of books and records can be ordered. Such grand juries must stay in session long enough to allow for the unusually long time required to build an organized crime case. The possibility of arbitrary termination of a grand jury by supervisory judges constitutes a danger to successful completion of an investigation.

The Commission recommends:

At least one investigative grand jury should be impaneled annually in each jurisdiction that has major organized crime activity.

If a grand jury shows the court that its business is unfinished at the end of a normal term, the court should extend that term a reasonable time in order to allow the grand jury to complete pending investigations. Judicial dismissal of grand juries with unfinished business should be appealable by the prosecutor and provision made for suspension of such dismissal orders during the appeal.

The automatic convening of these grand juries would force less than diligent investigators and prosecutors to explain their inaction. The grand jury should also have recourse when not satisfied with such explanations.

The Commission recommends:

The grand jury should have the statutory right of appeal to an appropriate executive official, such as an attorney general or governor, to replace local prosecutors or investigators with special counsel or special investigators appointed only in relation to mat-

394

ters that they or the grand jury deem appropriate for investigation.

When a grand jury terminates, it should be permitted by law to file public reports regarding organized crime conditions in the community.

Immunity. A general immunity statute as proposed in chapter 5 on the courts is essential in organized crime investigations and prosecutions. There is evidence to indicate that the availability of immunity can overcome the wall of silence that so often defeats the efforts of law enforcement to obtain live witnesses in organized crime cases. Since the activities of criminal groups involve such a broad scope of criminal violations, immunity provisions covering this breadth of illicit actions are necessary to secure the testimony of uncooperative or criminally involved witnesses. Once granted immunity from prosecution based upon their testimony, such witnesses must testify before the grand jury and at trial, or face jail for contempt of court.

Federal, State, and local coordination of immunity grants, and approval by the jurisdiction's chief law enforcement officer before immunity is granted, are crucial in organized crime investigations. Otherwise, without such coordination and approval, or through corruption of officials, one jurisdiction might grant immunity to someone about to be arrested or indicted in another jurisdiction.

The Commission recommends:

A general witness immunity statute should be enacted at Federal and State levels, providing immunity sufficiently broad to assure compulsion of testimony. Immunity should be granted only with the prior approval of the jurisdiction's chief prosecuting officer. Efforts to coordinate Federal, State, and local immunity grants should be made to prevent interference with existing investigations.

Perjury. Many prosecutors believe that the incidence of perjury is higher in organized crime cases than in routine criminal matters. Immunity can be an effective prosecutive weapon only if the immunized witness then testifies truthfully. The present special proof requirements in perjury cases, detailed in chapter 5, inhibit prosecutors from seeking perjury indictments and lead to much lower conviction rates for perjury than for other crimes. Lessening of rigid proof requirements in perjury prosecutions would strengthen the deterrent value of perjury laws and present a greater incentive for truthful testimony.

The Commission recommends:

Congress and the States should abolish the rigid two-witness and direct-evidence rules in perjury prosecutions, but retain the requirement of proving an intentional false statement.

WIRETAPPING AND EAVESDROPPING

In connection with the problems of securing evidence against organized crime, the Commission considered issues relating to electronic surveillance, including wiretapping and "bugging"—the secret installation of mechanical devices at specific locations to receive and transmit conversations.

Significance to Law Enforcement. The great majority of law enforcement officials believe that the evidence necessary to bring criminal sanctions to bear consistently on the higher echelons of organized crime will not be obtained without the aid of electronic surveillance techniques. They maintain these techniques are indispensable to develop adequate strategic intelligence concerning organized crime, to set up specific investigations, to develop witnesses, to corroborate their testimony, and to serve as substitutes for them—each a necessary step in the evidence-gathering process in organized crime investigations and prosecutions.

As previously noted, the organizational structure and operational methods employed by organized crime have created unique problems for law enforcement. High-ranking organized crime figures are protected by layers of insulation from direct participation in criminal acts, and a rigid code of discipline inhibits the development of informants against them. A soldier in a family can complete his entire crime career without ever associating directly with his boss. Thus, he is unable, even if willing, to link the boss directly to any criminal activity in which he may have engaged for their mutual benefit. Agents and employees of an organized crime family, even when granted immunity from prosecution, cannot implicate the highest level figures, since frequently they have neither spoken to, nor even seen them.

Members of the underworld, who have legitimate reason to fear that their meetings might be bugged or their telephones tapped, have continued to meet and to make relatively free use of the telephone—for communication is essential to the operation of any business enterprise. In legitimate business this is accomplished with written and oral exchanges. In organized crime enterprises, however, the possibility of loss or seizure of an incriminating document demands a minimum of written communication. Because of the varied character of organized criminal enterprises, the large numbers of persons employed in them, and frequently the distances separating elements of the organization, the telephone remains an essential vehicle for communication. While discussions of business matters are held on a face-to-face basis whenever possible, they are never conducted in the presence of strangers. Thus, the content of these conversations, including the planning of new illegal activity, and transmission of policy decisions or operating instructions for existing enterprises, cannot be detected. The extreme scrutiny to which potential members are subjected and the necessity for them to engage in criminal activity have precluded law enforcement infiltration of organized crime groups.

District Attorney Frank S. Hogan, whose New York County office has been acknowledged for over 27 years as one of the country's most outstanding, has testified that electronic surveillance is:

the single most valuable weapon in law enforcement's fight against organized crime . . . It has permitted us to undertake major investigations of organized crime. Without it, and I confine myself to top figures in the underworld, my own office could not have convicted Charles "Lucky" Luciano, Jimmy Hines, Louis "Lepke" Buchalter, Jacob "Gurrah" Shapiro, Joseph "Socks" Lanza, George Scalise, Frank Erickson, John "Dio" Dioguardi, and Frank Carbo . . .

Over the years New York has faced one of the Nation's most aggravated organized crime problems. Only in New York have law enforcement officials achieved some level of continuous success in bringing prosecutions against organized crime. For over 20 years, New York has authorized wiretapping on court order. Since 1957, bugging has been similarly authorized. Wiretapping was the mainstay of the New York attack against organized crime until Federal court decisions intervened. Recently chief reliance in some offices has been placed on bugging, where the information is to be used in court. Law enforcement officials believe that the successes achieved in some parts of the State are attributable primarily to a combination of dedicated and competent personnel and adequate legal tools; and that the failure to do more in New York has resulted primarily from the failure to commit additional resources of time and men. The debilitating effect of corruption, political influence, and incompetence, underscored by the New York State Commission of Investigation, must also be noted.

In New York at one time, Court supervision of law enforcement's use of electronic surveillance was sometimes perfunctory, but the picture has changed substantially under the impact of pretrial adversary hearings on motions to suppress electronically seized evidence. Fifteen years ago there was evidence of abuse by low-rank policemen. Legislative and administrative controls, however, have apparently been successful in curtailing its incidence.

The Threat to Privacy. In a democratic society privacy of communication is essential if citizens are to think and act creatively and constructively. Fear or suspicion that one's speech is being monitored by a stranger, even without the reality of such activity, can have a seriously inhibiting effect upon the willingness to voice critical and constructive ideas. When dissent from the popular view is discouraged, intellectual controversy is smothered, the process for testing new concepts and ideas is hindered and desirable change is slowed. External restraints, of which electronic surveillance is but one possibility, are thus repugnant to citizens of such a society.

Today, in addition to some law enforcement agents, numerous private persons are utilizing these techniques. They are employed to acquire evidence for domestic relations cases, to carry on industrial espionage and counter-espionage, to assist in preparing for civil litigation, and for personnel investigations, among others. Technological advances have produced remarkably sophisticated devices, of which the electronic cocktail olive is illustrative, and continuing price reductions have expanded their markets. Nor has man's ingenuity in the development of surveillance equipment been exhausted with the design and manufacture of electronic devices for wiretapping or for eavesdropping within buildings or vehicles. Parabolic microphones that pick up conversations held in the open at distances of hundreds of feet are available commercially, and some progress has been made toward utilizing the laser beam to pick up conversations within a room by focusing upon the glass of a convenient window. Progress in microminiaturizing electronic components has resulted in the production of equipment of extremely small size. Because it can detect what is said anywhere— not just on the telephone—bugging presents especially serious threats to privacy.

Detection of surveillance devices is difficult, particularly where an installation is accomplished by a skilled agent. Isolated instances where equipment is discovered in operation therefore do not adequately reflect the volume of such activity; the effectiveness of electronic surveillance depends in part upon investigators who do not discuss their activities. The current confusion over the legality of electronic surveillance compounds the assessment problem since many agents feel their conduct may be held unlawful and are unwilling to report their activities. It is presently impossible to estimate with any accuracy the volume of electronic surveillance conducted today. The Commission is impressed, however, with the opinions of knowledgeable persons that the incidence of electronic surveillance is already substantial and increasing at a rapid rate. *Present Law and Practice.* In 1928 the U. S. Supreme Court decided that evidence obtained by wiretapping a defendant's telephone at a point outside the defendant's premises was admissible in a Federal criminal prosecution. The Court found no unconstitutional search and seizure under the Fourth Amendment. Enactment of Section 605 of the Federal Communications Act in 1934 precluded interception and disclosure of wire communications. The Department of Justice has interpreted this section to permit interception so long as no disclosure of the content outside the Department is made. Thus, wiretapping may presently be conducted by a Federal agent, but the results may not be used in court. When police officers wiretap and disclose the information obtained, in accordance with State procedure, they are in violation of Federal Law.

Law enforcement experience with bugging has been much more recent and more limited than the use of the traditional wiretap. The legal situation with respect to bugging is also different. The regulation of the national telephone communication network falls within recognized national powers, while legislation attempting to authorize the placing of electronic equipment even under a warrant system would break new and uncharted ground. At the present time there is no Federal legislation explicitly dealing with bugging. Since the decision of the Supreme Court in *Silverman* v. *United States,* 365 U.S. 505 (1961), use of bugging equipment that involves an unauthorized physical entry into a constitutionally protected private area violates the Fourth Amendment, and evidence thus obtained is inadmissible. If eavesdropping is unaccompanied by such a trespass, or if the communication is recorded with the consent of one of the parties, no such prohibition applies.

The confusion that has arisen inhibits cooperation between State and Federal law enforcement agencies because of the fear that information secured in one investigation will legally pollute another. For example, in New York City prosecutors refuse to divulge the contents of wire communications intercepted pursuant to State court orders because of the Federal proscription but do utilize evidence obtained by bugging pursuant to court order. In other sections of New York State, however, prosecutors continue to introduce both wiretapping and eavesdropping evidence at trial.

Despite the clear Federal prohibition against disclosure of wiretap information no Federal prosecutions of State officers have been undertaken, although prosecutions of State officers under State laws have occurred.

One of the most serious consequences of the present state of the law is that private parties and some law enforcement officers are invading the privacy of many citizens without control from the courts and reasonable legislative standards. While the Federal prohibition is a partial deterrent against divulgence, it has no effect on interception, and the lack of prosecutive action against violators has substantially reduced respect for the law.

The present status of the law with respect to wiretapping and bugging is intolerable. It serves the interests neither of privacy nor of law enforcement. One way or the other, the present controversy with respect to electronic surveillance must be resolved.

The Commission recommends:

Congress should enact legislation dealing specifically with wiretapping and bugging.

All members of the Commission agree on the difficulty of striking the balance between law enforcement benefits from the use of electronic surveillance and the threat to privacy its use may entail. Further, striking this balance presents important constitutional questions now pending before the U. S. Supreme Court in *People* v. *Berger,* and any congressional action should await the outcome of that case.

All members of the Commission believe that if authority to employ these techniques is granted it must be granted only with stringent limitations. One form of detailed regulatory statute that has been suggested to the Commission is outlined in the appendix to the Commission's organized crime task force volume. All private use of electronic surveillance should be placed under rigid control, or it should be outlawed.

A majority of the members of the Commission believe that legislation should be enacted granting carefully circumscribed authority for electronic surveillance to law enforcement officers to the extent it may be consistent with the decision of the Supreme Court in *People* v. *Berger,* and, further, that the availability of such specific authority would significantly reduce the incentive for, and the incidence of, improper electronic surveillance.

The other members of the Commission have serious doubts about the desirability of such authority and believe that without the kind of searching inquiry that would result from further congressional consideration of electronic surveillance, particularly of the problems of bugging, there is insufficient basis to strike this balance against the interests of privacy.

Matters affecting the national security not involving criminal prosecution are outside the Commission's mandate, and nothing in this discussion is intended to affect the existing powers to protect that interest.

Katz v. United States*

This "electronic eavesdropping case" concerns the Federal Bureau of Investigation (F.B.I.) bugging a public telephone booth with the desire and ultimate goal of securing evidence against one Charles Katz. The F.B.I. possessed information that Katz was using a certain public phone for the purpose of transmitting gambling information, bets, etc. On this basis they bugged the telephone booth in question. An electronic device was hidden on top of the booth which permitted agents to overhear that portion of any conversation spoken by the person using the booth. As a result of statements made by Katz on the phone he was prosecuted for a statutory offense relating to the interstate transmission of gaming information.

At Katz's trial it was determined that the F.B.I. had not obtained a warrant which authorized the bugging. The agents testified that they only listened to the conversations of Katz and that once they had the information sought, the bugging was abandoned. Katz was convicted.

On review before the Supreme Court his conviction was reversed. In a seven to one decision, written by Mr. Justice Stewart, the Court held that the bugging of a telephone booth without a warrant is an unreasonable search and seizure. However, the Court made it explicit that it was not prohibiting the issuance of a search warrant for bugging purposes. Indeed the Court indicated that had a warrant been sought in this case a magistrate would have been more than justified in issuing one. The absolute necessity of obtaining a warrant in this area lies in the desirability of having an impartial party pass on the reasonableness of the proposed eavesdropping.

Implicit in the Court's decision are guidelines relative to when a magistrate may properly issue a warrant authorizing bugging. They are found in the language of the Court to the effect that had a warrant been sought by the F.B.I. in this case it would have been proper to issue one. These guidelines may be summarized as follows:

1. The magistrate must be properly notified of the need for such a search.

2. He must be specifically informed of the basis on which it is to proceed.

3. The surveillance must be narrowly circumscribed. The magistrate must be clearly apprized of the precise intrusion.

---

* 389 U.S. 347, 88 S.Ct. 507 (Dec. 18, 1967)

If this procedure is used, a magistrate may properly issue a warrant to permit bugging in an appropriate case.*

The Omnibus Crime Control and Safe Streets Act of 1968 was passed on June 19, 1968, some six months after the *Katz case*. Title III of that Act is entitled: "Wiretapping and Electronic Surveillance." The problems raised in *Katz* relative to the circumstances under which electronic surveillance is permissible are answered in this federal statute. It sets forth with exacting detail the circumstances under which court permission to conduct such a search may be obtained and the procedures for obtaining it. The statute is included in section C of this chapter which follows this case.

Text of Case

Petitioner was convicted under an indictment charging him with transmitting wagering information by telephone across state lines in violation of 18 U. S. C. § 1084. Evidence of petitioner's end of the conversations, overheard by FBI agents who had attached an electronic listening and recording device to the outside of the telephone booth from which the calls were made, was introduced at the trial. The Court of Appeals affirmed the conviction, finding that there was no Fourth Amendment violation since there was "no physical entrance into the area occupied by" petitioner.

Burton Marks and *Harvey A. Schneider* argued the cause and filed briefs for petitioner.

John S. Martin, Jr., argued the cause for the United States. With him on the brief were *Acting Solicitor General Spritzer, Assistant Attorney General Vinson* and *Beatrice Rosenberg*.

Mr. Justice Stewart delivered the opinion of the Court.

The petitioner was convicted in the District Court for the Southern District of California under an eight-count indictment charging him with transmitting wagering information by telephone from Los Angeles to Miami and Boston, in violation of a federal statute.[1] At

---

* The phrase "in an appropriate case" refers to the magistrate's agreement that *need* for the search exists. The mere notification by the law enforcement officials on this point is not enough. They must furnish the magistrate with information on which he can determine if need does in fact exist. He makes this determination by applying standards applicable to the issuance of a regular search warrant—a warrant to search a person, home, etc.

[1] 18 U. S. C. § 1084. That statute provides in pertinent part:

"(a) Whoever being engaged in the business of betting or wagering knowingly uses a wire communication facility for the transmission in interstate or foreign commerce of bets or wagers or information assisting in the placing of bets or wagers on any sporting event or contest, or for the transmission of a wire communication which entitles the recipient to receive money or credit as a result of bets or wagers, or for information assisting in the placing of bets or wagers, shall be fined not more than $10,000 or

trial the Government was permitted, over the petitioner's objection, to introduce evidence of the petitioner's end of telephone conversations, overheard by FBI agents who had attached an electronic listening and recording device to the outside of the public telephone booth from which he had placed his calls. In affirming his conviction, the Court of Appeals rejected the contention that the recordings had been obtained in violation of the Fourth Amendment, because "[t]here was no physical entrance into the area occupied by [the petitioner]."[2] We granted certiorari in order to consider the constitutional questions thus presented.[3]

The petitioner has phrased those questions as follows:

"A. Whether a public telephone booth is a constitutionally protected area so that evidence obtained by attaching an electronic listening recording device to the top of such a booth is obtained in violation of the right to privacy of the user of the booth.

"B. Whether physical penetration of a constitutionally protected area is necessary before a search and seizure can be said to be violative of the Fourth Amendment to the United States Constitution."

imprisoned not more than two years, or both.

"(b) Nothing in this section shall be construed to prevent the transmission in interstate or foreign commerce of information for use in news reporting of sporting events or contests, or for the transmission of information assisting in the placing of bets or wagers on a sporting event or contest from a State where betting on that sporting event or contest is legal into a State in which such betting is legal."

[2] 369 F.2d 130, 134.

[3] 386 U. S. 954. The petition for certiorari also challenged the validity of a warrant authorizing the search of the petitioner's premises. In light of our disposition of this case, we do not reach that issue.

We find no merit in the petitioner's further suggestion that his indictment must be dismissed. After his conviction was affirmed by the Court of Appeals, he testified before a federal grand jury concerning the charges involved here. Because he was compelled to testify pursuant to a grant of immunity, 48 Stat. 1096, as amended, 47 U. S. C. § 409(l), it is clear that the

fruit of his testimony cannot be used against him in any future trial. But the petitioner asks for more. He contends that his conviction must be vacated and the charges against him dismissed lest he be "subjected to [a] penalty . . . on account of [a] . . . matter . . . concerning which he [was] compelled . . . to testify . . . ." 47 U. S. C. § 409 (l). Frank v. United States, 347 F. 2d 486. We disagree. In relevant part, § 409 (l) substantially repeats the language of the Compulsory Testimony Act of 1893, 27 Stat. 443, 49 U. S. C. § 46, which was Congress' response to this Court's statement that an immunity statute can supplant the Fifth Amendment privilege against self-incrimination only if it affords adequate protection from future prosecution or conviction. Counselman v. Hitchcock, 142 U. S. 547, 585–586. The statutory provision here involved was designed to provide such protection, see Brown v. United States, 359 U. S. 41, 45–46, not to confer immunity from punishment pursuant to a prior prosecution and adjudication of guilt. Cf. Reina v. United States, 364 U. S. 507, 513–514.

We decline to adopt this formulation of the issues. In the first place, the correct solution of Fourth Amendment problems is not necessarily promoted by incantation of the phrase "constitutionally protected area." Secondly, the Fourth Amendment cannot be translated into a general constitutional "right to privacy." That Amendment protects individual privacy against certain kinds of governmental intrusion, but its protections go further, and often have nothing to do with privacy at all.[4] Other provisions of the Constitution protect personal privacy from other forms of governmental invasion.[5] But the protection of a person's *general* right to privacy—his right to be let alone by other people[6]—is, like the protection of his property and of his very life, left largely to the law of the individual States.[7]

Because of the misleading way the issues have been formulated, the parties have attached great significance to the characterization of the telephone booth from which the petitioner placed his calls. The petitioner has strenuously argued that the booth was a "constitutionally protected area." The Government has maintained with equal vigor that it was not.[8] But this effort to decide whether or not a given "area," viewed in the abstract, is "constitutionally pro-

---

[4] "The average man would very likely not have his feelings soothed any more by having his property seized openly than by having it seized privately and by stealth. . . . And a person can be just as much, if not more, irritated, annoyed and injured by an unceremonious public arrest by a policeman as he is by a seizure in the privacy of his office or home." *Griswold* v. *Connecticut*, 381 U. S. 479, 509 (dissenting opinion of MR. JUSTICE BLACK).

[5] The First Amendment, for example, imposes limitations upon governmental abridgment of "freedom to associate and privacy in one's associations." *NAACP* v. *Alabama*, 357 U. S. 449, 462. The Third Amendment's prohibition against the unconsented peacetime quartering of soldiers protects another aspect of privacy from governmental intrusion. To some extent, the Fifth Amendment too "reflects the Constitution's concern for . . . '. . . the right of each individual "to a private enclave where he may lead a private life." ' " *Tehan* v. *Shott*, 382 U. S. 406, 416. Virtually every governmental action inter-

feres with personal privacy to some degree. The question in each case is whether that interference violates a command of the United States Constitution.

[6] See Warren & Brandeis, The Right to Privacy, 4 Harv. L. Rev. 193 (1890).

[7] See, *e. g., Time, Inc.* v. *Hill*, 385 U. S. 374. Cf. *Breard* v. *Alexandria*, 341 U.S. 622; *Kovacs* v. *Cooper*, 336 U. S. 77.

[8] In support of their respective claims, the parties have compiled competing lists of "protected areas" for our consideration. It appears to be common ground that a private home is such an area, *Weeks* v. *United States*, 232 U. S. 383, but that an open field is not. *Hester* v. *United States*, 265 U.S. 57. Defending the inclusion of a telephone booth in his list the petitioner cites *United States* v. *Stone*, 232 F. Supp. 396, and *United States* v. *Madison*, 32 L. W. 2243 (D. C. Ct. Gen. Sess.). Urging that the telephone booth should be excluded, the Government finds support in *United States* v. *Borgese*, 235 F. Supp. 286.

tected" deflects attention from the problem presented by this case.[9] For the Fourth Amendment protects people, not places. What a person knowingly exposes to the public, even in his own home or office, is not a subject of Fourth Amendment protection. See *Lewis* v. *United States*, 385 U. S. 206, 210; *United States* v. *Lee*, 274 U. S. 559, 563. But what he seeks to preserve as private, even in an area accessible to the public, may be constitutionally protected. See *Rios* v. *United States*, 364 U. S. 253; *Ex parte Jackson*, 96 U. S. 727, 733.

The Government stresses the fact that the telephone booth from which the petitioner made his calls was constructed partly of glass, so that he was as visible after he entered it as he would have been if he had remained outside. But what he sought to exclude when he entered the booth was not the intruding eye—it was the uninvited ear. He did not shed his right to do so simply because he made his calls from a place where he might be seen. No less than an individual in a business office,[10] in a friend's apartment,[11] or in a taxicab,[12] a person in a telephone booth may rely upon the protection of the Fourth Amendment. One who occupies it, shuts the door behind him, and pays the toll that permits him to place a call is surely entitled to assume that the words he utters into the mouthpiece will not be broadcast to the world. To read the Constitution more narrowly is to ignore the vital role that the public telephone has come to play in private communication.

The Government contends, however, that the activities of its agents in this case should not be tested by Fourth Amendment requirements, for the surveillance technique they employed involved no physical penetration of the telephone booth from which the petitioner placed his calls. It is true that the absence of such penetration was at one time thought to foreclose further Fourth Amendment inquiry, *Olmstead* v. *United States*, 277 U. S. 438, 457, 464, 466; *Goldman* v. *United States*, 316 U. S. 129, 134–136, for that Amendment was thought to limit only searches and seizures of tangible property.[13] But "[t]he premise that property interests control the right of the Government to search and seize has been discredited." *Warden* v. *Hayden*, 387 U. S. 294, 304. Thus, although a

---

[9] It is true that this Court has occasionally described its conclusions in terms of "constitutionally protected areas," see, *e. g., Silverman* v. *United States*, 365 U.S. 505, 510, 512; *Lopez* v. *United States*, 373 U.S. 427, 438–439; *Berger* v. *New York*, 388 U.S. 41, 57, 59, but we have never suggested that this concept can serve as a talismanic solution to every Fourth Amendment problem.

[10] *Silverthorne Lumber Co.* v. *United States*, 251 U.S. 385.

[11] *Jones* v. *United States*, 362 U.S. 257.

[12] *Rios* v. *United States*, 364 U.S. 253.

[13] See *Olmstead* v. *United States*, 277 U.S. 438, 464–466. We do not deal in this case with the law of detention or arrest under the Fourth Amendment.

closely divided Court supposed in *Olmstead* that surveillance without any trespass and without the seizure of any material object fell outside the ambit of the Constitution, we have since departed from the narrow view on which that decision rested. Indeed, we have expressly held that the Fourth Amendment governs not only the seizure of tangible items, but extends as well to the recording of oral statements, overheard without any "technical trespass under . . . local property law." *Silverman* v. *United States*, 365 U.S. 505, 511. Once this much is acknowledged, and once it is recognized that the Fourth Amendment protects people—and not simply "areas"—against unreasonable searches and seizures, it becomes clear that the reach of that Amendment cannot turn upon the presence or absence of a physical intrusion into any given enclosure.

We conclude that the underpinnings of *Olmstead* and *Goldman* have been so eroded by our subsequent decisions that the "trespass" doctrine there enunciated can no longer be regarded as controlling. The Government's activities in electronically listening to and recording the petitioner's words violated the privacy upon which he justifiably relied while using the telephone booth and thus constituted a "search and seizure" within the meaning of the Fourth Amendment. The fact that the electronic device employed to achieve that end did not happen to penetrate the wall of the booth can have no constitutional significance.

The question remaining for decision, then, is whether the search and seizure conducted in this case complied with constitutional standards. In that regard, the Government's position is that its agents acted in an entirely defensible manner: They did not begin their electronic surveillance until investigation of the petitioner's activities had established a strong probability that he was using the telephone in question to transmit gambling information to persons in other States, in violation of federal law. Moreover, the surveillance was limited, both in scope and in duration, to the specific purpose of establishing the contents of the petitioner's unlawful telephonic communications. The agents confined their surveillance to the brief periods during which he used the telephone booth,[14] and they took great care to overhear only the conversations of the petitioner himself.[15]

---

[14] Based upon their previous visual observations of the petitioner, the agents correctly predicted that he would use the telephone booth for several minutes at approximately the same time each morning. The petitioner was subjected to electronic surveillance only during this predetermined period. Six recordings, averaging some three minutes each, were obtained and admitted in evidence. They preserved the petitioner's end of conversations concerning the placing of bets and the receipt of wagering information.

[15] On the single occasion when the statements of another person were

Accepting this account of the Government's actions as accurate, it is clear that this surveillance was so narrowly circumscribed that a duly authorized magistrate, properly notified of the need for such investigation, specifically informed of the basis on which it was to proceed, and clearly apprised of the precise intrusion it would entail, could constitutionally have authorized, with appropriate safeguards, the very limited search and seizure that the Government asserts in fact took place. Only last Term we sustained the validity of such an authorization, holding that, under sufficiently "precise and discriminate circumstances," a federal court may empower government agents to employ a concealed electronic device "for the narrow and particularized purpose of ascertaining the truth of the . . . allegations" of a "detailed factual affidavit alledging the commission of a specific criminal offense." *Osborn* v. *United States,* 385 U. S. 323, 329–330. Discussing that holding, the Court in *Berger* v. *New York,* 388 U. S. 41, said that "the order authorizing the use of the electronic device" in *Osborn* "afforded similar protections to those . . . of convential warrants authorizing the seizure of tangible evidence." Through those protections, "no greater invasion of privacy was permitted than was necessary under the circumstances." *Id.,* at 57.[16] Here, too, a similar judicial

---

inadvertently intercepted, the agents refrained from listening to them.

[16] Although the protections afforded the petitioner in *Osborn* were *"similar* . . . to those . . . of conventional warrants," they were not identical. A conventional warrant ordinarily serves to notify the suspect of an intended search. But if Osborn had been told in advance that federal officers intended to record his conversations, the point of making such recordings would obviously have been lost; the evidence in question could not have been obtained. In omitting any requirement of advance notice, the federal court that authorized electronic surveillance in *Osborn* simply recognized, as has this Court, that officers need not announce their purpose before conducting an otherwise authorized search if such an announcement would provoke the escape of the suspect or the destruction of critical evidence. See *Ker* v. *California,* 374 U.S. 23, 37–41.

Although some have thought that this "exception to the notice requirement where exigent circumstances are present," *id.,* at 39, should be deemed inapplicable where police enter a home before its occupants are aware that officers are present, *id.,* at 55–58 (opinion of MR. JUSTICE BRENNAN), the reasons for such a limitation have no bearing here. However true it may be that "[i]nnocent citizens should not suffer the shock, fright or embarrassment attendant upon an unannounced police intrusion," *id.,* at 57, and that "the requirement of awareness . . . serves to minimize the hazards of the officers' dangerous calling," *id.,* at 57–58, these considerations are not relevant to the problems presented by judicially authorized electronic surveillance.

Nor do the Federal Rules of Criminal Procedure impose an inflexible requirement of prior notice. Rule 41(d) does require federal officers to serve upon the per-order could have accommodated "the legitimate needs of law enforcement"[17] by authorizing the carefully limited use of electronic surveillance.

The Government urges that, because its agents relied upon the decisions in *Olmstead* and *Goldman,* and because they did no more here than they might properly have done with prior judicial sanction, we should retroactively validate their conduct. That we cannot do. It is apparent that the agents in this case acted with restraint. Yet the inescapable fact is that this restraint was imposed by the agents themselves, not by a judicial officer. They were not required, before commencing the search, to present their estimate of probable cause for detached scrutiny by a neutral magistrate. They were not compelled, during the conduct of the search itself, to observe precise limits established in advance by a specific court order. Nor were they directed, after the search had been completed, to notify the authorizing magistrate in detail of all that had been seized. In the absence of such safeguards, this Court has never sustained a search upon the sole ground that officers reasonably expected to find evidence of a particular crime and voluntarily confined their activities to the least intrusive means consistent with that end. Searches conducted without warrants have been held unlawful "notwithstanding facts unquestionably showing probable cause," *Agnello* v. *United States,* 269 U. S. 20, 33, for the Constitution requires "that the deliberate, impartial judgment of a judicial officer . . . be interposed between the citizen and the police . . . ." *Wong Sun* v. *United States,* 371 U. S. 471, 481–482. "Over and again this Court has emphasized that the mandate of the [Fourth] Amendment requires adherence to judicial processes," *United States* v. *Jeffers,* 342 U. S. 48, 51, and that searches conducted outside the judicial process, without prior approval by judge or magistrate, are *per se* unreasonable under the Fourth Amendment[18]—

son searched a copy of the warrant and a receipt describing the material obtained, but it does not invariably require that this be done before the search takes place. *Nordelli* v. *United States,* 24 F.2d 665, 666–667.

Thus the fact that the petitioner in *Osborn* was unaware that his words were being electronically transcribed did not prevent this Court from sustaining his conviction, and did not prevent the Court in *Berger* from reaching the conclusion that the use of the recording device sanctioned in *Osborn* was entirely lawful. 388 U.S. 41, 57.

[17] *Lopez* v. *United States,* 373 U.S. 427, 464 (dissenting opinion of MR. JUSTICE BRENNAN).

[18] See, *e. g., Jones* v. *United States,* 357 U.S. 493, 497–499; *Rios* v. *United States,* 364 U.S. 253, 261; *Chapman* v. *United States,* 365 U.S. 610, 613–615; *Stoner* v. *California,* 376 U.S. 483, 486–487.

subject only to a few specifically established and well-delineated exceptions.[19]

It is difficult to imagine how any of those exceptions could ever apply to the sort of search and seizure involved in this case. Even electronic surveillance substantially contemporaneous with an individual's arrest could hardly be deemed an "incident" of that arrest.[20] Nor could the use of electronic surveillance without prior authorization be justified on grounds of "hot pursuit."[21] And, of course, the very nature of electronic surveillance precludes its use pursuant to the suspect's consent.[22]

The Government does not question these basic principles. Rather, it urges the creation of a new exception to cover this case.[23] It argues that surveillance of a telephone booth should be exempted from the usual requirement of advance authorization by a magistrate upon a showing of probable cause. We cannot agree. Omission of such authorization

"bypasses the safeguards provided by an objective predetermination of probable cause, and substitutes instead the far less reliable procedure of an after-the-event justification for the . . . search, too likely to be subtly influenced by the familiar shortcomings of hindsight judgment." *Beck* v. *Ohio*, 379 U. S. 89, 96.

---

[19] See, e. g., *Carroll* v. *United States*, 267 U.S. 132, 153, 156; *McDonald* v. *United States*, 335 U.S. 451, 454–456; *Brinegar* v. *United States*, 338 U.S. 160, 174–177; *Cooper* v. *California*, 386 U.S. 58; *Warden* v. *Hayden*, 387 U.S. 294, 298–300.

[20] In *Agnello* v. *United States*, 269 U.S. 20, 30, the Court stated:
"The right without a search warrant contemporaneously to search persons lawfully arrested while committing crime and to search the place where the arrest is made in order to find and seize things connected with the crime as its fruits or as the means by which it was committed, as well as weapons and other things to effect an escape from custody, is not to be doubted." Whatever one's view of "the longstanding practice of searching for other proofs of guilt within the control of the accused found upon arrest," *United States* v. *Rabinowitz*, 339 U.S. 56, 61; cf. *id.*, at 71–79 (dissenting opinion of Mr. Justice Frankfurter), the concept of an "incidental" search cannot readily be extended to include sur-

reptitious surveillance of an individual either immediately before, or immediately after, his arrest.

[21] Although "[t]he Fourth Amendment does not require police officers to delay in the course of an investigation if to do so would gravely endanger their lives or the lives of others," *Warden* v. *Hayden*, 387 U.S. 294, 298–299, there seems little likelihood that electronic surveillance would be a realistic possibility in a situation so fraught with urgency.

[22] A search to which an individual consents meets Fourth Amendment requirements, *Zap* v. *United States*, 328 U.S. 624, but of course "the usefulness of electronic surveillance depends on lack of notice to the suspect." *Lopez* v. *United States*, 373 U.S. 427, 463 (dissenting opinion of MR. JUSTICE BRENNAN).

[23] Whether safeguards other than prior authorization by a magistrate would satisfy the Fourth Amendment in a situation involving the national security is a question not presented by this case.

And bypassing a neutral predetermination of the *scope* of a search leaves individuals secure from Fourth Amendment violations "only in the discretion of the police." *Id.,* at 97.

These considerations do not vanish when the search in question is transferred from the setting of a home, an office, or a hotel room to that of a telephone booth. Wherever a man may be, he is entitled to know that he will remain free from unreasonable searches and seizures. The government agents here ignored "the procedure of antecedent justification . . . that is central to the Fourth Amendment,"[24] a procedure that we hold to be a constitutional precondition of the kind of electronic surveillance involved in this case. Because the surveillance here failed to meet that condition, and because it led to the petitioner's conviction, the judgment must be reversed.

It is so ordered.

MR. JUSTICE MARSHALL took no part in the consideration or decision of this case.

MR. JUSTICE DOUGLAS, with whom MR. JUSTICE BRENNAN joins, concurring.

While I joined the opinion of the Court, I feel compelled to reply to the separate concurring opinion of my Brother WHITE, which I view as a wholly unwarranted green light for the Executive Branch to resort to electronic eavesdropping without a warrant in cases which the Executive Branch itself labels "national security" matters.

Neither the President nor the Attorney General is a magistrate. In matters where they believe national security may be involved they are not detached, disinterested, and neutral as a court or magistrate must be. Under the separation of powers created by the Constitution, the Executive Branch is not supposed to be neutral and disinterested. Rather it should vigorously investigate and prevent breaches of national security and prosecute those who violate the pertinent federal laws. The President and Attorney General are properly interested parties, cast in the role of adversary, in national security cases. They may even be the intended victims of subversive action. Since spies and saboteurs are as entitled to the protection of the Fourth Amendment as suspected gamblers like petitioner, I cannot agree that where spies and saboteurs are involved adequate protection of Fourth Amendment rights is assured when the President and Attorney General assume both the position of adversary-and-prosecutor and disinterested, neutral magistrate.

---

[24] See *Osborn* v. *United States,* 385 U.S. 323, 330.

There is, so far as I understand constitutional history, no distinction under the Fourth Amendment between types of crimes. Article III, § 3, gives "treason" a very narrow definition and puts restrictions on its proof. But the Fourth Amendment draws no lines between various substantive offenses. The arrests in cases of "hot pursuit" and the arrests on visible or other evidence of probable cause cut across the board and are not peculiar to any kind of crime.

I would respect the present lines of distinction and not improvise because a particular crime seems particularly heinous. When the Framers took that step, as they did with treason, the worst crime of all, they made their purpose manifest.

MR. JUSTICE HARLAN, concurring.

I join the opinion of the Court, which I read to hold only (a) that an enclosed telephone booth is an area where, like a home, *Weeks* v. *United States*, 232 U. S. 383, and unlike a field, *Hester* v. *United States*, 265 U. S. 57, a person has a constitutionally protected reasonable expectation of privacy; (b) that electronic as well as physical intrusion into a place that is in this sense private may constitute a violation of the Fourth Amendment; and (c) that the invasion of a constitutionally protected area by federal authorities is, as the Court has long held, presumptively unreasonable in the absence of a search warrant.

As the Court's opinion states, "the Fourth Amendment protects people, not places." The question, however, is what protection it affords to those people. Generally, as here, the answer to that question requires reference to a "place." My understanding of the rule that has emerged from prior decisions is that there is a twofold requirement, first that a person have exhibited an actual (subjective) expectation of privacy and, second, that the expectation be one that society is prepared to recognize as "reasonable." Thus a man's home is, for most purposes, a place where he expects privacy, but objects, activities, or statements that he exposes to the "plain view" of outsiders are not "protected" because no intention to keep them to himself has been exhibited. On the other hand, conversations in the open would not be protected against being overheard, for the expectation of privacy under the circumstances would be unreasonable. Cf. *Hester* v. *United States, supra*.

The critical fact in this case is that "[o]ne who occupies it, [a telephone booth] shuts the door behind him, and pays the toll that permits him to place a call is surely entitled to assume" that his conversation is not being intercepted. *Ante*, at 352. The point is not that the booth is "accessible to the public" at other times, *ante*, at 351, but that it is a temporarily private place whose momentary occupants' expectations of freedom from intrusion are recognized as reasonable. Cf. *Rios* v. *United States,* 364 U. S. 253.

In *Silverman* v. *United States,* 365 U. S. 505, we held that eavesdropping accomplished by means of an electronic device that penetrated the premises occupied by petitioner was a violation of the Fourth Amendment. That case established that interception of conversations reasonably intended to be private could constitute a "search and seizure," and that the examination or taking of physical property was not required. This view of the Fourth Amendment was followed in *Wong Sun* v. *United States,* 371 U. S. 471, at 485, and *Berger* v. *New York,* 388 U. S. 41, at 51. Also compare *Osborn* v. *United States,* 385 U. S. 323, at 327. In *Silverman* we found it unnecessary to re-examine *Goldman* v. *United States,* 316 U. S. 129, which had held that electronic surveillance accomplished without the physical penetration of petitioner's premises by a tangible object did not violate the Fourth Amendment. This case requires us to reconsider *Goldman,* and I agree that it should now be overruled.* Its limitation on Fourth Amendment protection is, in the present day, bad physics as well as bad law, for reasonable expectations of privacy may be defeated by electronic as well as physical invasion.

Finally, I do not read the Court's opinion to declare that no interception of a conversation one-half of which occurs in a public telephone booth can be reasonable in the absence of a warrant. As elsewhere under the Fourth Amendment, warrants are the general rule, to which the legitimate needs of law enforcement may demand specific exceptions. It will be time enough to consider any such exceptions when an appropriate occasion presents itself, and I agree with the Court that this is not one.

MR. JUSTICE WHITE, concurring.

I agree that the official surveillance of petitioner's telephone conversations in a public booth must be subjected to the test of reasonableness under the Fourth Amendment and that on the record now before us the particular surveillance undertaken was unreasonable absent a warrant properly authorizing it. This application of the Fourth Amendment need not interfere with legitimate needs of law enforcement.†

---

* I also think that the course of development evinced by *Silverman, supra, Wong Sun, supra, Berger, supra,* and today's decision must be recognized as overruling *Olmstead* v. *United States,* 277 U.S. 438, which essentially rested on the ground that conversations were not subject to the protection of the Fourth Amendment.

† In previous cases, which are undisturbed by today's decision, the Court

In joining the Court's opinion, I note the Court's acknowledgment that there are circumstances in which it is reasonable to search without a warrant. In this connection, in footnote 23 the Court points out that today's decision does not reach national security cases. Wiretapping to protect the security of the Nation has been authorized by successive Presidents. The present Administration would apparently save national security cases from restrictions against wiretapping. See *Berger* v. *New York,* 388 U. S. 41, 112–118 (1967) (WHITE, J., dissenting). We should not require the warrant procedure and the magistrate's judgment if the President of the United States or his chief legal officer, the Attorney General, has considered the requirements of national security and authorized electronic surveillance as reasonable.

MR. JUSTICE BLACK, dissenting.

If I could agree with the Court that eavesdropping carried on by electronic means (equivalent to wiretapping) constitutes a "search" or "seizure," I would be happy to join the Court's opinion. For on that premise my Brother STEWART sets out methods in accord with the Fourth Amendment to guide States in the enactment and enforcement of laws passed to regulate wiretapping by government. In this respect today's opinion differs sharply from *Berger* v. *New York,* 388 U. S. 41, decided last Term, which held void on its face a New York statute authorizing wiretapping on warrants issued by magistrates on showings of probable cause. The *Berger* case also set up what appeared to be insuperable obstacles to the valid passage of such wiretapping laws by States. The Court's opinion in this case, however, removes the doubts about

---

has upheld, as reasonable under the Fourth Amendment, admission at trial of evidence obtained (1) by an undercover police agent to whom a defendant speaks without knowledge that he is in the employ of the police, *Hoffa* v. *United States,* 385 U.S. 293 (1966); (2) by a recording device hidden on the person of such an informant, *Lopez* v. *United States,* 373 U.S. 427 (1963); *Osborn* v. *United States,* 385 U.S. 323 (1966); and (3) by a policeman listening to the secret micro-wave transmissions of an agent conversing with the defendant in another location, *On Lee* v. *United States,* 343 U.S. 747 (1952). When one man speaks to another he takes all the risks ordinarily inherent in so doing, including the risk that the man to whom he speaks will make public what he has heard. The Fourth Amendment does not protect against unreliable (or law-abiding) associates. *Hoffa* v. *United States, supra.* It is but a logical and reasonable extension of this principle that a man take the risk that his hearer, free to memorize what he hears for later verbatim repetitions, is instead recording it or transmitting it to another. The present case deals with an entirely different situation, for as the Court emphasizes the petitioner "sought to exclude . . . the uninvited ear," and spoke under circumstances in which a reasonable person would assume that uninvited ears were not listening.

state power in this field and abates to a large extent the confusion and near-paralyzing effect of the *Berger* holding. Notwithstanding these good efforts of the Court, I am still unable to agree with its interpretation of the Fourth Amendment.

My basic objection is twofold: (1) I do not believe that the words of the Amendment will bear the meaning given them by today's decision, and (2) I do not believe that it is the proper role of this Court to rewrite the Amendment in order "to bring it into harmony with the times" and thus reach a result that many people believe to be desirable.

While I realize that an argument based on the meaning of words lacks the scope, and no doubt the appeal, of broad policy discussions and philosophical discourses of such nebulous subjects as privacy, for me the language of the Amendment is the crucial place to look in construing a written document such as our Constitution. The Fourth Amendment says that

"The right of the people to be secure in their persons, houses, papers, and effects, against unreasonable searches and seizures, shall not be violated, and no Warrants shall issue, but upon probable cause, supported by Oath or affirmation, and particularly describing the place to be searched, and the persons or things to be seized." The first clause protects "persons, houses, papers, and effects, against unreasonable searches and seizures . . . ." These words connote the idea of tangible things with size, form, and weight, things capable of being searched, seized, or both. The second clause of the Amendment still further establishes its Framers' purpose to limit its protection to tangible things by providing that no warrants shall issue but those "particularly describing the place to be searched, and the persons or things to be seized." A conversation overheard by eavesdropping, whether by plain snooping or wiretapping, is not tangible and, under the normally accepted meanings of the words, can neither be searched nor seized. In addition the language of the second clause indicates that the Amendment refers not only to something tangible so it can be seized but to something already in existence so it can be described. Yet the Court's interpretation would have the Amendment apply to overhearing future conversations which by their very nature are nonexistent until they take place. How can one "describe" a future conversation, and, if one cannot, how can a magistrate issue a warrant to eavesdrop one in the future? It is argued that information showing what is expected to be said is sufficient to limit the boundaries of what later can be admitted into evidence; but does such general information really meet the specific language of the Amendment which says "particularly describing"? Rather than using language in a completely artificial way, I must conclude that the Fourth Amendment simply does not apply to eavesdropping.

Tapping telephone wires, of course, was an unknown possibility at the time the Fourth Amendment was adopted. But eavesdropping (and wiretapping is nothing more than eavesdropping by telephone) was, as even the majority opinion in *Berger, supra,* recognized, "an ancient practice which at common law was condemned as a nuisance. 4 Blackstone, Commentaries 168. In those days the eavesdropper listened by naked ear under the eaves of houses or their windows, or beyond their walls seeking out private discourse." 388 U. S., at 45. There can be no doubt that the Framers were aware of this practice, and if they had desired to outlaw or restrict the use of evidence obtained by eavesdropping, I believe that they would have used the appropriate language to do so in the Fourth Amendment. They certainly would not have left such a task to the ingenuity of language-stretching judges. No one, it seems to me, can read the debates on the Bill of Rights without reaching the conclusion that its Framers and critics well knew the meaning of the words they used, what they would be understood to mean by others, their scope and their limitations. Under these circumstances it strikes me as a charge against their scholarship, their common sense and their candor to give to the Fourth Amendment's language the eavesdropping meaning the Court imputes to it today.

I do not deny that common sense requires and that this Court often has said that the Bill of Rights' safeguards should be given a liberal construction. This principle, however, does not justify construing the search and seizure amendment as applying to eavesdropping or the "seizure" of conversations. The Fourth Amendment was aimed directly at the abhorred practice of breaking in, ransacking and searching homes and other buildings and seizing people's personal belongings without warrants issued by magistrates. The Amendment deserves, and this Court has given it, a liberal construction in order to protect against warrantless searches of buildings and seizures of tangible personal effects. But until today this Court has refused to say that eavesdropping comes within the ambit of Fourth Amendment restrictions. See, *e. g., Olmstead* v. *United States,* 277 U. S. 438 (1928), and *Goldman* v. *United States,* 316 U. S. 129 (1942).

So far I have attempted to state why I think the words of the Fourth Amendment prevent its application to eavesdropping. It is important now to show that this has been the traditional view of the Amendment's scope since its adoption and that the Court's decision in this case, along with its amorphous holding in *Berger* last Term, marks the first real departure from that view.

The first case to reach this Court which actually involved a clear-cut test of the Fourth Amendment's applicability to eavesdropping through a wiretap was, of course, *Olmstead, supra.* In holding that the interception of private telephone conversations by means of wiretapping was not a violation of the Fourth Amendment, this Court, speaking through Mr. Chief Justice Taft, examined the language of the Amendment and found, just as I do now, that the words could not be stretched to encompass overheard conversations:

"The Amendment itself shows that the search is to be of material things—the person, the house, his papers or his effects. The description of the warrant necessary to make the proceeding lawful, is that it must specify the place to be searched and the person or *things* to be seized. . . .

* * * * * * * * * *

"Justice Bradley in the *Boyd* case [*Boyd* v. *United States,* 116 U. S. 616], and Justice Clark[e] in the *Gouled* case [*Gouled* v. United States, 255 U. S. 298], said that the Fifth Amendment and the Fourth Amendment were to be liberally construed to effect the purpose of the framers of the Constitution in the interest of liberty. But that can not justify enlargement of the language employed beyond the possible practical meaning of houses, persons, papers, and effects, or so to apply the words search and seizure as to forbid hearing or sight." 277 U. S., at 464–465.

Goldman v. *United States,* 316 U.S. 129, is an even clearer example of this Court's traditional refusal to consider eavesdropping as being covered by the Fourth Amendment. There federal agents used a detectaphone, which was placed on the wall of an adjoining room, to listen to the conversation of a defendant carried on in his private office and intended to be confined within the four walls of the room. This Court, referring to *Olmstead,* found no Fourth Amendment violation.

It should be noted that the Court in *Olmstead* based its decision squarely on the fact that wiretapping or eavesdropping does not violate the Fourth Amendment. As shown, *supra,* in the cited quotation from the case, the Court went to great pains to examine the actual language of the Amendment and found that the words used simply could not be stretched to cover eavesdropping. That there was no trespass was not the determinative factor, and indeed the Court in citing *Hester* v. *United States,* 265 U.S. 57, indicated that even where there was a trespass the Fourth Amendment does not automatically apply to evidence obtained by "hearing or sight." The *Olmstead* majority characterized *Hester* as holding "that the

416

testimony of two officers of the law who trespassed on the defendant's land, concealed themselves one hundred yards away from his house and saw him come out and hand a bottle of whiskey to another, was not inadmissible. While there was a trespass, there was no search of person, house, papers or effects." 277 U.S., at 465. Thus the clear holding of the *Olmstead* and *Goldman* cases, undiluted by any question of trespass, is that eavesdropping, in both its original and modern forms, is not violative of the Fourth Amendment.

While my reading of the *Olmstead* and *Goldman* cases convinces me that they were decided on the basis of the inapplicability of the wording of the Fourth Amendment to eavesdropping, and not on any trespass basis, this is not to say that unauthorized intrusion has not played an important role in search and seizure cases. This Court has adopted an exclusionary rule to bar evidence obtained by means of such intrusions. As I made clear in my dissenting opinion in *Berger* v. *New York*, 388 U.S. 41, 76, I continue to believe that this exclusionary rule formulated in *Weeks* v. *United States*, 232 U.S. 383, rests on the "supervisory power" of this Court over other federal courts and is not rooted in the Fourth Amendment. See *Wolf* v. *Colorado*, concurring opinion, 338 U.S. 25, 39, at 40. See also *Mapp* v. *Ohio*, concurring opinion, 367 U.S. 643, 661–666. This rule has caused the Court to refuse to accept evidence where there has been such an intrusion regardless of whether there has been a search or seizure in violation of the Fourth Amendment. As this Court said in *Lopez* v. *United States*, 373 U.S. 427, 438–439, "The Court has in the past sustained instances of 'electronic eavesdropping' against constitutional challenge, when devices have been used to enable government agents to overhear conversations which would have been beyond the reach of the human ear [citing *Olmstead* and *Goldman*]. It has been insisted only that the electronic device not be planted by an unlawful physical invasion of a constitutionally protected area. *Silverman* v. *United States*."

To support its new interpretation of the Fourth Amendment, which in effect amounts to a rewriting of the language, the Court's opinion concludes that "the underpinnings of *Olmstead* and *Goldman* have been . . . eroded by our subsequent decisions . . . ." But the only cases cited as accomplishing this "eroding" are *Silverman* v. *United States*, 365 U.S. 505, and *Warden* v. *Hayden*, 387 U.S. 294. Neither of these cases "eroded" *Olmstead* or *Goldman*. *Silverman* is an interesting choice since there the Court expressly refused to re-examine the rationale of *Olmstead* or *Goldman* although such a re-examination was strenuously urged upon the Court by the petitioners' counsel. Also it is significant that in *Silverman*, as the Court described it, "the eavesdropping was accomplished by means of an unauthorized physical penetration into the premises occupied by the petitioners," 365 U.S., at 509, thus calling into play the supervisory exclusionary rule of evidence. As I have pointed out above, where there is an unauthorized intrusion, this Court has rejected admission of evidence obtained regardless of whether there has been an unconstitutional search and seizure. The majority's decision here relies heavily on the statement in the opinion that the Court "need not pause to consider whether or not there was a technical trespass under the local property law relating to party walls." (At 511.) Yet this statement should not becloud the fact that time and again the opinion emphasizes that there has been an unauthorized intrusion: "For a fair reading of the record in this case shows that the eavesdropping was accomplished by means of an *unauthorized physical penetration* into the premises occupied by the petitioners." (At 509, emphasis added.) "Eavesdropping accomplished by means of such a *physical intrusion* is beyond the pale of even those decisions . . . ." (At 509, emphasis added.) "Here . . . the officers overheard the petitioners' conversations only by *usurping* part of the petitioners' house or office . . . ." (At 511, emphasis added.) "[D]ecision here . . . is based upon the reality of an *actual intrusion* . . . ." (At 512, emphasis added.) "We find no occasion to re-examine *Goldman* here, but we decline to go beyond it, *by even a fraction of an inch*." (At 512, emphasis added.) As if this were not enough, Justices Clark and Whittaker concurred with the following statement: "In view of the determination by the majority that the *unauthorized physical penetration* into petitioners' premises constituted sufficient trespass to remove this case from the coverage of earlier decisions, we feel obliged to join in the Court's opinion." (At 513, emphasis added.) As I made clear in my dissent in *Berger*, the Court in *Silverman* held the evidence should be excluded by virtue of the exclusionary rule and "I would not have agreed with the Court's opinion in *Silverman* . . . had I thought that the result depended on finding a violation of the Fourth Amendment . . . ." 388 U.S., at 79–80. In light of this and the fact that the Court expressly refused to re-examine *Olmstead* and *Goldman*, I cannot read *Silverman* as overturning the interpretation stated very plainly in *Olmstead* and followed in *Goldman* that eavesdropping is not covered by the Fourth Amendment.

The other "eroding" case cited in the Court's opinion is *Warden* v. *Hayden*, 387 U.S. 294. It appears that this case is cited for the proposition that the Fourth Amendment applies to "intangibles," such as conversation, and the following ambiguous statement is quoted from the opinion: "The premise that property interests control the right of the Government to search and seize has been discredited." 387 U.S., at 304. But far from being concerned with eavesdropping, *Warden* v. *Hayden* upholds the seizure of *clothes*, certainly tangibles by any definition. The discussion of property interests was involved only with the common-law rule that the right to seize property depended upon proof of a superior property interest.

Thus, I think that although the Court attempts to convey the impression that for some reason today *Olmstead* and *Goldman* are no longer good law, it must face up to the fact that these cases have never been overruled or even "eroded." It is the Court's opinions in this case and *Berger* which for the first time since 1791, when the Fourth Amendment was adopted, have declared that eavesdropping is subject to Fourth Amendment restrictions and that conversations can be "seized."* I must align myself with all those judges who up to this year have never been able to impute such a meaning to the words of the Amendment.

Since I see no way in which the words of the Fourth Amendment can be construed to apply to eavesdropping, that closes the matter for me. In interpreting the Bill of Rights, I willingly go as far as a liberal construction of the language takes me, but I simply cannot in good conscience give a meaning to words which they have never before been thought to have and which they certainly do not have in common ordinary usage. I will not distort the words of the Amendment in order to "keep the Constitution up to date" or "to bring it into harmony with the times." It was never meant that this

---

* The first paragraph of my Brother HARLAN's concurring opinion is susceptible of the interpretation, although probably not intended, that this Court "has long held" eavesdropping to be a violation of the Fourth Amendment and therefore "presumptively unreasonable in the absence of a search warrant." There is no reference to any long line of cases, but simply a citation to *Silverman*, and several cases following it, to establish this historical proposition. In the first place, as I have indicated in this opinion, I do not read *Silverman* as holding any such thing; and in the second place, *Silverman* was decided in 1961. Thus, whatever it held, it cannot be said it "has [been] long held." I think my Brother HARLAN recognizes this later in his opinion when he admits that the Court must now overrule *Olmstead* and *Goldman*. In having to overrule these cases in order to establish the holding the Court adopts today, it becomes clear that the Court is promulgating new doctrine instead of merely following what it "has long held." This is emphasized by my Brother HARLAN's claim that it is "bad physics" to adhere to *Goldman*. Such an assertion simply illustrates the propensity of some members of the Court to rely on their limited understanding of modern scientific subjects in order to fit the Constitution to the times and give its language a meaning that it will not tolerate.

Court have such power, which in effect would make us a continuously functioning constitutional convention.

With this decision the Court has completed, I hope, its rewriting of the Fourth Amendment, which started only recently when the Court began referring incessantly to the Fourth Amendment not so much as a law against *unreasonable* searches and seizures as one to protect an individual's privacy. By clever word juggling the Court finds it plausible to argue that language aimed specifically at searches and seizures of things that can be searched and seized may, to protect privacy, be applied to eavesdropped evidence of conversations that can neither be searched nor seized. Few things happen to an individual that do not affect his privacy in one way or another. Thus, by arbitrarily substituting the Court's language, designed to protect privacy, for the Constitution's language, designed to protect against unreasonable searches and seizures, the Court has made the Fourth Amendment its vehicle for holding all laws violative of the Constitution which offend the Court's broadest concept of privacy. As I said in *Griswold* v. *Connecticut*, 381 U.S. 479, "The Court talks about a constitutional 'right of privacy' as though there is some constitutional provision or provisions forbidding any law ever to be passed which might abridge the 'privacy' of individuals. But there is not." (Dissenting opinion, at 508.) I made clear in that dissent my fear of the dangers involved when this Court uses the "broad, abstract and ambiguous concept" of "privacy" as a "comprehensive substitute for the Fourth Amendment's guarantee against 'unreasonable searches and seizures.' " (See generally dissenting opinion, at 507–527.)

The Fourth Amendment protects privacy only to the extent that it prohibits unreasonable searches and seizures of "persons, houses, papers, and effects." No general right is created by the Amendment so as to give this Court the unlimited power to hold unconstitutional everything which affects privacy. Certainly the Framers, well acquainted as they were with the excesses of governmental power, did not intend to grant this Court such omnipotent lawmaking authority as that. The history of governments proves that it is dangerous to freedom to repose such powers in courts.

For these reasons I respectfully dissent.

Omnibus Crime Control and Safe Streets Act*

TITLE III—WIRETAPPING AND ELECTRONIC SURVEILLANCE
FINDINGS

SEC. 801. On the basis of its own investigations and of published studies, the Congress makes the following findings:

(a) Wire communications are normally conducted through the use of facilities which form part of an interstate network. The same facilities are used for interstate and intrastate communications. There has been extensive wiretapping carried on without legal sanctions, and without the consent of any of the parties to the conversation. Electronic, mechanical, and other intercepting devices are being used to overhear oral conversations made in private, without the consent of any of the parties to such communications. The contents of these communications and evidence derived therefrom are being used by public and private parties as evidence in court and administrative proceedings, and by persons whose activities affect interstate commerce. The possession, manufacture, distribution, advertising, and use of these devices are facilitated by interstate commerce.

(b) In order to protect effectively the privacy of wire and oral communications, to protect the integrity of court and administrative proceedings, and to prevent the obstruction of interstate commerce, it is necessary for Congress to define on a uniform basis the circumstances and conditions under which the interception of wire and oral communications may be authorized, to prohibit any unauthorized interception of such communications, and the use of the contents thereof in evidence in courts and administrative proceedings.

(c) Organized criminals make extensive use of wire and oral communications in their criminal activities. The interception of such communications to obtain evidence of the commission of crimes or to prevent their commission is an indispensable aid to law enforcement and the administration of justice.

(d) To safeguard the privacy of innocent persons, the interception of wire or oral communications where none of the parties to the communication has consented to the interception should be allowed only when authorized by a court of competent jurisdiction and should remain under the control and supervision of the authorizing court. Interception of wire and oral communications

---

*18 U.S.C. § 2501 et seq.

should further be limited to certain major types of offenses and specific categories of crime with assurances that the interception is justified and that the information obtained thereby will not be misused.

SEC. 802. Part I of title 18, United States Code, is amended by adding at the end the following new chapter:

"Chapter 119. WIRE INTERCEPTION AND INTERCEPTION OF ORAL COMMUNICATIONS

"Sec.

"2510. Definitions.
"2511. Interception and disclosure of wire or oral communications prohibited.
"2512. Manufacture, distribution, possession, and advertising of wire or oral communication intercepting devices prohibited.
"2513. Confiscation of wire or oral communication intercepting devices.
"2514. Immunity of witnesses.
"2515. Prohibition of use as evidence of intercepted wire or oral communications.
"2516. Authorization for interception of wire or oral communications.
"2517. Authorization for disclosure and use of intercepted wire or oral communications.
"2518. Procedure for interception of wire or oral communications.
"2519. Reports concerning intercepted wire or oral communications.
"2520. Recovery of civil damages authorized.

"§ 2510. Definitions

"As used in this chapter—

"(1) 'wire communication' means any communication made in whole or in part through the use of facilities for the transmission of communications by the aid of wire, cable, or other like connection between the point of origin and the point of reception furnished or operated by any person engaged as a common carrier in providing or operating such facilities for the transmission of interstate or foreign communications;

"(2) 'oral communication' means any oral communication uttered by a person exhibiting an exceptation that such communication is not subject to interception under circumstances justifying such expectation;

"(3) 'State' means any State of the United States, the District of Columbia, the Commonwealth of Puerto Rico, and any territory or possession of the United States;

"(4) 'intercept' means the aural acquisition of the contents of any wire or oral communication through the use of any electronic, mechanical, or other device.

"(5) 'electronic, mechanical, or other device' means any device or apparatus which can be used to intercept a wire or oral communication other than—

"(a) any telephone or telegraph instrument, equipment or facility, or any component thereof, (i) furnished to the subscriber or user by a communications common carrier in the ordinary course of its business and being used by the subscriber or user in the ordinary course of its business; or (ii) being used by a communications common carrier in the ordinary course of its business, or by an investigative or law enforcement officer in the ordinary course of his duties;

"(b) a hearing aid or similar device being used to correct subnormal hearing to not better than normal;

"(6) 'person' means any employee, or agent of the United States or any State or political subdivision thereof, and any individual, partnership, association, joint stock company, trust, or corporation;

"(7) 'Investigative or law enforcement officer' means any officer of the United States or of a State or political subdivision thereof, who is empowered by law to conduct investigations of or to make arrests for offenses enumerated in this chapter, and any attorney authorized by law to prosecute or participate in the prosecution of such offenses;

"(8) 'contents', when used with respect to any wire or oral communication, includes any information concerning the identity of the parties to such communication or the existence, substance, purport, or meaning of that communication;

"(9) 'Judge of competent jurisdiction' means—

"(a) a judge of a United States district court or a United States court of appeals; and

"(b) a judge of any court of general criminal jurisdiction of a State who is authorized by a statute of that State to enter orders authorizing interceptions of wire or oral communications;

"(10) 'communication common carrier' shall have the same meaning which is given the term 'common carrier' by section 153 (h) of title 47 of the United States Code; and

"(11) 'aggrieved person' means a person who was a party to any intercepted wire or oral communication or a person against whom the interception was directed.

"§ 2511. Interception and disclosure of wire or oral communications prohibited

"(1) Except as otherwise specifically provided in this chapter any person who—

"(a) willfully intercepts, endeavors to intercept, or procures any other person to intercept or endeavor to intercept, any wire or oral communication;

"(b) willfully uses, endeavors to use, or procures any other person to use or endeavor to use any electronic, mechanical, or other device to intercept any oral communication when—

"(i) such device is affixed to, or otherwise transmits a signal through, a wire, cable, or other like connection used in wire communication; or

"(ii) such device transmits communications by radio, or interferes with the transmission of such communication; or

"(iii) such person knows, or has reason to know, that such device or any component thereof has been sent through the mail or transported in interstate or foreign commerce; or

"(iv) such use or endeavor to use (A) takes place on the premises of any business or other commercial establishment the operations of which affect interstate or foreign commerce; or (B) obtains or is for the purpose of obtaining information relating to the operations of any business or other commercial establishment the operations of which affect interstate or foreign commerce; or

"(v) such person acts in the District of Columbia, the Commonwealth of Puerto Rico, or any territory or possession of the United States;"

"(c) willfully discloses, or endeavors to disclose, to any other person the contents of any wire or oral communication, knowing or having reason to know that the information was obtained through the interception of a wire or oral communication in violation of this subsection; or

"(d) willfully uses, or endeavors to use, the contents of any wire or oral communication, knowing or having reason to know that the information was obtained through the interception of a wire or oral communication in violation of this subsection;

shall be fined not more than $10,000 or imprisoned not more than five years, or both.

"(2) (a) It shall not be unlawful under this chapter for an operator of a switchboard, or an officer, employee, or agent of any communication common carrier, whose facilities are used in the transmission of a wire communication, to intercept, disclose, or use that communication in the normal course of his employment while engaged in any activity which is a necessary incident to the rendition of his service or to the protection of the rights or property of the carrier of such communication: *Provided,* That said communication common carriers shall not utilize service observing or random monitoring except for mechanical or service quality control checks.

"(b) It shall not be unlawful under this chapter for an officer, employee, or agent of the Federal Communications Commission, in

424

the normal course of his employment and in discharge of the monitoring responsibilities exercised by the Commission in the enforcement of chapter 5 of title 47 of the United States Code, to intercept a wire communication, or oral communication transmitted by radio, or to disclose or use the information thereby obtained.

"(c) It shall not be unlawful under this chapter for a person acting under color of law to intercept a wire or oral communication, where such person is a party to the communication or one of the parties to the communication has given prior consent to such interception.

"(d) It shall not be unlawful under this chapter for a person not acting under color of law to intercept a wire or oral communication where such person is a party to the communication or where one of the parties to the communication has given prior consent to such interception unless such communication is intercepted for the purpose of committing any criminal or tortious act in violation of the Constitution or laws of the United States or of any State or for the purpose of committing any other injurious act.

"(3) Nothing contained in this chapter or in section 605 of the Communications Act of 1934 (48 Stat. 1143; 47 U.S.C. 605) shall limit the constitutional power of the President to take such measures as he deems necessary to protect the Nation against actual or potential attack or other hostile acts of a foreign power, to obtain foreign intelligence information deemed essential to the security of the United States, or to protect national security information against foreign intelligence activities. Nor shall anything contained in this chapter be deemed to limit the constitutional power of the President to take such measures as he deems necessary to protect the United States against the overthrow of the Government by force or other unlawful means, or against any other clear and present danger to the structure or existence of the Government. The contents of any wire or oral communication intercepted by authority of the President in the exercise of the foregoing powers may be received in evidence in any trial hearing, or other proceeding only where such interception was reasonable, and shall not be otherwise used or disclosed except as is necessary to implement that power.

"§ 2512. **Manufacture, distribution, possession, and advertising of wire or oral communication intercepting devices prohibited**

"(1) Except as otherwise specifically provided in this chapter, any person who willfully—

"(a) sends through the mail, or sends or carries in interstate or foreign commerce, any electronic, mechanical, or other de-

425

vice, knowing or having reason to know that the design of such device renders it primarily useful for the purpose of the surreptitious interception of wire or oral communications;

"(b) manufactures, assembles, possesses, or sells any electronic, mechanical, or other device, knowing or having reason to know that the design of such device renders it primarily useful for the purpose of the surreptitious interception of wire or oral communications, and that such device or any component thereof has been or will be sent through the mail or transported in interstate or foreign commerce; or

"(c) places in any newspaper, magazine, handbill, or other publication any advertisement of—

"(i) any electronic, mechanical, or other device knowing or having reason to know that the design of such device renders it primarily useful for the purpose of the surreptitious interception of wire or oral communications; or

"(ii) any other electronic, mechanical, or other device, where such advertisement promotes the use of such device for the purpose of the surreptitious interception of wire or oral communications,

knowing or having reason to know that such advertisement will be sent through the mail or transported in interstate or foreign commerce,

shall be fined not more than $10,000 or imprisoned not more than five years, or both.

"(2) It shall not be unlawful under this section for—

"(a) a communications common carrier or an officer, agent, or employee of, or a person under contract with, a communications common carrier, in the normal course of the communications common carrier's business, or

"(b) an officer, agent, or employee of, or a person under contract with, the United States, a State, or a political subdivision thereof, in the normal course of the activities of the United States, a State, or a political subdivision thereof, to send through the mail, send or carry in interstate or foreign commerce, or manufacture, assemble, possess, or sell any electronic, mechanical, or other device knowing or having reason to know that the design of such device renders it primarily useful for the purpose of the surreptitious interception of wire or oral communications.

"§ 2513. Confiscation of wire or oral communication intercepting devices

"Any electronic, mechanical, or other device used, sent, carried, manufactured, assembled, possessed, sold, or advertised in violation of section 2511 or section 2512 of this chapter may be seized and forfeited to the United States. All provisions of law relating to (1) the seizure, summary and judicial forfeiture, and condemnation of vessels, vehicles, merchandise, and baggage for violations of the customs laws contained in title 19 of the United States Code, (2) the disposition of such vessels, vehicles, merchandise, and baggage or the proceeds from the sale thereof, (3) the remission or mitigation of such forfeiture, (4) the compromise of claims, and (5) the award of compensation to informers in respect of such forfeitures, shall apply to seizures and forfeitures incurred, or alleged to have been incurred, under the provisions of this section, insofar as applicable and not inconsistent with the provisions of this section; except that such duties as are imposed upon the collector of customs or any other person with respect to the seizure and forfeiture of vessels, vehicles, merchandise, and baggage under the provisions of the customs laws contained in title 19 of the United States Code shall be performed with respect to seizure and forfeiture of electronic, mechanical, or other intercepting devices under this section by such officers, agents, or other persons as may be authorized or designated for that purpose by the Attorney General.

"§ 2514. Immunity of witnesses

"Whenever in the judgment of a United States attorney the testimony of any witness, or the production of books, papers, or other evidence by any witness, in any case or proceeding before any grand jury or court of the United States involving any violation of this chapter or any of the offenses enumerated in section 2516, or any conspiracy to violate this chapter or any of the offenses enumerated in section 2516 is necessary to the public interest, such United States attorney, upon the approval of the Attorney General, shall make application to the court that the witness shall be instructed to testify or produce evidence subject to the provisions of this section, and upon order of the court such witness shall not be excused from testifying or from producing books, papers, or other evidence on the ground that the testimony or evidence required of him may tend to incriminate him or subject him to a penalty or forfeiture. No such witness shall be prosecuted or subjected to any penalty or forfeiture for or on account of any transaction, matter or thing concerning which he is compelled, after having claimed his privilege against self-incrimination, to testify or produce evidence, nor shall testimony so compelled be used as evidence in any criminal proceeding (except in a proceeding described in the next sentence) against him in any court. No witness shall be exempt under this section from prosecution for perjury or contempt committed while giving testimony or producing evidence under compulsion as provided in this section.

"§ 2515. Prohibition of use as evidence of intercepted wire or oral communications

"Whenever any wire or oral communication has been intercepted, no part of the contents of such communication and no evidence derived therefrom may be received in evidence in any trial, hearing, or other proceeding in or before any court, grand jury, department, officer, agency, regulatory body, legislative committee, or other authority of the United States, a State, or a political subdivision thereof if the disclosure of that information would be in violation of this chapter.

"§ 2516. Authorization for interception of wire or oral communications

"(1) The Attorney General, or any Assistant Attorney General specially designated by the Attorney General, may authorize an application to a Federal judge of competent jurisdiction for, and such judge may grant in conformity with section 2518 of this chapter an order authorizing or approving the interception of wire or oral communications by the Federal Bureau of Investigation, or a Federal agency having responsibility for the investigation of the offense as to which the application is made, when such interception may provide or has provided evidence of—

"(a) any offense punishable by death or by imprisonment for more than one year under sections 2274 through 2277 of title 42 of the United States Code (relating to the enforcement of the Atomic Energy Act of 1954), or under the following chapters of this title: chapter 37 (relating to espionage), chapter 105 (relating to sabotage), chapter 115 (relating to treason), or chapter 102 (relating to riots) ;

"(b) a violation of section 186 or section 501(c) of title 29, United States Code (dealing with restrictions on payments and loans to labor organizations), or any offense which involves murder, kidnapping, robbery, or extortion, and which is punishable under this title;

"(c) any offense which is punishable under the following sections of this title: section 201 (bribery of public officials and witnesses), section 224 (bribery in sporting contests), section 1084 (transmission of wagering information), section 1503 (influencing or injuring an officer, juror, or witness generally), section 1510 (obstruction of criminal investigations), section 1751 (Presidential assassinations, kidnapping, and assault), section 1951 (interference with commerce by threats or violence), section 1952 (interstate and foreign travel or transportation in aid of racketeering enterprises), section 1954 (offer, acceptance, or solicitation to influence operations of employee benefit plan), section 659 (theft from interstate shipment), section 664 (embezzlement from pension and welfare funds), or sections 2314 and 2315 (interstate transportation of stolen property);

"(d) any offense involving counterfeiting punishable under section 471, 472, or 473 of this title;

"(e) any offense involving bankruptcy fraud or the manufacture, importation, receiving, concealment, buying, selling, or otherwise dealing in narcotic drugs, marihuana, or other dangerous drugs, punishable under any law of the United States;

"(f) any offense including extortionate credit transactions under sections 892, 893, or 894 of this title; or

"(g) any conspiracy to commit any of the foregoing offenses.

"(2) The principal prosecuting attorney of any State, or the principal prosecuting attorney of any political subdivision thereof, if such attorney is authorized by a statute of that State to make application to a State court judge of competent jurisdiction for an order authorizing or approving the interception of wire or oral communications, may apply to such judge for, and such judge may grant in conformity with section 2518 of this chapter and with the applicable State statute an order authorizing, or approving the interception of wire or oral communications by investigative or law enforcement officers having responsibility for the investigation of the offense as to which the application is made, when such interception may provide or has provided evidence of the commission of the offense of murder, kidnapping, gambling, robbery, bribery, extortion, or dealing in narcotic drugs, marihuana or other dangerous drugs, or other crime dangerous to life, limb, or property, and punishable by imprisonment for more than one year, designated in any applicable State statute authorizing such interception, or any conspiracy to commit any of the foregoing offenses.

"§ 2517. Authorization for disclosure and use of intercepted wire or oral communications

"(1) Any investigative or law enforcement officer who, by any means authorized by this chapter, has obtained knowledge of the contents of any wire or oral communication, or evidence derived therefrom, may disclose such contents to another investigative or law enforcement officer to the extent that such disclosure is appropriate to the proper performance of the official duties of the officer making or receiving the disclosure.

"(2) Any investigative or law enforcement officer who, by any means authorized by this chapter, has obtained knowledge of the contents of any wire or oral communication or evidence derived therefrom may use such contents to the extent such use is appropriate to the proper performance of his official duties.

"(3) Any person who has received, by any means authorized by this chapter, any information concerning a wire or oral communication, or evidence derived therefrom intercepted in accordance with the provisions of this chapter may disclose the contents of that communication or such derivative evidence while giving testimony under oath or affirmation in any criminal proceeding in any court of the United States or of any State or in any Federal or State grand jury proceeding.

"(4) No otherwise privileged wire or oral communication intercepted in accordance with, or in violation of, the provisions of this chapter shall lose its privileged character.

"(5) When an investigative or law enforcement officer, while engaged in intercepting wire or oral communications in the manner authorized herein, intercepts wire or oral communications relating to offenses other than those specified in the order of authorization or approval, the contents thereof, and evidence derived therefrom, may be disclosed or used as provided in subsections (1) and (2) of this section. Such contents and any evidence derived therefrom may be used under subsection (3) of this section when authorized or approved by a judge of competent jurisdiction where such judge finds on subsequent application that the contents were otherwise intercepted in accordance with the provisions of this chapter. Such application shall be made as soon as practicable.

"§ 2518. Procedure for interception of wire or oral communications

"(1) Each application for an order authorizing or approving the interception of a wire or oral communication shall be made in writing upon oath or affirmation to a judge of competent jurisdiction and shall state the applicant's authority to make such application. Each application shall include the following information:

"(a) the identity of the investigative or law enforcement officer making the application, and the officer authorizing the application;

"(b) a full and complete statement of the facts and circumstances relied upon by the applicant, to justify his belief that an order should be issued, including (i) details as to the particular offense that has been, is being, or is about to be committed,

(ii) a particular description of the nature and location of the facilities from which or the place where the communication is to be intercepted, (iii) a particular description of the type of communications sought to be intercepted, (iv) the identity of the person, if known, committing the offense and whose communications are to be intercepted;

"(c) a full and complete statement as to whether or not other investigative procedures have been tried and failed or why they reasonably appear to be unlikely to succeed if tried or to be too dangerous;

"(d) a statement of the period of time for which the interception is required to be maintained. If the nature of the investigation is such that the authorization for interception should not automatically terminate when the described type of communication has been first obtained, a particular description of facts establishing probable cause to believe that additional communications of the same type will occur thereafter;

"(e) a full and complete statement of the facts concerning all previous applications known to the individual authorizing and making the application, made to any judge for authorization to intercept, or for approval of interceptions of, wire or oral communications involving any of the same persons, facilities or places specified in the application, and the action taken by the judge on each such application; and

"(f) where the application is for the extension of an order, a statement setting forth the results thus far obtained from the interception, or a reasonable explanation of the failure to obtain such results.

"(2) The judge may require the applicant to furnish additional testimony or documentary evidence in support of the application.

"(3) Upon such application the judge may enter an ex parte order, as requested or as modified, authorizing or approving interception of wire or oral communications within the territorial jurisdiction of the court in which the judge is sitting, if the judge determines on the basis of the facts submitted by the applicant that—

"(a) there is probable cause for belief that an individual is committing, has committed, or is about to commit a particular offense enumerated in section 2516 of this chapter;

"(b) there is probable cause for belief that particular communications concerning that offense will be obtained through such interception;

"(c) normal investigative procedures have been tried and have failed or reasonably appear to be unlikely to succeed if tried or to be too dangerous;

431

"(d) there is probable cause for belief that the facilities from which, or the place where, the wire or oral communications are to be intercepted are being used, or are about to be used, in connection with the commission of such offense, or are leased to, listed in the name of, or commonly used by such person.

"(4) Each order authorizing or approving the interception of any wire or oral communication shall specify—

"(a) the identity of the person, if known, whose communications are to be intercepted;

"(b) the nature and location of the communications facilities as to which, or the place where, authority to intercept is granted;

"(c) a particular description of the type of communication sought to be intercepted, and a statement of the particular offense to which it relates;

"(d) the identity of the agency authorized to intercept the communications, and of the person authorizing the application; and

"(e) the period of time during which such interception is authorized, including a statement as to whether or not the interception shall automatically terminate when the described communication has been first obtained.

"(5) No order entered under this section may authorize or approve the interception of any wire or oral communication for any period longer than is necessary to achieve the objective of the authorization, nor in any event longer than thirty days. Extensions of an order may be granted, but only upon application for an extension made in accordance with subsection (1) of this section and the court making the findings required by subsection (3) of this section. The period of extension shall be no longer than the authorizing judge deems necessary to achieve the purposes for which it was granted and in no event for longer than thirty days. Every order and extension thereof shall contain a provision that the authorization to intercept shall be executed as soon as practicable, shall be conducted in such a way as to minimize the interception of communications not otherwise subject to interception under this chapter, and must terminate upon attainment of the authorized objective, or in any event in thirty days.

"(6) Whenever an order authorizing interception is entered pursuant to this chapter, the order may require reports to be made to the judge who issued the order showing what progress has been made toward achievement of the authorized objective and the need for continued interception. Such reports shall be made at such intervals as the judge may require.

"(7) Notwithstanding any other provision of this chapter, any investigative or law enforcement officer, specially designated by the Attorney General or by the principal prosecuting attorney of any State or subdivision thereof acting pursuant to a statute of that State, who reasonably determines that—

"(a) an emergency situation exists with respect to conspiratorial activities threatening the national security interest or to conspiratorial activities characteristic of organized crime that requires a wire or oral communication to be intercepted before an order authorizing such interception can with due diligence be obtained, and

"(b) there are grounds upon which an order could be entered under this chapter to authorize such interception,
may intercept such wire or oral communication if an application for an order approving the interception is made in accordance with this section within forty-eight hours after the interception has occurred, or begins to occur. In the absence of an order, such interception shall immediately terminate when the communication sought is obtained or when the application for the order is denied, whichever is earlier. In the event such application for approval is denied, or in any other case where the interception is terminated without an order having been issued, the contents of any wire or oral communication intercepted shall be treated as having been obtained in violation of this chapter, and an inventory shall be served as provided for in subsection (d) of this section on the person named in the application.

"(8) (a) The contents of any wire or oral communication intercepted by any means authorized by this chapter shall, if possible, be recorded on tape or wire or other comparable device. The recording of the contents of any wire or oral communication under this subsection shall be done in such way as will protect the recording from editing or other alterations. Immediately upon the expiration of the period of the order, or extensions thereof, such recordings shall be made available to the judge issuing such order and sealed under his directions. Custody of the recordings shall be wherever the judge orders. They shall not be destroyed except upon an order of the issuing or denying judge and in any event shall be kept for ten years. Duplicate recordings may be made for use or disclosure pursuant to the provisions of subsections (1) and (2) of section 2517 of this chapter for investigations. The presence of the seal provided for by this subsection, or a satisfactory explanation for the absence thereof, shall be a prerequisite for the

433

use or disclosure of the contents of any wire or oral communication or evidence derived therefrom under subsection (3) of section 2517.

"(b) Applications made and orders granted under this chapter shall be sealed by the judge. Custody of the applications and orders shall be wherever the judge directs. Such applications and orders shall be disclosed only upon a showing of good cause before a judge of competent jurisdiction and shall not be destroyed except on order of the issuing or denying judge, and in any event shall be kept for ten years.

"(c) Any violation of the provisions of this subsection may be punished as contempt of the issuing or denying judge.

"(d) Within a reasonable time but not later than ninety days after the filing of an application for an order of approval under section 2518(7)(b) which is denied or the termination of the period of an order or extensions thereof, the issuing or denying judge shall cause to be served, on the persons named in the order or the application, and such other parties to intercepted communications as the judge may determine in his discretion that is in the interest of justice, an inventory which shall include notice of—

"(1) the fact of the entry of the order or the application;

"(2) the date of the entry and the period of authorized, approved or disapproved interception, or the denial of the application; and

"(3) the fact that during the period wire or oral communications were or were not intercepted.

The judge, upon the filing of a motion, may in his discretion make available to such person or his counsel for inspection such portions of the intercepted communications, applications and orders as the judge determines to be in the interest of justice. On an ex parte showing of good cause to a judge of competent jurisdiction the serving of the inventory required by this subsection may be postponed.

"(9) The contents of any intercepted wire or oral communication or evidence derived therefrom shall not be received in evidence or otherwise disclosed in any trial, hearing, or other proceeding in a Federal or State court unless each party, not less than ten days before the trial, hearing, or proceeding, has been furnished with a copy of the court order, and accompanying application, under which the interception was authorized or approved. This ten-day period may be waived by the judge if he finds that it was not possible to furnish the party with the above information ten days before the trial, hearing, or proceeding and that the party will not be prejudiced by the delay in receiving such information.

"(10) (a) Any aggrieved person in any trial, hearing, or proceeding in or before any court, department, officer, agency, regulatory body, or other authority of the United States, a State, or a political subdivision thereof, may move to suppress the contents of any intercepted wire or oral communication, or evidence derived therefrom, on the grounds that—

"(i) the communication was unlawfully intercepted;

"(ii) the order of authorization or approval under which it was intercepted is insufficient on its face; or

"(iii) the interception was not made in conformity with the order of authorization or approval.

Such motion shall be made before the trial, hearing, or proceeding unless there was no opportunity to make such motion or the person was not aware of the grounds of the motion. If the motion is granted, the contents of the intercepted wire or oral communication, or evidence derived therefrom, shall be treated as having been obtained in violation of this chapter. The judge, upon the filing of such motion by the aggrieved person, may in his discretion make available to the aggrieved person or his counsel for inspection such portions of the intercepted communication or evidence derived therefrom as the judge determines to be in the interests of justice.

"(b) In addition to any other right to appeal, the United States shall have the right to appeal from an order granting a motion to suppress made under paragraph (a) of this subsection, or the denial of an application for an order of approval, if the United States attorney shall certify to the judge or other official granting such motion or denying such application that the appeal is not taken for purposes of delay. Such appeal shall be taken within thirty days after the date the order was entered and shall be diligently prosecuted.

"§ 2519. Reports concerning intercepted wire or oral communications

"(1) Within thirty days after the expiration of an order (or each extension thereof) entered under section 2518, or the denial of an order approving an interception, the issuing or denying judge shall report to the Administrative Office of the United States Courts—

"(a) the fact that an order or extension was applied for;

"(b) the kind of order or extension applied for;

"(c) the fact that the order or extension was granted as applied for, was modified, or was denied;

"(d) the period of interceptions authorized by the order, and the number and duration of any extensions of the order;

"(e) the offense specified in the order or application, or extension of an order;

435

"(f) the identity of the applying investigative or law enforcement officer and agency making the application and the person authorizing the application; and

"(g) the nature of the facilities from which or the place where communications were to be intercepted.

"(2) In January of each year the Attorney General, an Assistant Attorney General specially designated by the Attorney General, or the principal prosecuting attorney of a State, or the principal prosecuting attorney for any political subdivision of a State, shall report to the Administrative Office of the United States Courts—

"(a) the information required by paragraphs (a) through (g) of subsection (1) of this section with respect to each application for an order or extension made during the preceding calendar year;

"(b) a general description of the interceptions made under such order or extension, including (i) the approximate nature and frequency of incriminating communications intercepted, (ii) the approximate nature and frequency of other communications intercepted, (iii) the approximate number of persons whose communications were intercepted, and (iv) the approximate nature, amount, and cost of the manpower and other resources used in the interceptions;

"(c) the number of arrests resulting from interceptions made under such order or extension, and the offenses for which arrests were made;

"(d) the number of trials resulting from such interceptions;

"(e) the number of motions to suppress made with respect to such interceptions, and the number granted or denied;

"(f) the number of convictions resulting from such interceptions and the offenses for which the convictions were obtained and a general assessment of the importance of the interceptions; and

"(g) the information required by paragraphs (b) through (f) of this subsection with respect to orders or extensions obtained in a preceding calendar year.

"(3) In April of each year the Director of the Administrative Office of the United States Courts shall transmit to the Congress a full and complete report concerning the number of applications for orders authorizing or approving the interception of wire or oral communications and the number of orders and extensions granted or denied during the preceding calendar year. Such report shall include a summary and analysis of the data required to be filed with the Administrative Office by subsections (1) and (2) of this section. The Director of the Administrative Office of the United States Courts is authorized to issue binding regulations dealing with the content and form of the reports required to be filed by subsections (1) and (2) of this section.

"§ 2520. Recovery of civil damages authorized

"Any person whose wire or oral communication is intercepted, disclosed, or used in violation of this chapter shall (1) have a civil cause of action against any person who intercepts, discloses, or uses, or procures any other person to intercept, disclose, or use such communications, and (2) be entitled to recover from any such person—

"(a) actual damages but not less than liquidated damages computed at the rate of $100 a day for each day of violation or $1,000, which ever is higher;

"(b) punitive damages; and

"(c) a reasonable attorney's fee and other litigation costs reasonably incurred.

A good faith reliance on a court order or on the provisions of section 2518(7) of this chapter shall constitute a complete defense to any civil or criminal action brought under this chapter."

SEC. 803. Section 605 of the Communications Act of 1934 (48 Stat. 1103; 47 U.S.C. 605) is amended to read as follows:

"UNAUTHORIZED PUBLICATION OF COMMUNICATIONS

"SEC. 605. Except as authorized by chapter 119, title 18, United States Code, no person receiving, assisting in receiving, transmitting, or assisting in transmitting, any interstate or foreign communication by wire or radio shall divulge or publish the existence, contents, substance, purport, effect, or meaning thereof, except through authorized channels of transmission or reception, (1) to any person other than the addressee, his agent, or attorney, (2) to a person employed or authorized to forward such communication to its destination, (3) to proper accounting or distributing officers of the various communicating centers over which the communication may be passed, (4) to the master of a ship under whom he is serving, (5) in response to a subpena issued by a court of competent jurisdiction, or (6) on demand of other lawful authority. No person not being authorized by the sender shall intercept any radio communication and divulge or publish the existence, contents, substance, purport, effect, or meaning of such intercepted communication to any person. No person not being entitled thereto shall receive or assist in receiving any interstate or foreign communication by radio and use such communication (or any information therein contained) for his own benefit of for the benefit of another not entitled thereto. No person having received any inter-

437

cepted radio communication or having become acquainted with the contents, substance, purport, effect, or meaning of such communication (or any part thereof) knowing that such communication was intercepted, shall divulge or publish the existence, contents, substance, purport, effect, or meaning of such communication (or any part thereof) or use such communication (or any information therein contained) for his own benefit or for the benefit of another not entitled thereto. This section shall not apply to the receiving, divulging, publishing, or utilizing the contents of any radio communication which is broadcast or transmitted by amateurs or others for the use of the general public, or which relates to ships in distress."

SEC. 804. (a) There is hereby established a National Commission for the Review of Federal and State Laws Relating to wiretapping and Electronic Surveillance (hereinafter in this section referred to as the "Commission").

(b) The Commission shall be composed of fifteen members appointed as follows:

(A) Four appointed by the President of the Senate from Members of the Senate;

(B) Four appointed by the Speaker of the House of Representatives from Members of the House of Representatives; and

(C) Seven appointed by the President of the United States from all segments of life in the United States, including lawyers, teachers, artists, businessmen, newspapermen, jurists, policemen, and community leaders, none of whom shall be officers of the executive branch of the Government.

(c) The President of the United States shall designate a Chairman from among the members of the Commission. Any vacancy in the Commission shall not affect its powers but shall be filled in the same manner in which the original appointment was made.

(d) It shall be the duty of the Commission to conduct a comprehensive study and review of the operation of the provisions of this title, in effect on the effective date of this section, to determine the effectiveness of such provisions during the six-year period immediately following the date of their enactment.

(e) (1) Subject to such rules and regulations as may be adopted by the Commission, the Chairman shall have the power to—

(A) appoint and fix the compensation of an Executive Director, and such additional staff personnel as he deems necessary, without regard to the provisions of title 5, United States Code, governing appointments in the competitive service, and without regard to the provisions of chapter 51 and subchapter III of chapter 53 of such title relating to classification and General

Schedule pay rates, but at rates not in excess of the maximum rate for GS–18 of the General Schedule under section 5332 of such title; and

(B) procure temporary and intermittent services to the same extent as is authorized by section 3109 of title 5, United States Code, but at rates not to exceed $100 a day for individuals.

(2) In making appointments pursuant to paragraph (1) of this subsection, the Chairman shall include among his appointment individuals determined by the Chairman to be competent social scientists, lawyers, and law enforcement officers.

(f) (1) A member of the Commission who is a Member of Congress shall serve without additional compensation, but shall be reimbursed for travel, subsistence, and other necessary expenses incurred in the performance of duties vested in the Commission.

(2) A member of the Commission from private life shall receive $100 per diem when engaged in the actual performance of duties vested in the Commission, plus reimbursement for travel, subsistence, and other necessary expenses incurred in the performance of such duties.

(g) Each department, agency, and instrumentality of the executive branch of the Government, including independent agencies, is authorized and directed to furnish to the Commission, upon request made by the Chairman, such statistical data, reports, and other information as the Commission deems necessary to carry out its functions under this section. The Chairman is further authorized to call upon the departments, agencies, and other offices of the several States to furnish such statistical data, reports, and other information as the Commission deems necessary to carry out its functions under this section.

(h) The Commission shall make such interim reports as it deems advisable, and it shall make a final report of its findings and recommendations to the President of the United States and to the Congress within the one-year period following the effective date of this subsection. Sixty days after submission of its final report, the Commission shall cease to exist.

(i) (1) Except as provided in paragraph (2) of this subsection, any member of the Commission is exempted, with respect to his appointment, from the operation of sections 203, 205, 207, and 209 of title 18, United States Code.

(2) The exemption granted by paragraph (1) of this subsection shall not extend—

(A) to the receipt of payment of salary in connection with the appointee's Government service from any source other than the private employer of the appointee at the time of his appointment, or

439

(B) during the period of such appointment, to the prosecution, by any person so appointed, of any claim against the Government involving any matter with which such person, during such period, is or was directly connected by reason of such appointment.

(j) There is authorized to be appropriated such sum as may be necessary to carry out the provisions of this section.

(k) The foregoing provisions of this section shall take effect upon the expiration of the six-year period immediately following the date of the enactment of this Act.

Capital Punishment

*Witherspoon v. Illinois**

Capital punishment is one of the most controversial subjects in criminal jurisprudence. The right of the state to take the life of a criminal has been argued both for and against, on moral, ethical, and legal grounds. Those in favor of capital punishment no longer extol the virtue of retribution, an eye for an eye and a tooth for a tooth, but talk in terms of its effect as a deterrent. Those opposed to the ultimate in punishment refer to it as barbaric and unconstitutional, arguing that it is violative of the Eighth Amendment which prohibits the infliction of cruel and unusual punishment. The Supreme Court does not accept the Eighth Amendment argument. But in *Witherspoon* it has gone a long way to reduce the probability of the death penalty being inflicted. Therein lies the significance of this case.

Witherspoon committed the one crime from which very few evade detection. He shot and killed a policeman acting in the line of duty. At his trial, the defendant made no argument that the jury was partial, nor did he make such a contention in the first appeals he took through the State and Federal courts. It was not until some six years after his conviction that he raised the issue in a new petition filed in an Illinois State Court in which he requested whatever form of remedy is "provided for by Illinois law".

In this petition Witherspoon charged that the selection of his jury was unconstitutional. Any individuals with conscientious or religious scruples against the infliction of the death penalty were excluded from that jury by the trial judge; and Witherspoon contended that this exclusion deprived him of the impartial jury to which he was entitled.

In a six to three decision, the Supreme Court held that Witherspoon's sentence of death could not be carried out. The position of

* 391 U.S. 510, 88 S.Ct. 1770 (June 3, 1968)

the justices in this six to three holding is somewhat unusual. Mr. Justice Stewart who in most other cases expanding the rights of the accused, had been a dissenter, wrote the majority opinion. Mr. Justice Stewart had participated in a dissent in the *Mallory,*[1] *Escobedo,*[2] *Miranda*[3] and *Wade*[4] cases. Mr. Justice Black shifted in the opposite direction. Black, who participated in the majority in the above mentioned cases, dissented in *Witherspoon.*

There is an additional point worth noting relative to the judicial complexion of *Witherspoon.* Notwithstanding the single shift in both directions the balance of liberal and conservative views has changed. *Mallory, Escobedo* and *Miranda* were five to four decisions. *Witherspoon* was a six to three decision. This change is the result of Mr. Justice Clark's retirement. Clark had been one of the dissenters in the above three cases. Mr. Justice Thurgood Marshall was appointed to the vacancy on October 2, 1967. In this case, Mr. Justice Marshall has taken the liberal view relative to the rights of an accused.

This case opens the door for many convicted felons, now on death row, to apply for a new trial on the basis of an improper jury selection at their first trial. If only those veniremen who believed in capital punishment had been allowed to sit on the jury such a defendant might very well obtain relief. If not a reversal of his conviction, at least a reversal of the death sentence.[5]

Text of Case

Petitioner was adjudged guilty of murder and the jury fixed his penalty at death. An Illinois statute provided for challenges for cause in murder trials "of any juror who shall, on being examined, state that he has conscientious scruples against capital punishment, or that he is opposed to the same." At petitioner's trial the prosecution, under that statute, eliminated nearly half the venire of prospective jurors by challenging all who expressed qualms about the death penalty. Most of the veniremen thus challenged for cause were excluded with no effort to find out whether their scruples would invariably compel them to vote against capital punishment. The Illinois Supreme Court denied post-conviction relief.

Albert E. Jenner, Jr. argued the cause for petitioner. With him on the briefs were *Thomas P. Sullivan, Jerold S. Solovy,* and *John C. Tucker.*

---

[1] 378 U.S. 1, 84 S.Ct. 1489 (1964).
[2] 378 U.S. 478, 84 S.Ct. 1758 (1964).
[3] 384 U.S. 436, 86 S.Ct. 1602 (1966).
[4] 388 U.S. 218, 87 S.Ct. 1926 (1967).

[5] Witherspoon's conviction was not reversed. The Supreme Court only ruled that his sentence could not be carried out.

Donald J. Veverka, Assistant Attorney General, argued the cause for respondent State of Illinois. With him on the brief were *William G. Clark,* Attorney General, and *John J. O'Toole,* Assistant Attorney General. *James B. Zagel* argued the cause for respondent Woods, *pro hac vice.* With him on the brief were *John J. Stamos, Elmer C. Kissane,* and *Joel Flaum.*

Robert R. Granucci, Deputy Attorney General, argued the cause for the State of California, as *amicus curiae.* With him on the brief were *Thomas C. Lynch,* Attorney General, *Albert W. Harris, Jr.,* Assistant Attorney General, and *George R. Nock,* Deputy Attorney General, joined by the Attorneys General for their respective States as follows: *MacDonald Gallion* of Alabama, *Darrell F. Smith* of Arizona, *Joe Purcell* of Arkansas, *Duke W. Dunbar* of Colorado, *David P. Buckson* of Delaware, *Earl Faircloth* of Florida, *Arthur K. Bolton* of Georgia, *Allan G. Shepard* of Idaho, *Robert C. Londerholm* of Kansas, *John B. Breckinridge* of Kentucky, *Jack P. F. Gremillion* of Louisiana, *Norman H. Anderson* of Missouri, *Clarence A. H. Meyer* of Nebraska, *George S. Pappagianis* of New Hampshire, *Boston E. Witt* of New Mexico, *Helgi Johanneson* of North Dakota, *William B. Saxbe* of Ohio, *G. T. Blankenship* of Oklahoma, *William C. Sennett* of Pennsylvania, *Daniel R. McLeod* of South Carolina, *Frank L. Farrar* of South Dakota, *George F. McCanless* of Tennessee, *Crawford C. Martin* of Texas, *Robert Y. Button* of Virginia, *John J. O'Connell* of Washington, and *James E. Barrett* of Wyoming; and by *Marion O. Gordon,* Assistant Attorney General of Georgia, *Frank P. Lawley,* Deputy Attorney General of Pennsylvania, *Reno S. Harp III,* Assistant Attorney General of Virginia, and *Howard L. McFadden.*

Briefs of *amici curiae* were filed by *Elmer Gertz* for the Illinois Division, American Civil Liberties Union; by *Jack Greenberg, James M. Nabrit III, Michael Meltsner, Leroy D. Clark, Norman C. Amaker,* and *Charles S. Ralston* for the NAACP Legal Defense and Educational Fund, Inc., et al.; by *Alex Elson, Willard J. Lassers,* and *Marvin Braiterman* for the American Friends Service Committee et al.; by *F. Lee Bailey, pro se;* by *Joel W. Westbrook* for Turner, and by *John P. Frank* and *John J. Flynn* for Madden.

MR. JUSTICE STEWART delivered the opinion of the Court.

The petitioner was brought to trial in 1960 in Cook County, Illinois, upon a charge of murder. The jury found him guilty and fixed his penalty at death. At the time of his trial an Illinois statute provided:

"In trials for murder it shall be a cause for challenge of any juror who shall, on being examined, state that he has conscientious scruples against capital punishment, or that he is opposed to the same."[1] Through this provision the State of Illinois armed the prosecution with unlimited challenges for cause in order to exclude those jurors who, in the words of the State's highest court, "might hesitate to return a verdict inflicting [death]."[2] At the petitioner's trial, the prosecution eliminated nearly half the venire of prospective jurors by challenging, under the authority of this statute, any venireman who expressed qualms about capital punishment. From those who remained were chosen the jurors who ultimately found the petitioner guilty and sentenced him to death. The Supreme Court of Illinois denied post-conviction relief,[3] and we granted certiorari[4] to decide whether the Constitution permits a State to execute a man pursuant to the verdict of a jury so composed.

I.

The issue before us is a narrow one. It does not involve the right of the prosecution to challenge for cause those prospective jurors who state that their reservations about capital punishment would prevent them from making an impartial decision as to the defendant's guilt.[5] Nor does it involve the State's assertion of a right to

---

[1] Ill. Rev. Stat., c. 38, § 743 (1959). The section was re-enacted in 1961 but was not expressly repeated in the Code of Criminal Procedure of 1963. Ill.Rev.Stat., c. 38, § 115–4 (d) (1967) now provides only that "[e]ach party may challenge jurors for cause," but the Illinois Supreme Court has held that § 115–4 (d) incorporates former § 743. *People* v. *Hobbs*, 35 Ill. 2d 263, 274, 220 N. E. 2d 469, 475.

[2] "In the trial of the case where capital punishment may be inflicted a juror who has religious or conscientious scruples against capital punishment *might hesitate to return a verdict inflicting such punishment*, and in the present proceedings [a post-sentence sanity hearing] a juror having such scruples might likewise hesitate in returning a verdict finding [the defendant] sane, which in effect confirms the death sentence." *People* v. *Carpenter*, 13 Ill. 2d 470, 476, 150 N. E. 2d 100, 103. (Emphasis added.)

[3] 36 Ill. 2d 471, 224 N. E. 2d 259.

[4] 389 U. S. 1035.

[5] Unlike the statutory provision in this case, statutes and rules disqualifying jurors with scruples against capital punishment are often couched in terms of reservations against finding a man *guilty* when the penalty might be death. See, *e. g.*, Cal. Penal Code, § 1074, subd. 8. Yet, despite such language, courts in other States have sometimes permitted the exclusion for cause of jurors opposed to the death penalty even in the absence of a showing that their scruples would have interfered with their ability to determine guilt in accordance with the evidence and the law. See, *e. g.*, *State* v. *Thomas*, 78 Ariz. 52, 58, 275 P.2d 408, 412; *People* v. *Nicolaus*, 65 Cal. 2d 866, 882, 423 P.2d 787, 798; *Piccott* v. *State*, 116 So. 2d 626, 628 (Fla.); *Commonwealth* v. *Ladetto*, 349 Mass. 237, 246, 207 N. E. 2d 536, 542; *State* v. *Williams*, 50 Nev. 271, 278, 257 P. 619, 621; *Smith* v. *State*, 5 Okla. Cr. 282, 284, 114 P. 350, 351; *State* v. *Jensen*, 209 Ore. 239, 281, 296 P. 2d 618, 635; *State* v. *Leuch*, 198 Wash. 331, 333–337, 88 P. 2d 440, 441–442.

exclude from the jury in a capital case those who say that they could never vote to impose the death penalty or that they would refuse even to consider its imposition in the case before them. For the State of Illinois did not stop there, but authorized the prosecution to exclude as well all who said that they were opposed to capital punishment and all who indicated that they had conscientious scruples against inflicting it.

In the present case the tone was set when the trial judge said early in the *voir dire*, "Let's get these conscientious objectors out of the way, without wasting any time on them." In rapid succession, 47 veniremen were successfully challenged for cause on the basis of their attitudes toward the death penalty. Only five of the 47 explicitly stated that under no circumstances would they vote to impose capital punishment.[6] Six said that they did not "believe in the death penalty" and were excused without any attempt to determine whether they could nonetheless return a verdict of death.[7] Thirty-nine veniremen, including four of the six who indicated that they did not believe in capital punishment, acknowledged having "conscientious or religious scruples against the infliction of the death penalty" or against its infliction "in a proper case" and were excluded without any effort to find out whether their scruples would invariably compel them to vote against capital punishment.

Only one venireman who admitted to "a religious or conscientious scruple against the infliction of the death penalty in a proper case" was examined at any length. She was asked: "You don't believe in the death penalty?" She replied: "No. It's just I wouldn't want to be responsible." The judge admonished her not to forget her "duty as a citizen" and again asked her whether she had "a religious or conscientious scruple" against capital punishment. This time, she replied in the negative. Moments later, however, she repeated that she would not "like to be responsible for . . . decid-

---

[6] The State stresses the fact that the judge who presided during the *voir dire* implied several times that only those jurors who could *never* agree to a verdict of death should deem themselves disqualified because of their scruples against capital punishment. The record shows, however, that the remarks relied upon by the State were not made within the hearing of every venireman ultimately excused for cause under the statute. On the contrary, three separate venires were called into the courtroom, and it appears that at least 30 of the 47 veniremen eliminated in this case were not even present when the statements in question were made.

[7] It is entirely possible, of course, that even a juror who believes that capital punishment should never be inflicted and who is irrevocably committed to its abolition could nonetheless subordinate his personal views to what he perceived to be his duty to abide by his oath as a juror and to obey the law of the State. See *Commonwealth* v. *Webster*, 59 Mass. 295, 298. See also *Atkins* v. *State*, 16 Ark. 568, 580; *Williams* v. *State*, 32 Miss. 389, 395–396; *Rhea* v. *State*, 63 Neb. 461, 472–473, 88 N. W. 789, 792.

ing somebody should be put to death."[8] Evidently satisfied that this elaboration of the prospective juror's views disqualified her under the Illinois statute, the judge told her to "step aside."[9]

II.

The petitioner contends that a State cannot confer upon a jury selected in this manner the power to determine guilt. He maintains that such a jury, unlike one chosen at random from a cross-section of the community, must necessarily be biased in favor of conviction, for the kind of juror who would be unperturbed by the prospect of sending a man to his death, he contends, is the kind of juror who would too readily ignore the presumption of the defendant's innocence, accept the prosecution's version of the facts, and return a verdict of guilt. To support this view, the petitioner refers to what he describes as "competent scientific evidence

---

[8] Compare *Smith* v. *State*, 55 Miss. 410, 413–414: "The declaration of the rejected jurors, in this case, amounted only to a statement that they would not like . . . a man to be hung. Few men would. Every right-thinking man would regard it as a painful duty to pronounce a verdict of death upon his fellow-man. . . . for the error in improperly rejecting [these] two members of the special *venire* the case must be reversed."

[9] As the *voir dire* examination of this venireman illustrates, it cannot be assumed that a juror who describes himself as having "conscientious or religious scruples" against the infliction of the death penalty or against its infliction "in a proper case" (see *People* v. *Bandhauer*, 66 Cal. 2d 524, 531, 426 P. 2d 900, 905) thereby affirms that he could never vote in favor of it or that he would not consider doing so in the case before him. See also the *voir dire* in *Rhea* v. *State*, 63 Neb. 461, 466–468, 88 N. W. 789, 790. Cf. *State* v. *Williams*, 50 Nev. 271, 278, 257 P. 619, 621. Obviously many jurors "could, notwithstanding their conscientious scruples [against capital punishment], return . . . [a] verdict [of death] and . . . make their scruples subservient to their duty as jurors." *Stratton* v. *People*, 5 Colo. 276, 277. Cf. *Commonwealth* v. *Henderson*, 242 Pa. 372, 377, 89 A. 567, 569. Yet such jurors have frequently been deemed unfit to serve in a capital case. See, *e. g.*, *Rhea* v. *State*, *supra*, 63 Neb., at 470–471, 88 N. W., at 791–792. See generally Oberer, Does Disqualification of Jurors for Scruples Against Capital Punishment Constitute Denial of Fair Trial on Issue of Guilt?, 39 Tex. L. Rev. 545, 547–548 (1961); Comment, 1968 Duke L. J. 283, 295–299.

The critical question, of course, is not how the phrases employed in this area have been construed by courts and commentators. What matters is how they might be understood—or misunderstood—by prospective jurors. Any "layman . . . [might] say he has scruples if he is somewhat unhappy about death sentences. . . . [Thus] a general question as to the presence of . . . reservations [or scruples] is far from the inquiry which separates those who would never vote for the ultimate penalty from those who would reserve it for the direst cases." *Id.*, at 308–309. Unless a venireman states unambiguously that he would automatically vote against the imposition of capital punishment no matter what the trial might reveal, it simply cannot be assumed that that is his position.

that death-qualified jurors are partial to the prosecution on the issue of guilt or innocence."[10]

The data adduced by the petitioner, however, are too tentative and fragmentary to establish that jurors not opposed to the death penalty tend to favor the prosecution in the determination of guilt.[11] We simply cannot conclude, either on the basis of the record now before us or as a matter of judicial notice, that the exclusion of jurors opposed to capital punishment results in an unrepresentative jury on the issue of guilt or substantially increases the risk of conviction. In light of the presently available information, we are not prepared to announce a *per se* constitutional rule requiring the reversal of every conviction returned by a jury selected as this one was.

III.

It does not follow, however, that the petitioner is entitled to no relief. For in this case the jury was entrusted with two distinct responsibilities: first, to determine whether the petitioner was innocent or guilty; and second, if guilty, to determine whether his

---

[10] In his brief, the petitioner cites two surveys, one involving 187 college students, W. C. Wilson, Belief in Capital Punishment and Jury Performance (Unpublished Manuscript, University of Texas, 1964), and the other involving 200 college students, F. J. Goldberg, Attitude Toward Capital Punishment and Behavior as a Juror in Simulated Capital Cases (Unpublished Manuscript, Morehouse College, undated). In his petition for certiorari, he cited a study based upon interviews with 1,248 jurors in New York and Chicago. A preliminary, unpublished summary of the results of that study stated that "a jury consisting only of jurors who have no scruples against the death penalty is likely to be more prosecution prone than a jury on which objectors to the death penalty sit," and that "the defendant's chances of acquittal are somewhat reduced if the objectors are excluded from the jury." H. Zeisel, Some Insights Into the Operation of Criminal Juries 42 (Confidential First Draft, University of Chicago, November 1957).

[11] During the post-conviction proceedings here under review, the petitioner's counsel argued that the prosecution-prone character of "death-qualified" juries presented "purely a legal question," the resolution of which required "no additional proof" beyond "the facts . . . disclosed by the transcript of the voir dire examination . . . ." Counsel sought an "opportunity to submit evidence" in support of several contentions unrelated to the issue involved here. On this issue, however, no similar request was made, and the studies relied upon by the petitioner in this Court were not mentioned. We can only speculate, therefore, as to the precise meaning of the terms used in those studies, the accuracy of the techniques employed, and the validity of the generalizations made. Under these circumstances, it is not surprising that the *amicus curiae* brief filed by the NAACP Legal Defense and Educational Fund finds it necessary to observe that, with respect to bias in favor of the prosecution on the issue of guilt, the record in this case is "almost totally lacking in the sort of factual information that would assist the Court."

sentence should be imprisonment or death.[12] It has not been shown that this jury was biased with respect to the petitioner's guilt. But it is self-evident that, in its role as arbiter of the punishment to be imposed, this jury fell woefully short of that impartiality to which the petitioner was entitled under the Sixth and Fourteenth Amendments. See *Glasser* v. *United States,* 315 U.S. 60, 84–86; *Irvin* v. *Dowd,* 366 U.S. 717, 722–723; *Turner* v. *Louisiana,* 379 U.S. 466, 471–473.

The only justification the State has offered for the jury-selection technique it employed here is that individuals who express serious reservations about capital punishment cannot be relied upon to vote for it even when the laws of the State and the instructions of the trial judge would make death the proper penalty. But in Illinois, as in other States,[13] the jury is given broad discretion to decide whether or not death *is* "the proper penalty" in a given case, and a juror's general views about capital punishment play an inevitable role in any such decision.

A man who opposes the death penalty, no less than one who favors it, can make the discretionary judgment entrusted to him by the State and can thus obey the oath he takes as a juror. But a jury from which all such men have been excluded cannot perform the task demanded of it. Guided by neither rule nor standard, "free to select or reject as it [sees] fit,"[14] a jury that must choose between life imprisonment and capital punishment can do little more—and must do nothing less—than express the conscience of the community on the ultimate question of life or death.[15] Yet, in a nation less

---

[12] At the time of the petitioner's trial, the jury's penalty determination was binding upon the judge. Ill. Rev.Stat., c. 38, §§ 360, 801 (1959). That is no longer the case in Illinois, for the trial judge is now empowered to reject a jury recommendation of death, Ill. Rev. Stat., c. 38, § 1–7 (c) (1) (1967), but nothing in our decision turns upon whether the judge is bound to follow such a recommendation.

[13] See generally H. Kalven & H. Zeisel, The American Jury 435, 444, 448–449 (1966).

[14] *People* v. *Bernette,* 30 Ill. 2d 359, 370, 197 N. E. 2d 436, 443.

[15] It is suggested in a dissenting opinion today that the State of Illinois might "impose a particular penalty, including death, on all persons convicted of certain crimes." *Post,* at 541. But Illinois has attempted no such thing. Nor has it defined a category of capital cases in which "death [is] the *preferred* penalty." *People* v. *Bernette, supra,* at 369, 197 N. E. 2d, at 442. (Emphasis added.) Instead, it has deliberately "made . . . the death penalty . . . an optional form of punishment which [the jury remains] free to select or reject as it [sees] fit." 30 Ill. 2d, at 370, 197 N. E. 2d, at 443. And one of the most important functions any jury can perform in making such a selection is to maintain a link between contemporary community values and the penal system—a link without which the determination of punishment could hardly reflect "the evolving standards of decency that mark the progress of a maturing society." *Trop* v. *Dulles,* 356 U.S. 86, 101 (opinion of The Chief Justice, joined by Mr. Justice Black, Mr. Justice Douglas, and Mr. Justice Whittaker). Cf. n. 19, *infra.*

than half of whose people believe in the death penalty,[16] a jury composed exclusively of such people cannot speak for the community. Culled of all who harbor doubts about the wisdom of capital punishment—of all who would be reluctant to pronounce the extreme penalty—such a jury can speak only for a distinct and dwindling minority.[17]

If the State had excluded only those prospective jurors who stated in advance of trial that they would not even consider returning a verdict of death, it could argue that the resulting jury was simply "neutral" with respect to penalty.[18] But when it swept from the jury all who expressed conscientious or religious scruples against capital punishment and all who opposed it in principle, the State crossed the line of neutrality. In its quest for a jury capable of imposing the death penalty, the State produced a jury uncommonly willing to condemn a man to die.[19]

It is, of course, settled that a State may not entrust the determination of whether a man is innocent or guilty to a tribunal "organized to convict," *Fay* v. *New York*, 332 U.S. 261, 294. See *Tumey* v. *Ohio*, 273 U.S. 510. It requires but a short step from that principle to hold, as we do today, that a State may not entrust the determination of whether a man should live or die to a tribunal

[16] It appears that, in 1966, approximately 42% of the American public favored capital punishment for convicted murderers, while 47% opposed it and 11% were undecided. Polls, International Review on Public Opinion, Vol. II, No. 3, at 84 (1967). In 1960, the comparable figures were 51% in favor, 36% opposed, and 13% undicided. *Ibid.*

[17] Compare Arthur Koestler's observation:
"The devision is not between rich and poor, highbrow and lowbrow, Christions and atheists: it is between those who have charity and those who have not. . . . The test of one's humanity is whether one is able to accept this fact—not as lip service, but with the shuddering recognition of a kinship: here but for the grace of God, drop I." Koestler, Reflections on Hanging 166–167 (1956).

[18] Even so, a defendant convicted by such a jury in some future case might still attempt to establish that the jury was less than neutral with respect to *guilt*. If he were to succeed in that effort, the question would then arise whether the State's interest in submitting the penalty issue to a jury capable of imposing capital punishment may be vindicated at the expense of the defendant's interest in a completely fair determination of guilt or innocence—given the possibility of accommodating both interests by means of a bifurcated trial, using one jury to decide guilt and another to fix punishment. That problem is not presented here, however, and we intimate no view as to its proper resolution.

[19] The *amicus curiae* brief filed in this case by the American Friends Service Committee et al. notes that the number of persons under sentence of death in this country climbed from 300 at the end of 1963 to 406 at the end of 1966, while the number of persons actually executed fell from 21 in 1963 to 15 in 1964, seven in 1965, and one in 1966. The brief suggests that this phenomenon might be explained in part by society's "deep reluctance actually to inflict the death sentence" and by a widening "divergence of belief between the juries we select and society generally."

organized to return a verdict of death.[20] Specifically, we hold that a sentence of death cannot be carried out if the jury that imposed or recommended it was chosen by excluding veniremen for cause simply because they voiced general objections to the death penalty or expressed conscientious or religious scruples against its infliction.[21] No defendant can constitutionally be put to death at the

---

[20] It should be understood that much more is involved here than a simple determination of sentence. For the State of Illinois empowered the jury in this case to answer "yes" or "no" to the question whether this defendant was fit to live. To be sure, such a determination is different in kind from a finding that the defendant committed a specified criminal offense. Insofar as a determination that a man should be put to death might require "that there be taken into account the circumstances of the offense together with the character and propensities of the offender," *Pennsylvania* v. *Ashe*, 302 U.S. 51, 55, for example, it may be appropriate that certain rules of evidence with respect to penalty should differ from the corresponding evidentiary rules with respect to guilt. See, *e. g.*, *Williams* v. *New York*, 337 U.S. 241. But this does not mean that basic requirements of procedural fairness can be ignored simply because the determination involved in this case differs in some respects from the traditional assessment of whether the defendant engaged in a proscribed course of conduct. See, *e. g.*, *Specht* v. *Patterson*, 386 U.S. 605. Cf. *Mempa* v. *Rhay*, 389 U.S. 128. One of those requirements, at least, is that the decision whether a man deserves to live or die must be made on scales that are not deliberately tipped toward death. It was in part upon such a premise that the Fourth Circuit recently invalidated a North Carolina murder conviction, noting that a juror who felt it his "duty" to sentence *every* convicted murderer to death was allowed to serve in that case, "while those who admitted to scruples against capital punishment were dismissed without further interrogation." This "double standard," the court concluded, "inevitably resulted in [a] denial of due process." *Crawford* v. *Bounds*, 395 F. 2d 297, 303–304 (alternative holding). Cf. *Stroud* v. *United States*, 251 U.S. 15, 20–21; on petition for rehearing, *id.*, at 380, 381 (dictum).

[21] Just as veniremen cannot be excluded for cause on the ground that they hold such views, so too they cannot be excluded for cause simply because they indicate that there are some kinds of cases in which they would refuse to recommend capital punishment. And a prospective juror cannot be expected to say in advance of trial whether he would in fact vote for the extreme penalty in the case before him. The most that can be demanded of a venireman in this regard is that he be willing to *consider* all of the penalties provided by state law, and that he not be irrevocably committed, before the trial has begun, to vote against the penalty of death regardless of the facts and circumstances that might emerge in the course of the proceedings. If the *voir dire* testimony in a given case indicates that veniremen were excluded on any broader basis than this, the death sentence cannot be carried out even if applicable statutory or case law in the relevant jurisdiction would appear to support only a narrower ground of exclusion. See nn. 5 and 9, *supra*.

We repeat, however, that nothing we say today bears upon the power of a State to execute a defendant sentenced to death by a jury from which the only veniremen who were in fact excluded for cause were those who made unmistakably clear (1) that they would *automatically* vote against the imposition of capital punishment without regard to any evidence that might be developed at the trial of the case before them, or (2) that their attitude toward the death penalty would prevent

hands of a tribunal so selected.[22]

Whatever else might be said of capital punishment, it is at least clear that its imposition by a hanging jury cannot be squared with the Constitution. The State of Illinois has stacked the deck against the petitioner. To execute this death sentence would deprive him of his life without due process of law.

Reversed.

MR. JUSTICE DOUGLAS.

My difficulty with the opinion of the Court is a narrow but important one. The Court permits a State to eliminate from juries some of those who have conscientious scruples against the death penalty; but it allows those to serve who have no scruples against it as well as those who, having such scruples, nevertheless are deemed able to determine after a finding of guilt whether the death penalty or a lesser penalty should be imposed. I fail to see or understand the constitutional dimensions of those distinctions.

The constitutional question is whether the jury must be "impartially drawn from a cross-section of the community," or whether it can be drawn with systematic and intentional exclusion of some qualified groups, to use Mr. Justice Murphy's words in his dissent in *Fay* v. *New York*, 332 U.S. 261, 290.

Fay v. *New York*, which involved a conviction of union leaders for extortion, was the "blue ribbon" jury case in which the jury was weighted in favor of propertied people more likely to convict for certain kinds of crimes. The decision was 5–4, Mr. Justice Murphy speaking for MR. JUSTICE BLACK, Mr. Justice Rutledge, and myself:

---

them from making an impartial decision as to defendant's *guilt*. Nor does the decision in this case affect the validity of any sentence *other* than one of death. Nor, finally, does today's holding render invalid the *conviction*, as opposed to the *sentence*, in this or any other case.

[22] We have considered the suggestion, advanced in an *amicus curiae* brief filed by 27 States on behalf of Illinois, that we should "give prospective application only to any new constitutional ruling in this area," particularly since a dictum in an 1892 decision of this Court approved the practice of challenging for cause those jurors who expressed "conscientious scruples in regard to the infliction of the death penalty for crime." *Logan* v. *United States*, 144 U.S. 263, 298. But we think it clear, *Logan* notwithstanding, that the jury-selection standards employed here necessarily undermined "the very integrity of the . . . process" that decided the petitioner's fate, see *Linkletter* v. *Walker*, 381 U.S. 618, 639, and we have concluded that neither the reliance of law enforcement officials, cf. *Tehan* v. *Shott*, 382 U.S. 406, 417; *Johnson* v. *New Jersey*, 384 U.S. 719, 731, nor the impact of a retroactive holding on the administration of justice, cf. *Stovall* v. *Denno*, 388 U.S. 293, 300, warrants a decision against the fully retroactive application of the holding we announce today.

"There is no constitutional right to a jury drawn from a group of uneducated and unintelligent persons. Nor is there any right to a jury chosen solely from those at the lower end of the economic and social scale. But there is a constitutional right to a jury drawn from a group which represents a cross-section of the community. And a cross-section of the community includes persons with varying degrees of training and intelligence and with varying economic and social positions. Under our Constitution, the jury is not to be made the representative of the most intelligent, the most wealthy or the most successful, nor of the least intelligent, the least wealthy or the least successful. It is a democratic institution, representative of all qualified classes of people." *Id.*, at 299–300.

The idea that a jury should be "impartially drawn from a cross-section of the community"[1] certainly should not mean a selection of only those with a predisposition to impose the severest sentence or with a predisposition to impose the least one that is possible.

The problem is presented in different postures under several types of state laws. Many States, including Illinois, specifically grant the jury discretion as to penalty;[2] in some, this discretion is exercised at a special penalty trial, convened after a verdict of guilt has been returned.[3] In other States, death is imposed upon a conviction of first degree murder unless the jury recommends mercy or life imprisonment,[4] although in these States the jury is allowed

---

[1] "It is part of the established tradition in the use of juries as instruments of public justice that the jury be a body truly representative of the community." *Smith* v. *Texas*, 311 U.S. 128, 130. And see *Ballard* v. *United States*, 329 U.S. 187, 191; *Thiel* v. *Southern Pacific Co.*, 328 U.S. 217, 220 ("The American tradition of trial by jury, considered in connection with either criminal or civil proceedings, necessarily contemplates an impartial jury drawn from a cross-section of the community"); *Glasser* v. *United States*, 315 U.S. 60, 85–86.

[2] Ala. Code, Tit. 14, § 318 (1958); Ariz. Rev. Stat. Ann. § 13–453 (1956); Colo. Rev. Stat. Ann. § 40–2–3 (1963); Haw. Rev. Laws § 291–5 (1955); Idaho Code Ann. § 18–4004 (1948); Ill. Rev. Stat., c. 38, § 1–7 (c) (1) (1967); Ind. Ann. Stat. § 9–1819 (1956); Kan. Stat. Ann. § 21–403 (1964); Ky. Rev. Stat. § 435.010 (1962), Ky. Rule Crim. Proc. 9.84 (1965); Mo. Rev. Stat. § 559.030 (1959); Neb. Rev.

Stat. § 28–401 (1964); Nev. Rev. Stat. § 200.030 (1963); Okla. Stat. Ann., Tit. 21, § 707 (1958); Tenn. Code Ann. § 39–2406 (1955); Tex. Pen. Code Ann., Art. 1257 (1961), Tex. Code Crim. Proc., Art. 37.07 (1967 Supp.); Va. Code Ann. §§ 18.1–22, 19.1–291 (1960). In most of these States, a jury decision of death is binding on the court. In a few States, however, the judge may overrule the jury and impose a life sentence. Ill. Rev. Stat., c. 38, § 1–7 (c) (1) (1967); *State* v. *Anderson*, 384 S.W.2d 591 (Mo. 1964); S.D. Code § 13.2012 (1960 Supp.).

[3] Cal. Pen. Code § 190.1 (1967 Supp.); N. Y. Pen. Law §§ 125.30, 125.35 (1967); Pa. Stat., Tit. 18, § 4701 (1963). And see S. D. Code § 13.2012 (1960 Supp.) (trial court may ask jury to retire to deliberate on penalty after verdict of guilt returned).

[4] Ark. Stat. Ann. §§ 41–2227, 43–2153 (1964); Conn. Gen. Stat. Rev. § 53–10 (1965 Supp.); Del. Code Ann.,

to find a lesser degree of murder (or to find manslaughter, if under state law there are no degrees of murder), if the evidence will permit, without regard to the formal charge.[5] In some States, the death penalty is mandatory for certain types of crimes.[6] In still others, it has been abolished either in whole or in part.[7] And a few

Tit. 11, §§ 571, 3901 (1966 Supp.); Fla. Stat. §§ 782:04, 919.23 (1965); Ga. Code Ann. § 26–1005 (1953); La. Rev. Stat. § 14:30 (1950); Md. Ann. Code, Art. 27, § 413 (1967); Mass. Gen. Laws Ann., c. 265, § 2 (1959); Miss. Code Ann. § 2217 (1957); Mont. Rev. Codes Ann. § 94 2505 (1949); N. J. Rev. Stat. § 2A:113–4 (1953); N. M. Stat. Ann. § 40A–29–2 (1953); N. C. Gen. Stat. § 14–17 (1953); Ohio Rev. Code Ann. § 2901.01 (1954); S. C. Code Ann. § 16–52 (1962); Utah Code Ann. § 76–30–4 (1953); Wyo. Stat. Ann. § 6–54 (1959). In two of these States, the court possesses discretion to impose a life sentence despite the failure of the jury to recommend mercy. Ga. Code Ann. § 26–1005 (1953) (if conviction based solely on circumstantial evidence); Md. Ann. Code, Art. 27, § 413 (1967). In Delaware and Utah the court may overrule a jury recommendation of life imprisonment and impose the death penalty. Del. Code Ann., Tit. 11, §§ 571, 3901 (1966 Supp.); Utah Code Ann. § 76–30–4 (1953), State v. Romeo, 42 Utah 46, 128 P. 530 (1912).

[5] Arkansas: Ark. Stat. Ann. § 43–2152 (1964); Connecticut: Conn. Gen. Stat. Rev. § 53–9 (1965 Supp.); Delaware: State v. Price, 30 Del. 544, 108 A. 385 (1919); Florida: Brown v. State, 124 So. 2d 481 (1960); Georgia: (no degrees of murder) Graham v. State, 34 Ga. App. 598, 130 S. E. 354 (1925); Louisiana: (no degrees of murder) State v. Goodwin, 189 La. 443, 179 So. 591 (1938); Maryland: Md. Ann. Code, Art. 27, § 412 (1967), and see Chisley v. State, 202 Md. 87, 95 A. 2d 577 (1953), Gunther v. State, 228 Md. 404, 179 A. 2d 880 (1962); Massachusetts: Commonwealth v. Kavalauskas, 317 Mass. 453, 58 N. E. 2d 819 (1945), Commonwealth v. Di Stasio, 298 Mass. 562, 11 N. E. 2d 799 (1937); Mis-

sissippi: (no degrees of murder) Anderson v. State, 199 Miss. 885, 25 So. 2d 474 (1946); Montana: State v. Le Duc, 89 Mont. 545, 300 P. 919 (1931), State v. Miller, 91 Mont. 596, 9 P. 2d 474 (1932); New Jersey: State v. Sullivan, 43 N. J. 209, 203 A.2d 177 (1964), State v. Wynn, 21 N. J. 264, 121 A. 2d 534 (1956); New Mexico: State v. Smith, 26 N. M. 482, 194 P. 869 (1921); North Carolina: State v. Lucas, 124 N. C. 825, 32 S. E. 962 (1899); Ohio: State v. Muskus, 158 Ohio St. 276, 109 N. E. 2d 15 (1952); South Carolina: (no degrees of murder) State v. Byrd, 72 S. C. 104, 51 S. E. 542 (1905); Utah: State v. Mewhinney, 43 Utah 135, 134 P. 632 (1913); Wyoming: Brantley v. State, 9 Wyo. 102, 61 P. 139 (1900).

[6] Ala. Code, Tit. 14, § 319 (1958) (person serving life term at time of commission of offense); Ariz. Rev. Stat. Ann. § 13–701 (1956) (treason); Mass. Gen. Laws Ann., c. 265, § 2 (1959) (rape murders); Miss. Code Ann. § 2397 (1957) (treason); Ohio Rev. Code Ann. §§ 2901.09, 2901.10 (1954) (murder of President, Vice-President, Governor, or Lieutenant Governor); R. I. Gen. Laws Ann. § 11–23–2 (1956) (person serving life term at time of commission of offense).

[7] Alaska Stat. § 11.15.010 (1962); Iowa Code Ann. § 690.2 (1967 Supp.); Me. Rev. Stat. Ann., Tit. 17, § 2651 (1964); Mich. Stat. Ann. § 28.548, Comp. Laws 1948, § 750.316 (1954); Minn. Stat. § 609.185 (1965); Ore. Rev. Stat. § 163.010 (1967); W. Va. Code Ann. § 61–2–2 (1966); Wis. Stat. § 940.01 (1965). In North Dakota the death penalty has been abolished except in the case of murder committed while under a life sentence for murder, in which case the death penalty may be imposed at the jury's discretion. N. D. Cent. Code §§ 12–27–13, 12–27–22 (1960). Ver-

States have special rules which do not fit precisely into the above categories.[8]

A fair cross-section of the community may produce a jury almost certain to impose the death penalty if guilt were found; or it may produce a jury almost certain not to impose it. The conscience of the community is subject to many variables, one of which is the attitude toward the death sentence. If a particular community were overwhelmingly opposed to capital punishment, it would not be able to exercise a discretion to impose or not impose the death sentence. A jury representing the conscience of that community would do one of several things depending on the type of state law governing it: it would avoid the death penalty by recommending mercy or it would avoid it by finding guilt of a lesser offense.

In such instance, why should not an accused have the benefit of that controlling principle of mercy in the community? Why should his fate be entrusted exclusively to a jury that was either enthusiastic about capital punishment or so undecided that it could exercise a discretion to impose it or not, depending on how it felt about the particular case?

I see no constitutional basis for excluding those who are so opposed to capital punishment that they would never inflict it on a defendant. Exclusion of them means the selection of jurors who are either protagonists of the death penalty or neutral concerning it. That results in a systematic exclusion of qualified groups, and the deprivation to the accused of a cross-section of the community for decision on both his guilt and his punishment.

The Court in *Logan* v. *United States,* 144 U.S. 263, 298, held that prospective jurors who had conscientious scruples concerning in-

---

mont has also abolished the death penalty except in the cases of an unrelated second offense of murder or the killing of a peace officer or prison official, in which cases the death penalty may be imposed at the jury's discretion. Vt. Stat. Ann., Tit. 13, § 2303 (1967 Supp.). In Rhode Island the death penalty has been abolished except that it is mandatory in cases of murder committed while under a life sentence for murder. R. I. Gen. Laws Ann. § 11–23–2 (1956). In Georgia the death penalty may not be imposed if the person convicted was under 17 years of age at the time of the offense. Ga. Code Ann. § 26–1005 (1967 Supp.). In California it may not be imposed if the person was under 18 years of age. Cal. Pen. Code § 190.1 (1967 Supp.). In New York capital punishment has been abolished except that it may be imposed at the jury's discretion in cases of the murder of a peace officer while in the course of performing his official duties or of murder committed while under a life sentence for murder. N. Y. Pen. Law § 125.30 (1967).

[8] New Hampshire and Washington provide for life imprisonment unless the jury recommends death. N. H. Rev. Stat. Ann. § 585:4 (1955); Wash. Rev. Code § 9.48.030 (1956). Maryland permits the trial court alone to decide the penalty in its discretion without submitting the matter to the jury in cases of rape and aggravated kidnapping, Md. Ann. Code, Art. 27, §§ 461, 338 (1967).

fliction of the death penalty were rightly challenged by the prosecution for cause, stating that such jurors would be prevented "from standing indifferent between the government and the accused, and from trying the case according to the law and the evidence. . . ." That was a federal prosecution, the requirement being "an impartial jury" as provided in the Sixth Amendment, a requirement now applicable to the States by reason of the incorporation of the Jury Clause of the Sixth Amendment into the Due Process Clause of the Fourteenth. *Duncan* v. *Louisiana, ante,* p. 145.

But where a State leaves the fixing of the penalty to the jury, or provides for a lesser penalty on recommendation of mercy by the jury, or gives the jury power to find guilt in a lesser degree, the law leaves the jury great leeway. Those with scruples against capital punishment can try the case "according to the law and the evidence," because the law does not contain the inexorable command of "an eye for an eye." Rather "the law" leaves the degree of punishment to the jury. *Logan* v. *United States* in the setting of the present case[9] does not state what I believe is the proper rule. Whether in other circumstances it states a defensible rule is a question we need not reach. Where the jury has the discretion to impose the death penalty or not to impose it, the *Logan* rule is, in my opinion, an improper one. For it results in weeding out those members of the community most likely to recommend mercy and to leave in those most likely not to recommend mercy.[10]

Challenges for cause and peremptory challenges do not conflict with the constitutional right of the accused to trial by an "impartial jury." No one is guaranteed a partial jury. Such challenges generally are highly individualized not resulting in depriving the trial

---

[9] The ruling on the "impartial jury" in *Logan* v. *United States,* seems erroneous on the facts and the applicable law of that case. The governing statute (a Texas statute), 144 U. S., at 264, n. 1, left to the jury "the degree of murder, as well as the punishment."

[10] [T]he gulf between the community and the death-qualified jury grows as the populace becomes the more infected with modern notions of criminality and the purpose of punishment. Accordingly, the community support for the death verdict becomes progressively narrower, with all that this connotes for the administration of justice. Moreover, as the willingness to impose the death penalty—that is, *to be sworn as a juror in a capital* *case*—wanes in a particular community, the prejudicial effect of the death-qualified jury upon the issue of guilt or innocence waxes; to man the capital jury, the resort must increasingly be to the extremists of the community—those least in touch with modern ideas of criminal motivation, with the constant refinement of the finest part of our cultural heritage, the dedication to human charity and understanding. The due-process implications of this flux seem obvious. Yesterday's practice becomes less and less relevant to today's problem." Oberer, Does Disqualification of Jurors for Scruples Against Capital Punishment Constitute Denial of Fair Trial on Issue of Guilt?, 39 Tex. L. Rev. 545, 556–557 (1961).

of an entire class or of various shades of community opinion or of the "subtle interplay of influence" of one juror on another. *Ballard* v. *United States,* 329 U.S. 187, 193. In the present case, however, where the jury is given discretion in fixing punishment,[11] the wholesale exclusion of a class that makes up a substantial portion of the population[12] produces an unrepresentative jury.[13]

Although the Court reverses as to penalty, it declines to reverse the verdict of guilt rendered by the same jury. It does so on the ground that petitioner has not demonstrated on this record that the jury which convicted him was "less than neutral with respect to *guilt,*" *ante,* at 520, n. 18, because of the exclusion of all those opposed in some degree to capital punishment. The Court fails to find on this record "an unrepresentative jury on the issue of guilt." *Ante,* at 518. But we do not require a showing of specific prejudice when a defendant has been deprived of his right to a jury representing a cross-section of the community. See *Ballard* v. *United States,* 329 U.S. 187, 195; *Ware* v. *United States,* 123 U.S. App. D. C. 34, 356 F.2d 787 (1965). We can as easily assume that the absence of those opposed to capital punishment would rob the jury of certain peculiar qualities of human nature as would the exclusion of women from juries. *Ballard* v. *United States,* 329 U.S., at 193–194. I would not require a specific showing of a likelihood of prejudice, for I feel that we must proceed on the assumption that in many, if not most, cases of class exclusion on the basis of beliefs or attitudes some prejudice does result and many times will not be subject to precise measurement. Indeed, that prejudice "is so subtle, so intangible, that it escapes the ordinary methods of proof." *Fay* v. *New York,* 332 U.S., at 300 (dissenting opinion).

---

[11] In the words of the Illinois Supreme Court, the death penalty is "an optional form of punishment which [the jury is] free to select or reject as it [sees] fit." *People* v. *Bernette,* 30 Ill. 2d 359, 370, 197 N. E. 2d 436, 443 (1964). See also *People* v. *Dukes,* 12 Ill. 2d 334, 146 N. E. 2d 14 (1957); *People* v. *Weisberg,* 396 Ill. 412, 71 N. E. 2d 671 (1947); *People* v. *Martellaro,* 281 Ill. 300, 117 N. E. 1052 (1917).

[12] As the Court points out, a substantial number of the veniremen (47 out of 95), who we may assume represented a fair cross-section of the community, were excluded because of their opposition to the death penalty.

[13] In *Rudolph* v. *Alabama,* 375 U.S. 889, I joined the opinion of Mr. Justice Goldberg, dissenting from the Court's denial of certiorari, who expressed the view that this Court should consider the question whether the Eighth Amendment prohibits "the imposition of the death penalty on a convicted rapist who has neither taken nor endangered human life." *Ibid.* In contrast, the instant case concerns a convicted murderer who has been sentenced to death for his crime. The requirement imposed by the Sixth and the Fourteenth Amendments that a jury be representative of a cross-section of the community is, of course, separate and distinct from the question whether the death penalty offends the Eighth Amendment.

In my view, that is the essence of the requirement that a jury be drawn from a cross-section of the community.

MR. JUSTICE BLACK, with whom MR. JUSTICE HARLAN and MR. JUSTICE WHITE join, dissenting.

The Court closes its reversal of this murder case with the following graphic paragraph:

"Whatever else might be said of capital punishment, it is at least clear that its imposition by a hanging jury cannot be squared with the Constitution. The State of Illinois has stacked the deck against the petitioner. To execute this death sentence would deprive him of his life without due process of law."

I think this charge against the Illinois courts is completely without support in the record. The opinion affirming this conviction for a unanimous Illinois Supreme Court was written by Justice Walter Schaefer, a judge nationally recognized as a protector of the constitutional rights of defendants charged with crime. It seems particularly unfortunate to me that this Court feels called upon to charge that Justice Schaefer and his associates would let a man go to his death after the trial court had contrived a "hanging jury" and, in this Court's language, "stacked the deck" to bring about the death sentence for petitioner. With all due deference it seems to me that one might much more appropriately charge that this Court has today written the law in such a way that the States are being forced to try their murder cases with biased juries. If this Court is to hold capital punishment unconstitutional, I think it should do so forthrightly, not by making it impossible for States to get juries that will enforce the death penalty.

Now to the case.

On April 29, 1959, *more than nine years ago,* petitioner shot and killed a policeman in order to escape arrest. Petitioner had been struggling on the street with a woman whom he had met in a tavern when a police patrol car assigned to the vicinity stopped at a nearby traffic light. The woman was able to free herself from petitioner's grasp and rushed to the patrol car where she told the two policemen in it that petitioner was carrying a gun. Petitioner overheard this conversation and fled to a nearby parking lot and hid in one of the many parked trailers and tractors. It was while one of the policemen was searching this trailer that petitioner shot him. There is no doubt that petitioner killed the policeman since the dying officer himself identified petitioner at the hospital, and petitioner later lectured the police on using such young and inexperienced officers. And as I read the majority's opinion, even those who

457

agreed to it are unwilling to cast any doubt on petitioner's conviction. See n. 21, majority opinion.

At his trial for murder petitioner was represented by three appointed counsel, the chief of whom was the then Chairman of the Chicago Bar Association Committee for the Defense of the Indigent. It is important to note that when those persons who acknowledged having "conscientious or religious scruples against the infliction of the death penalty" were excluded from the jury, defense counsel made no attempt to show that they were nonetheless competent jurors. In fact, when the jurors finally were accepted by defense counsel, the defense still had three peremptory challenges left to exercise. In the past this has frequently been taken as an indication that the jurors who were impaneled were impartial. See cases collected in *United States* v. *Puff*, 211 F.2d 171, 185 (C.A.2d Cir. 1954). And it certainly amounts to a clear showing that in this case petitioner's able and distinguished counsel did not believe petitioner was being tried by a biased, much less a "hanging," jury.

After petitioner's conviction, another very distinguished attorney was appointed to prosecute his appeal, and an extensive brief alleging some 15 separate trial errors was filed in the Supreme Court of Illinois. Again, however, there was no indication that anyone thought petitioner had been convicted by a biased jury. On March 25, 1963, the Supreme Court of Illinois affirmed petitioner's conviction in a lengthy opinion. *People* v. *Witherspoon*, 27 Ill. 2d 483, 190 N.E.2d 281. Petitioner attacked his conviction by pursuing both habeas corpus relief and the statutory post-conviction remedy. Again no mention was made of any alleged bias in the jury. When the Supreme Court of Illinois on January 17, 1964, refused the requested relief, petitioner sought federal habeas corpus, and was assisted by a third court-appointed attorney. As in his previous attacks no claim was made that petitioner was denied an impartial jury. Petitioner was unsuccessful in this federal habeas corpus bid, *Witherspoon* v. *Ogilvie*, 337 F.2d 427 (C.A. 7th Cir. 1964), and we denied certiorari. *Witherspoon* v. *Ogilvie*, 379 U.S. 950. Then in February 1965, petitioner filed a petition in the state courts requesting whatever form of remedy is "provided for by Illinois law." Among other claims, now appeared the contention that petitioner's constitutional rights were violated when the trial court excused for cause prospective jurors having scruples against capital punishment. The state trial judge dismissed the petition on the ground that it failed to set forth facts sufficient to entitle the petitioner to relief. Petitioner then appealed to the Illinois Supreme Court where he was appearing for the third time in this case and where, more than six years after his trial, he argued that the disqualification for cause of jurors having conscientious or religious scruples against capital punishment was unconstitutional.[1] That court disallowed petitioner's claim concluding that "we adhere to the system in which each side is allowed to examine jurors and eliminate those who can not be impartial." 36 Ill.2d, at 476, 224 N.E.2d, at 262. This Court subsequently granted certiorari to review the decision of the Illinois Supreme Court.

At the time of petitioner's trial, § 743 of Ill. Rev. Stat., c. 38, provided:

"In trials for murder it shall be a cause for challenge of any juror who shall, on being examined, state that he has conscientious scruples against capital punishment, or that he is opposed to the same."

The obvious purpose of this section is to insure, as well as laws can insure such a thing, that there be an impartial jury in cases in Illinois where the death sentence may be imposed. And this statute recognizes that the people as a whole, or as they are usually called, "society" or "the state," have as much right to an impartial jury as do criminal defendants. This Court itself has made that quite clear:

"It is to be remembered that such impartiality requires not only freedom from any bias against the accused, but also from any prejudice against his prosecution. Between him and the state the scales are to be evenly held." *Hayes* v. *Missouri*, 120 U.S. 68, 70. See also *Swain* v. *Alabama*, 380 U.S. 202, 219–220.

As I see the issue in this case, it is a question of plain bias. A person who has conscientious or religious scruples against capital punishment will seldom if ever vote to impose the death penalty. This is just human nature, and no amount of semantic camouflage can cover it up. In the same manner, I would not dream of foisting on a criminal defendant a juror who admitted that he had conscientious or religious scruples against not inflicting the death sentence on any person convicted of murder (a juror who claims, for example, that he adheres literally to the Biblical admonition of "an eye for an eye"). Yet the logical result of the majority's holding is that such persons must be allowed so that the "conscience of the community" will be fully represented when it decides "the ultimate question of life or death." While I have always advocated that the jury be as fully representative of the community as possible, I would never carry this so far as to require that those

---

[1] Certainly long delays in raising objections to trial proceedings should not be condoned except to prevent intolerable miscarriages of justice. Cf. *Fay* v. *Noia*, 372 U.S. 391.

459

biased against one of the critical issues in a trial should be represented on a jury. I still subscribe to the words of this Court written over 75 years ago in *Logan* v. *United States*, 144 U.S. 263, 298:

"As the defendants were indicted and to be tried for a crime punishable with death, those jurors who stated on *voir dire* that they had 'conscientious scruples in regard to the infliction of the death penalty for crime' were rightly permitted to be challenged by the government for cause. A juror who has conscientious scruples on any subject, which prevent him from standing indifferent between the government and the accused, and from trying the case according to the law and the evidence, is not an impartial juror. This court has accordingly held that a person who has a conscientious belief that polygamy is rightful may be challenged for cause on a trial for polygamy. *Reynolds* v. *United States*, 98 U.S. 145, 147, 157; *Miles* v. *United States*, 103 U.S. 304, 310. And the principle has been applied to the very question now before us by Mr. Justice Story in *United States* v. *Cornell*, 2 Mason, 91, 105, and by Mr. Justice Baldwin in *United States* v. *Wilson*, Baldwin, 78, 83, as well as by the courts of every State in which the question has arisen, and by express statute in many States. Whart. Crim. Pl. (9th ed.) § 664."

The majority opinion attempts to equate those who have conscientious or religious scruples against the death penalty with those who do not in such a way as to balance the allegedly conflicting viewpoints in order that a truly representative jury can be established to exercise the community's discretion in deciding on punishment. But for this purpose I do not believe that those who have conscientious or religious scruples against the death penalty and those who have no feelings either way are in any sense comparable. Scruples against the death penalty are commonly the result of a deep religious conviction or a profound philosophical commitment developed after much soul-searching. The holders of such scruples must necessarily recoil from the prospect of making possible what they regard as immoral. On the other hand, I cannot accept the proposition that persons who do not have conscientious scruples against the death penalty are "prosecution prone."[2] With regard to this group, I would agree with the following statement of the Court of Appeals for the District of Columbia Circuit:

"No proof is available, so far as we know, and we can imagine none, to indicate that, generally speaking, persons not opposed to capital punishment are so bent in their hostility to criminals as to be incapable of rendering impartial verdicts on the law and the

---

[2] See *Bumper* v. *North Carolina*, *post*, p. 554 (dissenting opinion).

evidence in a capital case. Being not opposed to capital punishment is not synonymous with favoring it. Individuals may indeed be so prejudiced in respect to serious crimes that they cannot be impartial arbiters, but that extreme is not indicated by mere lack of opposition to capital punishment. The two antipathies can readily coexist; contrariwise either can exist without the other; and, indeed, neither may exist in a person. It seems clear enough to us that a person or a group of persons may not be opposed to capital punishment and at the same time may have no particular bias against any one criminal or, indeed, against criminals as a class; people, it seems to us, may be completely without a controlling conviction one way or the other on either subject . . . ." *Turberville* v. *United States,* 112 U.S. App. D. C. 400, 409–410, 303 F.2d 411, 420–421 (1962), cert. denied, 370 U.S. 946.

It seems to me that the Court's opinion today must be read as holding just the opposite from what has been stated above. For no matter how the Court might try to hide it, the implication is inevitably in its opinion that people who do not have conscientious scruples against the death penalty are somehow callous to suffering and are, as some of the commentators cited by the Court called them, "prosecution prone." This conclusion represents a psychological foray into the human mind that I have considerable doubt about my ability to make, and I must confess that the two or three so-called "studies" cited by the Court on this subject are not persuasive to me.

Finally, I want to point out that the *real* holding in this case is, at least to me, very ambiguous. If we are to take the opinion literally, then I submit the Court today has decided nothing of substance, but has merely indulged itself in a semantic exercise. For as I read the opinion, the new requirement placed upon the States is that they cease asking prospective jurors whether they have "conscientious or religious scruples against the infliction of the death penalty," but instead ask whether "they would *automatically* vote against the imposition of capital punishment without regard to any evidence that might be developed at the trial of the case before them." (See majority opinion, n. 21.) I believe that this fine line the Court attempts to draw is based on a semantic illusion and that the practical effect of the Court's new formulation of the question to be asked state juries will not produce a significantly different kind of jury from the one chosen in this case. And I might add that the States will have been put to a great deal of trouble for nothing. Yet, as I stated above, it is not clear that this is all the Court is holding. For the majority opinion goes out of its way to state that in some future case a defendant might well estab-

461

lish that a jury selected in the way the Illinois statute here provides is "less than neutral with respect to *guilt.*" (Majority opinion, n. 18.) This seems to me to be but a thinly veiled warning to the States that they had better change their jury selection procedures or face a decision by this Court that their murder convictions have been obtained unconstitutionally.

I believe that the Court's decision today goes a long way to destroying the concept of an impartial jury as we have known it. This concept has been described most eloquently by Justice Story: "To insist on a juror's sitting in a cause when he acknowledges himself to be under influences, no matter whether they arise from interest, from prejudices, or from religious opinions, which will prevent him from giving a true verdict according to law and evidence, would be to subvert the objects of a trial by jury, and to bring into disgrace and contempt, the proceedings of courts of justice. We do not sit here to produce the verdicts of partial and prejudiced men; but of men, honest and indifferent in causes. This is the administration of justice [which is required]." *United States* v. *Cornell,* 25 Fed. Cas. 650, 655–656 (No. 14,868) (1820).

It is just as necessary today that juries be impartial as it was in 1820 when Justice Story made this statement. I shall not contribute in any way to the destruction of our ancient judicial and constitutional concept of trial by an impartial jury by forcing the States through "constitutional doctrine" laid down by this Court to accept jurors who are bound to be biased. For this reason I dissent.

MR. JUSTICE WHITE, dissenting.

The Court does not hold that imposition of the death penalty offends the Eighth Amendment. Nor does it hold that a State Legislature may not specify only death as the punishment for certain crimes, so that the penalty is imposed automatically upon a finding of guilt, with no discretion in judge or jury. Either of these holdings might furnish a satisfactory predicate for reversing this judgment. Without them, the analytic basis of the result reached by the Court is infirm; the conclusion is reached because the Court says so, not because of reasons set forth in the opinion.

The Court merely asserts that this legislative attempt to impose the death penalty on some persons convicted of murder, but not on everyone so convicted, is constitutionally unsatisfactory:

"It is, of course, settled that a State may not entrust the determination of whether a man is innocent or guilty to a tribunal 'organized to convict.' It requires but a short step from that principle to hold, as we do today, that a State may not entrust the determination of whether a man should live or die to a tribunal organized

462

to return a verdict of death." *Ante,* at 521. (Citations and footnote omitted.)

The sole reason connecting the two sentences is the raw assertion that the situations are closely related. Yet the Constitution, which bars a legislative determination that everyone indicted should be convicted, and so requires the judgment of a guilt-determining body unprejudiced as to the result,[1] speaks in entirely different terms to the determination of sentence, even when that sentence is death. The Court does not deny that the legislature can impose a particular penalty, including death, on all persons convicted of certain crimes. Why, then, should it be disabled from delegating the penalty decision to a group who will impose the death penalty more often than would a group differently chosen?

All Illinois citizens, including those who oppose the death penalty, are assured by the Constitution a fair opportunity to influence the legislature's determinations about criminal sentences. *Reynolds* v. *Sims,* 377 U.S. 533 (1964), and succeeding cases. Those opposing the death penalty have not prevailed in that forum, however. The representatives of the people of Illinois have determined that the death penalty decision should be made in individual cases by a group of those citizens without conscientious scruples about one of the sentencing alternatives provided by the legislature. This method of implementing the majority's will was presumably related to a desire to preserve the traditional policy of requiring that jury verdicts be unanimous. The legislature undoubtedly felt that if all citizens could serve on the jury, and if one citizen with especially pronounced "scruples" could prevent a decision to impose death, the penalty would almost never be imposed.[2] We need not decide today whether any possible delegation of the sentencing decision, for example a delegation to the surviving relatives of the victim, would be constitutionally impermissible because it would offend the conscience of civilized men, *Rochin* v. *California,* 342 U.S. 165, 172 (1952). The delegation by Illinois, which merely excludes those with doubts in policy about one of the punishments among which the

---

[1] While I agree generally with the opinion of MR. JUSTICE BLACK, and so have joined it, I would not wholly foreclose the possibility of a showing that certain restrictions on jury membership imposed because of jury participation in penalty determination produce a jury which is not constitutionally constituted for the purpose of determining guilt.

[2] The States should be aware of the ease with which they can adjust to today's decision. They continue to be permitted to impose the penalty of death on all who commit a particular crime. And replacing the requirement of unanimous jury verdicts with majority decisions about sentence should achieve roughly the same result reached by the Illinois Legislature through the procedure struck down today.

legislature sought to have them choose, seems an entirely reasonable and sensible legislative act.

The Court may have a strong dislike for this particular sentence, and it may desire to meet Mr. Koestler's standards of charity. Those are laudable motives, but hardly a substitute for the usual processes of reasoned analysis. If the Court can offer no better constitutional grounds for today's decision than those provided in the opinion, it should restrain its dislike for the death penalty and leave the decision about appropriate penalties to branches of government whose members, selected by popular vote, have an authority not extended to this Court.

V

Freedom of Speech and Press

The First Amendment guarantees of freedom of speech and press have long been the subject of deep controversy. At one extreme are those individuals who feel that these freedoms have been construed in such a manner so as to pollute the minds of decent law abiding citizens. At the other end of the spectrum are those who feel that any censorship is an affront to their intelligence and an attempt by the government to dictate taste. The Supreme Court has balanced the interests of each of these groups in making determinations relative to whether these guarantees have been infringed in specific cases.

Let the reader not be mislead. We are concerned with much more than the censorship of sex in this area (although certainly this is an important aspect of the problem and three cases pertaining thereto have been included in this chapter). Whenever the individual's freedom to express himself is curtailed in any way you have a First Amendment problem. This is true whether the restraint involves sexual matters or not. However, such a violation does not necessarily mean there has been an invasion of First Amendment rights. It has long been settled that a person has no right to yell fire in a crowded theater just for kicks. But what about less obvious publications? Are cigarette manufacturers to be allowed to advertise cigarettes in an unrestricted fashion notwithstanding the considerable medical evidence that they may be fatal to the user? Although this question has yet to face the Supreme Court many other problems involving this area have been before it. Several cases which illustrate the difficulties encountered in construing the freedom of speech and press guarantees, are included in this chapter.

Estes v. Texas*

The *Estes* decision is noteworthy for its contribution to the fair trial—free press debate. The constitution provides that trials shall be public. The press qualifies as part of the public. Therefore, reporters will be accepted into the courtroom. What tools may the reporters bring with them? The notepad and pencil have always been permitted. But what about the reporter who desires to use a different tool, the television camera? The *Estes* opinion deals with this problem.

Billie Sol Estes was a nationally known figure at the time of the Texas trial which the Supreme Court reviews in this case. Allegations that he was the master mind of a multi-million dollar confidence game aroused interest throughout the country. At this trial it was alleged that Estes, through false pretenses and fraudulent representations, induced certain farmers to purchase fertilizer tanks and accompanying equipment which in fact did not exist.[1] Because of his public notoriety the case received considerable press coverage.

A substantial portion of the reporting was via the television camera. Texas was one of two states which at that time permitted the televising of judicial proceedings. Estes was not only on trial, he was on stage. The courtroom was frequently a maze of cables, cameras and cameramen.[2]

Estes was convicted and sentenced to eight years in prison. On review before the Supreme Court, counsel argued that Estes had been deprived of his Fourteenth Amendment right to due process of law. It was contended that the televising of the trial so disrupted the proceedings that a fair and impartial determination was impossible.

---

* 381 U.S. 532, 85 S.Ct. 1628 (June 7, 1965)

[1] This state prosecution involved local charges arising out of a fraudulent scheme which was national in scope. Estes had fraudulently induced many farmers, in Texas and other states, to purchase the non-existent tanks and equipment. To secure the purchase price he had them sign mortgages on the non-existent facilities. To encourage the farmers to sign he gave them 10% of the face amount of the mortgage and agreed to send them money with which to meet the payments. Estes then took the mortgages and sold them to finance companies throughout the nation. He used the proceeds to fund his own investments. In an effort to conceal the fact that the tanks did not exist he leased some and represented them to be the subject matter of the contracts. N.Y. Times, April 23, 1966, p. 12, col. 5.

[2] See exhibit "D-17" which appears at page 481 of this volume. This picture is from a glossy photograph which was part of the record before the Supreme Court. That exhibit and others from the record, which appear on pages 481 to 484 of this volume, were made available to the author by counsel for Estes, John D. Cofer and Hume Cofer of Austin, Texas.

The Supreme Court report is a lengthy discourse on the propriety of televising judicial proceedings. The Court, in this five to four holding, was divided on the issue in a rather complex fashion. There are five separate opinions contained in the decision.

Mr. Justice Clark wrote the majority opinion in which Justices Warren, Douglas, Harlan and Goldberg concurred. The conviction was reversed on the basis that the television coverage of Estes' trial resulted in a denial of due process of law. Mr. Chief Justice Warren wrote a separate concurring opinion in which Justices Douglas and Goldberg joined. This opinion expands the majority ruling. It expresses a view that televising any state trial is constitutionally prohibited. The majority opinion had addressed itself only to the propriety of televising the Estes' trial. Mr. Justice Harlan also wrote a separate concurring opinion. He emphasized that his determination relates only to the coverage of Estes' trial.

The dissent was written by Mr. Justice Potter. He was joined by Justices Black, White, and Brennan. Mr. Justice Brennan also wrote a separate opinion emphasizing that the majority did not hold that televising a judicial proceeding, in and of itself, was improper.

Billie Sol Estes may have won this battle but he lost the war. There were other prosecutions arising out of the same fraudulent scheme. One of the most notable was a federal prosecution for mail fraud in a twenty-four million dollar swindle of major finance companies. On March 28, 1963 Estes was convicted of this offense.[3] He was sentenced to fifteen years in prison.[4] Estes is presently serving that sentence in the federal penitentiary at Leavenworth, Kansas.[5]

Text of Case

Petitioner had been indicted by a Texas county grand jury for swindling. Massive pretrial publicity had given the case national notoriety. On the trial date, following a change of venue, a hearing commenced on petitioner's motion to prevent telecasting, radio broadcasting, and news photography. The hearing, conducted in the presence of some trial witnesses and veniremen later released, was carried live on television and radio, and news photography was permitted. The original jury panel, petitioner, counsel, and the trial judge were highly publicized during the two days the pretrial hearing lasted, emphasizing throughout the community the notorious character that the trial would take. Four of the jurors selected

---

[3] N.Y. Times, March 29, 1963, p. 1, col. 3.

[4] N.Y. Times, April 16, 1963, p. 1, col. 8.

[5] N.Y. Times, April 20, 1966, p. 28, col. 1.

later at the trial had seen or heard all or part of the broadcasts. The profusion of cameramen with their equipment in various parts of the crowded courtroom caused considerable disruption. The trial court denied petitioner's motion but granted a continuance of almost a month. During the interim a booth was erected in the rear of the courtroom to which television cameramen and equipment were restricted. Live telecasting was prohibited during most of the actual trial. The State's opening and closing arguments were carried live with sound (though because of mechanical difficulty there was no picture of the former), as were the return of the jury's verdict and its receipt by the judge. The court's order allowed videotapes without sound of the whole proceeding and the cameras operated intermittently during the three-day trial, which ended with petitioner's conviction. Film clips of the trial were shown largely on regularly scheduled news programs. Both the trial court and the appellate court rejected petitioner's claim of denial of due process in violation of the Fourteenth Amendment by the televising and broadcasting of the trial.

John D. Cofer and *Hume Cofer* argued the cause and filed a brief for petitioner.

Waggoner Carr, Attorney General of Texas, and *Leon Jaworski,* Special Assistant Attorney General, argued the cause for respondent. With them on the brief were *Hawthorne Phillips, Stanton Stone, Howard M. Fender* and *Gilbert J. Pena,* Assistant Attorneys General, and *Alton F. Curry,* Special Assistant Attorney General.

Briefs of *amici curiae,* urging reversal, were filed by *Whitney North Seymour, Richmond C. Coburn* and *John H. Yauch* for the American Bar Association, and by *Norman Dorsen* and *Melvin L. Wulf* for the American Civil Liberties Union et al.

Briefs of *amici curiae,* urging affirmance, were filed by *Davis Grant* for the State Bar of Texas, joined by *Duke W. Dunbar,* Attorney General of Colorado; and by *Douglas A. Anello, W. Theodore Pierson* and *Harold David Cohen* for the National Association of Broadcasters et al.

MR. JUSTICE CLARK delivered the opinion of the Court.*

The question presented here is whether the petitioner, who stands convicted in the District Court for the Seventh Judicial District of Texas at Tyler for swindling,[1] was deprived of his right under the

---

* MR. JUSTICE HARLAN concurs in this opinion subject to the reservations and to the extent indicated in his concurring opinion, *post,* p. 587.

[1] The evidence indicated that petitioner, through false pretenses and fraudulent representations, induced certain farmers to purchase fertilizer tanks and accompanying equipment, which in fact did not exist, and to sign and deliver to him chattel mortgages on the fictitious property.

Fourteenth Amendment to due process by the televising and broadcasting of his trial. Both the trial court and the Texas Court of Criminal Appeals found against the petitioner. We hold to the contrary and reverse his conviction.

I.

While petitioner recites his claim in the framework of Canon 35 of the Judicial Canons of the American Bar Association he does not contend that we should enshrine Canon 35 in the Fourteenth Amendment, but only that the time-honored principles of a fair trial were not followed in his case and that he was thus convicted without due process of law. Canon 35, of course, has of itself no binding effect on the courts but merely expresses the view of the Association in opposition to the broadcasting, televising and photographing of court proceedings. Likewise, Judicial Canon 28 of the Integrated State Bar of Texas, 27 Tex. B. J. 102 (1964), which leaves to the trial judge's sound discretion the telecasting and photographing of court proceedings, is of itself not law. In short, the question here is not the validity of either Canon 35 of the American Bar Association or Canon 28 of the State Bar of Texas, but only whether petitioner was tried in a manner which comports with the due process requirement of the Fourteenth Amendment.

Petitioner's case was originally called for trial on September 24, 1962, in Smith County after a change of venue from Reeves County, some 500 miles west. Massive pretrial publicity totaling 11 volumes of press clippings, which are on file with the Clerk, had given it national notoriety. All available seats in the courtroom were taken and some 30 persons stood in the aisles. However, at that time a defense motion to prevent telecasting, broadcasting by radio and news photography and a defense motion for continuance were presented, and after a two-day hearing the former was denied and the latter granted.

These initial hearings were carried live by both radio and television, and news photography was permitted throughout. The videotapes of these hearings clearly illustrate that the picture presented was not one of that judicial serenity and calm to which petitioner was entitled. Cf. *Wood* v. *Georgia*, 370 U.S. 375, 383 (1962); *Turner* v. *Louisiana*, 379 U.S. 466, 472 (1965); *Cox* v. *Louisiana*, 379 U.S. 559, 562 (1965). Indeed, at least 12 cameramen were engaged in the courtroom throughout the hearing taking motion and still pictures and televising the proceedings. Cables and wires were snaked across the courtroom floor, three microphones were on the judge's bench and others were beamed at the jury box and the counsel table. It is conceded that the activities of the television crews and news photographers led to considerable disruption of the hearings. Moreover, veniremen had been summoned and were present in the courtroom during the entire hearing but were later released after petitioner's motion for continuance had been granted. The court also had the names of the witnesses called; some answered but the absence of others led to a continuance of the case until October 22, 1962. It is contended that this two-day pretrial hearing cannot be considered in determining the question before us. We cannot agree. Pretrial can create a major problem for the defendant in a criminal case. Indeed, it may be more harmful than publicity during the trial for it may well set the community opinion as to guilt or innocence. Though the September hearings dealt with motions to prohibit television coverage and to postpone the trial, they are unquestionably relevant to the issue before us. All of this two-day affair was highly publicized and could only have impressed those present, and also the community at large, with the notorious character of the petitioner as well as the proceeding. The trial witnesses present at the hearing, as well as the original jury panel, were undoubtedly made aware of the peculiar public importance of the case by the press and television coverage being provided, and by the fact that they themselves were televised live and their pictures rebroadcast on the evening show.

When the case was called for trial on October 22 the scene had been altered. A booth had been constructed at the back of the courtroom which was painted to blend with the permanent structure of the room. It had an aperture to allow the lens of the cameras an unrestricted view of the courtroom. All television cameras and newsreel photographers were restricted to the area of the booth when shooting film or telecasting.

Because of continual objection, the rules governing live telecasting, as well as radio and still photos, were changed as the exigencies of the situation seemed to require. As a result, live telecasting was prohibited during a great portion of the actual trial. Only the opening[2] and closing arguments of the State, the return of the jury's verdict and its receipt by the trial judge were carried live with sound. Although the order allowed videotapes of the entire proceeding without sound, the cameras operated only intermittently, recording various portions of the trial for broadcast on regularly scheduled newscasts later in the day and evening. At the request of the petitioner, the trial judge prohibited coverage

---

[2] Due to mechanical difficulty there was no picture during the opening argument.

of any kind, still or television, of the defense counsel during their summations to the jury.

Because of the varying restrictions placed on sound and live telecasting the telecasts of the trial were confined largely to film clips shown on the stations' regularly scheduled news programs. The news commentators would use the film of a particular part of the day's trial activities as a backdrop for their reports. Their commentary included excerpts from testimony and the usual reportorial remarks. On one occasion the videotapes of the September hearings were rebroadcast in place of the "late movie."

II.

In *Rideau v. Louisiana*, 373 U.S. 723 (1963), this Court constructed a rule that the televising of a defendant in the act of confessing to a crime was inherently invalid under the Due Process Clause of the Fourteenth Amendment even without a showing of prejudice or a demonstration of the nexus between the televised confession and the trial. See *id.*, at 729 (dissenting opinion of CLARK, J.). Here, although there was nothing so dramatic as a home-viewed confession, there had been a bombardment of the community with the sights and sounds of a two-day hearing during which the original jury panel, the petitioner, the lawyers and the judge were highly publicized. The petitioner was subjected to characterization and minute electronic scrutiny to such an extent that at one point the photographers were found attempting to picture the page of the paper from which he was reading while sitting at the counsel table. The two-day hearing and the order permitting television at the actual trial were widely known throughout the community. This emphasized the notorious character that the trial would take and, therefore, set it apart in the public mind as an extraordinary case or, as Shaw would say, something "not conventionally unconventional." When the new jury was empaneled at the trial four of the jurors selected had seen and heard all or part of the broadcasts of the earlier proceedings.

III.

We start with the proposition that it is a "public trial" that the Sixth Amendment guarantees to the "accused." The purpose of the requirement of a public trial was to guarantee that the accused would be fairly dealt with and not unjustly condemned. History had proven that secret tribunals were effective instruments of oppression. As our Brother BLACK so well said in *In re Oliver*, 333 U.S. 257 (1948):

"The traditional Anglo-American distrust for secret trials has been variously ascribed to the notorious use of this practice by the Spanish Inquisition, to the excesses of the English Court of Star Chamber, and to the French monarchy's abuse of the *lettre de cachet* . . . . Whatever other benefits the guarantee to an accused that his trial be conducted in public may confer upon our society, the guarantee has always been recognized as a safeguard against any attempt to employ our courts as instruments of persecution." At 268–270. (Footnotes omitted.)

It is said, however, that the freedoms granted in the First Amendment extend a right to the news media to televise from the courtroom, and that to refuse to honor this privilege is to discriminate between the newspapers and television. This is a misconception of the rights of the press.

The free press has been a mighty catalyst in awakening public interest in governmental affairs, exposing corruption among public officers and employees and generally informing the citizenry of public events and occurrences, including court proceedings. While maximum freedom must be allowed the press in carrying on this important function in a democratic society its exercise must necessarily be subject to the maintenance of absolute fairness in the judicial process. While the state and federal courts have differed over what spectators may be excluded from a criminal trial, 6 Wigmore, Evidence § 1834 (3d ed. 1940), the *amici curiae* brief of the National Association of Broadcasters and the Radio Television News Directors Association, says, as indeed it must, that "neither of these two amendments [First and Sixth] speaks of an unlimited right of access to the courtroom on the part of the broadcasting media . . . ." At 7. Moreover, they recognize that the "primary concern of all must be the proper administration of justice"; that "the life or liberty of any individual in this land should not be put in jeopardy because of actions of any news media"; and that "the due process requirements in both the Fifth and Fourteenth Amendments and the provisions of the Sixth Amendment require a procedure that will assure a fair trial . . . ." At 3–4.

Nor can the courts be said to discriminate where they permit the newspaper reporter access to the courtroom. The television and raido reporter has the same privilege. All are entitled to the same rights as the general public. The news reporter is not permitted to bring his typewriter or printing press. When the advances in these arts permit reporting by printing press or by television without their present hazards to a fair trial we will have another case.

IV.

Court proceedings are held for the solemn purpose of endeavoring to ascertain the truth which is the *sine qua non* of a fair trial. Over the centuries Anglo-American courts have devised careful safeguards by rule and otherwise to protect and facilitate the performance of this high function. As a result, at this time those safeguards do not permit the televising and photographing of a criminal trial, save in two States and there only under restrictions. The federal courts prohibit it by specific rule. This is weighty evidence that our concepts of a fair trial do not tolerate such an indulgence. We have always held that the atmosphere essential to the preservation of a fair trial—the most fundamental of all freedoms—must be maintained at all costs. Our approach has been through rules, contempt proceedings and reversal of convictions obtained under unfair conditions. Here the remedy is clear and certain of application and it is our duty to continue to enforce the principles that from time immemorial have proven efficacious and necessary to a fair trial.

V.

The State contends that the televising of portions of a criminal trial does not constitute a denial of due process. Its position is that because no prejudice has been shown by the petitioner as resulting from the televising, it is permissible; that claims of "distractions" during the trial due to the physical presence of television are wholly unfounded; and that psychological considerations are for psychologists, not courts, because they are purely hypothetical. It argues further that the public has a right to know what goes on in the courts; that the court has no power to "suppress, edit, or censor events which transpire in proceedings before it," citing *Craig* v. *Harney,* 331 U.S. 367, 374 (1947); and that the televising of criminal trials would be enlightening to the public and would promote greater respect for the courts.

At the outset the notion should be dispelled that telecasting is dangerous because it is new. It is true that our empirical knowledge of its full effect on the public, the jury or the participants in a trial, including the judge, witnesses and lawyers, is limited. However, the nub of the question is not its newness but, as MR. JUSTICE DOUGLAS says, "the insidious influences which it puts to work in the administration of justice." Douglas, The Public Trial and the Free Press, 33 Rocky Mt. L. Rev. 1 (1960). These influences will be detailed below, but before turning to them the State's argument that the public has a right to know what goes on in the courtroom should be dealt with.

473

It is true that the public has the right to be informed as to what occurs in its courts, but reporters of all media, including television, are always present if they wish to be and are plainly free to report whatever occurs in open court through their respective media. This was settled in *Bridges* v. *California,* 314 U.S. 252 (1941), and *Pennekamp* v. *Florida,* 328 U.S. 331 (1946), which we reaffirm. These reportorial privileges of the press were stated years ago:

"The law, however, favors publicity in legal proceedings, so far as that object can be attained without injustice to the persons immediately concerned. The public are permitted to attend nearly all judicial inquiries, and there appears to be no sufficient reason why they should not also be allowed to see in print the reports of trials, if they can thus have them presented as fully as they are exhibited in court, or at least all the material portion of the proceedings impartially stated, so that one shall not, by means of them, derive erroneous impressions, which he would not have been likely to receive from hearing the trial itself." 2 Cooley's Constitutional Limitations 931–932 (Carrington ed. 1927).

The State, however, says that the use of television in the instant case was "without injustice to the person immediately concerned," basing its position on the fact that the petitioner has established no isolatable prejudice and that this must be shown in order to invalidate a conviction in these circumstances. The State paints too broadly in this contention, for this Court itself has found instances in which a showing of actual prejudice is not a prerequisite to reversal. This is such a case. It is true that in most cases involving claims of due process deprivations we require a showing of identifiable prejudice to the accused. Nevertheless, at times a procedure employed by the State involves such a probability that prejudice will result that it is deemed inherently lacking in due process. Such a case was *In re Murchison,* 349 U.S. 133 (1955), where MR. JUSTICE BLACK for the Court pointed up with his usual clarity and force:

"A fair trial in a fair tribunal is a basic requirement of due process. Fairness of course requires an absence of actual bias in the trial of cases. But our system of law has always endeavored to prevent even the *probability* of unfairness . . . . [T]o perform its high function in the best way 'justice must satisfy the appearance of justice.' *Offutt* v. *United States,* 348 U.S. 11, 14." At 136. (Emphasis supplied.)

And, as Chief Justice Taft said in *Tumey* v. *Ohio,* 273 U.S. 510, almost 30 years before:

"the requirement of due process of law in judicial procedure is not satisfied by the argument that men of the highest honor and the greatest self-sacrifice could carry it on without danger of injustice. Every procedure which would offer a *possible* temptation to the average man . . . to forget the burden of proof required to convict the defendant, or which might lead him not to hold the balance nice, clear and true between the State and the accused, denies the latter due process of law." At 532. (Emphasis supplied.)

This rule was followed in *Rideau, supra,* and in *Turner* v. *Louisiana,* 379 U.S. 466 (1965). In each of these cases the Court departed from the approach it charted in *Stroble* v. *California,* 343 U.S. 181 (1952), and in *Irvin* v. *Dowd,* 366 U.S. 717 (1961), where we made a careful examination of the facts in order to determine whether prejudice resulted. In *Rideau* and *Turner* the Court did not stop to consider the actual effect of the practice but struck down the conviction on the ground that prejudice was inherent in it. Likewise in *Gideon* v. *Wainwright,* 372 U.S. 335 (1963), and *White* v. *Maryland,* 373 U.S. 59 (1963), we applied the same rule, although in different contexts.

In this case it is even clearer that such a rule must be applied. In *Rideau, Irvin* and *Stroble,* the pretrial publicity occurred outside the courtroom and could not be effectively curtailed. The only recourse other than reversal was by contempt proceedings. In *Turner* the probability of prejudice was present through the use of deputy sheriffs, who were also witnesses in the case, as shepherds for the jury. No prejudice was shown but the circumstances were held to be inherently suspect, and, therefore, such a showing was not held to be a requisite to reversal. Likewise in this case the application of this principle is especially appropriate. Television in its present state and by its very nature, reaches into a variety of areas in which it may cause prejudice to an accused. Still one cannot put his finger on its specific mischief and prove with particularity wherein he was prejudiced. This was found true in *Murchison, Tumey, Rideau* and *Turner.* Such untoward circumstances as were found in those cases are inherently bad and prejudice to the accused was presumed. Forty-eight of our States and the Federal Rules have deemed the use of television improper in the courtroom. This fact is most telling in buttressing our conclusion that any change in procedure which would permit its use would be inconsistent with our concepts of due process in this field.

VI.

As has been said, the chief function of our judicial machinery is to ascertain the truth. The use of television, however, cannot be said to contribute materially to this objective. Rather its use amounts to the injection of an irrelevant factor into court proceedings. In addition experience teaches that there are numerous situations in which it might cause actual unfairness—some so subtle as to defy detection by the accused or control by the judge. We enumerate some in summary:

1. The potential impact of television on the jurors is perhaps of the greatest significance. They are the nerve center of the fact-finding process. It is true that in States like Texas where they are required to be sequestered in trials of this nature the jurors will probably not see any of the proceedings as televised from the courtroom. But the inquiry cannot end there. From the moment the trial judge announces that a case will be televised it becomes a *cause célèbre*. The whole community, including prospective jurors, becomes interested in all the morbid details surrounding it. The approaching trial immediately assumes an important status in the public press and the accused is highly publicized along with the offense with which he is charged. Every juror carries with him into the jury box these solemn facts and thus increases the chance of prejudice that is present in every criminal case. And we must remember that realistically it is only the notorious trial which will be broadcast, because of the necessity for paid sponsorship. The conscious or unconscious effect that this may have on the juror's judgment cannot be evaluated, but experience indicates that it is not only possible but highly probable that it will have a direct bearing on his vote as to guilt or innocence. Where pretrial publicity of all kinds has created intense public feeling which is aggravated by the telecasting or picturing of the trial the televised jurors cannot help but feel the pressures of knowing that friends and neighbors have their eyes upon them. If the community be hostile to an accused a televised juror, realizing that he must return to neighbors who saw the trial themselves, may well be led "not to hold the balance nice, clear and true between the State and the accused . . . ."

Moreover, while it is practically impossible to assess the effect of television on jury attentiveness, those of us who know juries realize the problem of jury "distraction." The State argues this is *de minimis* since the physical disturbances have been eliminated. But we know that distractions are not caused solely by the physical presence of the camera and its telltale red lights. It is the awareness of the fact of telecasting that is felt by the juror throughout the trial. We are all self-conscious and uneasy when being televised. Human nature being what it is, not only will a juror's eyes be fixed on the camera, but also his mind will be preoccupied with the telecasting rather than with the testimony.

476

Furthermore, in many States the jurors serving in the trial may see the broadcasts of the trial proceedings. Admittedly, the Texas sequestration rule would prevent this occurring there.[3] In other States following no such practice jurors would return home and turn on the TV if only to see how they appeared upon it. They would also be subjected to re-enactment and emphasis of the selected parts of the proceedings which the requirements of the broadcasters determined would be telecast and would be subconsciously influenced the more by that testimony. Moreover, they would be subjected to the broadest commentary and criticism and perhaps the well-meant advice of friends, relatives and inquiring strangers who recognized them on the streets.

Finally, new trials plainly would be jeopardized in that potential jurors will often have seen and heard the original trial when it was telecast. Yet viewers may later be called upon to sit in the jury box during the new trial. These very dangers are illustrated in this case where the court, due to the defendant's objections, permitted only the State's opening and closing arguments to be broadcast with sound to the public.

2. The quality of the testimony in criminal trials will often be impaired. The impact upon a witness of the knowledge that he is being viewed by a vast audience is simply incalculable. Some may be demoralized and frightened, some cocky and given to overstatement; memories may falter, as with anyone speaking publicly, and accuracy of statement may be severely undermined. Embarrassment may impede the search for the truth, as may a natural tendency toward overdramatization. Furthermore, inquisitive strangers and "cranks" might approach witnesses on the street with jibes, advice or demands for explanation of testimony. There is little wonder that the defendant cannot "prove" the existence of such factors. Yet we all know from experience that they exist.

In addition the invocation of the rule against witnesses is frustrated. In most instances witnesses would be able to go to their homes and view broadcasts of the day's trial proceedings, notwithstanding the fact that they had been admonished not to do so. They could view and hear the testimony of preceding witnesses, and so shape their own testimony as to make its impact crucial. And even in the absence of sound, the influences of such viewing on the attitude of the witness toward testifying, his frame of mind

---

[3] Only six States, in addition to Texas, require sequestration of the jury prior to its deliberations in a non-capital felony trial. The great majority of jurisdictions leave the matter to the trial judge's discretion, while in at least one State the jury will be kept together in such circumstances only upon a showing of cause by the defendant.

upon taking the stand or his apprehension of withering cross-examination defy objective assessment. Indeed, the mere fact that the trial is to be televised might render witnesses reluctant to appear and thereby impede the trial as well as the discovery of the truth.

While some of the dangers mentioned above are present as well in newspaper coverage of any important trial, the circumstances and extraneous influences intruding upon the solemn decorum of court procedure in the televised trial are far more serious than in cases involving only newspaper coverage.

3. A major aspect of the problem is the additional responsibilities the presence of television places on the trial judge. His job is to make certain that the accused receives a fair trial. This most difficult task requires his undivided attention. Still when television comes into the courtroom he must also supervise it. In this trial, for example, the judge on several different occasions—aside from the two days of pretrial—was obliged to have a hearing or enter an order made necessary solely because of the presence of television. Thus, where telecasting is restricted as it was here, and as even the State concedes it must be, his task is made much more difficult and exacting. And, as happened here, such rulings may unfortunately militate against the fairness of the trial. In addition, laying physical interruptions aside, there is the ever-present distraction that the mere awareness of television's presence prompts. Judges are human beings also and are subject to the same psychological reactions as laymen. Telecasting is particularly bad where the judge is elected, as is the case in all save a half dozen of our States. The telecasting of a trial becomes a political weapon, which, along with other distractions inherent in broadcasting, diverts his attention from the task at hand—the fair trial of the accused.

But this is not all. There is the initial decision that must be made as to whether the use of television will be permitted. This is perhaps an even more crucial consideration. Our judges are high-minded men and women. But it is difficult to remain oblivious to the pressures that the news media can bring to bear on them both directly and through the shaping of public opinion. Moreover, where one judge in a district or even in a State permits telecasting, the requirement that the others do the same is almost mandatory. Especially is this true where the judge is selected at the ballot box.

4. Finally, we cannot ignore the impact of courtroom television on the defendant. Its presence is a form of mental—if not physical—harrassment, resembling a police line-up or the third degree. The inevitable close-ups of his gestures and expressions during the ordeal of his trial might well transgress his personal sensibilities,

his dignity, and his ability to concentrate on the proceedings before him—sometimes the difference between life and death—dispassionately, freely and without the distraction of wide public surveillance. A defendant on trial for a specific crime is entitled to his day in court, not in a stadium, or a city or nationwide arena. The heightened public clamor resulting from radio and television coverage will inevitably result in prejudice. Trial by television is, therefore, foreign to our system. Furthermore, telecasting may also deprive an accused of effective counsel. The distractions, intrusions into confidential attorney-client relationships and the temptation offered by television to play to the public audience might often have a direct effect not only upon the lawyers, but the judge, the jury and the witnesses. See Pye, The Lessons of Dallas—Threats to Fair Trial and Free Press, National Civil Liberties Clearing House, 16th Annual Conference.

The television camera is a powerful weapon. Intentionally or inadvertantly it can destroy an accused and his case in the eyes of the public. While our telecasters are honorable men, they too are human. The necessity for sponsorship weighs heavily in favor of the televising of only notorious cases, such as this one, and invariably focuses the lens upon the unpopular of infamous accused. Such a selection is necessary in order to obtain a sponsor willing to pay a sufficient fee to cover the costs and return a profit. We have already examined the ways in which public sentiment can affect the trial participants. To the extent that television shapes that sentiment, it can strip the accused of a fair trial.

The State would dispose of all these observations with the simple statement that they are for psychologists because they are purely hypothetical. But we cannot afford the luxury of saying that, because these factors are difficult of ascertainment in particular cases, they must be ignored. Nor are they "purely hypothetical." They are no more hypothetical than were the considerations deemed controlling in *Tumey*, *Murchison*, *Rideau* and *Turner*. They are real enough to have convinced the Judicial Conference of the United States, this Court and the Congress that television should be barred in federal trials by the Federal Rules of Criminal Procedure; in addition they have persuaded all but two of our States to prohibit television in the courtroom. They are effects that may, and in some combination almost certainly will, exist in any case in which television is injected into the trial process.

VII.

The facts in this case demonstrate clearly the necessity for the application of the rule announced in *Rideau*. The sole issue before the court for two days of pretrial hearing was the question now before us. The hearing was televised live and repeated on tape in the same evening, reaching approximately 100,000 viewers. In addition, the courtroom was a mass of wires, television cameras, microphones and photographers. The petitioner, the panel of prospective jurors, who were sworn the second day, the witnesses and the lawyers were all exposed to this untoward situation. The judge decided that the trial proceedings would be telecast. He announced no restrictions at the time. This emphasized the notorious nature of the coming trial, increased the intensity of the publicity on the petitioner and together with the subsequent televising of the trial beginning 30 days later inherently prevented a sober search for the truth. This is underscored by the fact that the selection of the jury took an entire week. As might be expected, a substantial amount of that time was devoted to ascertaining the impact of the pretrial televising on the prospective jurors. As we have noted, four of the jurors selected had seen all or part of those broadcasts. The trial, on the other hand, lasted only three days.

Moreover, the trial judge was himself harassed. After the initial decision to permit telecasting he apparently decided that a booth should be built at the broadcasters' expense to confine its operations; he then decided to limit the parts of the trial that might be televised live; then he decided to film the testimony of the witnesses without sound in an attempt to protect those under the rule; and finally he ordered that defense counsel and their argument not be televised, in the light of their objection. Plagued by his original error—recurring each day of the trial—his day-to-day orders made the trial more confusing to the jury, the participants and to the viewers. Indeed, it resulted in a public presentation of only the State's side of the case.

As Mr. Justice Holmes said in *Patterson* v. *Colorado*, 205 U.S. 454, 462 (1907):
"The theory of our system is that the conclusions to be reached in a case will be induced only by evidence and argument in open court, and not by any outside influence, whether of private talk or public print."

It is said that the ever-advancing techniques of public communication and the adjustment of the public to its presence may bring about a change in the effect of telecasting upon the fairness of criminal trials. But we are not dealing here with future developments in the field of electronics. Our judgment cannot be rested on the hypothesis of tomorrow but must take the facts as they are presented today.

The judgment is therefore

Reversed.

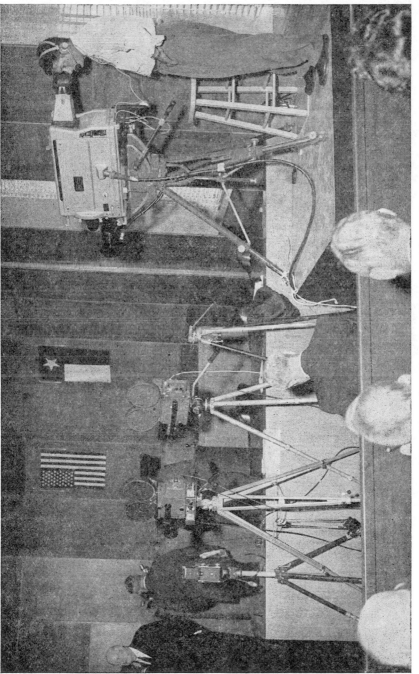

Pictures taken September 24, 1962 while the trial was in progress.

These pictures were also taken on September 24, 1962 during the progress of the trial. Billie Sol Estes can be seen in the picture on the left. He is sitting just to the left of the table resting his cheek on his right hand.

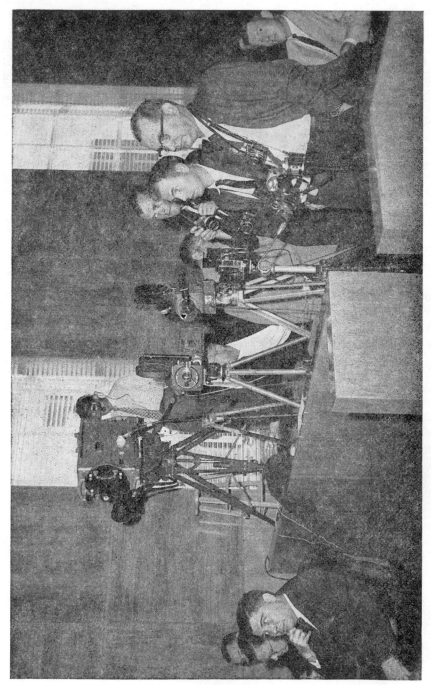

MR. CHIEF JUSTICE WARREN, whom MR. JUSTICE DOUGLAS and MR. JUSTICE GOLDBERG join, concurring.

While I join the Court's opinion and agree that the televising of criminal trials is inherently a denial of due process, I desire to express additional views on why this is so. In doing this, I wish to emphasize that our condemnation of televised criminal trials is not based on generalities or abstract fears. The record in this case presents a vivid illustration of the inherent prejudice of televised criminal trials and supports our conclusion that this is the appropriate time to make a definitive appraisal of television in the courtroom.

I.

Petitioner, a much-publicized financier, was indicted by a Reeves County, Texas, grand jury for obtaining property through false pretenses. The case was transferred to the City of Tyler, in Smith County, Texas, and was set for trial on September 24, 1962. Prior to that date petitioner's counsel informed the trial judge that he would make a motion on September 24 to exclude all cameras from the courtroom during the trial.

On September 24, a hearing was held to consider petitioner's motion to prohibit television, motion pictures, and still photography at the trial. The courtroom was filled with newspaper reporters and cameramen, television cameramen, and spectators. At least 12 cameramen with their equipment were seen by one observer, and there were 30 or more people standing in the aisles. An article appearing in the New York Times the next day stated:

"A television motor van, big as an intercontinental bus, was parked outside the courthouse and the second-floor courtroom was a forest of equipment. Two television cameras had been set up inside the bar and four more marked cameras were aligned just outside the gates . . . . [C]ables and wires snaked over the floor."[1] With photographers roaming at will through the courtroom, petitioner's counsel made his motion that all cameras be excluded. As he spoke, a cameraman wandered behind the judge's bench and snapped his picture. Counsel argued that the presence of cameras would make it difficult for him to consult with his client, make his client ill at ease, and make it impossible to obtain a fair trial since the cameras would distract the jury, witnesses and lawyers. He also expressed the view that televising selected cases tends to give the jury an impression that the particular trial is different

---

[1] N. Y. Times, Sept. 25, 1962, p. 46, col. 4. See Appendix, Photographs 1, 2, 3.

from ordinary criminal trials. The court, however, ruled that the taking of pictures and televising would be allowed so long as the cameramen stood outside the railing that separates the trial participants from the spectators. The court also ruled that if a complaint was made that any camera was too noisy, the cameramen would have to stop taking pictures; that no pictures could be taken in the corridors outside the courtroom; and that those with microphones were not to pick up conversations between petitioner and his lawyers. Subsequent to the court's ruling petitioner arrived in the courtroom,[2] and the defense introduced testimony concerning the atmosphere in the court on that day. At the conclusion of the day's hearing the judge reasserted his earlier ruling. He then ordered a roll call of the prosecution witnesses, at least some of whom had been in the courtroom during the proceedings.

The entire hearing on September 24 was televised live by station KLTV of Tyler, Texas, and station WFAA–TV of Dallas, Texas. Commercials were inserted when there was a pause in the proceedings. On the evening of Monday, September 24, both stations ran an edited tape of the day's proceedings and interrupted the tape to play the commercials ordinarily seen in the particular time slot. In addition to the live television coverage there was also a live radio pickup of the proceedings by at least one station.

The proceedings continued on September 25. There was again a significant number of cameramen taking motion pictures, still pictures and television pictures. The judge once more ordered cameramen to stay on the other side of the railing and stated that this order was to be observed even during court recesses. The panel from which the petit jury was to be selected was then sworn in the presence of the cameramen. The panel was excused to permit counsel to renew his motion to prohibit photography in the courtroom. The court denied the motion, but granted a continuance of trial until October 22 and dismissed the jury panel. At the suggestion of petitioner's counsel the trial judge warned the prosecution witnesses who were present not to discuss the case during the continuance. The proceedings were televised live and portions of the television tape were shown on the regularly scheduled evening news programs. Live radio transmission apparently occurred as on the day before.

On October 1, 1962, the trial judge issued an order explaining what coverage he would permit during the trial. The judge delivered the order in his chambers for the benefit of television cameramen so that they could film him. The judge ruled that although he

---

[2] Counsel explained to the trial court that he desired to protect petition- er from the cameras until the court had made its ruling.

would permit television cameras to be present during the trial, they would not be permitted to present live coverage of the interrogation of prospective jurors or the testimony of witnesses. He ruled that each of the three major television networks, NBC, CBS, ABC, and the local television station KLTV could install one camera not equipped to pick up sound and the film would be available to other television stations on a pooled basis. In addition, he ruled that with respect to the news photographers only cameramen for the local press, Associated Press, and United Press would be permitted in the courtroom. Photographs taken were also to be made available to others on a pooled basis. The judge did not explain how he decided which television cameramen and which still photographers were to be permitted in the courtroom and which were to be excluded.

For the proceedings beginning on October 22, station KLTV, at its own expense, and with the permission of the court, had constructed a booth in the rear of the courtroom painted the same or near the same color as the courtroom. An opening running lengthwise across the booth permitted the four television cameras to photograph the proceedings. The courtroom was small and the cameras were clearly visible to all in the courtroom.[3] The cameras were equipped with "electronic sound on camera" which permitted them to take both film and sound. Upon entering the courtroom the judge told all those with television cameras to go back to the booth; asked the press photographers not to move around any more than necessary; ordered that no flashbulbs or floodlights be used; and again told cameramen that they could not go inside the railing. Defense counsel renewed his motion to ban all "sound equipment . . . still cameras, movie cameras and television; and all radio facilities" from the courtroom. Witnesses were again called on this issue, but at the conclusion of the hearing the trial judge reaffirmed his prior ruling to permit cameramen in the courtroom. In response to petitioner's argument that his rights under the Constitution of the United States were being violated, the judge remarked that the "case [was] not being tried under the Federal Constitution."

None of the proceedings on October 22 was televised live. Television cameras, however, recorded the day's entire proceedings with sound for later showings. Apparently none of the October 22 proceedings was carried live on radio, although the proceedings were recorded on tape. The still photographers admitted by the court were free to take photographs from outside the railing.

On October 23 the selection of the jury began. Overnight an ad-

---

[3] See Appendix, Photograph 6.

ditional strip had been placed across the television booth so that the opening for the television cameras was reduced, but the cameras and their operators were still quite visible.[4] A panel of 86 prospective jurors was ready for the *voir dire*. The judge excused the jurors from the courtroom and made still another ruling on news coverage at the trial. He ordered the television recording to proceed from that point on without an audio pickup, and, in addition, forbade radio tapes of any further proceedings until all the evidence had been introduced. During the course of the trial the television cameras recorded without sound whatever matters appeared interesting to them for use on later newscasts; radio broadcasts in the form of spot reports were made from a room next to the court room. There was no live television or radio coverage until November 7 when the trial judge permitted live coverage of the prosecution's arguments to the jury, the return of the jury's verdict and its acceptance by the court. Since the defense objected to being photographed during the summation, the judge prohibited television cameramen or still photographers from taking any pictures of the defense during its argument. But the show went on, and while the defense was speaking the cameras were directed at the judge and the arguments were monitored by audio equipment and relayed to the television audience by an announcer. On November 7 the judge, for the first time, directed news photographers desiring to take pictures to take them only from the back of the room. Up until this time the trial judge's orders merely limited news photographers to the spectator section.

II.

The decision below affirming petitioner's conviction runs counter to the evolution of Anglo-American criminal procedure over a period of centuries. During that time the criminal trial has developed from a ritual practically devoid of rational justification[5] to a fact-finding process, the acknowledged purpose of which is to provide a fair and reliable determination of guilt.[6]

An element of rationality was introduced into the guilt-determining process in England over 600 years ago when a rudimentary trial by jury became "the principal institution for criminal cases."[7] Initially members of the jury were expected to make their own

---

[4] See Appendix, Photograph 7.
[5] Jenks, A Short History of English Law 46–47 (6th ed. 1949); I Stephen, A History of the Criminal Law of England 51–74 (1883).
[6] See, *e. g., Craig* v. *Harney*, 331 U. S. 367, 378; *Irvin* v. *Dowd*, 366 U. S. 717, 728; *Brady* v. *Maryland*, 373 U. S. 83, 87; *Jackson* v. *Denno*, 378 U. S. 368, 391.
[7] See *Singer* v. *United States*, 380 U. S. 24, 27.

examinations of the cases they were to try and come to court already familiar with the facts,[8] which made it impossible to limit the jury's determination to legally relevant evidence. Gradually, however, the jury was transformed from a panel of witnesses to a panel of triers passing on evidence given by others in the court-room.[9] The next step was to insure the independence of the jury, and this was accomplished by the decision in the case of *Edward Bushell,* 6 How. St. Tr. 999 (1670), which put an end to the practice of fining or otherwise punishing jury members who failed to reach the decision directed by the court. As the purpose of trial as a vehicle for discovering the truth became clearer, it was recognized that the defendant should have the right to call witnesses and to place them under oath,[10] to be informed of the charges against him before the trial,[11] and to have counsel assist him with his defense.[12] All these protections, and others which could be cited, were part of a development by which "the administration of criminal justice was set upon a firm and dignified basis."[13]

When the colonists undertook the responsibility of governing themselves, one of their prime concerns was the establishment of trial procedures which would be consistent with the purpose of trial. The Continental Congress passed measures designed to safeguard the right to a fair trial,[14] and the various States adopted constitutional provisions directed to the same end.[15] Eventually the Sixth Amendment incorporated into the Constitution certain provisions dealing with the conduct of trials:

"In all criminal prosecutions, the accused shall enjoy the right to a speedy and public trial, by an impartial jury of the State and district wherein the crime shall have been committed, which district shall have been previously ascertained by law, and to be informed of the nature and cause of the accusation; to be confronted with the witnesses against him; to have compulsory process for obtaining witnesses in his favor, and to have the Assistance of Counsel for his defence."

Significantly, in the Sixth Amendment the words "speedy and public" qualify the term *trial* and the rest of the Amendment defines specific protections the accused is to have at his *trial.* Thus, the Sixth Amendment, by its own terms, not only requires that the accused have certain specific rights but also that he enjoy them

---

[8] II Pollock and Maitland, The History of English Law 621–622 (2d ed. 1909).

[9] I Stephen, *supra,* note 5, at 260.

[10] See 7 Will. 3, c. 3 (1695).

[11] *Ibid.*

[12] *Ibid.*; 6 & 7 Will. 4, c. 114 (1836).

[13] I Stephen, *supra,* note 5, at 427.

[14] I Journals of the Continental Congress 1774–1789, 69 (Ford ed. 1904).

[15] Radin, The Right to a Public Trial, 6 Temple L. Q. 381, 383, n. 5a (1932).

at a *trial*—a word with a meaning of its own, see *Bridges* v. *California*, 314 U.S. 252, 271.

The Fourteenth Amendment which places limitations on the States' administration of their criminal laws also gives content to the term *trial*. Whether the Sixth Amendment as a whole applies to the States through the Fourteenth,[16] or the Fourteenth Amendment embraces only those portions of the Sixth Amendment that are "fundamental,"[17] or the Fourteenth Amendment incorporates a standard of "ordered liberty" apart from the specific guarantees of the Bill of Rights,[18] it has been recognized that state prosecutions must, at the least, comport with "the fundamental conception" of a fair *trial*.[19]

It has been held on one or another of these theories that the fundamental conception of a fair trial includes many of the specific provisions of the Sixth Amendment, such as the right to have the proceedings open to the public, *In re Oliver*, 333 U.S. 257; the right to notice of specific charges, *Cole* v. *Arkansas*, 333 U.S. 196; the right to confrontation, *Pointer* v. *Texas*, 380 U.S. 400; *Douglas* v. *Alabama*, 380 U.S. 415; and the right to counsel, *Gideon* v. *Wainwright*, 372 U.S. 335. But it also has been agreed that neither the Sixth nor the Fourteenth Amendment is to be read formalistically, for the clear intent of the amendments is that these specific rights be enjoyed at a constitutional trial. In the words of Justice Holmes, even though "every form [be] preserved," the forms may amount to no "more than an empty shell" when considered in the context or setting in which they were actually applied.[20]

In cases arising from state prosecutions this Court has acted to prevent the right to a constitutional trial from being reduced to a formality by the intrusion of factors into the trial process that tend to subvert its purpose. The Court recognized in *Pennekamp* v. *Florida*, 328 U.S. 331, 334, that the "orderly operation of courts" is "the primary and dominant requirement in the administration of justice." And, in *Moore* v. *Dempsey*, 261 U.S. 86, 90–91, it was held that the atmosphere in and around the courtroom might be so hostile as to interfere with the trial process, even though an exam-

---

[16] *Adamson* v. *California*, 332 U.S. 46, 71–72 (dissenting opinion of MR. JUSTICE BLACK).

[17] *Gideon* v. *Wainwright*, 372 U. S. 335, 342.

[18] *Pointer* v. *Texas*, 380 U. S. 400, 408 (opinion of MR. JUSTICE HARLAN, concurring in the result).

[19] *Cox* v. *Louisiana*, 379 U. S. 559, 562; *Frank* v. *Mangum*, 237 U. S. 309,

347 (dissenting opinion of Justice Holmes). See *Adamson* v. *California*, 332 U. S. 46, 53; *In re Murchison*, 349 U. S. 133, 136; *Irvin* v. *Dowd*, 366 U. S. 717, 722; *Jackson* v. *Denno*, 378 U. S. 368, 377 (Court opinion), 424 (dissenting opinion of MR. JUSTICE CLARK), 428 (dissenting opinion of MR. JUSTICE HARLAN).

[20] *Frank* v. *Mangum*, 237 U. S. 309, 346 (dissenting opinion).

ination of the record disclosed that all the forms of trial conformed to the requirements of law: the defendant had counsel, the jury members stated they were impartial, the jury was correctly charged, and the evidence was legally sufficient to convict. Moreover, in *Irvin* v. *Dowd*, 366 U.S. 717, a conviction was reversed where extensive pretrial publicity rendered a fair trial unlikely despite the observance of the formal requisites of a legal trial. We commented in that case:

"No doubt each juror was sincere when he said that he would be fair and impartial to petitioner, but the psychological impact requiring such a declaration before one's fellows is often its father." *Id.*, at 728.

To recognize that disorder can convert a trial into a ritual without meaning is not to pay homage to order as an end in itself. Rather, it recognizes that the courtroom in Anglo-American jurisprudence is more than a location with seats for a judge, jury, witnesses, defendant, prosecutor, defense counsel and public observers; the setting that the courtroom provides is itself an important element in the constitutional conception of trial, contributing a dignity essential to "the integrity of the trial" process. *Craig* v. *Harney*, 331 U.S. 367, 377. As MR. JUSTICE BLACK said, in another context: "The very purpose of a court system is to adjudicate controversies, both criminal and civil, in the calmness and solemnity of the courtroom according to legal procedures."[21] In light of this fundamental conception of what the term *trial* means, this Court has recognized that often, despite widespread, hostile publicity about a case, it is possible to conduct a trial meeting constitutional standards. Significantly, in each of these cases, the basic premise behind the Court's conclusion has been the notion that judicial proceedings can be conducted with dignity and integrity so as to shield the trial process itself from these irrelevant, external factors, rather than to aggravate them as here. Thus, in reversing contempt convictions for out-of-court statements, this Court referred to "the power of courts to protect themselves from disturbances and disorder *in the court room*," *Bridges* v. *California*, 314 U.S. 252, 266 (emphasis added) ; "the necessity for fair adjudication, free from interruption of its processes," *Pennekamp* v. *Florida*, 328 U.S. 331, 336; "the integrity of the trial," *Craig* v. *Harney*, 331 U.S. 367, 377. And, in upholding a conviction against a claim of unfavorable publicity, this Court commented "that petitioner's trial was conducted in a calm judicial manner," *Darcy* v. *Handy*, 351 U.S. 454, 463.

---

[21] *Cox* v. *Louisiana*, 379 U.S. 559, 583 (dissenting opinion).

Similarly, when state procedures have been found to thwart the purpose of trial this Court has declared those procedures to be unconstitutional. In *Tumey* v. *Ohio*, 273 U.S. 510, the Court considered a state procedure under which judges were paid for presiding over a case only if the defendant was found guilty and costs assessed against him. An argument was made that the practice should not be condemned broadly, since some judges undoubtedly would not let their judgment be affected by such an arrangement. However, the Court found the procedure so inconsistent with the conception of what a trial should be and so likely to produce prejudice that it declared the practice unconstitutional even though no specific prejudice was shown.

In *Lyons* v. *Oklahoma*, 322 U.S. 596, this Court stated that if an involuntary confession is introduced into evidence at a state trial the conviction must be reversed, even though there is other evidence in the record to justify a verdict of guilty. We explained the rationale behind this judgment in *Payne* v. *Arkansas*, 356 U.S. 560, 568:

"[W]here . . . a coerced confession constitutes a part of the evidence before the jury and a general verdict is returned, no one can say what credit and weight the jury gave to the confession." Similar reasoning led to the decision last Term in *Jackson* v. *Denno*, 378 U.S. 368. We held there that when the voluntariness of a confession is at issue there must be a procedure adopted which provides "a reliable and clearcut determination of . . . voluntariness." *Id.*, at 391. We found insufficient a procedure whereby the jury heard the confession but was instructed to disregard it if the jury found the confession involuntary:

"[T]he New York procedure poses substantial threats to a defendant's constitutional rights to have an involuntary confession entirely disregarded and to have the coercion issue fairly and reliably determined. These hazards we cannot ignore." *Id.*, at 389.

Earlier this Term, in *Turner* v. *Louisiana*, 379 U.S. 466, we considered a case in which deputy sheriffs, who were the prosecution's principal witnesses, were in charge of a sequestered jury during the trial. The Supreme Court of Louisiana criticized the practice but said that in the absence of a showing of prejudice there was no ground for reversal. We reversed because the "extreme prejudice inherent" in the practice required its condemnation on constitutional grounds.

Finally, the Court has on numerous other occasions reversed

convictions, where the formalities of trial were observed, because of practices that negate the fundamental conception of trial.[22]

This line of cases does not indicate a disregard for the position of the States in our federal system. Rather, it stands for the proposition that the criminal trial under our Constitution has a clearly defined purpose, to provide a fair and reliable determination of guilt, and no procedure or occurrence which seriously threatens to divert it from that purpose can be tolerated.

III.

For the Constitution to have vitality, this Court must be able to apply its principles to situations that may not have been foreseen at the time those principles were adopted. As was said in *Weems* v. *United States*, 217 U.S. 349, 373, and reaffirmed in *Brown* v. *Board of Education*, 347 U.S. 483, 492-493:

"Legislation, both statutory and constitutional, is enacted, it is true, from an experience of evils, but its general language should not, therefore, be necessarily confined to the form that evil had theretofore taken. Time works changes, brings into existence new conditions and purposes. Therefore a principle to be vital must be capable of wider application than the mischief which gave it birth . . . . In the application of a constitution, therefore, our contemplation cannot be only of what has been but of what may be. Under any other rule a constitution would indeed be as easy of application as it would be deficient in efficacy and power. Its general principles would have little value and be converted by precedent into impotent and lifeless formulas. Rights declared in words might be lost in reality."

I believe that it violates the Sixth Amendment for federal courts and the Fourteenth Amendment for state courts to allow criminal trials to be televised to the public at large. I base this conclusion on three grounds: (1) that the televising of trials diverts the trial from its proper purpose in that it has an inevitable impact on all the trial participants; (2) that it gives the public the wrong impression about the purpose of trials, thereby detracting from the dignity of court proceedings and lessening the reliability of trials; and (3) that it singles out certain defendants and subjects them to trials under prejudicial conditions not experienced by others.

I have attempted to show that our common-law heritage, our Constitution, and our experience in applying that Constitution have

---

[22] See *Mooney* v. *Holohan*, 294 U. S. 103; *Alcorta* v. *Texas*, 355 U. S. 28; *Napue* v. *Illinois*, 360 U. S. 264; and *Brady* v. *Maryland*, 373 U. S. 83.

committed us irrevocably to the position that the criminal trial has one well-defined purpose—to provide a fair and reliable determination of guilt. In *Tumey* v. *Ohio, supra,* at 532, this Court condemned the procedure there employed for compensating judges because it offered a "possible temptation" to judges "not to hold the balance nice, clear and true between the State and the accused." How much more harmful is a procedure which not only offers the temptation to judges to use the bench as a vehicle for their own ends, but offers the same temptation to every participant in the trial, be he defense counsel, prosecutor, witness or juror! It is not necessary to speak in the abstract on this point. In the present case, on October 1, the trial judge invited the television cameras into his chambers so they could take films of him reading one of his pretrial orders. On this occasion, at least, the trial judge clearly took the initiative in placing himself before the television audience and in giving his order, and himself, the maximum possible publicity. Moreover, on October 22, when trial counsel renewed his motion to exclude television from the courtroom on the ground that it violated petitioner's rights under the Federal Constitution, the trial judge made the following speech:
"This case is not being tried under the Federal Constitution. This Defendant has been brought into this Court under the state laws, under the State Constitution.

. . . . .

"I took an oath to uphold this Constitution; not the Federal Constitution but the State Constitution; and I am going to do my best to do that as long as I preside on this Court, and if it is distasteful in following my oath and upholding the constitution, it will just have to be distasteful."
One is entitled to wonder if such a statement would be made in a court of justice by any state trial judge except as an appeal calculated to gain the favor of his viewing audience. I find it difficult to believe that this trial judge, with over 20 years' experience on the bench, was unfamiliar with the fundamental duty imposed on him by Article VI of the Constitution of the United States:
"This Constitution, and the Laws of the United States which shall be made in Pursuance thereof; and all Treaties made, or which shall be made, under the Authority of the United States, shall be the supreme Law of the Land; and the Judges in every State shall be bound thereby, any Thing in the Constitution or Laws of any State to the Contrary notwithstanding."
This is not to say that all participants in the trial would distort it by deliberately playing to the television audience, but some un-

494

doubtedly would. The even more serious danger is that neither the judge, prosecutor, defense counsel, jurors or witnesses would be able to go through trial without considering the effect of their conduct on the viewing public. It is admitted in dissent that "if the scene at the September hearing had been repeated in the courtroom during this jury trial, it is difficult to conceive how a fair trial in the constitutional sense could have been afforded the defendant." *Post,* p. 612. But it is contended that what went on at the September hearing is irrelevant to the issue before us. With this I cannot agree. We granted certiorari to consider whether petitioner was denied due process when he was required to submit to a televised trial. In this, as in other cases involving rights under the Due Process Clause, we have an obligation to make an independent examination of the record, *e. g., Watts* v. *Indiana,* 338 U.S. 49, 51; *Norris* v. *Alabama,* 294 U.S. 587, 590; and the limited grant of certiorari does not prohibit us from considering all the facts in this record relevant to the question before us. The parties to this case, and those who filed briefs as *amici curiae,* recognize this, since they treat the televising of the September proceedings as a factor relevant to our consideration. Our decisions in *White* v. *Maryland,* 373 U.S. 59, and *Hamilton* v. *Alabama,* 368 U.S. 52, clearly hold that an accused is entitled to procedural protections at pretrial hearings as well as at actual trial and his conviction will be reversed if he is not accorded these protections. In addition, in *Pointer* v. *Texas,* 380 U.S. 400, we held that a pretrial hearing can have a profound effect on the trial itself and effectively prevent an accused from having a fair trial. Petitioner clearly did not have a fair determination of his motion to exclude cameras from the courtroom. The very presence of the cameras at the September hearing tended to impress upon the trial judge the power of the communications media and the criticism to which he would have been subjected if he had ruled that the presence of the cameras was inconsistent with petitioner's right to a fair trial. The prejudice to petitioner did not end here. Most of the trial participants were present at the September hearing—the judge, defense counsel, prosecutor, prosecution witnesses and defendant himself—and they saw for themselves the desecration of the courtroom. After undergoing this experience it is unrealistic to suppose that they would come to the October trial unaware that court procedures were being sacrificed in this case for the convenience of television. The manner in which the October proceedings were conducted only intensified this awareness. It was impossible for any of the trial participants ever to be unaware of the presence of television cameras in court for the actual trial.[23] The snouts of the four television cameras protruded through the opening in the booth, and the cameras and their operators were not only readily visible but were impossible to ignore by all who were surveying the activities in this small courtroom. No one could forget that he was constantly in the focus of the "all-seeing eye." Although the law of Texas purportedly permits witnesses to object to being televised, it is ludicrous to place this burden on them. They would naturally accept the conditions of the courtroom as the judge establishes them, and feel that it would be as presumptuous for them to object to the court's permitting television as to object to the court reporter's recording their testimony. Yet, it is argued that no witnesses objected to being televised. This is indeed a slender reed to rely on, particularly in view of the trial judge's failure, in the course of his self-exculpating statements justifying his decision to allow television, to advise the witnesses or the jurors that they had the right to object to being televised. Defense counsel, however, stated forcefully that he could not concentrate on the case because of the distraction caused by the cameras. And the trial judge's attention was distracted from the trial since he was compelled to make seven extensive rulings concerning television coverage during the October proceedings alone, when he should, instead, have been concentrating on the trial itself.

It is common knowledge that "television . . . can . . . work profound changes in the behavior of the people it focuses on."[24] The present record provides ample support for scholars who have claimed that awareness that a trial is being televised to a vast, but unseen audience, is bound to increase nervousness and tension,[25] cause an increased concern about appearances,[26] and bring to

---

[23] See Appendix, Photograph 7.
[24] Keating, "Not 'Bonanza,' Not 'Peyton Place,' But the U. S. Senate," N. Y. Times Magazine, April 25, 1965, 67, 72. See, e. g., N. Y. Times, April 22, 1965, p. 43, col. 2 (in describing a televised stockholders' meeting the Times reported, "Some stockholders seemed very much aware they were on camera"); Tinkham, Should Canon 35 be Amended? A Question of Proper Judicial Administration, 42 A. B. A. J. 843, 845 (1956) (in giving examples of how people react when they know they are on television, the author describes the reactions of a television audience when the camera was turned on it as "contorted, grimacing"); Gould, N. Y.

Times, March 11, 1956, § 2, p. X 11, col. 2 ("The most experienced performers in show business know the horrors of stage fright before they go on TV. This psychological and emotional burden must not be placed on a layman whose testimony may have a bearing on whether, in a murder trial, another human being is to live or die.").
[25] See, e. g., Douglas, The Public Trial and the Free Press, 46 A. B. A. J. 840, 842 (1960). In *United States* v. *Kleinman*, 107 F. Supp. 407 (D. C. D. C. 1952), the court refused to hold in contempt witnesses in a congressional hearing who refused to answer questions while television cameras were focused on them. The court stated:

the surface latent opportunism that the traditional dignity of the courtroom would discourage. Whether they do so consciously or subconsciously, all trial participants act differently in the presence of television cameras. And, even if all participants make a conscientious and studied effort to be unaffected by the presence of television, this effort in itself prevents them from giving their full attention to their proper functions at trial. Thus, the evil of televised trials, as demonstrated by this case, lies not in the noise and appearance of the cameras, but in the trial participants' awareness that they are being televised. To the extent that television has such an inevitable impact it undercuts the reliability of the trial process.

In the early days of this country's development, the entertainment a trial might provide often tended to obfuscate its proper role.

"The people thought holding court one of the greatest performances in the range of their experience. . . . The country folks would crowd in for ten miles to hear these 'great lawyers' plead; and it was a secondary matter with the client whether he won or lost his case, so the 'pleading' was loud and long."[27]

"In early frontier America, when no motion pictures, no television, and no radio provided entertainment, trial day in the country was like fair day, and from near and far citizens young and old converged on the county seat. The criminal trial was the theater and *spectaculum* of old rural America. Applause and cat calls were not infrequent. All too easily lawyers and judges became part-time actors at the bar. . . ."[28]

"The only reason for having a witness on the stand, either before a committee of Congress or before a court, is to get a thoughtful, calm, considered and, it is to be hoped, truthful disclosure of facts. That is not always accomplished, even under the best of circumstances. But at least the atomosphere of the forum should lend itself to that end.

"In the cases now to be decided, the stipulation of facts discloses that there were, in close proximity to the witness, television cameras, newsreel cameras, news photographers with their concomitant flashbulbs, radio microphones, a large and crowded hearing room with spectators standing along the walls, etc. The obdurate stand taken by these two defendants must be viewed in the context of all these conditions. The concentration of all of these elements seems to me necessarily so to disturb and distract any witness to the point that he might say today something that next week he will realize was erroneous. And the mistake could get him in trouble all over again." *Id.*, at 408.

[26] See, *e. g.*, Douglas, *supra*, note 25, at 842; Yesawich, Televising and Broadcasting Trials, 37 Cornell L. Q. 701, 717 (1952).

[27] Wigmore, A Kaleidoscope of Justice 487 (1941).

[28] Mueller, Problems Posed by Publicity to Crime and Criminal Proceedings, 110 U. Pa. L. Rev. 1, 6 (1961).

I had thought that these days of frontier justice were long behind us, but the courts below would return the theater to the courtroom.

The televising of trials would cause the public to equate the trial process with the forms of entertainment regularly seen on television and with the commercial objectives of the television industry. In the present case, tapes of the September 24 hearing were run in place of the "Tonight Show" by one station and in place of the late night movie by another. Commercials for soft drinks, soups, eyedrops and seatcovers were inserted when there was a pause in the proceedings. In addition, if trials were televised there would be a natural tendency on the part of broadcasters to develop the personalities of the trial participants, so as to give the proceedings more of an element of drama. This tendency was noticeable in the present case. Television commentators gave the viewing audience a homey, flattering sketch about the trial judge, obviously to add an extra element of viewer appeal to the trial:

"Tomorrow morning at 9:55 the WFAA T. V. cameras will be in Tyler to telecast live [the trial judge's] decision whether or not he will permit live coverage of the Billie Sol Estes trial. If so, this will be the first such famous national criminal proceeding to be televised in its entirety live. [The trial judge] was appointed to the bench here in Tyler in 1942 by [the Governor]. The judge has served every two years since then. This *very* beautiful Smith County Courthouse was built and dedicated in 1954, but before that [the trial judge] had made a reputation for himself that reached not only throughout Texas, but throughout the United States as well. It is said that [the trial judge], who is now 53 years old, has tried more cases than any other judge during his time in office."

The television industry might also decide that the bareboned trial itself does not contain sufficient drama to sustain an audience. It might provide expert commentary on the proceedings and hire persons with legal backgrounds to anticipate possible trial strategy, as the football expert anticipates plays for his audience. The trial judge himself stated at the September hearing that if he wanted to see a ball game he would turn on his television set, so why not the same for a trial.

Moreover, should television become an accepted part of the courtroom, greater sacrifices would be made for the benefit of broadcasters. In the present case construction of a television booth in the courtroom made it necessary to alter the physical layout of the courtroom and to move from their accustomed position two benches reserved for spectators.[29] If this can be done in order better to

---

[29] Compare Appendix, Photograph 5,
with Appendix, Photograph 6.

accommodate the television industry, I see no reason why another court might not move a trial to a theater, if such a move would provide improved television coverage. Our memories are short indeed if we have already forgotten the wave of horror that swept over this country when Premier Fidel Castro conducted his prosecutions before 18,000 people in Havana Stadium.[30] But in the decision below, which completely ignores the importance of the courtroom in the trial process, we have the beginnings of a similar approach toward criminal "justice." This is not an abstract fear I am expressing because this very situation confronted the Nebraska Supreme Court in *Roberts* v. *State*, 100 Neb. 199, 203, 158 N. W. 930, 931–932 (1916):

"The court removed the trial from the court-room to the theater, and stated as a reason therefor: 'By reason of the insufficiency of the court-room to seat and accommodate the people applying for admission . . . it is by the court ordered that the further trial of this cause be had at the Keith Theater, and thereupon the court was adjourned to Keith Theater, where trial proceeded.' The stage was occupied by court, counsel, jury, witnesses, and officers connected with the trial. The theater proper was crowded with curious spectators. Before the trial was completed it was returned to the court-room and concluded there. At the adjournment of court on one occasion the bailiff announced from the stage: 'The regular show will be tomorrow; matinee in the afternoon and another performance at 8:30. Court is now adjourned until 7:30.' "

There would be a real threat to the integrity of the trial process if the television industry and trial judges were allowed to become partners in the staging of criminal proceedings. The trial judge in the case before us had several "conferences [with] representatives of the news media." *Post,* p. 606. He then entered into a joint enterprise with a television station for the construction of a booth in his courtroom. The next logical step in this partnership might be to schedule the trial for a time that would permit the maximum number of viewers to watch and to schedule recesses to coincide with the need for station breaks. Should the television industry become an integral part of our system of criminal justice, it would not be unnatural for the public to attribute the shortcomings of the industry to the trial process itself. The public is aware of the television industry's consuming interest in ratings, and it is also aware of the steps that have been taken in the past to maintain viewer interest in television programs. Memories still recall vividly the scandal caused by the disclosure that quiz programs had been cor-

---

[30] N. Y. Times, Jan. 23, 1959, p. 1, col. 1.

rupted in order to heighten their dramatic appeal. Can we be sure that similar efforts would not be made to heighten the dramatic appeal of televised trials? Can we be sure that the public would not inherently distrust our system of justice because of its intimate association with a commercial enterprise?

Broadcasting in the courtroom would give the television industry an awesome power to condition the public mind either for or against an accused. By showing only those parts of its films or tapes which depict the defendant or his witnesses in an awkward or unattractive position, television directors could give the community, state or country a false and unfavorable impression of the man on trial. Moreover, if the case should end in a mistrial, the showing of selected portions of the trial, or even of the whole trial, would make it almost impossible to select an impartial jury for a second trial. Cf. *Rideau* v. *Louisiana*, 373 U.S. 723. To permit this powerful medium to use the trial process itself to influence the opinions of vast numbers of people, before a verdict of guilt of innocence has been rendered, would be entirely foreign to our system of justice.

The sense of fairness, dignity and integrity that all associate with the courtroom would become lost with its commercialization. Thus, the televising of trials would not only have an effect on those participating in the trials that are being televised, but also on those who observe the trials and later become trial participants.

It is argued that television not only entertains but also educates the public. But the function of a trial is not to provide an educational experience; and there is a serious danger that any attempt to use a trial as an educational tool will both divert it from its proper purpose and lead to suspicions concerning the integrity of the trial process. The Soviet Union's trial of Francis Gary Powers provides an example in point. The integrity of the trial was suspect because it was concerned not only with determining the guilt of the individual on trial but also with providing an object lesson to the public. This divided effort undercut confidence in the guilt-determining aspect of the procedure and by so doing rendered the educational aspect self-defeating.

"Was it prejudicial to [Powers] that the trial took place in a special hall with over 2,000 spectators, that it was televised, that prominent representatives of many organizations in various countries were invited to attend, that simultaneous oral translations of the proceedings . . . were provided, and that detailed . . . reports of the case in various languages were distributed to the press before, during and after the trial?"

". . . [T]he Soviet legal system . . . consciously and explicitly

uses the trial, and indeed the very safeguards of justice themselves, as instruments of the social and political objectives of the
state. . . .

". . . A Soviet trial is supposed to be correct, impartial, just,
reasonable, and at the same time it is supposed to serve as an object-lesson to society, a means of teaching the participants, the
spectators and the public generally to be loyal, obedient, disciplined
fighters for Communist ideals. . . .

". . .[T]he tension between the demands of justice and the demands of politics can never be entirely eliminated. The fate of the
accused is bound to be influenced in one way or another when the
trial is lifted above its individual facts and deliberately made an
object-lesson to the public."

". . . [T]he deliberate use of a trial as a means of political education threatens the integrity of the judicial process."[31]

Finally, if the televising of criminal proceedings were approved,
trials would be selected for television coverage for reasons having
nothing to do with the purpose of trial. A trial might be televised
because a particular judge has gained the fancy of the public by
his unorthodox approach; or because the district attorney has decided to run for another office and it is believed his appearance would
attract a large audience; or simply because a particular courtroom
has a layout that best accommodates television coverage.[32] For the
most part, however, the most important factor that would draw
television to the courtroom would be the nature of the case. The
alleged perpetrator of the sensational murder, the fallen idol, or
some other person who, like petitioner, has attracted the public interest would find his trial turned into a vehicle for television. Yet,
these are the very persons who encounter the greatest difficulty in
securing an impartial trial, even without the presence of television.
This Court would no longer be able to point to the dignity and calmness of the courtroom as a protection from outside influences. For
the television camera penetrates this protection and brings into the
courtroom tangible evidence of the widespread interest in a case—
an interest which has often been fanned by exhaustive reports in
the newspapers, television and radio for weeks before trial. The

---

[31] Berman, Introduction to the Trial
of the U 2 xiii, xii–xiii, xxix (1960).

[32] A revealing dialogue took place in
the present case between defense
counsel and one of the television
executives present in the courtroom
during the September 24 hearing.

"Q. The camera on the other side
of the room has to look over a corner of the jury box and past the

jurors to be aimed at the witness
box, does it not?

"A. I think that is pretty clear,
sir. I don't think the jurors would
be in the way there.

"Q. You don't think the jurors
would get in the way of your operations?

"A. I don't mean that exactly,
sir."

present case presents a clear example of this danger. In the words of petitioner's counsel:

"The Saturday Evening Post, The Readers Digest, Time, Life all had feature stories upon [petitioner's] story giving in detail his life history and the details of . . . alleged fraudulent transactions. . . .

"The metropolitan papers throughout the country featured the story daily. Each day for weeks the broadcasts carried some features of the story."[33]

After living in the glare of this publicity for weeks, petitioner came to court for a legal adjudication of the charges against him. As he approached the courthouse he was confronted by an army of photographers, reporters and television commentators shoving microphones in his face.[34] When he finally made his way into the courthouse it was reasonable for him to expect that he could have a respite from this merciless badgering and have his case adjudicated in a calm atmosphere. Instead, the carnival atmosphere of the September hearing served only to increase the publicity surrounding petitioner and to condition further the public's mind against him. Then, upon his entrance into the courtroom for his actual trial he was confronted with the sight of the television camera zeroed in on him and the ever-present still photographers snapping pictures of interest. As he opened a newspaper waiting for the proceedings to begin, the close-up lens of a television camera zoomed over his shoulder in an effort to find out what he was reading. In no sense did the dignity and integrity of the trial process shield this petitioner from the prejudicial publicity to which he had been exposed, because that publicity marched right through the courtroom door and made itself at home in heretofore unfamiliar surroundings. We stated in *Gideon* v. *Wainwright*, 372 U.S. 335, 344, "From the very beginning, our state and national constitutions and laws have laid great emphasis on procedural and substantive safeguards designed to assure fair trials before impartial tribunals in which every defendant stands equal before the law." This principle was not applied by the courts below.

I believe petitioner in this case has shown that he was actually prejudiced by the conduct of these proceedings, but I cannot agree with those who say that a televised trial deprives a defendant of a fair trial only if "actual prejudice" can be shown. The prejudice of television may be so subtle that it escapes the ordinary methods of proof,[35] but it would gradually erode our fundamental conception

---

[33] Petition for writ of certiorari, 35a.
[34] See Appendix, Photograph 4.

[35] See, *e. g.*, Douglas, *supra*, note 25, at 844.

of trial.[36] A defendant may be unable to prove that he was actually prejudiced by a televised trial, just as he may be unable to prove that the introduction of a coerced confession at his trial influenced the jury to convict him when there was substantial evidence to support his conviction aside from the confession, *Payne* v. *Arkansas, supra;* that the jury refrained from making a clear-cut determination on the voluntariness question, *Jackson* v. *Denno, supra;* that a particular judge was swayed by a direct financial interest in his conviction, *Tumey* v. *Ohio, supra;* or that the jury gave additional weight to the testimony of certain prosecution witnesses because of the jury's repeated contacts with those witnesses during the trial, *Turner* v. *Louisiana, supra.* How is the defendant to prove that the prosecutor acted differently than he ordinarily would have, that defense counsel was more concerned with impressing prospective clients than with the interests of the defendant, that a juror was so concerned with how he appeared on television that his mind continually wandered from the proceedings, that an important defense witness made a bad impression on the jury because he was "playing" to the television audience, or that the judge was a little more lenient or a little more strict than he usually might be? And then, how is petitioner to show that this combination of changed attitudes diverted the trial sufficiently from its purpose to deprive him of a fair trial? It is no answer to say that an appellate court can review for itself tapes or films of the proceedings. In the first place, it is not clear that the court would be able to obtain unedited tapes or films to review. Even with the cooperation of counsel on both sides, this Court was unable to obtain films of this trial which were in any sense complete. In addition, time limitations might restrict the television companies to taking pictures only of those portions of the trial that are most newsworthy and most likely to attract the attention of the viewing audience. More importantly, the tapes or films, even if unedited, could give a wrong impression of the proceedings. The camera which takes pictures cannot take a picture of itself. In addition, the camera cannot possibly cover the actions of all trial participants during the trial. While the camera is focused on the judge who is apparently acting properly, a juror may be glancing up to see where the camera is pointing and counsel may be looking around to see whether he can confer with his client without the close-up lens of the camera focusing on them. Needless to say, the camera cannot penetrate the minds of the trial participants and show their awareness that they may at that moment be the subject

---

[36] Cf. *Fay* v. *New York,* 332 U.S. 261, 300 (dissenting opinion of Mr. Justice Murphy).

of the camera's focus. The most the camera can show is that a formally correct trial took place, but our Constitution requires more than form.

I recognize that the television industry has shown in the past that it can be an enlightening and informing institution, but like other institutions it must respect the rights of others and cannot demand that we alter fundamental constitutional conceptions for its benefit. We must take notice of the inherent unfairness of television in the courtroom and rule that its presence is inconsistent with the "fundamental conception" of what a trial should be. My conviction that this is the proper holding in this case is buttressed by the almost unanimous condemnation of televised court proceedings by the judiciary in this country and by the strong opposition to the practice by the organized bar in this country. Canon 35 of the American Bar Association's Canons of Judicial Ethics prohibits the televising of court trials.[37] With only two, or possibly three exceptions,[38] the highest court of each State which has considered the question has declared that televised criminal trials are inconsistent with the Anglo-American conception of "trial."[39] Similarly, Rule 53

---

[37] The Canon provides in pertinent part:

"Proceedings in court should be conducted with fitting dignity and decorum. The taking of photographs in the court room, during sessions of the court or recesses between sessions, and the broadcasting or televising of court proceedings detract from the essential dignity of the proceedings, distract participants and witnesses in giving testimony, and create misconceptions with respect thereto in the mind of the public and should not be permitted."

[38] Colorado, *In re Hearings Concerning Canon 35 of the Canons of Judicial Ethics*, 296 P. 2d 465 (Colo. Sup. Ct. 1956), and Texas permit televising of trials in the discretion of the trial judge. The current situation in Oklahoma is unclear. In *Lyles* v. *State*, 330 P. 2d 734 (1958), the Criminal Court of Appeals of Oklahoma stated that the televising of proceedings was in the discretion of the trial judge. In 1959, however, the Supreme Court adopted a rule prohibiting television during actual proceedings. Okla. Stat. Ann., Tit. 5, at 65–66 (1963 Supp.). Nevertheless, in 1961 the court again stated

that the televising of trials is a matter for the trial judge's discretion. *Cody* v. *State*, 361 P. 2d 307 (Ct. Crim. App. Okla. 1961).

[39] With the exceptions stated in note 38, *supra*, no State affirmatively permits televised trials. It has been stated that Canon 35 is in effect in 30 States. 48 J. Am. Jud. Soc. 80 (1964); Brief for Petitioner, p. 39. It is difficult to verify this figure because of the lack of uniformity among the States in reporting their court rules. However, the following States have clearly adopted Canon 35, or its equivalent: Alaska, Alaska Rules Crim. Proc. 48; Arizona, Ariz. Sup. Ct. Rule 45, 17 Ariz. Rev. Stat. Ann., at 40; Connecticut, Conn. Practice Book 27 (1963); Delaware, Del. Sup. Ct. Rule 33, 13 Del. Code Ann., at 23 (1964 Supp.) (adopted Canon 35 in its pre-1952 form, which does not explicitly prohibit television, but does prohibit "the taking of photographs" and "broadcasting of court proceedings"); Florida, Code of Ethics, Rule A35, 31 Fla. Stat. Ann., at 285 (1964 Supp.), see *Brumfield* v. *State*, 108 So. 2d 33 (Fla. Sup. Ct. 1958); Hawaii, Hawaii Sup. Ct. Rule 16, 43 Haw. 450; Illinois, 1964 Ann. Rep. of the Ill.

of the Federal Rules of Criminal Procedure prohibits the "broadcasting" of trials,[40] and the Judicial Conference of the United States has unanimously condemned televised trials.[41] This condemnation rests on more than notions of policy; it arises from an understanding of the constitutional conception of the term "trial." Such a general consensus is certainly relevant to this Court's determination of the question. See *Mapp* v. *Ohio,* 367 U.S. 643, 651.

Judicial Conference 168–169, see *People* v. *Ulrich,* 376 Ill. 461, 34 N. E. 2d 393 (1941), *People* v. *Munday,* 280 Ill. 32, 117 N. E. 286 (1917); Iowa, Iowa Sup. Ct. Rule 119, 40 Iowa Code Ann., c. 610 (1964 Supp.); Kansas, Kansas Sup. Ct. Rule 117, 191 Kan. xxiv (1963) (does not refer specifically to television); Kentucky, Ky. Ct. App. Rule 3.170, Russell's Kentucky Practice and Service 21 (1964); Louisiana, Canon of Judicial Ethics XXIII, 242 La. LI (1960); Michigan, Canon of Judicial Ethics 35, Callaghan's Michigan Pleading and Practice, Rules at 422–423 (2d ed. 1962); New Jersey Canon of Judicial Ethics 35, 1 Wallzinger, New Jersey Practice 299 (Rev. ed. 1954); New Mexico, N. M. Sup. Ct. Rule 27, 4 N. M. Stat. Ann., at 95 (1963 Supp.); New York, N. Y. Rules of the Administrative Board of the Judicial Conference, Rule 5, N. Y. Judiciary Law, at 320 (1964 Supp.); Ohio, 176 Ohio St. lxiv (1964), see *State* v. *Clifford,* 162 Ohio St. 370, 123 N.E. 2d 8 (1954), cert. denied, 349 U. S. 929; Tennessee, Tenn. Sup. Ct. Rule 38, 209 Tenn. 818 (1961); Virginia, 201 Va. cvii (1960) (prohibits taking of photographs and broadcasting, although it does not refer specifically to television); Washington, 61 Wash. 2d xxviii (1963); West Virginia, 141 W. Va. viii (1955).

In addition, Brand, Bar Associations, Attorneys and Judges (1956 and 1959 Supp.) reports that the Idaho Supreme Court adopted Canon 35 in its present form and the Supreme Courts of Oregon, South Dakota and Utah adopted the Canon when it merely prohibited "photographing" and "broadcasting" without specifically mentioning television. It has also been reported that the Supreme Court of Arkansas adopted Canon 35. 44 J. Am. Jud. Soc. 120 (1960).

Moreover, the Supreme Court of California assumed it was "improper" to televise criminal proceedings in *People* v. *Stroble,* 36 Cal. 2d 615, 226 P. 2d 330 (1951), affirmed 343 U. S. 181, rehearing denied 343 U. S. 952; see the rule adopted by the Conference of California Judges, 24 Cal. State Bar J. 299 (1949); the Court of Appeals of Maryland in *Ex parte Sturm,* 152 Md. 114, 122, 136 A. 312, 315 (1927), used language indicating that Maryland would probably bar television from the courtroom if faced with the problem; and the Supreme Court of Pennsylvania cited with approval Canon 35 in *Mack Appeal,* 386 Pa. 251, 257, n. 5, 126 A. 2d 679, 681–682, n.4 (1956), cert. denied, 352 U.S. 1002, see 48 J. Am. Jud. Soc. 200 (1965).

[40] Rule 53 provides:
"The taking of photographs in the court room during the progress of judicial proceedings or radio broadcasting of judicial proceedings from the court room shall not be permitted by the court."

[41] "Resolved, That the Judicial Conference of the United States condemns the taking of photographs in the courtroom or its environs in connection with any judicial proceedings, and the broadcasting of judicial proceedings by radio, television, or other means, and considers such practices to be inconsistent with fair judicial procedure and that they ought not to be permitted in any federal court." Annual Report of the Proceedings of the Judicial Conference of the United States, March 8–9, 1962, p. 10.

IV.

Nothing in this opinion is inconsistent with the constitutional guarantees of a public trial and the freedoms of speech and the press.

This Court explained in *In re Oliver*, 333 U.S. 257, 266, 270, that the public trial provision of the Sixth Amendment is a "guarantee to an accused" designed to "safeguard against any attempt to employ our courts as instruments of persecution." Clearly the openness of the proceedings provides other benefits as well: it arguably improves the quality of testimony, it may induce unknown witnesses to come forward with relevant testimony, it may move all trial participants to perform their duties conscientiously, and it gives the public the opportunity to observe the courts in the performance of their duties and to determine whether they are performing adequately.[42] But the guarantee of a public trial confers no special benefit on the press, the radio industry or the television industry. A public trial is a necessary component of an accused's right to a fair trial and the concept of public trial cannot be used to defend conditions which prevent the trial process from providing a fair and reliable determination of guilt.

To satisfy the constitutional requirement that trials be public it is not necessary to provide facilities large enough for all who might like to attend a particular trial, since to do so would interfere with the integrity of the trial process and make the publicity of trial proceedings an end in itself. Nor does the requirement that trials be public mean that observers are free to act as they please in the courtroom, for persons who attend trials cannot act in such a way as to interfere with the trial process, see *Moore* v. *Dempsey, supra*. When representatives of the communications media attend trials they have no greater rights than other members of the public. Just as an ordinary citizen might be prohibited from using field glasses or a motion picture camera in the courthouse because by so doing he would interfere with the conduct of the trial, representatives of the press and broadcasting industries are subject to similar limitations when they attend court. Since the televising of criminal trials diverts the trial process from its proper end, it must be prohibited. This prohibition does not conflict with the constitutional guarantee of a public trial, because a trial is public, in the constitutional sense, when a courtroom has facilities for a reasonable number of the public to observe the proceedings, which facilities are not so small as to render the openness negligible and not so large as to distract the

---

[42] See, *e. g.*, 3 Blackstone, Commentaries on the Laws of England 372–373 (15th ed. 1809); 6 Wigmore, Evidence 332–335 (3d ed. 1940).

trial participants from their proper function, when the public is free to use those facilities, and when all those who attend the trial are free to report what they observed at the proceedings.

Nor does the exclusion of television cameras from the courtroom in any way impinge upon the freedoms of speech and the press. Court proceedings, as well as other public matters, are proper subjects for press coverage.

"A trial is a public event. What transpires in the court room is public property. If a transcript of the court proceedings had been published, we suppose none would claim that the judge could punish the publisher for contempt. And we can see no difference though the conduct of the attorneys, of the jury, or even of the judge himself, may have reflected on the court. Those who see and hear what transpired can report it with impunity. There is no special perquisite of the judiciary which enables it, as distinguished from other institutions of democratic government, to suppress, edit, or censor events which transpire in proceedings before it."[43]

So long as the television industry, like the other communications media, is free to send representatives to trials and to report on those trials to its viewers, there is no abridgment of the freedom of press. The right of the communications media to comment on court proceedings does not bring with it the right to inject themselves into the fabric of the trial process to alter the purpose of that process.

In summary, television is one of the great inventions of all time and can perform a large and useful role in society. But the television camera, like other technological innovations, is not entitled to pervade the lives of everyone in disregard of constitutionally protected rights.[44] The television industry, like other institutions, has a proper area of activities and limitations beyond which it cannot go with its cameras. That area does not extend into an American courtroom. On entering that hallowed sanctuary, where the lives, liberty and property of people are in jeopardy, television representatives have only the rights of the general public, namely, to be present, to observe the proceedings, and thereafter, if they choose, to report them.

---

[43] *Craig* v. *Harney*, 331 U.S. 367, 374. See *Bridges* v. *California*, 314 U. S. 252; *Pennekamp* v. *Florida*, 328 U.S. 331.

[44] Compare *Olmstead* v. *United States*, 277 U.S. 438, 471 (dissenting opinion of Mr. Justice Brandeis); *On* *Lee* v. *United States*, 343 U.S. 747, 762 (dissenting opinion of Mr. JUSTICE DOUGLAS); *Silverman* v. *United States*, 365 U. S. 505; *Lopez* v. *United States*, 373 U. S. 427, 445–446 (opinion concurring in the result), 465 (dissenting opinion of MR. JUSTICE BRENNAN).

Mr. JUSTICE HARLAN, concurring.

I concur in the opinion of the Court, subject, however, to the reservations and only to the extent indicated in this opinion.

The constitutional issue presented by this case is far reaching in its implications for the administration of justice in this country. The precise question is whether the Fourteenth Amendment prohibits a State, over the objection of a defendant, from employing television in the courtroom to televise contemporaneously, or subsequently by means of videotape, the courtroom proceedings of a criminal trial of widespread public interest. The issue is no narrower than this because petitioner has not asserted any isolatable prejudice resulting from the presence of television apparatus within the courtroom or from the contemporaneous or subsequent broadcasting of the trial proceedings. On the other hand, the issue is no broader, for we are concerned here only with a criminal trial of great notoriety, and not with criminal proceedings of a more or less routine nature.

The question is fraught with unusual difficulties. Permitting television in the courtroom undeniably has mischievous potentialities for intruding upon the detached atmosphere which should always surround the judicial process. Forbidding this innovation, however, would doubtless impinge upon one of the valued attributes of our federalism by preventing the States from pursuing a novel course of procedural experimentation. My conclusion is that there is no constitutional requirement that television be allowed in the courtroom, and, at least as to a notorious criminal trial such as this one, the considerations against allowing television in the courtroom so far outweigh the countervailing factors advanced in its support as to require a holding that what was done in this case infringed the fundamental right to a fair trial assured by the Due Process Clause of the Fourteenth Amendment.

Some preliminary observations are in order: All would agree, I am sure, that at its worst, television is capable of distorting the trial process so as to deprive it of fundamental fairness. Cables, kleig lights, interviews with the principal participants, commentary on their performances, "commercials" at frequent intervals, special wearing apparel and makeup for the trial participants—certainly such things would not conduce to the sound administration of justice by any acceptable standard. But that is not the case before us. We must judge television as we find it in this trial—relatively unobtrusive, with the cameras contained in a booth at the back of the courtroom.

I.

No constitutional provision guarantees a right to televise trials. The "public trial" guarantee of the Sixth Amendment, which reflects a concept fundamental to the administration of justice in this Country, *In re Oliver*, 333 U.S. 257, certainly does not require that television be admitted to the courtroom. See *United Press Assns*. v. *Valente*, 308 N.Y. 71, 123 N.E.2d 777. Essentially, the public-trial guarantee embodies a view of human nature, true as a general rule, that judges, lawyers, witnesses, and jurors will perform their respective functions more responsibly in an open court than in secret proceedings. *In re Oliver, supra,* at 266–273. A fair trial is the objective, and "public trial" is an institutional safeguard for attaining it.

Thus the right of "public trial" is not one belonging to the public, but one belonging to the accused, and inhering in the institutional process by which justice is administered. Obviously, the public-trial guarantee is not violated if an individual member of the public cannot gain admittance to a courtroom because there are no available seats. The guarantee will already have been met, for the "public" will be present in the form of those persons who did gain admission. Even the actual presence of the public is not guaranteed. A public trial implies only that the court must be open to those who wish to come, sit in the available seats, conduct themselves with decorum, and observe the trial process. It does not give anyone a concomitant right to photograph, record, broadcast, or otherwise transmit the trial proceedings to those members of the public not present, although to be sure, the guarantee of public trial does not of itself prohibit such activity.

The free speech and press guarantees of the First and Fourteenth Amendments are also asserted as embodying a positive right to televise trials, but the argument is greatly overdrawn. Unquestionably, television has become a very effective medium for transmitting news. Many trials are newsworthy, and televising them might well provide the most accurate and comprehensive means of conveying their content to the public. Futhermore, television is capable of performing an educational function by acquainting the public with the judicial process in action. Albeit these are credible policy arguments in favor of television, they are not arguments of constitutional proportions. The rights to print and speak, over television as elsewhere, do not embody an independent right to bring the mechanical facilities of the broadcasting and printing industries into the courtroom. Once beyond the confines of the courthouse, a news-gathering agency may publicize, within wide limits, what its representatives have heard and seen in the courtroom. But the line is drawn at the courthouse door; and within, a reporter's constitutional rights are no greater than those of any other member of the public. Within the courthouse the only relevant constitutional consideration is that the accused be accorded a fair trial. If the presence of television substantially detracts from that goal, due process requires that its use be forbidden.

I see no force in the argument that to exclude television apparatus from the courtroom, while at the same time permitting newspaper reporters to bring in their pencils and notebooks, would discriminate in favor of the press as against the broadcasting services. The distinctions to be drawn between the accouterments of the press and the television media turn not on differences of size and shape but of function and effect. The presence of the press at trials may have a distorting effect, but it is not caused by their pencils and notebooks. If it were, I would not hesitate to say that such physical paraphernalia should be barred.

II.

The probable impact of courtroom television on the fairness of a trial may vary according to the particular kind of case involved. The impact of television on a trial exciting wide popular interest may be one thing; the impact on a run-of-the-mill case may be quite another. Furthermore, the propriety of closed circuit television for the purpose of making a court recording or for limited use in educational institutions obviously presents markedly different considerations. The Estes trial was a heavily publicized and highly sensational affair. I therefore put aside all other types of cases; in so doing, however, I wish to make it perfectly clear that I am by no means prepared to say that the constitutional issue should ultimately turn upon the nature of the particular case involved. When the issue of television in a non-notorious trial is presented it may appear that no workable distinction can be drawn based on the type of case involved, or that the possibilities for prejudice, though less severe, are nonetheless of constitutional proportions. Compare *Powell* v. *Alabama,* 287 U.S. 45; *Betts* v. *Brady,* 316 U.S. 455; *Gideon* v. *Wainwright,* 372 U.S. 335. The resolution of those further questions should await an appropriate case; the Court should proceed only step by step in this unplowed field. The opinion of the Court necessarily goes no further, for only the four members of the majority who unreservedly join the Court's opinion would resolve those questions now.

I do not deem the constitutional inquiry in this case ended by the finding, in effect conceded by petitioner's counsel, that no isolatable prejudice was occasioned by the manner in which television was employed in this case.[1] Courtroom television introduces into the conduct of a criminal trial the element of professional "showmanship," an extraneous influence whose subtle capacities for serious mischief in a case of this sort will not be underestimated by any lawyer experienced in the elusive imponderables of the trial arena. In the context of a trial of intense public interest, there is certainly a strong possibility that the timid or reluctant witness, for whom a court appearance even at its traditional best is a harrowing affair, will become more timid or reluctant when he finds that he will also be appearing before a "hidden audience" of unknown but large dimensions. There is certainly a strong possibility that the "cocky" witness having a thirst for the limelight will become more "cocky" under the influence of television. And who can say that the juror who is gratified by having been chosen for a front-line case, an ambitious prosecutor, a publicity-minded defense counsel, and even a conscientious judge will not stray, albeit unconsciously, from doing what "comes naturally" into pluming themselves for a satisfactory television "performance"?

Surely possibilities of this kind carry grave potentialities for distorting the integrity of the judicial process bearing on the determination of the guilt or innocence of the accused, and, more particularly, for casting doubt on the reliability of the fact-finding process carried on under such conditions. See Douglas, The Public Trial and the Free Press, 46 A. B. A. J. 840 (1960). To be sure, such distortions may produce no telltale signs, but in a highly publicized trial the danger of their presence is substantial, and their effects may be far more pervasive and deleterious than the physical disruptions which all concede would vitiate a conviction. A lively public interest could increase the size of the viewing audience immensely, and the masses of spectators to whom the trial is telecast would have become emotionally involved with the case through the dissemination of pretrial publicity, the usual concomitant of such a case. The presence of television would certainly emphasize to the trial participants that the case is something "special." Particularly treacherous situations are presented in cases where pretrial publicity has been massive[2] even when jurors positively state they will not be influenced by it; see *Rideau* v. *Louisiana*, 373 U.S. 723; *Irvin* v. *Dowd*, 366 U.S. 717. To increase the possibility of influence

---

[1] The trial judge ordered that there was to be no audio transmission of the witnesses' testimony. The witnesses, however, were present at the September hearing when everything was broadcast, and the record does not show affirmatively that they were aware that the microphone which confronted them during the actual trial was not being used for the same purpose.

[2] Petitioner in this case amassed 11 volumes of pretrial press clippings.

and the danger of a "popular verdict" by subjecting the jurors to the view of a mass audience whose approach to the case has been conditioned by pretrial publicity can only make a bad situation worse. The entire trust of rules of evidence and the other protections attendant upon the modern trial is to keep extraneous influences out of the courtroom. *Turner* v. *Louisiana,* 379 U.S. 466, 472–473. As we recently observed in *Turner,* "Mr. Justice Holmes stated no more than a truism when he observed that 'Any judge who has sat with juries knows that in spite of forms they are extremely likely to be impregnated by the environing atmosphere.' *Frank* v. *Mangum,* 237 U.S. 309, at 349 (dissenting opinion)." *Id.,* at 472.[3] The knowledge on the part of the jury and other trial participants that they are being televised to an emotionally involved audience can only aggravate the atmosphere created by pretrial publicity.

The State argues that specific prejudice must be shown for the Due Process Clause to apply. I do not believe that the Fourteenth Amendment is so impotent when the trial practices in question are instinct with dangers to constitutional guarantees. I am at a loss to understand how the Fourteenth Amendment can be thought not to encompass protection of a state criminal trial from the dangers created by the intrusion of collateral and wholly irrelevant influences into the courtroom. The Court has not hesitated in the past to condemn such practices, even without any positive showing of isolatable prejudice. In *Turner* v. *Louisiana, supra,* decided just this Term, we held that the "potentialities" for distortion of the trial created by a key witness serving as bailiff to a sequestered jury were sufficient to violate the Due Process Clause of the Fourteenth Amendment. In *Jackson* v. *Denno,* 378 U.S. 368, the Court made the judgment that a trial judge's determination of a coerced-confession issue is more likely to avoid prejudice than a jury determination, a judgment which indeed overrode a long-standing contrary state practice. And in *Irvin* v. *Dowd,* 366 U.S. 717, we held that flamboyant pretrial publicity cast sufficient doubt on the impartiality of the jury to vitiate a conviction, even in the face of statements by all the jurors that they were not subject to its influence. See 366 U.S., at 729 (Frankfurter, J., concurring). Other examples of instances in which the Court has exercised its judgment as to the effects of one thing or another on human behavior are plentiful. See, *e. g., Griffin* v. *California,* 380 U.S. 609; *Tancil* v. *Woolls,* 379 U.S. 19; *Mapp* v. *Ohio,* 367 U.S. 643 (compare *People* v. *Defore,*

---

[3] The Court had occasion to recognize in *Cox* v. *Louisiana,* 379 U.S. 559, 565, that even "judges are human" and not immune from outside environmental influences.

242 N.Y. 13, 150 N.E. 585); *Avery* v. *Georgia*, 345 U.S. 559; *Brown* v. *Board of Education*, 347 U.S. 483; *Tumey* v. *Ohio*, 273 U.S. 510.

The judgment that the presence of television in the courtroom represents a serious danger to the trial process is supported by a vast segment of the Bar of this country, as evidenced by Canon 35 of the Canons of Judicial Ethics of the American Bar Association, counseling against such practices,[4] the views of the Judicial Conference of the United States (*infra,* p. 601), Rule 53 of the Federal Rules of Criminal Procedure, and even the "personal views" (*post,* pp. 601–602) of the Justices on the dissenting side of the present case.

The arguments advanced against the constitutional banning of televised trials seem to me peculiarly unpersuasive. It is said that the pictorial broadcasting of trials will serve to educate the public as to the nature of the judicial process. Whatever force such arguments might have in run-of-the-mill cases, they carry little weight in cases of the sort before us, where the public's interest in viewing the trial is likely to be engendered more by curiosity about the personality of the well-known figure who is the defendant (as here), or about famous witnesses or lawyers who will appear on the television screen, or about the details of the particular crime involved, than by innate curiosity to learn about the workings of the judicial process itself. Indeed it would be naive not to suppose that it would be largely such factors that would qualify a trial for commercial television "billing," and it is precisely that kind of case where the risks of permitting television coverage of the proceedings are at their greatest.

It is also asserted that televised trials will cause witnesses to be more truthful, and jurors, judges, and lawyers more diligent. To say the least this argument is sophistic, for it is impossible to believe that the reliability of a trial as a method of finding facts and determining guilt or innocence increases in relation to the size of the crowd which is watching it. Attendance by interested spectators in the courtroom will fully satisfy the safeguards of "public trial." Once openness is thus assured, the addition of masses of spectators would, I venture to say, detract rather than add to the reliability of the process. See *Cox* v. *Louisiana*, 379 U.S. 559, 562. A trial in Yankee Stadium, even if the crowd sat in stony silence, would be a substantially different affair from a trial in a traditional courtroom under traditional conditions, and the difference would not, I

---

[4] The consistent position of the American Bar Association is set out in the Appendix.

think, be that the witnesses, lawyers, judges, and jurors in the stadium would be more truthful, diligent, and capable of reliably finding facts and determining guilt or innocence.[5] There will be no disagreement, I am sure, among those competent to judge that precisely the opposite would likely be the case.

Finally, we should not be deterred from making the constitutional judgment which this case demands by the prospect that the day may come when television will have become so commonplace an affair in the daily life of the average person as to dissipate all reasonable likelihood that its use in courtrooms may disparage the judicial process. If and when that day arrives the constitutional judgment called for now would of course be subject to re-examination in accordance with the traditional workings of the Due Process Clause. At the present juncture I can only conclude that televised trials, at least in cases like this one, possess such capabilities for interfering with the even course of the judicial process that they are constitutionally banned. On these premises I concur in the opinion of the Court.

APPENDIX TO OPINION OF MR. JUSTICE HARLAN, CONCURRING.

The development of Canon 35 is set out at length in the *amicus curiae* brief of the American Bar Association, pp. 3–8, as follows: "It [Canon 35] was originally adopted on September 30, 1937 by the House of Delegates[1] in the following form:

" 'Proceedings in court should be conducted with fitting dignity and decorum. The taking of photographs in the court room, during sessions of the court or recesses between sessions, and the broadcasting of court proceedings are calculated to detract from the essential dignity of the proceedings, degrade the court and create misconceptions with respect thereto in the mind of the public and should not be permitted.' 62 A. B. A. REP. 1134–35 (1937).

---

[5] There may, of course, be a difference in impact upon the atmosphere and trial participants between the physical presence of masses of people and the presence of a camera lens which permits masses of people to observe the process remotely. However, the critical element is the knowledge of the trial participants that they are subject to such visual observation, an element which is, of course, present in this case.

[1] "The House of Delegates is not only the governing body of the American Bar Association; because of the presence of representatives of all State Bar Associations, the largest and most important local bar associations, and of other important national professional groups, it is in fact a broadly representative policy forum for the profession as a whole."

"A Special Committee on Cooperation Between Press, Radio and Bar, as to Publicity Interfering with Fair Trial of Judicial and Quasi-Judicial Proceedings had reported to the Association its grave concern with the dangers attendant upon the use of radio in connection with trials, particularly in light of the spectacular publicity and broadcast of the trial of Bruno Hauptmann.[2] The Committee specifically referred to the evil of 'trial in the air'.[3] 62 A. B. A. REP. 860 (1937).

"After the adoption of Judicial Canon 35, the direct radio broadcasting of court proceedings was disapproved by the Association's Committee on Professional Ethics and Grievances in its Opinion No. 212, March 15, 1941, as being specifically condemned. The Committee quoted with approval the following statement of the Michigan and Detroit Bar Associations:

" 'Such broadcasts are unfair to the defendant and to the witnesses. The natural embarrassment and confusion of a citizen on trial should not be increased by a realization that his voice and his difficulties are being used as entertainment for a vast radio audience. The fear expressed by most persons when facing an audience or microphone is a matter of common knowledge, and but few defendants or witnesses can properly concentrate on facts and testify fully and fairly when so handicapped. . . . Such broadcasts are unfair to the Judge, who should be permitted to devote his undivided attention to the case, unmindful of the effect which his comments or decision may have upon the radio audience.' American Bar Association, Opinion of the Committee on Professional Ethics and Grievances 426 (1957).

"In 1952, the growing prominence of television as a medium of mass communication was dealt with in a report of the Special Committee on Televising and Broadcasting Legislative and Judicial Proceedings [headed by the late John W. Davis]. 77 A. B. A. REP. 607 (1952). In condemning the practice of televising judicial proceedings, the Committee called attention to the fact that:

---

[2] "See *State* v. *Hauptmann*, 155 N. J. L. 412, 180 Atl. 809 (Ct. Err. & App.), *cert. denied*, 296 U. S. 649 (1935)."

[3] "Prior to the adoption of Judicial Canon 35, the impropriety of permitting radio broadcasts of court proceedings was recognized by the Committee on Professional Ethics and Grievances of the Association in its Opinion No. 67, March 21, 1932. The Committee had recourse to Judicial Canon 34 which provides that a judge should not administer his office 'for the purpose of advancing his personal ambitions or increasing his popularity.' The Committee found that radio broadcasting of a trial changes 'what should be the most serious of human institutions either into an enterprise for the entertainment of the public or of one for promoting publicity for the judge.' AMERICAN BAR ASSOCIATION, OPINIONS OF THE COMMITTEE ON PROFESSIONAL ETHICS AND GRIEVANCES 163 (1957)."

" 'The attention of the court, the jury, lawyers and witnesses should be concentrated upon the trial itself and ought not to be divided with the television or broadcast audience who for the most part have merely the interest of curiosity in the proceedings. It is not difficult to conceive that all participants may become over-concerned with the impression their actions, rulings or testimony will make on the absent multitude.' *Id.* at 610.

"As a result of this report, and the recommendation of the Committee on Professional Ethics and Grievances, Judicial Canon 35 was amended by inserting a ban on the 'televising' of court proceedings and inserting the descriptive phrase 'distract the witness in giving his testimony' before the phrase 'degrade the court.' In addition, a second paragraph was added providing for the televising and broadcasting of certain ceremonial proceedings. *Id.* at 110–11.

"In October, 1954, the Board of Governors authorized the appointment of a Special Bar-Media Conference Committee on Fair Trial-Free Press to meet with representatives of the press, radio, and television. The views of both sides were thoroughly explored and were presented in detail in the September, 1956 issue of the American Bar Association Journal.[4] After extensive joint debate, no solutions or agreements were reached. 83 A. B. A. REP. 790–91 (1958). The Committee did report that it was convinced that

" 'courtroom photographing or broadcasting or both would impose undue police duties upon the trial judge[,] . . . that the broadcasting and the photographing in the courtroom might have an adverse phychological effect upon trial participants, judges, lawyers, witnesses and juries[,] . . . [and] that partial broadcasts of trials, particularly on television, might influence public opinion which in turn might influence trial results. . . .' *Id.* at 645.

"Following the presentation of the Bar-Media Conference Committee report and in connection with the consideration of a report and recommendation of a Special Committee of the American Bar Foundation created in July, 1955 (83 A.B.A. REP. 643–45 (1958)), the House of Delegates conducted a hearing as a 'Committee of the Whole' during its February, 1958 session at which proponents and opponents of Judicial Canon 35 were fully heard. 83 A.B.A. REP. 648–69 (1958). Thereafter, at the August, 1958 meeting of the House of Delegates, it was decided to have a Special Committee study Canon 35 and

" 'conduct further studies of the problem, including the obtaining of a body of reliable factual data on the experience of judges and lawyers in those courts where either photography, televising or broadcasting, or all of them, are permitted. . . . The fundamental ob-

---

4 "42 A.B.A.J. 834, 838, 843 (1956)."

jective of the Committee and of all others interested must be to consider and make recommendations which will preserve the right of fair trial.' 83 A. B. A. REP. 284 (1958).

"The Special Committee filed an Interim Report and Recommendations with the House of Delegates in August, 1962 setting forth the 'Area and Perspective' of its survey and studies. The report included portions of testimony by media representatives taken at a hearing held in Chicago on February 18, 1962, as well as a summary of the Committee's informal conference with certain representatives from Colorado and Texas. In addition, the report included written comments by officers of State Bar Associations responding to a Committee survey, and certain general correspondence received by the Committee regarding Judicial Canon 35. The report also listed significant publications favoring either revision or retention of the Canon. . . . [Hereinafter cited *Int. Rep.*]

"The Special Committee thereafter submitted its final report and recommendations, concluding that the substantive provisions of Judicial Canon 35 remain valid and 'should be retained as essential safeguards of the individual's inviolate and personal right of fair trial.' . . . The Committee did recommend certain minor deletions . . . and changes . . . which were adopted by the House of Delegates, after full debate, on February 5, 1963:

" 'The taking of photographs in the courtroom, during sessions of the court or recesses between sessions, and the broadcasting or televising of court proceedings [are calculated to] detract from the essential dignity of the proceedings, distract [the] *participants and witnesses* in giving [his] testimony, [degrade the court] and create misconceptions with respect thereto in the mind of the public and should not be permitted.' [5]

"A vast majority of the states have voluntarily adopted Judicial Canon 35 in one form or another, and it has been embodied in principle in Rule 53 of the Federal Rules of Criminal Procedure.

---

[5] "The full text of Judicial Canon 35, as amended, is as follows:

" 'IMPROPER PUBLICIZING OF COURT PROCEEDINGS

" 'Proceedings in court should be conducted with fitting dignity and decorum. The taking of photographs in the court room, during sessions of the court or recesses between sessions, and the broadcasting or televising of court proceedings detract from the essential dignity of the proceedings, distract participants and witnesses in giving testimony, and create misconceptions with respect thereto in the mind of the public and should not be permitted.

" 'Provided that this restriction shall not apply to the broadcasting or televising, under the supervision of the court, of such portions of naturalization proceedings (other than the interrogation of applicants) as are designed and carried out exclusively as a ceremony for the purpose of publicly demonstrating in an impressive manner the essential dignity and the serious nature of naturalization.' "

In a recent Resolution of the Judicial Conference of the United States, the philosophy of Canon 35 was unanimously reaffirmed:

" 'Resolved, That the Judicial Conference of the United States condemns the taking of photographs in the courtroom or its environs in connection with any judicial proceeding, and the broadcasting of judicial proceedings by radio, television, or other means, and considers such practices to be inconsistent with fair judicial procedure and that they ought not to be permitted in any federal court.' *Int. Rep.* p. 97."

(Footnotes numbered and partially omitted.)

MR. JUSTICE STEWART, whom MR. JUSTICE BLACK, MR. JUSTICE BRENNAN, and MR. JUSTICE WHITE join, dissenting.

I cannot agree with the Court's decision that the circumstances of this trial led to a denial of the petitioner's Fourteenth Amendment rights. I think that the introduction of television into a court room is, at least in the present state of the art, an extremely unwise policy. It invites many constitutional risks, and it detracts from the inherent dignity of a courtroom. But I am unable to escalate this personal view into a *per se* constitutional rule. And I am unable to find, on the specific record of this case, that the circumstances attending the limited televising of the petitioner's trial resulted in the denial of any right guaranteed to him by the United States Constitution.

On October 22, 1962, the petitioner went to trial in the Seventh Judicial District Court of Smith County, Texas, upon an indictment charging him with the offenses of (1) swindling, (2) theft by false pretenses, and (3) theft by a bailee. After a week spent in selecting a jury, the trial itself lasted some three and a half days. At its conclusion the jury found the petitioner guilty of the offense of swindling under the first count of the indictment. The trial judge permitted portions of the trial proceedings to be televised, under the limitations described below. He also gave news photographers permission to take still pictures in the courtroom under specified conditions.

The Texas Court of Criminal Appeals affirmed the petitioner's conviction, and we granted certiorari, limited to a single question. The question, as phrased by the petitioner, is this:

"Whether the action of the trial court, over petitioner's continued objection, denied him due process of law and equal protection of the laws under the Fourteenth Amendment to the Constitution of the United States, in requiring petitioner to submit to live television of his trial, and in refusing to adopt in this all out publicity

518

case, as a rule of trial procedure, Canon 35 of the Canons of Judicial Ethics of the American Bar Association, and instead adopting and following, over defendant's objection, Canon 28 of the Canons of Judicial Ethics, since approved by the Judicial Section of the integrated (State agency) State Bar of Texas."

The two Canons of Judicial Ethics referred to in the petitioner's statement of the question presented are set out in the margin.[1] But, as the Court rightly says, the problem before us is not one of choosing between the conflicting guidelines reflected in these Canons of Judicial Ethics. It is a problem rooted in the Due Process Clause of the Fourteenth Amendment. We deal here with matters subject to continuous and unforeseeable change—the techniques of public communication. In an area where all the variables may be modified

---

[1] Canons of Judicial Ethics. American Bar Association: Judicial Canon 35. Improper publicizing of Court proceedings.

"Proceedings in court should be conducted with fitting dignity and decorum. The taking of photographs in the court room, during sessions of the court or recesses between sessions, and the broadcasting or televising of court proceedings detract from the essential dignity of the proceedings, distract participants and witnesses in giving testimony, and create misconceptions with respect thereto in the mind of the public and should not be permitted.

"Provided that this restriction shall not apply to the broadcasting or televising, under the supervision of the court, of such portions of naturalization proceedings (other than the interrogation of applicants) as are designed and carried out exclusively as a ceremony for the purpose of publicly demonstrating in an impressive manner the essential dignity and the serious nature of naturalization."

Canons of Judicial Ethics, Integrated State Bar of Texas: Judicial Canon 28. Improper Publicizing of Court Proceedings.

"Proceedings in court should be conducted with fitting dignity and decorum. The taking of photographs in the court room, during sessions of the court or recesses between sessions, and the broadcasting or televising of court proceedings unless properly supervised and controlled, may detract from the essential dignity of the proceedings, distract participants and witnesses in giving testimony, and create misconceptions with respect thereto in the mind of the public. The supervision and control of such trial coverage shall be left to the trial judge who has the inherent power to exclude or control coverage in the proper case in the interest of justice.

"In connection with the control of such coverage the following declaration of principles is adopted:

"(1) There should be no use of flash bulbs or other artificial lighting.

"(2) No witness, over his expressed objection, should be photographed, his voice broadcast or be televised.

"(3) The representatives of news media must obtain permission of the trial judge to cover by photograph, broadcasting or televising, and shall comply with the rules prescribed by the judge for the exercise of the privilege.

"(4) Any violation of the Court's Rules shall be punished as a contempt.

"(5) Where a judge has refused to allow coverage or has regulated it, any attempt, other than argument by representatives of the news media directly with the Court, to bring pressure of any kind on the judge, pending final disposition of the cause in trial, shall be punished as a contempt."

tomorrow, I cannot at this time rest my determination on hypothetical possibilities not present in the record of this case. There is no claim here based upon any right guaranteed by the First Amendment. But it is important to remember that we move in an area touching the realm of free communication, and for that reason, if for no other, I would be wary of imposing any *per se* rule which, in the light of future technology, might serve to stifle or abridge true First Amendment rights.

I.

The indictment was originally returned by a grand jury in Reeves County, Texas, and it engendered widespread publicity. After some preliminary proceedings there, the case was transferred for trial to Smith County, more than 500 miles away. The trial was set for September 24, 1962, but it did not commence on that date. Instead, that day and the next were spent in hearings on two motions filed by defense counsel: a motion to bar television and news cameras from the trial, and a motion to continue the trial to a later date. Those proceedings were themselves telecast "live," and news photographers were permitted to take pictures in the courtroom. The activities of the television crews and news photographers led to considerable disruption of the hearings.[2] At the conclusion of the hearings the motion for a continuance was granted, and the case reset for trial on October 22. The motion to bar television and news photographers from the trial was denied.[3]

---

[2] A contemporary newspaper account described the scene as follows:

"A television motor van, big as an intercontinental bus, was parked outside the courthouse and the second-floor courtroom was a forest of equipment. Two television cameras had been set up inside the bar and four more marked cameras were aligned just outside the gates.

"A microphone stuck its 12-inch snout inside the jury box, now occupied by an overflow of reporters from the press table, and three microphones confronted Judge Dunagan on his bench. [C]ables and wires snaked over the floor." The New York Times, September 25, 1962, p. 46, col. 4.

[3] In ruling on the motion, the trial judge stated:

"In the past, it has been the policy of this Court to permit televising in the court room under the rules and supervision of the Court.

Heretofore, I have not encountered any difficulty with it. I was unable to observe any detraction from the witnesses or the attorneys in those cases. We have watched television, of course, grow up from its infancy and now into its maturity; and it is a news media. So I really do not see any justified reason why it should not be permitted to take its proper seat in the family circle. However, it will be under the strict supervision of the Court. I know there has been pro and con about televising in the court room. I have heard some say that it makes a circus out of the Court. I had the privilege yesterday morning of sitting in my home and viewing a sermon by the First Baptist Church over in Dallas and certainly it wasn't any circus in that church; and I feel that if it is a proper instrument in the house of the Lord, it is not out of place

On October 1, the trial judge issued an order delineating what coverage he would permit during the trial.[4] As a result of that order and ensuing conferences between the judge and representatives of the news media, the environment for the trial, which began on

in the court room, if properly supervised.

"Now, television is going to be televising whatever the scene is here. If you want to watch a ball game and that is what they televise, you are going to see a ball game. If you want to see a preacher and hear a sermon, you tune in on that and that is what you are going to get. If the Court permits a circus in this court room, it will be televised, that is true, but they will not be creating a circus.

"Now, the most important point is whether or not it would interfere with a fair and impartial trial of this Defendant. That is the most important point, and that is the purpose, or will be the primary purpose of the Court, to insure that he gets that fair trial.

. . . . .

"There is not anything the Court can do about the interest in this case, but I can control your activities and your conduct here; and I can assure you now that this Court is not going to be turned into a circus with TV or without it. Whatever action is necessary for the Court to take to insure that, the Court will take it.

. . . . .

"There has been one consideration that the Court has given and it is that this is a small court room and there will be hundreds of people trying to get into this court room to witness this trial. I believe we would have less confusion if they would stay at home and stay out of the court room and look in on the trial. With all of those people trying to crowd in and push into this court room, that is another consideration I have given to it."

[4] "In my statement of September 24, 1962, admitting television and other cameras in the court room during the trial of Billie Sol Estes, I said cameras would be allowed

under the control and direction of the Court so long as they did not violate the legal rights of the Defendant or the State of Texas.

. . . . .

"In line with my statement of September 24, 1962, I am at this time informing both television and radio that live broadcasting or telecasting by either news media cannot and will not be permitted during the interrogation of jurors in testing their qualifications, or of the testimony given by the witnesses, as to do so would be in violation of Art. 644 of the Code of Criminal Procedure of Texas, which provides as follows: 'At the request of either party, the witnesses on both sides may be sworn and placed in the custody of an officer and removed out of the court room to some place where they can not hear the testimony as delivered by any other witness in the case. This is termed placing witnesses under rule.'

". . . [E]ach television network and the local television station will be allowed one film camera without sound in the court room and the film will be made available to other television stations on a pool basis. Marshall Pengra, manager of Television Station KLTV, Tyler, will be in charge of the independent pool and independent stations may contact him. The same will be true of cameras for the press, which will be limited to the local press, Associated Press and United Press.

. . . . .

"I am making this statement at this time in order that the two news media affected may have sufficient notice before the case is called on October 22nd.

"The rules I have set forth above concerning the use of cameras are subject to change if I find that they are too restrictive or not workable, for any reason."

521

October 22, was in sharp contrast to that of the September hearings. The actual extent of television and news photography in the courtroom was described by the judge, after the trial had ended, in certifying the petitioner's bill of exceptions. This description is confirmed by my understanding of the entire record and was agreed to and accepted by defense counsel:

"Prior to the trial of October 22, 1962, there was a booth constructed and placed in the rear of the courtroom painted the same or near the same color as the courtroom with a small opening across the top for the use of cameras . . . .

"Live telecasting and radio broadcasting were not permitted and the only telecasting was on film without sound, and there was not any broadcasting of the trial by radio permitted. Each network, ABC, NBC, CBS, and KRLD [KLTV] Television in Tyler was allowed a camera in the courtroom . . . . The telecasting on film of this case was not a continuous camera operation and only pictures being taken at intervals during the day to be used on their regular news casts later in the day. There were some days during the trial that the cameras of only one or two stations were in operation, the others not being in attendance upon the Court each and every day. The Court did not permit any cameras other than those that were noiseless nor were flood lights and flash bulbs allowed to be used in the courtroom. The Court permitted one news photographer with Associated Press, United Press International and Tyler Morning Telegraph and Courier Times. However, they were not permitted inside the Bar; and the Court did not permit any telecasting or photographing in the hallways leading into the courtroom or on the second floor of the courthouse where the courtroom is situated, in order that the Defendant and his attorneys would not be hindered, molested or harassed in approaching or leaving the courtroom. The Court did permit live telecasting of the arguments of State's counsel and the returning of the verdict by the Jury and its acceptance by the Court. The opening argument of the District Attorney of Smith County was carried by sound and because of transmission difficulty, there was not any picture. The closing argument for the State by the District Attorney of Reeves County was carried live by both picture and sound. The arguments of attorneys for Defendant, John D. Cofer and Hume Cofer, were not telecast or broadcast as the Court granted their Motion that same not be permitted.

"There was not any televising at any time during the trial except from the booth in the rear of the courtroom, and during the argument of counsel to the jury, news photography was required

522

to operate from the booth so that they would not interfere or detract from the attention of either the jurors or the attorneys.

"During the trial that began October 22nd, there was never at any time any radio broadcasting equipment in the courtroom. There was some equipment in a room off of the courtroom where there were periodic news reports given; and throughout the trial that began October 22nd, not any witness requested not to be televised or photographed while they were testifying. Neither did any juror, while being interrogated on voir dire or at any other time, make any request of the Court not to be televised."

Thus, except for the closing arguments for the prosecution and the return of the jury's verdict, there was no "live" telecasting of the trial. And, even for purposes of delayed telecasting on later news programs, no words or other sounds were permitted to be recorded while the members of the jury were being selected or while any witness was testifying. No witnesses and no jurors were televised or photographed over their objection.[5]

Finally, the members of the jury saw no telecasts and no pictures of anything that went on during the trial. In accord with Texas law, the jurors were sequestered, day and night, from the beginning of the trial until it ended.[6] The jurors were lodged each night in quarters provided for that purpose in the courthouse itself. On the evening of November 6, by agreement of counsel and special permission of the court, the members of the jury were permitted to watch the election returns on television for a short period. For this purpose a portable television was brought into the jury's quarters by a court officer, and operated by him. Otherwise the jurors were not permitted to watch television at any time during the trial. The only newspapers permitted the jury were ones from which all coverage of the trial had been physically removed.

II.

It is important to bear in mind the precise limits of the question before us in this case. The petition for a writ of certiorari asked us to review four separate constitutional claims. We declined to review three of them, among which was the claim that the members of the jury "had received through the news media damaging and prejudicial evidence . . . ."[7] We thus left undisturbed the determination of the Texas Court of Criminal Appeals that the mem-

[5] There were nine witnesses for the prosecution and no witnesses for the defense.
[6] Arts. 668, 745, and 725, Tex. Code Crim. Proc.
[7] Petition for Writ of Certiorari, Question 3, p. 3.

bers of the jury were *not* prejudiced by the widespread publicity which preceded the petitioner's trial. One ingredient of this pretrial publicity was the telecast of the September hearings. Despite the confusion in the courtroom during those hearings, all that a potential juror could have possibly learned from watching them on television was that the petitioner's case had been called for trial, and that motions had been made and acted upon for a continuance, and to exclude cameras and television. At those hearings, there was no discussion whatever of anything bearing on the petitioner's guilt or innocence. This was conceded by the petitioner's counsel at the trial.[8]

Because of our refusal to review the petitioner's claim that pretrial publicity had a prejudicial effect upon the jurors in this case, and because, insofar as the September hearings were an element of that publicity, the claim is patently without merit, that issue is simply not here. Our decision in *Rideau* v. *Louisiana*, 373 U.S. 723, therefore, has no bearing at all in this case. There the record showed that the inhabitants of the small Louisiana parish where the trial was held had repeatedly been exposed to a television film showing "Rideau, in jail, flanked by the sheriff and two state troopers, admitting in detail the commission of the robbery, kidnapping, and murder, in response to leading questions by the sheriff." 373 U.S., at 725. We found that "[a]ny subsequent court proceedings in a community so pervasively exposed to such a spectacle could be but a hollow formality." *Id.*, at 726. See also *Irvin* v. *Dowd*, 336 U.S. 717.

The *Rideau* case was no more than a contemporary application of enduring principles of procedural due process, principles reflected in such earlier cases as *Moore* v. *Dempsey*, 261 U.S. 86; *Brown* v. *Mississippi*, 297 U.S. 278; and *Chambers* v. *Florida*, 309 U.S. 227, 235–241. "Under our Constitution's guarantee of due process," we said, "a person accused of committing a crime is vouchsafed basic minimal rights. Among these are the right to counsel, the right to plead not guilty, and the right to be tried in a courtroom presided over by a judge." 373 U.S., at 726–727. We had occasion to apply the same basic concepts of procedural due process earlier this Term in *Turner* v. *Louisana*, 379 U.S. 466. "In the con-

---

[8] "A. [Mr. Hume Cofer, counsel for petitioner] . . . . The publicity that was given this trial on the last occasion and the number of cameras here, I think was sufficient to spread the news of this case throughout the county, to every available juror; and it is my opinion that on that occasion, there were so many cameras and so much paraphernalia here that it gave an opportunity for every prospective juror in Smith County to know about this case.

"Q. Not about the facts of the case?

"A. No, sir; not about the facts, nor any of the evidence."

stitutional sense, trial by jury in a criminal case necessarily implies at the very least that the 'evidence developed' against a defendant shall come from the witness stand in a public courtroom where there is full judicial protection of the defendant's right of confrontation, of cross-examination, and of counsel." 379 U.S., at 472–473.

But we do not deal here with mob domination of a courtroom, with a kangaroo trial, with a prejudiced judge or a jury inflamed with bias. Under the limited grant of certiorari in this case, the sole question before us is an entirely different one. It concerns only the regulated presence of television and still photography at the trial itself, which began on October 22, 1962. Any discussion of pretrial events can do no more than obscure the important question which is actually before us.

III.

It is obvious that the introduction of television and news cameras into a criminal trial invites many serious constitutional hazards. The very presence of photographers and television cameramen plying their trade in a courtroom might be so completely and thoroughly disruptive and distracting as to make a fair trial impossible. Thus, if the scene at the September hearing had been repeated in the courtroom during this jury trial, it is difficult to conceive how a fair trial in the constitutional sense could have been afforded the defendant.[9] And even if, as was true here, the television cameras are so controlled and concealed as to be hardly perceptible in the courtroom itself, there are risks of constitutional dimensions that lurk in the very process of televising court proceedings at all.

Some of those risks are catalogued in the *amicus curiae* brief filed in this case by the American Bar Association: "[P]otential or actual jurors, in the absence of enforceable and effective safeguards, may arrive at certain misconceptions regarding the defendant and his trial by viewing televised pre-trial hearings and motions from which the jury is ordinarily excluded. Evidence otherwise inadmissible may leave an indelible mark .... Once the trial begins, exposure to nightly rebroadcasts of selected portions of the day's proceedings will be difficult to guard against, as jurors spend frequent evenings before the television set. The obvious impact of witnessing repeated trial episodes and hearing accompanying commentary, episodes admittedly chosen for their news value and not for evidentiary purposes, can serve only to distort the ju-

---

[9] See note 2.

rors' perspective . . . . Despite the court's injunction not to discuss the case, it seems undeniable that jurors will be subject to the pressure of television-watching family, friends and, indeed, strangers . . . . It is not too much to imagine a juror being confronted with his wife's television-oriented viewpoint . . . . Additionally, the jurors' daily television appearances may make them recognizable celebrities, likely to be stopped by passing strangers, or perhaps harried by intruding telephone calls . . . ." Constitutional problems of another kind might arise if a witness or juror were subjected to being televised over his objection.

The plain fact of the matter, however, is that none of these things happened or could have happened in this case. The jurors themselves were prevented from seeing any telecasts of the trial, and completely insulated from association with any members of the public who did see such telecasts. This case, therefore, does not remotely resemble *Turner* v. *Louisiana*, 379 U.S. 466, where, during the trial, the jurors were subjected outside the courtroom to unmeasured and unmeasurable influences by key witnesses for the prosecution.

In the courtroom itself, there is nothing to show that the trial proceeded in any way other than it would have proceeded if cameras and television had not been present. In appearance, the courtroom was practically unaltered. There was no obtrusiveness and no distraction, no noise and no special lighting. There is no indication anywhere in the record of any disturbance whatever of the judicial proceedings. There is no claim that the conduct of the judge, or that any deed or word of counsel, or of any witness, or of any juror, was influenced in any way by the presence of photographers or by television.

Furthermore, from a reading of the record it is crystal clear that this was not a trial where the judge was harassed or confused or lacking in command of the proceedings before the jury. Not once, after the first witness was called, was there any interruption at all of the trial proper to secure a ruling concerning the presence of cameramen in the courtroom. There was no occasion, during the entire trial—until after the jury adjourned to reach its verdict—for any cautionary word to members of the press in the courtroom. The only time a motion was made, the jury was not in the courtroom. The trial itself was a most mundane affair, totally lacking in the lurid and completely emotionless. The evidence related solely to the circumstances in which various documents had been signed and negotiated. It was highly technical, if not downright dull. The petitioner called no witnesses, and counsel for petitioner made only a brief closing argument to the jury. There is nothing to indicate

526

that the issues involved were of the kind where emotion could hold sway. The transcript of the trial belies any notion that frequent interruptions and inconsistent rulings communicated to the jury any sense that the judge was unable to concentrate on protecting the defendant and conducting the trial in a fair manner, in accordance with the State and Federal Constitutions.

IV.

What ultimately emerges from this record, therefore, is one bald question—whether the Fourteenth Amendment of the United States Constitution prohibits all television cameras from a state courtroom whenever a criminal trial is in progress. In the light of this record and what we now know about the impact of television on a criminal trial, I can find no such prohibition in the Fourteenth Amendment or in any other provision of the Constitution. If what occurred did not deprive the petitioner of his constitutional right to a fair trial, then the fact that the public could view the proceeding on television has no constitutional significance. The Constitution does not make us arbiters of the image that a televised state criminal trial projects to the public.

While no First Amendment claim is made in this case, there are intimations in the opinions filed by my Brethren in the majority which strike me as disturbingly alien to the First and Fourteenth Amendments' guarantees against federal or state interference with the free communication of information and ideas. The suggestion that there are limits upon the public's right to know what goes on in the courts causes me deep concern. The idea of imposing upon any medium of communications the burden of justifying its presence is contrary to where I had always thought the presumption must lie in the area of First Amendment freedoms. See *Speiser* v. *Randall*, 357 U.S. 513, 525. And the proposition that nonparticipants in a trial might get the "wrong impression" from unfettered reporting and commentary contains an invitation to censorship which I cannot accept. Where there is no disruption of the "essential requirement of the fair and orderly administration of justice," "[f]reedom of discussion should be given the widest range." *Pennekamp* v. *Florida*, 328 U.S. 331, 347; *Bridges* v. *California*, 314 U.S. 252. Cf. *Cox* v. *Louisiana*, 379 U.S. 559, 563.

I do not think that the Constitution denies to the State or to individual trial judges all discretion to conduct criminal trials with television cameras present, no matter how unobtrusive the cameras may be. I cannot say at this time that it is impossible to have a constitutional trial whenever any part of the proceedings is televised or recorded on television film. I cannot now hold that the

527

Constitution absolutely bars television cameras from every criminal courtroom, even if they have no impact upon the jury, no effect upon any witness, and no influence upon the conduct of the judge.

For these reasons I would affirm the judgment.

MR. JUSTICE WHITE, with whom MR. JUSTICE BRENNAN joins, dissenting.

I agree with MR. JUSTICE STEWART that a finding of constitutional prejudice on this record entails erecting a flat ban on the use of cameras in the courtroom and believe that it is premature to promulgate such a broad constitutional principle at the present time. This is the first case in this Court dealing with the subject of television coverage of criminal trials; our cases dealing with analogous subjects are not really controlling, cf. *Rideau* v. *Louisiana,* 373 U.S. 723; and there is, on the whole, a very limited amount of experience in this country with television coverage of trials. In my view, the currently available materials assessing the effect of cameras in the courtroom are too sparse and fragmentary to constitute the basis for a constitutional judgment permanently barring any and all forms of television coverage. As was said in another context, " we know too little of the actual impact . . . to reach a conclusion on the bare bones of the . . . evidence before us." *White Motor Co.* v. *United States,* 372 U.S. 253, 261. It may well be, however, that as further experience and informed judgment do become available, the use of cameras in the courtroom, as in this trial, will prove to pose such a serious hazard to a defendant's rights that a violation of the Fourteenth Amendment will be found without a showing on the record of specific demonstrable prejudice to the defendant. Compare *Wolf* v. *Colorado,* 338 U.S. 25, with *Mapp* v. *Ohio,* 367 U.S. 643; *Betts* v. *Brady,* 316 U.S. 455, with *Gideon* v. *Wainwright,* 372 U.S. 335; *Stein* v. *New York,* 346 U.S. 156, with *Jackson* v. *Denno,* 378 U.S. 368, 389–390.

The opinion of the Court in effect precludes further opportunity for intelligent assessment of the probable hazards imposed by the use of cameras at criminal trials. Serious threats to constitutional rights in some instances justify a prophylactic rule dispensing with the necessity of showing specific prejudice in a particular case. *Rideau* v. *Louisiana,* 373 U.S. 723, 727; *Jackson* v. *Denno,* 378 U.S. 368, 389. But these are instances in which there has been ample experience on which to base an informed judgment. Here, although our experience is inadequate and our judgment correspondingly infirm, the Court discourages further meaningful study of the use of television at criminal trials. Accordingly, I dissent.

MR. JUSTICE BRENNAN.

I write merely to emphasize that only four of the five Justices voting to reverse rest on the proposition that televised criminal trials are constitutionally infirm, whatever the circumstances. Although the opinion announced by my Brother CLARK purports to be an "opinion of the Court," my Brother HARLAN subscribes to a significantly less sweeping proposition. He states:
"The Estes trial was a heavily publicized and highly sensational affair. I therefore put aside all other types of cases . . . . The resolution of those further questions should await an appropriate case; the Court should proceed only step by step in this unplowed field. *The opinion of the Court necessarily goes no farther, for only the four members of the majority who unreservedly join the Court's opinion would resolve those questions now.*" Ante, pp. 590–591. (Emphasis supplied.)

Thus today's decision is *not* a blanket constitutional prohibition against the televising of state criminal trials.

While I join the dissents of my Brothers STEWART and WHITE, I do so on the understanding that their use of the expressions "the Court's opinion" or "the opinion of the Court" refers only to those views of our four Brethren which my Brother HARLAN explicitly states he shares.

Sheppard v. Maxwell*

One could reasonably argue that *Sheppard v Maxwell* is the most important case in the fair trial—free press area. The trial court was called upon to make several decisions which necessitated weighing the right of the accused to a fair trial against the right of the press to be free. In almost each instance the decision was an improper one with the scales of justice continually tilted against the accused. Because of this fact the trial judge's performance constitutes a model: a model of what shouldn't be done.

Marilyn Sheppard had been bludgeoned to death in her Bay Village home just outside of Cleveland, Ohio. From the very beginning the Cleveland papers pointed an accusing finger at her husband, Doctor Sam Sheppard, with editorials demanding that he be brought to the bar of justice. And this was just the start of a campaign against Sheppard for other news media soon joined the attack. The detailed facts need not be repeated here as they are examined in detail in the text of the opinion. It suffices to say that preju-

---

* 384 U.S. 333, 86 S.Ct. 1507 (June 6, 1966)

dicial news accounts flooded the news media prior to and during the course of the trial. In this atmosphere characterized by one judge as a "Roman Holiday for the news media",[1] Sam Sheppard stood trial for his life.

From the very inception of the proceedings the trial judge, Judge Edward Blythin, announced that neither he nor anyone else could restrict prejudicial publicity.[2] Herein lay the fundamental error of the trial court which was compounded on each occasion when defense counsel sought the imposition of some restraint on the news media.

What were the circumstances that lead Judge Blythin to make this fundamental legal error? Judge Blythin, who was elected to his judgeship, was coming up for re-election just two weeks after the commencement of the trial.[3] A favorable press at this time was something that would be desirable from the Judge's standpoint. Certainly this factor could have had an influence on Judge Blythin's attitude toward the press. Any consideration on the merits of elected judges versus appointed judges should consider this point, the elected judge's need for a favorable press and its effect on the administration of justice.

Another possible cause of the Judge's laissez-faire policy relative to the press is judicial bias. Substantially all judges attempt to administer justice in a fair and impartial manner. But being human they are subject to prejudices and bias as is the rest of mankind. The ruling of a judge may unconsciously be affected by his bias. Could this factor have played any part in Judge Blythin's ruling? In an unsworn statement made several years after the conviction and six years after Blythin's death, Dorothy Kilgallen, noted columnist, asserted that the Judge had told her prior to Sheppard's conviction, "It's an open and shut case . . . he is guilty as hell."[4]

It could be that neither of these factors had a causal connection with the Judge's ruling. Maybe it was just a matter of judgment. It could be that both contributed to it. The answers to these questions we will never know. Whatever the cause, eight of the nine justices on the Supreme Court, Justice Black dissenting, agreed that Sheppard's constitutional rights had been violated.

After the reversal of his conviction Sheppard was released from the Ohio State Penitentiary where he had spent the past nine years. But his freedom was still restricted as he was released on $10,000

[1] 165 Ohio St., at 294, 135 N.E.2d, at 342.
[2] Sheppard v. Maxwell, 86 S. Ct. 1507, at 1519.
[3] Same as above, at 1512.
[4] Same as above, at 1520, N. 11.

bail.[5] The State of Ohio had decided to prosecute him a second time. The second trial began October 24, 1966 and on November 17, 1966, he was acquitted of Marilyn Sheppard's murder.[6]

Doctor Sheppard is still in the news. His present wife, whom he married after his release, is suing him for divorce. She filed a divorce petition on December 4, 1968 in the Common Pleas Court of Cuyahoga County, Ohio. The petition charged gross neglect and extreme cruelty and asked the court to enjoin Sheppard from "touching the person of the plaintiff . . . for her protection."

Text of Case

Petitioner's wife was bludgeoned to death July 4, 1954. From the outset officials focused suspicion on petitioner, who was arrested on a murder charge July 30 and indicted August 17. His trial began October 18 and terminated with his conviction December 21, 1954. During the entire pretrial period virulent and incriminating publicity about petitioner and the murder made the case notorious, and the news media frequently aired charges and counter-charges besides those for which petitioner was tried. Three months before trial he was examined for more than five hours without counsel in a televised three-day inquest conducted before an audience of several hundred spectators in a gymnasium. Over three weeks before trial the newspapers published the names and addresses of prospective jurors causing them to receive letters and telephone calls about the case. The trial began two weeks before a hotly contested election at which the chief prosecutor and the trial judge were candidates for judgeships. Newsmen were allowed to take over almost the entire small courtroom, hounding petitioner, and most of the participants. Twenty reporters were assigned seats by the court within the bar and in close proximity to the jury and counsel, precluding privacy between petitioner and his counsel. The movement of the reporters in the courtroom caused frequent confusion and disrupted the trial; and in the corridors and elsewhere in and around the courthouse they were allowed free rein by the trial judge. A broadcasting station was assigned space next to the jury room. Before the jurors began deliberations they were not sequestered and had access to all news media though the court made "suggestions" and "requests" that the jurors not expose themselves to comment about the case. Though they were sequestered during the five days and four nights of their delibera-

---

[5] N.Y. Times, November 17, 1966, p. 1, col. 7.
[6] Same as 5.

[7] N.Y. Times, December 4, 1968, p. 22, col. 8.

tions, the jurors were allowed to make inadequately supervised telephone calls during that period. Pervasive publicity was given to the case throughout the trial, much of it involving incriminating matter not introduced at the trial, and the jurors were thrust into the role of celebrities. At least some of the publicity deluge reached the jurors. At the very inception of the proceedings and later, the trial judge announced that neither he nor anyone else could restrict the prejudicial news accounts. Despite his awareness of the excessive pretrial publicity, the trial judge failed to take effective measures against the massive publicity which continued throughout the trial or to take adequate steps to control the conduct of the trial. The petitioner filed a habeas corpus petition contending that he did not receive a fair trial. The District Court granted the writ. The Court of Appeals reversed.

F. Lee Bailey argued the cause for petitioner. With him on the brief were Russell A. Sherman and Benjamin L. Clark.

William B. Saxbe, Attorney General of Ohio, and John T. Corrigan argued the cause for respondent. With Mr. Saxbe on the brief was David L. Kessler, Assistant Attorney General.

Bernard A. Berkman argued the cause for the American Civil Liberties Union et al., as amici curiae, urging reversal. With him on the brief was Melvin L. Wulf.

John T. Corrigan and Gertrude Bauer Mahon filed a brief for the State of Ohio, as amicus curiae, urging affirmance.

MR. JUSTICE CLARK delivered the opinion of the Court.

This federal habeas corpus application involves the question whether Sheppard was deprived of a fair trial in his state conviction for the second-degree murder of his wife because of the trial judge's failure to protect Sheppard sufficiently from the massive, pervasive and prejudicial publicity that attended his prosecution.[1] The United States District Court held that he was not afforded a fair trial and granted the writ subject to the State's right to put Sheppard to trial again, 231 F.Supp. 37 (D.C.S.D. Ohio 1964). The Court of Appeals for the Sixth Circuit reversed by a divided vote, 346 F.2d 707 (1965). We granted certiorari, 382 U.S. 916 (1965). We have concluded that Sheppard did not receive a fair trial consistent with the Due Process Clause of the Fourteenth Amendment and, therefore, reverse the judgment.

[1] Sheppard was convicted in 1954 in the Court of Common Pleas of Cuyahoga County, Ohio. His conviction was affirmed by the Court of Appeals for Cuyahoga County, 100 Ohio App. 345, 128 N. E. 2d 471 (1955), and the Ohio Supreme Court, 165 Ohio St. 293, 135 N. E. 2d 340 (1956). We denied certiorari on the original application for review. 352 U. S. 910 (1956).

I.

Marilyn Sheppard, petitioner's pregnant wife, was bludgeoned to death in the upstairs bedroom of their lakeshore home in Bay Village, Ohio, a suburb of Cleveland. On the day of the tragedy, July 4, 1954, Sheppard pieced together for several local officials the following story: He and his wife had entertained neighborhood friends, the Aherns, on the previous evening at their home. After dinner they watched television in the living room. Sheppard became drowsy and dozed off to sleep on a couch. Later, Marilyn partially awoke him saying that she was going to bed. The next thing he remembered was hearing his wife cry out in the early morning hours. He hurried upstairs and in the dim light from the hall saw a "form" standing next to his wife's bed. As he struggled with the "form" he was struck on the back of the neck and rendered unconscious. On regaining his senses he found himself on the floor next to his wife's bed. He rose, looked at her, took her pulse and "felt that she was gone." He then went to his son's room and found him unmolested. Hearing a noise he hurried downstairs. He saw a "form" running out the door and pursued it to the lake shore. He grappled with it on the beach and again lost consciousness. Upon his recovery he was lying face down with the lower portion of his body in the water. He returned to his home, checked the pulse on his wife's neck, and "determined or thought that she was gone."[2] He then went downstairs and called a neighbor, Mayor Houk of Bay Village. The Mayor and his wife came over at once, found Sheppard slumped in an easy chair downstairs and asked, "What happened?" Sheppard replied: "I don't know but somebody ought to try to do something for Marilyn." Mrs. Houk immediately went up to the bedroom. The Mayor told Sheppard, "Get hold of yourself. Can you tell me what happened?" Sheppard then related the above-outlined events. After Mrs. Houk discovered the body, the Mayor called the local police, Dr. Richard Sheppard, petitioner's brother, and the Aherns. The local police were the first to arrive. They in turn notified the Coroner and Cleveland police. Richard Sheppard then arrived, determined that Marilyn was dead, examined his brother's injuries, and removed him to the nearby clinic operated by the Sheppard family.[3] When the Coroner, the Cleveland police and other officials arrived, the house and surrounding area were thoroughly searched, the

---

[2] The several witnesses to whom Sheppard narrated his experiences differ in their description of various details. Sheppard claimed the vagueness of his perception was caused by his sudden awakening, the dimness of the light, and his loss of consciousness.

[3] Sheppard was suffering from severe pain in his neck, a swollen eye, and shock.

rooms of the house were photographed, and many persons, including the Houks and the Aherns, were interrogated. The Sheppard home and premises were taken into "protective custody" and remained so until after the trial.[4]

From the outset officials focused suspicion on Sheppard. After a search of the house and premises on the morning of the tragedy, Dr. Gerber, the Coroner, is reported—and it is undenied—to have told his men, "Well, it is evident the doctor did this, so let's go get the confession out of him." He proceeded to interrogate and examine Sheppard while the latter was under sedation in his hospital room. On the same occasion, the Coroner was given the clothes Sheppard wore at the time of the tragedy together with the personal items in them. Later that afternoon Chief Eaton and two Cleveland police officers interrogated Sheppard at some length, confronting him with evidence and demanding explanations. Asked by Officer Shotke to take a lie detector test, Sheppard said he would if it were reliable. Shotke replied that it was "infallible" and "you might as well tell us all about it now." At the end of the interrogation Shotke told Sheppard: "I think you killed your wife." Still later in the same afternoon a physician sent by the Coroner was permitted to make a detailed examination of Sheppard. Until the Coroner's inquest on July 22, at which time he was subpoenaed, Sheppard made himself available for frequent and extended questioning without the presence of an attorney.

On July 7, the day of Marilyn Sheppard's funeral, a newspaper story appeared in which Assistant County Attorney Mahon—later the chief prosecutor of Sheppard—sharply criticized the refusal of the Sheppard family to permit his immediate questioning. From there on headline stories repeatedly stressed Sheppard's lack of cooperation with the police and other officials. Under the headline "Testify Now In Death, Bay Doctor Is Ordered," one story described a visit by Coroner Gerber and four police officers to the hospital on July 8. When Sheppard insisted that his lawyer be present, the Coroner wrote out a subpoena and served it on him. Sheppard then agreed to submit to questioning without counsel and the subpoena was torn up. The officers questioned him for several hours. On July 9, Sheppard, at the request of the Coroner, re-enacted the tragedy at his home before the Coroner, police officers, and a group of newsmen, who apparently were invited by the Coroner. The home was locked so that Sheppard was obliged to wait outside until the Coroner arrived. Sheppard's performance was reported in detail by

---

[4] But newspaper photographers and reporters were permitted access to Sheppard's home from time to time and took pictures throughout the premises.

the news media along with photographs. The newspapers also played up Sheppard's refusal to take a lie detector test and "the protective ring" thrown up by his family. Front-page newspaper headlines announced on the same day that "Doctor Balks At Lie Test; Retells Story." A column opposite that story contained an "exclusive" interview with Sheppard headlined: " 'Loved My Wife, She Loved Me,' Sheppard Tells News Reporter." The next day, another headline story disclosed that Sheppard had "again late yesterday refused to take a lie detector test" and quoted an Assistant County Attorney as saying that "at the end of a nine-hour questioning of Dr. Sheppard, I felt he was now ruling [a test] out completely." But subsequent newspaper articles reported that the Coroner was still pushing Sheppard for a lie detector test. More stories appeared when Sheppard would not allow authorities to inject him with "truth serum."[5]

On the 20th, the "editorial artillery" opened fire with a front-page charge that somebody is "getting away with murder." The editorial attributed the ineptness of the investigation to "friendships, relationships, hired lawyers, a husband who ought to have been subjected instantly to the same third-degree to which any other person under similar circumstances is subjected . . . ." The following day, July 21, another page-one editorial was headed: "Why No Inquest? Do It Now, Dr. Gerber." The Coroner called an inquest the same day and supoenaed Sheppard. It was staged the next day in a school gymnasium; the Coroner presided with the County Prosecutor as his advisor and two detectives as bailiffs. In the front of the room was a long table occupied by reporters, television and radio personnel, and broadcasting equipment. The hearing was broadcast with live microphones placed at the Coroner's seat and the witness stand. A swarm of reporters and photographers attended. Sheppard was brought into the room by police who searched him in full view of several hundred spectators. Sheppard's counsel were present during the three-day inquest but were not permitted to participate. When Sheppard's chief counsel attempted to place some documents in the record, he was forcibly ejected from the room by the Coroner, who received cheers, hugs, and kisses from ladies in the audience. Sheppard was questioned for five and one-half hours about his actions on the night of the murder, his married life, and a love affair with Susan Hayes.[6] At

---

[5] At the same time, the newspapers reported that other possible suspects had been "cleared" by lie detector tests. One of these persons was quoted as saying that he could not understand why an innocent man would refuse to take such a test.

[6] The newspapers had heavily emphasized Sheppard's illicit affair with Susan Hayes, and the fact that he had initially lied about it.

the end of the hearing the Coroner announced that he "could" order Sheppard held for the grand jury, but did not do so.

Throughout this period the newspapers emphasized evidence that tended to incriminate Sheppard and pointed out discrepancies in his statements to authorities. At the same time, Sheppard made many public statements to the press and wrote feature articles asserting his innocence.[7] During the inquest on July 26, a headline in large type stated: "Kerr [Captain of the Cleveland Police] Urges Sheppard's Arrest." In the story, Detective McArthur "disclosed that scientific tests at the Sheppard home have definitely established that the killer washed off a trail of blood from the murder bedroom to the downstairs section," a circumstance casting doubt on Sheppard's accounts of the murder. No such evidence was produced at trial. The newspapers also delved into Sheppard's personal life. Articles stressed his extramarital love affairs as a motive for the crime. The newspapers portrayed Sheppard as a Lothario, fully explores his relationship with Susan Hayes, and named a number of other women who were allegedly involved with him. The testimony at trial never showed that Sheppard had any illicit relationships besides the one with Susan Hayes.

On July 28, an editorial entitled "Why Don't Police Quiz Top Suspect" demanded that Sheppard be taken to police headquarters. It described him in the following language:

"Now proved under oath to be a liar, still free to go about his business, shielded by his family, protected by a smart lawyer who has made monkeys of the police and authorities, carrying a gun part of the time, left free to do whatever he pleases . . . ."

A front-page editorial on July 30 asked: "Why Isn't Sam Sheppard in Jail?" It was later titled "Quit Stalling—Bring Him In." After calling Sheppard "the most unusual murder suspect ever seen around these parts" the article said that "[e]xcept for some superficial questioning during Coroner Sam Gerber's inquest he has been scot-free of any official grilling . . . ." It asserted that he was "surrounded by an iron curtain of protection [and] concealment."

That night at 10 o'clock Sheppard was arrested at his father's home on a charge of murder. He was taken to the Bay Village City Hall where hundreds of people, newscasters, photographers and reporters were awaiting his arrival. He was immediately arraigned —having been denied a temporary delay to secure the presence of counsel—and bound over to the grand jury.

---

[7] A number of articles calculated to evoke sympathy for Sheppard were printed, such as the letters Sheppard wrote to his son while in jail. These stories often appeared together with news coverage which was unfavorable to him.

The publicity then grew in intensity until his indictment on August 17. Typical of the coverage during this period is a front-page interview entitled: "DR. SAM: 'I Wish There Was Something I Could Get Off My Chest—but There Isn't.' " Unfavorable publicity included items such as a cartoon of the body of a sphinx with Sheppard's head and the legend below: " 'I Will Do Everything In My Power to Help Solve This Terrible Murder.' —Dr. Sam Sheppard." Headlines announced, *inter alia*, that: "Doctor Evidence is Ready for Jury," "Corrigan Tactics Stall Quizzing," "Sheppard 'Gay Set' Is Revealed By Houk," "Blood Is Found In Garage," "New Murder Evidence Is Found, Police Claim," "Dr. Sam Faces Quiz At Jail On Marilyn's Fear Of Him." On August 18, an article appeared under the headline "Dr. Sam Writes His Own Story." And reproduced accross the entire front page was a portion of the typed statement signed by Sheppard: "I am not guilty of the murder of my wife, Marilyn. How could I, who have been trained to help people and devoted my life to saving life, commit such a terrible and revolting crime?" We do not detail the coverage further. There are five volumes filled with similar clippings from each of the three Cleveland newspapers covering the period from the murder until Sheppard's conviction in December 1954. The record includes no excerpts from newscasts on radio and television but since space was reserved in the courtroom for these media we assume that their coverage was equally large.

II.

With this background the case came on for trial two weeks before the November general election at which the chief prosecutor was a candidate for common pleas judge and the trial judge, Judge Blythin, was a candidate to succeed himself. Twenty-five days before the case was set, 75 veniremen were called as prospective jurors. All three Cleveland newspapers published the names and addresses of the veniremen. As a consequence, anonymous letters and telephone calls, as well as calls from friends, regarding the impending prosecution were received by all of the prospective jurors. The selection of the jury began on October 18, 1954.

The courtroom in which the trial was held measured 26 by 48 feet. A long temporary table was set up inside the bar, in back of the single counsel table. It ran the width of the courtroom, parallel to the bar railing, with one end less than three feet from the jury box. Approximately 20 representatives of newspapers and wire services were assigned seats at this table by the court. Behind the bar railing there were four rows of benches. These seats were likewise assigned by the court for the entire trial. The first row was

537

occupied by representatives of television and radio stations, and the second and third rows by reporters from out-of-town newspapers and magazines. One side of the last row, which accommodated 14 people, was assigned to Sheppard's family and the other to Marilyn's. The public was permitted to fill vacancies in this row on special passes only. Representatives of the news media also used all the rooms on the courtroom floor, including the room where cases were ordinarily called and assigned for trial. Private telephone lines and telegraphic equipment were installed in these rooms so that reports from the trial could be speeded to the papers. Station WSRS was permitted to set up broadcasting facilities on the third floor of the courthouse next door to the jury room, where the jury rested during recesses in the trial and deliberated. Newscasts were made from this room throughout the trial, and while the jury reached its verdict.

On the sidewalk and steps in front of the courthouse, television and newsreel cameras were occasionally used to take motion pictures of the participants in the trial, including the jury and the judge. Indeed, one television broadcast carried a staged interview of the judge as he entered the courthouse. In the corridors outside the courtroom there was a host of photographers and television personnel with flash cameras, portable lights and motion picture cameras. This group photographed the prospective jurors during selection of the jury. After the trial opened, the witnesses, counsel, and jurors were photographed and televised whenever they entered or left the courtroom. Sheppard was brought to the courtroom about 10 minutes before each session began; he was surrounded by reporters and extensively photographed for the newspapers and television. A rule of court prohibited picture-taking in the courtroom during the actual sessions of the court, but no restraints were put on photographers during recesses, which were taken once each morning and afternoon, with a longer period for lunch.

All of these arrangements with the news media and their massive coverage of the trial continued during the entire nine weeks of the trial. The courtroom remained crowded to capacity with representatives of news media. Their movement in and out of the courtroom often caused so much confusion that, despite the loudspeaker system installed in the courtroom, it was difficult for the witnesses and counsel to be heard. Furthermore, the reporters clustered within the bar of the small courtroom made confidential talk among Sheppard and his counsel almost impossible during the proceedings. They frequently had to leave the courtroom to obtain privacy. And many times when counsel wished to raise a point

538

with the judge out of the hearing of the jury it was necessary to move to the judge's chambers. Even then, news media representatives so packed the judge's ante-room that counsel could hardly return from the chambers to the courtroom. The reporters vied with each other to find out what counsel and the judge had discussed, and often these matters later appeared in newspapers accessible to the jury.

The daily record of the proceedings was made available to the newspapers and the testimony of each witness was printed verbatim in the local editions, along with objections of counsel, and rulings by the judge. Pictures of Sheppard, the judge, counsel, pertinent witnesses, and the jury often accompanied the daily newspaper and television accounts. At times the newspapers published photographs of exhibits introduced at the trial, and the rooms of Sheppard's house were featured along with relevant testimony.

The jurors themselves were constantly exposed to the news media. Every juror, except one, testified at *voir dire* to reading about the case in the Cleveland papers or to having heard broadcasts about it. Seven of the 12 jurors who rendered the verdict had one or more Cleveland papers delivered in their home; the remaining jurors were not interrogated on the point. Nor were there questions as to radios or television sets in the jurors' homes, but we must assume that most of them owned such conveniences. As the selection of the jury progressed, individual pictures of prospective members appeared daily. During the trial, pictures of the jury appeared over 40 times in the Cleveland papers alone. The court permitted photographers to take pictures of the jury in the box, and individual pictures of the members in the jury room. One newspaper ran pictures of the jurors at the Sheppard home when they went there to view the scene of the murder. Another paper featured the home life of an alternate juror. The day before the verdict was rendered—while the jurors were at lunch and sequestered by two bailiffs—the jury was separated into two groups to pose for photographs which appeared in the newspapers.

III.

We now reach the conduct of the trial. While the intense publicity continued unabated, it is sufficient to relate only the more flagrant episodes:

1. On October 9, 1954, nine days before the case went to trial, an editorial in one of the newspapers criticized defense counsel's random poll of people on the streets as to their opinion of Sheppard's guilt or innocence in an effort to use the resulting statistics to show the necessity for change of venue. The article said the

survey "smacks of mass jury tampering," called on defense counsel to drop it, and stated that the bar association should do something about it. It characterized the poll as "non-judicial, non-legal, and nonsense." The article was called to the attention of the court but no action was taken.

2. On the second day of *voir dire* examination a debate was staged and broadcast live over WHK radio. The participants, newspaper reporters, accused Sheppard's counsel of throwing roadblocks in the way of the prosecution and asserted that Sheppard conceded his guilt by hiring a prominent criminal lawyer. Sheppard's counsel objected to this broadcast and requested a continuance, but the judge denied the motion. When counsel asked the court to give some protection from such events, the judge replied that "WHK doesn't have much coverage," and that "[a]fter all, we are not trying this case by radio or in newspapers or any other means. We confine ourselves seriously to it in this courtroom and do the very best we can."

3. While the jury was being selected, a two-inch headline asked: "But Who Will Speak for Marilyn?" The front-page story spoke of the "perfect face" of the accused. "Study that face as long as you want. Never will you get from it a hint of what might be the answer . . . ." The two brothers of the accused were described as "Prosperous, poised. His two sisters-in-law. Smart, chic, well-groomed. His elderly father. Courtly, reserved. A perfect type for the patriarch of a staunch clan." The author then noted Marilyn Sheppard was "still off stage," and that she was an only child whose mother died when she was very young and whose father had no interest in the case. But the author—through quotes from Detective Chief James McArthur—assured readers that the prosecution's exhibits would speak for Marilyn. "Her story," McArthur stated, "will come into this courtroom through our witnesses." The article ends:

"Then you realize how what and who is missing from the perfect setting will be supplied.

"How in the Big Case justice will be done.

"Justice to Sam Sheppard.

"And to Marilyn Sheppard."

4. As has been mentioned, the jury viewed the scene of the murder on the first day of the trial. Hundreds of reporters, cameramen and onlookers were there, and one representative of the news media was permitted to accompany the jury while it inspected the Sheppard home. The time of the jury's visit was revealed so far in advance that one of the newspapers was able to rent a helicopter and fly over the house taking pictures of the jurors on their tour.

5. On November 19, a Cleveland police officer gave testimony that tended to contradict details in the written statement Sheppard made to the Cleveland police. Two days later, in a broadcast heard over Station WHK in Cleveland, Robert Considine likened Sheppard to a perjurer and compared the episode to Alger Hiss' confrontation with Whittaker Chambers. Though defense counsel asked the judge to question the jury to ascertain how many heard the broadcast, the court refused to do so. The judge also overruled the motion for continuance based on the same ground, saying:

"Well, I don't know, we can't stop people, in any event, listening to it. It is a matter of free speech, and the court can't control everybody . . . . We are not going to harass the jury every morning . . . . It is getting to the point where if we do it every morning, we are suspecting the jury. I have confidence in this jury . . . ."

6. On November 24, a story appeared under an eight-column headline: "Sam Called A 'Jekyll-Hyde' by Marilyn, Cousin To Testify." It related that Marilyn had recently told friends that Sheppard was a "Dr. Jekyll and Mr. Hyde" character. No such testimony was ever produced at the trial. The story went on to announce: "The prosecution has a 'bombshell witness' on tap who will testify to Dr. Sam's display of fiery temper—countering the defense claim that the defendant is a gentle physician with an even disposition." Defense counsel made motions for change of venue, continuance and mistrial, but they were denied. No action was taken by the court.

7. When the trial was in its seventh week, Walter Winchell broadcast over WXEL television and WJW radio that Carole Beasley, who was under arrest in New York City for robbery, had stated that, as Sheppard's mistress, she had borne him a child. The defense asked that the jury be queried on the broadcast. Two jurors admitted in open court that they had heard it. The judge asked each: "Would that have any effect upon your judgment?" Both replied, "No." This was accepted by the judge as sufficient; he merely asked the jury to "pay no attention whatever to that type of scavenging. . . . Let's confine ourselves to this courtroom, if you please." In answer to the motion for mistrial, the judge said:

"Well, even, so, Mr. Corrigan, how are you ever going to prevent those things, in any event? I don't justify them at all. I think it is outrageous, but in a sense, it is outrageous even if there were no trial here. The trial has nothing to do with it in the Court's mind, as far as its outrage is concerned, but—

"Mr. CORRIGAN: I don't know what effect it had on the mind of any of these jurors, and I can't find out unless inquiry is made.

541

"The COURT: How would you ever, in any jury, avoid that kind of thing?"

8. On December 9, while Sheppard was on the witness stand he testified that he had been mistreated by Cleveland detectives after his arrest. Although he was not at the trial, Captain Kerr of the Homicide Bureau issued a press statement denying Sheppard's allegations which appeared under the headline: " 'Bare-faced Liar,' Kerr Says of Sam." Captain Kerr never appeared as a witness at the trial.

9. After the case was submitted to the jury, it was sequestered for its deliberations, which took five days and four nights. After the verdict, defense counsel ascertained that the jurors had been allowed to make telephone calls to their homes every day while they were sequestered at the hotel. Although the telephones had been removed from the jurors' rooms, the jurors were permitted to use the phones in the bailiffs' rooms. The calls were placed by the jurors themselves; no record was kept of the jurors who made calls, the telephone numbers or the parties called. The bailiffs sat in the room where they could hear only the jurors' end of the conversation. The court had not instructed the bailiffs to prevent such calls. By a subsequent motion, defense counsel urged that this ground alone warranted a new trial, but the motion was overruled and no evidence was taken on the question.

IV.

The principle that justice cannot survive behind walls of silence has long been reflected in the "Anglo-American distrust for secret trials." *In re Oliver*, 333 U.S. 257, 268 (1948). A responsible press has always been regarded as the handmaiden of effective judicial administration, especially in the criminal field. Its function in this regard is documented by an impressive record of service over several centuries. The press does not simply publish information about trials but guards against the miscarriage of justice by subjecting the police, prosecutors, and judicial processes to extensive public scrutiny and criticism. This Court has, therefore, been unwilling to place any direct limitations on the freedom traditionally exercised by the news media for "[w]hat transpires in the court room is public property." *Craig* v. *Harney*, 331 U.S. 367, 374 (1947). The "unqualified prohibitions laid down by the framers were intended to give to liberty of the press . . . the broadest scope that could be countenanced in an orderly society." *Bridges* v. *California*, 314 U.S. 252, 265 (1941). And where there was "no threat or menace to the integrity of the trial," *Craig* v. *Harney*, *supra*, at 377, we have consistently required that the press have a free hand, even though we sometimes deplored its sensationalism.

But the Court has also pointed out that "[l]egal trials are not like elections, to be won through the use of the meeting-hall, the radio, and the newspaper." *Bridges* v. *California, supra,* at 271. And the Court has insisted that no one be punished for a crime without "a charge fairly made and fairly tried in a public tribunal free of prejudice, passion, excitement, and tyrannical power." *Chambers* v. *Florida,* 309 U.S. 227, 236–237 (1940). "Freedom of discussion should be given the widest range compatible with the essential requirement of the fair and orderly administration of justice." *Pennekamp* v. *Florida,* 328 U.S. 331, 347 (1946). But it must not be allowed to divert the trial from the "very purpose of a court system . . . to adjudicate controversies, both criminal and civil, in the calmness and solemnity of the courtroom according to legal procedures." *Cox* v. *Louisiana,* 379 U.S. 559, 583 (1965) (BLACK, J., dissenting). Among these "legal procedures" is the requirement that the jury's verdict be based on evidence received in open court, not from outside sources. Thus, in *Marshall* v. *United States,* 360 U.S. 310 (1959), we set aside a federal conviction where the jurors were exposed "through news accounts" to information that was not admitted at trial. We held that the prejudice from such material "may indeed be greater" than when it is part of the prosecution's evidence "for it is then not tempered by protective procedures." At 313. At the same time, we did not consider dispositive the statement of each juror "that he would not be influenced by the news articles, that he could decide the case only on the evidence of record, and that he felt no prejudice against petitioner as a result of the articles." At 312. Likewise, in *Irvin* v. *Dowd,* 366 U.S. 717 (1961), even though each juror indicated that he could render an impartial verdict despite exposure to prejudicial newspaper articles, we set aside the conviction holding: "With his life at stake, it is not requiring too much that petitioner be tried in an atmosphere undisturbed by so huge a wave of public passion . . . ." At 728.

The undeviating rule of this Court was expressed by Mr. Justice Holmes over half a century ago in *Patterson* v. *Colorado,* 205 U.S. 454, 462 (1907): "The theory of our system is that the conclusions to be reached in a case will be induced only by evidence and argument in open court, and not by any outside influence, whether of private talk or public print."

Moreover, "the burden of showing essential unfairness . . . as a demonstrable reality," *Adams* v. *United States ex rel. McCann,*

317 U.S. 269, 281 (1942), need not be undertaken when television has exposed the community "repeatedly and in depth to the spectacle of [the accused] personally confessing in detail to the crimes with which he was later to be charged." *Rideau* v. *Louisiana*, 373 U.S. 723, 726 (1963). In *Turner* v. *Louisiana*, 379 U.S. 466 (1965), two key witnesses were deputy sheriffs who doubled as jury shepherds during the trial. The deputies swore that they had not talked to the jurors about the case, but the Court nonetheless held that, "even if it could be assumed that the deputies never did discuss the case directly with any members of the jury, it would be blinking reality not to recognize the extreme prejudice inherent in this continual association . . . ." At 473.

Only last Term in *Estes* v. *Texas*, 381 U.S. 532 (1965), we set aside a conviction despite the absence of any showing of prejudice. We said there:

"It is true that in most cases involving claims of due process deprivations we require a showing of identifiable prejudice to the accused. Nevertheless, at times a procedure employed by the State involves such a probability that prejudice will result that it is deemed inherently lacking in due process." At 542–543.

And we cited with approval the language of MR. JUSTICE BLACK for the Court in *In re Murchison*, 349 U.S. 133, 136 (1955), that "our system of law has always endeavored to prevent even the probability of unfairness."

V.

It is clear that the totality of circumstances in this case also warrants such an approach. Unlike Estes, Sheppard was not granted a change of venue to a locale away from where the publicity originated; nor was his jury sequestered. The Estes jury saw none of the television broadcasts from the courtroom. On the contrary, the Sheppard jurors were subjected to newspaper, radio and television coverage of the trial while not taking part in the proceedings. They were allowed to go their separate ways outside of the courtroom, without adequate directions not to read or listen to anything concerning the case. The judge's "admonitions" at the beginning of the trial are representative:

"I would suggest to you and caution you that you do not read any newspapers during the progress of this trial, that you do not listen to radio comments nor watch or listen to television comments, insofar as this case is concerned. You will feel very much better as the trial proceeds . . . . I am sure that we shall all feel very much better if we do not indulge in any newspaper reading or listening to any comments whatever about the matter while the case is in progress. After it is all over, you can read it all to your heart's content . . . ."

At intervals during the trial, the judge simply repeated his "suggestions" and "requests" that the jurors not expose themselves to comment upon the case. Moreover, the jurors were thrust into the role of celebrities by the judge's failure to insulate them from reporters and photographers. See *Estes* v. *Texas, supra,* at 545–546. The numerous pictures of the jurors, with their addresses, which appeared in the newspapers before and during the trial itself exposed them to expressions of opinion from both cranks and friends. The fact that anonymous letters had been received by prospective jurors should have made the judge aware that this publicity seriously threatened the jurors' privacy.

The press coverage of the Estes trial was not nearly as massive and pervasive as the attention given by the Cleveland newspapers and broadcasting stations to Sheppard's prosecution.[8] Sheppard stood indicted for the murder of his wife; the State was demanding the death penalty. For months the virulent publicity about Sheppard and the murder had made the case notorious. Charges and countercharges were aired in the news media besides those for which Sheppard was called to trial. In addition, only three months before trial, Sheppard was examined for more than five hours without counsel during a three-day inquest which ended in a public brawl. The inquest was televised live from a high school gymnasium seating hundreds of people. Furthermore, the trial began two weeks before a hotly contested election at which both Chief Prosecutor Mahon and Judge Blythin were candidates for judgeships.[9]

While we cannot say that Sheppard was denied due process by the judge's refusal to take precautions against the influence of

---

[8] Many more reporters and photographers attended the Sheppard trial. And it attracted several nationally famous commentators as well.

[9] At the commencement of trial, defense counsel made motions for continuance and change of venue. The judge postponed ruling on these motions until he determined whether an impartial jury could be impaneled. *Voir dire* examination showed that with one exception all members selected for jury service had read something about the case in the newspapers. Since, however, all of the jurors stated that they would not be influenced by what they had read or seen, the judge overruled both of the motions. Without regard to whether the judge's actions in this respect reach dimensions that would justify issuance of the habeas writ, it should be noted that a short continuance would have alleviated any problem with regard to the judicial elections. The court in *Delaney* v. *United States,* 199 F. 2d 107, 115 (C. A. 1st Cir. 1952), recognized such a duty under similar circumstances, holding that "if assurance of a fair trial would necessitate that the trial of the case be postponed until after the election, then we think the law required no less than that."

pretrial publicity alone, the court's later rulings must be considered against the setting in which the trial was held. In light of this background, we believe that the arrangements made by the judge with the news media caused Sheppard to be deprived of that "judicial serenity and calm to which [he] was entitled." *Estes* v. *Texas, supra,* at 536. The fact is that bedlam reigned at the courthouse during the trial and newsmen took over practically the entire courtroom, hounding most of the participants in the trial, especially Sheppard. At a temporary table within a few feet of the jury box and counsel table sat some 20 reporters staring at Sheppard and taking notes. The erection of a press table for reporters inside the bar is unprecedented. The bar of the court is reserved for counsel, providing them a safe place in which to keep papers and exhibits, and to confer privately with client and co-counsel. It is designed to protect the witness and the jury from any distractions, intrusions or influences, and to permit bench discussions of the judge's rulings away from the hearing of the public and the jury. Having assigned almost all of the available seats in the courtroom to the news media the judge lost his ability to supervise that environment. The movement of the reporters in and out of the courtroom caused frequent confusion and disruption of the trial. And the record reveals constant commotion within the bar. Moreover, the judge gave the throng of newsmen gathered in the corridors of the courthouse absolute free rein. Participants in the trial, including the jury, were forced to run a gantlet of reporters and photographers each time they entered or left the courtroom. The total lack of consideration for the privacy of the jury was demonstrated by the assignment to a broadcasting station of space next to the jury room on the floor above the courtroom, as well as the fact that jurors were allowed to make telephone calls during their five-day deliberation.

VI.

There can be no question about the nature of the publicity which surrounded Sheppard's trial. We agree, as did the Court of Appeals, with the findings in Judge Bell's opinion for the Ohio Supreme Court:

"Murder and mystery, society, sex and suspense were combined in this case in such a manner as to intrigue and captivate the public fancy to a degree perhaps unparalled in recent annals. Throughout the preindictment investigation, the subsequent legal skirmishes and the nine-week trial, circulation-conscious editors catered to the insatiable interest of the American public in the bizarre . . . . In this atmosphere of a 'Roman holiday' for the news media, Sam Sheppard stood trial for his life." 165 Ohio St., at 294, 135 N.E.2d, at 342.

Indeed, every court that has considered this case, save the court that tried it, has deplored the manner in which the news media inflamed and prejudiced the public.[10]

Much of the material printed or broadcast during the trial was never heard from the witness stand, such as the charges that Sheppard had purposely impeded the murder investigation and must be guilty since he had hired a prominent criminal lawyer; that Sheppard was a perjurer; that he had sexual relations with numerous women; that his slain wife had characterized him as a "Jekyll-Hyde"; that he was "a bare-faced liar" because of his testimony as to police treatment; and, finally, that a woman convict claimed Sheppard to be the father of her illegitimate child. As the trial progressed, the newspapers summarized and interpreted the evidence, devoting particular attention to the material that incriminated Sheppard, and often drew unwarranted inferences from testimony. At one point, a front-page picture of Mrs. Sheppard's bloodstained pillow was published after being "doctored" to show more clearly an alleged imprint of a surgical instrument.

Nor is there doubt that this deluge of publicity reached at least some of the jury. On the only occasion that the jury was queried, two jurors admitted in open court to hearing the highly inflammatory charge that a prison inmate claimed Sheppard as the father of her illegitimate child. Despite the extent and nature of the publicity to which the jury was exposed during trial, the judge refused defense counsel's other requests that the jurors be asked whether they had read or heard specific prejudicial comment about the case, including the incidents we have previously summarized. In these circumstances, we can assume that some of this material reached members of the jury. See *Commonwealth* v. *Crehan*, 345 Mass. 609, 188 N.E.2d 923 (1963).

---

[10] Typical comments on the trial by the press itself include:

"The question of Dr. Sheppard's guilt or innocence still is before the courts. Those who have examined the trial record carefully are divided as to the propriety of the verdict. But almost everyone who watched the performance of the Cleveland press agrees that a fair hearing for the defendant, in that area, would be a modern miracle."

Harrison, "The Press vs. the Courts," The Saturday Review (Oct. 15, 1955).

"At this distance, some 100 miles from Cleveland, it looks to us as though the Sheppard murder case was sensationalized to the point at which the press must ask itself if its freedom, carried to excess, doesn't interfere with the conduct of fair trials." Editorial, The Toledo Blade (Dec. 22, 1954).

VII.

The court's fundamental error is compounded by the holding that it lacked power to control the publicity about the trial. From the very inception of the proceedings the judge announced that neither he nor anyone else could restrict prejudicial news accounts. And he reiterated this view on numerous occasions. Since he viewed the news media as his target, the judge never considered other means that are often utilized to reduce the appearance of prejudicial material and to protect the jury from outside influence. We conclude that these procedures would have been sufficient to guarantee Sheppard a fair trial and so do not consider what sanctions might be available against a recalcitrant press nor the charges of bias now made against the state trial judge.[11]

The carnival atmosphere at trial could easily have been avoided since the courtroom and courthouse premises are subject to the control of the court. As we stressed in *Estes*, the presence of the press at judicial proceedings must be limited when it is apparent that the accused might otherwise be prejudiced or disadvantaged.[12] Bearing in mind the massive pretrial publicity, the judge should have adopted stricter rules governing the use of the courtroom by newsmen, as Sheppard's counsel requested. The number of reporters in the courtroom itself could have been limited at the first sign that their presence would disrupt the trial. They certainly should not have been placed inside the bar. Furthermore, the judge should have more closely regulated the conduct of newsmen in the courtroom. For instance, the judge belatedly asked them not to handle and photograph trial exhibits lying on the counsel table during recesses.

Secondly, the court should have insulated the witnesses. All of the newspapers and radio stations apparently interviewed prospective witnesses at will, and in many instances disclosed their testimony. A typical example was the publication of numerous statements by Susan Hayes, before her appearance in court, regarding her love affair with Sheppard. Although the witnesses were barred from the courtroom during the trial the full verbatim testimony

[11] In an unsworn statement, which the parties agreed would have the status of a deposition, made 10 years after Sheppard's conviction and six years after Judge Blythin's death, Dorothy Kilgallen asserted that Judge Blythin had told her: "It's an open and shut case . . . he is guilty as hell." It is thus urged that Sheppard be released on the ground that the judge's bias infected the entire trial. But we need not reach this argument, since the judge's failure to insulate the proceedings from prejudicial publicity and disruptive influences deprived Sheppard of the chance to receive a fair hearing.

[12] The judge's awareness of his power in this respect is manifest from his assignment of seats to the press.

was available to them in the press. This completely nullified the judge's imposition of the rule. See *Estes* v. *Texas, supra,* at 547.

Thirdly, the court should have made some effort to control the release of leads, information, and gossip to the press by police officers, witnesses, and the counsel for both sides. Much of the information thus disclosed was inaccurate, leading to groundless rumors and confusion.[13] That the judge was aware of his responsibility in this respect may be seen from his warning to Steve Sheppard, the accused's brother, who had apparently made public statements in an attempt to discredit testimony for the prosecution. The judge made this statement in the presence of the jury:

"Now, the Court wants to say a word. That he was told—he has not read anything about it at all—but he was informed that Dr. Steve Sheppard, who has been granted the privilege of remaining in the court room during the trial, has been trying the case in the newspapers and making rather uncomplimentary comments about the testimony of the witnesses for the State.

"Let it be now understood that if Dr. Steve Sheppard wishes to use the newspapers to try his case while we are trying it here, he will be barred from remaining in the court room during the progress of the trial if he is to be a witness in the case.

"The Court appreciates he cannot deny Steve Sheppard the right of free speech, but he can deny him the . . . privilege of being in the court room, if he wants to avail himself of that method during the progress of the trial."

Defense counsel immediately brought to the court's attention the tremendous amount of publicity in the Cleveland press that "misrepresented entirely the testimony" in the case. Under such circumstances, the judge should have at least warned the newspapers to check the accuracy of their accounts. And it is obvious that the judge should have further sought to alleviate this problem by imposing control over the statements made to the news media by counsel, witnesses, and especially the Coroner and police officers. The prosecution repeatedly made evidence available to the news

---

[13] The problem here was further complicated by the independent action of the newspapers in reporting "evidence" and gossip which they uncovered. The press not only inferred that Sheppard was guilty because he "stalled" the investigation, hid behind his family, and hired a prominent criminal lawyer, but denounced as "mass jury tampering" his efforts to gather evidence of community prejudice caused by such publications. Shep-

pard's counterattacks added some fuel but, in these circumstances, cannot preclude him from asserting his right to a fair trial. Putting to one side news stories attributed to police officials, prospective witnesses, the Sheppards, and the lawyers, it is possible that the other publicity "would itself have had a prejudicial effect." Cf. Report of the President's Commission on the Assassination of President Kennedy, at 239.

549

media which was never offered in the trial. Much of the "evidence" disseminated in this fashion was clearly inadmissible. The exclusion of such evidence in court is rendered meaningless when news media make it available to the public. For example, the publicity about Sheppard's refusal to take a lie detector test came directly from police officers and the Coroner.[14] The story that Sheppard had been called a "Jekyll-Hyde" personality by his wife was attributed to a prosecution witness. No such testimony was given. The further report that there was "a 'bombshell witness' on tap" who would testify as to Sheppard's "fiery temper" could only have emanated from the prosecution. Moreover, the newspapers described in detail clues that had been found by the police, but not put into the record.[15]

The fact that many of the prejudicial news items can be traced to the prosecution, as well as the defense, aggravates the judge's failure to take any action. See *Stroble* v. *California*, 343 U.S. 181, 201 (1952) (Frankfurter, J., dissenting). Effective control of these sources—concededly within the court's power—might well have prevented the divulgence of inaccurate information, rumors, and accusations that made up much of the inflammatory publicity, at least after Sheppard's indictment.

More specifically, the trial court might well have proscribed extrajudicial statements by any lawyer, party, witness, or court official which divulged prejudicial matters, such as the refusal of Sheppard to submit to interrogation or take any lie detector tests; any statement made by Sheppard to officials; the identity of prospective witnesses or their probable testimony; any belief in guilt or innocence; or like statements concerning the merits of the case. See *State* v. *Van Duyne*, 43 N.J. 369, 389, 204 A.2d 841, 852 (1964), in which the court interpreted Canon 20 of the American Bar Association's Canons of Professional Ethics to prohibit such statements. Being advised of the great public interest in the case, the mass coverage of the press, and the potential prejudicial impact of publicity, the court could also have requested the appropriate city and county officials to promulgate a regulation with respect to dissemination of information about the case by their em-

---

[14] When two police officers testified at trial that Sheppard refused to take a lie detector test, the judge declined to give a requested instruction that the results of such a test would be inadmissible in any event. He simply told the jury that no person has an obligation "to take any lie detector test."

[15] Such "premature disclosure and weighing of the evidence" may se-

riously jeopardize a defendant's right to an impartial jury. "[N]either the press nor the public had a right to be contemporaneously informed by the police or prosecuting authorities of the details of the evidence being accumulated against [Sheppard]." Cf. Report of the President's Commission, *supra*, at 239, 240.

ployees.[16] In addition, reporters who wrote or broadcast prejudicial stories, could have been warned as to the impropriety of publishing material not introduced in the proceedings. The judge was put on notice of such events by defense counsel's complaint about the WHK broadcast on the second day of trial. See p. 346, *supra*. In this manner, Sheppard's right to a trial free from outside interference would have been given added protection without corresponding curtailment of the news media. Had the judge, the other officers of the court, and the police placed the interest of justice first, the news media would have soon learned to be content with the task of reporting the case as it unfolded in the courtroom— not pieced together from extrajudicial statements.

From the cases coming here we note that unfair and prejudicial news comment on pending trials has become increasingly prevalent. Due process requires that the accused receive a trial by an impartial jury free from outside influences. Given the pervasiveness of modern communications and the difficulty of effacing prejudicial publicity from the minds of the jurors, the trial courts must take strong measures to ensure that the balance is never weighed against the accused. And appellate tribunals have the duty to make an independent evaluation of the circumstances. Of course, there is nothing that proscribes the press from reporting events that transpire in the courtroom. But where there is a reasonable likelihood that prejudicial news prior to trial will prevent a fair trial, the judge should continue the case until the threat abates, or transfer it to another county not so permeated with publicity. In addition, sequestration of the jury was something the judge should have raised *sua sponte* with counsel. If publicity during the proceedings threatens the fairness of the trial, a new trial should be ordered. But we must remember that reversals are but palliatives; the cure lies in those remedial measures that will prevent the prejudice at its inception. The courts must take such steps by rule and regulation that will protect their processes from prejudicial outside interferences. Neither prosecutors, counsel for defense, the accused, witnesses, court staff nor enforcement officers coming under the jurisdiction of the court should be permitted to frustrate its function. Collaboration between counsel and the press as to information affecting the fairness of a criminal trial is not only subject to regulation, but is highly censurable and worthy of disciplinary measures.

---

[16] The Department of Justice, the City of New York, and other governmental agencies have issued such regulations. *E. g.*, 28 CFR § 50.2 (1966). For general information on this topic see periodic publications (*e. g.*, Nos. 71, 124, and 158) by the Freedom of Information Center, School of Journalism, University of Missouri.

Since the state trial judge did not fulfill his duty to protect Sheppard from the inherently prejudicial publicity which saturated the community and to control disruptive influences in the courtroom, we must reverse the denial of the habeas petition. The case is remanded to the District Court with instructions to issue the writ and order that Sheppard be released from custody unless the State puts him to its charges again within a reasonable time.

It is so ordered.

MR. JUSTICE BLACK dissents.

Freedom of Speech and Press
continued in volume two